. . . .

PRAGMATISM AND THE

POLITICAL ECONOMY OF

CULTURAL REVOLUTION,

1850–1940

PRAGMATISM AND THE POLITICAL ECONOMY OF CULTURAL REVOLUTION, 1850–1940

JAMES LIVINGSTON

THE UNIVERSITY OF NORTH CAROLINA PRESS

CHAPEL HILL AND LONDON

Library of Congress Cataloging-in-Publication Data
Livingston, James, 1949–
Pragmatism and the political economy of cultural revolution, 1850–1940 /
James Livingston.
p.   cm.—(Cultural studies of the United States)
Includes bibliographical references and index.
ISBN 0-8078-2157-8 (cloth : alk. paper)
1. United States—Civilization—19th century.   2. United States—Civilization—1865–
1918.   3. United States—Civilization—1918–1945.   4. United States—Economic
conditions—1865–1918.   5. United States—Economic conditions—1918–1945.
6. Pragmatism.   7. Consumer behavior—United States—History.   8. Industry—
Social aspects—United States—History.   9. Capitalism—United States—History.
I. Title.   II. Series.
E169.1.L58   1994
973—dc20   94-5736
CIP

The paper in this book meets the guidelines for permanence and durability of the
Committee on Production Guidelines for Book Longevity of the Council on Library
Resources.

98 97 96 95 94   5 4 3 2 1

For my parents

MARGARET CROSSLEY LIVINGSTON

LESLIE ARTHUR LIVINGSTON

CONTENTS

. . . .

FOREWORD

By its argument and its method, *Pragmatism and the Political Economy of Cultural Revolution, 1850–1940,* puts you to work as few books in American cultural history do. It's not that the argument is especially difficult or the method obscure. The book simply challenges us by its defiance of customary boundaries—the expected lines of demarcation among genres of history writing and among disciplines of thought and scholarship. "Interdisciplinary" gives one sort of name to Jim Livingston's way of drawing from political economy, social history, the history of thought and of formal philosophy, and literary criticism and theory in pursuit of his goal, which is to refurbish entirely our understanding of the relation between economic and cultural change in late nineteenth-century and early twentieth-century America. But "interdisciplinary" falls short of defining a usable category for this book. The term sounds too formulaic by now, too programmatic. Questions—raised by the book itself—regarding the kind of book this is refer us back to the experience of reading and emphasize the book's unexpected turns from one sort of discourse (a panorama of economic change) to another (an account of changing definitions of money) and yet another (the emergence of pragmatism as formal philosophy and political-ethical program). The reader has to *work* at discovering what more conventional books of history provide without any effort on our part: a reliable sense of where the author stands; in what "fields" his or her feet are planted; what the book is paraphrasably about. This unusually strenuous work of reading tells much of what Livingston's book is all about.

Jim Livingston practices here what can best be called a version of philosophical history. A particular philosophy, pragmatism, informs a large part of the book, explaining how William James and John Dewey engaged in dialogue with thinkers like Hegel and Kant and Schelling and Fichte. But the book's mode is not that of the history of thought as such. Nor is it a work of philosophy in itself. It is clearly, unmistakably, history, but history understood as an interpretive and critical account of meanings. It is philosophical history by virtue of its possessing both an argument about thought, the

xi

ties between thinking and living, and a theoretical method, the method of dialectic. The book offers to teach readers not just how to think anew about the monumental structural changes in the relation between thought and life in the new society that corporate capitalism had produced by early in this century, but how to think contextually, historically, about the relation between social change and human possibility. It offers to teach us how to think about the way things go together in the process of human and social development.

The book's originality takes measure of its ambition to revise some fundamental premises about the "new America," especially about the possibilities for personal growth and social transformation that accompany a modernity more typically described by critics and historians as grimly repressive and limiting of freedom. At the core of the book is an argument that takes a historical commonplace, which holds that between 1850 and 1940 the United States underwent a revolutionary change from proprietary to corporate capitalism, and transvalues the usual lament this change evokes among intellectuals. Against the conventional wisdom, Livingston argues that this transition enlarged rather than diminished the realm of human freedom. He argues that corporate capitalism entails the social death of the older capitalist order and that it does so by shrinking the realm of necessity in personal life, the realm governed by work, wage labor, and fixed class identities. Expressed like this, the point seems paradoxical in the extreme, for has not corporatism seemed the antithesis of freedom, the undoing of the older republican notion of a nation of self-governing, virtuous citizens? Livingston invites such a response, just as he invites controversy. Paradox runs through the book, a key figure and example of Livingston's dialectical method. Corporate capitalism, so the argument goes, overturns older categories of work, money, and personhood and produces an abundance of time free of labor (as important to the argument as the production of consumable goods), thereby opening the prospect of life lived outside and beyond the strictures and imperatives of the marketplace. The new forms of capital wrought by the corporation produce, in short, the material and social conditions for what Livingston (citing J. G. A. Pocock) calls "the ethos of historicist socialism." Livingston casts his book as a provocation toward that goal, the realization of the "socialist" potential within corporate capitalism. It is an argument, then, about transition, about the signs of fundamental change that Livingston detects, with the help of William James, John Dewey, and Theodore Dreiser, in the shifting winds of the turn-of-the-century era.

The book does not shy away from controversy, and it frequently adopts a polemical tone. Although Livingston implies that among the older categories, shaken by change so deep and fundamental it passes unnoticed by many, are the designations of right and left, his argument proceeds from the left. A summary account may make it appear that he wants to celebrate the corporate order, or at least exonerate it from the crimes against freedom with which it has been charged. Hardly. Livingston holds, in a dialectical perspective familiar to readers of Karl Marx, that corporatism gives birth to capacities and possibilities that will be its undoing, and that intellectuals might better serve the interests of the future by focusing on these—by helping society identify opportunities for new growth and responsible change. The "antimodernist irony" by which intellectuals (Lewis Mumford is a major example here) have defined their stance toward the present Livingston deplores as romantic evasion. Respectful of the idea of freedom the ironists cherish and protect, he mistrusts the practical effects of a rhetoric of lament.

Provocative, polemical, scolding, prophetic, Livingston's book proposes a brilliant new interpretation of the origins and character of modernity in the United States. *Sui generis*, as are many significant works of scholarship, it confronts a monumental theme and rises to the occasion with great erudition and much aplomb. However you take to the details of its argument, the book sweeps you up in its stunning analyses and surprising tangents. No small part of its challenge to the reader is the role in it of ethical questions such as what responsibility shares with freedom, the nature of choice, and the social grounds of personhood. An integrated work of criticism and history, *Pragmatism and the Political Economy of Cultural Revolution* raises a host of issues in the process of teaching its lessons, not least of which is its own example of cultural studies as history with an eye on the future.

Alan Trachtenberg

· ·

When I began thinking about how to write this book, my goal was to start a conversation between fields that stopped talking to each other around twenty years ago, when the "new economic history" and the "new social history" partitioned the discipline and encouraged new settlements in their respective territories. I wanted to show that each field required the other to complete its arguments about what is meaningful and significant in the historical record; for example, I wanted to show that consumer culture becomes intelligible only when we study it in terms of economic as well as social history. But I found that to keep this conversation going, I had to write as if the cultural moments and intellectual innovations that interested me (consumer culture, marginalist economics, pragmatism, and literary naturalism) were constituent elements in the transition from proprietary to corporate capitalism. In other words, I had to write as if economic change were one dimension of a larger social-cultural transformation or intellectual revolution; to put it in a way that William James would appreciate, I had to write as if thoughts were things, and vice versa. The study of pragmatism accordingly became something more than a chapter or case study in this book, and began to function as the regulative principle—the method and the sensibility—of my inquiry.

James and Dewey, I realized, had treated the emergence of "the trusts" and their correlate in "pacific cosmopolitan industrialism" as the warrant for intellectual innovation. So I asked, can we also treat these events, which we now summarize by reference to the rise of corporate capitalism, as something other than evidence of deviation or devolution from a more democratic past? If so, can we treat the transition from proprietary to corporate capitalism as an open question—as a transition that is still subject to our theories and practices, still revealing its consequences in the form of political possibilities?

Well, of course we can. But in doing so, we violate the narrative protocol now enforced by the "new social history" and its disciplinary armature, through which the rise of corporate capitalism appears as tragedy, as a betrayal of the "democratic promise" specific to subaltern social movements (especially but not only populism). There is no way to calculate the price we pay for our violations of that narrative protocol; even so, we can be sure that the valorization of subaltern studies has increased the professional costs, and the political risks, of investing our intellectual resources in narratives not sanctioned by social history. In this sense, social history has finally become a "barrier to entry" in the marketplace of ideas where historians circulate their stories. It would be an insignificant barrier if pragmatism itself did not originate as a narrative of the transition from proprietary to corporate capitalism. But it so happens that in the narrative form of pragmatism, the decline of proprietary capitalism loses its pathos, and the triumph of corporate capitalism appears as the first act of an unfinished comedy, not the residue of tragedy. To tell the story of this transition from the standpoint afforded by pragmatism is, then, to depart from the standpoint of the "new social history."

That is what I have tried to do in what follows: to tell a familiar story from the standpoint afforded by pragmatism. I do not ignore the empirical content of social history and its cognates; to do so would be to announce that what follows is idiocy, not apostasy. But I do take issue with the narrative form of social history—I do question the moral of the story now told about the transition from proprietary to corporate capitalism. If my story sounds unfamiliar, that is why.

In Part 1, "The Political Economy of Consumer Culture, 1850–1940," I begin by reconstructing Karl Marx's two-sector model of accumulation, through which he showed how industrialization entailed a relative restriction of the consumer goods sector and an absolute expansion of the capital goods sector. The point of this exercise in chapter 1 is neither to invoke the authority of Marx nor to rehabilitate the labor theory of value, but to see what we can learn about consumer goods as dimensions of economic growth and cultural development. I claim that Marx's two-sector model has long since entered the mainstream of economic theory; that it can be used to periodize the relation between consumption and investment because it is, among other things, a way of grasping economic events as effects of social movements and political conflicts; and, most significant, that the circulation of commodities in the nineteenth century is not the equivalent of twentieth-century consumer culture. I have banished the technical details and difficulties, so that readers who want to skip over chapter 1 will feel guilty.

Guilty or not, in chapter 2 they will find an application of the two-sector model to the economic history and theory of the nineteenth century. I claim that the Civil War, or rather the Republican Party, did effect a revolutionary reversal between the two sectors. But I also demonstrate that the changing relation between consumption and investment in the late nineteenth century was a contingent product of class struggle which became a central issue in American political discourse, and that, for all its odd abstractions—there are plenty of them—marginalist economic theory should be understood as an immediate dividend of that discourse.

In chapter 3, I begin by proposing that marginalism is the political economy of consumer culture because it treats mass consumption and corporate enterprise as equally significant and functionally related phenomena. I go on to claim that the young (and old) intellectuals of the early twentieth century believed they were witness to the advent of an "age of surplus" under the aegis of "the trusts," and refused accordingly to be bound by the categories of necessity, production, and class. I argue that they understood this new epoch as a threat to modern subjectivity, but conducted a search for alternatives to the modern subject in good faith, mainly by specifying the dimensions of the "social self" emerging from the intellectual currents and new social movements (e.g., feminism, socialism, progressivism, trade unionism) that were remaking political discourse. So I also argue that the subsequent search for such alternatives—the search we call the postmodern condition—has been blocked by the irony inscribed in the critique of consumer culture and its intellectual antecedents. I conclude Part 1 by showing, in chapter 4, that twentieth-century U.S. economic history can be read as the record of a passage beyond relations of production, thus as a reason to accredit the notion of an "age of surplus" and its corollaries.

In Part 2, "Naturalism, Pragmatism, and the Reconstruction of Subjectivity, 1890–1930," I begin, in chapter 5, by explaining the departure of social-cultural history from intellectual history in political terms, as if each camp represents a different stance toward the liberal tradition. Then I ask why, for all their differences, neither camp can account for the cultural change and intellectual innovation of the period 1890–1920. I propose to do so through a study of political-economic change as it was defined by the men and women who came of age around the turn of the century.

In chapter 6, I reintroduce the issues of subjectivity broached in chapter 3. I claim that the exemplary naturalist novel *Sister Carrie* should be read as a formal parody of realism—that is, as a romance of which we cannot ask, "given these characters, what will happen?" Carrie begins to sound like a character in a novel only at the end of this novel, I demonstrate, and her development as, or into, such a "character" is a consequence of her desires and disguises. So I ask, what can we do with this shortage of realistic characters, or, what does it mean to acknowledge that naturalism is not realism? I answer by suggesting that, when reworked by Theodore Dreiser and the other naturalists, the romance form accommodated the "social self" specified by philosophers, jurists, and social scientists in search of an alternative to the modern subject.

In chapter 7, I address Kenneth Burke's question—"Is not Whitman the poetic replica of James?"—as if it were more and less than rhetorical. In doing so, I try to suggest that the new genealogy of pragmatism, in which James appears as mere middleman between the more profound Peirce and the more democratic Dewey, needs rewriting. I also suggest that to look beyond the realm of necessity for the source of values, as James did in designating Whitman a "contemporary prophet," was to look into, not away from, the ongoing transformation of capitalism, and that this transformation is comparable to the transition from feudalism to capitalism.

In chapter 8, I show why it matters that pragmatists take the commodity form for granted, or rather take it seriously as a condition of their philosophical reconstruction. I claim that Dewey's appreciation of "speculation" is central to his intellectual experimentation, and show what it means for James to make "persistent use of financial metaphors," as Lewis Mumford claimed he did. Then I enlist the philosophers and poets of the early nineteenth century in explicating the James who speaks in *Pragmatism*. I conclude this chapter with a brief history of the moral personality in the Atlantic intellectual tradition, as a way of introducing the antinomies of modern subjectivity.

In chapter 9, I analyze the reception, or rather the repression, of pragmatism, by exploring the young intellectuals' response to James and Dewey from 1917 to 1934. Here my focus and foil is Mumford, who, by defining pragmatism as positivism or utilitarianism, could honestly hope to reinstate a romantic model of modern subjectivity. The point of this chapter is not to show how mistaken Mumford was, but to explain the sources of his opposition to pragmatism, and to suggest that insofar as his map of misreading still shapes the reception of pragmatism on the American Left, it still mutilates the historical consciousness of the American Left.

In chapter 10, I return to James via Dewey and Donald Davidson. Here I demonstrate that the essays in radical empiricism of 1904–5 compose a design for a postmodern subjectivity and that, so conceived, pragmatism represents a postrepublican "lesson of reception" through which the quarrel of the self with history can be ended. In doing so, I claim that Richard Rorty's unsatisfactory treatment of the problem of relativism derives from the privilege of radical discontinuity in his historical conspectus, and that relativism is a real problem which can be solved from within the pragmatist paradigm as James sketched it. I conclude by suggesting that only from the standpoint of his proposed departure from the tradition of Western philosophy—the departure announced in the essays on radical empiricism—does this tradition become intelligible, and remain useful, as a continuum of conflicts over the core issues of subjectivity.

In *What Is Philosophy?*, José Ortega y Gasset insisted that the poetry of the self should be treated as evidence of broader change: "But suppose that this idea of subjectivity which is the root of modernity should be superseded, suppose it should be invalidated in whole or in part by another idea, deeper and firmer. This would mean that a new climate, a new era, was beginning." I treat these remarks as working hypotheses in what follows. I claim that the idea of modern subjectivity was superseded by the forms of selfhood pragmatism authorized; that pragmatism functions as a narrative of the transition from proprietary to corporate capitalism—a "frame of acceptance," as Kenneth Burke would say—through which new shapes of solidarity and new species of the moral personality became recognizable; and that consumer culture resides in the same transition. In sum, I claim that the new climate, the new era which we have learned to call postmodern, and which we may yet learn to call postcapitalist, was beginning in the first decade of the twentieth century, when the "trust question" became our transition question.

ACKNOWLEDGMENTS

. . . .

This is not the book I set out to write. For that I am grateful to so many people that I am almost embarrassed to mention everyone who has tried to change my mind. My principal debts are to the people who had to live with this book when it was still a "project"—when they knew I wasn't making sense, but listened anyway. They gave me a kind of "talking cure." They are Patricia A. Rossi, my wife; Vincent J. Livingston and Julia Rossi Livingston, our children; Andrew J. Livingston, my brother; Leland Meredith Livingston, my sister-in-law; and three old friends, Mike Fennell, Raymond J. Michalowski, and Keith Haynes.

Colleagues from UNC-Charlotte, where I used to teach, have remained helpful critics in absentia. Steven Usselman is the youngest but the most demanding of them—he functions as my ideal reader from the "hard side" of our discipline. Robert Rieke, Julia Blackwelder, and Lyman Johnson have always insisted that we should loosen up and have more fun; they will be glad to know that in Part 2, I have tried.

I have written or rewritten all the chapters in this book since arriving at Rutgers in 1988. Several colleagues in the Department of History— Paul Clemens, William Connell, Gerald Grob, Traian Stoianovich, Donald Kelley, and Philip Pauly—have given me helpful comments on chapters I have shared with them. Two other colleagues, Thomas P. Slaughter and T. J. Jackson Lears, have decided to treat these chapters as contributions to our unfinished conversation on the future of American politics and culture. They are not persuaded by what I have to say; but they want to keep talking. They have taught me a great deal about the value of intellectual work and collegial exchange; each in his own way, they have also taught me how to rebuild our bridges and make our ideas clear. So, too, have the graduate students in history at Rutgers. The arguments of Part 2 started out as questions for discussion in a reading seminar I taught in the spring of 1990. Since then, conversations with Richard Moser, Eliza Reilly, Van Gosse, Randy Stearns, Trudi Abel, Joe Broderick, Regina Gramer, David Engerman, Arlene Kriv, Robert Mensel, Andrea Volpe, Joseph P. Moore III, J. Allen Douglas, and

Andrew Schroeder have been especially important in shaping my approach. I am particularly grateful to Eliza Reilly for long-distance discussions that revealed the limits and the possibilities of the arguments that follow.

Colleagues and friends from the Department of English at Rutgers have been quite generous as well. Richard Poirier gave me a close reading of the chapters on pragmatism which encouraged me to believe that they were worth revising in light of his searching questions and criticisms. I have not always agreed with what he writes about Emerson and James; but I have learned more from him than from anyone else who has written on the intellectual tradition we call pragmatism. Marc Manganaro and Alec Marsh gave me very different readings of the same chapters, but they, too, encouraged me to revise, often by sharing their ideas about modernist poetry with me. All along, Bruce Robbins has made me think about my purpose in writing, mainly by providing an unpretentious example of intellectual integrity and political commitment, but also by remaining skeptical about my most basic assumptions. I am deeply indebted to him and to our mutual friend John McClure for the many conversations in which my arguments with and about the American Left took shape.

The reading and writing that went into the book were made possible by two fellowships, one from the National Museum of American History, where my sponsor was Gary Kulik, the other from Rutgers University. My thanks to these institutions for making resources available when I needed them most. The reading and writing that went into Part 1 were made necessary by Victoria de Grazia, who asked me in 1989 to present a paper at a conference she was organizing on consumer cultures; three years later, as Director of the Rutgers Center for Historical Analysis, she made me finish what I had started. I hope these chapters reflect her uncanny ability to get stimulating results from unlikely sources.

Outside agitators have also had a hand in this book. For strong readings of chapters from Part 2, my thanks to Patricia A. Rossi, L. Moody Simms, Jr., Barbara Sicherman, Michael T. Gilmore, Michelle Bogart, Robert Sklar, Ann Fabian, Philip Scranton, Edward Hartman, and Martin J. Sklar. For equally strong readings of chapters from Part 1, my thanks to Steve Rosswurm, Keith Haynes, William Burr, Leon Fink, Gerald Berk; to the members of the Triangle Economic History Workshop convened in April 1990, especially Richard Sylla, Robert Gallman, Michael Bernstein, and Robert Korstad; and to my colleagues at the Rutgers Center for Historical Analysis, especially Leonardo Paggi, Ellen Furlough, and Diane Neumeier, who helped me to clarify the argument of chapter 3.

Since 1972, I have tried to live up to the standards of intellectual discipline and honesty that Martin J. Sklar and Carl P. Parrini set for students at Northern Illinois University. But I have learned to treat the education they provided as a gift, as a debt I cannot repay except by trying to follow their example. Since 1980, Harold D. Woodman and Stanley N. Katz have taken an active interest in my work and career. It is safe to say, in fact, that without their timely efforts, I would not have a career in academe. At long last, I can thank them properly by saying they made this second book possible. Alan Trachtenberg made it probable by signing it for his series, "Cultural Studies of the United States," and leading me to believe that he fully expected a completed manuscript. My thanks to him for his scholarship, his advice, his patience, and his sense of humor. Barbara Hanrahan, the editor-in-chief of UNC Press, reshaped and improved the manuscript at an early stage of its development; Pamela Upton expertly guided the manuscript through the production process; and D. Teddy Diggs patiently repaired my prose. They have made working with UNC Press a pleasure.

For good advice about (and permission to quote from) the collections in their care, my thanks to Leslie Morris of Harvard's Houghton Library and to Nancy Shawcross of the Van Pelt Library at the University of Pennsylvania. And for providing images from the Lewis Mumford collection at Monmouth College, my thanks to Vincent di Mattio.

Being a parent teaches you that you live forward but understand backward, as Kierkegaard claimed. You have to see the world from the standpoint of your children, but you can't become a child. From that weird perspective, you begin to see your own parents in new ways. At any rate that is what has happened to me. I now see that my parents gave me a love of words, ideas, and arguments. So I give them back a book that came to me as a gift—a book that got written after my son asked me what would happen if I did *not* write it, and I had to say, "Well, nothing, I guess."

PART 1

. . . .

THE POLITICAL ECONOMY

OF CONSUMER CULTURE,

1850–1940

But to the degree that large industry develops, the creation of real wealth comes to depend less on labour time and on the amount of labour employed than on the power of the agencies set in motion during labour time, whose "powerful effectiveness" is itself all out of proportion to the direct labour time spent on their production, but depends rather on the general state of science and on the progress of technology, or the application of this science to production. . . . As soon as labour in the direct form has ceased to be the great well-spring of wealth, labour-time ceases and must cease to be its measure, and hence exchange value of use value.—Karl Marx, 1858

Under modern conditions of production, no measurable relation can be found between work contributed and goods consumed. . . . A whole moral fabric is thus rent and torn, with the most alarming and far-reaching consequences.—Stuart Chase, 1934

Meanwhile we have lost our former proprietor and must go back to find him.
—Adolf A. Berle, Jr., 1958

CHAPTER 1

. . . .

MAKING USE OF MARX

Marx's Model and Its Echoes

In a famous essay of 1930, J. M. Keynes chided his Anglo-American audience for its obsession with the "economic problem," which he defined as the cultural corollaries of the "struggle for subsistence." He was afraid that the great slump would reinstate the social significance of that struggle, refurbish the reputation of economists, and so rehabilitate the "pseudo-moral principles" that had promoted the accumulation of capital. He concluded with this admonition: "But, chiefly, do not let us overestimate the importance of the economic problem, or sacrifice to its supposed necessities other matters of greater and more permanent significance."

The audience for this book is composed, I would guess, of those who share Keynes's fear of reiterated sacrifice to the "supposed necessities" of economic growth and who tend, therefore, to designate economists not as he had hoped—"as humble, competent people, on a level with dentists"—but as my friend Alec Marsh does, as the "court poets" of modern capitalism. Why, then, must we begin by attending the court society in which economists still celebrate the rule of dead matter and blind "market forces"?[1]

As I see it, we do not have much of a choice. If we do not read and interpret the deadly poetry of political economy, we cannot make sense of American culture; for Americans have typically derived political meanings and moral significance from the distribution of property and the production of value through work. I do not mean that Americans have agreed on how to do so, or on what the results should be. Instead I mean that until the mid-twentieth century, most Americans found the condition of salvation as well as self-determination under the sign of necessary or productive labor. To understand the culture they created is to understand how and why they could derive so much from what we would define as economic activities.

Perhaps it is more to the point to say that we cannot appreciate the intellectual innovations known as pragmatism and literary naturalism unless we attend to the cultural meaning and significance of economic activities— and vice versa. James and Dewey and Dreiser never tried to rise above the realm of necessity in the name of higher truths; they never treated the commodity form as the enemy of the spirit or, alternatively, as the solvent of things in themselves. Instead they tried to discover durable truths in and through what seem to be the most transient market phenomena. In this sense, they were responding to Emerson's complaint of 1842: "We have yet had no genius in America, with tyrannous eye, which knew the value of our incomparable materials, and saw, in the barbarism and materialism of the times, another carnival of the same gods whose picture he so much admires in Homer; then in the Middle Age; then in Calvinism."[2]

Like Whitman, the first writer to fit Emerson's specification of genius, James and Dewey and Dreiser did see this carnival in the barbarism and materialism of their times. They admired the "credit economy" of the late nineteenth century for its capacity to increase the stock of those fundamental truths that are contingent on the shape of the future. They also grasped the "trust movement" as the source of new truths about genuine selfhood. In other words, they treated the effects of nineteenth-century economic development as the causes of intellectual revolution—as a common fund of cultural capital from which they drew in speculating on the future of subjectivity. To understand their achievement is, then, to try on Emerson's tyrannous eye, to see what we can learn from the barbarism and materialism of the late nineteenth and early twentieth centuries.

That is what I have tried to do in part 1 of this book. But I do not want to claim that part 1 is a reinterpretation of U.S. economic history as such; for it is a contribution to the current debates on the periodization of consumer culture rather than a survey of economic growth and development from the mid-nineteenth century to the mid-twentieth. In short, it is more cultural than economic history. One of my principal purposes in restricting the scope of my inquiry is to demonstrate that the antagonism between saving or investment on the one hand and spending or consumption on the other is quite real under circumstances specific to the regime of capital accumulation. In my view, it follows that those nineteenth-century observers who designated the restriction of consumption as the necessary condition of economic growth and social progress (of "development"), or who treated the deferment of immediate gratification as the cause and effect of a specifically modern subject, were not merely inflating the commonplaces of middle-class morality in the age of anality. It also follows that if twentieth-century economists and policymakers do not understand development in the same or similar terms—for example, if they designate consumer expenditures, not investment out of saving, as the fulcrum of economic growth—then their departure from the nineteenth-century consensus requires a historical explanation that asks whether their outlook is consistent with, and perhaps ingredient in, the pattern of economic change since the nineteenth century. In effect, then, I am asking when, how, and why consumption became the fulcrum of economic growth, in theory and practice.

My procedure at the outset is to outline a model of accumulation drawn from the work of Marx and his latter-day interpreters, including "left Keynesians" such as Michal Kalecki and Anatol Murad but relying more immediately on Martin Sklar, Sydney Coontz, and Michio Morishima.[3] The model is, however, less eclectic than this odd list of theorists might suggest; for, as we shall see, modern theories of growth begin with the rediscovery (or reinvention) of Marx's two-sector reproduction schemes. Lineages and legacies aside, I adopt a Marxian model of accumulation for three reasons. First, it reveals the tension between saving and spending without abstracting from the social relations in which goods production and income distribution are embedded; that is, it allows us to examine economic phenomena without losing sight of the larger social or cultural context in which spending and saving are valorized. In this sense, the model produces more interesting results and significant facts than a theory of capitalist growth which is predicated on the notion of "concentration." For a model of accumulation acknowledges such concentration but does not elevate it to a regulative principle of analysis, and thereby does not entail a periodization of capitalism which is dominated, willy-nilly, by the question of scale.[4]

Second, a Marxian model of accumulation produces more significant facts than a theory of growth (or of "modernization") which is obsessed with change in the distribution of resources (including human resources) between agriculture and industry—mainly because a model of accumulation distinguishes between the production of consumer goods and capital goods within industry as such.[5] It thereby acknowledges the crucial limits on consumer expenditure and choice presumably represented by faster growth in the labor force and output of the capital goods industries. As W. Arthur Lewis points out: "At any level of income, people can consume only the quantity of consumer goods which exists. Since their incomes derive from producing consumer goods and investment [i.e., capital] goods, and since they can buy only the consumer goods, it follows that they must save a part of their income equal to the value of the investment goods which have been produced. . . . What they are thus forced to save may not, however, correspond to what they would like to save at that level of income."[6] For the same reason, a Marxian model produces more interesting results than a theory of growth which, because it makes no distinction between consumer and investment demand—and indeed designates change in consumer preferences as the cause of growth—simply ignores the difference between consumption and investment which not only characterizes modern industrial development but, in the form of a theoretical problem (what is the source and function of profit?), shapes the discipline of economics from the mid-nineteenth to the late twentieth century.[7]

Third, a Marxian model of accumulation has broader scope and utility than general equilibrium models that do not treat business cycles or economic crises as inevitable episodes in the course of growth under capitalism. For the point of the model of accumulation is precisely to relate secular and cyclical phenomena, to show how balanced growth is possible but not necessary; thus it does not force us to abandon the search for "covering laws" even while it allows us to acknowledge the fundamental contingency of capitalist accumulation.[8]

Marx developed his model of accumulation at two levels of abstraction, in volumes 1 and 2 of *Capital*. In the first volume, he establishes the indispensability of the "system of constants" available through the theory of value (part 1); sketches the historical stages or conditions—primitive accumulation, Manufacture, Modern Industry—that accompany and enforce capitalist growth (parts 3–5, 8); and introduces the "general law of accumulation" as both cause and effect of capitalist growth (part 7). In the second volume, the periodization of volume 1 is assumed; hence the analysis proceeds according to a sectoral disaggregation by "value composition" and economic function which is consistent with the previous statement and background of the general law of accumulation.[9]

Now the law of accumulation as Marx stated it was "change in the technical composition of capital by which the variable constituent becomes always smaller and smaller as compared with the constant" (1:685). By "the technical composition of capital," he meant the technologically determined relation between a given mass of means of production and the labor force necessary to operate it. The law of accumulation thus posits a relatively faster growth of the mass of means of production vis-à-vis the number of employees (or work hours) required to mobilize it for purposes of commodity production. At this level, the law is the necessary corollary of growth in labor productivity. "Whether condition or consequence, the growing extent of the means of production, as compared with the labour-power incorporated with them, is an expression of the growing productiveness of labour. The increase of the latter appears, therefore, in the diminution of the mass of labour in proportion to the mass of means of production moved by it, or in the diminution of the subjective factor of the labour process as compared with the objective factor" (1:682).

There is, according to Marx, a "strict correlation" between the technical composition and the value composition of capital—by the latter he meant the relation between the exchange value of past labor-time embodied in existing means of production ("constant capital") and the exchange value of current labor-time embodied in wage goods available for consumption by the employed labor force ("variable capital"). This strict correlation he termed the "organic composition of capital." So the law of accumulation also holds that the value relation between past and present labor-time will be increasingly skewed toward the former, that the value of means of production and intermediate goods (such as raw materials) will increase faster than the value of those commodities which compose the wage bill. In short, accumulation means the growth of "constant capital" both absolutely and relatively to "variable capital," whether accumulation itself is conceived in terms of use value (the technical composition) or exchange value (the value composition). The linkage between these forms of value is the labor process, or rather the productivity of labor as it is enforced and increased by the general law of accumulation. For growth in the productivity of labor implies the reduction in the exchange value (though not the use value) of wage goods, because a smaller amount of labor-time is necessary to produce a given quantity of wage goods; this in turn implies the availability of relatively more labor-time for purposes of accumulation, not consumption, that is, for production and reproduction of means of production which cannot be consumed as wage goods.

Before we turn to the formalization of the model in volume 2 of *Capital*, we should note two implications of the general law of accumulation and then, in the spirit of Marx's own inquiry, ask whether it is merely an article of faith that we might admire but also ignore. First, at the level of the firm, the rise in the organic composition of capital implies the displacement of labor, unless the firm's addition of plant or equipment to its existing capital stock requires an increase in the number of employees paid at prevailing wages (or in the number of hours worked by the existing labor force)—unless, that is, the expected increase in gross output which originally induced investment in additional plant and equipment is large enough to warrant additions to the payroll. But at the level of the economy as a whole, the rise in the organic composition of capital covered by the law of accumulation implies an increase in the demand for labor or an increase in employment as such. For as machines replace the skills and exertions of men or women in the central shops and the factories, the labor force producing those machines and their various inputs (raw materials, etc.) will necessarily grow. Here is how Marx explained it in *Theories of Surplus Value*: "As the constant capital grows, so also does the proportionate quantity of the total labour force which is engaged in its reproduction. . . . While for the individual capital the fall in the variable part of the capital as compared with the constant part takes the form of a reduction in the capital expended in wages, for the total capital—in its reproduction—this necessarily takes the form that a relatively greater part of the total labour force employed is engaged in the reproduction of means of production than is engaged in the production of products themselves" (1:219).

Second, as the passage just cited would suggest, the general law of accumulation implies, or rather entails, the "priority of Department I"—the priority, that is, of the capital goods sector in the growth pattern of capitalism. "That which distinguishes in this case capitalist society," as Marx announced in defending his reproduction schemes, is simply that it "employs more of its available annual labor in the production of means of production (and thus of constant capital) which are not convertible into revenue in the form of wages or surplus-value, but can serve only as capital" (2:509–10). The rise in the organic composition of capital means, in other words, that the rates of labor force growth and output in the capital goods sector will exceed those in the consumer goods sector (Department II), with all that implies for the distribution of income between profits and wages or investment and consumption. This asymmetry in the growth rates of Departments I and II ultimately makes the expansion of Department II the derivative of expansion in Department I. At this stage of development, the source of increasing demand for labor in Department II—the source of expanded operation of means of production in the consumer goods sector—becomes the increasing demand for wage goods represented by the more rapid growth of the labor force in Department I, that is, it becomes expanded production of means of production.

But the "priority of Department I" should not be exaggerated. The stage at which the expansion of Department II becomes a function of expansion of Department I has all the characteristics of industrialization as Walt Rostow, A. O. Hirschman, Lewis, and others have defined it, and of what Marx himself called the advent of "Modern Industry" (1:368–466).[10] Yet Marx did not treat accumulation and Modern Industry as interchangeable concepts or moments; instead he claimed that his general law covered three different (but overlapping) forms of accumulation. From this standpoint, the rise in the organic composition of capital presupposes a faster growth rate in Department I than in II, but does not stipulate that the relation between them which is observable under the regime of Modern Industry necessarily holds under all other forms or stages of accumulation.

We might then suppose that there is a stage before (or after) Modern Industry, one in which the rise in the organic composition of capital takes place as a consequence of a boom in the consumer goods sector, through which increased demand for and output of means of production, and a recognizable division of labor between Departments I and II, are created or enforced by the expansion of Department II. At this stage, the expansion of Department I would be the derivative of expansion in Department II—production would still presuppose a certain level of consumption—but accumulation would nevertheless be under way.[11] In any event, accumulation so conceived requires the creation of "surplus labor," or a labor force that is not needed to produce for purposes of immediate consumption. That division of labor presupposes the growth of the labor force as such: "Accumulation is, therefore, increase of the proletariat," as Marx suggested in analyzing the reproduction of the social relation between capital and labor (1:673). The corresponding growth of consumer demand—the new working class must buy the right not to die of starvation or exposure—presumably stimulates concentration, innovation, and greater investment in consumer goods industries; the result is not only larger output but also increased labor productivity in these industries. As productivity here continues to increase, the quantity of consumer goods required to sustain the total labor force can be produced by a decreasing proportion of that labor force, regardless of the scale of consumer demand; and so an increasing proportion of total labor force growth can be diverted from production for immediate consumption, thus devoted to purposes of accumulation. In this sense, the early stages of accumulation are necessarily predicated on and driven by the growth of consumer demand, that is, by the expansion of Department II.[12]

In the course of the nineteenth century—the age of industrialization—the expansion of Department II does, however, become a function of expansion in Department I, and the priority of the latter is accordingly inscribed in economic theory as well as in Victorian culture. In view of this reversal, the breathless announcements of "the birth of consumer society" in the late eighteenth or early nineteenth century sound premature at best, unless the only claim at issue in such announcements is that, with the breakdown of a household economy and the creation of a working class that spends what it gets in wages, the commodity form must reshape every dimension of social life. Even so, we should not be surprised to find that the inversion of the original relation between Departments I and II, at least in the United

States and the United Kingdom, is the result of that sudden or rapid growth in consumer demand now deemed "the birth of consumer society," in the absence of which much larger investment in expensive capital goods, to reduce costs per unit of expanded consumer goods output—that is, to increase labor productivity—would have been irrational.[13]

We will be returning to the question of the timing of this reversal in the United States. For now, the question before us is whether we should treat Marx's general law of accumulation as anything more than an article of faith that overdetermines the formal model of reproduction, thus making it the prototype of dogmatic Marxism. To begin with, we should note that the argument of the general law was aimed at the tendency in classical political economy to equate accumulation and labor force growth—that is, to equate the value of the annual wage bill and the value of total annual output. Adam Smith, James Mill, David Ricardo, and other early theorists of capitalism did not usually treat accumulation as a matter of producing, purchasing, and maintaining means of production as well as labor power, and did not, therefore, perceive any limits on the share of national income available for purposes of consumption.[14] In short, they saw no contradiction between accumulation and consumption. Marx did. He argued that the increasing significance of "constant capital"—as both physical input and bearer of value—required the diversion of an increasing proportion of available resources to the production, purchase, and maintenance of means of production; since these resources included the income generated by past production, this diversion meant, among other things, that an increasing share of national income would be withheld from consumption. Growth enforced by the "priority of Department I" would, then, exact an opportunity cost in the form of foregone consumption, or, as Lewis would put it, in the form of forced saving equal to the value of gross investment (i.e., equal to the value of the capital goods used up and newly produced by labor plus the related costs of employing that labor). Marx's argument with classical political economy thus introduced the functional distinction between investment and consumption which animates all modern theories of economic growth (as against programs of stabilization), particularly those that emphasize the role of capital formation or rates of investment.[15] To that extent, the departure from Smith, Mill, and Ricardo announced in the general law of accumulation has become an axiom of economic theory.

Historical studies of economic growth are by and large based on this same axiom. For example, the notion that growth involves change in "factor proportions," or a rise in the ratio of capital to labor, is a commonplace of economic history (it is often cited as a cause of the increasing scale of industrial operation). So, too, is the related idea that an increase in capital-output ratios characterizes modern economic development. These ratios, which are calculated in value terms, show that in the United States, capital inputs per unit of total industrial output increased dramatically until about 1919. But this is only a way of saying that the "value composition of capital" in the United States changed precisely as predicted by Marx's law of accumulation.[16] For a rise in capital-output ratios means simply that "the industries that sell to other industries grow faster than the industries that sell to consumers," as Peter Temin puts it, or—as Albert O. Hirschman would have it—that the degree of industrial linkage and interdependence increases faster than the overall rate of economic growth, resulting in a rise in the proportion of total output "that does not go to final demand but rather to other industries."[17]

To be sure, historical studies of changes in the functional distribution of the labor force are more equivocal. Here the premises and purposes of disaggregation were largely determined by economists' engagement with the postwar foreign policy issues of modernization and political stabilization in countries susceptible to statist modes of industrialization. The difference between agricultural and industrial (or primary and tertiary) employment accordingly became the organizing principle of their compilation of occupational statistics for the nineteenth century, when the United States was itself undergoing modernization enforced by industrialization.[18] Even so, the enthusiastic reception given to Walter Hoffmann's studies of "types and stages of industrialization" in the late 1950s would suggest that many economists recognized the need to differentiate between capital goods and consumer goods industries—as Hoffmann did—in depicting the division of labor specific to capitalist growth. Hoffmann's work, which was completed in 1932 but not translated and widely disseminated until 1958, is analogous to the innovations of "the years of high theory" (1926–39) in at least two respects. First, the more pressing issues of fascism, world war, and decolonization delayed its assimilation by economists and historians until the late 1950s. Second, and more important, it was an innovation predicated on the recovery or reinvention of an unclaimed theoretical legacy. In the case of Hoffmann, as in that of J. M. Keynes, Roy Harrod, Wassily Leontief, and Kalecki—most of the "high theorists" of the interwar period—this legacy was the two-sector model of accumulation.[19]

The filial relation between the Marxian model and Leontief's input-output tableaux or Kalecki's essays on growth is quite clear because both these theorists began their careers, in the 1920s, with formal training in Marxian economics. Joan Robinson attributed Kalecki's head start on the

Keynesian revolution to this training. "Keynes could never make head or tail of Marx. . . . But starting from Marx would have saved him a lot of trouble. [R. F.] Kahn, at the 'circus' where we discussed [Keynes's] Treatise in 1931, explained the problem of saving and investment by imagining a cordon around the capital-good industries and then studying the trade between them and the consumption-good industries; he was struggling to rediscover Marx's schema. Kalecki began at that point."[20]

The relation between the Marxian model of accumulation and Harrod's "dynamic economics," which he outlined in the late 1930s and elaborated in the late 1940s and 1950s, is less obvious, notwithstanding Robinson's claim of an essential identity between Harrod's mathematics of "warranted growth" and Marx's arithmetic of extended reproduction. But Evsey Domar, who invented a mathematical model of growth which is so similar to Harrod's that economists normally refer to the Harrod-Domar model, openly acknowledged his debt to Marx and to Soviet theorizing of the 1920s. In that sense, the relation between Marx and the modern mainstream of growth theory is perhaps as direct as Robinson would have it. Shigeto Tsuru's summary of their convergence does, in any event, suggest the possibility that, in the 1950s, economists were just catching up with Marx. "In both cases, that of Marx and Harrod, the question implicitly asked is the same; namely, what are the factors which determine the proportion in which the national product is divided between consumers' goods and producers' goods as the economy advances steadily. Since the two men dealt with basically the same problem, it is not at all accidental that the correspondence between them appears to be almost perfect."[21]

Comparisons of Marx and Keynes are usually more ambiguous. Yet the latter's crucial innovation was not so much the rejection of Say's Law or the specification of effective demand as the key problem of macroeconomics— on both counts, there were plenty of precedents in neoclassical theory— as it was the disaggregation of income, and thus demand, into the functional components of investment and consumption. If a two-sector model is only implicit in this disaggregation, its subsequent articulation in Keynesian theories of growth nevertheless justifies the remark of A. K. DasGupta: "Keynes dynamized would look pretty much like Marx." For Keynes dynamized looks exactly like Kalecki or Harrod and Domar.[22]

To my knowledge, Hoffmann does not acknowledge Marx's model of accumulation as the theoretical source or rationale for his studies of the division of labor under capitalist industrialization. For that matter, neither did Keynes, Harrod, or Leontief (although the last did not have to, and has in any case written on Marx and modern economics). But the question at hand is not whether every model of growth should be judged by its possible affiliation with or conscious derivation from Marx, as if he were the one great economist from whom all theories flow; it is instead whether, in view of economic theory and history since the mid-nineteenth century, we can treat his general law of accumulation as something more than an article of faith, as something like an indispensable insight into the growth pattern peculiar to capitalism. It now seems fair to answer that Marx's general law and its implications are in fact consistent with and indeed embedded in the modern mainstream of both economic theory and economic history. This is not to say that we are all Marxists now—merely that if we want to understand economic growth since 1750, it is practically impossible, and certainly pointless, to avoid Marx's model of accumulation.

Social Origins of Economic Growth

We can finally turn to the formal version of that model secure in the knowledge that it is not simply sectarian dogma. Marx presented it in terms of value relations because he was trying to demonstrate the linkage between the volume of physical production in each department (supply) and the conditions of realization (demand) by reference to labor-time, that is, to proportionate quantities of employment. Each element in his equations accordingly functions as both cost of and demand for products. In this way, he illustrated that the costs of employing labor also constituted demand for consumer goods, or, to put it another way, that the condition of the receipt of income in the form of wages—thus of an effective claim to a share of consumer goods—was implication in the production and reproduction of value through work.[23] But the disaggregation into two departments was carried out on the assumption that each department's final output had unique material functions or use values, either as capital goods or as consumer goods. Thus Marx decomposed the value of each department into "constant capital," "variable capital," and "surplus value" (C + V + S) and proceeded to the depiction of the interdepartmental commerce that would create equilibrium.

Under the conditions of *simple* reproduction, no net additions to the capital stock are made because capitalists consume the entire surplus value accruing to them as owners of the means of production: there is no net investment—and no accumulation—because the supply of constant capital produced in Department I corresponds in value only to the constant capital used up and requiring replacement in both departments. The quantity of labor-time and the productivity of labor in Department I must then be such as to produce only the equivalent of the value of, or the cost of replacing and maintaining, the constant capital used in Department II.

Under the conditions of *expanded* reproduction, the supply of constant capital produced in Department I exceeds replacement requirements because capitalists have invested a portion of the surplus value accruing to them—that is, they have purchased supplies of raw materials and means of production (constant capital), but also of labor power (variable capital), over and above those supplies needed to replace existing plant and equipment or to maintain existing levels of output. They have incurred the costs, including the labor costs, of making net additions to the capital stock, and so have provided for net investment. The system is in balance if the quantity of labor-time and the productivity of labor in Department I are sufficient to provide for the growth of demand for constant capital from Department II.

But expanded reproduction or accumulation as such is the cause of a rise in the organic composition of capital ($C:V$)—and thus of a relative decline in the value of variable capital or a fall in the share of wages in national income.[24] The effect of expanded reproduction will then be a declining rate of growth in demand for the output of Department II and, consequently, a declining rate of growth in demand for the output of Department I. At that point, the system is caught in a "low-level equilibrium trap," or in a generalized overproduction crisis. In the long run, therefore, the sufficient condition of expanded reproduction must be something other than the growth of demand for constant capital represented by the growth of Department II. For when the system approaches its equilibrium condition, it verges on crisis.

What is that sufficient condition? We might say that it resides in the reversal of the original relation between Departments I and II. But the question then becomes, how is this reversal accomplished? To ask either question is to suggest that we need to specify the sources of disequilibrium, and to provide some account of how they are introduced and enforced over time. Now we know that in Marx's model, the crucial source of disequilibrium is investment: the system moves according to how the surplus accruing to capitalists is divided between consumption and investment, while investment itself is conceived in terms of expenditures for both means of production and labor power. We also know that economists and economic historians of radically different political propensities have converged on the idea that "self-sustaining growth" involves a "once-over savings rate change" which in turn allows "autonomous investment." In other words, they agree that the sufficient condition of expanded reproduction—of escape from a "low-level equilibrium trap"—is the shift in income shares which allows Department I to grow faster than the increase in demand from Department II would warrant. But this is only a way of saying that the reversal of the original or equilibrium relation between the two departments is, or became, the sufficient condition of expanded reproduction. Lewis describes such a reversal as follows: "All the countries which are now relatively developed have at some time in the past gone through a period of rapid acceleration, in the course of which their rate of annual net investment has moved from 5 per cent or less to 12 per cent or more. This is what we mean by an Industrial Revolution." Rostow concurs in his analysis of the stages of growth, of course, but so do neoclassical economists such as Jeffrey G. Williamson and Marxists such as Coontz. The latter, for example, proposes that capitalists' investment in Department I becomes "autonomous"—that is, it becomes independent of the growth of demand for constant capital originating in Department II—when "potential demand for producer goods is increased by the rise in the share of entrepreneurial income." [25]

But the questions that follow from this consensus are not themselves susceptible to strictly economic or quantitative analysis, as Rostow argued thirty years ago: "The rise in the rate of investment—which the economist conjures up to summarize the transition [to self-sustaining growth]—requires a radical shift in the society's effective attitude toward fundamental and applied science; toward the initiation of change in productive technique; toward the taking of risk; and toward the conditions and methods of work. One must say a change in effective attitude . . . because what is involved here is not some vague change in psychological or sociological orientation, but a change translated into working institutions and procedures." And so economists must appeal to other disciplines if they would explain these sudden or significant shifts in income shares and rates of investment as both effects of past development and causes of future growth; at that point, economic theory gives way to social or cultural history, and a theory of growth becomes a theory of "modernization" if not a philosophy of history. Certainly Moses Abramovitz admitted as much in 1952, in a survey of growth theory which, following the Keynesian lead, stressed that capital formation and investment were the key variables: "The foundation of an adequate theory of capital formation does, in fact, involve grappling with a complex sociological tangle which can hardly be unraveled with the aid of such concepts and hypotheses as economics now furnishes." [26]

Here, too, Marx's model meets the requirements of explanatory adequacy, because it presupposes a theory of capitalist society. For example, the key variable in the reproduction schemes, as in modern theories of growth, is investment. But the distribution of income between capital and labor is not given or determined by the model—as it is in the production functions of modern economics—except insofar as the model is designed to show how the rise in the organic composition of capital and the corresponding shift in income shares are made possible by exchange between the two departments. In short, the model shows what is necessary if accumulation is to proceed smoothly, not that it will proceed smoothly. For Marx, distribution was determined by the relation between income claimants construed as social classes. Thus the "rate of exploitation"—the ratio between surplus value and variable capital—would determine how large a share of the value produced by employed labor could be appropriated and invested by capitalists. But Marx insisted that this ratio, which we would now translate as the relation between labor productivity growth and real wages, was itself a social product subject to the changing contours and balance of class power.[27]

In such perspective, the distribution of value or income sufficient to sustain expanded reproduction over the long run is contingent on the production and reproduction of those social relations that validate an increasing rate of exploitation through the subjection of labor to capital. As Rostow would put it, "the rise in the rate of investment"—in other words, the reversal of the original relation between Departments I and II—is contingent on political, social, and cultural change embodied in "working institutions and procedures." In the United States, as elsewhere in the world after 1790, such change sooner or later assumed revolutionary proportions. But if political, social, and cultural phenomena sooner or later become dimensions of economic growth, the requirements of economic growth will meanwhile redefine the imaginable range of political, social, and cultural possibilities. The distribution of value or income sufficient to sustain expanded reproduction, for example, can enforce the subjection of labor to capital and thus constrain the emergence of a different set of social relations. For if "the rise in the rate of investment" signifies a shift in the balance of social power, and if opportunities are thereafter allocated according to the distribution of income, then to maintain the higher rate of investment and its corresponding claims on future incomes is to maintain the new balance of power. The diversion of resources from production for immediate consumption, in other words, is not an economic event that has certain political and cultural consequences or connotations; it is itself a political and cultural event.

In sum, the Marxian model depicts economic growth or expanded reproduction in social terms, as a social process. So conceived, growth—implicitly defined as increasing output, labor productivity, and per capita incomes—requires increasing inputs of the labor-time necessary to produce means of production in excess of replacement requirements, and to operate that increment of means of production. To put it more plainly, accumulation simply is this process through which an ever greater proportionate share of an increasing quantity of socially necessary labor-time is devoted to purposes other than production for immediate consumption.[28] At a certain point in the process, therefore, the condition of continued quantitative increase in that proportionate share becomes qualitative change in the inherited relation between production and consumption, in the absence of which a reversion to "proto-industrial" production of consumer goods within a household or family economy, not capitalist industrialization, will ensue. If effected, the maintenance of the new relation depends fundamentally on a distribution of income that increases effective demand for the output of the capital goods sector by increasing surplus value or profits vis-à-vis variable capital or wages; which is to say, yet again, that the restriction of consumption eventually becomes both condition and consequence of capital accumulation.

By this account, economic growth as enforced by capital accumulation has been anything but laborsaving. According to Marx, there is a necessary correlation between growth and accumulation, and accumulation itself is conceived as the increase of socially necessary labor-time. Now in the nineteenth century, the broad application of complex machines to goods production did in fact enlarge the meaning and scope of necessary labor by creating whole new industries that produced the machines and their intermediate or unfinished inputs; to that extent, Marx's model provides indispensable insights into capitalist industrialization. But do these correlations hold for the twentieth century? Many economists and historians have noted that since about 1910, economic growth has proceeded as a function of a decline in socially necessary labor-time (due to electrification, instrumentation, "automation," etc.), or have suggested that the apparent atrophy of net private investment in the interwar period (and after) signifies the attainment, or at least the possibility, of growth without the attributes of accumulation.[29] If they are correct, on what grounds can we say that Marx's model remains applicable to the twentieth century? Is it so narrowly focused on the production of value through necessary labor that it cannot help us grasp the very epoch in which the realm of necessity has been receding? Or does it retain a certain relevance after all?

A persuasive answer to such questions would require yet another discourse on Marx's method. A provisional but plausible defense of his relevance to the twentieth century would require only that we acknowledge his explicit anticipation of an end to accumulation (and not merely in the "revolutionary" asides that were never excised from the unfinished manuscripts). In view of his contempt for economists who treated capitalism as a transhistorical or natural social order, it would be surprising to find that he had not attempted to describe the beginnings of this end. But we have already encountered one attempt along these lines in *Capital*, where Marx notes that the growth of labor productivity appears "in the diminution of the mass of labour in proportion to the mass of means of production moved by it, or in the diminution of the subjective factor of the labour process as compared with the objective factor." If accumulation means the increase of necessary labor in every sense, he seems to claim, it also promises to extricate human labor from goods production, to reduce the "subjective factor of the labour process" to virtually nothing. These perverse possibilities are realized "to the degree that large industry develops," as Marx argued in the preliminary studies for *Capital*: "The creation of real wealth comes to depend less on labour time and on the amount of labour employed than on the power of the agencies set in motion during labour time, whose 'powerful effectiveness' is itself in turn out of all proportion to the direct labour time spent on their production, but depends rather on the general state of science and technology, or the application of this science to production." The "monstrous disproportion" between the increasing quantity of current labor-time applied to goods production and the exponentially increasing quantity of goods produced is reiterated in the "qualitative imbalance between labour, reduced to a pure abstraction, and the power of the production process it superintends." [30]

This new distance between labor and the labor process—this abstraction or impending extrication—implies two new realities that Marx treats as already manifest within modern-industrial production. First, the nature of work itself changes. "Labour no longer appears so much to be included within the production process; rather, the human being comes to relate more as watchman and regulator to the production process itself. . . . No longer does the worker insert a modified natural thing [a tool?] as middle link between the object and himself; rather, he inserts the process of nature, transformed into an industrial process, as a means between himself and inorganic nature, mastering it. He steps to the side of the production process instead of being its chief actor." Second, the class relation between labor and capital changes (and with it the larger relations of production that compose modern-industrial civil society?) insofar as "the mass of direct labour time, the quantity of labour employed" loses its role as the "determinant factor in the production of wealth"—insofar, that is, as "large industry" develops and transmutes "general social knowledge" into fixed capital, a "direct force of production." For the presupposition of the class relation between labor and capital ("the exchange of living labour for objectified labour") is the difference between necessary and surplus labor-time, the difference between the value of labor power and the value of the products of labor, the difference that accumulation enlarges over time. But when workers can "step to the side of the production process" because fixed capital—the "objective factor" in that process—has supplanted or reduced their active input, the increase of necessary forms of labor and of socially necessary labor-time has ceased. By definition, so, too, has accumulation. At any rate Marx suggests as much. "As soon as labour in the direct form has ceased to be the great well-spring of wealth, labour time ceases and must cease to be its measure, and hence exchange value [must cease to be the measure] of use value. . . . With that, production based on exchange value breaks down, and the direct, material production process is stripped of the form of penury and antithesis."[31]

Production based on exchange value has of course not broken down: penury and antithesis are still very much with us. But Marx should not be ridiculed or dismissed because he believed that the end of accumulation would signal the beginning of the end of capitalism. In this he resembles nothing so much as the "stagnationists," those peculiarly Keynesian pessimists led by Alvin Hansen, who believed that if remunerative investment opportunities would not increase because capital requirements per unit of output were not rising as they had in the nineteenth century—and indeed were falling—then capitalism could not last beyond the mid-twentieth century without fundamental reconstruction.[32] What neither Marx nor the stagnationists could imagine was a capitalist society in which surplus value had lost its investment function—in which capitalists appropriate but do not (need to) accumulate out of the surplus value accruing to them as owners of the means of production, because growth in output and labor productivity does not require net investment. But Marx did posit a decline in socially necessary labor-time as the inevitable consequence of its increase under the aegis of accumulation. So it is fair to say that he recognized the impending inversion, and indeed that his model of accumulation enabled him to recognize its significance. For the model takes as its point of departure the difference between the production of labor power and the productivity of human labor which capitalism creates and enforces. "Though the existence of surplus-labour presupposes that the productivity of labour has reached a certain level, the mere possibility of this surplus-labour . . . does not in itself make it a reality. For this to occur, the labourer must first be compelled to work in excess of the [necessary labor] time, and this compulsion is exerted by capital."[33]

The theoretical comprehension of a capitalist society in which surplus value has lost its investment function should, then, begin at the ending Marx identified with the development of "large industry." This is precisely where Martin Sklar did begin in 1969, when he argued that corporate capitalism, which emerged ca. 1890–1920 in the United States, should be understood in terms of the "disaccumulation" of capital. His abbreviated analysis of this fundamental transformation warrants our close attention because it illuminates, as no other theory has, the new relation between production and consumption which characterizes twentieth-century "mass society," which gives Keynesian economics its lease on policy, and which not incidentally animates modern consumer culture. Sklar claimed that his analysis flowed directly from Marx's theory of value. Accordingly, he defined accumulation and disaccumulation as a social relation, in terms of "the ratio between the labor-time represented by [wage earners] exercising labor-power, and the social labor-time embodied in the means of production." As we have seen, this ratio is what Marx termed the value relation between variable capital and constant capital. "The relationship is one of capital accumulation," Sklar then explained, "so long as an increased production and operation of means of production requires an increased employment of living human labor-power measured in man-hours of socially necessary labor."[34]

Disaccumulation is simply the inversion of accumulation so defined. "At the point where there is no such increased employment of labor-power in the production and operation of the means of production, that is, where the production and operation of the means of production results in expanded production of goods without the expansion of such employment of labor-power, capital accumulation has entered the process of transformation to disaccumulation. In other words, disaccumulation means that the expansion of goods-production capacity proceeds as a function of the sustained decline of required, and possible, labor-time employment in goods-production." As usual, the implications are more interesting than the mere statement of the theory. In this case, there are two implications that are especially pertinent to the question of the political economy of consumer culture. First, the passage from the phase of accumulation to the phase of disaccumulation, ca. 1910–30, "coincides with the partial and progressing extrication of human labor from the immediate goods-production process." That passage also coincides, then, with the emergence of a society in which the "directly effective determinant of general social relations" is not necessarily relations of production. Second, the onset of disaccumulation dissolves the contradiction between production and consumption which had hitherto characterized the theory and practice of capitalist industrialization: "The necessity of deferring immediate consumption as the condition of expanded production capacity falls away."[35]

Construed as a social process with economic consequences, disaccumulation means that the growth of the labor force in Department I practically ceases; all subsequent labor force growth must, then, be absorbed by Department II, the consumer goods sector, with all that suggests for the structure of demand and the distribution of income required to sustain growth. Construed as an economic phenomenon with social consequences, disaccumulation means that the functional relation between capitalist appropriation of surplus value or profit and the expansion of productive capacity is attenuated if not dissolved, because making net additions to the total capital stock and to the labor force of Department I—in a word, net investment— is no longer the necessary condition of increasing either output or labor productivity. The celebration of private investment out of profit as the critical source of growth accordingly becomes absurd; so, too, does the related claim that capitalists and private enterprise are the indispensable agents of progress.

Composition of Capital, Decomposition of Capitalism

We can now proceed on the assumption that a Marxian model of accumulation is immediately relevant to the study of the political economy of consumer culture because it allows us to specify the role of consumption in capitalist growth. To be more precise, that model warrants the following claims, which can hereafter be elaborated, modified, or abandoned in light of the available historical evidence.

1. In the initial ("proto-industrial") stage of accumulation, ca. 1790– 1850, the division of labor between the capital goods and consumer goods sectors is relatively undeveloped; demand for the output of Department I is largely derived from the growth of Department II, which is in turn a function of (a) proletarianization of agricultural populations and urban working-class formation, and (b) the commercialization of agriculture and the breakdown of a household economy, through which markets and money come to mediate exchanges of goods hitherto negotiated more directly, through forms of barter. In short, growth as such is consumer-led.

2. In the second stage of accumulation—capitalist industrialization, ca. 1840–1920—the rate and morphology of growth are determined by "autonomous investment," which is in turn contingent on a reversal of the original ("proto-industrial") relation between Departments I and II. The condition and consequence of that reversal is a new distribution of income, which increases effective demand for the output of Department I and thereby enforces the "rise in the rate of investment." So conceived, the reversal presupposes (a) the rapid growth of consumer demand in the 1830s and 1840s ("the birth of consumer society" in the United States), which justifies the greater outlay on plant and equipment summarized in the "rise in the rate of investment," and (b) political, social, and cultural change ca. 1846–70, culminating in the abdication of merchant capital— the power behind King Cotton's throne—and the Republican revolution in fiscal-economic policy ca. 1863–70.

3. In this second stage of accumulation, we can specify three separate phases of growth, each of which is characterized by a different balance of social power and a corresponding distribution of income: (a) 1846–73, the moment of the great inversion—the "rise in the rate of investment"— which makes industrial capital the source of economic strategy or policy for the United States and institutionalizes, as it were, the "priority of Department I"; (b) 1873–97, the "Great Stalemate," during which phase a relative stagnation in the capital goods sector is created and enforced by the divergence of labor productivity and real wages in the nonfarm sector, as a result of which the distribution of income between profits and wages necessary to sustain "autonomous investment" cannot be realized; the corresponding growth of labor's share of national income vis-à-vis capital is reflected not only in a boom in the consumer goods sector—the movement toward mass marketing through integrated retail firms is specific to the 1880s—but also in the increasing consternation of capitalists with respect to the distribution of income as such; (c) 1897–1919, the triumph of corporate-industrial capital, through which the distribution of income specific to (a) above is reinstated and the "priority of Department I" is reinscribed in the pattern of economic growth.

4. In the third stage of accumulation—capital disaccumulation, ca. 1910– 70—the rate and morphology of growth come increasingly to be determined by consumer expenditures, as net investment necessarily atrophies and labor force growth is concentrated almost exclusively in the consumer goods sector (and of course in its adjunct, the so-called services). Here, too, we can specify separate phases in the decomposition of capital(ism): (a) 1919–29, the first period in which the tendencies characteristic of disaccumulation

were manifested (and also perceived), but in which the distribution of income was increasingly skewed toward capital, resulting inevitably in the crash of 1929 and the Great Depression—the first business cycle whose contours were defined and complicated by the fact that recovery (ca. 1933–37) did not require rising rates of investment; the key to the buoyancy of the 1920s, in such perspective, was the constraint on the underlying shift to profits represented by the rapid growth of a salaried, white-collar middle class, whose income was in effect a deduction from surplus value and thus a component of capitalist consumption; (b) 1929–41, the Great Depression proper, which, precisely because it comprised such an enormous social-political crisis, could accommodate the fundamental shift of income shares—the promotion of mass consumption—demanded by growth under disaccumulation; if it did not threaten the sanctity of private investment as the arbiter of growth, this shift did require that the receipt of wage income be detached from the capital-labor relation and the production of value through work ("detached," e.g., by welfare, public works, social security, etc.); (c) 1941–54, the interregnum of war economy and world reconstruction, through which the terms of debate on the role of private investment in economic growth were recast by confrontation with the statist alternative at home and abroad, not by reconsideration of investment as such, and in which consumption was deferred according to politico-military purposes, not the perceived requirements of economic growth; and (d) 1954–73, recapitulation of the themes of the 1920s, except that mass consumption now becomes, and is widely defined as, the fulcrum of economic growth, and the question of investment becomes increasingly problematic in both theory and practice.

Even when rendered in such schematic fashion, these claims do not sound controversial. But that is one of their virtues. For I want to suggest that there is a way to reconcile the older periodization of consumer culture, which held that it emerged in the twentieth century, and the newer periodization, which holds that it is synonymous with the generalization of the commodity form or the creation of a market in labor. I want to suggest, in other words, that if we are to appreciate consumer culture, we must understand the development of capitalism. We must then understand that markets and commodities are not specific to capitalism, and presumably will not disappear even when it becomes impossible to distinguish between the development of postindustrial society and the decomposition of capitalism.

CHAPTER 2

. . . .

CONSUMER GOODS AND

CONTINENTAL INDUSTRIALIZATION,

1850–1900

Households into Markets

Evsey Domar has observed that a society's propensity to consume may be low, and its propensity to save accordingly high, and yet its rate of investment might be comparatively low because its capital goods sector is relatively backward. "A closed economy without well-developed metal, machinery, and subsidiary industries (the complex of the so-called heavy industries) is unable to produce a sizable quantity of capital goods and thus to invest a high fraction of its income, however high its potential saving propensity may be."[1] Domar made this observation with reference to the Soviet planning debates of the 1920s, but it can serve as an apt characterization of the American economy before 1850. It was only toward the middle of the century that the potential savings of the United States could be channeled into industries producing capital goods, and only during and after the Civil War that public policy and private-sector financial institutions validated this diversion of resources away from the established consumer goods industries of the Northeast.

But the capital goods industries that came of age at midcentury were themselves spawned by the rapid development of established consumer goods industries; and this development was the effect of fundamental demographic and social changes summarized by historians under the heading of the breakdown of the household or family economy. The turning point in the process came between 1846 and 1857, when the mechanization of prairie farming, the sudden increase of immigration, the completion of the east-west trunk lines, and the collapse of the outwork system in New England combined to change the composition as well as the level of final demand, and to justify a scale of investment which, in turn, fostered the growth of industries geared strictly to the production of capital goods. If they were not all situated in the area bounded by Pittsburgh and Chicago, these new industries were peculiarly dependent on the continued expansion of mechanized prairie farming and, in effect, on the development of a continental market for their output. Moreover, they were subject, as the established (and once-protected) consumer goods industries were not, to the price competition of British manufacturers; and yet they had virtually no access to the financial resources long available (since 1808) to the northeastern consumer goods industries.[2]

So the chances were slim that these new capital goods industries would continue to develop without a radical reorientation of federal economic policy. In this sense, the political choices made in the late 1850s and the 1860s determined the pace and contours of American economic growth in the late nineteenth century. When economists announce that "America had successfully overcome the problem of industrialization by 1860"—that is, before a Republican-controlled Congress created a unitary labor-property system, a new financial apparatus, and a protected continental market through nonmilitary legislation—we should therefore be skeptical, especially in view of their reverence for the economies of scale made possible by large markets. When historians claim that the Civil War somehow "retarded" industrialization, or that the events of the 1860s do not matter much in any case, we should be equally skeptical.[3] For it was not until the 1860s that the long-standing federal policy of promoting a free-trade, Atlantic economy—a policy that presupposed the extension of slave labor and King Cotton—was finally replaced by the alternative program of the radical, trans-Allegheny wing of the Republican Party, which promoted continental, not metropolitan, industrialization, and afforded the "heavy industries" the kind of protection once reserved for textiles. The turning point of 1846–57 can be defined as such, then, because the new industrial possibilities impending, but only impending, in this moment were realized by the revolutionary politics that followed.

Let us examine this moment more closely, to see how these new industrial possibilities became political choices. The transformation in question was not a linear process. The breakdown of the household economy, for example, was both cause and effect of the boom in the consumer goods industries which dominated antebellum development, and which meanwhile permitted the emergence of capital goods industries. It was a cause insofar as the appropriation of goods necessary to the reproduction of the household increasingly required money or store credit—that is, the mediation of the merchant—and represented demand for the output of distant producers. It was an effect insofar as the lower unit costs of new and highly capitalized farms that were immediately implicated in interregional markets placed the older farms of the Northeast at the margin of going concerns, and thus forced them to find new sources of income, often in the labor market. For my purposes, however, what is most interesting about the recent debates on the household economy is the agreement on its chronological scope: according to its chroniclers, its breakdown (in the North) was specific to the late 1830s and early 1840s. This suggests that the first crisis of the emerging market economy (the depression of 1837–44) coincided with the new contours of internal migration, which quickly changed the patterns of both supply and demand for the nation as a whole.[4]

Until the late 1830s, the farm economy of the Northwest was largely a subsistence economy, a close replica of what the emigrants had left behind in the border states. The farms created in Ohio, Indiana, and Illinois in the 1820s were cleared on relatively steep grades from forestland. Their proprietors marketed a surplus of corn and hogs (bacon, ham, pork) downriver only if household requirements had already been met. That surplus did grow quite rapidly in the 1820s, at a rate even faster than the remarkable rate of population growth in the Northwest. But these subsistence farmers did not represent comparable growth in demand for manufactured goods from the Northeast. The costs of creating their farms out of the forested land of the Ohio River valley were not such as to implicate them immediately in debt and therefore in producing cash crops for sale in distant markets (the greater labor costs of clearing forestland did not have to be recouped quickly in money because they were incurred in the form of the household's labor, or through exchange in kind with other households, and the timber then served as materials for a dwelling). And they had no need for expensive machinery to plow the land or harvest the crop, since they were not raising small grains on flat land and large farms, but corn and hogs on small farms in the hills. In short, they produced limited surpluses for the limited markets of the South; the commodities they appropriated by means of their money incomes were accordingly a small fraction of the goods they needed and used.[5]

Things changed with the development of prairie farming in the Northwest states after 1840, but more particularly with the mechanization of such farming in the late 1840s and the 1850s. The families that created the new farms came from or through areas already in transition to a market economy—they were culturally prepared to act on the greater psychological costs of producing for the market, and thus to accept the higher monetary costs of farm making on the prairie. Between the mid-1830s and the early 1850s, the costs of farm making as such doubled or tripled, due mainly to higher prices for land (the speculators had arrived early) but also to the requirements of fencing, housing, and well-digging on land without trees or rivers. The corresponding burden of debt created irresistible incentives for specialized, mechanized cash crop production—that is, for rational market behavior—on an astonishing scale. In the 1850s, 250,000 new farms were established in the Northwest, adding 19 million acres of improved farmland, usually on larger farms, to the nation's total; in Illinois, for example, where improved acreage increased 163 percent, average farm size increased 40 percent in the decade, but even more in the northern counties, where the land was almost devoid of contour and the soil was particularly rich. Between 1849 and 1854, moreover, the value of improvements to farmland tripled; for the decade of the 1850s, the increase in the value of farm implements and machinery was 61 percent, greater than for any other decade of the nineteenth century. Meanwhile, grain prices rose much faster than farm labor costs—a result of increasing demand from both the seaboard cities, where the new immigrants congregated, and Great Britain, which had repealed its tariffs on imports of grain in 1846—so that the immediate savings in labor costs made possible by use of reapers, threshers, mowers, and seed drills made up for the considerable outlay on the new machines. Moreover, the "terms of trade" for northwestern produce improved radically, by 76 percent between 1846 and 1859, because the prices of consumer goods shipped to the Northwest did not increase as fast as grain prices did.[6]

This improvement meant a corresponding increase in demand for those goods, which the prairie farmers bought because, in the new context of production for eastern markets, the opportunity cost of diverting a significant portion of their household's labor to the domestic production of such goods was lower output of cash crops and thus lower revenue with which to cover debts, to increase future output, and to purchase the insignia of prosperity. But the composition as well as the level of demand was changing—or rather the composition of demand was changing because the level of demand was. For example, the entrepreneurs of Lynn who were trying desperately to increase the output of boots and shoes in the mid-to-late 1840s understood perfectly well that they were trying to meet the new demands of urban and western markets. Between 1845 and 1850, they hired enough labor to double output. By the end of the decade, however, they faced a severe shortage of labor—the limits of the outwork system had finally been reached—and productivity was stagnant if not declining. Their response was to adapt sewing machines to the tasks of stitching and binding, thus increasing output in line with the new contours of consumer demand while reducing costs per unit of output. In doing so, these entrepreneurs invented factory discipline in shoemaking, but, in their drive to profit from the increase of consumer expenditures, they also created a demand for companies and industries that would produce the sewing machines and their inputs. The transformation in question was virtually completed between 1852 and 1860. The "disintegration" of textile machinery production—its detachment from textile companies and its emergence as an industry in its own right—was not incidentally completed in the same decade.[7]

The possibility of meeting the new demands of western markets would never have arisen in the absence of east-west trunk lines that could move goods to and from areas in which water transport was unavailable or inadequate. In this sense, it is probably impossible to overestimate the importance of the railroads in creating and enforcing the new patterns of production and consumption which characterized the turning point of 1846–57. Even so, we should not insist on the kind of either/or proposition Alfred Chandler occasionally indulges, through which the level or composition of demand becomes irrelevant and the key constraint on or cause of economic change becomes technological (a matter of supply). The weaknesses of this approach are evident in his treatment of coal. According to Chandler, the opening of the Pennsylvania anthracite fields in the 1830s lifted the "most significant" technological constraint on economic innovation of the antebellum period. But the technology of anthracite-fired iron was widely understood as early as the 1820s. Very few entrepreneurs acted on this knowledge and invested in costly anthracite furnaces until the mid-to-late 1840s, when the demand for high-quality, easily malleable, charcoal-fired "merchant bar" declined, and the demand for cheaper, more brittle, anthracite-fired iron—for use in machine construction (and reconstruction, i.e., replacing wooden parts with metal)—began to increase.[8]

That new demand came largely from industries that produced agricultural machinery (by 1860, 20 percent of all machinery produced in the United States was agricultural machinery), from industries that sold machines to companies that processed raw agricultural output (one of every three steam engines in use before 1860 was housed in a flour and grist mill), and from industries that were building specialized machines to replace learned skills in the production of consumer goods (as in shoemaking). The part played by mechanized prairie farming in creating such derived demand for capital goods is probably even more significant than this list would suggest. For if the proletarianization of eastern farmers and the consequent migration from the countryside produced more city dwellers than did immigration ca. 1846–60, and if the phenomenal growth of the urban population in the same period—it increased about three times as fast as the general population—accounts for a large share of the growth of consumer demand, then mechanized prairie farming, which supplied the new urban population with necessary foodstuffs, created the conditions of its own expansion by producing more efficiently than eastern farmers and eventually driving them (or their sons and daughters) into the cities, where, as proletarians, they had to buy what they had once been able to produce at home or to appropriate through local exchange in kind. From this standpoint, it is not surprising that the rate of urbanization in the two antebellum decades exceeds any subsequent rates, and that the growth of small towns (those with populations of twenty-five hundred to twenty-five thousand) peaked between 1852 and 1860, at the moment immigration began to slow and mechanized prairie farming came into its own.[9]

In any event, it is worth repeating that the composition of demand changed because the level of consumer demand increased. To illustrate the point, let us reconsider the iron industry. The initial investment for furnaces that used coal to heat iron ore was about 50 percent higher than required for charcoal furnaces; but the capacity of the anthracite furnaces was about double, sometimes triple, that of comparable charcoal plants. Thus the use of anthracite promised lower capital costs per unit of output only if there was enough remunerative demand for the doubled or tripled output of which the new furnaces were capable. To be cost-effective, in other words, the switch to anthracite (then to coked coal) had to be predicated on an enormous increase in demand for cheap, low-quality iron, which would be sold not to country stores and blacksmiths but directly to metalworking industries.[10] Now the metalworking industries par excellence are those that produce machines which function as capital equipment. But it was the boom in the consumer goods sector that permitted the growth of such industries; most of the specialized machines in use before 1860—reapers, threshers, sewing machines, steam engines, drawing frames, spinning throstles and mules, mechanical looms, etc.—functioned as capital equipment in the production of food (raw grain, flour), clothing, and home furnishings (cotton or wool textiles, boots and shoes), for which demand had increased as the household economy gave way to an increasingly urban labor market and money incomes came to define or mediate social relations. So the antebellum iron industry survived, and even prospered until 1857, not because of growing demand for rails (British manufacturers supplied the bulk of them before 1861) but because the commercialization of agriculture took the form of mechanized prairie farming and thus enforced "the birth of consumer society" in the United States.

It is not possible to specify even the broad contours of consumption in this period, however much statistical studies might tell us about the gross output of consumer goods. But we can safely claim that the decade of the 1840s was the watershed between a household and a market economy, and that the increasing quantity and variety of consumption expenditures in the two antebellum decades did contribute to a qualitative change in American life. At least this was the case in the North, which ultimately imposed its new way of life on the South. Of the raw statistical materials available, perhaps the most suggestive is the increase of "services flowing to consumers" in national income accounts. Between 1830 and 1870, this component of net national product rises from about 15 percent to almost 27 percent, reflecting not only the commodification of labor-time—the creation of a market in labor—but also the declining importance of social relations and economic transactions conducted without reference to value expressed in monetary terms and symbols. In view of the South's self-sufficiency as late as the 1850s (and its subsequent separation), the increase of the value of "services flowing to consumers" indicates the rapid growth of northern markets in and for specialized labor skills. This increase is consistent with the enlarged use of paper money before the war: in 1846, the volume of banknotes in circulation was about the same as it had been in 1839 and was lower than it had been in 1837; by 1857, that volume had doubled.[11]

Meanwhile, the real wages of the employed labor force on the farms and in the cities were increasing in the 1850s, but particularly for nonfarm workers. For the period 1840–60, there is related evidence to suggest that the proportion of earnings spent on the "bare necessities" of food and shelter declined sharply, even though the reconstruction of the residential landscape—in both the towns and the countryside—was specific to the 1850s. This new distribution of expenditure was due in part to the total collapse of the supply of household-produced clothing by the late 1840s or early 1850s, which augmented the demand for "ready-made" clothes accordingly. In that sense, the quantity of consumer expenditures increased insofar as the availability of goods and services came to be determined by, but also reduced to, what the market could accommodate in the form of commodities. Even so, the quantity and variety of consumer goods available through the market economy did increase enormously after the mid-1840s.[12]

That increase multiplied the imaginable passages between present and future precisely because these goods were commodities that necessarily had more than local meanings or particular use values: their profusion complicated and enlarged the perceptible relation between the interior and the exterior of the self—the unstable frontier on which patent medicines, that most modern of consumer goods, suddenly flourished in the 1850s—especially since the production of the self and the production of goods no longer converged in the patriarchal household. The revolution in domestic architecture at midcentury, which fed on and into the boom in the consumer goods sector by providing the setting for a greater density of durable familial goods, was animated by this new sense of permeability, this new confusion of inner and outer spheres. It did not so much reflect a sentimental "cult of domesticity" as it suggested that the boundary between the home and the widening world of the market had become more porous, more fluid, more open to question and reconsideration.[13]

The Politics of Continental Industrialization

By the 1850s, North America had, then, reached a verge that qualifies as its first industrial divide. In effect, the choice was between metropolitan and continental industrialization. The related choices were clearly drawn by 1857 or 1858 because the leadership of the new Republican Party had made slavery the central issue in political debates at the national level—and thus had foreclosed any change in federal economic policy that was not articulated in terms of that issue. This realignment of American political discourse tends, therefore, to obscure the inner civil war between the mercantile elite of the seaboard cities and the new entrepreneurs of the trans-Allegheny industrial towns who were trying in every sense to capitalize their concerns. For the centrality of slavery in the politics of the 1850s makes the debates over developmental strategy *in the North* seem insignificant by comparison to the larger conflict between North and South. But it is in the context of these debates that most Republican leaders went beyond criticism of the "Slave Power" and offered a positive alternative to further expansion of the Atlantic economy—an economy predicated on the export of agricultural raw materials and the import, mainly from the United Kingdom, of manufactured goods—in which both southern slaveholders and northeastern merchants had a vested interest. It is in the same context that we can begin to assess the effects of economic policy on the path of U.S. economic growth; it is here, in other words, that we can grasp "the rise in the rate of investment" as the product of social and political purpose, not an accident of economic history.

The difference between the Republican platforms of 1856 and 1860 suggests the nature of the alternative in the making. In 1856, the familiar "no extension" slogan was the entire platform on which John C. Frémont ran for president. In 1860, the party cast a wider net by adding several demands that appealed directly to the new "agro-industrial complex" that had come of age in the 1850s. These planks were supposed to swing Pennsylvania, which the party had lost to James Buchanan or Millard Fillmore in 1856, but also the Great Lakes states, which, in view of Stephen A. Douglas's popularity on the middle border, could not be carried simply by putting a "western moderate" on the ticket. The key demands in the new platform were for a protective tariff, federal aid to transcontinental railroads (and other "internal improvements"), and a homestead bill based on preemption. Taken together, these demands would reverse the trend of federal economic policy since 1833; more immediately, they would reverse the policies of the Buchanan administration, which had supported the "free-trade" tariff of 1857, vetoed several homestead bills, and tied legislation on railroad rights-of-way to the constitutional protection of slavery in all territories. In effect, then, the Republican platform promised to prevent the impending encirclement of the northern states and to create a continental market on the legal-constitutional basis of free labor—but also to change the sectional and social sources of political-economic power *in the North* by subsidizing the emerging agro-industrial complex as against the "moneyed capitalists" of the seaboard cities, whose regime required free trade as well as the further expansion of the South's labor system and agricultural output.

Abraham Lincoln, that "western moderate," certainly understood the political crisis of the 1850s, and the Republican Party's mission, in exactly these terms. His "House Divided" speech of 1858, for example, dwells on the fact that the legal-constitutional groundwork of encirclement was already laid, in the form of the *Dred Scott* decision. In his speeches of 1856 on behalf of Frémont, moreover, he treated the disposition of the territories as both a moral and a political-economic problem. "Have we no interest in the free Territories of the United States—that they should be kept open for the homes of free white people? As our Northern States are growing more and more in wealth and population, we are continually in want of an outlet, through which it [*sic*] may pass out to enrich our country. In this we have an interest—a deep and abiding interest." The meaning of growth that Lincoln conveys here is not simply spatial or territorial; it is economic in a strictly modern sense. So the expansion of the agricultural sector— this is no frontier he has in mind—functions not merely as a "safety valve" for surplus population, but as a field of investment and a source of demand, without which the political economy of the North, including the settled states, would wither.[14]

The link between Lincoln's criticism of the status quo ante and his commitment to the positive alternative in the platform of 1860 was a notion of "productive labor" that he shared with Republicans such as Henry C. Carey, the influential economist, and William D. "Pig Iron" Kelley, the self-made attorney, judge, and congressman. "Productive labor," by their account, was labor that produced new value, or added value to natural or unfinished materials, and thus created the wealth (or the surplus) by which the possibilities of social mobility and future growth were realized. The merchant and the slaveholder were accordingly and equally parasites on productive labor—they consumed without creating or adding value. They appropriated or transferred wealth in the form of revenue from the sale of commodities they had no part in producing. Carey insisted, therefore, that "with every diminution in the quantity of the machinery of exchange, wealth will still more rapidly increase." In such terms, consumption was authorized by production: one's right to appropriate the fruits of labor as such presupposed one's own expenditure of labor-power in the production of commodities, because no individual had the right to consume the fruits of another's labor unless that other had somehow relinquished his or her *natural* right to them.[15]

From this standpoint, the impending "union between the slave capitalists of the South and the moneyed capitalists of the North," announced by Horace Greeley, was a logical and fitting collaboration between social classes with a vested interest in an Atlantic economy. For each set of "capitalists" was a "heavy pensioner" on productive labor, Lincoln claimed. The profits of the northern merchant who organized the distribution of finished manufactures that could (eventually) be produced with equal or less amounts of American labor were as much a "heavy burden upon the useful labor connected [with] such articles" as were the costs of supporting the slaveholders' ostentation. Neither kind of burden could be tolerated by a political coalition that assumed the proper end of government was, as Lincoln put it, "to secure to each laborer the whole product of his labor." The blueprint for modern America outlined in the Republican platform of 1860 (and enacted thereafter) was, then, the programmatic form of an ideology or developmental strategy designed to save, in every sense, the costs of commodity circulation, and to reduce the corresponding margin of consumption accruing to "moneyed capitalists" and slaveholders. The pivotal role of the protective tariff in the platform and rhetoric of 1860 becomes explicable in these terms: it was the critical device through which the resources hitherto consumed by the managers and beneficiaries of an Atlantic economy would be diverted to and invested in a home market.[16]

Most influential merchants and commercial bankers of the North understood the Republican threat to their hegemony quite as well as the leading slaveholders of the South did. These "gentlemen of property and standing" knew that federal policy oriented toward the reciprocal expansion of prairie agriculture and heavy industries would fundamentally alter the sectional and social sources of power in the United States. For such a policy would reduce the volume and the value of raw material exports and of manufactured imports, and thus would tend to reduce the incomes and demean the functions of established merchants and commercial bankers, especially those in the eastern seaboard cities.[17] Until 1866, therefore, these men actively opposed the Republican program with remarkable unanimity.

The response of northern merchant capital to the economic legislation of Civil War Congresses provides forceful illustration of its stance toward the new developmental strategy. The suspension of specie payments in December 1861 by the major banks of New York was, as the historian Leonard Curry suggests, "a declaration of their unwillingness to support the government's financial policy." By then, however, the banks' refusal to continue purchasing (or trying to sell) the government's notes at par gold prices was part of the mercantile elite's broader resistance to Republican economic policy as such. The commercial and financial leaders of New York had already given notice that they would ally with New England textile manufacturers against a protective tariff. In 1862–63, with support from their counterparts in Boston and Philadelphia, they would denounce the legal tender acts, which powerfully reinforced the new tariff's protection of heavy industries by devaluing the U.S. currency vis-à-vis gold, and the National Banking Act, which threatened to undercut the financial supremacy of the seaboard cities, or at least to change the economic criteria of bankers and banking.[18]

This is not to suggest that northern merchant capital was unanimous in its support for the Democracy or inflexible in its opposition to the nonmilitary legislation of Civil War Congresses. In fact, the ideological conflict over developmental strategy was played out within the Republican coalition as well as between the two parties. Radical Republicans and western "moderates" were likely to be articulate supporters of the new, continental-industrial strategy, whereas conservative Republicans and eastern moderates were likely to be suspicious of it. Eastern moderates were by and large more sympathetic and susceptible to the appeals of established merchants and commercial bankers than were their western counterparts; so they accepted the new strategy piecemeal, only as each of its legislative components became a necessary means of prosecuting war against the South.[19] The eastern moderates' mercantile constituency did not give up so quickly. In 1865 and 1866, the commercial and financial leaders of the seaboard cities hailed Andrew Johnson's plans for a speedy restoration of the South, urged Congress to lower or abolish the new tariffs, and supported the Treasury Department's determined contraction of the outstanding legal tenders. They clung, for the moment, to a developmental strategy founded on American (re)integration into an Atlantic economy, which required the resumption of cotton exports, lower tariffs, and monetary stability founded on the international gold-exchange standard.[20]

But the mercantile elite was not immune to the forces that were transforming both the Republican coalition and the larger society. Indeed, the revolutionary political-economic changes wrought by Civil War and Reconstruction eventually undermined the older elite's commitment to an Atlantic economy, and finally led it to embrace the new developmental strategy outlined by increasingly radical Republican Congresses. This social-ideological realignment made allies of the erstwhile mercantile elite and the new corps of industrial entrepreneurs that came of age after 1860; it was the turning point in the making of a new bourgeois ethic that sanctioned not "productive labor" but capital accumulation in an industrial mode. In other words, it signified the abdication of merchant capital.

The political-economic changes that made this realignment possible are familiar enough to historians and economists. The unprecedented experiment known as Reconstruction, which began in earnest in 1863, was perhaps the most important, for not even men of large capital accustomed to commercial uses for that capital could avoid cultivating western markets and investment outlets so long as Congress kept the South out of the Union.[21] Positive incentives to this shift in investment patterns came, of course, in the form of the Homestead Act (1862) and subsidies to railroads (beginning in 1864). Such legislation made continental industrialization a realistic business proposition.

The fiscal and monetary aspects of the Republicans' revolution enforced and ultimately validated that momentous shift. The interest-bearing federal debt that was necessary to finance total war against the South probably slowed capital formation between 1860 and 1865. But the retirement of that debt after 1865 rapidly redistributed national income toward large propertyholders on a massive scale; the protective tariff and the larger tax system meanwhile encouraged the flow of these savings into industrial production, for their effect was to dramatically reduce the price of producers' durables—that is, capital goods—vis-à-vis finished manufactured goods. Investment in hitherto undercapitalized U.S. industries, including capital goods industries, thus became significantly more profitable than it had ever been before the war. Highly profitable investment opportunities in such industries, and the volume of savings necessary to exploit them, appeared, then, at the very moment that the restoration of the southern market became virtually impossible.[22]

Moreover, federal war-debt management had already created an entirely new relationship between capital markets and domestic industries other than textiles, and so made a shift in investment patterns toward undercapitalized areas of manufacturing that much easier. "Before the war," Glenn Porter and Harold Livesay point out, "formal financial agencies that pooled the savings of the public at large rarely supplied capital to manufacturers outside the textile industry." Federal debt management changed this situation in two ways. First, the new national banking system, which had fiscal as well as developmental purposes, created a corps of financiers without a vested interest in the commercial possibilities of an Atlantic economy—these were men whose idea of a profitable portfolio centered on the local production and regional distribution of specialized manufactured goods, not the export of cotton or sugar and the import of finished goods from the United Kingdom. Second, manufacturers found that the certificates of indebtedness with which the government often paid them could be discounted for cash at local banks already accustomed to purchasing federal paper. The fiscal revolution of the Civil War had thus made capital markets the ally, if not the servant, of undercapitalized domestic industries; they were no longer merely the handmaidens of international commerce.[23]

That revolution also fostered the development of banking technique and institutions that could efficiently underwrite large-scale enterprise in transportation and manufacturing. The innovations required to sell an unprecedented volume of government securities, and the enormity of the transcontinental rail projects sponsored by Civil War Congresses, made modern investment banking—and the postwar linkage between it and large industrial enterprise—both possible and necessary. The firms that dominated investment banking in 1900 were not the partnerships formed in the 1850s to sell railroad bonds through their European connections; rather, they were the firms founded or reorganized between 1860 and 1870 to underwrite and refund the federal war debt, and to exploit the potential of a market in railroad securities (both bonds and stocks) now undergirded by the financial commitment of governments at every level.[24]

The monetary aspects of the Republicans' revolution were equally important in redefining the methods and objects of American business enterprise. To begin with, the issue of $450 million in legal tender notes enforced the protective effects of the tariff by creating a "premium" on gold—by making the money of account in international trade more expensive in terms of U.S. currency. The greenbacks were, then, especially popular among small entrepreneurs in general and undercapitalized manufacturers in particular, not least because the injection of the greenbacks into the North's money supply destroyed the merchant-dominated financial system that had constrained the expansion of heavy industries before the war. Domestic business shifted to a cash basis in late 1862 because, as a contemporary observer put it, "the fluctuating value of the depreciated currency made long credits quite hazardous." Undercapitalized industries such as iron and steel received a substantial boost once this transition was completed, for working capital could now be supplied almost immediately from cash sales, and new construction could be undertaken without recourse to loans from merchant-wholesalers.[25]

In sum, then, each aspect of the Republicans' revolution contributed to the redistribution of national income and investment toward those domestic industries that, unlike textiles, had hitherto received little or no special attention and subsidies from the federal government. The ideological realignment or abdication of merchant capital—its acceptance and advocacy of a developmental strategy oriented toward continental industrialization—was, in this sense, one more consequence of Civil War and Reconstruction. That realignment may now be traced against the background of conflict over postwar monetary policy. We have already seen that, in 1866, the leadership of the seaboard's commercial-financial community favored restoration (not reconstruction) of the South, tariff reduction, and contraction of the greenbacks, so that interconvertibility between gold and U.S. currency (specie payments) could be resumed—so that the American economy could be reintegrated into an Atlantic economy. By late 1867, this consensus had begun to dissolve as the exigencies of economic crisis and the opportunities of lucrative investment in the "great and growing West" combined to make the mercantile elite's rationale for resumption and restoration less plausible. Eastern investment bankers involved in railroad and/or federal bond promotion were among the first to dissent. For example, Jay Cooke, Henry Clews, and John J. Cisco reversed their stand on greenback contraction and resumption of gold payments between 1866 and 1867. For that matter, so did most New England and Middle State Republicans in Congress, who were falling into line behind their midwestern colleagues.[26] But these eastern moderates in Congress were soon followed by a majority of the mercantile elite. By 1870, the mercantile consensus of 1866 had all but disappeared in a wave of enthusiasm for the developmental effects of fiat money.

The best evidence of this realignment is found in the deliberations of the New York Chamber of Commerce and the National Board of Trade. In 1868, the New York Chamber noted, "The inconveniences of a depreciated currency are most seriously felt on the seaboard, and the restraints and losses incidental to an abnormal condition of our foreign exchanges are most patent to those who are brought in contact with the pecuniary systems of England and continental Europe." The accompanying resolution in favor of greenback contraction and resumption of gold payments assumed the propriety of restoring the status quo ante bellum, which was necessarily predicated, according to merchant capital, on the expansion of European markets for agricultural raw materials and the expansion of American markets for manufactured imports. The National Board of Trade, which Irwin Unger claims was "the nearest thing to a country-wide gauge of commercial attitudes," endorsed similar resolutions in 1868 and in 1869. In 1870, however, both the New York Chamber and the National Board of Trade *defeated* resolutions endorsing contraction and its corollaries.[27]

Simeon B. Chittenden, who was among the most prominent and influential of the seaboard's merchant capitalists—and who, not incidentally, supported greenback contraction and gold payments resumption until 1870—based his new opposition to contraction on what he saw as the promise of continental-industrial development, which had been realized almost overnight, it seems, in the immediate aftermath of the war itself. "Had we resumed [in 1866] we should not have had the great development of railroads which has come as an incident to our paper money, and which may yet prove, contrary to all history, that a great war and paper money may possibly be a great blessing [and] that the magnificent development of our country was an incident of the great rebellion and of the prodigious amount of paper which consequently circulated through the country." It can be argued, of course, that Chittenden merely suffered a brief attack of economic opportunism in 1870—that, as Unger suggests, "scruples momentarily yielded to expediency." But it is more plausible to argue that Chittenden genuinely believed that his postwar experience required the revision of his prewar outlook, and that his revisionism was neither eccentric nor momentary. He was supported, after all, by a majority of his mercantile colleagues from New York, Baltimore, and Philadelphia—the very men who had been denouncing the greenbacks and their effects since the end of the war. It is more plausible, in other words, to interpret Chittenden's conversion as part of the broader realignment of the seaboard's mercantile elite, through which merchant capital signified its acceptance of the developmental strategy residing in nonmilitary legislation of the 1860s and its willingness to abandon an Atlantic economy in favor of continental industrialization.[28]

The abdication of merchant capital meant that the antagonistic social classes that had contended for control of federal economic policy between 1857 and 1870 could now begin to identify their common interests as different functional elements of a capitalist class, as against other social classes in the making. This was a peculiarly fortuitous event for the Republican Party, because it coincided with and compensated for the Democracy's "New Departure" of 1871, which, by acknowledging the legitimacy of the Reconstruction Amendments, allowed Democrats to recruit certain fragments of what had been solidly Republican constituencies in the North (e.g., native-born urban laborers, prairie farmers). By the early 1870s, these once-reliable Republican partisans were ready to believe local or state politicians who argued that the legislation of the war decade had transferred income and wealth from the majority of the working population—from the people who had fought the war—to the minority that was interested only in acquiring more income and wealth.[29]

They had good reasons to believe this argument, which radical Republicans as well as midwestern Democrats pursued as political doctrine through the 1870s. For the "incomes of the savers" were in fact significantly increased between 1850 and 1870, apparently at the expense of the working population's share of national income, and certainly at the expense of its ability to make its demands effective through labor organization or collective action. What the Republicans' working-class constituencies objected to, in other words, was "the rise in the rate of investment" made possible by nonmilitary legislation of the 1860s—not because they were ignorant of the requirements of economic growth or envious of the men of capital, but because they understood that the transfer of income enforced by the new economic policies threatened to concentrate social power in the hands of capital(ists) and to foreclose the possibility of social mobility for wage earners. They understood, in short, that the emergence of class society threatened republican politics and popular government.

Now "the rise in the rate of investment" and the corresponding shift in income shares on which it was predicated over the period 1850–70 are not matters of controversy among economists. Robert Gallman's widely used estimates of the ratio of gross domestic capital formation (GDCF) to gross domestic product (GDP) show an increase of about 40 percent between 1849–58 and 1869–78. Simon Kuznets's earlier estimates suggest that GDCF was 21.6 percent of gross national product (GNP) in the latter decade and almost 19 percent of GDP, a rate never subsequently equaled. For my purposes, it is even more significant that the internal composition of investment as such also changed drastically. According to Gallman and others, the share of manufactured producers' durables in net investment—or the constant price share of producers' durables investment in GDCF—more than doubled between the mid-1850s and the late 1870s. Here is how Gallman himself characterizes this new composition: "Investment in durables increased relative to investment in improvements, and the movement appears to be very general, affecting all the main industrial sectors . . . suggesting that the supply schedules for these goods must have been shifting outward with unusual speed, presumably due to exceptionally fruitful technical innovation, improved material supplies, or the like (e.g. improved supplies of machine tools)." Meanwhile, that is, between 1850 and 1870, the share of wages and salaries in the value of net output fell 12 percent, even though the number of gainful workers increased 37 percent. The broader trend toward sharply higher real yields on equity capital and government bonds, ca. 1867–78, suggests the same underlying shift of income shares, which in turn allowed much higher investment rates because it raised the "incomes of the savers." [30]

In the absence of incentives to investment in heavy industries—in metal mining as well as metalworking industries—the increase of potential demand for producers' durables represented by this rise in the "incomes of the savers" would not have been realized in the form of continental industrialization. But in fact the "priority of Department I" was inscribed in the economic policies—particularly the tariff—sanctioned by the victors in the inner civil war, whose developmental strategy required a break from the Atlantic economy. Accordingly, demand for capital goods would not be derived from, or limited by, metropolitan industrialization, that is, from or by the growth of consumer goods industries in the seaboard cities on the social basis of handicraft and petty manufacture. Instead, demand for consumer goods would increasingly be driven by expanded output of capital goods. In this sense, the reversal in the original relation between the consumer goods and the capital goods sectors centered critically in, and was a crucial consequence of, the epoch of Civil War and Reconstruction.

Production and Consumption as Political Culture

And yet the political-economic record of the late nineteenth century does not conform to the quasi-teleological accounts of those historians who render the period in terms of the reign of the robber barons, the rise of big business, or the inevitable demise of popular politics. In other words, the "priority of Department I" was inscribed in the radical shifts of economic policy and income shares, ca. 1857–70, but the future was not therefore or thereby overdetermined. Accumulation did proceed, of course, and did entail the restriction of consumption expenditures as against saving and investment; but it proceeded fitfully and cyclically, in accordance with the changing balance of class power and the corresponding distribution of income between investment and consumption, that is, between capital and labor.

The capitalist class born in the inner civil war tried desperately in the late nineteenth century to maintain the distribution of income specific to the moment of its birth and understood, by the 1880s, that this task required its acquisition of political and cultural authority as well as the formalization of its economic prerogatives. Meanwhile, the working classes tried with no little success to change that distribution of income by acting on two related claims. First, the meaning of labor was not comprehended by the categories of political economy; by the same token, the social roles and political obligations of members of the working class could not be wholly determined by their economic functions or occupations. Second, and consequently, their incomes and social standing—their standard of living— could not properly be defined by the technical requirements of economic growth as these were gauged by capitalists and their allies. In effect, then, the deepening contradiction between production and consumption became the pivot of political and cultural conflict between capital and labor. Since this conflict both registered and determined the distribution of income, and was not resolved one way or another until about 1900, it is immediately relevant to understanding the rate and contours of accumulation in the late nineteenth century.

From the standpoint of capital, the period was more nightmare than golden age. According to informed and influential observers of the economic scene as well as the business press, the cycles of 1873–97 constituted one long depression in which prices and profits moved consistently downward, in the opposite direction of money and real wages. By 1890, the distribution of income between capital and labor had become a virtual obsession of both capitalists and economists—indeed by then the problem of distribution, which was typically expressed in the juxtaposition of "progress and poverty," dominated the political imagination of all social classes and strata, including the proprietary middle class on the farms and in the cities. None of them seemed satisfied with its share of national income. But we should not dismiss the complaints of capitalists as the product of "money illusion," through which they confused falling prices and lower profits, or as the poor-mouthing propaganda of robber barons. For the trends of real wages and labor productivity in the nonfarm sector did diverge from the early 1880s until the mid-1890s and did, therefore, reduce capital's share of nonfarm income—and this at the very moment that growing competitive pressures demanded greater investment in fixed capital as the condition of retaining market share through lower unit costs and prices.

The obvious solutions to the problem of distribution so conceived were to increase labor productivity by reconstructing and mechanizing the labor process (thus to increase output and revenues vis-à-vis the wage bill); to bring supply into line with effective demand by limiting output (thus to raise prices and presumably profits vis-à-vis wages); or simply to reduce wages. But these solutions were not available to capitalists in the period because each presupposed either the solidarity of capital or the weakness of labor. To limit output in the name of reasonable returns on investment, for example, required the kind of interfirm cooperation that was illegal or impossible in an era of juridical confusion in regard to the rights of property, of popular antipathy to concentrated economic power, and of falling prices enforced by fierce competition. But to reconstruct and mechanize the labor process or to reduce wages was equally difficult, if not impossible, at least in the 1880s and the early 1890s. At the level of the firm, skilled workers' control of the division of labor and rates of output was enforced by employers' ignorance of what actually happened on the shop floor; when employers tried to remedy their ignorance by introducing new machines and reshaping work rules, they often faced resistance in the form of strikes that united not only the skilled and the unskilled but also local officials, editors, shopkeepers, and sympathetic workers in other trades. Similar results were produced by wage cuts, particularly after 1884. So there was no microeconomic solution to the problem of distribution as capital itself had defined it. For any initiative at the level of the firm immediately implicated populations that invoked extra-local political loyalties and languages to deny or question the legitimacy of large capital.[31]

The distribution of income between profits and wages or investment and consumption was, then, a political and cultural issue as well as a macroeconomic puzzle. "The contests of interest between capitalists and laborers are intensified by counter-claims in equity," the economist John Bates Clark explained in 1887, "and the problem thrust upon society is not merely how to divide a sum, but how to adjust rights and obligations." Certainly the "producing classes" understood it in these terms. They adapted the language once directed at merchants and slaveholders to identify capitalists as parasites on the body politic, as those who produced nothing and yet who controlled and consumed a disproportionate share of the products of labor. But their criticism of capitalists, and for that matter of capitalism, did not entail a rejection of commodity production and circulation—that is, of the market in goods to which their labor and incomes gave them access. Their political ideology and programs were not compromised as a result; in fact they were sharpened by commitment to the "self-regulating" or simple market society valorized by the American political tradition.[32] In this sense, the plebeian or popular culture created by the "producing classes" was commercial(ized) long before Coney Island became its modern emblem. But it was not animated by acknowledgment of a disjuncture between production and consumption. To see how and why this was so, we need to retrace the relation between the political culture of the nineteenth-century United States and the grievances of the "producing classes."

To begin with, we should note the uncanny coherence of such grievances. Between the 1870s and the turn of the century, "jackleg" farmers, industrial workers, small entrepreneurs, and even certain proprietary capitalists used the same inherited language of "productive labor" to argue that consumption was authorized only by production—in other words, one's receipt and expenditure of income required one's production of real value through work. Any division of labor that separated these social functions was a betrayal of republican politics and popular government because it presupposed hierarchy and privilege. By this account, the division of mental and manual labor, which capitalists cited to justify their incomes and to explain the need for managerial control of a mechanized labor process, merely accommodated the unjust asymmetry of social power that enabled capitalist appropriation of the products of labor, or consumption without production. It was intolerable precisely because it recalled and reconstituted the premodern specification of the relation between necessity and freedom, which the "Slave Power" had tried to reinstate at midcentury.

Until the advent of modernity in the form of market society, ca. 1450–1650, that relation was invariably construed as a fundamental contradiction. Those people immersed in the production of goods, in the realm of necessity, could not be free, for if they worked, they did so at another's behest:

they were by definition slaves or serfs. Consumption or control of goods beyond what was necessary to sustain life as such was the insignia, then, of the free man or citizen who did not produce those goods. So, too, was the life of the mind—only men free of the claims of necessity could be philosophers or priests. The practical and the aesthetic accordingly identified different levels of social life as well as different orders of truth and rhetoric.[33] The collapse of these distinctions or divisions—of this contradiction—was one result of the great bourgeois revolutions of the seventeenth and eighteenth centuries. The citizens of bourgeois society defined themselves as free and fit to rule because they worked on and produced the material conditions of their new world. In their view, the realms of freedom and necessity intersected in that bustling area of life they learned to call "civil society"—the new social space opened up between the paradigmatic realms of power or coercion, the state and the family. Those who consumed without producing were parasites on civil society, on those who, by mixing their labor with their property, made it productive and themselves free. So the functional separation of production and consumption by social class or rank was dangerous at best. The life of the mind, as a corollary of this social-functional separation, was similarly problematic. But the cultural standards or values of bourgeois society as it emerged in England and North America were more or less *mechanical*. To that extent, they abolished the rhetorical distinction between the practical and the aesthetic (or the useful and the beautiful), and repudiated the social differentiation it ratified; to the same extent, the life of the mind did not represent an immediate threat to the vitality of civil society.[34]

The perceived unity or interpenetration of necessity and freedom, production and consumption, the practical and the aesthetic, was nowhere more pronounced than in the culture of eighteenth- and nineteenth-century North America; for it was the extremity in every sense of bourgeois society.[35] Hence the articulation of a division of manual and mental labor, in fact and as value, was nowhere more difficult. The typically American fear of "middlemen," bureaucrats, bankers, lawyers, and all other forms of apparently unproductive mental labor ultimately derives from the assumption that they consume the wealth created by productive labor. In the nineteenth century, this fear extended to, or rather focused on, capitalists, the modern-industrial version of a many-layered aristocracy that consumed and controlled wealth without producing anything. "The capitalist performs no productive labor himself," a striking telegraph operator explained to a Senate committee in 1883. A young machinist who testified before the same committee was more pointed: "Jay Gould never earned a great deal, but he owns a terrible lot." Capitalists somehow invaded and inverted the proper relationship between personality and property by making the personalities of producers the means to the unlimited accumulation of property. They accordingly destroyed the intersection of freedom and necessity in civil society by creating and dominating a mass of propertyless workers, a class of "wage slaves" or "industrial serfs" which had only its manual dexterity to sell in the labor market.[36]

This at any rate was the view of those Americans who interpreted their world and unconsciously narrated their futures in terms of the republican tradition sanctified by Civil War and Reconstruction. In denying the legitimacy of a division of mental and manual labor, they were denying the legitimacy of the social differentiation—the inequality—it presupposed. They were also protesting the consequent dissolution of the nexus between property in productive labor and self-determining personality, which had served as the groundwork of bourgeois political theory and practice since the seventeenth century. If they did not constitute a majority, it is difficult to explain much of the legislation, jurisprudence, and political language of the late nineteenth century. But their numbers almost did not matter, for the same republican tradition weighed like a nightmare on the minds of their opponents.[37] Certainly it offered no idiom in which to explain or justify unilateral capitalist control of production, and so to make capital's claim to a share of national income effective. The power and authority of large capital, whether at the point of production, at the law, or in the larger society, would be decisively limited, therefore, until the republican tradition was supplanted as the political culture of the United States, or at least until it was acknowledged but contained by an alternative.

For their part, the men of large capital clearly understood the area of their culture to be a small and fragmented part of the linguistic territory they shared with their social inferiors. In the 1880s, most of that territory seemed positively foreign, an unexplored and inexplicable dark continent residing within the nation yet reaching beyond the capacities of a language that still could not reconcile "urban masses and moral order." Hence the fearful hyperbole of most upper-class pronouncements on the lower classes. But the fear was greater than mere ignorance of that Other could produce. For the possibility of reconciling "urban masses and moral order" presupposed an agent of moral order—or cultural authority—that was external to the masses. "Moral reform must come from the top," Carroll D. Wright, the esteemed commissioner of labor from Massachusetts, explained to the Senate Committee on Labor and Education in 1883. Yet capitalists seemed to have no sense of collectivity or solidarity, no lived culture of their own that would allow them to see themselves and act as the purposeful agents or exemplars of moral order, of cultural authority. For until the 1880s, they were in fact divided by economic interest and function, and by a fiercely competitive or individualistic ethic that fit the circumstances and explained the imperatives of business enterprise only too well. So they would have to rehabilitate themselves, in effect begin to constitute themselves as a social class, before they could recognize and depict themselves as a potential source of cultural integration—before they could articulate an alternative to what seemed the impending hegemony of the lower classes.[38]

From this standpoint, the "turn of the wheel" that economists date from the late 1890s—the sudden increase in growth rates, labor productivity, prices, and profits—was predicated on the reorientation of American culture, which consolidated the area of "high culture" to the point where its creators could begin to explore and to reclaim the territory inhabited by the lower classes. The reorientation of American culture in that sense began in earnest in the late 1880s, when the new men of capital in the nation's largest cities first tried to redefine the moral sensibilities of the urban masses and thus to create a new, educational relationship between upper and lower classes. In creating this new relationship, they realized that insofar as their latent social power did not take the form of cultural authority, but was instead exercised only as paramilitary force, the lower classes would not accept that social power as legitimate. Lyman Gage, the president of Chicago's First National Bank (who would in 1897 become William McKinley's secretary of the treasury) explained, for example, that the anarchy and the violence of 1886 were cause for rethinking these critical matters: "The facts led me and others of like mind to consider whether repression by force ought not to be supplemented by moral methods." Such methods centered on the endowment and establishment of new cultural institutions and events—museums, research libraries, universities, orchestras, exhibitions, civic bodies, and fairs. Chicago was accordingly transformed between the mid-1880s and the mid-1890s by a small group of railroad executives, bankers, publishers, merchants, and corporate lawyers which invented the Art Institute, the Symphony Orchestra, the University of Chicago, the Field Museum, the Newberry Library, and the Columbian Exposition.[39]

These institutions were representations of a hidden text or unspoken language that identified the high arts and imposing artifacts of the Old World as the inheritance of modern American capitalists. The enormous mass, classical balance, and vast interior spaces of the buildings that contained the emblems of the Old World's cultural tradition challenged—and were meant to challenge—the unruliness of the city's streets: they announced an alternative to the class conflict, partisan division, and incessant strife that characterized the New World. But the men of capital did not recall a specific segment of the European past as a way of rejecting or escaping from modern-industrial civilization in North America; in other words, the impulse to violate the ordinary scale and reshape the everyday sensibilities of the urban scene was not "antimodern." It was a way of evoking the sources or possibilities of social unity on the unlikely site of modernity itself; it proposed and ratified a new urban-industrial order, an impending future, in which capitalists were the legitimate heirs to the "high tradition" of western Europe and thus, at least by implication, to "civilization" as such.[40]

Perhaps because he did not experience it as it happened, Henry James understood this process better than anyone else; at any rate he was willing, in *The American Scene*, to offer a close reading of the texts he found in the changed urban landscape. For he assumed that all the "recent expensive construction . . . had cost thought as well as money, that [it] had taken birth presumably as a serious demonstration" of something. And he saw that the "frontage and cornice and architrave" reproduced from European models were reconstituted in the New World to tell the "great cold calculated story" of modernity, not medievalism.[41] The moral of that story apparently could be discovered in any of the "Palladian piles" that seemed to have erupted in the nation's largest city. But it was particularly obvious in New York's "palace of art," the Metropolitan Museum, a cultural institution rebuilt and in effect refounded by the city's business leaders between the mid-1880s and the late 1890s. "Education, clearly, was going to seat herself in these marble halls—admirably prepared for her, to all appearances—and issue her instructions without regard to cost." Here the story of modernity was told in a manner that somehow consecrated the losses its dramatis personae had suffered. "It is a palace of art, truly, that sits there on the edge of the Park, rearing itself with a radiance. . . . It spoke with a hundred voices of that huge process of historic waste that the place in general keeps putting before you; but showing it a light that drew out the harshness or the sadness, the pang, whatever it had seemed elsewhere, of the reiterated sacrifice to pecuniary profit. For the question here was to be of the advantage to the spirit, not to the pocket; to be of the aesthetic advantage involved in the wonderful clearance to come."

But how did the museum convey this extraordinary impression to someone who, like most Americans, was not disposed to believe that great wealth conferred ability or legitimacy on its holder? James thought it succeeded because it boldly claimed that the "reiterated sacrifice to pecuniary profit," the ever larger accumulations of capital, even the grotesque "grope of wealth" he ridiculed, were the necessary conditions of a more generous, a more civilized American future: "There was money in the air, ever so much money—that was, grossly expressed, the sense of the whole intimation. And the money was to be for all the most exquisite things—for all the most exquisite except creation, which was to be kept off the scene altogether; for art, selection, criticism, for knowledge, piety, taste. The intimation—which was somehow, after all, so pointed—would have been detestable if interests other, and smaller, than these had been in question."[42]

In terms of American culture, this was a new idea of progress; for if it did not celebrate accumulation as an end in itself, it did define money as something more than a means of exchange—in the "palace of art," it became both signifier and signified—and did suggest that the men who had grasped its mysteries and controlled its sources were, after all, the agents of progress toward the jubilee that would be advertised, on the eve of the apocalypse, as the last clearance sale ever. More to the point, to define money in this way was to suggest that production and consumption were not immediately or necessarily connected. James said as much when he emphasized that creation "was to be kept off the scene altogether."

The "high culture" the new institutions mapped was, then, a territory from which the facts of production had been banished, a realm of life already so complete that imagining how to live in or to create it was out of the question, even for its creators; passive contemplation or consumption of it was the only appropriate response. To see the physical artifacts this museum culture enclosed in silence as products of past labor that combined manual dexterity and mental skills was virtually impossible. They appeared to be, and in effect became, the products of the wealthy donors whose names were a prominent feature of the ubiquitous labels that defined the artifacts as such. In this sense, the new cultural institutions codified a break between the practical and the aesthetic by celebrating a division of manual and mental labor—by removing production from the scene of knowledge, piety, and taste. In the same sense, they represented a break from the political culture that insisted these dimensions of social life were indissoluble. To the extent that culture per se became what the new men of capital claimed it was—the life of the consuming aesthete, not the life of productive labor—maintaining the unity of craft knowledge and craft skill at the point of production became a form of nostalgia. But so, too, did insisting on the integrity of productive labor and personality, of necessity and freedom, or of production and consumption.[43]

From our standpoint in the late twentieth century, we can see clearly that American culture never has become what the new men of capital claimed it was, even if we suppose that the notion of "consumer culture" describes a large part of the territory in question. For we can also see that the political culture residing in the republican tradition has never been entirely extinguished. It was revived in the form of syndicalism in the early twentieth century; it was rehabilitated under the auspices of the Congress of Industrial Organizations and the Communist Party in the 1930s and 1940s; and in our own time it reappears in the political languages and cultural criticisms of "antimodern" conservatives on the Right as well as "progressive" radicals on the Left. In this sense, the consumer culture of the twentieth century is an unstable isotope that contains trace elements of the political positions articulated in the late nineteenth century by social classes still in the process of formation. At one extreme is the position that production of value through work authorizes consumption of goods. The corollary of this position is that, as the unambiguous sign of real value embodied in commodities, money is merely a means of exchange, a realistic representation of objects "out there" in the "real world." At the other extreme is the position that consumption needs no authorization by production of value through work unless both value and work are so broadly defined that they lose the connotations conferred on them by wage labor under the regime of capital accumulation. The corollary of this position is that money is a floating signifier that ultimately refers to or represents not objects "out there" in the "real world" but itself, or rather *the* self; money, like mind and language, is the sign of a sign. The difference between these positions is the political distance between the anticapitalist "producing classes" and the protocapitalist class of the late nineteenth century. The recognizably "modernist" position is of course the latter's, and should be attributed accordingly.[44] But again, it does not exhaust the meanings of twentieth-century consumer culture, just as it does not regulate every aspect of modern American culture. For its opponents never proposed to abolish the market in consumer goods which revolutionized family life in the late nineteenth century, and never suggested that civil society, the site of commodity production and circulation, should be reabsorbed by the family or controlled by the state.

Mass Consumption and Marginalist Economics

If there is still a middle ground between these original positions, it was first articulated at the same moment, in the course of the late-nineteenth-century debates that gave birth to modern economic theory in the United States. Those debates turned on the relevance of the labor theory of value under modern-industrial conditions, and, as in Europe, they led toward the break with classical political economy called the "marginalist revolution in economics." The crux of the argument based on marginalist principles was that commodities had more or less value not because they cost more or less in human labor—this is what the classical political economy had supposed—but because consumers found more or less utility in them. The value of a commodity was greater or smaller according to the state of demand for it, then, not the quantity of labor-time necessary to produce it. Since less demand naturally followed from increased consumption of the same commodity, its utility would fall as its supply increased; the final or marginal unit demanded would therefore determine the utility—the value—of the entire supply.[45]

The marginalists assumed their first task was to discredit the labor theory of value because they understood themselves to be shifting the focus of political economy from the sphere of production to the sphere of consumption, from the supply side to the demand side. Their starting point was not the social relations between individuals or functional groups engaged in producing goods but the "psychological relation between individuals and finished goods," as Ronald Meek suggested in 1957. Even so, the marginalists did not deny that the category of value had social meaning and determinants. To be sure, they claimed that individual or "subjective" or particular desires of consumers were more significant than quantities of social labor-time in the determination of any commodity's value; to be more exact, they claimed that unless effective demand validated the prior expenditure of labor-power, commodities would have no value regardless of the labor-time contained in them. In short, they argued that if production was the necessary condition of value, demand was the sufficient condition. Yet the category of effective demand did not become unwieldy or inexplicable because it appeared to be the sum of innumerable and incomparable desires. In terms of marginalist theory, every individual was a composite or social self, whose identity and desires were powerfully shaped if not wholly determined by the expectations of the others who embodied the social-cultural context in which he or she lived and worked. If pure subjectivity was therefore implausible, so was the related possibility that desire, and thus value as such, were purely subjective.[46]

In any event, the mere statement of marginalist principles suggested that production and consumption were not different aspects of the same phenomenon, and so were not directly connected in theory or practice. By focusing their theory on the demand side, the marginalists were announcing that the problem of supply (or production) had been solved, that the critical issue of the times was distribution (or consumption). In doing so, they were acknowledging the evidence of late-nineteenth-century business cycles, which, as interpreted by economic theorists and businessmen alike, suggested that supply simply did not create its own demand. For my purposes, however, the significant fact is that the marginalists' focus on the issues of demand and distribution represented, or implied the possibility of, a new orientation toward the working class; the habits, desires, and demands of the majority—in effect, mass consumption—had become the proper object of high theory.

Here, too, the evidence was readily available. Influential observers of the "great depression" of the late nineteenth century, which plagued Europe as well as North America, generally agreed that the cause of falling prices was "overproduction," that is, production beyond effective or remunerative demand. The results of overproduction were not the same, however, across class lines or economic sectors. Most pro-capitalist observers emphasized that after 1873, money and real wages had increased dramatically, especially for skilled labor in the metalworking or heavy industries, and therefore that wage earners were the principal beneficiaries of economic development under conditions approximating depression. For example, David A. Wells, who was probably the most influential of all observers of the economic scene, announced in 1890: "Profits and prices of commodities have fallen, except in a few special departments. Consequently the purchasing power of wages has risen, and this has given to the wage-earning class a greater command over the necessaries of life." Charles A. Conant, perhaps the most accomplished and prolific theoretician of modern business enterprise in the late nineteenth century, was more cautious yet more pointed. "Those laborers who continue to earn their customary wages are benefited materially in a period of low prices, because of the greatly increased purchasing power of their earnings. An industrial enterprise which continues to operate without profit or at a loss during a depression . . . transfers all its benefits, therefore, to the wage earners, and their wealth is enhanced at the expense of the owners of inherited or accumulated capital." In effect, what Wells and Conant were describing (and denouncing) was a transfer of income from capital to labor, from profits to wages—and a corresponding diversion of resources from production for production to production for consumption.[47]

And indeed the 1880s look in retrospect like a golden age for the consumer goods industries. This was the moment at which companies such as Procter & Gamble, Libbey Foods, General Mills, Duke Tobacco, Johnson & Johnson, and Coca-Cola reorganized and adopted a "mass market" strategy predicated on high volume, low margins, new packaging, and recognizably modern advertising campaigns. It was also the moment at which visionaries such as A. Montgomery Ward and Richard Sears invented the retail mail-order business, in the belief that they might eventually sell every imaginable household item C.O.D. to every household. And it was of course the moment at which the metropolitan press and the department store finally came of age; the consummation of their relationship in the 1880s, which had been impending since the 1850s, not incidentally created both journalism and advertising as we still experience them, as the situation of the scandalous or the spectacular in everyday life. The first major department stores in New York and Chicago began in the 1860s and 1870s as subsidiary enterprises in far-flung wholesale operations; but by the 1880s, the retail end had become more profitable, and founding fathers such as Marshall Field acted accordingly. Other firms that grew out of small retail operations established at midcentury (e.g., Macy's, Bloomingdale's, Abraham & Straus, Wanamaker's) did not become full-scale department stores until the 1880s or 1890s, when the reconstruction of their facades and the construction of new physical plants for larger stores—these were "palaces of art" or expositions in their own right—began in earnest.[48]

If we can rely on the calculations of William H. Shaw for the period 1869–1919, the percentage increase in output of consumer durables between 1879 and 1889 is matched or exceeded only by the increase between 1914 and 1919. The increase in personal and household furnishings—precisely the commodities featured by the new department stores—is especially striking. Since Shaw's figures are presented in dollar amounts, and since the 1880s was a decade of severe deflation, the increase is all the more striking. It suggests that to the familiar list of causes for the new stage of mass marketing reached in the 1880s, we might add the distribution of income, which validated the phenomenal growth of consumer goods industries and, to the same extent, worried those who believed that workers' "greater command of the necessaries of life" constituted a moral as well as an economic problem because it challenged the role of saving, profits, and investment in the rate and pattern of economic growth—that is, because it challenged the social functions of capital(ists).[49]

The new professional economists were among those who worried about the moral implications of the distribution of income; in fact their interest in the issue of distribution defined their professional activities and signified their opposition to the "old economics." Yet they were just as interested in the possibility of integrating the evidence of mass consumption into the theory of value and the discipline of political economy. For they believed that such evidence indicated a new stage of social development, one in which the inherited antagonism between production and consumption was dissolving; to comprehend the meanings of consumption was, then, to demonstrate that political economy was the stuff of social theory as well as practical politics. If the antagonism between production and consumption was dissolving, for example, the possibility of redefining—and pacifying—the social relation between capital and labor would no longer seem quite so remote, because the wages of labor could be advertised in such terms as something more than cost of production, as something other than a threat to profits. Moreover, if value was conferred on commodities by activity that did not qualify as "production" in the political languages of American social movements (of farmers as well as workers), the obvious difficulties of reconciling republicanism and modern-industrial capitalism—of integrating capitalists into the body politic—would no longer seem insurmountable. To comprehend the meanings of consumption was, then, to discover new authorization for consumption as such, whether by capital or labor; to accomplish that task, however, was to explain and justify the distribution of income (the condition of consumption) without recourse to the language of productive labor residing in the republican tradition.

At least this was how John Bates Clark, the leading American marginalist, conceived his intellectual agenda in the 1880s and 1890s. Like most of his colleagues among professional economists, Clark understood the popular appeal of socialism as the consequence of its close relation to the republican tradition. Indeed he called it "economic republicanism" because he believed that its creators and proponents had recast the familiar language of productive labor in terms that fit the circumstances of modern-industrial capitalism. In such perspective, the labor theory of value was merely the formalization of a popular cultural tradition. Thus Clark also understood that the marginalist departure from this tradition narrated a passage between past, present, and future which opened onto moral reformation and social reconstruction, not class conflict and socialist revolution. But he was aware that his own departure would seem an eccentric detour unless he could show how wealth was constituted if not created by those who played no visible or active role in the production of commodities, and thus why their claim to a share of those commodities was both rational and just. So he began his first major work, *The Philosophy of Wealth* (1887), by announcing that because existing economic theory "found no adequate place for the intellectual activities of men," it was deficient, and possibly dangerous. His task was then to rectify political economy by rehabilitating mental labor.[50]

In the opening chapters, Clark rejected the classical distinction between productive and unproductive labor as the source of confusion about the meaning of wealth, and repudiated the labor theory of value. His method was to replace the problem of valuation—the problem of relating quantities of output and quantities of value—with the more expansive notion of utility, by claiming that wealth was a "condition of relative well-being" with no conceivable objective or transhistorical measure; as such, it could be "produced only by that which, besides satisfying wants, is capable of appropriation." Mental labor was crucial to the creation of wealth because if "one class of laborers" produced "specific useful commodities" with the attribute of utility, the other "general class" produced laws, principles, and procedures that gave objects the "attribute of appropriability," in effect by bringing them to market, or simply by naming them, as consumable commodities. This implicit division of society into classes with different productive functions was immediately obscured by Clark's repudiation of the labor theory of value on the grounds that it reduced labor to its measurable, manual element, and thus could not grasp the value of its "mental and moral" elements. But if readers were confused by the discursive form of the argument, its content and its object were unmistakable. "In view of the constant presence of these three elements in labor, the physical, the mental, and the moral, any effort, in the supposed interest of the working classes, to depreciate mental labor in comparison with physical is unintelligent." The republican tradition, like the working class itself, was apparently trapped in the body. At any rate Clark suggested that both had to be modified or contained by the "higher" elements of human nature discovered and articulated in "the state of actual development" which transcended the "primitive paradise" of the physical and the natural. So modified or contained—in short, once sublimated—neither the republican tradition nor the working class would represent a threat to the further development of the larger social organism.[51]

Clark was not proposing, then, to forget or repress the republican tradition, just as he was not proposing to subjugate the working class. He was exploring the middle ground between labor and capital, trying to find an alternative to their positions on the relation between production and consumption of wealth, staking out an area that included both positions without becoming either. He secured only a foothold in *The Philosophy of Wealth* because his argument was more assault on than resettlement of contested terrain. He did include a chapter entitled "The Law of Distribution," which promised to solve the problem of "how to justly divide the gain" in total wealth or income. But at this crucial moment, Clark reverted to the radical criticism of cutthroat competition which had become the stock-in-trade of the "new economics." He did not yet have a language or a voice that was consistent with the dispassionate or "scientific" solution he sought: his foothold was the moral high ground. It was almost as if Clark were waiting for the historical tendencies of "centralization" and "solidarity" to validate a lawful distribution of wealth. For every time he approached the original problem—"how to justly divide the gain"—he immediately veered toward discussion of the impending stage of economic development in which the organized solidarity of both capital and labor would replace or modulate the brute force of "individualistic competition," and thus provide a new basis for the distribution of wealth among legitimate claimants. The privileged place of truth he claimed was not, then, his theory of distribution, but the civilization of the future.[52]

Yet there were hints of the position Clark would finally establish in *The Distribution of Wealth* (1899); and the author himself treated the later work as the completion of the earlier. In the chapter following "The Law of Distribution," for example, he insisted that "in the primary sense of the term," wages were a "quantity of wealth" equal to labor's share of value added in a given industry—in other words, wages equaled the distinguishable product of labor, "a payment regarded as a mass of concrete commodities of a kind adapted to the laborer's use." Here Clark was elaborating on the grand claim of the pivotal second chapter: "The law of wages, the subject of desperate controversy, is, as we shall soon see, placed in a new and clear light when one apprehends, in its full bearing, the principle that the wage of labor is the market value of its product." What he ignored, of course, was the possibility of a difference between the exchange value of labor-power construed as a commodity and the exchange value of the commodities that constituted the output of wage-laborers. But he did so because he had already dismissed the labor theory of value. His premises throughout were that the value of any commodity was determined by its "effective utility"—what we would now call "opportunity cost"—and that the addition of capital to any given mix of productive inputs would increase the output of labor ("capital" was left undefined, but its implicit meanings were both material and mental, i.e., it could be understood as an amount of fixed capital or as the supervisory functions of capitalists).[53] The question Clark could not answer in *The Philosophy of Wealth* was how that gain of output was, or ought to be, divided between capital and labor.

He tried again in *The Distribution of Wealth*.[54] This time he assumed that adding on to the edifice of classical political economy, by illustrating the role of demand or consumption in the determination of market value, would not produce satisfying results. "The indictment that hangs over society is that of 'exploiting labor,'" Clark noted at the outset. "If this charge were proved, every right-minded man should become a socialist." To stay above the fray—to remain in the realm of consumption—was to admit the truth of the socialist position. So the "new economics" had to *include* the old, not dismiss it or ignore it. "If we are to test the charge, however, we must enter the realm of production."[55] Clark's entry was, then, by way of marginal productivity, not utility. In effect, he assumed that the realms of production and consumption required different methods or categories of analysis because each operated according to unique principles. He did not drop the idea that "effective utility" determined the value of commodities. But he did attempt to explain capital as both a material input and a functional role in production, both of which could be measured in monetary terms as investment.

Thus he could claim that "pure profit" was the temporary, residual gain due entrepreneurs for their organizational innovations, whereas "interest" represented the earnings of capital construed as an enduring input and the condition of secular increase in labor productivity. The marginal "product" of capital, in this sense, was the difference between the total output of a given labor force before and after investment in and installation of new plant and equipment. The increase in the marginal product of labor—and so in the wages of labor—was now theoretically dependent on the maintenance of productive investment, which was itself a function of past income accruing to capital (interest).[56]

Capital could hereafter appear as a factor of *production*. Far from being a parasite on productive labor, it was, according to Clark, the condition of labor's productivity and the linchpin of what we would now call total factor productivity. As such, "capital" was a figure whose income derived from a quantifiable contribution to the production of commodities; yet its function was not "productive labor" according to the republican dispensation. It was, moreover, a figure whose consumption was authorized by a "marginal product"; and so its role was not that of the "consuming aesthete" valorized in the "new vistas of silence" which defined the high culture invented by the upper class. This figure stood between the extremities of a culture in the making—but it was much more than a middleman because it seemed to synthesize the economic functions and social positions of capital and labor. It did not, then, represent a new class so much as it symbolized the possibility of an end to class conflict between capital and labor.

CHAPTER 3

. . . .

BETWEEN CONSUMERS AND

CORPORATIONS

Economists and Cultural Critics

By any measure, Clark's achievement was extraordinary. He had defined the problem of income distribution as a fundamentally political or ideological problem and had consistently engaged it at that level, where microeconomic applications—the normal science of his emerging profession—were almost incidental to the larger argument. For he wanted to show "not merely how to divide a sum, but how to adjust rights and obligations." Like most of his contemporaries among the new professional economists, he was more or less obsessed with meeting the challenge issued by the moral philosopher Henry Sidgwick, in his review of Francis A. Walker's pioneering work, *The Wages Question* (1877). "While Professor Walker's argument gives a coup de grace to the wages-fund theory, it supplies no substitute for it; it leaves us with no theoretical determination whatever for the average proportions in which produce is divided between capital and labor." Walker himself established the pattern of response with an essay of 1887, "The Source of Business Profits." Here he overthrew the empiricist dictum of *The Wages Question*—"what we need is not a nice theoretical classification, but a just and strong exhibition of the great groups of our modern industrial society"—and offered a down payment on "a complete and consistent body of doctrine regarding the distribution of wealth." Clark's efforts may be viewed as either further installments or final payments.[1]

In 1903, J. H. Hollander of Johns Hopkins suggested that Walker's investment in a theory of distribution was "a reaction born of intimate acquaintance with American economic conditions [against] the traditional doctrines of the English classical political economy." But Walker's purpose was not to exempt the U.S. from the corollaries and consequences of industrial capitalism as these were revealed by a Ricardian theory of value; instead, he wanted to understand and to explain industrial capitalism as it had developed in the United States. So his concerns were never strictly practical or narrowly historical. Even the proximity to political power which purchased his "intimate acquaintance with American economic conditions" was afforded by his intellectual attainments, and fed into his theoretical project. Walker taught political economy at Yale from 1873 to 1881, then served as president of the Massachusetts Institute of Technology until his death in 1897. Meanwhile, he supervised the ninth and the tenth censuses as director of the U.S. Bureau of Statistics and consulted with the Senate Finance Committee during its investigations of wages and prices in the early 1890s. The most significant of the American economic conditions to be discovered from these various positions seemed to be that capitalists had become, or were fast becoming, public servants. As Hollander put it, in the United States "the laborer, and not the entrepreneur received, or might receive if he asserted his claim thereto, whatever economic surplus or unearned increment resulted from industry."[2]

The question that followed for Walker, and for the new generation of economists which included Clark, Hollander, Richard Ely, John R. Commons, E.R.A. Seligman, Irving Fisher, Franklin Giddings, and Simon Patten, was this: assuming it is possible for wage earners to receive "whatever economic surplus" results from industrial production—presumably because almost everyone agreed that consumption was authorized by the creation of new values through "productive labor," not by the "unproductive" mental labor of the middleman or the manager—on what grounds can entrepreneurs or capitalists justify their claims to a share of national income? Like his successors, Walker hoped that his answer, his new theory of distribution, would have broadly political consequences. For example, here is how he concluded his essay of 1887: "The bearing of this view of the source of business profits upon the socialist assumption that profits are but unpaid wages is too manifest to require exposition. That this view . . . would have a truly reconciling influence upon the always strained and often hostile relations between employer and employed, cannot be doubted."[3]

Walker's successors, who shared his fears of class conflict and his hopes for economic theory, were the original American marginalists. By the 1920s, scholars generally agreed that these New World innovators excelled within the province of theory that attempted to explain the distribution of income between the "factors of production" (i.e., land/rent, labor/wages, capital/profit). Scholars could agree on this because the American marginalists were the first to articulate an elaborate conception of the capitalist's creative function in commodity production as well as distribution and, on that basis, to propose theories of cost, profit, and interest which fit the new "subjective" bent of political economy. Since the marginalist theory of value was essentially a theory of demand, it required as a condition of its coherence a theory of income distribution—that is, some account of how demand was made effective. The American marginalists provided this account. That is why contestants in the recent debate over modern capital theory so often cite the work of John Bates Clark.[4]

But from their standpoint in the late twentieth century, his faith in the moral weight and healing power of economic theory seems quaint at best. For example, Lionel Lord Robbins, the eminent economist, accepts marginal productivity as an analytical technique but dismisses the ethical import its inventors attributed to it. "It has sometimes been argued—J. B. Clark is perhaps the chief culprit—that a proof that, under competitive conditions, productive agents are paid according to the value of their marginal physical product is a proof that such a society is just. This of course is a complete *non sequitur*."[5] And yet Clark and his allies within the marginalist vanguard did not see it that way. So before we decide that we can detach the "scientific" content of marginal productivity from its original "ideological" form—as if we could extrude the essence of economic theory from the base alloy of language in which it happens to be embedded—we should ask why its American inventors never noticed the logical contradiction in which they had apparently implicated themselves and their students.

To do so is to ask why the marginalists in the United States saw the need for a new language, a new model, of political obligation, or, what is the same thing, why they believed they had to specify new conditions of mutuality, harmony, and equality among the interests or agents that constituted civil society. To begin with, the American marginalists assumed that natural right—what Thorstein Veblen called the principle of "natural liberty"— was no longer adequate to explain or to justify capitalist conduct and income. Alfred Marshall, the English economist with whom Walker and Clark had the most in common, stated that assumption forthrightly: "The tendency of careful economic study is to base the rights of private property not on any abstract principle, but on the observation that in the past they have been inseparable from solid economic progress." In other words, so long as the natural right of property went unquestioned, the classical economists' "failure to realize a positive service of capital in production," as Hollander put it, was not a serious omission.[6]

But once civil society was no longer an assembly of individual proprietors who were equally subject to the anonymous laws of the market—

once a certain concentration of wealth and the permanence of a property-less "wages class" were evident to all interested observers—any expectation of agreement among civil society's constituent elements on the most basic rights and obligations (e.g., of property) became dangerously naive. Arthur Hadley, the authority on (and director of) railroads from Yale who adapted marginalist principles in his *Economics* of 1896, explained the problem in this way: "A republican government is organized on the assumption that all men are free and equal. If the political power is . . . equally distributed while the industrial power is concentrated in the hands of a few, it creates dangers of class struggles and class legislation which menace both our political and our industrial order."[7]

From his standpoint, the search for a theory of distribution which attributed to capitalists a "positive service in production" was a search for the principles and sources of mutuality, harmony, and equality among individuals aggregated according to economic function. It was, then, a search made possible and necessary by the rise of the "labor problem"—by the demise of equality among individuals and the concurrent emergence of a modern class society. In that sense, or to that extent, we can say that the marginalists faced the question of class struggle squarely. It is precisely because they did not try to avoid the issues raised by the "socialistic writers," as Hadley called them, that they were successful in enunciating a new language of political obligation which stressed the active service and progressive functions of capital.[8]

At this metatheoretical level, marginalism was an unquestionably realistic approach to the key issues of modern, corporate-industrial society in the United States. As such, it constitutes a significant contribution to what we know as modern liberalism. For modern liberalism acknowledges the equity of functional groups as a *potential* principle of political obligation in a society characterized by the concentration of wealth and power.[9] But it is difficult to account in these terms for the success of marginalism as a teaching device in the universities and as a policy-relevant model in private-sector planning. We need, therefore, to ask what made it appear realistic in the realm of microeconomic applications.

Another way to pose the same question is to ask why it was not until the 1890s that marginal utility (or productivity) was deemed "useful in solving practical economic problems," as C.D.W. Goodwin puts it. In effect we are asking what, if any, practical economic problems emerging in or by the 1890s seemed uniquely susceptible to marginalist assumptions and methods. If we can judge from discussions among the leaders of the American business community—who were increasingly drawn from the new corporate sector of this community—the late-nineteenth-century order of events had defined the relation between costs, prices, and returns on capital investment as the critical microeconomic problem, but had also demonstrated that the economic problem so conceived was one symptom of unanswered social, cultural, and political questions. Their solution was to consolidate competing firms, to integrate separate industries, thus to stabilize prices and reinstate reasonable profits—in other words, to use the possibilities of the corporate legal form as an answer to such questions. This strategy of corporate "rationalization" would reduce fixed costs vis-à-vis the price of finished products, and in the longer run would allow the conscious adjustment of supply to demand and price to cost.[10]

But if supply rather than price or profit was to be the new variable in a new corporate-industrial investment system, the technical or administrative problem of cost allocation among different kinds and different uses of capital assets acquired a practical significance it did not—and could not— have as long as the determination of prices and profits was left to the demand side. And here marginalist analysis became particularly relevant and useful. Its theorem of opportunity cost, for example, by which one calculates the utilities that could have been produced with the same resources that went into what was actually produced, is essentially a method of establishing priorities in economic planning; for it presumes that one can choose between at least two different uses of assets. The principle of substitution (capital for labor and vice versa), which not incidentally animates neoclassical capital theory, is similarly predicated on the assumption that investment decisions are not forced on capitalists by external circumstances, as Jeremiah Jenks, the Cornell economist and authority on "the trust question," claimed they were as late as 1890. "No sooner has the capitalist fairly adopted one improved machine, than it must be thrown away for a still later and better invention, which must be purchased at dear cost, if the manufacturer would not see himself eclipsed by his rival."[11]

Marginal utility or productivity could not, then, become useful in solving the practical economic problems of cost allocation and long-term investment planning until the corporate alternative to unrestricted competition among capitalists made them practical economic possibilities. By the same token, the marginalist view of capital's active function in producing value would seem implausible unless managers had effectively challenged skilled workers' control of the division of labor within the factory, and until pro-capitalist intellectuals had proposed realistic alternatives to the category of productive labor. From this standpoint, the marginalists carried the day after 1890 because they designed a model that posited—that presupposed *and* promoted—those changes through which capitalist solidarity and managerial discretion would become the conditions of renewed economic growth and social development. We now summarize those changes by reference to the rise of corporate (or managerial or monopoly) capitalism. Clark's generation summarized them in terms of "the trust question," and used the new theory of marginal productivity to explain them. As Hollander claimed, "The successive aspects of the theory become intelligible as the interpretation . . . of contemporary industrial life."[12] Clark and his colleagues in the marginalist vanguard understood that the point was to change it; and they were able to help change it because their theories did in fact comprehend their times.

Or did they? I have been arguing that the marginalist model allowed economists to narrate—to examine, to explain, to justify—the emergence of both mass consumption and corporate enterprise. In effect I have been arguing that the marginalist model amounts to the political economy of consumer culture, and should be appreciated as such. I want to clarify this argument by demonstrating that consumer culture resides in the transition from proprietary to corporate capitalism. So I must begin by insisting that we define consumer culture as something more than the negotiation of meanings through the display of goods, or rather through the commodity form; otherwise we have no incentive to treat consumption as both economic and cultural activity, and thus no reason to believe that qualitative and quantitative changes in consumption after 1800 signify either economic or cultural change.

Perhaps I protest too much. To be sure, much of the recent work on the topic does tend to equate "the birth of consumer society" and the generalization of the commodity form; that is why debates among scholars who assume the validity of this equation often sound both portentous and pointless. But Richard Fox and Jackson Lears, the editors of the pathbreaking collection *The Culture of Consumption*, do, after all, define consumer culture as a "value system," as a "new set of sanctions for the elite control" of twentieth-century American society, as "an ethic, a standard of living, and a power structure," and finally as "an ideology and a way of seeing."[13] They also claim that this complex came of age between 1880 and 1930, as a consequence of convergence between the "maturation of the national marketplace," the "emergence of a new stratum of professionals and managers," and the "rise of a new gospel of therapeutic release" (xi). So their periodization of consumer culture is certainly consistent with what I will propose hereafter; for they argue that the new culture was convened by a constellation of economic, social, and intellectual events (mature market-place, new stratum, new gospel) specific to the late nineteenth century.

Yet for all their doubts about earlier scholarship, which perfected a paranoid style in explaining the political effects of mass consumption, Fox and Lears define the culture in question as the invention of persuaders hidden between labor and capital.

> In this time of cultural consternation, the new professional-managerial corps appeared with a timely dual message. On the one hand they proposed a new managerial efficiency, a new regime of administration by experts for business, government, and other spheres of life. On the other hand, they preached a new morality that subordinated the old goal of transcendence to new ideals of self-fulfillment and immediate gratification. This late-nineteenth-century link between individual hedonism and bureaucratic organizations—a link that has been strengthened in the twentieth century—marks the point of departure for modern American consumer culture. (xii)

They also treat the "maturation of the national marketplace" as a self-evident summary of economic change in the period. So the historical perspective they bring to the study of consumer culture cannot address the questions of periodization raised by scholars who claim that "the birth of consumer society" is an eighteenth-century phenomenon.

In effect, Fox, Lears, and their coauthors argue that the culture emerging in the United States at the turn of the twentieth century should be understood as the extremity of what Georg Lukács called "reification"; for it completes the "commodification" of social life which began with the rise of capitalism, by making every social relation, personal attribute, and political principle subject to the "cash nexus," to the laws of value that regulate the circulation of commodities. They designate this new complex a "consumer" culture because everything, even subjectivity as such, is finally and fully implicated in the price system—*because the self-determining personality now becomes a consumer good*, the elements of which are for sale in the market as beauty, cleanliness, sincerity, and autonomy. Here is how Lukács put it: "The transformation of the commodity relation into a thing of 'ghostly objectivity' . . . stamps its imprint upon the whole consciousness of man; his qualities and abilities are no longer an organic part of his personality, they are things which he can 'own' or 'dispose of' like the various objects of the external world." So conceived, consumer culture becomes the frontier of commodity fetishism opened by the "maturation of the national marketplace" and mapped by the new professional persuaders—it requires the negotiation of all meanings, even the meanings of selfhood, through the display of those goods that the commodity form can accommodate. As Fox, Lears, and their coauthors define and criticize it, twentieth-century consumer culture is, then, the fulfillment of eighteenth-century "consumer society" as John McKendrick, J. H. Plumb, and others define and celebrate it. According to both camps, the difference between these notions and periods is of degree rather than kind; for both camps assume that the generalization of the commodity form must be the proximate cause of what they propose to explain.[14]

I want to sketch an alternative to this unlikely historiographical consensus by defining consumer culture more broadly, in terms of the development of capitalism—that is, by reopening the question of "reification" or "commodification." I do not mean to suggest that we can safely ignore the generalization of the commodity form. But I think John Dewey was correct to say that "because we are such materialists," we tend to focus our attention "upon the rigid thing instead of upon the moving act." We tend, in other words, to treat commodities as if they were external objects, not moments in a circuit of thoughts as well as things, of language as well as labor. We do so because we know, from reading Marx among others, that capitalism enlarges the dominion of dead matter, by enforcing the social power of past labor-time congealed in capital goods or represented by money and its surrogates. But we also know, from reading Dewey among others, that the development of capitalism enables an active, experimental attitude toward truth, which demands purposeful production and manipulation of objects as the condition of certainty in knowledge. Insofar as we treat the commodity form accordingly—insofar, that is, as we treat it pragmatically, as a "moving act" instead of a "rigid thing"—we can begin to grasp its meaning for and significance in different historical epochs. We might then be able to use the notion of "reification" as if it was something more than a synonym for alienation from the human condition.[15]

If I understand them correctly, Fox and Lears have claimed that the defining characteristic of twentieth-century consumer culture is the commodification of personality or selfhood. But to my knowledge, they have not explained how and why this phenomenon is specific to the late nineteenth or early twentieth century. Indeed I would say there are at least two reasons that they cannot do so. First, if we know that private property serves as the foundation of the self-determining personality in postfeudal society, but also that property must be an alienable commodity to serve as such, then we can assume that the commodification of personality or selfhood is the moral and political problem that determines the modern condition and defines the transition from feudalism to capitalism. As C. B. Macpherson, J.G.A. Pocock, and Jean-Christophe Agnew have demonstrated, the increasing mobility of property in the eighteenth-century aftermath of the financial revolution complicates but not does not create this problem.[16] Second, if the ethical principle that regulates the critique of consumer culture is the integrity of the "natural individual," the self-determining personality, and if the condition of that integrity is abstention from the historical process through which social relations, personal attributes, and political principles are commodified in theory and practice, then the critique becomes incoherent. For it posits as ethical principle precisely what it repudiates as historical event—it posits the "natural individual," the self-determining personality, created in and by the transition from feudalism to capitalism, that is, in and by the commodification of personality or selfhood which reached a critical stage with "the birth of consumer society" in the eighteenth century.

So I would suggest that the critique of consumer culture according to Fox, Lears, and others should be understood as a moral polemic against the proletarianization of the small producer which remains perfectly consistent with possessive individualism; in other words, it should be understood as a more or less populist protest against the bureaucratization of bourgeois society by corporate-industrial business enterprise. But I do not want to suggest that their critique is insignificant because it is animated by populist politics. I would instead insist that it is indispensable because it begins by asking this question: if the personality has no fixed location, no real foundation in property or in a community of producers, can we imagine the possibility of genuine selfhood and, for that matter, of an intelligible morality? Like the Populists, Fox, Lears, and their coauthors answer with an almost thunderous "No!" In doing so, they threaten to exclude most of the twentieth-century population from full citizenship in the moral and political universe they valorize. But the question is more important than the answer; for it leads us back to the late nineteenth century, when the fact of a permanent proletarian majority became a salient issue in American political discourse—that is, when people asked the same question as if their answers would determine the future of popular government.

I am not claiming that more was at stake back then, or that the political discourse of the late nineteenth century was superior to that of the late twentieth century. I *am* claiming that until the mid-1920s, the sources of the genuine self were open to serious question and political answers. When artists and intellectuals asked whether subjectivity could survive its expulsion from the private Eden of the inner self, the question was not merely rhetorical, and the answers were not invariably elegiac, as they have since become for almost all writers on the Left. They treated the characteristic changes of their epoch—the reconstruction of business enterprise, the confusion of cultural spheres, and the remaking of class relations—not only as threats to modern subjectivity but also as sources of a new, *social* self. So they saw promise and possibility where the contemporary critics of consumer culture see only problems. Where the latter see the commodification of social relations as such, for example, the former saw both the possibility of a passage beyond the realm of necessity and the promise of rewarding work that was nevertheless "unproductive" labor from the standpoint of subaltern social movements.[17]

Note, however, that both generations of young intellectuals agree that the characteristic changes of the epoch beginning around 1890 do represent threats to modern subjectivity or possessive individualism. They also agree that questions of political economy are central to all others if only because the division of mental and manual labor—a division that defines the "new social stratum" of professional persuaders—is itself determined by the mechanization of commodity production and the bureaucratization of the labor process under corporate auspices. This broad area of agreement makes the differences between the generations all the more striking; surely it makes examination and explanation of these differences all the more essential. Let us return, then, to the generation that came of age at the turn of the century. Why did it believe that the problem of production had been solved, and how did it express that belief?

Advent of the "Age of Surplus"

By the end of the nineteenth century, observers of the American scene—not just the economists and the academic intellectuals but also the politicians and the larger public—had several good reasons to believe that the existing capacity to produce commodities far exceeded the effective demand for those commodities. The notion of "overproduction" had already supplanted or subsumed monetary explanations of economic crisis, and not simply because the Populists had lost their electoral gamble of 1896. For the pro-corporate goldbugs had turned the labor theory of value against its presumed partisans among the "toiling millions," mainly by pointing out that prices of commodities fell as did the labor-time required to produce them: monetary factors alone could not account for the available evidence. In the

1890s and after, the question of demand or distribution accordingly became a central political issue as well as a problem for macroeconomic theory.[18]

Indeed the inventors of the new industrial corporations depicted them as means by which this question could be properly addressed. So conceived, the corporations appeared as a device through which supply could be adjusted to demand without state-centered planning, and demand itself could be enlarged, reshaped, or even created. If you were a Populist, this capacity of the corporations represented a threat to the liberties of the people because it presupposed the centralization of market power and the manipulation of market forces; if you were not a Populist, it represented the possibility of treating the market as something other than a self-regulating externality that limited the liberties of most people. But everyone agreed that the corporations were both symptom and attempted cure of "overproduction," and would succeed insofar as they found answers to the question of distribution.

So the corporations announced the advent of the age of surplus. In populist perspective, everything about "the trusts" was superfluous, including— or rather especially—the new social stratum that inhabited, and managed, the relation between the "producing classes" and the capitalists. This stratum produced nothing of its own, nothing of value in the strict sense determined by the category of "productive labor," except perhaps the laws and the rules that would regulate the disposition of *excess* values. In short, the corporations were the equivalent—the cause and the effect—of the unproductive and the unnecessary. From a different standpoint than that afforded by the Peoples' Party, however, this equivalence was a reason to celebrate, or to contemplate, the effects and implications of business enterprise as it had been redefined by corporate innovation. At any rate it was an invitation to think about the meaning of necessity, and perhaps to rethink the significance of the "social surplus" that corporate enterprise had appeared to allocate.[19]

By 1914, so many writers had accepted this invitation that the notion of an "age of surplus" had become a commonplace if not a cliché. The utility of the notion was due in part to the efforts of Simon Patten, the University of Pennsylvania economist who began describing an impending "economic revolution" in the 1890s. He mapped the promised land most clearly in a popular book of 1907, *The New Basis of Civilization*, where he charted the passage from a "pain economy" to a "pleasure economy," or from the "age of deficit" to the "age of surplus." Long stretches of this book are barren ground on which nothing but superficial speculations could flourish; elsewhere the tone and style are so anxiously prophetic as to make the argument a parody of a seventeenth-century jeremiad. Yet Patten himself was a perfectly respectable member of several professional communities; in 1908, for example, he served as president of the American Economic Association. Moreover, his book's immediate influence was considerable—by which I mean not that it went through eight editions before 1923, although this is indicative of its popularity, but that it quickly became a lexicon for all kinds of writers who were looking for a way to specify the relation between the "economic revolution" residing in the "trust movement" and the cultural revolution residing in the redefinition of subjectivity. Among these writers were Van Wyck Brooks, the most influential of the so-called young intellectuals who rewrote nineteenth-century American literary history between 1915 and 1929; Mary Roberts Smith Coolidge, the Stanford sociologist who became an authority on both immigration and feminism; and William James, who understood more clearly than anyone else that subjectivity would survive the transition to what he called a "pacific cosmopolitan industrialism." [20]

But the notion of an "age of surplus" was even more pervasive and reputable than these examples would suggest. Economists in the mainstream of both theoretical developments and practical policy-making had been dealing with the implications of surplus capital since the mid-1890s. By the second decade of the twentieth century, they had also begun to consider the limits to growth represented by social and psychological constraints on consumption, not investment. For example, in 1912, Wesley C. Mitchell of Columbia, who had been a student of Thorstein Veblen's at the University of Chicago—he later became a founder of the National Bureau of Economic Research and the dean of business cycle theorists in the United States—published an essay entitled "The Backward Art of Spending Money" in the *American Economic Review*. Here Mitchell followed contemporary feminist usage by defining the family as a constraint on the increase of consumption recently made possible and necessary by the "gigantic increase in the volume of goods produced and in the aggregate incomes earned." He claimed that North Americans were already "reorganizing certain forms of family expenditure on the basis of large groups"—for example, through "socialized spending of money" on parks, playgrounds, nurseries, libraries—and proposed to enlarge on these "promising experiments" in the organization of consumption. [21]

Jeremiah Jenks also wondered about the effects of this new relation between production and consumption—new because the practical question it raised was no longer how to restrict consumption or contain the growth of wage income in the name of greater investment and expanded production, but how to enlarge consumption or maintain the growth of wage income when the growth of employment (hence wage income) no longer seemed to be the function of expanded production enforced by greater private investment. In 1913, at the moment social scientists were beginning to worry about what they now call structural unemployment, Jenks addressed this question in the context of a study of the demand for labor as it would be determined by patterns of immigration. If employment was no longer growing proportionately to the increase of output because corporations had economized on labor-time (and labor costs) by fully mechanizing the production process, he noted, then the continuation of immigration at existing rates would create an unprecedented problem of unemployment. He proposed to reconsider if not revise immigration policies, and left it at that. But my point is that Jenks noticed what later economists and social theorists would grasp as the characteristic problem, or promise, of twentieth-century corporate capitalism—he noticed that one effect of the "trust movement" was the extrication of human labor as such from commodity production, and he wondered what to make of it.[22]

Since then, we have all been wondering about the same thing, whether we know it or not. The bottom line of recent debates about government spending, for example, is reached when we realize that both sides in the debate agree that the demand for labor determined by *private* investment cannot create full employment; in other words, everyone agrees that "public investment" in the form of government spending is necessary to the growth of wage income (hence consumption) because growth of employment can no longer be defined as a function of expanded production enforced by private investment.[23] I do not want to suggest that Jenks and Mitchell or Patten and Coolidge or Brooks and James stated the case in this way, or that they were fully aware of what the ongoing "economic revolution" entailed. But I do want to insist that they made significant contributions to the political economy of consumer culture—that they studied the social and cultural questions of their time as if these were also economic questions raised by the advent of the "age of surplus."

Certainly Walter Lippmann did so in what remains his most provocative and political book, *Drift and Mastery: An Attempt to Diagnose the Current Unrest* (1914).[24] "We do no longer regard it as 'sordid' to take an interest in economic problems" (143), he announced, as if to remind his readers that he had already defined new social movements and cultural possibilities as symptoms of political-economic change. In the opening chapters of part 1, Lippmann summarized such change by noting that "the cultural basis of property is radically altered," and by suggesting how inherited ideas about the relation between property and personality would have to be altered accordingly; throughout he assumed that the "trust movement" was the proximate cause of these alterations (32–51). In the closing chapters of part 3, Lippmann moved to a different level of abstraction, where Patten's lexicon became the vernacular, and began to treat symptomatic social movements as if they were also cures for American economic ailments. For example, he concluded chapter 12 by predicting a future in which "mankind will have emerged from a fear economy" (138). This was not incidentally a paraphrase of James, who had quoted Patten in "The Moral Equivalent of War."

In the next chapter, Lippmann claimed that the "desire for self-government has become vivid with the accumulation of a great surplus of wealth" (140–41), and went on to define the labor movement and the "women's awakening" as symptoms of this modern, democratic desire. Indeed he called them the "two greatest forces for human emancipation"—here he followed Ibsen's lead—because they were "pointed away from submissive want, balked impulse, and unquestioned obedience" (142–43). They were expressions, he suggested, of an impending passage beyond necessity. "In the midst of plenty, the imagination becomes ambitious, rebellion against misery is at last justified, and dreams have a basis in fact" (141). From this standpoint, the related results of the renunciation of desire—social control and character formation—looked like residues of repression which had become unnecessary in view of "a great surplus of wealth"; in other words, the reform of the body politic required the resurrection of the body, but both presupposed the advent of the age of surplus. "So, too, the day is passing when the child is taught to regard the body as a filthy thing. . . . Our interest in sex is no longer to annihilate it, but to educate it, to find civilized opportunities for its expression. We hope to organize industry and housekeeping so that normal mating shall not be a monstrously difficult problem" (143).[25]

By Lippmann's account, "the accumulation of a great surplus of wealth" undermined the older incentives for increased production under the auspices of "modern industry" (35–44) and accordingly enlarged the cultural significance of consumption. "We hear a great deal about the class-consciousness of labor; my own observation is that in America to-day consumers' consciousness is growing very much faster" (55). This correlation of "great surplus" and "consumers' consciousness" logically entailed the growth of feminism, or at least some increase in the economic and cultural significance of women, apparently because female experience had not been shaped by production for profit or work for wages. "The mass of women do not look at the world as workers; in America, at least their prime interest is as consumers" (54). Other close observers of the American scene used a similar gauge to measure the same dimension of the age of surplus. In 1910, for example, William James explained the appeal of war by reference to the lack of necessary labor or meaningful work under the stupefying regime of "pacific cosmopolitan industrialism." The age of surplus was creating "a world of clerks and teachers, of co-education and zo-ophily, of 'consumer's leagues' and 'associated charities,' of industrialism unlimited, and feminism unabashed"—in other words, a world over which women presided. Edward Devine, one of Patten's more energetic and influential students from the University of Pennsylvania, was perhaps more explicit in "The Economic Function of Woman," an essay published in 1894: "If acquisition is the idea which in the past history of economics has been all but unduly emphasized, expenditure is the idea which the future of the science will place beside it. It is this change which involves a revolution in the attitude of the science toward the economic function of woman." [26]

When Lippmann, James, and Devine suggested that women embodied or represented the principle of consumption (as against production), they were drawing on common knowledge; for the gendered division of labor between household and market which characterized capitalist industrialization in the nineteenth century had already expelled manhood and productive labor from the symbolic property of the home, where feminine domesticity could become a consumer good. [27] But when they claimed that consumption had or would become the regulative principle of life under "pacific cosmopolitan industrialism," and deduced the increasing significance of females (or feminism) from that claim, they were remaking common sense. For they were suggesting that the relation between the "economic revolution" residing in the "trust movement" (that is, the advent of the "age of surplus" under corporate auspices) and the cultural revolution residing in the redefinition of subjectivity was transacted in the figure of the New Woman.

From their standpoint, I would then conclude, the New Woman represented not only the principle of consumption but the promise of subjectivity under circumstances that seemed to have cast the "social self" as the new paradigm of personality. James is more ambiguous than the others—mainly, I think, because his critique of modern subjectivity authorizes several alternatives. Even so, we should remember that it was James who spoke as if pragmatism were a woman. "Ought we ever not to believe what it is better for us to believe? And can we then keep the notion of what is better for us, and what is true for us, permanently apart? Pragmatism says no, and I fully agree with her." [28] Since James and his ambiguities are the main characters in part 2 of this book, there is no need to develop them here. But I do want to reexamine Lippmann's argument about selfhood as a way of testing my conclusion on the representative capacities of the New Woman, and recalling my question about the differences between generations of young intellectuals.

There are three moments in this argument. First, Lippmann notes that the rise of the large corporations has radically changed the meaning and significance of private property. "The trust movement is doing what no conspirator or revolutionist could ever do: it is sucking the life out of private property. For the purposes of modern industry the traditional notions have become meaningless: the name continues, but the fact is disappearing. You cannot conduct the great industries and preserve intact the principles of private property. And so the trusts are organizing private property out of existence, are altering its nature so radically that very little remains but the title and the ancient theory" (45). This verdict on property may sound demented or apocalyptic to citizens of the late twentieth century. But it was both unexceptional and unexceptionable in 1914. As Alfred Marshall had suggested, those who were engaged in "careful economic study" did not invoke natural right when explaining or defending the purposes to which private property was put by that legal artifice known as the large corporation; they already knew better. Lippmann's verdict should be allowed to stand in any event. For the separation of ownership and direct control of corporate assets implies that the right to manage such assets cannot be derived from its traditional source in the natural right of property, and that the performance of corporate managers need not be evaluated according to strictly economic criteria such as profit and loss.[29]

Second, Lippmann claims that under circumstances defined by the "trust movement," property ownership cannot be posited as the necessary condition of self-determination. The civilizing "magic of property" simply will not work in the laboratory of the "largescale corporation," where "capital shall be impersonal, 'liquid,' 'mobile' "—not the material means to authentic individuality. "For where in the name of sanity have all the courage, foresight, initiative gone to, what has happened to all the rugged virtues that are supposed to be inherent in the magic of property? They have gone a-glimmering with the revolutionary change that the great industry has produced. Those personal virtues belong to an earlier age when men really had some personal contact with their property" (47). The cause-effect relation between property ownership and the virtues of self-determination ("courage, foresight, initiative")—a relation normally represented in American political discourse by the figure of the freeholder or the small producer—was, then, attenuated if not adjourned under social conditions defined by corporate enterprise. The freeholder, the small producer, had escaped the vicissitudes of historical time by virtue of his fixed location in the body politic, his unique place in relation to his property; he had served accordingly as the model of the modern subject, the "inner-directed" individual. This modern individual also appeared as the moral personality because he was both autonomous and rational: he could neither be appropriated by others—he was not a wage slave—nor dominated by his own desires. So he was something more than the creature of social or natural circumstances; he had *character*. He was the "man of reason."[30] But insofar as the relation between property and personality became an open question, as it did in Lippmann's argument, so, too, did this "man of reason"; for he was the product of the relation in question.

The third moment in Lippmann's argument is reached when he addresses this open question as if there might be an answer, that is, when alternatives to the dessicated figure of the freeholder or the small producer appear to complicate its correlates in the modern subject, the moral personality, the "man of reason." Those alternatives appear at the cutting edge of the movement for democracy—in the labor movement and through the "women's awakening." I cannot claim that Lippmann proposes the proletarian and the female as new models of subjectivity. But I can claim that these are the figures he associates with "social property," and with solutions to the "problem of collectivism" which emerges when private property becomes "too abstract, too scattered, too fluctuating" to constitute subjectivity in singular form, as the male proprietor.

For example, in concluding his analysis of the waning "magic of property," Lippmann remarks: "What has happened to the railroads is merely a demonstration of what is likely to happen to the other great industries. . . . Private property will melt away; its functions will be taken over by the salaried men who direct them, by government commissions, by developing trade unions" (49). But at that point the movement toward social democracy has only begun. "The real problem of collectivism is the difficulty of combining popular control with administrative power. Private property is no part of the issue. . . . What would remain for discussion would be the conflict between democracy and centralized authority" (50). So the labor movement becomes the key to resolving this conflict. "It is the development of a citizenship in industry that the labor movement has before it. It will have to work out the intricate problem of popular control in relation to technical administration" (66). For its purpose is to create a collective identity, a social subjectivity. "Only through the union can the wage-earner participate in the control of industry, and only through the union can he obtain the discipline needed for self-government" (59). Or again: "Labor is still fighting to be admitted to the sphere of human society where it is possible to talk of adjusting difficulties. A few workers, like the skilled railroad men, have just about climbed in. But the great mass has not been made part of that world where decisions are made and policies are formulated. The unions are struggling to give the wage-earners representation [in this domain], and that is why the hopes of democracy are bound up with the labor movement" (67).

Lippmann is even more emphatic about the civilizing function of the social movement convened by feminism. "The awakening of women points straight to the discipline of cooperation. And so it is laying the real foundations for the modern world" (133–34). Here again the pivot of the argument is the redefinition of property; for that is what creates both the possibility of and the necessity for collective identities through cooperation. "Now in the complicated civilization upon which we are now entering," Lippmann predicts, "it will be impossible for many people to enjoy the primitive sense of absolute possession. We shall need men and women who can take an interest in collective property, who can feel personally and vividly about it" (130). By redefining the home and the family, feminism promises to meet this need for adults who can imagine selfhood in the absence of absolute proprietary rights. "One of the supreme values of feminism is that it will have to socialize the home. When women seek a career they have to specialize. When they specialize they have to cooperate. They have to abandon more and more the self-sufficient individualism of the older family" (131).

As that older family recedes, Lippmann suggests, so, too, will the notion of property that served as its ego-boundary. "The sense of property may be a deep instinct. But surely the nineteenth century home stimulated the instinct to the point of morbidity. For it did almost nothing to bring the child into contact with the real antidote to acquisitiveness—a sense of social property" (130). This antidote is contained, then, in the feminist family, which, by its deepening implication in the social division of labor, can produce "people who can feel that they possess the parks, the libraries, the museums of their city, [who] are likely to be far more civilized people than those who want a park which they can enclose, and who want to own a masterpiece all by themselves" (130). So, while "the trusts" are busily "sucking the life out of private property," the women's movement inspired by feminism is breathing life into "a sense of social property"; in the same breath, Lippmann claims, it is announcing an alternative to "the self-sufficient individualism of the older family," wherein the female "learns to obey, to wait on the lordly male" (130).

He does, then, suggest that there are new models of subjectivity emerging from the labor movement and the "women's awakening." In both cases, the "social self" or the collective identity forged by cooperation appears as the alternative to the morbid isolation of the lordly male proprietor who still believes in the illusion of individualism, the magic of private property. But Lippmann expects the feminists to build the "real foundations" of a more civilized future; in his view, the New Woman represents the promise of subjectivity as well as the principle of consumption under circumstances defined by corporate enterprise. "For one fact is written across the whole horizon, the prime element in any discussion," he insists. "That fact is the absolute necessity for a readjusting of woman's position" (125). In Lippmann's argument, the moving figure of that woman already transacts the relation between the "economic revolution" residing in the "trust movement" and the cultural revolution residing in the redefinition of subjectivity.

But why and how did the New Woman become this middle term, this metaphor of movement beyond the modern subject, the moral personality, and the "man of reason" as these were engendered, in every sense, by the figure of the freeholder or the small producer? Why not the working class— or rather how did the figure of the female come to connote a broader range of possibility than the labor movement? In Lippmann's case, I think it is fair to say that he used this figure to interrogate the theory and practice of socialism. In 1914, he was dissatisfied not with socialism as such but with a socialist movement that gave priority to the principle of class by assuming that relations of production—the scene of "socially necessary labor"—still determined or regulated all social relations. So conceived, socialism merely replicated the outlook of the labor movement; it was not yet a cross-class ideology that could address the concerns and accommodate the constituencies of other social movements, for example those animated by more or less feminist issues. "We hear a great deal about the class-consciousness of labor," Lippmann noted. "My own observation is that in America to-day consumers' consciousness is growing very much faster."[31]

Most of the young intellectuals who came together as writers on the Left before the war did not study socialism as carefully as Lippmann had; certainly none of them had his practical experience as an assistant to the socialist mayor of Schenectady. Even so, most of them were socialists of a similar sort. They were committed to the labor movement; they treated the profit motive—what Henry James called the "grope of wealth"—as hopelessly regressive; and they understood socialism as the infrastructural or "economic" dimension of a broader cultural movement beyond the parochialisms of the Puritan, the pioneer, and the Philistine.[32]

Van Wyck Brooks is a good example of the type. In *America's Coming-of-Age*, published a year after Lippmann's *Drift and Mastery*, Brooks noted, "A familiar distinction between the nineteenth and the twentieth centuries is that the problem of civilization is no longer the problem of want but the problem of surplus." It followed, he claimed, that "economic self-assertion ('enterprise') has become to a large extent a vicious anachronism." Indeed, so long as entrepreneurial self-assertion set the standards for selfhood, the articulation of "personality"—the fulfillment of the self through art, religion, literature—would be impossible. According to Brooks, socialism was the means by which Americans could set these standards aside and begin to make other, less aggressive alternatives available in the culture at large; in that sense, socialism was the necessary (but not the sufficient) condition for a reconstruction of subjectivity.

> It will remain of the least importance to patch up politics, to become infected with social consciousness, or to do any of the other easy popular contemporary things unless, in some way, personality can be made to release itself on a middle plane between vaporous idealism and self-interested practicality; unless, in short, self-fulfillment as an ideal can be substituted for self-assertion as an ideal. On the economic plane, this implies socialism; on every other plane it implies something which a majority of Americans in our day certainly do not possess—an object in living.[33]

In the end, Brooks suggested that this release of personality "on a middle plane" required the release of subjectivity from the grip of the male proprietor; in other words, he suggested that the reconstruction of subjectivity as such required the incorporation of the feminine. At any rate he invoked the figure of the female in completing his argument. Throughout his new literary history, Brooks had insisted that the map of American culture was split between "highbrow" and "lowbrow" regions—for example, between "the cultivated public and the business public, the public of theory and the public of activity." One region was "largely feminine, the other largely masculine." The middle ground, where Walt Whitman had camped out and cooked up "a fresh democratic ideal, based upon the whole personality," was, then, both a usable literary past and a promising future for self-fulfillment. As past or future, this middle ground was an area where feminine and masculine mingled, where the male prerogative of "economic self-assertion" did not exhaust the meanings of selfhood. But Brooks had argued that if settlement of this area was made *possible* in view of Whitman's nineteenth-century survey, it was made *necessary* in view of the twentieth-century "problem of surplus"; for the mere existence of surplus meant that Americans were now "faced with the problem not of making money but of spending it."[34] As the designation or consumption of values became more significant than the production of values, the "feminine" regions on the map of American culture began to look like central places, not marginal enclaves.

The Priority of Class and the Production of Irony

So far I have made three claims. I have claimed that the young intellectuals who came of age between 1910 and 1920 posited a reconstruction of subjectivity which they hoped would allow the articulation of the "whole personality"—of the "social self" whose ego-boundaries would be determined neither by ownership of private property nor by "economic self-assertion" but by association with others in managing the "collective property" of culture (e.g., parks, libraries, museums; religion, art, literature). I have also claimed that they understood this ongoing reconstruction as one dimension of a passage beyond the "socially necessary labor" residing in relations of production, a passage they described as the product of the "trust movement" and defined, with uncanny uniformity, in terms of surplus. I have claimed, finally, that they used the figure of the New Woman, or of the female, to express both their dissatisfaction with the *priority* of the principle of class and their sense of the possibilities waiting to be discovered in the regions beyond the realm of necessity, where consumption and its connotations would matter more than production and its requirements.

Let me clarify this last claim before returning to the question of differences between generations of young intellectuals. Like the marginalists who confronted the "socialistic writers," the young intellectuals of the early twentieth century did not avoid the category of class or ignore the reality of class struggle; they merely recognized the limits of class analysis and refused accordingly to accept, or to reinstate, the priority of class as a principle of social theory and practice. In effect, they were following the lead of the economists, who had already shifted the focus of theory from the scene of "socially necessary labor" in relations of production—where Marx had insisted it belonged under the regime of modern industry—to a wider range of transactions, where the meanings of work and the values determined by mental labor were still unknown or unsettled. In this sense, the young intellectuals represented the implications of the new economics; they wanted a similar change of scene. They proposed to look beyond the realm of necessity for the sources of the self, but not because they wanted to escape the domain of "socially necessary labor" ruled by the laws of political economy; like the marginalists, they believed that the boundaries of this domain were contracting, and that nineteenth-century notions of the "socially necessary" were probably too narrow, and too rigid, for use in the "age of surplus."

So I am suggesting that where Nancy Cott sees privilege, the young intellectuals saw something else. Here is how she analyzes the "systematic prejudice" in the language of women who gave priority to the principle of gender:

> The woman's rights tradition was historically initiated by, and remains prejudiced toward, those who perceive themselves first and foremost as "woman," who can gloss over their class, racial, and other status identifications because they are culturally dominant and therefore relatively invisible. The privilege—or self-deception—of making gender more important than its attendant attributes has not been available, most obviously, to women of color in the United States, where race has been such a crucial marker, but neither does that angle of vision wholly match most women's experience.[35]

Now if Cott is correct to suggest that class and race are the "culturally dominant" principles of social organization in the United States, and if class, like gender, is the product of difference, conflict, and struggle, then making gender more important than its "attendant attributes" should become less than a privilege—indeed it should become the norm—when class is not, or is no longer, the characteristic (or "culturally dominant") product of difference, conflict, and struggle, as it clearly was in the late nineteenth century under the regime of modern industry. The question that follows, I think, is why and how class gives way in this sense to alternative principles of social organization such as race and gender. Does it recede when or where relations of production do not regulate all other social relations? Or is the *priority* of the principle of class a transhistorical feature of human experience?

If we take the ontological priority of class for granted, we will eventually need words like *privilege* and *self-deception* to explain those who would act on alternative principles of social theory and practice—to explain, for example, not only the feminists and the young intellectuals of the early twentieth century but also the "new social movements" of the late twentieth century. But if we do not take this priority for granted, we will not need such words and their connotations of "false consciousness." What is more important, we can then acknowledge that the priority of the principle of class was determined by the development of capitalism. At any rate we can acknowledge that the development of capitalism was animated as well as accompanied by an enormous expansion in the social and cultural significance of relations of production. It was here, in the realm of necessity, in the "callings" through which the curse of labor became the cause of civilization, that the citizens of bourgeois society located their human nature and their political capacities. They treated political economy as if it were social theory; they learned accordingly to aggregate individuals and to define social roles in terms of their different productive functions. In other words, they invented class analysis as a way of making sense of their new civilization, in which commodity production could (and finally did) characterize or mediate or reshape all forms of social intercourse. Marx simply followed *their* lead—he gave theoretical priority to the principle of class because he wanted to comprehend a society in which relations of production had become the regulative form of all social relations.[36]

But this was a provisional priority in the works that succeeded the *Manifesto* of 1848. As we have seen (in chapter 1), Marx believed that the beginning of the end of class society was announced in the perfection of commodity production under the regime of "large industry." In his view, the reproduction of the class relation between labor and capital, and with it the priority of the principle of class, required the continual "exchange of living labour for objectified labour [i.e., capital]." But this exchange was attenuated, he argued, by the appearance of "large industry," which developed by transmuting science into fixed capital and demanding that "living labour" give up the role of "chief actor" in the drama of commodity production. Insofar as "living labour" was extricated from that drama, either by its assumption of ancillary roles—"the human being comes to relate more as watchman and regulator to the production process"—or by its expulsion from commodity production at the automatic extremity of "large industry," the social and cultural significance of relations of production had to decline, or to change in ways that would tend to reduce the salience of class in everyday experience.[37]

If we adopted this approach, and assumed accordingly that the principle of class must recede when or where relations of production do not regulate all other social relations, we would not be confused or surprised or dismayed to find that the principle of class gives way to alternative principles of social theory and practice soon after the turn of the century; for the promises of "large industry" were realized at this moment, in the development of corporate capitalism—or so I will presently argue. Nor would we be confused or surprised or dismayed to find that the most influential intellectuals of the early twentieth century identified with an international socialist movement, yet refused to accept the priority of the principle of class in theory or practice; for we would not expect them to insist on the ontological priority of class any more than we would expect the "new social movements" of our own time to insist on the political priority of class struggle at the point of production.

But if this periodization of the principle of class is plausible, it follows, I think, that the important differences between generations of young intellectuals must be matters not of historical experience and consciousness but of sensibility and interpretation. In other words, if the impending passage beyond the categories of necessity, production, and class defines the twentieth century as a unitary epoch, then what distinguishes the late-twentieth-century critics of "mass society" and consumer culture is the form in which they have cast their historical narratives. On the basic historical facts, they do not disagree with their counterparts among the young intellectuals of the early twentieth century. So their distance from the "age of surplus" is more political (or aesthetic) than temporal; it is a distance determined by irony, not incommensurability.

For example, all contestants agree that modern subjectivity as represented by the male proprietor, the figure of the freeholder, became an open question—even a political issue—around the turn of the century, when the proletarianization of males was practically complete. Then as now, the choices available to those who would reconstitute subjectivity as a way of reinstating the possibility of the moral personality were to situate the self in historical time or to reclaim the extratemporal space—the political economy of populism—in which the figure of the freeholder once flourished. To situate the self in historical time was, however, to acknowledge that subjectivity was more effect than cause of social circumstances created in and by the past; it was to acknowledge the communities, solidarities, and traditions within which selfhood could become a goal. The question that followed was whether this "social self" could be autonomous and rational. Could it have "character," or would it be appropriated by others, and dominated by its desires?

The mid-twentieth-century critics of "mass society" answered by equating the "social self" and the "other-directed self" of advertisers' dreams. The late-twentieth-century critics of consumer culture have answered in much the same way; they call this hybrid the "managed self." But in the early twentieth century, the leaders of the labor movement, the original feminists, the young intellectuals—and for that matter the older philosophers and social scientists like Royce, James, and Dewey, Cooley, Angell, and Mead, Ely, Clark, and Patten—were much more ambiguous in addressing the same question.[38] They were more ambitious as well. In fact they answered by changing the subject, by trying to redraw the boundary between self and society, reason and desire, mind and body, science and ideology. They claimed that rationality and its correlate in "character" were not the effects of abstraction or abstention from social context and purpose but the effects of implication in and engagement with particular communities, solidarities, and traditions. In short, they proposed to substitute the "social self" for the "man of reason." But they did not merely retouch the portrait of the republican citizen—in sketching the context and purpose of the "social self," they did not reinstate the classical notion of the political community as the scene of self-consciousness and self-mastery. Instead, they looked into the communities, solidarities, and traditions taking shape in civil society, where the commodity form already reigned; in doing so, they designed a postrepublican model of selfhood.[39]

I do not mean to suggest that the young (and old) intellectuals of the early twentieth century settled the significant questions raised by their reconstruction of subjectivity—only we can do that. I mean that they addressed such questions in good faith, as if genuine selfhood could be salvaged from the wreckage of modern subjectivity by their efforts, and that we still have more to learn from their efforts than from the critique of consumer culture. I would claim, for example, that their notion of a "social self" was more inclusive than anything afforded by the inherited tradition, because it cast the proletarian male and the New Woman in the role of the moral personality hitherto monopolized by the male proprietor. At the very least, we can safely say that their studies of the "social self" reopened the question of "character" and allowed for consideration of alternatives to the "man of reason." But why, then, do we not simply take these studies for granted, and get on with the search for a postmodern subjectivity?

The short answer (part 2 is the long version) is that the critics of consumer culture have reduced the "social self" to the "other-directed" or the "managed self"—the cousin, I take it, of the "authoritarian personality." By doing so, they have foreclosed discussion of the question of "character" and disallowed consideration of alternatives to the "man of reason" along lines drawn in the early twentieth century. We do not usually notice these "secondary" effects because the reduction of the social to the managed self is an ideological implication rather than an empirical operation. I mean that the critics of consumer culture begin not by arguing but by assuming that there is no alternative to modern subjectivity except the loss of selfhood as such. The irony that regulates their critique derives, in turn, from that unstated assumption. For once they have assumed that the search for a postmodern subjectivity is pointless, and probably dangerous, the motives of the search party must seem either unintelligible or naive; if the narrative they write to explain the search is not, strictly speaking, a satire, in which they feign ignorance of the search party's naïveté, it must be a story from which effective action is excluded, and in which most significant consequences are unintended. This "non-heroic residue of tragedy" represents a world without illusions, to be sure, but only because its ironic form denies the possibility of redemption through effective action in the world.[40]

If we are to learn from the intellectual innovation of the early twentieth century, we must then go beyond the irony that condescends to this past and accordingly keeps us in exile from the present. That means going beyond the critique of consumer culture as it is currently conceived—as a moral polemic against proletarianization—and moving toward a position from which we may answer the question of "character" by changing the subject, that is, by recognizing alternatives to the "man of reason" who happens to be the male proprietor. In part 2, I argue that pragmatism is the postrepublican "frame of acceptance" we need to complete our inventory of these alternatives. But we have already begun taking stock of the possibilities as soon as we realize that those who witnessed the completion of proletarianization in the late nineteenth century defined it as both problem and prospect. By all accounts, it was an event that challenged or discredited inherited ways of thinking about American society and conducting American politics. By some accounts, however, and perhaps most, it was a promising condition of social and political progress precisely because it challenged or discredited the received tradition and made intellectual innovation necessary. And these accounts were not only or even mainly the handiwork of pro-capitalist hacks and "positive thinkers." In the 1890s, for example, John Dewey argued that the factory was an appropriate setting for the development of the moral personality. At this early stage of his career, Dewey was particularly interested in both the promise of an ethical theory animated by acknowledgment of the "social self"—the urban-industrial worker served as his ideal type—and the meaning of epistemology if "speculation" in the markets by "the trusts" had become the paradigm of thought as such. His philosophical agenda was already a kind of cross-class construction.[41]

Notice that going beyond the critique of consumer culture turns out to mean moving back in time, toward the positions established by the generation that came of age around the turn of the century—toward the positions forgotten by the generation that came of age after midcentury. In the next chapter, I will try to demonstrate that this return *to* what has been repressed by historiographical irony is the best way to diagnose the symptoms of consumer culture (and these would include its critics) as attempted cures of the ailments specific to corporate capitalism.

I do not mean that we must somehow remove ourselves from our own time and regress to the standpoint of the turn of the century. We cannot abolish irony any more than we can prove that the young (and old) intellectuals of the early twentieth century are immune to critical interrogation from our standpoint in the late twentieth century. But we can test their claims against the available evidence, by asking whether their notion of an "age of surplus" complicates our definition and completes our periodization of consumer culture.

CHAPTER 4

. . . .

CORPORATE CAPITALISM

AND CONSUMER CULTURE,

1890–1940

From Cultural to Economic History

We already know that both generations of young intellectuals agree that the central and characteristic event in the nation's coming of cultural age (ca. 1890–1930) is the reconstruction of selfhood or subjectivity. One generation treats this event as the erosion of genuine selfhood, the other as the articulation of new models for subjectivity; but both agree that it defines the cultural transformation in question and sets the agenda for subsequent debates on related events. We also know that both generations agree that political-economic changes associated with (if not caused by) the large industrial corporations are key moments in the cultural history they have to write. One generation treats these changes as the "maturation of the national marketplace" enforced by "bureaucratic organizations," the other as an "age of surplus" devised by the "trust movement." Aside, then, from the crucial differences on how to interpret the threat to modern subjectivity residing in the completion of proletarianization under corporate auspices, what still separates the two generations is the difference between their accounts of the same political-economic changes. Both sides evidently agree that we need to understand the emergence of corporate-industrial bureaucracies if we are to explain the cultural transformation in question. So we have to ask, which economic history makes for better cultural history?

Since I have already claimed that the promises of what Marx called "large industry" were realized in the development of corporate enterprise, and that consumer culture resides in the transition from proprietary to corporate capitalism, I have already revealed my preference for the economic history implied in the notion of an "age of surplus." I need, then, to demonstrate that the passage beyond the proprietary stage of capitalism contains a passage beyond the categories of necessity, production, and class, and that this moment in the larger transition authorizes the articulation of alternatives to modern subjectivity. I propose to do so by identifying and examining two distinct but overlapping phases in the development of corporate capitalism: *emergence*, ca. 1890–1920, and *consolidation*, ca. 1910–40.

Perhaps the best way to understand the emergent phase is to think of it as the corporate innovators themselves did—as an attempt to validate their claims on a share of national income, to enlarge their social prerogatives and economic functions, and accordingly to preclude the development of capitalism without capitalists. They wanted to preserve the civilizing content of capitalism by changing its social form. But to think of their bid for power in this way requires that we recall their complaints about the character of late-nineteenth-century economic growth. Without exception, influential observers of the American scene—whether populist or socialist or pro-capitalist—emphasized that economic growth after 1870 was simply phenomenal if measured in absolute terms. For example, in 1889, David A. Wells, the most influential of all observers, noted that since 1870, economic change was unquestionably "more important and varied than during any former corresponding period of the world's history." The "greater control over the forces of nature" produced by such change was self-evident. But like every other observer—again regardless of political propensities—he insisted that the question raised by rapid growth was the distribution of income. From his standpoint, the real problem revealed by late-nineteenth-century "overproduction" was that capital did not, and probably could not, receive appropriate remuneration for its significant contribution to economic growth. According to Wells, the primary beneficiary of that growth was skilled labor in the metalworking trades, not the more familiar figures from the ranks of "big business."[1]

When equipped with modern economic theory, we can revisit the winters of his discontent with a means of testing his claims. The relation between growth in real wages and in labor productivity is what concerns us, as Clarence D. Long explained in his 1960 monograph on late-nineteenth-century wages and earnings in the United States. "So large is labor's share of national income that any substantial disparity between productivity and real wages would exert great impact on the other shares—either largely expropriating them or presenting them with huge windfalls." If real wages are increasing rapidly as a result of drastic price deflation, for instance, and labor productivity is not meanwhile increasing at a comparable rate, capital's share of national income will be "expropriated" (in Long's sense) by labor.[2]

Insofar as we can rely on professional economists and government research volumes, we can say that this hypothetical situation corresponds to the historical reality of the late-nineteenth-century United States—that is, to the historical reality denounced by Wells and his allies. Price deflation and the consequent growth of real wages were not offset, it seems, by a comparable growth of labor productivity in the industrial sector (or by the effects of unemployment on the aggregate wage bill). But the disparity between growth in real wages and labor productivity is most noticeable in the later stages of the period, between 1884 and 1894. Productivity in the non-farm sector barely improved over these ten years (0.6 percent per annum), yet real wages continued to increase rapidly (3 to 4 percent per annum), at a rate five or six times faster than productivity (see tables 1 and 2). This divergence of productivity and real wages is astonishing in view of what we know about absolute rates of growth in the late nineteenth century. What makes it even more astonishing is that the 1880s saw not only a doubling of the capital endowment per worker but the beginnings of a movement in industry toward the "rationalization" of work routines and cost control though "systematic management."[3]

So we can safely say that concern about a transfer of income from capital to labor was becoming eminently reasonable by 1890, and that labor productivity did not suffer for lack of trying by capitalists. Surely it is no accident that economists and capitalists alike repeatedly cited Wells as their authority in defining the central problem of economic development as a disturbing distribution of income between profits and wages. In retrospect, the solutions to the problem of economic development so conceived seem obvious. On the supply side, capitalists who hoped to bring the growth of real wages and labor productivity into line had to reduce money wages, improve productivity by completing the mechanization of production, or increase prices by adjusting output to effective demand. But until the mid-1890s, capitalists in the industrial sector were price-takers, not price-makers, unless they had resorted to some form of extralegal combination in restraint of trade (e.g. pools and trusts). On the demand side, their only hope—at least for the time being—was foreign markets; that is why empire seemed so inviting a prospect in the 1890s. But late-nineteenth-century economists who studied European empires and American companies operating abroad stressed that the development of foreign markets was practically impossible without the economies of scale promised in large corporate enterprise

TABLE 1.

Declining Annual Growth in GNP

1869–78 to 1874–83	5.58%
1874–83 to 1879–88	4.76%
1879–88 to 1884–93	3.68%
1884–93 to 1889–98	2.55%

Source: Robert E. Gallman, "Gross National Product in the United States, 1834–1909," *Output, Employment, and Productivity in the United States after 1800* (New York: National Bureau of Economic Research, 1966), tables 2 (p. 9), 6 (p. 22).

TABLE 2.

Annual Growth in GNP, by Categories

Decade	Per Capita	Per Work-Hour
1874–84	3.8%	3.2%
1884–94	0.6%	0.6%
1889–99	2.3%	2.3%

Overlapping Decades*	Per Worker
1878–82 to 1888–92	1.0 %
1883–87 to 1893–97	0.58%
1888–92 to 1898–1902	1.5 %
1893–97 to 1903–7	2.36%

Sources: U.S. Bureau of Economic Analysis, *Long-Term Growth, 1860–1970* (Washington, D.C.: GPO, 1973), pt. 5, charts 18 (p. 107), 20 (p. 109); Simon Kuznets, "Notes on the Pattern of U.S. Economic Growth," in *Economic Growth and Structure* (New York: National Bureau of Economic Research, 1965), table 1 (p. 305).
*Kuznets presumably used overlapping decades to reduce the statistical salience of unique events and to emphasize long-term trends.

(the reform of the banking system and the mobilization of the state's fiscal powers were salient but political entailments of empire).[4]

Capital's effective control of the supply side appeared, then, as the first step toward solving the problem of economic development as Wells and his allies had defined it, as a problem of distribution determined by the relation between labor and capital. As a practical question, however, effective control of the supply side meant effective control of that social relation, of the labor process itself. And here capitalists had only two choices—either to reduce money wages or to complete the mechanization of production. In the long run, mechanization was the more promising policy because it would simultaneously increase productivity and abolish or reduce the high labor costs associated with craft skill. In the short run, capitalists favored wage reductions. As Arthur T. Lyman, the treasurer of the Lowell Manufacturing Co., put it, "When profits disappear, wages must fall." But either policy embroiled capitalists in struggles they could not seem to win.[5]

For until the mid-to-late 1890s, skilled workers were able to enforce those social norms that sanctioned their control of machine production. Before then, the extent of the division of labor and the pace of mechanization at the point of production were largely determined not by management's technical rules of efficiency and profitability, but by work rules first enacted spontaneously by skilled craftsmen, then codified in union contracts, and ultimately enforced by strikes. John Frey, an experienced iron molder and a leading labor journalist, ascribed this power of skilled workers at the point of production to the indivisibility of mental and manual labor they maintained. "It is this unique *possession* of craft knowledge and craft skill on the part of a body of wage workers, that is, their *possession* of these things and the employers' ignorance of them, that has enabled the workers to organize and force better terms from the employers." From his standpoint, the mechanization of industrial production was the higher education of the employers, because it presupposed and promoted a "separation of craft knowledge from craft skill"—in other words, it promised to reconstitute and routinize in specialized machines the "scattered craft knowledge" of skilled workers, leaving them with only their "manual skill and dexterity" to sell in the labor market. "The machinery instead of the man is the brains," as a young machinist explained the result to a Senate committee in 1883.[6]

It was this fundamental division of mental and manual labor, not machine production or "industrialism" as such, that skilled workers and their allies fought with remarkable tenacity in the 1880s and 1890s. There are three ways to measure their success. First, money wages were not reduced to the extent that capitalists and managers wanted or sought between 1886 and 1894, largely because they could not impose longer hours on the labor force. Second, the "gross surplus" available to manufacturers—the share of revenue from value added that industrial capitalists could retain after covering the wage bill—declined noticeably over the same years. Third, productivity growth virtually ceased until 1896.[7]

TABLE 3.
TABLE 3.
Reasons for Strikes, 1881–1905

Years	Working Conditions* (excluding wages)	Working Conditions (excluding union recognition)
1881–85	30.6%	22.8%
1886–90	51.1%	37.1%
1891–95	49.7%	34.3%
1896–1900	50.2%	34.3%
1901–5	60.7%	31.6%

Source: Adapted from P. K. Edwards, Strikes in the United States, 1881–1974 (New York: St. Martin's, 1981), table 4.3 (p. 92).
*Working conditions = hours, union recognition and rules, employment of certain persons, method and time of payment, work rules, discipline, etc.

But skilled workers were "successful" in this limited economic sense because they did not have to rely on the resources they could bring to bear at the point of production. They did not ignore or misuse their ultimate weapon, the strike—in fact, they struck more often as the battle over control of the workplace intensified in the late 1880s and early 1890s (see tables 3 and 4). Even so, skilled workers could not have succeeded in any sense if their identification with and access to the sources of political power and cultural authority had not protected or enlarged the meaning of their strikes. External forces of "law and order" could not determine the outcome of strikes in the 1880s, for example, because local officeholders, editors, and shopkeepers often supported striking workers (skilled and unskilled) against the large employers. To be sure, workers and local leaders convened this solidarity across class lines only insofar as they remained unable to acknowledge the market power of corporate capital as a permanent or legitimate dimension of American society. But no matter how or why convened, such solidarity made strikebreaking and union busting much more difficult than they would soon become; skilled workers' claims at the point of production were accordingly less difficult to make, or to accept as plausible premises of local political action.[8]

As the old and new labor history has shown, the winners of the battle against "systematic management" lost their subsequent war against the scientific managers and the new industrial corporations. The corporate innova-

TABLE 4.
Strikes and Their Resolutions, 1881–1905

	Number		Results for Labor (%)		
Years	Strikes	Establishments	Won	Compromised	Lost
1881–85	2,491	12,443	56.1	8.7	35.2
1886–89	4,849	27,270	44.2	13.1	42.8
1890–93	6,153	27,653	43.7	9.8	46.5
1894–97	4,668	29,123	53.0	15.1	31.9
1898–1901	7,556	35,282	54.4	15.0	30.6
1902–5	11,040	52,990	38.5	19.1	42.4

Sources: *Twenty-First Annual Report of the U.S. Commissioner of Labor: Strikes and Lockouts, 1881–1905* (Washington, D.C.: GPO, 1906), 15; Edwards, *Strikes*, table 2.6 (p. 42).

tors were ultimately able to abolish any formal control of machine production by skilled or unionized workers—they succeeded, in short, where the smaller firms of the late nineteenth century had failed. When they explained their success, moreover, these innovators cited the social capacities of the corporate legal form. Frank Vanderlip, a vice-president of the National City Bank who became something of an expert on "the trusts," claimed in 1905, for example, that the new corporations represented the "means to industrial managers to combat unfair demands on the part of labor organizations," for they were "better united and able to meet organization with organization."[9] We can of course say that the emergence of the large corporations coincides with the mechanization or "homogenization" of the labor process and the eclipse of skilled workers' control of machine production (ca. 1890–1920). But can we also say that the emergence of the corporations made these social changes possible and necessary? Did the corporate innovators grasp their creations as the cause, in every sense, of mechanization at the point of production?

From the standpoint of capital in the late nineteenth century, coming to terms with labor meant solving the persistent problem of "overproduction." For as long as the determination of prices was left to the demand side, profits could be raised or reinstated only by cutting wages and breaking unions; bitter class conflict appeared to be the unavoidable consequence, so that even when capital won a local struggle, it did not appear as a legitimate victor. The vice-chairman of the Chicago Conference on Trusts, convened in 1899, explained the dilemma this way: "A large part of the friction that has existed between capital and labor, causing strikes, lockouts and riots, was the result, in part, of overproduction. The product was unloaded at a loss, the owners tried to recompense themselves by cutting the wages of their workmen."[10]

The solution to the labor problem so conceived was not higher wages and more consumption, as the labor movement proposed, but the reclamation of income transferred from profits to wages as a result of prolonged overproduction. By 1896, in view of decisions in the federal courts on the scope of the Sherman Anti-Trust Act, corporate consolidation of control over investment and output appeared to be the most promising way to stem this tide, that is, to reinstate reasonable profits. Jeremiah Jenks claimed, for example, that overproduction exemplified the "waste of competition." Since it derived "from the inability of adapting one's plants and output to the needs of the market," the costs it imposed could be "partly saved by combination of many manufacturing establishments in one industry under one management." On this adaptive potential of "combination," the economists and the capitalists were practically unanimous.[11] For if prices were stabilized at a level that allowed reasonable profits—if supply could be adjusted to demand, and overproduction was accordingly adjourned—capitalists would not have to treat wages as the crucial variable in calculating the difference between costs and prices that equaled profits. Resort to class war would no longer represent the best alternative to operating at a loss.

But this solution to the macroeconomic problem of overproduction did not evade the social questions—and these included the question of class struggle—raised by economic growth; instead, it offered a new way of addressing them. On the one hand, it announced that small entrepreneurs and proprietary capitalists would have to accept a secondary role in resource allocation if overproduction was not to be reinstated from the supply side. "They are the ones who have been caught between the upper and the nether mill stones," as James J. Hill, the founding father of the Great Northern Railway, put it. "They are the middlemen, and the small competitor who was unable to meet the larger concern in the open market."[12]

On the other hand, the corporate solution to overproduction announced that managers would have to play the lead at the point of production, where skilled workers still acted as if they were the main characters. At least that is how the corporate innovators saw it. In their view, bringing an end to "ruinous competition" was pointless unless the fixed capital that was not scrapped after a merger or reorganization could be made more efficient and productive. But if wage rates were not very flexible (as indeed they were not), and would in any case remain higher than European levels, the condition of greater efficiency and productivity was the completion of the mechanization of the labor process. Charles R. Flint, a founder of the U.S. Rubber Company in 1891 and an active promoter of the "new industrials" created in the merger wave of 1898–1902, explained how corporate combination met this condition. "The American workingman to-day earns higher wages than are paid in any other country . . . because [he] produces more, and he produces more because he has been supplied with the most perfect system of labor-saving machinery on earth. To supply this machinery, large capital is necessary. The individual manufacturer, standing alone, is not in a position to perfect his machinery in the same measure as the consolidated enterprise." [13]

Of the "various economies" residing in the large scale of the corporations, Flint and his cohorts emphasized this above all others: "In general, centralized manufacture permits the largest use of special machinery." From their standpoint, the corporation was, then, a means to the end of mechanizing, and thus reshaping, the labor process. Both parties to the class struggle certainly understood that technological innovation at the point of production was a preeminently social process that would determine whether employers or employees controlled the labor process. The U.S. commissioner of labor's 1898 survey of production methods in industry found, for example, that cutting leather parts for shoes and boots could be (and was) done by hand in about half the time it took by machine. The apparent anomaly bothered the commissioner, Carroll D. Wright of Massachusetts, enough to query the respondent. "When called to the attention of the manufacturer he stated that the time was correct, and that a smart cutter unhampered by 'union rules' could perform the work in the time specified." The commissioner's report duly noted that the "greatest efficiency is obtained under the primitive method." But by the turn of the century, "efficiency" could mean more than a reduction of the labor-time, and thus of the labor costs, required for the profitable production of commodities. As the response to Wright implied, it could begin to mean the removal of labor from its leading role as "chief actor" in commodity production as such.[14]

Workers and unions had a role to play in the new scenario animated by corporate consolidation, but they could not be allowed to exercise any meaningful control of machine production. If they somehow limited the use of new labor-saving machinery, the "economies of scale" promised in the mechanization of production under corporate auspices could not be realized. This possibility seemed especially worrisome when the architects of empire contemplated the international capacities of the corporations. For example, in 1903 Vanderlip declared that "controlling the world's industrial markets" was the obvious destiny of the United States. "The only serious obstacle in the way of that," he noted, "will be our labor organizations." Unions that sought increased wages through contracts with employers were perfectly acceptable; but if they continued to insist on a significant role in production—that is, in determining rates of output—they would hamstring American enterprise in world markets: "We are surrounded by conditions that will permit us to pay two or three times as much wages as our foreign competitors and still meet successfully their competition, but we cannot, in addition to that handicap, permit the workers to limit production and hope for a successful outcome in a world contest." [15]

By this account, scientific management was the pure expression of the corporate solution to late-nineteenth-century overproduction and class war; for its purpose was to create a new relation between workers and the mechanical conditions of work, through which capitalist control of the labor process could be effected and labor productivity growth—that is, the end of "soldiering" on the job—guaranteed. In 1912, Frederick W. Taylor himself claimed, "This type of management has been in process of evolution during a period of about 30 years." It emerged, he suggested, as an alternative to deepening conflict in the late nineteenth century over the distribution of income between profits and wages. "In the past it has been in the division of [the] surplus that the great labor troubles have come between employers and employees." For the "old type of management" often resorted to wage cuts as a way of maintaining profits: "Frequently, when the management have found the selling price going down they have turned toward a cut in the wages—toward reducing the workman's share of the surplus—as their way of getting out whole, of preserving their profits intact." The workers of course resisted, and the result was overt class conflict. "In the extreme cases this has been the cause of serious disagreements and strikes." [16]

Scientific management aimed to increase labor productivity and per capita income so that disagreement over the shares of industrial income accruing respectively to labor and capital would not continue to broaden, or devolve, into class struggle. Here is how Taylor put it: "The great revolution that takes place in the mental attitude of the two parties under scientific management is that both sides take their eyes off of the division of the surplus as the all-important matter, and together turn their attention to increasing the size of the surplus until this surplus becomes so large that it is unnecessary to quarrel over how it shall be divided." Scientific management was, then, "the equivalent of a labor-saving device"—it was a "human mechanism." As such, it required as a condition of its realization the social resources only the corporations could mobilize on a large scale; at any rate Taylor insisted that it required "a degree of cooperation, coupled with a kind of leadership on the management's side, which is entirely impossible with the independent individualism which characterizes the old type of management."[17]

Taylor accordingly emphasized that the "new type of management" involved something more than supervision of workers, but something other than ownership of the means of production; from its ambiguous position between capital and labor, its role was to convene what economists like John Bates Clark were already calling the production function. "Neither Labor nor Capital can co-operate effectively save under the guiding genius of Management," as W. L. Mackenzie King, who invented the "human relations" brand of industrial psychology, put it in 1919. "Capital's contribution to industry is in the nature of material substance loaned by way of investment. Its possessor may be any kind of person. . . . Managerial ability, on the other hand, is in the nature of a personal service of the very highest order, and is wholly necessary . . . to bring about efficient co-operation between Labor and Capital in the work of production." Taylor spoke the vernacular of time and motion studies, but the point was the same. "All day long every workman's acts are dovetailed in between some corresponding act of the management."[18]

So conceived, scientific management signified much more than Taylor's compulsive clockwork. As both the "latest word in the sheer mechanics of production"—this is how Robert Hoxie labeled it in his *Scientific Management and Labor* of 1915—and the original manifesto of the managerial revolution, it represented a profound threat to the category and the corollaries of "productive labor." From the standpoint of the skilled workers who were the organized sector of the metalworking trades, for example, it looked dangerous at best. Certainly John Frey thought so. In his view, the "greatest blow that could be delivered against trade unionism and the organized workers would be the separation of craft knowledge from craft skill." But that separation had "actually taken place in an ever-widening area and with an ever-increasing acceleration." It took "two main forms," according to Frey. One was mechanization, which he understood as a social question raised by mass production and large-scale enterprise. "The first of these is the introduction of machinery and standardization of tools, materials, products and process, which make production possible on a large scale, and the specialization of the workmen." The other form was "more insidious and dangerous than the first" because it worked by "systematizing [craft knowledge] and concentrating it in the hands of the employer and then doling it out again only in the form of minute instructions."[19]

Frey feared scientific management (the second form) more than mechanization as such because it dismembered the oral tradition through which organized workers had preserved craft knowledge and protected their prerogatives under the modern-industrial conditions of the factory. But he recognized that the division of labor was increasingly driven by the symbiosis of large-scale enterprise and scientific management in the organizational complex of the large industrial corporations; that is why he referred to an "ever-widening area" of concern, and believed the cause of trade unionism was endangered. He was wrong about trade unionism, or rather he was wrong to believe that the preservation of craft knowledge would remain its purpose and its method. But I think he was right to worry about the "ever-widening area" over which the corporations were extending their bureaucratic suzerainty. For insofar as the corporations did reshape the division of labor along the lines Frey described, the notion of "productive labor" would lose its explanatory adequacy. When that happened, the idea of socially necessary labor and the received tradition of trade unionism would become problematic. At the same moment, the disjuncture between production and consumption impending in the late-nineteenth-century shortfall of effective demand would finally acquire factual standing in popular culture and political discourse. In other words, consumer culture would take root when the notion of "productive labor" stopped making sense as a way of designating values, allocating social roles, and explaining class relations or political conflicts. But these claims will sound odd unless we revisit the scenes of genuine selfhood as they were framed by "productive labor."

In the late nineteenth century, there were two major variations on this theme of self-mastery in a market society, each of which animated a subaltern social movement that spoke for the "producing classes" and the "toiling millions." In the variation proposed by the small holders, labor leaders, and tenant farmers who became Greenbackers and/or Populists, ownership of self presupposed ownership of productive property. In their view, consumption of goods was authorized by the creation of new values through work—through an investment of labor-time in the raw materials of one's trade and through the production of commodities that were both real and necessary. Those who deducted their incomes from the sum of values created by others, that is, who consumed without producing, were the middlemen, the bankers, the lawyers, and the speculators. Their superfluous presence, their socially unnecessary labor, served the illegitimate purposes of "artificial persons"—the railroad corporations and other "trusts."[20]

In the variation proposed by the working people, trade unionists, and labor reformers who joined the Knights of Labor and organized the federated trades in the 1880s, self-mastery was conceivable even in the absence of a "competency." By their account, ownership of self required not ownership of productive property but membership in—and access to the powers of—the community whose boundaries were defined by the scope of "productive labor." Entrepreneurs from the industrial sector were candidates for admission to this community; but so were operatives and unskilled laborers. Capitalists and "heads of large establishments" were not. Again, consumption was authorized only by the creation of new values through work that was recognizable as socially necessary labor because it produced real and useful goods. When asked, for example, whether a capitalist "ought to have some share in the benefits derived from the improved machinery for which he pays," John S. McClelland, a telegraph operator and member of the Knights from Hoboken, answered his senatorial interlocutor as follows: "If he has accumulated money to build the machine it must have been taken from labor, because the capitalist performs no productive labor himself." At the same Senate hearings, Thomas B. McGuire, who identified himself as a truck driver from New York, noted: "[The] poor unfortunate laborer is just like the kernel of wheat between the upper and the lower millstone; in any case he is certain to be ground. He *produces* all the wealth while the men who produce nothing *have* all the wealth."[21]

In populist perspective, proletarianization as such was the solvent of self-determination: "wage slaves" and "industrial serfs" were not free men. But the redivision of mental and manual labor from which the corporate innovators hoped to profit was no less a threat to the meanings of work—and selfhood—contained in (and by) the urban-industrial variation on the theme of "productive labor." In the form of mechanization, that redivision promised to move skilled workers to the margins of commodity production, where they would set up, maintain, and repair increasingly specialized machines and processes under the close supervision of white-collared managers who would claim, as it turned out, to be the main characters in the drama of production. In the form of scientific management, that redivision promised to validate the growth of those very economic functions and social strata which could not be accommodated by the category of "productive labor" because they accrued income but did not add to the sum of values.

More often than not, organized workers resisted this redivision of labor, even though it meant increased wages; for, among other things, it demanded that they locate the origins of their collective and political identities (vis-à-vis capital) outside the sphere of production and the realm of socially necessary labor. To meet that demand was to revise their view of capitalists, who had hitherto appeared as parasites on the body politic, and to see themselves in a different light as well. Little wonder, than, that the results of revisionism in the early twentieth century were profoundly ambiguous. For example, one of these results was the so-called pure and simple trade unionism of the American Federation of Labor. It pointed beyond the category of "productive labor" by acknowledging the legitimacy of "the trusts"—of their claims to income as well as their redivision of labor—and by restricting the scope of "workers' control" at the point of production to union control of job classifications and wage bargains; so its contribution to the reconstruction of subjectivity was not limited to a practical demonstration of the social self. But this "pure and simple" approach was part of a larger syndicalist sensibility (the Industrial Workers of the World was its left-wing extreme) through which social roles were allocated according to economic functions; so it was—and is—the middle term between "productive labor" and consumer culture, which serves to remind us that relations of production did not dissolve when the corporations appeared.[22]

The corporate innovators, another cadre of revisionists from the early twentieth century, would remind us in any case. As they saw it, their task was to rehabilitate capitalism by retrieving income transferred from profits to wages, or from investment to consumption, in the course of late-nineteenth-century development. The corporation was the institutional device by which they hoped to install a new division of labor determined by the capacities of mechanized production and to correct the distribution of income between capital and labor. In this sense, the corporation was a means to the ends of reinstating the cultural salience and enlarging the social significance of relations of production. The corporate innovators wanted to restrict the circulation of income revenue, or rather to reclaim revenue that had circulated in the form of wages, as consumer demand; they wanted to invest that revenue in new plant and specialized machines that would increase output but reduce costs per unit of output. To get what they wanted, they had, then, to reverse the late-nineteenth-century relation between demand for consumer goods (wages) and demand for capital goods (profits); and in trying to get what they wanted, in the 1890s and after, they discovered that what they needed was formal control of the "human element" in the production process.

Historians now generally agree that the corporate innovators got pretty much what they wanted, and then some. By 1920, it seems, they had invented a new labor system, or at any rate a new relation between capital and labor, by means of mechanization and scientific management; they had improved labor productivity and stabilized prices, thus increasing the share of national income accruing to capital; they had reshaped the law and redefined the role of the federal government in regulating economic development, yet had not resorted to state capitalism; and with the help of the "new social stratum" that emerged between labor and capital, they had convened a "culture of consumption."[23] But since the mid-1960s, historians have concentrated their interpretive energies on what they define as deviations from this mainstream of Progressive reform and corporate-industrial development; indeed the mainstream normally appears in their accounts as the residue of the tragedy residing in the defeat of the deviations, that is, in the failure of populism and the "fall of the house of labor." We take these accounts seriously because we know that history written from the counterfactual standpoint of what might have been is indispensable. As Roberto Unger puts it, "Insight into lines of development that were halted or reversed is crucial to understanding the main direction events in fact took."[24]

But let us suppose that the crucial insight to which Unger commits us is not the exclusive property of subaltern social movements and their chroniclers. We will then want to know what the standpoint of capital discloses. In other words, we will want to know if the consolidation of corporate capitalism (ca. 1910–40) halted or reversed certain lines of development that the corporate innovators themselves cited as the promise of industrial combination. If so, we might interpret the completed transition from proprietary to corporate capitalism as the first act of an unfinished comedy rather than the residue of tragedy. We might also cast ourselves as something other than its audience or its critics.

The Human Element

From the standpoint of capital in the late nineteenth century, the real danger to be averted by corporate-industrial combination was the social death of capitalists. "The manufacturers are tired of working for the public," E. S. Meade, an authority on trust finance from the University of Pennsylvania (he later worked for the Department of Agriculture under the New Deal), noted in 1900. "They want a larger profit without such a desperate struggle to get it." They designed or embraced the corporate form of legal personality and managerial organization with this "desperate struggle" in mind—they hoped to prevent the demotion of capitalists to public servants by increasing productivity, prices, and profits in the manufacturing sector, and by providing dividends to stockholders in the new, vertically integrated companies that took shape after the initial merger wave of 1897–98.[25]

As late as 1900, when John Moody finally launched his "manual" of industrial securities, only 14 percent of all manufacturing establishments were corporations. By 1905, corporations represented just 24 percent of all manufacturing establishments; but they controlled 83 percent of the capital and employed 71 percent of the wage earners in manufacturing. These were the immediate results of what Alfred Chandler calls the "most significant merger movement in American history"—the great "trust movement" of 1898–1902. It created over three hundred new manufacturing firms worth about $5 billion as well as the small number of giant corporations that would dominate the metal, machinery, and chemical industries associated with late-nineteenth-century innovations in science and engineering (in 1909, 5 percent of manufacturing establishments employed 62 percent of wage earners in manufacturing). As Martin Sklar points out, the "trust movement" enacted a transfer of property on a scale unmatched by any previous confiscation under revolutionary conditions—including the emancipation of 1863–65, which canceled all legal claims on $4 billion of property in slaves—and offered a new model for the redivision of labor in the twentieth century. By 1920, virtually all manufacturing and mining firms had participated somehow in this movement toward integrated operation, either by merger or by internal reorganization and "rationalization."[26]

But did it work then and thereafter as the corporate innovators claimed? More specifically, did the "trust movement" allow for the completion of mechanization at the point of production? Did it reinstate the cultural salience and enlarge the social significance of relations of production? Were capitalists rehabilitated by the increase of productivity and profits? Or did the corporations underwrite the development of capitalism without capitalists? As it turns out, our answers will—or should—depend on the period we choose as the paradigm of twentieth-century development. If we treat the emergent phase of corporate capitalism as the relevant historical record, our answers will probably be consistent with the historiographical consensus through which the Progressive Era and its aftermath appear as the residue of tragedy. But if we take a longer view, we will have to qualify these answers.

Indeed I would suggest that the best answer to the last two questions is ambiguous even if we confine ourselves to evidence from the emergent phase. For the fundamental division of labor produced by the corporate form of enterprise was not the new contradiction between mental and manual labor but the separation between ownership of and control over corporate assets. That separation was recognized in various ways long before James Burnham, Adolf Berle, and Gardiner Means made it the pivot of their political theories in the 1930s. It was recognized, for example, in Taylor's implicit and King's explicit distinction between the functions of capital and management; it was recognized by the law, in limits on the claims of common stockholders to the assets of corporations; and by 1919 it was recognized by social scientists as the source of modern-industrial bureaucracies. We have already seen that as early as 1914, Walter Lippmann described the separation of ownership and control by reference to the "cultural basis" of property. "The real news about business," he proclaimed, "is that it is being administered by men who are not profiteers. The managers are on salary, divorced from ownership and bargaining. They represent the revolution in business incentives at its very heart." [27]

In the late twentieth century, this proclamation sounds jarring not because we doubt that corporate capitalism is predicated on the development of managerial capacities and hierarchies but because, unlike Lippmann, we doubt that capitalism has an ending we can narrate. If we recall, however, that the English Revolution codified epochal changes in the rights of property and the common law which had been under way for three centuries, we might compare ourselves to the Machiavellians who doubted that the decadent rule of the landed nobility had an ending they could narrate until the mid-seventeenth century—when they realized that the nobility's rights to property in the land and the products of peasant labor were no longer absolute, and in some areas not even actionable, because enterprising commoners had inherited the earth. At any rate they had changed the meaning of rights to property in the land, both at the law and as a matter of fact. To make this comparison is of course to suggest that the transition from proprietary to corporate capitalism entails the social (not the literal) death of capitalists in the same sense that the transition from feudalism to capitalism entailed the social death of the landed nobility; for it is to suggest that the rise of corporations controlled by salaried managers rehabilitated capitalism in the same sense that the growth of estates controlled by rent-paying commoners rehabilitated feudalism. In the short run, these transfers of control over property reinstated the incomes of the original owners and renewed their lease on an uncertain future; in the long run, they would make the original owners more superfluous than the rhetoric of Puritans or Populists could convey. [28]

To see how the longer view might qualify our answers to the remaining questions—and how it might also produce a comic "frame of acceptance" through which the "trust movement" appears as the beginning of the ending we want to narrate—we need to trace the connections between the consolidation of corporate capitalism and the completion of mechanization at the point of production; then we need to map the scope and significance of relations of production. At that point, we can finally return to the question of consumer culture.

By the late 1920s, the young intellectuals who had carved out careers in journalism and academia were creating a new genre of cultural critique organized around the metaphor of the machine, or as they preferred, "the machine age." Everyone, from the literary critics to the economists, was fascinated by the extraordinary capacities of manufacturing technique in mass production (typified by automobiles), and was trying to gauge the effects of that technique on everything from consumer demand to sexual desire. *Middletown* (1929), the Lynds' study of social-cultural change in Muncie, Indiana, between the 1890s and the 1920s, is only the most obvious and famous example of the genre. Among the many others are Floyd Dell, *Love in the Machine Age* (1930), Stuart Chase, *Men and Machines* (1929) and *The Economy of Abundance* (1934), Rexford G. Tugwell, *Industry's Coming of Age* (1927), Lewis Mumford, *Technics and Civilization* (1934), Harry Jerome, *Mechanization in Industry* (1934), Frederick C. Mills, *Economic Tendencies in the U.S.* (1932), and the volumes produced by the President's Conference on Unemployment, *Recent Economic Changes* (1929) and *Recent Social Trends* (1934).[29]

These and other works in the same genre (e.g., Joseph Schumpeter's *Business Cycles* [1939]) converge on three conclusions that, notwithstanding the problem of periodization presented by the World War, establish a certain continuity in the period 1910–30. First, they agree on the sudden increase in the scale of industrial operation after 1900; the decade of the 1920s appears in these accounts as predictable aftershocks of the prewar earthquake. Second, they agree or assume that this increase in scale accelerated the mechanization of the production process, inaugurated "the machine age" proper, and enforced startling improvements in labor productivity, ca. 1910–30. Third, they agree that the "human element" in the production process changes drastically after 1907 or 1910, and seems, at least in manufacturing, to recede from view after 1920. They agree, then, that management's control of the labor process was finally realized by corporate-industrial consolidation, and that the "capital intensity" of an increasingly mechanized production process was a technological effect of social causes residing in the organizational complex of the large industrial corporations.

By these accounts, the "trust movement" did allow for the completion of mechanization at the point of production. But their authors also insist, in various ways, that quantitative changes—in the degree of mechanization and in the demand for labor—became qualitative at some moment in the second or third decade of the twentieth century, and that these changes are the most interesting chapters in the story they have to tell.[30]

Let us read these chapters in conjunction with later works of the same genre, to see how and why (or whether) they still bear interest. The question we need to address at the outset is, if industrialization as such is characterized by the mobilization of inanimate sources of power like steam—by the advent of "machine production"—what can studies in the mechanization of commodity production under corporate auspices tell us about cultural change or revolution in the twentieth century? A detailed answer can be found in my reconstruction of Marx's two-sector model of accumulation, which appears as the introduction to part 1 of this book. Here I need note only that industrialization in the nineteenth century does not "displace" or reduce demand for labor except in the sense that it entails the recomposition of the labor force. Modern industry reduces the labor-time required for the production of finished consumer goods by installing complex machines where simple tools and craft traditions had sufficed; but it expands output and continues to develop only by enlarging that proportion of the labor force which is engaged in the production of those machines *and their inputs* in the form of raw materials (e.g., coal, iron ore), intermediate goods (e.g., rolled steel), and services (e.g., railroad transportation). So conceived, industrialization is a social process that implicates greater amounts and kinds of labor in production that is preparation for production—in production of commodities that cannot be consumed because they are means of production. It enforces a mechanization of production that enlarges the domain of socially necessary labor even though it reduces the labor-time necessary to produce a given quantity of finished consumer goods. As Peter Temin summarizes the process, "The industries that sell to other industries grow faster than the industries that sell to consumers."[31]

Until the second decade of the twentieth century, the mechanization of production under corporate auspices conforms to this pattern, and confirms the claims of the innovators who defined the corporations as the device by which income transferred from profits to wages—that is, from investment to consumption—could be recovered, and capitalist control of economic development could be established. The proportion of the labor force engaged in production of means of production increased dramatically between 1890 and 1920, in line with the increase of profits which derived, in turn, from the reversal of the late-nineteenth-century relation between growth in real wages and labor productivity. Meanwhile, the pace of mechanization at the point of production accelerated. Horsepower per worker in manufacturing more than doubled between 1900 and 1930, about 40 percent faster than the increase of the period 1870–1900, when "machine production" came of age.[32]

This power was both generated and allocated in new ways. After 1905, when plants could begin to purchase electric power from central stations, electricity quickly replaced steam as the prime mover in the larger factories and on the capital-intensive cutting edge of the second industrial revolution. For the central stations made the "fractionalization" of power a practical proposition—for example, small, specialized, high-speed machine tools driven by electricity, unlike general-purpose tools powered by steam, could be used periodically at full capacity without loss of efficiency or waste of power, and could be placed for optimum product flow rather than near the shafts and belts that carried steam power from the basement boiler to the factory floor. The costs of power to industry fell accordingly, by 70 to 80 percent, at the same moment that the costs of labor per unit of industrial output were reduced by a redivision of labor in which electric motors looked natural.[33]

"For a number of years past," the commissioners of the British Iron Trade Association noted as early as 1902, "the aim of the American manufacturing engineer and inventor has been to make machinery as far as possible automatic." So they were especially worried about the impending competition from steel producers in the United States. "The tendency in the American steel industry is to reduce by every possible means the number of highly-skilled men employed and more and more to establish the general wage on the basis of common unskilled labor. This is not a new thing, but it becomes every year more accentuated as a result of the use of automatic appliances which unskilled labor is usually competent to control." The measurable effects of mechanization in steel, by their account, were higher wages but lower labor costs expressed as a percentage of total costs; they calculated that between 1890 and 1900, the wage bill had increased about $30 million, average wages had risen 11.5 percent, and the percentage of wages in total costs had fallen from 20.2 to 17.1. Carnegie Steel's victory at the battle of Homestead in 1892 had paid a dividend after all. And yet the war was not over. Steel workers were organizing locally, sometimes even striking, between 1909 and 1916, often enough without the assistance or the approval of the Amalgamated Association; soon thereafter, with help from the American Federation of Labor, they would begin organizing on a nationwide basis, and would finally confront the steel companies in 1919.[34]

The "human element" in the new automobile industry was no more pliable, even though the technological transformation of the labor process went further here than anywhere else. Between 1903 and 1907, when autos were still a luxury or novelty item, skilled labor and general-purpose machine tools were the predominant factors of production—indeed, skilled workers represented about 60 percent of the labor force in the auto plants until 1909 or 1910. As demand for autos steadily rose and shortages of skilled labor began to appear, money and real wages in the industry increased; unit costs began to rise accordingly. When the crisis of 1907 struck, therefore, the owners, managers, and engineers at the larger automobile companies were already looking for ways to increase labor productivity as well as output; the financial rigors of the crisis simply convinced them that they were looking in the right direction. Like their counterparts in steel, and for that matter in the larger industrial sector, they settled on the redivision of labor enforced by mechanization at the point of production. But they moved more quickly. In 1915, only 26 percent of Ford employees (and only 13 percent of the labor force in Cleveland's auto plants) were classified as "skilled operators." Two years later, "skilled trades" accounted for just 2.4 percent of Ford employees. Specialized machine tools equipped with automatic feed, clamping, and indexing had moved them to the margins of the production process, where they served in ancillary roles, as watchmen and regulators. The wage bill in the automobile industry increased, to be sure, as the companies hired more semiskilled "specialists" in response to increasing demand for moderately priced cars, ca. 1909–19; but unit labor costs were meanwhile reduced by a 400 percent increase in labor productivity.[35]

Even these extraordinary achievements did not satisfy Ford and his fellow capitalists. For if auto workers did not organize and strike, they often left their jobs in single file: as late as 1913, annual labor turnover in the automobile industry was between 100 and 200 percent (at Ford it was 370 percent). Owners, managers, and engineers began, then, to rethink the "human element." On the one hand, they devised new personnel policies and departments, through which "human relations" experts were able to redraw the lines between the worlds inside and outside the plants—between work, home, and neighborhood—as well as the worlds inside and outside each worker. On the other hand, they began to imagine a production process without producers, or rather without workers. They began to speak the language of "automation." Here is an example of that language from 1929: "Wherever output is a function of speed and accuracy, mechanisms, which are simply standardized laborers, will eventually displace the human element." The speaker is the National Industrial Conference Board, whose president, Magnus Alexander, had conducted the original labor turnover studies of the automobile industry between 1911 and 1913. The auto-innovators themselves spoke the vernacular version of this language as early as 1909; but they did not spread the word until their experiments in mechanization began to bear fruit, around 1916, when the president of A. O. Smith, the steel-frame manufacturer of Milwaukee, decided it was possible "to build automobile frames without men." [36]

By 1919, "the human element" had already become a familiar part of auto-speech, the wage-earning correlate of which was destined, it seemed, for "elimination." In 1915, for example, *The Automobile*, a trade publication, described a new spring-making machine by claiming, "Not only is the new process quicker, but the human element is eliminated." In 1919, *Automotive Industries*, another trade publication, explained the advantages of specialized machine tools by using the same language: "Special machinery, special jigs and special fixtures, supplemented by the especially designed gages, leave no room for the human element which is the foe to interchangeability in manufactured products." [37] Taken literally, these claims sound exaggerated at best. But if we suppose that the point of installing specialized machine tools was to incorporate both craft knowledge and modern science in the machines themselves—to inscribe the very idea of scientific management in things, in the equipment representing past labor—then the "elimination" of the "human element" in the auto plants begins to sound like the fulfillment of the promise of mechanization at the point of production. The automobile industry begins to look like the extremity of, not the exception to, the labor-saving tendencies specific to the consolidation of corporate capitalism.

This view of things is verified, I believe, by comparison to other capital-intensive industries, and by examination of capital formation as such from 1915 to 1940. At any rate my summary of findings from these forays into the territory of the economist would emphasize three claims. First, the savings of labor-time and costs made possible by mechanization at the point of production now become practically universal. By 1920, the process was no longer characterized by the introduction of compound or specialized machines and the consequent reconfiguration of work, but by the replacement or improvement of existing machinery at lower cost. The demand for labor and the recomposition of the labor force changed accordingly. Until the second decade of the twentieth century—from about 1840 to about 1910—any displacement of labor through mechanized production of finished consumer goods almost certainly increased demand for labor in the capital goods sector by increasing demand for machinery and its myriad inputs. Thereafter, net displacements of labor in the capital goods sector outstripped those in the booming consumer goods sector, as technical (including organizational) innovation permitted greater output in both sectors without increased investment of resources in preparation for production—that is, without the monetary or social costs of increasing both the past labor-time embodied in plant or equipment and the current labor-time ("living labour," as Marx would say) represented in the wage bill. In short, expanded production of commodities no longer required that capital mobilize more labor-time, living or dead.[38]

Second, the consolidation of corporate capitalism takes the mechanization of production to its logical conclusion by turning labor-saving machinery into capital-saving technique. When the current labor-time necessary to expand output of commodities as such began to contract, at some point between 1915 and 1925, the commodities that took the form of capital goods were affected like most others—they became cheaper because they required diminishing quantities of resources to produce. Some economists acknowledge this tendency by measuring a decline in capital-output ratios after 1909 or 1919 (there is general agreement on an increase in capital-output ratios before then, or at least from ca. 1850 to ca. 1920), or by calling attention to a related decline in net investment after 1910. Others do so by proposing a distinction between innovation and investment, and by arguing that after 1919, and perhaps even before, technical change was far more important than capital formation as a source of economic growth. Either way, the obsolescence of capital's historic functions—of saving, investing, and enforcing the increasing productivity of social labor—is implied in the developmental dynamic ascribed to the mechanization of production, which now appears as an autonomous process of technological change.[39]

Third, the conflict between capital formation and consumption, the conflict that had characterized the political culture of accumulating America, is now complicated, and perhaps superseded, by a pattern of economic growth determined, or rather accompanied, by declining capital-output ratios and rates of net investment. For when the expansion of industrial output and productivity requires only the replacement or maintenance of existing plant and equipment, profits lose their function as the fund out of which increased investment must be financed—in fact, their withdrawal from the income stream that represents aggregate demand for consumer goods now becomes a constraint on, not a condition of, economic growth. Before Keynes provided a theoretical rationale for an attack on the "fallacy of saving," certain

American economists had recognized and grappled with this problem, by citing the disproportionate relation between growth of profits and wages, or between rates of output in the capital goods and consumer goods sectors, in the 1920s. In the early 1930s, still without benefit of Keynes's *General Theory*, they would express similar concerns by proposing to close the gap between the nation's capacities for production and consumption.[40]

Let me flesh out these claims as a way of surveying the domain of socially necessary labor residing in relations of production. By the late 1920s, "the displacement of men by machines" had become almost a cliché of the new cultural critique. It seemed that the "human element" was on the verge of elimination from manufacturing after all. Stuart Chase, for example, began the decade by classifying the appeals of print advertising (to vanity, shame, "sex curiosity," etc.) and ended it with this announcement: "Factory population—our biggest item—has been steadily declining since 1920. Mass production and the automatic function are relentlessly substituting machines for machine tenders. Between 1923 and 1928, total factory employees declined by 1,250,000." Wesley Mitchell argued along similar lines in 1929: "The supply of new jobs has not been equal to the number of new workers plus the old workers displaced. Hence there has been a net increase of unemployment, between 1920 and 1927, which exceeds 650,000 people." By 1932, at the trough of the depression, the chorus had swelled to the size of a social movement; the intellectuals' earlier interest in automation and mass production was compounded when unemployment became the rule in manufacturing. Lewis Mumford was only one of many writers—among them were Mills, Schumpeter, Jerome, David Weintraub, Louis Fraina (a.k.a. Lewis Corey), Elizabeth F. Baker, and Archibald MacLeish—who wondered whether such unemployment in the 1930s was the completion of the tendency toward displacement of industrial workers in the 1920s rather than a symptom of deviation from normal patterns of growth.[41]

Later studies of the 1920s, from George Soule's monograph of 1947 to Michael Bernstein's synthesis of 1988, have raised the same questions. By all accounts, there was a net displacement of about 1 million workers in manufacturing, mining, and railroads, ca. 1920–29 (if construction is omitted, the number of workers in capital goods industries fell from 3.3 million in 1919 to 2.9 million in 1929). These were the industrial sites on which most new jobs—that is, most of the increase in the demand for labor—had been created since the 1840s. They could not function as such in the 1920s because gigantic increases in output (255 percent in automobiles and 156 percent in petroleum products) did not increase demand for labor enough to offset the effects of productivity growth. Labor productivity in manufacturing, for example, increased 43 percent from 1919 to 1929 (but 98 percent in automobiles); in the nonfarm sector, output per unit of labor input increased 56 percent for the decade. Meanwhile, overall output in manufacturing rose 64 percent—a substantial amount, but not enough to require net additions to the labor force in manufacturing. Future growth of the total labor force would have to be accommodated elsewhere, for example in the bureaucracies of the private and public sectors, where white-collar, "lower salaried" employees congregated.[42]

Savings of labor-time also appeared in the guise of "capital-improving" innovation, which reduced the costs of maintaining and increasing productive capacity. For example, petroleum refining was revolutionized, at least in a technical sense, by the replacement of straight-run distillation with continuous thermal cracking of crude oil. The new process was perfected and patented in several versions between 1910 and 1920. By 1929, when two of every three families owned a car, and gasoline had long since replaced kerosene as the primary product of petroleum refiners, continuous thermal cracking accounted for 90 percent of the gasoline refined in the United States. It had almost quadrupled the yield of gasoline per barrel of crude yet had cut refinery construction costs in half; capital inputs per unit of refined output declined accordingly, by 12.3 percent between 1910 and 1930. Similar patterns hold in other capital-intensive industries. In iron and steel, for example, there was no increase in the value of fixed capital or in the number of wage earners, ca. 1919–29, but output rose 40 percent because productivity per man-hour increased 63 percent for the decade. In motor vehicle and parts manufacturing, which the Department of Commerce identified as the largest American industry of 1925, the value of fixed capital declined after 1926—that is, after Ford's extensive retooling in preparation for production of the Model A—while productivity per man-hour kept rising.[43]

More generally it is clear, from Robert Gordon's calculations as well as studies of "instrumentation," that expenditures on industrial plant and equipment declined across the board from 1921 to 1929. In manufacturing and mining, there was a decline in gross investment between 1926 and 1929, when, as Gordon notes, "manufacturing as a whole displayed the most vigorous expansion." By 1929, the economy resembled a self-regulating mechanism; for the mechanization of commodity production now threatened to eliminate the "human element" at both ends of the capital-labor relation. At any rate the simple location of socially necessary labor was no longer obvious. But then neither was the meaning of the difference between production and consumption.[44]

The Limits of Consumer Culture

In a 1930 study of consumer credit sponsored by the Twentieth Century Fund (the fund's president, Edward A. Filene, had a vested interest in consumers), Evans Clark noted that the need for new markets had created a demand for what he called the "new economics": "The working masses of the world's population—the men and women who streamed into factories and shops in the morning and out again at night—have been thought of in the past primarily as *producers*. Today they are being visualized more as *consumers*: as business men or women in their own right." Throughout his study, Clark's narrative strategy was to identify these consumers as "going concerns" that deserved the "extension of reasonable credits" which had once financed the expansion of industrial production. "If markets are to be maintained," he insisted, "they must be able to buy more and more goods. But they can do this only if they are solvent, going concerns, with a constantly growing excess of net income from which further purchases can be made." The rhetorical reduction of consumers to small producers was completed by Clark's treatment of consumer durables as the key to the expansion of installment credit in the 1920s. He began with an unqualified assertion. "Mr. and Mrs. Jones can borrow . . . to finance the purchase of their automobile, their piano and radio, their washing machine and vaccuum cleaner[,] but they cannot pay the grocer or the landlord on the instalment plan, or their doctor's bills or taxes." Then he explained why such current expenses could not be financed. "Most economists would agree that it would be unsound for them to do so as a general practice. It is now generally assumed that consumer credit is economically justified only on goods which the buyer is actually using during the period over which credit is extended."[45]

Durable goods such as automobiles lasted at least as long as the loan did; unlike food, for example, they were supposed to retain a certain solidity, a value in use, even after the period or moment of expenditure. To that extent, they were comparable to the income-producing assets that small business firms typically purchased by borrowing from commercial banks. But Clark argued that consumer credit, not higher real wages, would have to supply the "growing excess of net income" which he defined as the necessary condition of growth in legitimate demand for these consumer durables; and no stretch of the accountant's imagination could turn consumer credit into a "growing excess of net income" for anyone except the finance companies and the acceptance corporations (e.g., GMAC). On the one hand, then, he recognized that consumption was more significant than production in determining economic growth and development—the maintenance of markets required that consumers "be able to buy more and more goods." On the other hand, he assumed that the wages and salaries of the "working masses" would not provide the margin of increase in net income which enabled them to do so—"to buy more and more goods"—and therefore could not enforce economic growth as such. Consumer credit made up the difference between actual and remunerative demand for consumer goods.

Clark's conflation of producers and consumers, which he used to drape consumption with the moral fiber that once clothed production, became a familiar convention among economists. In the late twentieth century, it animates criticism of government spending by letting us believe that there are no important differences between the budgets of households, business firms, and governments. But his approach to the problem of economic growth still deserves our attention; for it reveals the limits of consumer demand even as it acknowledges the "sovereignty of the consumer" in determining the rate and pattern of growth under conditions specific to corporate capitalism. At least it makes an issue of those limits. In Clark's account, "credit" represents the increased demand for goods which is necessary to economic growth. It is equivalent, we might say, to the difference between the current market value of available goods and the current income of business firms and consumers alike; in effect, Clark proposes that "credit" is the mechanism that clears the market at remunerative prices. The net increase of business profits presumably provides the funds necessary to repay loans used for the purchase of income-producing assets, whereas the net increase of wages and salaries presumably provides the funds necessary to repay loans used for the purchase of consumer durables.

So far, so good. But let us suppose, following Clark (and more recent economists), that economic growth is increasingly driven by the growth of consumer expenditures as financed out of wages and salaries; that any net increase of wages and salaries is a function of growing demand for labor (of growth in employment, of more jobs at prevailing wage rates); and that, in the absence of public spending, demand for labor is a function of changes in private investment. If we make these suppositions, we can see that the real threat to the extension of consumer credit is the unprecedented combination of rapid labor productivity growth and declining net private investment which reduced demand for labor in the 1920s and after.[46] We can see, in other words, that the real threat to the expansion of consumer demand, and thus to growth as such, is the consolidation of corporate capitalism, which restricts the scope of socially necessary labor by completing the mechanization of production—by extricating the "human element" from production of capital goods as well as consumer goods. We can also see that the real threat to the expansion of private investment resides in the same event, in the consolidation of corporate capitalism, which makes the pursuit of profit pointless by allowing rapid growth without increasing net investment. But can we have it both ways? Can we say that the consolidation of corporate capitalism is the cause of and the constraint on economic growth in the twentieth century—that is, the cause of and the constraint on the expansion of consumer demand? If so, does it follow that the limits of consumer culture are the limits determined by political economy?

I do think we can have it both ways. The consolidation of corporate capitalism is a powerful impetus to economic growth in the twentieth century precisely because it allows a more efficient or productive use of existing resources. As the economist Edmund S. Phelps has pointed out, under the aegis of the large industrial corporations, "technical progress becomes organizational in the sense that its effect on productivity does not require any change in the quantity of inputs." Indeed the completion of the transition from proprietary to corporate capitalism broke the social and cultural connections between the expansion of necessary labor-time and the increase of goods production or wealth—the connections codified in the exchange of money wages for labor-power, contained in the notion of "productive labor," and formalized in the labor theory of value. In 1934, Stuart Chase summarized the confusion that resulted: "Under modern conditions of production, no measurable relation can be found between work contributed and goods consumed. . . . A whole moral fabric is thus rent and torn, with the most alarming and far-reaching consequences." This confusion of spheres is not exactly what the corporate innovators originally intended; they had hoped to reinstate the significance of relations of production, to restrict the growth of real wages and consumption in favor of higher profits and greater investment. But the mechanization of production over which they presided had such a remarkable impact on labor productivity that the terms of political conflict between labor and capital over shares of national income changed radically. Meanwhile, ca. 1919–29, the social scope of production in preparation for production began to contract, making production for consumption the only dynamic sector of the "mature economy" and the indispensable condition of economic growth as such; for as the labor-time engaged in the production and operation of means of production declined, the labor-time available for production of consumer goods and services increased.[47]

I would, then, claim that the consolidation of corporate capitalism makes consumer demand the key variable in economic growth and that, by reducing the significance of relations of production, it underwrites a culture in which value is constituted by the varieties of subject positions or social relations required to appreciate goods, not measured by the quantities of labor-time required to produce commodities; in which consumption is authorized by the articulation of desire and the criterion of need as well as the production of value through work; and in which the integrity of the self finally becomes a function of the modern subject's fragmentation and reconstruction. This is a consumer culture because it presupposes the ubiquity of the commodity form but supersedes the categories of necessity, production, and class. I would also claim that the consolidation of corporate capitalism constrains the growth of consumer demand, by validating capital's share of national income and by reducing the scope of socially necessary labor. So conceived, it is the cause of both the "consumer durables revolution" in the 1920s and the Great Depression of the 1930s; by the same token, it is the condition and the limit of consumer culture. For if the consolidation of corporate capitalism validates our refusal to be bound by the categories of necessity, production, or class because it reduces the scope of socially necessary labor, it also constrains the emergence of alternatives to alienated labor.

Let us see if these claims are consistent with the most recent and authoritative books on both events; if they are, we may be in a position to conclude this study of the political economy of consumer culture. In *Buy Now, Pay Later* (1991), Martha Olney establishes the empirical contours of the "consumer durables revolution" in the 1920s, and attempts to explain it by reference to a fundamental postwar shift in demand rather than to changes in the relation between prices and incomes or to the availability of consumer credit. In *The Great Depression* (1988), which is largely an analysis of "investment failure" and changing demand in the 1920s, Michael Bernstein argues that recovery was delayed because the dynamic new "industrial blocs" in the consumer goods sector suffered most from the lasting income effects of the financial crisis that deranged markets after 1929. Taken together, these books constitute a definitive account of interwar economic development in the United States.[48]

My claims are consistent with this account in the sense that they address the evidence Olney and Bernstein have acknowledged or adduced; but they reproduce neither their explanations nor their contradictions. Olney argues

that American households "allocated more disposable income toward consumption in general" after World War I, that "durable goods substituted for
saving in the 1920s." The personal savings rate was almost halved in the
1920s, she demonstrates, while debt as a percentage of income doubled and
installment debt on consumer durables tripled (consumer debt for car purchases increased 500 percent between 1922 and 1929). She explains these
changes by reference to the decay of "moral prohibitions against being in
debt," which, when combined with relatively higher postwar prices for consumer goods and with new appetites for expensive items like automobiles,
vacuum cleaners, and radios, made for a "consumer durables revolution" on
the installment plan. And yet Olney insists that by spending with borrowed
money on consumer goods, households were simply "saving differently"—
not less—than before the war; for she equates saving, investment, and
consumption. She defines the purchase of a durable good "as household
investment in a capital asset that produces a stream of services over that
asset's productive lifetime."[49]

By doing so, she almost dismisses the questions her important book helps
us answer. For example, why did higher prices and "moral prohibitions"
not preclude the shift in demand toward consumer durables, especially in
view of the concurrent decline in wages and salaries vis-à-vis the value of
both total and industrial output? We know that consumers' outlay rose 37
percent between 1922 and 1929 (14 percent per capita), propelling a 51 percent increase in the output of consumer durables; but we also know that
over 90 percent of tax-payers had *less* disposable income in 1929 than in
1922. Does the combination of consumer credit and high-end consumption
explain this apparent anomaly? Did the extraordinary increase in consumer
spending "offset a decline in the ratio of business investment to income,"
as Thomas Juster and Robert Lipsey have argued—in other words, did it
compensate for the shortfall in aggregate demand determined by declining
net investment—and thus open up new paths of development as well as
possibilities of growth? Or is the "consumer durables revolution" of the
1920s an illusion conjured by our anachronistic distinction between saving
and consumption?[50]

Olney's *Buy Now, Pay Later* functions, in part, as an empirical test of
Bernstein's *Great Depression*. At any rate it confirms the shift in demand
during the 1920s on which his argument turns, and illustrates the long-
term significance of the new "industrial blocs" emerging from the consumer
goods sector. In addressing Bernstein's ambitious argument, therefore, we
are addressing both authors. The key to that argument, I believe, is the
relation it specifies between the "secular transformation" of the 1920s and

the "cyclical" events that composed the "financial crisis" of 1929: "The Great Depression in America thus appears to have been the result of two mechanisms, one cyclical, the other secular." The crash halted the secular trend toward new demand patterns and the maturation of industries "dependent on consumer markets for their growth," mainly, it seems, by reducing effective demand for consumer goods: "An unprecedented derangement of financial markets, and the resultant fall in consumer purchasing power, interrupted the long-term development process." But Bernstein treats the intersection of the "short-term" or cyclical event (the financial crisis) and the long-term "secular transformation" as an accident. "The Great Depression must be viewed as an event triggered by random historical and institutional circumstances but prolonged by the timing of the process of long-term industrial development in the U.S." So the financial crisis is exempt from historical explanation because it is a random, cyclical phenomenon; it nonetheless bears a crushing explanatory load: "Had there been no financial disruption in 1929, the secular transformation I have outlined would have proceeded relatively smoothly."[51]

To be persuaded by Bernstein's argument as it appears in this book, we must, then, assume that there is no intelligible relation between the secular trends of the 1920s and the cyclical events of 1929–33, and that the Great Depression interrupted the emergence of an economy oriented toward and animated by consumer demand. But if we adopt these assumptions, we do not need to be persuaded by the argument. I would, then, propose that we remake the argument, and complete Bernstein's account of interwar economic development, by turning these assumptions into questions. What is the relation between the secular trends and the cyclical events, ca. 1919–38? Did the depression interrupt the "secular transformation" of the 1920s—or enforce it?

One clue to the financial debacle of 1929 was offered by the president of Sun Oil Co. in an annual report of 1932: "If a larger share of prosperity's profits had gone to wages, there would have been more consumption and less speculation." In other words, a different distribution of income might have reduced the volume of savings available for speculation in real estate and financial markets. Between 1922 and 1929, the share of wages in total revenues of manufacturing corporations fell from 52 percent to 43 percent; meanwhile, corporate profits rose 62 percent, dividends doubled, and the top 1 percent of tax-payers increased their disposable income by 63 percent. But net investment was declining, as we have already seen, even though productivity and output were increasing rapidly. A shift to profits coincided, then, with a shrinking field of remunerative outlets for domestic capital investment (and after 1927, for foreign capital investment). According to Moody's Investors Service, for example, the proportion of net new corporate securities issues which was used "productively," for capital construction, declined from 62 to 29 percent between 1924 and 1929. Some of the "unproductive" proceeds probably found their way into the time (not demand) deposits at commercial banks on which corporations now earned interest, and from which the banks drew in loaning "on call" against the collateral of securities listed by the stock exchange; between 1921 and 1929, member banks of the Federal Reserve more than doubled their loans against stock exchange collateral. In 1928, when the banks began to look elsewhere for investment outlets, "other" institutions, including industrial corporations with idle surpluses, started to meet the demand for money in the brokers' call loan market; by October 1929, these "other" institutions had increased their loans in that market by 260 percent (to $6.6 billion). A 1932 memorandum for Adolph Miller of the Federal Reserve Board summarized the process in a postmortem on the 1920s. "As early as 1925, there was some evidence that the out-of-the ordinary profits accruing temporarily to common stock equities were laying the basis for an extraordinarily speculative stock market. This movement continued during 1926 and 1927 and culminated in fantastic markets in 1928 and 1929."[52]

Between 1926 and 1929, aggregate demand for consumer durables began to wane. Sales of new automobiles and residential construction declined after 1926, for example, as growth in total earnings of wage workers stagnated. But the speculative boom in the stock market fed on itself, and into high-end consumption, for two more years. As the Miller memorandum explained: "Holders of common stocks found themselves with sudden profits which enabled them to splurge, a condition which overstimulated the market for the higher-priced automobile, the tourist industry, and other luxury industries. . . . There was a tremendous growth in the number of persons employed by investment trusts and by brokers in merchandising securities, and there was also a further increase in the demand for office buildings to house appropriately these staffs." The number of white-collar, "lower salaried" employees who earned around $2,500 annually did grow rapidly in the 1920s, becoming an important source of increasing per capita consumption even after consumer credit had reached the point of diminishing returns, in 1927—the disposable income of these tax-payers rose 23 percent between 1923 and 1929. Their bubble burst when the non-banking institutions that had moved into the call loan market in 1928 pulled out in October of 1929, having realized that increasing profits from common stock trading were even less likely than improving profits on automobile production.[53]

By this account, the origin of stock market speculation was the surplus capital generated by the shift to profits after 1922; but the shift to profits in the 1920s was one dimension of the decline in capital requirements per unit of industrial output, that is, the sudden decline in demand for past labor as well as "living labour." It was yet another symptom of the spectacular increases in labor productivity made possible by the consolidation of corporate capitalism and the completion of mechanization at the point of production. So the stock market speculation that finally created the financial crisis of 1929 was itself caused by the "secular transformation" of the 1920s—by a pattern of employment and a distribution of income that could not sustain increased demand for consumer durables, and could not validate the impending transition to a new, consumer-led path of economic development, because they were determined by private investment.

How, then, do we define the Great Depression? Let us begin by recalling two salient facts about the recovery of the 1930s. First, it was genuine. The Federal Reserve Board's index of production rose from 64 in 1932 to 116 in the first nine months of 1937 (1929=121). According to the Department of Commerce, the national income rose from $40 billion in 1932 to $70 billion in 1937 (in 1929 it was $81 billion, but in 1937 prices were generally lower than in 1929, so $70 billion bought more); in 1939, GNP equaled that of 1929. The number of new automobiles annually registered declined from about 23 million in 1929 to less than 21 million in 1933, then increased to more than 25 million by 1937 when, thanks to the Congress of Industrial Organizations and federal relief, consumption expenditures as such nearly regained the level of 1929. Second, this recovery did not promote growing demand for capital goods—the proportion of replacement and maintenance expenditure in all investment, which had hovered around 80 percent in the 1920s, *increased* in the 1930s. Nor did it promote anything resembling the full employment of labor (in 1937, the unemployment rate was 14 percent, with about 8 million people out of work). As H. W. Arndt argued in 1944, it was a recovery unlike any other in the annals of American business cycles: "Whereas in the past cyclical recoveries had generally been initiated by a rising demand for capital goods in response to renewed business confidence and new investment opportunities, and had only consequentially led to increased consumers' income and demand for consumption goods, the recovery of 1933–7 seems to have been based and fed on rising demand for consumers' goods."[54]

The "secular transformation" of the 1920s, which Bernstein so ably out-lines, was, then, completed in the 1930s. In other words, the Great Depression of 1929–39 *enforced* the transition to consumer-led growth, mainly by shattering all confidence in a path of development determined exclusively by private investment. Hereafter, it would be impossible—or at least more difficult—to think of either consumer demand or economic growth as the derivative of private investment. In view of the New Deal's net contributions to consumer demand out of federal deficits, it would also be difficult or impossible to think of consumers' income as a simple function of employment in the private sector or, again, as the derivative of private investment. And so the central idea of the old republic—that consumption was authorized by the production of value through work, that only income earned in alienated labor gave individuals legitimate access to a share of the "social surplus" embodied in consumer goods—was finally tabled. At any rate it was challenged, in practice and in theory, by politicians, by intellectuals, and by unemployed workers. "With this alarming and wholesale denial of claims to consume based on productive labor," Chase explained in *The Economy of Abundance*, "and with power age industry roaring and strain-ing to produce goods, titles to consumption must be found elsewhere, and speedily." The Brookings Institution economists who produced *America's Capacity to Consume* (1934) did not altogether agree with Chase, but they thought policymakers did: "The same view is often expressed in the state-ment that the age of scarcity has been replaced by the era of abundance, an era in which the great problem is how to make effective use of the leisure time which the age of technology has thrust upon us. Of more significance than the mere expression of this view by individual observers is the fact that it is being embodied, more or less consciously, in governmental policies." And if policymakers did not agree with Chase on the need to detach income from wage labor, workers on the dole certainly did. "There is a noticeable tendency to regard obtaining relief as another way of earning a living," a Chicago social worker noted in 1934. In Washington, meanwhile, an aide to Harry Hopkins concurred: "The stigma of relief has almost disappeared except among white collar groups." [55]

In *The Economy of Abundance*, Chase often cited Rexford G. Tugwell, the Columbia professor of economics who was an outspoken admirer of Simon Patten—he edited a collection of Patten's essays for publication in 1924—and an accredited member of Franklin D. Roosevelt's "brains trust." Tugwell was a typical "technocrat" in the narrow sense that he wanted his "progressive" views embodied in governmental policies but did not believe that he could change public opinion and, for that matter, did not have much faith in the voting publics that elected Congress. For the time being, Chase was more interested in the making of opinion "out of doors," where he would not, as he thought, be bound by the conventions and sensibilities of the new men (and women) of power. Like Tugwell, he claimed Thorstein Veblen as a crucial source of his theoretical lineage; but until the 1940s, he shared his larger intellectual concerns with Edmund Wilson and Lewis Mumford—among other contributors to *The New Republic*—not with government officials and cabinet members like Henry Wallace, Harry Hopkins, and Frances Perkins. The fact remains that they all used the lexicon Patten had first made popular. Of course none of them believed that the meanings of "surplus" or "abundance" were self-evident, especially in the context of world depression. But they did believe that the new significance of consumption was evidence of a passage beyond necessity—beyond a society defined by relations of production—and they did try to map that passage for us. Now that we have surveyed the same area for ourselves, we do not have to treat this map as an interesting anachronism; we can instead use it as if we still inhabit the world it depicts, to choose a path of development and to decide on a political destination.[56]

PART 2

. . . .

NATURALISM, PRAGMATISM,

AND THE RECONSTRUCTION

OF SUBJECTIVITY,

1890–1930

Only Hegel is fit for America.
Walt Whitman, [1860?]

Is not Whitman the poetic replica of James?
Kenneth Burke, 1937

It may perhaps be enough for me to indicate the
beginning of the road to follow.
William James, 1905

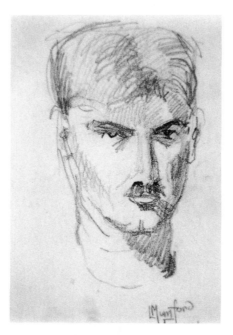

Lewis Mumford, self-portrait, 1920.
(Courtesy of Monmouth College)

CHAUTAUQUA.
Assembly Department
Program for Friday, July 24, 1896.

A. M.

7:45-10:00 C. N. E. C. A Study in Hebrews XI. Mr. W. N. Stearns. Museum.

8:00 College Prayers. Prof. W. D. McClintock. College Chapel.

8:30-12:00 Schools of the Collegiate Department in Session. See poster above. Office in C. L. S. C. building.

8:30 Boys and Girls' Meeting. Dr. B. T. Vincent. Temple.

8:30 Little People's Meeting. Mrs. B. T. Vincent. Kellogg Hall.

9:00 Chorus Drill. Dr. H. R. Palmer. Amphitheater.

9:00 "Junior Outlook Club." Miss Helen Bainbridge. C. L. S. C. Hall, Rear.

9:00 Women's Club. Mrs. B. T. Vincent, President. Hall.

10:00 "The Outlook." Young Women's Club. Miss Agnes Lathe. Higgins Memorial Hall.

10:15 Devotional Hall Hour. Hall.

11:00 Lecture: "Municipal Reform." Dr. Amos P. Wilder. Hall.

12:00 Noon-day Prayer Meeting. "The Work of the W. C. T. U. for Immigrants." W. C. T. U. Room, Kellogg Hall.

P. M.

1:30 Primary Chorus for Boys and Girls twelve years of age and under. Free. Mr. L. S. Leason. College Chapel.

2:00 Chautauqua Mandolin and Guitar Club. For players only. Mr. R. P. Loomis. Room 2, Amphitheater.

3:00 Lecture: "Co-operation of Home and School; The Educational Efficiency of the School." II. Prof. W. L. Bryan. Hall.

3:45 Lecture on Model of Palestine. Dr. H. B. Waterman. Palestine Park.

4:00 Chorus Drill. Dr. H. R. Palmer. Amphitheater.

4:00 Lecture: "Psychology and Relaxation." Prof. William James. Hall.

5:00 Lecture-Recital. Mr. Wm. H. Sherwood. Sherwood Hall. Extra Charge.

5:00 Lecture: "Glimpses of Old Southern Life and Humor." Prof. W. M. Baskerville. Hall.

7:00 Young Peoples' Prayer Meeting. "Seeing God in Nature." Hall.

7:00 Sight Singing Class. Sherwood Hall.

7:00 German Club. Prof. Henry Cohn. Higgins Hall.

7:00 Lecture: "The Psychology of Gesture." Mr. S. H. Clark. Normal Hall.

7:00 Twilight Concert. Rogers' Band. Miller Park.

8:00 Illustrated Lecture: "A Visit to Other Worlds." Prof. T. H. Dinsmore. Amphitheater.

9:00 C. E. Reception. Higgins Hall.

9:15 Electrical Display. Lake Front.

Chautauqua flyer, July 1896.
(By permission of the Houghton Library, Harvard University, bMSAm 1092.9)

William James, self-portrait, 1860s.
(By permission of the Houghton
Library, Harvard University,
FMSAm 1092.2)

William James, 1893.
(By permission of the Houghton
Library, Harvard University,
pfMSAm 1092)

CHAPTER 5

. . . .

GHOSTS IN THE

NARRATIVE MACHINE

The Politics of Historiography

Since 1960, with the appearance or assimilation of seminal books by Morton White, H. Stuart Hughes, and Henry May, we have been able to assume that the revision of intellectual agendas in western Europe and North America, ca. 1890–1920, was fundamental, even revolutionary. Indeed we might read these books as early examples of the attempt to reconstitute those turn-of-the-century agendas—the same attempt that characterizes or determines the work of artists and intellectuals in our own, more self-consciously "postmodern" moment.[1] Meanwhile, the new social-cultural history has emerged, and our sense of the changes in question has broadened accordingly, to include the life of the body as well as the mind, ultimately to include readers, consumers, and subaltern classes as well as novelists, artists, and intellectuals. But the social-cultural historians have been much more ambiguous than their predecessors among the intellectual historians. If they do not see turn-of-the-century changes in terms of loss or regression—as agendas to be repudiated—they do caution us against an embrace of the consumer culture that they define as the product of such changes. That is why the word *transformation* appears so often in their subtitles and texts: it conveys their ambiguity and focuses our attention on the unintended consequences of a moment that has all the attributes of a cultural revolution.[2]

My purpose in part 2 is to explore the middle ground between the transformation described by the social-cultural historians and the revolution described by the intellectual historians. In doing so, I hope to show that there is an unclaimed legacy residing in the extraordinary changes we associate with the turn of the century—that there is enormous potential in (not in spite of) the ambiguous character of these changes. My procedure is to mediate in two senses between the different approaches of the rival historiographical camps. I try to show that there is a contiguous relation between the domains they describe. And I try to show that to explore this borderland is to specify a historical relation between material circumstances and intellectual inscription without reducing one to the other. What I hope finally to illuminate is the political economy of cultural revolution in the United States, ca. 1890–1930.

I begin with a rough sketch of the differences between the intellectual and the social-cultural historians. I conclude this introduction by claiming that neither camp can account for the upheaval or assimilate the changes in question. With this claim in mind, I turn to the nature of intellectual and cultural innovation in the period. I argue that the transition from proprietary to corporate capitalism is comparable to the earlier transition from feudalism to capitalism because it points the way beyond relations of production as the effective determinant of social relations as such, and accordingly beyond modern class society as well. So conceived, the transition authorizes or allows the characteristic gesture of intellectuals in the period between 1890 and 1930—that is, their refusal to be bound by the categories of necessity, production, or class. I will claim in concluding that the virtue of the innovations specific to the turn of the century is to have demonstrated that a debate about the conditions and scope of selfhood or knowledge cannot be continued, let alone completed, unless we recognize that it is less philosophical or intellectual or linguistic than practical, cultural, and political— or rather that it becomes philosophical and intellectual because it is practical and cultural.

The real difference between the intellectual historians and the social-cultural historians is not that the former were prone to celebration of the "revolt against formalism" which united the deep thinkers and the rebellious bohemians; for White and May as well as Hughes were quite conscious of the evasions and equivocations that the new intellectual discourse indulged. It is instead that they defined the prewar revolt as both liberation from nineteenth-century constraints and promising groundwork for intellectual renovation at mid-twentieth century. What divides them from the social-cultural historians in this sense is a certain faith in the modern, liberal, broadly progressive outlook which they rightly claim was both cause and effect of turn-of-the-century innovation. For the most part, the social-cultural historians do not have and cannot muster any such faith; so they claim that the modern, liberal, broadly progressive mainstream was built on the ruins of genuine alternatives, that liberation—if it can be called that—

entailed still untold losses, and that intellectual renovation requires the recuperation of what modern liberalism has repressed or forgotten. The difference between the two camps is as much political as methodological, then, although their methods do in the end produce different domains of fact.

Before I map these domains, therefore, let me briefly and schematically trace this connection between the political and the methodological. I begin with the proposition that serious doubts about modern liberalism were pervasive and growing among leading intellectuals at the very beginning of the American century, ca. 1955–63. As evidence of these doubts, I would cite the following: the voter studies sponsored by the Survey Research Center at the University of Michigan, which demonstrated the apparent irrationality of American electoral behavior, and their correlates in political theorizing, most notably that of Philip Converse; the seminal works of Daniel Bell (*The End of Ideology*) and Richard Hofstadter (*The Age of Reform*), which were about the exhaustion, not the triumph, of liberalism; the discovery of "mass society" and the popularization of David Riesman's notion of the "other-directed self"; the ambitious studies in political philosophy by Sheldon Wolin, Hannah Arendt, and C. B. Macpherson, which led toward the rehabilitation of classical republicanism; the work of C. Wright Mills, particularly the essays collected as *The Sociological Imagination*, in which he announced the arrival of a postmodern and accordingly postliberal epoch; the appropriation and American inflection of European social theory in the works of Talcott Parsons, Robert Merton, Robert Bierstadt, Hans Gerth, William Appleman Williams, and many others; and finally, the studies in scientific revolutions by Thomas Kuhn, which, if nothing else, demonstrated the indissolubility of fact and value.[3]

I do not want to overstate the case by claiming that these intellectual currents amounted to a flood of anxiety about liberalism as social theory and system. Nevertheless, we should note that the doubts stirring in such currents ran deepest where the most influential academics and intellectuals congregated, and that everyone seized on the same facts as proof of the need to get beyond the status quo in theory if not in practice. According to both Mills and Hofstadter, for example, the rational, autonomous individual required—or at least posited—by liberal political theory was a thing of the past. Both claimed, moreover, that this death of the subject was a product of corporate-industrial bureaucratization. The modern (or, as Mills would have it, the postmodern) self was in any event contained and determined by structures and desires that liberal theory could not seem to acknowledge.[4]

Insofar as we can say that the indispensable assumption of liberalism is the ontological priority of the pure self, and that this assumption is authorized by acceptance of the principle of analysis—through which knowledge is secured only when the knower distinguishes between reason (mind) and desire (body) and represses the latter—we can also say that the findings of leading intellectuals in the 1950s and early 1960s were inconsistent with liberalism.[5] But the immediate results were not political, with the possible exception of the Port Huron Statement, largely because the intellectuals' heirs were themselves academics without constituencies beyond their graduate students. The immediate results were instead methodological, involving as such a search within academia for alternatives to the principle of analysis and the ontological priority of the pure self. The turn toward social and cultural history, for example, was driven by two arguments derived from the counterliberal findings of the late 1950s. First, if mind and body or reason and desire were not antithetical modes of apprehending reality, and if fact and value were accordingly indissoluble, there remained no rationally defensible privilege for the history of ideas over the history of popular culture—no privilege, that is, for the life of the mind over the body. The "physical complexity" of African-American culture, for example, could then appear as different from, not inferior to, the compulsive rationality of its European-American counterpart. Second, if the self was irretrievably embedded in social structures and irrational beliefs or rituals, then the inherited emphasis on the leading figures of the historical stage had to give way to an emphasis on the collective identities and practices in which all individuals, even the leading figures, were created or contained. The history of subaltern social movements could thereafter appear as the proper object of professional monographs and careers.[6]

The elaboration of these arguments in monographic forms eventually exhumed the historical alternatives to modern American liberalism—an exhaustive listing of which would only begin with republicanism, socialism, antimodernism, plebeian culture, working-class solidarity, and women's separate sphere. These alternatives now function as querulous ghosts out of Elizabethan tragedy, who keep reminding historians of what might have been had not the usurper appeared to steal their raiment and recast the genealogy of modern times. Indeed their voices are no longer heard from offstage; they have become the featured players. Where we once let Macbeth describe Banquo for us, we now listen only to the ghost.

So the historical drama in question has been complicated by the addition and amplification of new characters, new voices. The tentative or contingent quality of its ostensibly univocal conclusion—in favor of a modern, liberal, broadly progressive outlook—has accordingly been acknowledged by historians, even those who do not believe that the alternatives were as promising as modern liberalism. As a result, we have several useful studies of the segmentation of American culture at the turn of the century, of which the widening gulf between highbrow and lowbrow is only one manifestation.[7] But another result of the same attention to historical alternatives is our inability to explain either the convergence of discourses in the 1890s or the subsequent emergence of a cultural consensus—except by perfunctory reference to asymmetries in political-economic power that are themselves outcomes of struggle, or by more refined and bravely ironic reference to unintended consequences. That we no longer dismiss populism as atavism, or define skilled workers' control of output as "shirking," is of course a sign of historiographical progress. That we seem to have no way of appreciating the alternative to these alternatives would suggest that the social-cultural historians have produced a parody of the modern-liberal mainstream, one that does not intersect with or include this rival but instead runs parallel to it, as if the alternatives available, then and now, were mutually exclusive. Progress does have its price.

Again, I do not want to overstate the case. At its best, the new social-cultural history displays a fine dialectical or dialogical sense of how the actual is constituted by the potential, of how the content of the repressed is both annulled and preserved in a "hegemonic" symbolic order. Even so, the close attention to historical alternatives has finally made it impossible for us to understand why large numbers of workers, farmers, and middle-class intellectuals committed themselves to a future in which those alternatives were marginalized if not unavailable. For the "imagined extension of deviations" that Roberto Unger has demanded, and the corresponding insights "into lines of development that were halted or reversed," have gone so far that we have lost sight of those lines of development that still mark the boundaries of the mainstream. Thus we have not yet begun the project that Unger outlines as follows: "We must determine the extent to which particular deviations failed because they were suppressed by force and guile and the extent to which they were outdone by their rivals on the multiple terrain of practical, moral, and theoretical needs."[8]

I do not mean to suggest that the older intellectual history was superior to the newer social-cultural history in this sense. The intellectual historians have tended either to neglect or to trivialize the "deviations," on the assumption that the modern, liberal, broadly progressive outlook emerged the winner because it represented an obvious advance over Victorianism or populism or socialism. Indeed they did not (and do not) recognize these cultural formations and social movements as genuine alternatives to modern liberalism, in part at least because they believed, with good reason, that the American liberal tradition was invented by the revolutionaries of the eighteenth century, not by the progressives of the twentieth. In other words, the intellectual historians have treated liberalism as the inclusive mainstream of American political culture, not as one current among many. They have not bothered to deal with the alternatives because they have not and cannot see them as such.[9]

Let us turn, then, to the different domains of fact produced by the two camps. The intellectual historians would, I trust, agree that the significant changes or innovations of the period 1890–1920 could be adequately if provisionally summarized as follows:

1. A loss of faith in, and a new self-consciousness about, the assumptions and purposes of intellectual inquiry, political action, and received cultural tradition, which were due only in part to the Darwinian deconstruction of supernatural sanctions for inherited social norms[10]
2. A new sense of the relation between past and present animated by the recognition of a fundamental contingency or fluidity in the nature of knowledge, truth, and their deep structure in the self[11]
3. A reassessment or redefinition of individuality or subjectivity in terms of social, physical, and irrational modes of apprehension[12]
4. New ideas about and programs pertaining to the relation between civil society and state power, both flowing from intensified study of interfirm competition and the rights, scope, and obligations of property[13]
5. The articulation of new social roles and agendas for writers, artists, experts, academics, and intellectuals in and through the eruption of little magazines, commercial mass media, professional organizations and journals, modern universities, social movements, progressive politics, and government commissions or agencies[14]

For their part, the social-cultural historians would surely agree that significant change or innovation could be adequately if provisionally summarized as follows:

1. The decomposition of the genteel or Victorian cultural tradition, in which mind and body, reason and desire, realism and romance, self and other, male and female, occupied separate spheres [15]
2. The segmentation of cultures into highbrow and lowbrow, which recapitulates and validates the correlates of class society, that is, the division of mental and manual labor and the differentiation of social spaces (e.g., country and city, or upper- and lower-class urban enclaves) [16]
3. The emergence of spectacularly commercial cultural forms and practices (department stores, sports, movies, dance music, amusement parks) suited to "mass society," which eventually drained even the remaining backwaters of middle-class morality [17]
4. A shift in the site of self-discovery and determination from commodity production to consumption and, accordingly, a shift from character (or manhood) to personality (or self-realization) as the method and goal of psychological maturation and social mobility [18]
5. The eclipse of republicanism as both the political culture of subaltern social movements and the master plot of popular literature and, consequently, the rise of modern-liberal notions of citizenship and political action which complete the new "culture of consumption" implied at (3) and (4) [19]
6. The articulation of new social roles, political obligations, and sexual standards for women [20]

From either perspective, this was clearly a moment of extraordinary change and innovation. How, then, do we account for it? The intellectual historians do of course cite political-economic change as part of their explanations; but they correctly insist that they should be more interested in consequences—the content of new thinking—than causes, and that they run the risk of reductionism insofar as they fall back on the second industrial revolution of the late nineteenth century for explanations of the intellectual revolution that coincides with it. Accordingly they write their histories in terms of influential intellectual communities or biographies, and define significant change as a break with the methodological past constituted by faith or reason—that is, by religious revelation or by natural science. This procedure has produced extraordinary results, for example, the recent work of Bruce Kuklick, James Kloppenberg, and Thomas Haskell, as well as the earlier work of R. Jackson Wilson, Sidney Fine, White, and May.[21]

But this procedure elegantly elides two related questions. First, what are we to make of George Santayana's claim that the "subsoil" of American life—"the moods of the dumb majority"—found expression in the thought of William James and, by implication, in the broader "revolt against formalism" that characterized intellectual change in the period? We might dismiss it as the archetypal expression of European distaste for the American Philistine. But we would then have to dismiss the indigenous critical tradition founded by Van Wyck Brooks, Randolph Bourne, and Lewis Mumford—and later reinvigorated by Christopher Lasch—according to which the pragmatic plow was sunk too deep in the same subsoil, and so became a form of acquiescence to the imperatives of modern capitalism. We would also have to overlook Santayana's special status as a brilliant student of American culture, Western philosophy, and James himself.[22]

Second, how are we to specify the generally American character or qualities of intellectual change and innovation? In other words, how do we explain such change and innovation in terms of American history as such, rather than as the typical reflex of the "interdependence" experienced by the inhabitants of late-nineteenth-century Western civilization, or as the unique product of higher education in the United States? Why is it that the intellectual revolution here was broader, deeper, and more consequential than elsewhere? And why did its makers invoke the poets and the common people—the "dumb majority"—of their own culture in erecting their new barricades? So far the intellectual historians have not addressed, and cannot provide answers to, these questions. Accordingly they cannot yet account for the revolution in question.

The social-cultural historians are by and large more interested in giving voice to inarticulate forms of expression; they are in fact excavating the very subsoil out of which pragmatism is supposed to have grown. But these new Diggers invariably write as if the area of a culture is bounded by class (or gender), not language, thus as if there is no discernible relation between social and intellectual change, or between the particular political cultures of subaltern social strata and the liberal mainstream that, by most accounts, broadened in this period to include them. This procedure has also produced extraordinary results—in the recent work of Kathy Peiss, Roy Rosenzweig, and Carroll Smith-Rosenberg, as well as the earlier work of Herbert Gutman, John Kasson, and Lawrence Goodwyn.[23]

But it energetically elides the very questions it raises. For example, was this subsoil the ground on which modern liberalism and consumer culture were propagated? Or were new, artificially fertilized frontiers required to nurture these profuse hybrids? Or were the boundaries moved to include untried fields and allow new growth? To the extent that the social-cultural historians proceed on the assumption that the whole of the emergent culture was constituted by the sum of, not the relation between, its various parts or "subcultures," they beg such questions. Indeed they beg the question of culture itself. For a culture does not merely provide symbols, conventions, and rules that govern the designation of a given reality. It does not merely assign meaning to the *products* of mental and manual labor. It also assigns different meanings to these different *forms* of labor, and thus occupies the area between them—the area, as William James pointed out, in which reality itself is culturally remade over time. To the extent that the social-cultural historians have let the parts stand for the whole, they have not explored this area, and cannot yet account for the transformation in question.

Hereafter I will be attempting to account for cultural revolution by exploring the character of political-economic change as it was defined by the men and women who came of age at or near the turn of the century. But my goal is not to trace new ideas or practices to their origins within a transparent field of political-economic interests or functions. Rather, it is to show how different interpretations of the same changes shaped the most popular of American cultures—the political—and accordingly determined the possibilities of intellectual innovation.

. . . .

CHAPTER 6

THE SUBJECT OF NATURALISM

Language, Form, and Style in Character Building

In one of the original manifestoes of the new literary history—of what has become the "new historicism"—Hans Robert Jauss distinguishes between literature as an invented order of ideas and history as an inherited order of events. "In contrast to a political event, a literary event has no lasting results which succeeding generations cannot avoid. It can continue to have an effect only if future generations still respond to it or rediscover it."[1] If he is correct, as I think he is, then we need to ask how and why certain generations respond to or rediscover past "literary events."[2] We need, that is, to ask what circumstances enable these discoveries, these "acts of historical solidarity," as Roland Barthes calls them; otherwise we have removed readers and critics (ourselves included) from the historical time in which we have already situated the textual objects of our inquiry.[3]

In this chapter, I address the question of historical solidarity by asking a simpler one about *Sister Carrie* (1900), Theodore Dreiser's first novel: why did the author situate a realist style within the apparently archaic form of romance? I suggest that as the political-economic groundwork of the modern subject seemed to dissolve in the 1890s, with the completion of proletarianization and the emergence of a "credit economy," the finished characters posited by realism became problematic if not unintelligible. The rediscovery of romance—the literary form in which the line between self and society cannot be clearly drawn—accordingly became possible, and perhaps necessary. I claim that the writers, intellectuals, and artists of Dreiser's generation solved the problem of character or subjectivity by drawing on a broad range of cultural resources, including both the popular, theatrical forms from which romance had never been exiled and the older, more reputable works of the antebellum masters. In effect I claim that, when reworked by Dreiser and the other naturalists, the romance form accommodated the "social self" specified by philosophers, jurists, and social scientists in search of an alternative to the modern subject. I then turn to the contemporary relevance of their solutions as a way of proposing that the decade of the 1890s is the origin of our own time, of the "transition questions" that still concern us.[4] In concluding, I suggest that Whitman's claim about Hegel ("only Hegel is fit for America") should be taken seriously, if only because Hegel's theory of the transitive subject, the discursive self, helps us understand why we still recognize Carrie as our sister.

I do not mean to suggest that the period between the mid-nineteenth and the late twentieth centuries is a unitary epoch, although I do try to salvage Harold Bloom's notion of a "post-Enlightenment crisis" by sketching some historical foundations for this castle in the air.[5] Nor do I mean to suggest that between the 1850s and our own time there has been a linear or cumulative movement in the realm of literary events, through which narrative forms regulated by realism were replaced by better ones. Instead, I mean to explain how and why Dreiser chose to be influenced by the very writers William Dean Howells sought to displace, and why we still respond to Dreiser's choice. But I also want to demonstrate that the question of character or subjectivity became a pressing, practical question at the turn of the century. Having done so, I can more plausibly claim in subsequent chapters that naturalism and pragmatism are different versions of the same answer.

At the outset, my procedure is to show that Bloom's notion of the "American Sublime"—the "acceptance or affirmation of discontinuities in the self"—is necessary but not sufficient to understanding the novelty and consequences of naturalism as Dreiser developed it in *Sister Carrie*. Bloom invokes Whitman and Emerson to illustrate his argument, implying that these writers deserve their canonical standing because they founded the tradition that defines modern American letters by inventing the "American Sublime."[6] Of course Whitman and Emerson, like Melville and Hawthorne, did celebrate or investigate the discursive self who thrives in nonrealistic literary forms. But an American literary canon that included all these figures did not take shape until the second or third decade of the twentieth century, when their works were defined as equally original moments in the making of a usable past by Van Wyck Brooks, D. H. Lawrence, and Lewis Mumford. Before then, these works were not commensurable literary events.[7] To explore the interregnum of the late nineteenth century would presumably be to recapture the terms of literary debate at the turn of the century, and thus to illuminate both the choices available to writers then *as* now and the possible continuities between writers then *and* now.

In effect I am asking why certain authors, forms, or styles had to be rediscovered or reappropriated at the turn of the century. One plausible response would be to cite the great post–Civil War divide between American life, where the new industrial entrepreneurs turned the world upside down, and American letters, where the new realist writers tried to meet the challenge to character—and to solve the problem of characterization—presented by rapidly changing social conditions. This is the explanatory procedure Mumford adopted in *The Golden Day* (1926). But the realists themselves repudiated both the legacy of the midcentury renaissance and the grotesque grope of wealth that (re)organized social life in the late nineteenth century. Howells, for example, who championed realism on moral as well as aesthetic grounds, criticized the "intense ethicism" of the antebellum masters, who excelled not in the novel as such but in poetry and romance. "They still helplessly pointed the moral in all they did . . . they felt their vocation as prophets too much for their good as poets." From this standpoint, Hawthorne's fiction was quite similar to the extremity of romance in *Uncle Tom's Cabin* (1852) by Harriet Beecher Stowe. Howells noted, "Its chief virtue, or its prime virtue, is in its address to the conscience, and not in its address to the taste; to the ethical sense, not the aesthetical sense."[8]

The shortcoming of romance as form, according to Howells, was its inversion of the proper relation between incident and character. The romance moved erratically along the surface of extraordinary events and allegorical figures, and thus never produced a recognizable individual about whom one could ask: given this character, what will happen? To this extent, romance lacked a citizenry that could grasp, or be obligated by, the moral law; hence its creators had to point the moral from outside the text, as authorial presence, rather than in and through their characters. The task of the novel was, then, to create these recognizable individuals, these characters, so that the moral law became intelligible as an active dimension of real, everyday life, as the truth embedded in and inseparable from an aesthetic sensibility or design—a form—that faithfully represented real, everyday life. Only by accomplishing this task could the novel unify the real and the ideal, the "is" and the "ought," or as Howells put it in 1887, the facts and the duties of humanity. "No one hereafter will be able to achieve greatness who is false to humanity, either in its facts or its duties. . . . no conscientious man can now set about painting an image of life without perpetual question of the verity of his work, and without feeling bound to distinguish so clearly that no reader of his may be misled, between what is right and what is wrong . . . in the actions and characters he portrays."[9]

The difficulty here, Howells knew, was to create finished characters with enough interiority to grasp the nuances of the moral law. Unless they were finished in this respect, they could not exemplify the moral issue(s) from within the text, and so could not validate the "ethical sense" of readers by appealing to their "aesthetical sense." But if they were finished—if their identities were fixed—they could not deal with the novel circumstances and new options that rapid social change, the hallmark of modernity, normally produces. To such characters, the incomplete present in which real life is necessarily lived would appear dangerous: it would become the source of delusion and the site of dissolution. In Howells's first major fiction—the work that signifies his attempt to make it as a novelist, not as an arbiter of taste from his editorial position at the *Atlantic*—this difficulty is powerfully illustrated by the characters themselves.[10] The following exchange takes place toward the end of *A Modern Instance* (1882), after Ben Halleck, who is in love with Bartley Hubbard's wife, has returned to the scene of his anguish (from which Hubbard has disappeared) and has tried to convince his perfectly priggish friend Atherton that he has had to repress his forbidden desire:

> Halleck lay back in his chair, and laughed wearily.
> "I wish I could convince somebody of my wickedness. . . . I suppose now, that if I took you by the button-hole and informed you confidentially that I had stopped long enough at 129 Clover street to put a knife into Hubbard in a quiet way, you wouldn't send for a policeman."
> "I should send for a doctor," said Atherton.
> "Such is the effect of character! And yet, out of the fulness of the heart the mouth speaketh. Out of the heart proceed all those unpleasant things enumerated in Scripture; but if you bottle them up there, and keep your label fresh, it's all that's required of you—by your fellow beings, at least. What an amusing thing morality would be if it were not—otherwise. Atherton, do you believe that such a man as Christ ever lived?"
> "I know you do, Halleck," said Atherton.
> "Well, that depends on what you call me. If what I was,—if my well Sunday-schooled youth—is I, I do. But if I, poising dubiously on the momentary present between the past and future, am I—I'm afraid I don't. And yet it seems to me that I have a fairish sort of faith. I know that, if Christ never lived on earth, some One lived who imagined him, and that One must have been a God. The historical fact oughtn't to matter."[11]

This last remark seems to contradict Halleck's attempt to locate his self in the momentary present; for the historical fact of his well-Sunday-schooled youth authorizes his belief in the possibility of genuine selfhood. But it is consistent with the fear of externality or otherness that characterizes his search for a groundwork of the moral law which, once discovered, will presumably secure his identity. From Halleck's standpoint, such externality takes two forms. It appears in space as the body, both his own ("out of the fulness of the heart," etc.) and that of Christ. The historical fact of the god-man's bodily presence on earth "oughtn't to matter," Halleck claims, as if the very existence of the body's particularity calls morality as such into question. Externality also appears as time itself, in the form of an incomprehensible relation between past, present, and future; so conceived, as irrational contingency, the order of events cannot, or rather should not, impinge on the order of ideas Halleck calls morality.[12]

Halleck's appeal to the past is nostalgic, then, since he immediately points out that past and present are incommensurable, and that the future is unbound. What remains is the dubious present. If it is momentary, as Halleck suggests, it is of course unknowable. But once we have decided there is no comprehensible relation between past and present, as Halleck has, we have in effect erased the boundaries between them and encouraged one to colonize the other. The pastness of the past, lacking representation in the here and now, will then give way before an imperial present in which everyone, from every time and place, is recognizable as the exemplar of an unchanged and unchanging "human nature." This present is eminently knowable, for it is the abiding present of the pure self who, as interiorized mind, as living abstraction, is undefiled by externality of any kind, and thus is not so much above as absent from history. This present is conclusive, closed, complete; and so characters such as Halleck can inhabit it without losing themselves in it. It becomes the groundwork for their metaphysic of morality.

That Howells, like Halleck, believed "the historical fact oughtn't to matter" is made clear in his criticism as well as in his fiction. By the turn of the century, he was engaged in a rearguard action against the new historical romances, in which the excesses of affect and incident effaced character altogether. His strategy was to defend the historical fictions of Leo Tolstoy and Mark Twain against the historical romances. His defense rested, however, on the grounds that the former depicted the past not as commensurable with but as identical to the present, and thereby preserved the sanctions of the moral law in the present.

> There [in *War and Peace*] a whole important epoch lives again, not in the flare of theatrical facts, but in motives and feelings so much like those of our own time, that I know them for the passions and principles of all times. . . . For a like reason our greatest romancer, Mark Twain, . . . is a true historical novelist because he represents humanity as we know it

must have been, since it is humanity as we know it is. . . . the moral law is as active in that fascinating dream world [of *A Connecticut Yankee*] as it is in this waking world, where sooner or later every man feels its power. I like Mark Twain's historical fiction above all for this supreme truth, just as I like Tolstoy's. . . . It is by some such test that we are to know the validity of any work of art. It is not by taking us out of ourselves, but by taking us into ourselves, that its truth, its worth, is manifest.[13]

Howells's obsession with "the moral law" as the cultural work of fiction should not be equated with narrow-minded prudery. Like every other serious writer of his time, he was attempting to confer meaning on a world that had only recently been desacralized, to find durable significance and purpose in lives that had only recently been liberated from the obligations and constraints of parochial communities. He was attempting, in other words, to illustrate the possibility of morality in the absence of all external authority, including the authority of God. This project required that he demonstrate the sovereignty of the self, yet not concede that morality is purely subjective and contingent, and thus strictly a matter of individual preference or "taste." Like Immanuel Kant, Howells posited a supersensible, extrahistorical realm of mind as a way of meeting both requirements. By taking us ever farther into this infinite present—"not by taking us out of ourselves, but by taking us into ourselves"—he hoped to grasp its truth.

Sister Carrie *as Romance*

But in such an interiorized realm of pure selves, desire has no place, or rather no function. For, as Hegel suggested, it is precisely desire that takes us "out of ourselves" into the forms of objectivity that realize ourselves; it implicates us in externality, drives us to identify with and become something we are not. Desire, in this sense, is the cunning of reason, the source and medium of the self construed as the "concrete actuality" of self-consciousness. Whitman demonstrated the proposition poetically, by constructing an autobiography of the discursive self which never ignores or represses the body, but instead treats its particularity—its insistent desires—as consistent with and ingredient in a movement toward new consciousness, new identity.[14]

This discursive self goes underground after the Civil War, as the realism of Howells and Twain carries the day. But it erupts from the exhausted soil of American letters in the 1890s, in the form of literary naturalism.

Art and philosophy are meanwhile revolutionized by the rediscovery of this same underground (wo)man.[15] Naturalism, like pragmatism, foregrounds the sensational, desiring body as the necessary and enduring condition of self-consciousness and selfhood. In doing so, it contributes to the inversion—or at least the interrogation—of stereotypes applying equally to women, workers, and African Americans (e.g., that their complexity is physical, "natural," sensational, thus beyond the pale of reason, character, and political deliberation). This naturalist notion of selfhood as the effect of entanglement in externality enables a new, discursive model of personality that lives another underground (or rather apolitical) existence from the 1930s to the 1950s, when, in the absence of official apartheid and an institutionalized Left, it reshapes the languages of both popular culture and radical politics.[16]

So the truth embedded in the old-fashioned idea that literary naturalists are vulgar Marxists—the truth that must be included in any reassessment of naturalism—is that they did grapple with the possibility of a correlation between entanglement in externality and external domination. They explored the same constraints on morality and freedom that had obsessed Howells, in other words, and yet remained equivocal about the effects of such constraints. The naturalists sought confirmation of this equivocal stance in the future, then, not in the present; but they wrote the history of that future by defining the archaic form of romance as their usable past, by adapting the style of realism to the formal properties and implications of romance.[17]

The best way to illustrate these propositions is to examine the exemplary naturalist novel *Sister Carrie*. Critics have noted that it contains many levels of writing, but they have invariably concluded that it is a species of realism. The typologies of form found in the work of Howells, Northrop Frye, and Fredric Jameson—three unlikely allies—suggest, however, that it should be read as romance. According to Frye, whose argument recalls that of Howells, the "essential difference" between the romance and the novel as a type of prose fiction is the absence of characterization in the former. In the novel, the "characters are prior to the plot," and the question both author and reader address is, "given these characters, what will happen?" Romance, by contrast, describes what happens to characters, "for the most part, externally." Jameson draws on Kenneth Burke and Martin Heidegger to enlarge Frye's account. "Romance is precisely that form in which the worldness of the world reveals or manifests itself, in which, in other words, world in the technical sense of the transcendental horizon of our experience becomes visible in an inner-worldly sense." More concretely, "in romance that category of Scene tends to capture and to appropriate the attributes of

Agency and Act, making the 'hero' over into something like a registering apparatus" of external change or movement. Hence romance heroes and heroines seem always to be "reaping the rewards of cosmic victory without ever having been quite aware of what was at stake in the first place."[18]

The other salient elements of romance are results of the absence of characters. As Howells noted, and as Frye emphasizes, romance plots extraordinary episodes discontinuously along a "vertical" axis. Its normal planes of existence are idyllic and demonic; or at least they are higher and lower than the everyday experience rendered "horizontally" in realist novels. Frye also points out that romance is closer to the mythic world of "total metaphor" than is the novel, because the population of romance is identified with and as the mysterious externality that constitutes its field of heroic action. From this standpoint, romance becomes the form in which desire cannot be effectively disciplined, evaded, or sublimated. Its heroes and heroines are always being projected beyond themselves by the force of their desires—since we cannot ask what these characters will do, but only what will happen to them, there is no story to be told unless they are so projected—and yet the worldness of the world they register is immediate, particular, almost invasive: it is otherness writ large. In romance, accordingly, there can be no abiding present in which the moral law becomes intelligible by virtue of its internalization; there can be no promise of release from the alienation, the perception of division, that is projected outward as desire. In this sense, the privileged place of truth in romance cannot be found outside of time; it lies at the beginning and at the end of time. Indeed the utopian agenda of romance—the morality of this form—finally derives from the fact that its "characters" are not contained by their world; instead they somehow contain it. As Frye puts it, "The desiring self finds fulfillment that delivers it from the anxieties of reality by containing that reality."[19]

Now let us suppose that our three unlikely allies have accounted for the differences between romance and the realist novel. From this supposition it follows that *Sister Carrie* is formally or structurally a romance. To begin with, the novel has no characters to speak of. As Julian Markels observed more than thirty years ago, "They do not make the story, the story manifests them."[20] Carrie, Drouet, and Hurstwood are "below the threshold of consciousness," and so we cannot at any point ask, given these characters, what will happen? These people are so inarticulate—so "vacant," to borrow Dreiser's favorite adjective for his heroine—that Agency and Act have almost no meaning in the novel. Their enclosure within the category of Scene is made explicit by their common source in the darkened theater that Carrie finds so appealing ("This new atmosphere was more friendly. . . .

Here was no illusion"). It is here, and only here, that each of the leading characters comes alive, comes to recognize the objects of his or her desire, and resolves to have them.

Certainly Carrie is a perfectly tuned registering apparatus for the particularity, the worldness of her world. Here she is on Lake Shore Drive at about five o'clock in the evening:

> There was a softness in the air which speaks with an infinite delicacy of feeling to the flesh as well as the soul. Carrie felt that it was a lovely day. She was ripened by it in spirit for many suggestions. . . . Across the broad lawns, now first freshening into green, she saw lamps faintly glowing upon rich interiors. Now it was but a chair, now a table, now an ornate corner, which met her eye, but it appealed to her as almost nothing else could. Such childish fancies as she had had of fairy palaces and kingly quarters now came back. She imagined that across these richly carved entrance-ways, where the globed and crystalled lamps shone upon panelled doors set with stained and designed panes of glass, was neither care nor unsatisfied desire. She was perfectly certain that here was happiness. . . . She gazed and gazed, wondering, delighting, longing, and all the while the siren voice of the unrestful was whispering in her ear. (94)

Markels also reminds us that *Sister Carrie* is organized around the kind of vertical axis usually found in romance. When our heroine loses her shoe factory job, for example, "Dreiser reverses direction again, leaving Carrie at the bottom and taking us to the 'top,' to witness a conversation between Drouet and Hurstwood in the 'truly swell saloon' of Fitzgerald and Moy's."[21] This reversible movement between higher and lower planes of existence is the narrative device by which we are forced to see, in vertical perspective, that Carrie's early career as a Chicago factory worker is the demonic parody of her later career as New York actress, and that Hurstwood's decline and fall in New York is the demonic parody of his "high life" in Chicago. That *Sister Carrie* is dominated by metaphors, as against more displaced, "horizontal," and representational similes, probably needs no emphasis beyond that provided by Walter Benn Michaels and Lester Cohen.[22] But it is worth noting that metaphors are foreign to the language— or level—of realism in the novel; they begin piling up only when Carrie's desire identifies her with the objects she does not but must have if she is to be herself. "She did not grow in knowledge so much as she awakened in the matter of desire," Dreiser notes as preface to the scene on Lake Shore Drive. And in fact Carrie's awakening desire determines her entire itinerary. In this sense, her rise in the real world from factory worker to celebrity actress is a demonic parody of the rise of Silas Lapham, whose moral integrity is secured as a consequence of his escape from the delusions of desire. Thus we can safely assume that the "economy of desire" that animates *Sister Carrie* is at the very least inconsistent with the fear, or absence, of desire that regulates realism as Howells defined and practiced it.[23] We can accordingly claim either that the tradition of social realism is not broad enough to contain the novel, or that a more appropriate formal designation for it is romance.

But the point is not to reclassify Dreiser's first novel; it is instead to recognize that both sentimentalism and realism are parodied by the romance form in which they are contained and criticized. This "dialogical" combination defines any choice between these forms as fundamentally false or as irrelevant to the possibilities of American life and letters. To put this another way, the transition from rhetoric to style that *Sister Carrie* reenacts by the juxtaposition of sentimental and realist passages is mediated and criticized by the morality of the novel's form; but the peculiar morality of the romance form is itself criticized by the realistic inversion of its conventions.[24] Thus the long-standing conflict between romance and realism is registered if not resolved in a fictional discourse that incorporates both without becoming either.

Surely the binary opposition of good and evil which Jameson defines as the "ideological core of the romance paradigm" is destroyed by Dreiser's use of realism.[25] Carrie's journey to the idyllic upper world, for example, begins with the loss of her virginity. Her sister Minnie narrates this crucial event in her dreams according to the traditional terms of romance, as a descent or fall that negates identity. But that Dreiser has nothing to say about it in his narrative capacity is emphasized by his answer to Carrie's question ("What is it I have lost?"): "Before this world-old proposition we stand, serious, interested, confused" (64–65, 74). The binary opposition that Minnie's romance dream depicts vertically is presented as archaic, as an axis that will not intersect at any point with Carrie's rise through the real worldliness of her world. But if it is fair to say that the ethical binary at the core of romance is in this manner displaced by realism, it is also fair to say that the serious, interested, and confused voice of realism is at critical moments replaced by a language, or a level of writing, that is neither grotesquely sentimental nor starkly realistic. This is the siren whisper of romance, which awakens the inertial Carrie and projects her toward new desires and dreams. This is the voice, as heard in chapter 12 on Lake Shore Drive, that disavows not the real but realism.

But how do we explain Dreiser's novel use of the romance form? Why does he resort to it? In other words, what is naturalized in *Sister Carrie* that lay beyond the scope of realism? I would suggest three possibilities. First, the incomplete present in which real life gets lived is reinstated under the sign of romance. But this is only a way of saying that the relation between past and present is recast as a developmental or cumulative sequence, through which self-consciousness or reason is realized, not posited as a property of mind in the form of finished characters. Second, desire becomes the medium of that discursive process of realization, so that illusion and alienation, the fall into time and space—and desire—become the sources of identity, not the obstacles to it; personality, consciousness, and character are construed as the results of entanglement in, not release from, the tyranny of external circumstances given by the past. Indeed, Carrie's desire is the medium through which her memory is restored, her consciousness is awakened, her personality is constructed—the means by which she begins to look and sound, at the end of the novel, like a character in a novel. Her externalization, her immersion in or absorption by the "worldness" of her world, objectifies her particular subjectivity, that is, it eventually makes her self-conscious.[26]

Dreiser concludes, in fact, where a realist novel might begin, at the moment that consciousness, hitherto "a kind of external relation," as William James would suggest in 1904, returns to itself.[27] It is almost as if Dreiser were writing the prehistory of the novel as a narrative form or—what amounts to the same thing—of the autonomous individual as a plausible fiction. But *Sister Carrie* is even more deeply and perversely "historical" than this. For the point at which it concludes is not just the historical moment at which a realist novel might begin; it is also the moment of memory, of self-consciousness, at which the recorded history of the species does begin. History is not, then, an absent cause in, or simply absent from, the novel; it is inscribed throughout as the product of desire. That is why it first appears under the fantastic sign of romance. "Such childish fancies as she had had of fairy palaces and kingly quarters now came back."

Third, the "chronotope"—the peculiar space-time—of the theater is recovered in and by Dreiser's use of the romance form.[28] To understand what is at stake here, we need to recall the special significance of the theatrical self in nineteenth-century American culture, particularly at midcentury. The most popular ritual in this culture was probably minstrelsy, the Yankee invention through which the desiring, sensational self was projected and objectified onstage in the form of the African American. Minstrelsy was in some ways the ambitious stepchild of melodrama, which was less conclusive, less strident, about the choices it offered between home, hearth, and "feminine" virtue on the one hand and market, money, and "masculine" worldliness on the other.[29] In any event, the theater as such foregrounded the new divisions and extensions of the self that had become possible and necessary under the regime of antebellum accumulation.

Within the receding household economy of agricultural subsistence and artisanal industrial production, there was no meaningful distinction to be drawn between economic function and domesticity as the foundation of personal identity; for there were no extrafamilial economic functions except those of incidental commerce, not production. When this economy finally gives way at midcentury (ca. 1846–57), the distinction can be grasped as impending historical disjuncture—as the terms of a choice—in the work of the popular women writers.[30] But where the market, or rather money, mediates all social relations and multiplies social roles, so that neither economic function (marketplace) nor domesticity (home) can serve as the foundation of personal identity, the self is divided, distended, dislocated. This is the problem that seizes the imagination of practically every writer, popular or not, at midcentury.

Some writers treat it as an opportunity as well as a problem (those who treat it as both are not incidentally our canonical writers). Whitman goes further than anyone else in treating it as such; his "lesson of reception" tends toward what we might justly criticize as pure tolerance. But Melville and Hawthorne also treat the dislocation of the self as something more (or less) than a threat to selfhood. And in their most self-conscious meditations on the romance form—*The Confidence-Man* (1857) and *The Blithedale Romance* (1852)—they do so in explicitly theatrical terms. Both fictions are deadly serious parodies of minstrelsy in which the self cannot escape its theatrically objectified Other.

Melville kept reminding his readers that the demand for consistency of character in fiction was unrealistic. "Is it not a fact, that, in real life, a consistent character is a rara avis?" Real life experience could not serve as an independent body of fact by which readers could test characterization; for "no one man can be coextensive with what is." Moreover, the stuff of experience was accumulated unevenly because the field of experience—space and time—was perceived and assimilated as disjuncture, as heterogeneous, not as simple location on a continuum. "That author who draws a character, even though to common view incongruous in its parts, as the flying squirrel, and, at different periods, as much at variance with itself as the butterfly is with the caterpillar into which it changes, may yet, in so doing, be not false but faithful to the facts." Thus the implosive chronotope of the theater was crucial to the realistic depiction of real lives. "And as, in real life, the proprieties will not allow people to act out themselves with that unreserve permitted to the stage; so, in books of fiction, they look not only for more entertainment, but, at bottom, even for more reality, than real life can show. Thus, though they want novelty, they want nature, too; but nature unfettered, exhilarated, in effect transformed. In this way of thinking, the people in a fiction, like the people in a play, must dress as nobody exactly dresses, talk as nobody exactly talks, act as nobody exactly acts."[31] The masquerade of the confidence man was this theatrical negation—this preservation by annulment—of the apparent stability of real lives; nobody on Melville's stage is exactly who he says he is because everybody is playing his role(s) with sincerity. Every one is false in reality because unity itself is impossible.

Hawthorne too announced that his purpose was to "establish a theatre, a little removed from the highway of ordinary travel," where he might gain a "foothold between fiction and reality." Miles Coverdale, the narrator, describes his own part as "that of the Chorus in a classic play," but he is in fact the director whose questions provide motives and whose staging creates the triangles of desire that destroy the masquerade at Blithedale. He is also one of the actors in the drama: the more he narrates, the more roles he plays.[32] In his concluding confession, at the point where we might expect some indication that the narrator is now beyond the narration, Coverdale divides and reinterprets himself again. "I have made but a poor and dim figure in my own narrative," he claims at the outset, "establishing no separate interest, and suffering my colorless life to take its hue from other lives." Then he cautions us: "The reader must not take my own word for it." But then he promises closure. "The confession, brief as it is, will throw a gleam of light over my behavior in the foregoing incidents, and is, indeed, essential to a full understanding of my story." And finally he confesses, making his behavior incomprehensible except as the effect of a wholly externalized self, whose life was pure projection through and total identification with other members of the Blithedale community.[33]

By their manipulation of the theatrical chronotope specific to a non-realistic narrative form—the romance—Melville and Hawthorne elucidate what Bloom calls the American Sublime. They use the "flare of theatrical facts," as Howells put it, to illuminate the discursive self, the transitive subject that is its Other. By his recovery and revision of the apparently archaic romance form, Dreiser reintroduces this self into American letters— or rather he revives the chronotope of the theater specific to romance as a way of foregrounding this self.[34]

I have already suggested that the theater is the site of characterization in *Sister Carrie*. Its centrality may be grasped once we recognize that the second half of the novel is a theatrical parody of realism as such. Hurst-wood, for example, is literally absorbed by the reality of the fugitive's life in New York. He becomes anonymous, in effect invisible, by virtue of his lack of employment, status, and income; ultimately he has no place in the real world except in the "grim, beast silence" of a "cold, shrunken, dis-gruntled mass" (396). But this loss of self may be read, Michaels has shown, as the result of his attempt to secure or stabilize his new identity in and through the paradigmatic realist text—the newspaper.[35] Hurstwood's death is the immediate consequence, then, of desire exhausted, or sublimated, by realism. The last time he rouses himself from his deepening lethargy is at Broadway and Thirty-Ninth Street, under a marquee featuring a life-size poster of "Carrie Madenda," the star of the Casino Company. " 'She's got it,' he said incoherently, thinking of money. 'Let her give me some.' He started around to the side door. Then he forgot what he was going for and paused, pushing his hands deeper to warm the wrists. Suddenly it returned. The stage door! That was it." He is of course shoved roughly out the door; without further ado, he reaches his "one distinct mental decision"—that is, to kill himself (391–92). He has no money because he can't get into the theater; his representational resources are exhausted; he is as good as dead. Carrie, meanwhile, has become a star, a celebrity, "an interesting figure in the public eye," mainly because she refuses to inhabit the realist text. The narrative movement in which she acts as the featured player is backward, as it were, in time and space—toward the older commercial city, away from the antic brutality of industrial Chicago. But this is the formal movement of the novel, too; as it moves "backward" toward romance, it moves beyond realism. In short, it moves back into the theater rebuilt by Hawthorne and Melville from materials available through melodrama and minstrelsy.

Like Hawthorne and Melville, Dreiser questions the choices that melo-drama (and minstrelsy) authorized without dismissing theatrical time and space as the proper setting for the realistic exploration of selfhood. In this sense, he draws on popular forms to replenish the raw materials of novel-istic signification, to broaden his constituency outside as well as inside the text, among readers as well as characters. But he does not do so uncritically. For the middle ground between social and individual, public and private, marketplace and home—the ground sanctified by melodrama and staked out by Hawthorne in *The House of Seven Gables* (1851)—did not exist for Dreiser. He was aware that modernity in the form of machine production had somehow invaded and reconstructed every kind of social intercourse; or at least it had destroyed the local grounds, the familiar places, that once supported it. As he explained in a piece on Salem published in 1898: "It is so modern in parts. Why, only a block from the now large and grimy railroad station, there stood in Hawthorne's time 'the town pump,' which gave forth such a dainty and inspiring rill of thought concerning its own vocation. Some seven trolley lines pass around that identical corner now! The very bowels of the earth from which it drew the sparkling liquid, have been torn out to make way for a smoky two-track tunnel, and steam cars now pass where once the darksome well held its cool treasure in store for man and beast."[36] The earth itself has been hollowed out since Hawthorne's time, Dreiser suggests; and so the middle ground available to the writers of midcentury offered no foothold to modern writers. The world "out there"— otherness writ large—had already moved, uninvited, into the most familiar realms.

The Political Economy of the Self

Carrie's immersion in commodity production (the shoe factory) and circulation (the department store) registers this invasion, and thereby announces that there is no choice to be made between domesticity and marketplace because there is no escape from the latter, not even for a young woman from the country. Minnie, the only representative of Carrie's family, is the character who dreams according to the older terms of choice established by melodrama and midcentury sentimentalism (and who lives according to the political-economic dictates of modernity); Carrie's worldly success, and her development as—or rather into—a character, violate these very terms. Again, each voice parodies the other. But Carrie, who as an actress plays the roles allocated by melodrama, embodies the absence of domesticity in her "real life" away from the factory and then the stage. There is no escape, then, from the phenomenology of the market: it cannot be displaced or dismissed as it was in the sentimental literature or in the larger highbrow culture of the nineteenth century.

The question that follows—for us as for Dreiser—is whether the self can be known, or can make itself, in this discursive milieu, where money creates but also contests the possibility of meaningful signification, of relating particular and universal, of unifying material circumstances and intellectual inscription. The great theorist of the puzzle is Karl Marx. But the immediate implications of the same puzzle obsessed most Americans for most of the nineteenth century because, as Marc Shell points out, "America was the birthplace of the widespread use of paper money in the Western world." Paper money complicates, intensifies, and enlarges the puzzle of meaningful signification that the use of coinage created first in antiquity, again in the twelfth century in western Europe, and yet again in the seventeenth century; for the relation between the substantial thing—the use value of the commodity—and its sign is recast by the appearance and generalization of banknotes as an everyday medium of exchange. "While a coin may be both symbol (as inscription or type) and commodity (as metallic ingot), paper is virtually all symbolic."[37]

Americans used paper money as early as the seventeenth century. But they did not become obsessed with the money question as a problem of representation, in both aesthetic and political terms, until the middle of the nineteenth century, when the collapse of the household economy was registered and reinforced by the doubling of the number of banks and the volume of banknotes in circulation, ca. 1846–54.[38] Hereafter, issues of money in every sense come to dominate political discourse, but also to invade if not enrich aesthetic discourse. These issues turn on the uses of money and the meanings of the self under conditions of capital accumulation—that is, under conditions that efface and reconstruct the inherited division between household and market.

Paper money, I would emphasize, is not necessarily a threatening or deconstructive medium so long as its ghostlike formlessness is contained and structured by material antecedents and objects at either end of its circuit, by specie in the bank vault and by use values in the shape of needed commodities. So long as the symbol remains reductive, in other words, and corresponds in theory and practice to real, substantial things, the problem of signification need not be, and is not, a pandemic crisis of representation. For at this level money functions as mind or language functions under the sign of Enlightenment: it is strictly a medium of exchange, by which the correspondence between unlike things—the underlying unity of particular objects—is realized, and the relation between outward existence and inner reflection is posited. Under such a monetary regime, production presupposes a certain level of consumption; money remains a means of exchange, an instrumental appearance that "fits" reality but is never mistaken for reality as such. The production of wealth or the creation of value is accordingly construed as a means to the end of reproducing a certain social-political type—that is, the self-determining head of household whose independence is guaranteed by his control of productive property and consequently of his own labor power.

Capital accumulation requires and enables a different monetary regime, for it makes the production of wealth in the abstract an end in itself. The multiplication of symbols, of weightless tokens of value without material referents, inherent limits, or external moorings, now becomes both method and object of goods production. Since production no longer presupposes a certain level of consumption, money can function as a "store of value," a floating signifier, a fund of potential claims on time and commodities. The mobility of property and the mobility of the self are, as J.G.A. Pocock suggests, constituted by this monetary regime, which emerges in Europe a generation before it does in the United States (1780–1820 as against 1840–80).[39] So it is probably neither incidental nor accidental that the autobiographical agenda of romanticism—its insistence that mind and language are fundamentally creative, for example, not instruments with which the artist copies the given structure of external reality—emerges in Europe and in the United States at the very moment that money is detached from its referential moorings by the advent of the accumulationist regime. Indeed I would suggest that this moment may be defined as the political economy of the post-Enlightenment crisis.

In the United States, at any rate, the debate over the definition and uses of money was in effect a debate over the conditions of selfhood or self-production. And the issues were not decided until the 1890s. By then, however, the value of substitutes for issues of currency, whether greenbacks, Treasury certificates, or national banknotes, was greater than the value of the outstanding currency. These substitutes took many forms, but among them were checks, drafts, bills, deposits, bank clearinghouse certificates, and, finally, securities listed on the stock exchange or contracts made through the produce exchanges ("futures"). Paper money was substantial stuff compared with these apparitions of "credit," many of which were never seen outside of the cities, perhaps even the larger cities with central reserve status in the national banking system (New York, Chicago, St. Louis). In *Looking Backward* (1888), the utopian novel that reached a circulation of over one million by the mid-1890s, Edward Bellamy summarized the "prodigious illusions"—the crisis of representation—that followed from this development of a credit economy. "Already accustomed to accept money for commodities, the people next accepted promises for money, and ceased to look at all behind the representative for the thing represented. Money was a sign of real commodities, but credit was but a sign of a sign."[40]

Meanwhile, the insular world of "real commodities" was colonized by modern advertising, which, like modern credit, referred less to any particular or substantial use values than to the imagined possibilities and unrealized desires that commodities signified as the apparatus of autobiography. Here were the rudiments of the language of demand that economists needed once they assigned the problem of the supply side to classical political economy. But advertising remained the delinquent stepchild of the new marginalist economics, even though these two relatives shared the hedonistic psychology and "subjectivist" bent of modernist discourse; for advertising continued to speak the vernacular of desire, and ignored—or redrew— the boundary between fact and fiction by valorizing consumers devoted to immediate gratification. Modern advertising was, then, the nonrealist language of illusion in which everyday life appeared, that is, became, theatrical.[41]

Carrie inhabits this commodified culture, this spectacle, wherein the suspension of disbelief is both necessary and impossible. "She drew near these things, Chicago, New York; Drouet, Hurstwood; the world of fashion and the world of stage—these were but incidents. Not them, but that which they represented, she longed for. Time proved the representation false" (397). But what exactly did these "incidents" represent? "If she wanted to do anything better or move higher she must have more—a great deal more" (362–63). More of what? Money, say the critics, in unison. But isn't Carrie "too full of wonder and desire to be greedy" (100)? What, then, is money to her? It does not represent substantial things, as if it were a medium of exchange: "Not them, but that which they represented, she longed for." It is an end in itself. "One of her order of mind would have been content to be cast away on a desert island with a bundle of money, and only the long strain of starvation would have taught her that in some cases it could have no value. Even then she would have had no conception of the relative value of the thing" (51). Or rather the not-thing, the insensible symbol that is money; it has no relative or referential value in this sense apart from its self-referential values. "She found, after all—as what millionaire has not?—that there was no realising, in consciousness, the meaning of large sums" (355). Symbolization as such is now detached from any substantial things: there are only signs of signs. In this sense, the worlds accredited in *Sister Carrie* and in modern advertising are animated by the same belief in the reality of illusion, appearance, representation.[42]

The Politics of the Poetry of the Self

What, then, becomes of my claim that Carrie's character is ultimately credible? This is not a strictly empirical question—in other words, to answer it is not simply a matter of presenting the textual evidence. For behind it stands the larger question that dominates modern political theory, moral philosophy, and cultural criticism. I have already alluded to that larger question, and will now merely rephrase it: can the self be known—can character be constructed—through entanglement in the externality peculiar to market society? According to Ann Douglas, the answer provided by the women writers of the mid-to-late nineteenth century was "No," but not exactly in thunder, since they had already been excluded from the market and were carving out a sphere of morality and spirituality that was by definition outside that dynamic, "masculine" preserve. Douglas claims that the "feminization" of American culture—its odd detachment from the hurly-burly of American capitalism—was the result.[43] The subsequent failure of our culture (including our political culture) to come to grips with modernity as such is one corollary of "feminization" so conceived. This is a powerful and persuasive argument, but, as Douglas understands, it applies with special force to those who, in the twentieth century, would be critical of the culture and politics specific to modern capitalism. For if these critics assume at the outset that the market in its modern manifestations is by definition defiling, as did their "feminine" precursors, they cannot locate a source of resistance to or transcendence of capitalism which resides within a present determined by the development of capitalism. More to the point, they cannot acknowledge the possibility that selfhood and market, or character and capitalism, are compatible. The unintended implication of their ostensibly critical stance is, then, the validation of business as usual except in those spheres of life that have somehow remained impervious to the corrosive effects of capital accumulation.

A good example of this implication may be found in the recent critique of the "culture of consumption" elaborated by that unruly discipline called American Studies. One of the most sophisticated contributions to the critique is that of Jean-Christophe Agnew, whose study of the "consuming vision" of Henry James is simply brilliant. But in this study of James, Agnew notes that his analysis of consumer culture is "deeply indebted" to the theoretical work of William Leiss. Now, according to Leiss, "the striving for satisfaction . . . is an 'intensive' dimension of experience involving the internal disposition of a person," that is, it does not involve or require the extroversion and objectification of desire as the condition of articulating (knowing) the possible forms of satisfaction; hence the "intensive character of needing suffers in proportion to the sheer extensiveness of the search [for satisfaction] carried out among the almost infinite possibilities."[44] The normative principle of Agnew's critique is, then, the pure self whose internal disposition—whose subjectivity or character—is created and experienced not in, through, and as externalized desire for particular objects and others but rather as release or abstention from the plenitude of possibilities circulating as commodities in the market. This is a self that can secure its identity and realize its own needs only by ignoring such circulation. In effect, therefore, the self as such is to be found only above and beyond the defiling realm of commodity production and distribution, where, according to Douglas, the women writers of the nineteenth century had already placed it and, for that matter, where the realists would leave it. And in this crucial sense, the contemporary debate about the character(s) of the "culture of consumption" formally recapitulates the literary debate at the turn of the century; for both debates center on the predicates of self-discovery and determination under conditions defined by the ubiquity of the commodity.

Dreiser's unique position within these debates is incomprehensible unless we recognize that both the sentimental and the realist traditions engender and finally entail the unargued assumption which now animates the critique of the "culture of consumption"—that is, the assumption that there is a necessary contradiction between the development of capitalism and the development of character. Taken at face value, it inspires cultural critique on *ethical* grounds: to discover the genuine self is to dismantle capitalism. But it also undermines political critique (or action) on *historical* grounds: to discover the genuine self is to recover the transparency of precapitalist social conditions or, failing that, to find an Archimedean point, a "clearing," outside of existing social relations, perhaps in the "culture of resistance" afforded by radical movements, perhaps in the "free social space" of the university. Future and past accordingly appear as fundamentally incommensurable because the ethical principle—the integrity of the self—does not seem to reside in or flow from the historical development of capitalism. In *Sister Carrie*, Dreiser turns the assumption into argument by entertaining the possibility that character is a consequence of capitalism. To that extent, he explores the possibility that the ethical and the historical are not antithetical but commensurable and interlocking planes of narrative or analysis.

I emphasize "possibility" because the novel is ambiguous at every level. But let us see where Carrie stands. At the conclusion, we note first, she has become neither a man nor a wife. That she remains a single woman may seem wholly unexceptional; and yet the playful confusion over identity that characterizes both romance and theater before the twentieth century often led to reversals that did not so much question an allocation of roles according to gender as confirm it, by giving the disguised woman who penetrates the public realm of politics and markets all the attributes of a man. Carrie's identity is never fixed; but she is still on her own at the end, and has not lost the "emotional greatness" that originally propelled her into the world of money, commodities, and the stage. Nor has she learned that she must have a husband. In fact she becomes more wary of men. "Experience of the world and of necessity was in her favour. No longer the lightest word of a man made her head dizzy. She had learned that men could change and fail" (343). After she leaves Hurstwood and moves in with her female friend from the chorus line, a member of the opera company "discovered a fancy for her." But Carrie "found herself criticising this man. He was too stilted, too self-opinionated. He did not talk of anything that lifted her above the common run of clothes and material success" (351).

She also becomes a reader of the novel, leaving behind sentimental romances such as *Dora Thorne* (246–50, 392–93). To that extent, Carrie fulfills the hopes of Howells: she becomes a recognizable character who grasps the nuances of the moral law (she acquires "character") insofar as she can identify with the population of the realist text, yet not confuse fiction and fact—a project that requires a certain cognitive distance, or abstraction, from both realms. But the novel that moves her, that suggests "how silly and worthless had been her earlier reading," is Honoré de Balzac's *Père Goriot* (1834), which Howells of course deemed the worst novel ever written. It is not my purpose to account for Howells's loathing, or to interpret *Père Goriot*. Even so, we should note that Carrie's new reading habits indicate, but also animate, her new capacity for introspection as well as abstraction. The "plague of poverty" that had "galled her" before she drew a star's salary, for example (318), is now projected outward through the medium of Balzac's fiction. From her "comfortable chambers at the Waldorf," her roommate hopes for enough snow to go sleigh riding. " 'Oh dear,' said Carrie, with whom the sufferings of Father Goriot were still keen. 'That's all you think of. Aren't you sorry for the people who haven't anything tonight?' " (393).

Briefly, then, what made old Goriot suffer? In what Howells claimed to be the worst of novels, Balzac has rewritten the Faust legend, setting it in Paris of 1819, and has cast Father Goriot as our Father, who is not in heaven. He is not there because he is on earth, trying to reestablish his presence among the living: "I shall go and come like a good fairy who makes himself felt everywhere without being seen, shall I not?" But the Devil (Vautrin) now rules the world—"there was nothing he did not know"—and, as Luther claimed, the Devil's word is money: Vautrin is the banker of the Parisian criminal underground. This Mephistopheles identifies Paris, where money rules society, not only as a cesspool—here he follows Luther's usage—but also as Europe's version of America, where money determines everything, including personal identity. The question that Vautrin asks, in striking his bargain with Rastignac, the provincial law student, is, "how are you to prosper if you do not discount your love," that is, if you do not cash in on your sentiments before they come due?[45] The student has no answer, for everyone, even Father Goriot, agrees that the "heart is a treasury" (69)—love, like paper money and credit, has value and confers success because, but only insofar as, it circulates and thereby organizes social intercourse as such. On his deathbed, waiting vainly for his daughters to arrive, Goriot explains their absence to poor Rastignac: "Ah, if I were rich still, if I had kept my money, if I had not given all to them, they would be with me now. . . . Money brings everything to you, even your daughters" (206). Such wisdom has already made his bargain with Rastignac essentially the same as Vautrin's, in both form and content—it is secured by a bill of credit.

So *Père Goriot* inhabits and articulates a world turned upside down by the power of money. It too is a demonic parody of sentimentalism, for it announces that the secret alliance enforcing the rule of money is forged between fathers and daughters (e.g., 68, 127, 175): they may occupy separate spheres—production/consumption, public/private, and so forth—but their agendas converge on the reproduction of capitalism. And yet it is not a strictly realist parody of sentimentalism. As Dreiser noted in an essay of 1896, "romance and realism blend and become one" under Balzac's narrative spell.[46] In *Père Goriot*, the peddler of realism, among other things, is the Devil. His proposed alternative to the secret alliance of fathers and daughters is the exclusively masculine preserve that he associates with the wilderness of the New World; only bachelorhood in the frontier forest, Vautrin implies, can disentangle men from the "effeminate age" defined by sentimentalism but enforced by capitalism (92–3, 130–31). In this sense, Natty Bumppo is the Devil's disciple. Rastignac is not because he does not rise above, or try to escape, the commodified world symbolized in and by the great city.

Neither does Carrie. She becomes a credible character not by ignoring or avoiding the illusions of the market and the theater—not by heading for the territory where the self's integrity is guaranteed by keeping the Other in its proper place—but by identifying with what she is not, indeed by becoming a sign of the signs specific to the symbolic universe of the stage. To put this another way, it is precisely Carrie's fictionalizing (her dreaming, acting, and identifying with others who are not "real people") that makes her a character because it eventually takes her beyond what is given and what she is at the outset; but the sources and materials of that fictionalizing—her money, her roles, her reading—are themselves fictional, symbolic, or lacking substance in the real world. Like the money she derives from the roles she plays, the consciousness that makes her a character has no objective correlate.

The Uses of Historicism

Is it false, then? I have already tried to suggest that our answer will depend as much on our extratextual evidence and assumptions as on our reading of the text. In this case, the evidence and assumptions will be consequences of a theory of knowledge, a notion of the truth, a model of the self. Thus we can and should turn to the language of philosophy for help in deciding the question. But which language? On what grounds, for example, should we choose Hegel over Kant? My own view is that we do not have much of a choice, because our first responsibility as intellectuals is to understand the relation between past and present—to explain, in other words, how past and present may be treated as commensurable, and thereby to explain why we are neither wholly determined nor simply unbound by the past. If these priorities are in order, we need a language that historicizes, that allows us to see extension in space and time as something other than irrational contingency or natural externality, and that accordingly allows us to periodize moral philosophies without succumbing to relativism. And so we are driven willy-nilly toward Hegel.[47]

In any event, he does address the problem of false consciousness in a manner that is immediately relevant to the question at hand. Hegel notes in his preface to *The Phenomenology* (1807): "Truth and falsehood as commonly understood belong to those sharply defined ideas which claim a completely fixed nature of their own, one standing in solid isolation on this side, the other on that, without any community between them. Against that view it must be pointed out, that truth is not like stamped coin that is issued ready from the mint and so can be taken up and used." The truth, in other words, works something like paper money but even more like modern credit in the form of interest-bearing securities, which preserve the original principal when canceled; for the truth implies the negation—the preservation by cancellation—of original principles.[48]

"Doubtless we can know in a way that is false," Hegel acknowledges. "To know something falsely means that knowledge is not adequate to, is not on equal terms with, its substance." But to identify falsehood in such terms would be to posit a correspondence between, a unity of, subject and object, or knowledge and its substance, which could in turn serve as normative principle for the evaluation of any form of knowledge. "Yet this very dissimilarity is the process of distinction in general, the essential moment in knowing. It is, in fact, out of this active distinction that its harmonious unity arises, and this identity, when arrived at, is truth." We cannot say that truth is "an original and primal unity as such" unless we are willing to derive it from the supernatural principle called God: it cannot be both an identity that somehow subsists beyond time and the criterion by which the living specify falsehood in human knowledge. "But it [this unity] is not truth in a sense which would involve the rejection of the discordance, the diversity, like dross from pure metal; nor, again, does truth remain detached from diversity, like a finished article from the instrument that shapes it. Difference itself continues to be an immediate element within truth as such, in the form of the principle of negation, in the form of the activity of the Self." Hegel summarizes, and emphasizes the historicizing movement of his argument, by claiming that "the false is no longer false as a moment of the true."[49]

So the divisions and dislocations of the discursive self cannot be construed as deviations from the truth of selfhood, and thus as falsehood; for they are the predicates of the attempt to realize the "harmonious unity" this self learns in time, in that attempt, to call the truth: they become not the proximate cause but the enduring conditions of identity in every sense. From that standpoint, the falsehoods, the illusions, the waking dreams in which Carrie posits herself, are moments in the truth of the character she is becoming. From the same standpoint, Hurstwood's early admonition to Carrie—"Don't you moralise until you see what becomes of the money" (80)—is a warning to readers who are looking for the bottom line.

With that warning in mind, let me demonstrate how two radically different political readings of *Sister Carrie* can be reconciled, or rather contained, by another, and thus how Dreiser forces us to treat this novel as a durable good that cannot be "consumed" or discarded, but does not pretend, in doing so, that it stands above or outside the commodified world it describes. In 1977, Sandy Petrey tried to explain what bad writing meant in *Sister Carrie*. He argued that the function of the realist passages Alfred Kazin admired was to subvert the sentimental discursions Leslie Fiedler detested. For Petrey, the "direct language capable of stating what industrialism meant" is the authentic language of the novel, because its blank realism invalidates the media of false consciousness—that is, the sentimental and melodramatic "linguistic forms which perpetuated myths." *Sister Carrie* belongs, accordingly, in the "great tradition of social realism" because it undermined the "ideologically significant myths" nourished by the sentimental tradition; it "made a certain way of lying so patent that it does not need exposure." In such perspective, Dreiser's "refusal to approve the new industrial order" is self-evident.[50]

In 1980, Walter Benn Michaels suggested that *Sister Carrie* could not be so interpreted, as a refusal to approve modern-industrial capitalism. He argued that the novel's "economy of desire" identifies Carrie with an inexhaustible commodity lust—an "involvement with the world [of objects] so central to one's sense of self that the distinction between what one is and what one wants tends to disappear." The equilibrium and individual autonomy celebrated in the republican and realist traditions of the nineteenth century are explicitly repudiated by such an economy, which defines desire that is "in principle never satisfied" as the condition of life itself. By this reading, Dreiser's doubts about the new industrial order are rather less than self-evident. Indeed Michaels claimed that the "unrestrained capitalism" of the turn of the century receives an "unequivocal endorsement" in *Sister Carrie*. He concluded by suggesting that what is "arguably the greatest American realist novel" remains popular because it celebrates the commodity fetishism and psychological desublimation peculiar to twentieth-century capitalism.[51]

It seems that these readings converge only on the name they give to the novel's form—realism. And yet they agree that realism is not the only level of writing in the novel. For Petrey, the language of realism par excellence is found in the shoe factory scenes; for Michaels, that language is the "literature of exhausted desire and economic failure" which corresponds to Hurstwood's decline. They might also agree that *Sister Carrie* is not merely a realist novel, then, simply because Carrie's career does not follow the path anticipated in the shoe factory and traced in Hurstwood's decline: ultimately she moves out of the neighborhood naturalized by realism. In any event, the reading I have proposed can accommodate those of both Petrey and Michaels, for it acknowledges but does not privilege the novel's realist level of writing. To put this another way, my reading would suggest that *both* Petrey and Michaels are correct, since *Sister Carrie* is critical of industrial capitalism, but not from the Archimedean standpoint of a self that remains undefiled by the commodity form.

Michaels is not wrong, for example, to claim that *Sister Carrie* represents an "unequivocal endorsement" of modern capitalism, because the novel embraces and endorses History as such, as the antecedent necessity or reality that is beyond criticism. Even so, the ethical or utopian principle of romance remains. For after all is said and done, Carrie is not contained by historical reality; she contains it. And so she stands between, and perhaps embodies, the transcendent truths realized in the epoch of accumulation. She is living proof that freedom resides in necessity, in the historically determined "worldness" of the world. But she also acts on the principle of hope residing in the knowledge that true freedom lies somewhere beyond necessity, in the posthistorical redefinition of work as Play. Since she is in this sense both object and subject of History, her story required the representation of the historical from the standpoint of the ethical, or more simply, realism in the narrative form of romance.

As Dreiser tells the story, Carrie becomes the "New Woman" of the twentieth century, in whom we can see a transitive subject taking shape in the movement away from the familiar social norms and roles of the nineteenth century. But it is precisely the movement away from the familiar that casts Carrie as our *sister*, as the lead in a "family romance" from which domesticity is altogether lacking. While Dreiser drafted this new kind of family romance in the late 1890s, William James was similarly engaged in a search for a nonrealist narrative form that could include the extremities of American life; he too worried about the limits of realism. In his talks to teachers of the 1890s, for example, he adopted the pose of the romancer to tell a story about the "laboring classes" in which they became "the very parents of our life." Let us turn, then, to a closer study of this family romance in the making, as a way of understanding why proletarian women and industrial workers could appear as its key figures.

. . . .

CHAPTER 7

TRANSITION QUESTIONS: WILLIAM JAMES AT THE

ORIGIN OF OUR OWN TIME

Speeding with the Train to Buffalo

The cultural revolution I want to elucidate resides in the fundamental reconstruction of subjectivity which was dramatized in Dreiser's first novel.
But to elucidate the results, the substance, of this reconstruction is to grasp
its standpoint, its method. To do so is, then, to recognize that its agents were
trying to revise if not reverse the perceived relation between philosophy and
common sense, between theory and practice, and so were prepared to corroborate their ideas by reference to current events—that is, by reference to
practical experience and historical circumstance. These agents believed, in
other words, that their theories could not be adequately assessed by recourse
to logic alone, by asking whether their new notions of self and knowledge
were internally coherent. They believed that these notions attained theoretical dignity and explanatory adequacy only by opening onto, only by
apprehending and promoting, the practical reconstruction of self and knowledge which, in the 1890s, seemed to them both obvious and unknown. They
believed that their ideas had cultural functions and political implications
precisely because they mediated in new ways between theory and practice;
such ideas had to be assessed accordingly, as if the relation between theory
and practice—between ideas and events—was what mattered in philosophy
as in politics. To acknowledge their achievement is, then, to realize their
methods: to show how their ideas both presupposed and pointed beyond the
events of their time. To do so is, finally, to suggest that such ideas became
the stuff of organic ideology because the subject positions they posited were
becoming increasingly legible in the social relations that emerged at the end
of the nineteenth century.

Let us begin with William James and John Dewey, whose political affinities, it seems to me, are just as evident and significant as their intellectual affinities. We should note at the outset that between 1890, when *The Principles of Psychology* appeared, and 1902, when *The Varieties of Religious Experience* appeared, James's books were collections of occasional essays or lectures delivered on different topics at different places or times. *The Varieties* was also a set of lectures, but, like *Pragmatism* (1907), it was planned and executed as a systematic exploration of limited themes. The books of the 1890s were more variegated and were designed to flesh out, in a more or less popular manner, the implications of *The Principles*. James himself understood that he was discovering these implications as he wrote and rewrote the lectures, as he played with the possibilities of his own ideas. The first products of this play were the lectures collected and published in 1899 as *Talks to Teachers on Psychology*. These were drafted and delivered in 1892, just after James abridged *The Principles* for a one-volume edition; in this sense, they precede *The Will to Believe*, a collection organized around the title address of 1896 and published in 1897.[1]

The tone of the *Talks* is almost conversational. "I have found by experience," James remarked in the preface, "that what my hearers seem least to relish is analytical technicality, and what they most care for is concrete practical application." So he "gradually weeded out" the technicalities and finally published lectures that were "practical and popular in the extreme" (iii). But we should not dismiss them as vulgarizations of the more strictly philosophical essays that were meanwhile appearing in the professional journals. For if James was playing with the possibilities of the ideas he originally developed in *The Principles*, he treated this play as serious work, as a kind of civic obligation. "In taking my cue from what has seemed to me to be the feeling of the audiences I believe that I am shaping my book so as to satisfy the more genuine public need" (iii). He was, after all, trying to educate the educators, by placing his ideas in contexts that would allow people who were neither philosophers nor psychologists to grasp their significance. In fact that was what he was trying to do in every essay, lecture, or book he published after *The Principles*—especially in *Pragmatism*, the fullest summary of his thought and by all accounts the key text in the elaboration of an essentially American philosophical tradition.

In the *Talks*, James was looking for, or rather sounding out, the contexts or connections that would enable his audiences to translate theory into practice. He announced, moreover, that the second and third of the "Talks to Students" which concluded the book were the climactic scene of this attempted mediation between philosophy and ideology. These two addresses "belong together," he noted, and then claimed that the first of them "connects itself with a definite view of the world and of our moral relations to the same." Hitherto that worldview had a technical appellation and a professional meaning. "Those who have done me the honor of reading my volume of philosophic essays [*The Will to Believe*] will recognize that I mean the pluralistic or individualistic philosophy" (v). Now, in these two "Talks to Students," James would clothe his philosophy with broader social, political, and aesthetic meanings, in the hope that its "practical consequence" would be grasped. In other words, he adopted the posture and gestures of the organic intellectual who realizes that political struggles are always rehearsed in and as contestant ideas, and who acts on the assumption that a privileged position within the division of labor does not preclude political commitment in the form of ideological articulation.

James opened each of the concluding "Talks to Students" with a "personal reminiscence"—a story that placed his audience within a narrative field and form. In the last of the talks, "What Makes a Life Significant?," this story is an abbreviated romance that summarizes the radical changes and extraordinary possibilities impending in everyday American life. James sets up his romance by examining the rationality of the love that unites the allegorical figures of Jack and Jill. "Jack realizes Jill concretely, and we do not" (266). Jack identifies with her—"he struggles toward a union with her inner life, divining her feelings, anticipating her desires"—and so corroborates her existence; in doing so, Jack corroborates himself, for his acknowledgment of Jill's subjectivity in this sense makes her recognition of his own concrete existence, as another self, an objective, observable fact (266–67). Desire for and identification with the Other—the irrational imperatives of love—make the genuine self possible.

This antirealist principle of the romance form regulates the story that follows. But James enlarges the field of its narrative operation to the margins of American life as such. He tells his audience—now readers as well as listeners—about his visit to an actually existing Altruria in upstate New York, "the Assembly Grounds on the borders of Chautauqua Lake," where he found in permanent session a "serious and studious picnic on a gigantic scale." James "went in curiousity for a day" but stayed for a week, "held spell-bound by the charm and ease of everything." Here he was steeped in culture, kindness, cheapness, equality—he stewed happily, he claims, in the same container with the "best fruits" of civilization.[2] In the Chautauqua brand of Utopia, James concludes, "You have a foretaste of what human society might be, were it all in the light, with no suffering and no dark corners" (268–70).

He was of course relieved to escape "from the Chautauquan enclosure."

James's physical departure from the suffocating routine of this "middle-class paradise" (270) reinstates his first-person narrative voice, and marks the beginning of his intellectual departure—his dissent—from the future it represents. But that departure did not lead to a simpler past; his dissent was not a form of antimodern protest against the iron cages commonly constructed in the name of modern utopia. Instead it led him toward a celebration of the unenlightened present—"the big outside worldly wilderness with all its sins and sufferings" (270)—from which the heroic representations of romance had not been expunged.

> I asked myself what the thing was that was so lacking in this Sabbatical city. . . . And I soon recognized that it was the element that gives to the wicked outer world all its moral style, expressiveness and picturesqueness,—the element of precipitousness, so to call it, of strength and strenuousness, intensity and danger. What excites and interests the looker-on at life, what the romances and the statues celebrate and the grim civic monuments remind us of, is the everlasting battle of the powers of light with darkness; with heroism, reduced to its bare chance, yet ever and anon snatching victory from the jaws of death. But in this unspeakable Chautauqua there was no potentiality of death in sight anywhere, and no point of the compass from which danger might possibly appear. . . . Sweat and effort, human nature strained to its uttermost and on the rack, yet getting through alive . . . this is the sort of thing the presence of which inspires us and the reality of which it seems to be the function of all the higher forms of literature and fine art to bring home to us and suggest. At Chautauqua there were no racks, even in the place's historical museum; and no sweat, except possibly the gentle moisture on the brow of some lecturer, or on the sides of some player in the ball-field. Such absence of human nature in extremis anywhere seemed, then, a sufficient explanation for Chautauqua's flatness and lack of zest. (271–73)

Note that James is still poised at the entrance to the "big outside worldly wilderness." In his mind's eye, he can still see the jagged edges of existence represented in romances, statues, monuments, literature; but they now appear as a strictly symbolic horizon, which recedes before the "dead level and quintessence of every mediocrity" realized by Chautauqua.

> An irremediable flatness is coming over the world. Bourgeoisie and mediocrity, church sociables and teachers conventions, are taking the place of the old heights and depths and romantic chiaroscuro. And, to get human life in its wild intensity, we must in future turn more and more away

from the actual, and forget it, if we can, in the romancer's or the poet's pages. The whole world, delightful and sinful as it may appear for a moment to one just escaped from the Chautauquan enclosure, is nevertheless obeying more and more just those ideals that are to make of it in the end a mere Chautauqua Assembly on an enormous scale. (273)

At this point, James's journey back into the "big outside worldly wilderness" actually begins. There he is, "speeding with the train to Buffalo," when he is overtaken by the epiphany that revises his sense of the realities impending in American life. But he understands, and tells us, that he was prepared to see the world differently—to see that the dead level of a middle-class paradise did not exhaust the possibilities of American culture—because he had already adopted the standpoint of the romancer. In other words, the cognitive distance James needs to escape Chautauqua in every sense is supplied by a departure from the narrative principles of realism. The reality of romance in the outside world becomes recognizable once he is able to *get* beyond the world as realism maps it, or as Chautauqua constitutes in the form of a middle-class paradise; but it is his prior recognition of the symbolic landscape drawn by the romancers and the poets that allows him to *look* beyond that paradise, to find another kind of reality.

With these thoughts in my mind, I was speeding with the train to Buffalo, when, near that city, the sight of a workman doing something on the dizzy edge of a sky-scaling iron construction brought me to my senses very suddenly. And now I perceived, by a flash of insight, that I had been steeping myself in pure ancestral blindness, and looking at life with the eyes of a remote spectator. Wishing for heroism and the spectacle of human nature on the rack, I had never noticed the great fields of heroism lying round about me, I had failed to see it present and alive. I could only think of it as dead and embalmed, labelled and costumed as it is in the pages of romance. And yet there it was before me in the daily lives of the laboring classes. Not in clanging fights and desperate marches only is heroism to be looked for, but on every railway bridge and fireproof building that is going up to-day. On freight trains, on the decks of vessels, in cattle-yards and mines, on lumber-rafts, among the firemen and the policemen, the demand for courage is incessant; and the supply never fails. There, every day of the year somewhere, is human nature in extremis for you. And wherever a scythe, an axe, a pick, or a shovel is wielded, you have it sweating and aching and with its powers of patient endurance racked to the utmost under the length of hours of the strain. . . . These are our soldiers, thought I, these our sustainers, these the very parents of our life. (274–75)

As James narrates it, the passage from realism to romance is the passage from the insipid scene of middle-class mediocrity to the heroic scene of working-class exertions. If he has not quite turned the world upside down, he has seen it from a subaltern standpoint; he has accordingly shifted his perspective on the past and changed his mind about the future. To forget the actual by turning to romances, he now suggests, is to forget that the reality of romance resides in the everyday life of the laboring classes; it is also to repress the memory of our parents, to act as if the past is a nightmare from which the living have only to wake.

James completes his extrarealist itinerary in two steps. First he invokes Leo Tolstoy's "deification of the bravery, patience, kindliness, and dumbness of the unconscious natural man," and laments the lack of an American author who might "bring the truth of all this home" (276). Then he asks whether the archrealist, William Dean Howells, could be that author. James answers with another rhetorical question: "Or [is he] still too deep in the ancestral blindness, and not humane enough for the inner joy and meaning of the laborer's existence to be really revealed" (277)? At this point, at the end of his story, the correlation between the narrative standpoint of romance and the phenomenal extremities of working-class existence—between aesthetic principle and subject position—becomes unmistakable. So we should ask whether that correlation is the moral of the story. Does James go on to show how it "connects itself with a definite view of the world"— with the philosophical principles enunciated in *The Will to Believe*? Or does he deconstruct his own story?

I would suggest that he does both. The remainder of the talk is "more impersonal," James notes (279). He becomes critic as well as author, commentator on as well as character in his own story. He compares his new appreciation of manual labor and working-class life to the celebrations of subaltern existence in both Tolstoy and Robert Louis Stevenson; it seems they tell stories similar to his (279–83). But the sympathies (or "social prejudices") that animate these stories obscure as much as they illuminate, James now suggests, for they displace the "phenomenal world," the "outer differences" through which meanings are constructed and transacted. "Tolstoi's philosophy, deeply enlightening though it certainly is, remains a false abstraction . . . [for it] declares the whole phenomenal world and its facts and their distinctions to be a cunning fraud" (284).

"Western common sense" is the proper antidote to such abstraction, according to James, because it instinctively reinstates the relation between inner existence and outward circumstances as the moving frontier on which the "meaning of life" gets created. This common sense tells us that the "total significance of a human being" is somehow a product of "his inner virtue *and* his outer place,—neither simply taken, but both conjoined" (284–85). Thus poverty and hard labor or great wealth and ease are meaningless in and of themselves. They take on meanings only in relation to ideals, those "communicable and publicly recognizable purposes" that become legible in the social intercourse of people whose outward circumstances are different (288–94). So an inert inventory of ideals is equally meaningless. "The more ideals a man has, the more contemptible, on the whole, do you continue to deem him, if the matter ends there for him, and if none of the laboring man's virtues are called into action on his part,—no courage shown, no privations undergone, no dirt or scars contracted in the attempt to get them realized" (293).

The tendency of Western common sense is to define meaning and significance as the translation of ideal into action, of theory into practice, of philosophy into ideology. "The thing of deepest—or, at any rate, of comparatively deepest—significance in life does seem to be its character of *progress*, or that strange union of reality with ideal novelty which it continues from one moment to another to present" (294). To abstain from experiment and experience in the phenomenal world, to take "mere possession of ideals," is, then, not only to defy common sense but also to deny its crucial insights into the continuity or indissolubility of thought and will. It is to adopt the standpoint of the scholastic, and thereby to make of college professors "the most absolutely and deeply significant of men" (293).

So the Tolstoyan deification of manual labor produces an exquisite irony. By abstracting from the phenomenal world, by denying its significance in the creation of meanings, it covertly establishes the moral priority of mental labor, or rather the epistemological priority of mind. This is the irony James excludes from his own story by interpreting it—by demonstrating that common sense or practical reason cannot and does not abstract from the phenomenal world. It therefore acknowledges that meaning, or the contingency of truth, resides in and flows from the changing relation between inner existence and outward circumstances, between the ideal and the real. James has accordingly demonstrated that manual labor, the work of the body, is neither extraneous nor equivalent to the work of the mind. Each is a moment on the cultural continuum summarized in but also constructed by Western common sense. Manual labor is not mindless; mental labor is never disembodied. Common sense or practical reason is the medium in which these truths are realized. To deny that fact, James suggests, is to become a professor or a philosopher like Tolstoy, someone who is content with "false abstraction" or the "mere possession of ideals." To accept it, however, is to recognize common sense as the usable past of philosophy—to make its criteria the criteria of philosophy, by assuming that ideals cannot be adequately assessed unless they can be shown to have practical, phenomenal effects.

The social text from which James quotes to illustrate these implications is not incidentally "the labor-question." "We are suffering to-day in America from what is called the labor-question," he notes, and then insists that no one can escape it: "When you go out into the world, you will each and all of you be caught up in its perplexities" (297). No one can find refuge in a middle-class paradise, whether it is found at Lake Chautauqua or in college. Sooner or later, everyone will approach the industrial city and there confront the phenomenal figure of the laboring classes. For the genteel culture of the middle class is already a backwater—not a city upon a hill, but "a city simmering in the tepid lakeside sun" (270).

James has finally announced that his middle-class, college-educated audience cannot go back in any sense to the safe enclosures of the past. But neither can it pretend to be a "remote spectator," as he did before he approached Buffalo. There is no vantage point above or even outside the industrial city. So the audience is now implicated in James's story. By quoting from the social text called the labor question, he has enlarged his own; his romance now includes readers and listeners alike. If they adopt his narrative standpoint from within the social text they already inhabit, they will be able to *see* beyond Chautauqua when they *get* beyond it. If they do not— if they do not become romancers—the laboring classes will for all practical purposes remain invisible. So too will the meaning and significance of the conflict between classes, because as long as "everybody remains outside of everybody else's sight," no one will recognize the "intellectual ideals" that inform the "external situation."

I use the brief term labor-question to cover all sorts of anarchistic discontents and socialistic projects, and the conservative resistances which they provoke. So far as this conflict is unhealthy and regrettable,—and I think it is so only to a limited extent,—the unhealthiness consists solely in the fact that one-half of our fellow-countrymen remain entirely blind to the internal significance of the lives of the other half. They miss the joys and sorrows, they fail to see the moral virtue, and they do not guess the presence of the intellectual ideals. . . . Each [side], in short, ignores the fact that happiness and unhappiness and significance are a vital mystery; each pins them absolutely on some ridiculous feature of the external situation; and everybody remains outside of everybody else's sight. (297–98)

After this, the concluding paragraphs seem inconsequential if not platitudinous. But James had already made his subaltern sympathies clear and could not, in any event, proceed as if the political corollaries were obvious. When there was a socialist movement on the American scene, James did explicitly identify with it. In the 1890s, however, even in the epochal election year of 1896, the available political choices could not appeal to someone who recognized, and celebrated, the reality of romance in the industrial city.[3]

Two of these concluding paragraphs are nevertheless significant, because they raise the question of political economy, and do so in a way that will come to characterize James's treatment of it. "Society has, with all this, undoubtedly got to pass toward some newer and better equilibrium," he notes, "and the distribution of wealth has doubtless slowly got to change" (298). But the point of redistribution is not to abolish time or to bring history to a close. In fact, to believe that political-economic change should take priority over other kinds of change is to miss the point altogether. It is to wish for a proletarian version of Chautauqua, a working-class paradise. "The altered equilibriums and redistributions only diversify our opportunities and open chances for new ideals" (300).

James does not, then, dismiss the question of political economy. But he is unwilling to inflate its importance. He is looking for a source of meanings or values or ideals which exists by virtue of something more than false abstraction from the phenomenal world, but which is not synonymous with the realm of necessity ruled by political economy. So he is not merely staking out a middle ground between nineteenth-century liberalism and socialism, which somehow corresponds to his middle-class position. The area James wants to explore lies beyond both, at least as they were constituted in theory and practice around the turn of the century. For he is in effect proposing to limit the expansion of the realm of necessity which characterized the ideologies of socialism no less than the development of capitalism before the twentieth century.

In the Anglo-American world, at any rate, this characteristic expansion took two forms in and after the seventeenth century. On the one hand, relations of production became the effective determinant of social relations as such. Class accordingly became the regulative principle of social organization. On the other hand, this realm of necessity residing in relations of production became the source of transcendent yet increasingly secular meanings. What distinguishes the development of industrial capitalism—in England after 1750 and in North America after 1840—is surely the expansion of socially necessary labor beyond every inherited limit, to the point where it seemed as if commodity production had become an end in itself. But what marks the earlier emergence of bourgeois (or "proto-industrial") society, and what not only reveals but determines the social content of capitalist industrialization in both countries, is the extraordinary *cultural* significance accorded this realm of necessity. It was here, under the sign of necessary labor, that the citizens of bourgeois society found the condition of salvation and the groundwork for the production of values in every sense. It was also here, under the sign of productive labor, that the Anglo-American radicals and Populists and socialists of the nineteenth century found the condition of self-determination and the source of values.[4]

When James suggests that a new social equilibrium conceived in political-economic terms—as the result of redistribution—cannot be very interesting because it ignores the derivation of "new ideals," he suggests, I think, that the realm of necessity constituted by necessary or productive labor will not serve as this groundwork and source of values. That is why he tries to look beyond it without abstracting from it. But he can do so only by assuming that the realm of necessity residing in relations of production is receding from view or that its cultural salience is no longer self-evident. Either way, he has discovered contingency where there was once condition of both salvation and self-determination.

Indeed that contingency turns out to be the medium in which the development of the self—"its character of progress"—is transacted. In the second of the "Talks to Students," about two-thirds of which is given over to long excerpts from other writers, James announces: "Only in some pitiful dreamer, some philosopher, poet, or romancer, or when the common practical man becomes a lover, does the hard externality give way, and a gleam of insight into the . . . vast world of inner life beyond us, so different from that of outer seeming, illuminate our mind. Then the whole scheme of our customary value gets confounded, then our self is riven and its narrow interests fly to pieces, then a new centre and a new perspective must be found" (241). The dislocation of the self, or rather its relocation from the sphere of practical concerns and interests, becomes the cause of its search for a new consciousness ("a new perspective"), which in turn invests outward circumstances ("the hard externality") with new meanings.

In this passage, "customary value" apparently resides in "hard externality." In a later passage that recalls the roll of visionaries who see through such externality, "customary value" is replaced by "commercial value," the kind that was customarily measured in hours of socially necessary labor. James quotes from the autobiography of Richard Jefferies, who, like Walt Whitman, once found himself invaded, inflated, and pretty much "carried away" by the "inexpressible beauty" of a grassy hilltop (246–47). James then comments as follows:

> Surely a worthless hour of life, when measured by the usual standards of commercial value. Yet in what other kind of value can the preciousness of any hour, made precious by any standard, consist, if it consist not in feelings of excited significance like these, engendered in some one, by what the hour contains? Yet so blind and dead does the clamor of our own practical interests make us to all other things [i.e., things without commercial value], that it seems almost as if it were necessary to become worthless as a practical being, if one is to hope to attain to any breadth of insight into the impersonal world of worths as such. Only your mystic, your dreamer, or your insolvent tramp or loafer, can afford so sympathetic an occupation, an occupation which will change the usual standards of human value in the twinkling of an eye. (247)

To establish an objective standard of value—"to attain to any breadth of insight into the impersonal world of worths as such"—is to depart from the domain of practical interests and commercial value, where the content of each hour is indistinguishable from that of all others because it is constituted by homogeneous quantities of time. To establish the grounds of objective judgment is, then, to escape the realm of necessity defined by socially necessary labor-time, "to become worthless as a practical being," to take up those occupations that do not produce value in the customary, commercial sense. But the characteristic output of those plainly unproductive occupations is the kind of sympathy that dissolves the self isolated by narrow, practical interests, and relocates it in "the vast world of inner life" which lies beyond that self. The grounds of objective judgment are established, it would seem, by the absence of stable grounds on which to erect a self—by entry into a world that is literally impersonal because none of its inhabitants is self-contained.

I suppose we could treat James's distaste for commercial value as the typical mugwump's response to the unsightly "grope of wealth" that seemed to have reshaped American life or, more generally, as a species of "romantic reaction" against the cash nexus and its sordid implications. But there are two good reasons not to do so. First, this account of self and knowledge is perfectly consistent with the account given in chapters 9 and 10 of *The Principles*.[5] The significant difference is that the social text in which knower and known are situated has become more concrete because James now uses metaphors of unemployment (the tramp, the loafer, the worthless practical being) to convey the contingent character of selfhood and consciousness. Second, James immediately invokes Whitman to illustrate his argument, and does so in a way that precludes the possibility of withdrawal from the phenomenally commercial world in the name of the truth or the integrity of the self.

Whitman was "a sort of ideal tramp," according to James, because in practical or academic terms, he was "a worthless, unproductive being" (248). Here James announces that his earlier reference to "your insolvent tramp" was not incidental, that he is drawing on and contributing to the meanings of this popular figure of the late-nineteenth-century American imagination. The tramp was not a mere figment of that imagination: he appeared as a social type and a narrative principle in the wake of the Great Strikes of the 1870s. But in the dime novels and the rhetoric of the social sciences alike, the tramp quickly became both social type and narrative principle—that is, an allegorical figure with largely metaphorical meanings. In the dime novels, he was the workingman disinherited by capital; in the rhetoric of the social sciences, he was the collective savage, the tool of the demagogue.[6]

In James's rendition, Whitman the tramp is more prodigal than dutiful son of the republic; he is "a worthless, unproductive being" by choice, not circumstance. So he fits the description of the tramp still favored in the 1890s, at least by those who were neither unemployed nor soldiers in Coxey's Army—he has no real occupation because he is apparently lazy and incorrigible and quite possibly depraved. When James calls him "this hoary loafer" (250), he is borrowing from this description, and from Whitman's own job description, with ironic intent. For what makes Whitman dangerous in a civilization devoted to the expansion of socially necessary labor (and accordingly of exchange value) is what makes him useful, and delightful, to James. He takes his sympathetic but unproductive occupation so seriously that it becomes practically impossible to distinguish between him and the scenes he observes. He is absorbed by them in every sense. As James points out, he "abolishes the usual human distinctions" (248), even the distinction between himself and the phenomenal world of others and objects.

Whitman never could abstract from that world; he exalts almost everything he encounters, including the evidence of wealth and commerce as well as work. From Brooklyn Ferry, as James quotes him, he sees "the sailors at work in the rigging," but also "the gray walls of the granite store-houses by the docks," "the fires from the foundry chimneys burning high." And from the Broadway omnibus, again as James quotes him, he sees "a sort of living, endless panorama—shops and splendid buildings and great windows: on the broad sidewalks crowds of women richly dressed continually passing, altogether different, superior in style and looks from any to be seen anywhere else—in fact a perfect stream of people—men too dressed in high style, and plenty of foreigners" (250–51). In a later lecture on Emerson, James would accuse Whitman of "indiscriminate hurrahing for the Universe."[7] He probably had these very passages in mind. But in this lecture, he insists that Whitman wrote the history of the future James himself would inhabit, and so must be designated "a contemporary prophet" (250).

I want to emphasize that the distinction between knower and known is collapsed in Whitman's conspectus; to be more precise, the knower is not exterior to the known. So the integrity of the knower, that is, of the self, cannot be guaranteed by its withdrawal or abstention from the phenomenal world; indeed the usual distinction between the phenomenal world and a point of view on that world—between object and subject—becomes untenable. And, as the passages from Whitman attest, that world includes the domain of "commercial value." The phenomenology of the market accordingly becomes inescapable for those who accept Whitman's terms.[8]

James's ambiguity in regard to Whitman's pure tolerance (his "indiscriminate hurrahing") would, then, suggest that he understood the difficult consequences of accepting those terms. In view of that ambiguity, and of his retort to the global claims of commercial value, we might be driven back to the conclusion that James was a typical mugwump, whose distaste for the crassly commercial dimensions of American life corroborated the "feminization" of American culture and contributed to the antimodern currents stirring in that culture. But, again, there are good reasons not to retreat. We should of course acknowledge James's ambiguity, for it is one source of his critical edge and aims. Even so, we must recognize that his strictures on contemporary American culture are predicated on a sense of its unknown yet evident possibilities—they are not derived from an Archimedean point outside of that culture, that historical moment, because James is already incapable of positing such a point. That is why he invokes Whitman the prophet, the poet of the moods of the dumb majority, who announced, "The Poetry of America lies in the future—what these States and their coming men and women are certainly to be."[9]

As we will see, James eventually embraced Whitman's "lesson of reception" and built a case for cultural revolution out of the political-economic materials and metaphorical possibilities provided by modern-industrial capitalism. Meanwhile, let us reexamine the lecture at hand, to see whether he does evade the phenomenology of the market. James speaks as if the distinction between productive and unproductive labor—the distinction that regulated the conflict between capital and labor in the late nineteenth century—is meaningless. There are three ways to explain his treatment of this crucial distinction. First, he was ignorant of it. Second, he rejected it because he was unsympathetic to the political position of subaltern social movements, through which unproductive labor appeared as the work of parasitic "middlemen" who merely distributed existing values or who otherwise deducted their incomes from the sum of values created by productive labor. Third, he assumed that it had been abolished in the course of nineteenth-century events.

The first explanation is inadequate because it must overlook James's repeated and ironic use of the word *unproductive*, to valorize activity that does not embody real value in material forms and so is neither socially necessary nor productive according to the customary definitions of subaltern social movements. He is clearly aware of the distinction as it was articulated in late-nineteenth-century political discourse. The second explanation is more plausible, then, because James does reject the distinction. In fact he suggests that the glorification of productive labor enables the expansion of the domain of commercial value and, consequently, the exclusion of other kinds of value. So it becomes necessary to ask why, or rather how, James rejects the distinction. Are his grounds theoretical or practical, philosophical or historical? In other words, what was the *form* of his argument?

I would suggest that it is more practical than theoretical, more historical than philosophical, because the designation of Whitman as a "contemporary prophet" is an indication of the position James thinks he occupies within the order of events. Note that Whitman plays two roles here. As a tramp and a romancer, he abolishes the usual human distinctions. As a prophet, he does more than that—he presumably predicts the actual abolition of such distinctions. Whitman's ideas have been validated, in this sense, by events to which James is witness; accordingly they become the method appropriate to the apprehension of those events, which constitute the historical moment that James inhabits. Once upon a time, Whitman was ahead of his time. But that was then and this is now. What was unknown, except to hoary loafers and unproductive beings like Whitman, is now obvious, and must be grasped in the terms he proposed. In sum, James assumed that the course of nineteenth-century events had abolished the customary distinction between productive and unproductive labor.

His rendition of the allegory of the tramp takes on new meaning in view of this historically determined assumption. Whitman the "ideal tramp" is still cast as son of and heir to the republic—he is, after all, a contemporary prophet—but, again, he is "a worthless, unproductive being" by choice, not circumstance. The moral of his story, it would then seem, is that there are more heirs to the republic than can be contained within the strenuously masculine category of productive labor. As Whitman would have it, the characters necessary to complete his narrative are all of "the coming men and women" of these United States, not just the dutiful sons who speak in reverent, republican accents of the Spartan world they have lost. As it turns out, James would have it the same way: the extravagant and liminal figures from the margins of society—the mystics, dreamers, tramps, and loafers—now look to be the main characters as well as the proper narrators of his romance. The category of productive labor, like the narrative scope of realism, was simply not inclusive enough to hold them.

And so James tries to look beyond it without abstracting from the larger phenomenal world in which it was embedded. But again, he can do so only be assuming that the realm of necessity residing in relations of production is receding from view or that its cultural salience is no longer self-evident. Insofar as we can say that the form of his argument is practical and historical, we can also say that *both* assumptions determined its content. In other words, he looks beyond the realm of necessity—and its political correlate, the category of productive labor—not because he is repelled by the phenomenology of the market but because he believes that these rhetorical domains describe a shrinking area of American society and culture.

Toward the Limits of Relations of Production

I will presently argue that this same belief animates the broader cultural revolution of which James is the unlikely prophet and Dewey the awkward exemplar. Meanwhile, I should explain why it was neither irresponsible nor idiotic to act as if the realm of necessity residing in relations of production was receding from view around the turn of the century.

Most historians would agree that American capitalism changed fundamentally between 1890 and 1930; many would also agree that the relevant changes can be summarized by reference to the decay of proprietary capitalism and the rise of corporate capitalism. Within this broad consensus, there is room for vigorous debate on the characteristic social structures, political practices, and cultural forms of modern American capitalism; but most historians now agree that the rise of corporate capitalism coincided with the creation of a recognizably modern "culture of consumption." Outside the discipline of history, moreover, invocations of "consumer capitalism" have become commonplace. So almost everyone now argues or assumes that the inherited relation between production and consumption was radically recast in the four decades after 1890, and that the social, economic, and cultural significance of consumption somehow superseded that of production by 1920 or 1930.[10]

Now if the inherited relation between production and consumption was changing after 1890 in ways that the notion of consumer culture (or "consumer capitalism") would prepare us to recognize, then we should not be surprised to find that close observers of the American scene believed that the realm of necessity was receding. But the fact is that historians and others have only prepared us to recognize such change. By and large, they have been content to assume, not argue, its importance; and so they have left open the question of the linkage between the rise of corporate capitalism and the emergence of a modern American culture. To address that question is, then, to make arguments rather than assumptions. But my arguments bear on the periodization of consumer culture only to the extent that such a culture presupposes the generalized perception of a radical disjuncture between production and consumption.[11] My aim, in short, is neither to trivialize nor to substantiate the notion of a "culture of consumption." I want instead to explain how it was possible and why it was reasonable for contemporaries to believe that they lived at a moment in which relations of production no longer seemed to regulate or describe the content of social relations, and in which the question of class relations could therefore be reopened.

If class is the product of political and ideological struggle, then the late nineteenth and early twentieth centuries should be construed as a moment of extraordinary debate on its significance for American society—a moment at which alternative principles of social organization and division of labor could be treated as realistic or practical alternatives. In that sense, this debate recapitulates an earlier and equally decisive moment in American history. Between 1848 and 1868, the electorate and the larger public defined class as the appropriate principle of social organization, but only because the alternatives—race and gender—were eventually excluded in the course of ideological, then political, and finally armed struggle. In other words, this prolonged struggle made relations of production the immediately effective determinant of social relations as such, and accordingly inscribed class in the everyday lives and languages of North Americans. But the outcome could not be predicted in the 1850s; indeed, if we may judge from the popular culture and the canonical literature of the decade, it was the moment of deepest doubt and debate about the meanings and principles of

American society. The choices were clearly drawn here, in fictional, the-atrical discourses that were not strictly or even consciously political; and the ideologues who were able to make those choices available in electoral contexts treated such discourses as the vernacular of politics. Abraham Lincoln is only the most obvious example of the ideologue who translated the metaphors of domesticity and the conventions of minstrelsy into a political language that displaced both gender and race as actionable or appropriate principles of social organization—and thereby sanctified the category of necessary or productive labor.[12]

By the end of the nineteenth century, however, the unitary principle of class was already beginning to give way, in theory and practice, to old *and* new alternatives. The transparent American society created in and through the looking glass of midcentury was increasingly occluded, distended, dis-torted, until it became a "land of contrasts," a house of mirrors. Even before the turn of the century, the principle of class was giving way to the principle of role in the quasi-bureaucratic form of professionalism, through which "merit," not assets or income or productive labor, becomes the source of legitimate opportunities and social mobility; thereafter class would also give way to race and gender, but in their strictly modern forms of nation and feminism.[13] Again, these were not moments of an "objective" process that somehow imposed itself on the consciousness of contemporaries. For the alternatives to the principle of class were themselves products of ideological struggle undertaken in full view of the relevant historical record.

The diversity of these principles becomes all the more remarkable in light of the relevant historical record as contemporaries understood it; for everyone pretty much agreed on how to define the central events of the nineteenth century, and therefore on how to define the key political issues of the 1890s and after. In other words, the important differences between political contestants were matters of historical interpretation, not conscious-ness. For example, what divided the Populists and their pro-capitalist oppo-nents—those who put their faith in "centralization"—was not whether industrial consolidation under the corporate legal form had occurred but whether it represented a condition of renewed social mobility and economic progress. Similarly, no one doubted that the problem of income distribu-tion demanded immediate resolution, or that the emergence of the large corporations presented either an opportunity for or an obstacle to its equi-table resolution. And everyone agreed that the labor question (are class society and republican government compatible?) and the money question (was there enough of it, and what did it represent, anyway?) were to be understood as consequences of nineteenth-century historical developments in which large business enterprise played a dominant role. Disagreements appeared when political contestants addressed these questions as problems or prospects, that is, as undeniable evidence of the body politic's corruption or as promising conditions of social-political development.[14]

Note that all contestants not only agreed on what the key issues of the 1890s were but also defined them in terms of their relation to the figure of the corporation, or "the trust," as the political vernacular named the phenomenon. In this sense, all contestants recognized that the critical and characteristic event of the times was the impending transformation of capitalism. In the same sense, they were confronted with a "transition question" of momentous proportions and understood that they had, in fact, reached a turning point in the history of Western civilization which became comprehensible by reference to the earlier transition. The ostensibly "antimodern" fascination with the Gothic that permeated popular literature as well as working-class politics, and that finally became Henry Adams's desperate obsession, is one indication of this search for an appropriate historical standard by which to gauge the enormous scope and probable consequences of contemporary change. So, too, are William James's comparison of pragmatism and Protestantism—the kind that erupted in the sixteenth century—and the methodical collection of artifacts from the Renaissance for display in the new museums founded by urban upper classes. For that matter, so is the development of a systematic theory of modernity or modernization within the new social sciences.[15]

There is a good reason to take these gestures seriously, as an attempt to find a narrative that could accommodate, not evade, the possibilities—that is, the characters and roles—being created by the transformation of capitalism. If we were to treat James Harrington and Karl Marx as the seminal theorists of the transition from feudalism to capitalism, we would probably say that the decisive moment in that transition came in the fifteenth and sixteenth centuries, when the landed nobility of England tried to reconstitute its prerogatives and maintain its income by turning over control of agricultural production to rent-paying commoners known first as peasants, then as yeomen. In retrospect, we can see that the long-term effects of this legal transfer were the social death of the landed nobility and the emergence of a modern, or postfeudal, society—but only in retrospect, because it took three centuries and at least that many revolutions for enterprising commoners to think through and work out the implications of their new status and functions.[16]

If we were to treat Max Weber, Gardiner Means, Adolf Berle, William A. Williams, Alfred Chandler, and Martin Sklar as the seminal theorists of the transition from proprietary to corporate capitalism, we would probably say that the decisive moment in that transition came between 1889 and 1909, when capitalists tried to reconstitute their prerogatives and reinstate their incomes by reconstructing production and distribution under the bureaucratic aegis of the corporations. They wanted to avoid the status of public servants, and used the corporate legal form to guarantee their private lease on the future. But of course they failed according to this account. They were quickly replaced by professional managers who control but do not own the resources which, as organized through large corporations, compose the crucial sectors and linkages of the twentieth-century economy.[17] In retrospect, we can see that the long-term effects of this legal transfer may well be the social death of capitalists and the emergence of a postmodern, or postcapitalist, society.

But only in retrospect? Or can we say that we have begun to theorize our own "transition question" because we have rediscovered the generation that witnessed its decisive moment? I do not doubt that the increasingly "postmodern" sensibility of our time is in fact predicated on the rediscovery of turn-of-the-century intellectual and cultural agendas—that is the premise with which I began this chapter as well as the conclusion I draw from recent scholarship on the period. But it is one thing to claim that we use the ideas of an earlier generation for our own purposes and quite another to claim that these purposes are consistent with the ideas. Nevertheless I would make the larger claim. For, notwithstanding the increase of class consciousness and conflict in the three decades after 1890, what distinguishes and characterizes the intellectual (and political) innovation of the period is its refusal to be bound by the categories of necessity, production, or class relations. But, again, that refusal is not an evasion of these categories; it is instead an acknowledgment of the confusion of spheres—the creation of new social spaces and roles—determined by the transformation of capitalism.

Before I return to the illustration of my larger claim, let me explain exactly how the transformation of capitalism pointed the way beyond relations of production and class society in this important sense. There are three moments in the process as I understand it. First, the accelerating separation of ownership and control within the legal and organizational structure of the corporate economy created new social strata—and the demand for new institutions—that stood between, or at the periphery of, labor and capital, and thus complicated or displaced the more transparent class relations of the nineteenth century. The Populists and the Knights of Labor understood this distension as the increase of unproductive, strictly mental labor, and worried about the political propensities of the liminal figures who occupied the thickening social space between the people and the plutocrats. For example, James B. Weaver, the Populist Party candidate for president in 1892, warned, "Universal uprising of the industrial forces will result in unifying the monopolistic and plutocratic forces also, and through the business and social influences of these potential and awakened forces, thousands of well-meaning professional and business men of all classes will be induced, for a time, to make common cause against us." His pro-capitalist opponents, on the other hand, hailed the new division of labor between owners and managers as the dawn of scientific procedure in business enterprise and the source of social mobility for the sons of the working class. In their view, the corporations would become the recruiting ground for talent from families without social connections or inherited wealth, and the business schools within the modern universities would become their adjunct.[18]

Either way, the class relation of capital and labor was now occluded by the insertion and expansion of a social stratum whose political position could not be deduced from or traced to its occupational or functional profile—not even if the corporation men could treat higher education as the bottom rung on the job ladder. For the colleges and universities (and for that matter the newspapers and the little magazines) were also turning out young intellectuals, men *and* women like Van Wyck Brooks, John Reed, Walter Lippmann, W.E.B. Du Bois, Florence Kelley, Jane Addams, and Jessie Taft, who resolved the vocational crisis that had afflicted their parents by ignoring it, by embracing—or rather inventing—social roles that neither the corporate bureaucracies nor the category of productive labor could accommodate. These men and women came of age in the first or second decade of the twentieth century and, with James and Dewey as their methodological mentors, made a cultural revolution by reopening old questions and asking new ones about the meaning and principles of American society. They were able to do so, I think, because the ambiguity of their class position—their status as "artificial persons" in every sense—allowed them to stand at the heart of contemporary change, and accordingly to grasp the possibilities residing in both the disintegrating past and the impending future. But they understood that the ambiguity of their class position was itself evidence of a transformation of capitalism through which the categories of necessity, production, and class were somehow receding. The "cultural basis of property is radically altered," Lippmann noted in 1914. "The real news about business, it seems to me, is that it is being administered by men who are not profiteers. The managers are on salary, divorced from ownership and bargaining. They represent the revolution in business incentives. . . . For they conduct gigantic enterprises and stand outside the higgling of the market. . . . The trust movement is doing what no conspirator or revolutionist could ever do: it is sucking the life out of private property."[19]

Second, the corporate reconstruction of production and distribution was designed to reinstate relations of production as the regulative principle of modern society; the goal of the corporate innovators was not only to pacify but also to reinscribe class relations as the sum of social relations and the locus of values as such. Indeed the corporations were conceived as the means by which capital could reassert control of the labor process and increase labor productivity through the mechanization of goods production. The watchwords of this movement, however, were "system," "science," and "efficiency." For the point was to increase "throughput" by reducing the labor-time and the associated costs required to produce a given volume of goods—that is, the point was to reduce the scope and the amount of socially necessary labor engaged in goods production. Until the early twentieth century, the general increase of labor productivity did not cause the displacement, or the absolute reduction, of socially necessary labor, because even as machines replaced the skills and bodily exertions of adults and children in the factories and on the farms, demand for the machines and their inputs (raw materials, fabricated metal parts, plant construction, etc.) increased overall demand for labor. But between 1890 and 1910, the increase in overall demand for labor slowed considerably as the new industrial corporations increased their output across the board without a corresponding or comparable increase of the industrial labor force; for under the corporate aegis, "technical progress [became] organizational in the sense that its effect on productivity [did] not require any change in the quantity of the inputs." To verify this argument of the economist Edmund S. Phelps, we need only consult the studies of social democracy and of "postindustrial society" in the advanced capitalist countries. These studies have emphasized the virtual cessation in the proportionate growth of the industrial working class at or near the turn of the century; but then so have studies of supervisory or "white-collar" employees in the United States. Thus the corporate reconstruction, which was undertaken in the name of class society, of increased productivity, and of exchange value, erected barriers to the expansion of relations of production, of socially necessary labor-time, and of exchange value.[20]

Third, the corporate reconstruction and mechanization of the labor process—a project that entailed the generalization of scientific management—not only promised to redefine work by extricating human labor from goods production but quickly delivered on that promise. By 1910, and certainly no later than 1919, the electrification of industrial plant and production had significantly reduced capital inputs per unit of industrial output; for it had reduced the energy waste inherent in steam power and had allowed the redesign of machine production and product flow in the factories. Meanwhile, technical innovations like continuous thermal cracking towers, which halved capital requirements per unit of refined oil, were patented and introduced in the manufacturing sector. In short, the secular increase in the capital-output ratio that had characterized the growth pattern of industrialization, especially after 1880, was halted or reversed between 1910 and 1920. In the 1920s, therefore, net investment declined as a percentage of national income, yet output and productivity in manufacturing rose at annual rates of 4 to 6 percent. Demand for labor changed accordingly between 1910 and 1930. As we have seen, the industrial labor force grew absolutely from 1890 to 1910, but its growth had slowed in relation to its previous rate and to that of other sectors, particularly commerce, communications, and other so-called services. After 1910, such growth was halted or reversed, although the new tendency would be obscured by war-induced demand on American capacity—then as now. In the 1920s, therefore, the number of industrial workers, and the total labor-time required to increase capacity and output in manufacturing by about 64 percent, declined absolutely.[21]

As I suggest in part 1, it was the great prophet of the modern class struggle, Karl Marx himself, who clearly recognized *and welcomed* these tendencies as the secret solvent of class relations and society. He claimed that under the regime of "large industry," which we might translate as corporate capitalism, "the creation of real wealth comes to depend less on labour time and on the amount of labour employed than on the power of the agencies set in motion during labour time, whose 'powerful effectiveness' is itself in turn out of all proportion to the direct labour time spent on their production, but depends rather on the general state of science and technology, or the application of this science to production." Labor is "reduced to a pure abstraction" under this regime. For it "no longer appears so much to be included within the production process; rather, the human being comes to relate more as watchman and regulator to the production process itself. . . . He steps to the side of the production process instead of being its chief actor." But "as soon as labour in the direct form has ceased to be the great well-spring of wealth, labour time ceases and must cease to be its measure, and hence exchange value [the measure] of use value." The class relation of labor and capital is thereby effaced or attenuated if not dissolved, because it presupposes the "exchange of living labour for objectified labour"—that is, the worker's expenditure of effort (and creation of value) in return for wages. So the emergence of "large industry" signifies the possibility of a passage beyond socially necessary labor-time as the "determinant factor in the production of wealth," and accordingly beyond relations of production as the regulative principle of general social relations.[22]

To look beyond the realm of necessity at or near the turn of the century was, then, to look into, not away from, the ongoing transformation of capitalism. For that transformation opened new social spaces and social roles. At any rate those who occupied them thought so. They also thought that this transformation produced new metaphorical possibilities that exceeded the inherited limits of rhetorical representation and so demanded either new narrative forms or—as James, Dewey, Frank Norris, Theodore Dreiser, and Lewis Mumford saw it—the recuperation of what appeared to be archaic forms. To see how this metaphorical surplus was produced, and where it could be invested, we need to recover the political languages in which the key issues of the 1890s (and after) were specified. Only then can we begin to make sense of the scandal of pragmatism.

CHAPTER 8

. . . .

MONEY QUESTIONS AND

MORAL EQUIVALENTS IN

THE FUTURE TENSE

Conflict from Consensus on a Credit Economy

In the late nineteenth century, the subaltern position on the question of distribution was determined by a straightforward application of the category of productive labor. The Populists and the Knights of Labor believed that the bankers, the merchants, and the lawyers—the middlemen and the capitalists—created no new or real values in the form of commodities that could be consumed or used for productive purposes; instead they merely manipulated existing values and deducted their incomes from the sum of values that would otherwise be available to those who actually produced it. The manufacturer as such was more or less exempt from this charge of "unproductive labor" unless the scale and scope of his operations placed him in the camp of "the trusts." Thus it was the small manufacturer who remained innocent of exploitation as the category of productive labor could explain it.[1]

So conceived, the question of distribution was one dimension of the labor question; for the discussion of distribution disclosed the relation between capital and labor by providing each a position on the level and the legitimacy of profits as against wages. But it had wider implications as well. Many small or tenant farmers embraced the political analysis and programs that flowed from the category of productive labor. They, too, assumed that the capitalists embodied the superfluous in every sense. For they, too, assumed that the problem of production had been solved—the problem was not how to produce use values but how to assign appropriate symbolic values to real, useful things, how to limit the creation and circulation of meanings by reference to the real, useful labor of the "producing classes." In this respect, subaltern social movements defined the question of distribution in terms of a symbolic surplus. There was more than enough human energy and material resources, they insisted, to produce what everyone deserved by virtue of his (or her) labor. Poverty and progress nevertheless coincided because the allocation of energy and resources was regulated not by principles derived from the category of productive labor but by the extraordinary powers of "artificial persons"—the railroad corporations, "the trusts," and their creatures—who could create legal claims on the future products of labor at will and therefore could deduct their current revenues from the values created by the productive labor of workers and farmers.[2]

The pro-capitalist opponents of the Populists and the Knights agreed that the question of distribution should be defined in terms of surplus. But they understood its connotations and consequences differently. For example, they claimed that "overproduction"—production beyond effective or remunerative demand—caused whatever problems of distribution were evident in the 1890s; that a shortage of profits, not wages, was the obvious symptom of those problems; and that the solution was to centralize control of industrial output under the corporate legal form, not to disperse such control, thus to rehabilitate the small entrepreneurs who represented the margin of supply and accordingly to reconstitute the social conditions of "overproduction." These pro-capitalist observers of the economic scene did, then, recognize a surplus of capital and capitalists; even so, they did not propose to get rid of capitalism. Instead they sought to modify it by organizing and accommodating new forms of capitalist production. But if in the end they argued that the problem of production had not been solved—that the possibilities of growth and development on the supply side had not yet been realized—they did assume that it was inseparable from the larger question of distribution. To this extent, their new order of business included the agendas outlined by subaltern social movements.[3]

The highly original contribution of pro-capitalist observers to the question of distribution was their defense of mental labor—that is, the work of the bankers, the merchants, the lawyers, the middlemen, and the managers. Here they directly confronted the category of productive labor by claiming that use values could not be appropriated unless they were first clothed with exchange value, with symbolic properties, and thus could circulate freely in the market as commodities. By creating and maintaining this symbolic matrix in which objects could acquire social-cultural meanings *and thereby become useful*, the unsung middlemen gave everyone immediate access to available use values. If it did not add to the sum of use values, their mental labor—their cultural work—did make such values recognizable, commensurable, and meaningful; thus, even though it could not be evaluated in terms of the received classical tradition of political economy, it was nonetheless necessary labor. In this sense, pro-capitalist observers of the economic scene gave theoretical sanction to new social roles, new forms of mental labor, new models of selfhood—precisely those roles, forms, and models that the sons and the daughters of the proprietary middle class were discovering and developing and, not incidentally, those that the category of productive labor could neither acknowledge nor accommodate.[4]

I have already suggested that the labor question intersected with and informed the discussion of distribution. In fact the problem of proletarianization shaped every kind and level of discourse in the 1890s, because almost all observers, regardless of their political preferences, agreed that a permanent working class and a republican form of government were probably incompatible. If James Madison had been correct to say that the "two cardinal objects" of republican government were "the rights of persons and the rights of property," and to suggest that the protection of one set of rights would not exclude protection of the other only so long as the majority had a vested interest in the rights of property, then political crisis would necessarily follow once the majority had become wage earners and thus could perceive no such interest. By all accounts, that crisis had been impending since 1877, had erupted in 1886, and had only intensified thereafter. "This separation of laborers and capitalists into distinct classes involves serious dangers to society as a whole," Arthur T. Hadley, the Yale economist and authority on railroads, noted in 1896. "It involves a contradiction between our political theories and the facts of industrial life."[5]

But the same historical perspective suggested that the political upheaval of the 1890s was symptomatic of a deeper cultural crisis. For the obvious fact and novel uses of working-class solidarity raised new questions about the social and legal groundwork of individualism and personal liberty—which were in effect questions about the conditions of character or selfhood as such. Those new questions turned on the plausibility of positing the ontological priority of the pure self and its political corollary, natural right. The responses were as ambiguous and contradictory as the political alignments, social movements, and cultural currents of the 1890s. But by the turn of the century, the notion of a "social self"—another apparently "artificial person" suspended in a collective web of historical contingency—had become a commonplace of social science, philosophy, and literature, and had become the subject of legal controversy as well (in the form of debate over the rights of individuals as against groups or corporate "persons"). In this crucial sense, the emergence of class society and its attendant forms of solidarity challenged or discredited inherited ways of thinking about American society and politics precisely because it seemed to have recast— or reopened—the relation between self and society. Certainly the debates of the 1890s on the questions of distribution and labor acknowledged the fluidity of this relation; indeed they constituted it by making its terms the immediate objects of political languages and programs. In the long run, self and society would be the consequences of these debates. The contestants understood that, and conducted themselves accordingly.[6]

In this light, debate on the money question seems less concrete and consequential. Perhaps that is why most historians have treated it as a strictly symbolic or ceremonial substitute for debate on the "real questions" raised by industrialization. But the contestants themselves treated it as if it were still the master text that made all others intelligible and meaningful in translation. The money question had become this metonymical device by which all issues were apparently joined or reduced because it allowed simultaneous discussion of the most mundane realities and the most abstruse possibilities. Spokesmen (and women) for industrial workers, small farmers, and large capital, for example, commonly adopted its familiar terms to explain the distribution of income, but in doing so, they assumed that they had to address the derivation of value and the problem of representation— to adduce the meanings of money—as if these issues were immediately practical, not academic or irrelevant.[7] Since the monetary forms specific to a modern "credit economy" (e.g., deposits, checks, bills of exchange, securities) approached the status of pure symbols precisely because they represented potential claims on future income—they were in fact "floating signifiers"—to adduce these meanings was to posit a certain relation between material circumstances and intellectual inscription, between object and subject, and to situate this hypothetical subject within a corresponding symbolic or rhetorical universe. Thus the money question was the idiom in which seemingly abstract philosophical or epistemological issues became the predicates of political arguments as well as popular fiction—and vice versa. For as we shall see, the philosophers, the people who made a living from epistemology, also recognized the pliability of money and credit as metaphors for mind, language, and thought.[8]

The subaltern position on the money question was shaped by two arguments specific to the late nineteenth century. First, the legal powers of the national banks, which gave them control of both interest rates and money supply, allowed private corporations to tax the incomes of the "toiling millions," making it impossible for these millions to acquire or maintain productive property and thereby to become or remain independent proprietors. From this standpoint, the problems of proletarianization and distribution were dimensions of the money question. The solution was to give the federal government the power to issue currency in quantities sufficient to lower interest rates and to maintain effective demand for the output of productive labor—hence the call for more greenbacks and for "free silver." Second, the national banks and "the trusts" had collaborated in creating a "credit economy," in which there was no discernible or reasonable relation between legal claims on income and tangible assets—that is, between the symbols of wealth that were the sources of income and the real wealth of the nation that was produced by the "toiling millions." These symbols of surplus or excess congregated in the markets for stocks, bonds, and "futures," where bankers and brokers—the creatures of large capital—merely manipulated them without regard to the real, useful commodities that were, in principle, their objective correlate. Here they represented nothing except other representations of a moment that did not yet exist. But these symbols dominated the nation's existence and imagination, because they were both origin and object of the gambling and speculation that ultimately caused economic crises. By this account, the solutions to the problem of a "credit economy" were to nationalize or closely regulate "the trusts," which were inconceivable without the stock market and its speculative consequences, and to reinstate an equivalence or correspondence between signifiers and signified—between the money supply and the things it was supposed to represent, not displace.[9]

Pro-capitalist observers acknowledged that the success of large corporate business enterprise depended on the use of new credit instruments and the specialized markets in which they were traded. They also acknowledged that stocks, bonds, and other fiduciary promises might represent intangible assets such as "good will" or the stream of future income to be realized by use of existing tangible assets. In this sense, pro-capitalist observers understood the new credit instruments to be titles to property as the federal courts had redefined it between 1886 and 1890—that is, not only as the material substance of existing assets but also as the "probable expectancy" of future income (future profits) from use of those assets. They agreed with their opponents that the relation between the symbols of wealth and the real wealth of the nation had changed; but they were not as fearful of the possibilities residing in this change. They were more likely to accept the radical contingency that resulted once these symbols had been detached from their moorings in tangible assets or real commodities, and accordingly circulated as if the symbolic universe of the financial markets was a world unto itself. From their standpoint, the risk borne by the speculator was an indispensable condition of development as such. That is why they proposed to regulate the financial and commodities markets—to minimize gambling, not to abort the "trust movement" by dismantling the "credit economy" on which it turned.[10]

So epistemological as well as political lines were clearly drawn in debates on the money question. The constituents of subaltern social movements argued that insofar as the paper symbols denominated as money did not correspond to tangible objects "out there" in the real world—insofar as money did not represent existing values by functioning as a medium of exchange, and only as a medium of exchange—something was amiss. For in that case, money had become a sign of a sign, an end in itself. It constituted a "credit economy," a symbolic universe that did not designate or stand for anything truly objective, unless symbols themselves were objective. In such a post-representational universe, the difference between symbol and symbolized apparently dissolved. But then so too did the distinction between knower and known. In this odd new world, everything could be artificial because nothing had an objective correlate.[11]

Pro-capitalist observers of the same "credit economy" admired its capacity to produce "substitutes for money"—that is, new and different signs of a sign—and to reduce demand for coin, cash, and the commodities customarily held as bank reserves. In other words, they admired it precisely because it was a fertile and flexible field of symbols, in which the representations of claims on property, income, or labor-power were not limited by the requirements of current consumption, by the perceived needs and inventories of the present; instead such representations could be indefinitely extended in time and space. From this standpoint, economic crises erupted when the symbolic field constituted by a "credit economy" collapsed because everyone wanted to know the cash value of existing inventories—when the correspondence between money and tangible objects "out there" in the real world was reasserted, and a representational equilibrium was momentarily restored.[12]

To speak of a "credit economy" in or after the 1890s was, then, to situate one's utterance in the popular, political discourse of the money question, and to assume that its metonymy made sense of nineteenth-century history. In doing so, however, one had to take a stand on the consequences of that history. In populist perspective, for example, approval of a "credit economy" was something like sympathy for the devil, because "the trusts" were cause and effect of speculation in the stock market; to be for the people and against the plutocrats was to be scandalized by the "credit economy" in which all manner of altogether artificial accretions accumulated. The phenomenology of the market determined by this perspective—the Populists never proposed to abolish markets as such—could acknowledge a future for neither the social nor the symbolic surplus generated by the emergence of corporate capitalism. To acknowledge these surpluses, and to suggest that they could be productively invested, was, then, to take a hopeful stand on the impending consequences of nineteenth-century history: it was to see genuine possibilities where the Populists could see only distressing problems. For those with subaltern sympathies, this revisionist stand must have been a difficult act of faith in the 1890s, because it did in fact require a certain sympathy for the devil.

John Dewey's Sympathy for the Devil

Consider the case of young John Dewey. Here was a prolific philosopher whose subaltern sympathies could not have been more evident. In his last three years at the University of Michigan (1891–94), he not only tried to establish a popular journal that would draw out the political implications of intellectual innovation, "to show that philosophy has some use"— this journal was the ill-fated *Thought News*, the product of Dewey's collaboration with Franklin Ford, a radical syndicalist—but also wrote articles for the *Inlander*, the university's monthly student magazine, in which he claimed that the popular rituals of American politics were not the objectionable "blots upon our character and repute" they appeared to be in the editorial jeremiads of the time but "some of the most poetic features of our American life." When he moved to the University of Chicago in 1894, he immediately began lecturing at the Working-People's Social Science Club, where Henry Demarest Lloyd, among others, also held forth, and at similar groups or meetings that flourished under the aegis of Jane Addams's Hull House. Wherever he appeared, he insisted that the truth was a social product to be more equally distributed among the people, "so that it becomes the Commonwealth."[13]

Meanwhile Dewey wrote dozens of scholarly articles, reviews, essays, and even a book, *Outlines of a Critical Theory of Ethics*, which was published in 1891. In doing so, he made his sympathies increasingly legible. For example, in the *Theory of Ethics*, he used the choices available to a striking streetcar conductor to illustrate the nature of moral dilemmas—to illustrate how worldly or practical ethical theory might be, and why working-class life in the modern-industrial world represented not the absence but the elements of philosophical discourse (176–79). The book is organized, however, around the revelation on which Hegel had built a critique of Kant and a positive (though speculative) system. That revelation was the consequence of Hegel's encounter with the political economy of Adam Smith and James Steuart, through which the youthful German philosopher realized that modern, commercial society and the abstract social labor of the factory could be conceived as *both* the negation and the conditions of political community.[14] Dewey summarized his Hegelian sources and posture as follows:

> In the realization of the law of social function [through which "self, or individuality, is essentially social"], conflict must occur between the desire as an immediate and direct expression of the individual—the desire in its isolation—and desire as an expression of the whole man; desire, that is, as wholly conformable to the needs of the surroundings. Such a conflict is real enough, as everyone's experience will testify, but it is a conflict which may be solved—which must be solved so far as morality is attained. And since it is a conflict within desire itself, its solution or morality, does not require any impossible obliteration of desire, nor any acting from an "ought" which has no relation to what "is." This, indeed, is *the* failure of the Kantian Ethics: in separating what should be from what is, it deprives the latter, the existing social world as well as the desires of the individual, of all moral value; while, by the same separation, it condemns that which should be to a barren abstraction. An "ought" which does not root in and flower from the "is," which is not the fuller realization of the actual state of social relationships, is a mere pious wish that things should be better. (151)

So Dewey would have to search within the "actual state of social relationships" for the democratic promise that the Populists and their champions, then as now, found in the simple market society of the past. His social sympathies were complicated and enlarged, in this sense, by his intellectual commitment to an outlook or method in which historical circumstance and ethical principle could not appear as antithetical categories of analysis or narrative. Accordingly he treated both business enterprise and the factory system as appropriate sites for the explication of the meanings of morality and moral community (112–13, 137). "The term 'moral community' can mean only a unity of action," he claimed, "made what it is by the cooperating activities of diverse individuals." It followed that "there is unity in the work of a factory, not in spite of, but *because of* the division of labor" (137). For the same reasons, he treated poetry as William James did—not as literary refuge from the issues addressed in philosophy and science but as the narrative form that contained them. "The importance and endurance of poetry, as of all art, are in its hold upon reality. We hear much, on this side and that, of realism. Well, we may let realism go, but we cannot let go reality."[15]

At any rate Dewey could neither let it go nor believe that it contained only the evidence of a fall from grace—not even if that reality included "the trusts" and their unholy, quasi-monetary symbols. He did believe that the new ideas he and his colleagues were developing could lead beyond the reality he observed, but only if they led through the "actual state of social relationships," and acknowledged that such relationships were determined by their depiction. "What life is found to be depends in large measure upon the prevailing theory of life," Dewey insisted. For social life "is not a raw, unworked material to which the poet may directly apply himself." Instead it is "already a universe of meanings, of interpretations."[16] To interpret this world differently was, then, to change it. "The social world exists spiritually, as conceived, and a new conception of it, [a] new perception of its scope and bearings, is, perforce, a change of that world" (207).

But Dewey's new perception turned, I think, on his assessment of the properties and possibilities of a "credit economy," through which he conceived the social world as, or in terms of, a new phenomenology of the market. I am claiming, in other words, that he used the epistemological or metaphorical surplus of the money question as the margin on which he speculated in the market of ideas, and that the profit he made as a result became the intellectual capital out of which he made his career as the "philosopher of democracy." To see if these claims bear anything more than interest, we need to examine the decisive moment in his intellectual development, which came between 1889 and 1892, *before* he moved to Chicago.[17]

By 1891, Dewey had spent three years discussing the political economy of "the trusts" with Franklin Ford and had decided to go ahead with *Thought News*, through which they hoped to illustrate the practical consequences of impending intellectual revolution. In effect, Dewey had embraced, and would now act on, Ford's optimistic yet political-economic periodization of modern life—even though the journal never did get started. So he had left Henry George behind and was already heading toward the political stage on which Henry Demarest Lloyd then played the leading role. Dewey had also moved beyond the familiar problem of reconciling the modes of apprehension specific to science and religion. Hereafter he would treat religious revelation as an annex of art, and would concern himself with the "present separation of science and art, [the] division of life into prose and poetry."

For he now believed it was art, not science or religion, that had "outrun the slower step of reflective thought" by capturing the recognizably modern "movement of life, of experience." Epistemology had to catch up to poetry. "We must, in the cold, reflective way of critical system, justify and organize the truth which poetry, with its quick, naive contacts, has already felt and reported."[18]

Dewey announced his new agenda by situating himself in the order of nineteenth-century events as it had been revealed to him by his collaboration with Ford. Like James, he designated a contemporary prophet whose methods allowed the comprehension of those events—this prophet was of course Hegel—and suggested that these methods were themselves events to be grasped as a dimension of the historical reality in question. But Dewey was more explicit than James in celebrating the political economy of contingency, at least until 1904. For he was more interested in, and more playful with, the metaphors of the money question.

Dewey outlined the new agenda in two articles of 1891. One was a piece for the *Monist*, entitled "The Present Position of Logical Theory."[19] It is almost incoherent because Dewey keeps reminding himself and his readers that, in the format of a professional journal, he cannot say exactly what is on his mind. For example: "And were it not somewhat out of my present scope, I should like to show that modern culture is thus a prepared victim for the skillful dialectician of the reactionary army" (129). He also acknowledges at several points that his argument is incomplete, and would require a great deal more evidence and explication to become convincing; for the time being, he says, we have to take it on faith. For example: "I shall not attempt here any defence of the 'transcendental' [i.e., Hegelian] logic; I shall not even attempt to show that the interpretation of it which I have given above is correct. It must go, for the present, simply as my individual understanding of the matter" (133–34).

But if this article is more manifesto than argument, the author's purposes are clear enough. Dewey makes three large claims. First, the medieval social context in which formal logic, the "foundation-stone" of scholasticism, became coherent and useful has disappeared; yet formal logic—"the notion that the mind has a faculty of thought apart from things, the notion that this faculty is constructed, in and of itself with a fixed framework, the notion that thinking is the imposing of this fixed framework on some unyielding matter called particular objects, or facts" (128)—still reigns as the dominant model of thought or inquiry in modern science as in philosophy. Second, scientific theory as such is inconsistent so long as it adheres to the scholastic model of thought or inquiry, because the practical conduct of modern science is predicated on the assumption that thought and will are indissoluble moments in the unitary project of mastering reality by consciously changing and shaping it. "Types of thought are simply the various forms which reality progressively takes as it is progressively mastered as to its meaning,—that is, understood. Methods of thought are simply the various active attitudes into which intelligence puts itself in order to detect and grasp the fact" (133). Third, and most interesting, Hegel represents "the quintessence of the scientific spirit" (134) because he treated thought as this very movement of active attitudes. "When Hegel calls thought objective he means just what he says: that there is no special, apart faculty of thought belonging to and operated by a mind existing separate from the outer world" (136–37).

Hegel is consistently misinterpreted, Dewey claims, because his interpreters assume that he began where they do—with the "scholastic" notion of mind as a closed system bound by the rules of formal logic and forever exiled from the external world of objects (134–40). But the legacy of nineteenth-century events allows a different and better interpretation, that is, a recuperation of the "transcendental" Hegelian logic. The "rationality of fact had not been sufficiently realised in detail in the early decades of the century to admit of the principle of the 'transcendental' movement being other than misunderstood. That is to say, the development of science and, more particularly, its application to the specific facts of the world was comparatively rudimentary" (139). What Dewey is struggling to say here, I think, is that the "objective significance" of mind could not be recognized until science in its practical, mechanical, industrial forms had visibly and irrevocably changed the world. "However certain it may be that there are no real types or methods of thought excepting those of the object-matter itself as it comes to be understood, yet to man this objective significance cannot be real till he has made it *out* in the details of the scientific processes, and *made* it in applied science, in invention" (140). By the end of the century, at any rate, it is obvious that human beings have remade the world of object-matter through "practical invention, as the manifestation of the rationality of fact" (140). Having done so—having turned themselves inside out in the form of mechanical devices that make scientific methods of thought productive—they are finally able to treat thought or mind exactly as Hegel had proposed, as intrinsically objective. "It seems to me that we are already at this stage, or are at the point of getting to it" (140).

As James used Whitman, so Dewey used Hegel to suggest that the knower is not exterior to the known, and that the standpoint afforded by the accumulation of nineteenth-century events is necessarily as "transcendental" as these figures had insisted it must be. Since it was Whitman who announced that "only Hegel is fit for America," Dewey was in effect claiming James's intellectual lineage as his own; his family tree had deeper (or different) roots in European soil, but he was now out on the same limb. "I would point out," he concluded, "that the constant detailed work of science upon the world in theory and in invention, must in time give that world an evident meaning in human consciousness. . . . The whole set of external, or non-immanent entities, is now on the point of falling away, of dissolving" (140). Here we are, Dewey suggests, on the verge of realizing that we are already immanent in or absorbed by the scenes we supposedly observe from outside, that the form and content of consciousness are unknowable before, or apart from, their embodiment in the world. When we do realize these facts, what happens? "What then?" he asks (141). In 1904, James would reply by claiming that consciousness as such does not exist except as "a kind of external relation," except as practical, observable consequences in and on the world. Dewey answers, "It will be seen that logic is no revived, redecked scholasticism, but a complete abandonment of scholasticism." Logic will then become history, it seems, and "will be free to ask after that structure of meanings making up the skeleton of the world of knowledge" (141).

Later in 1891, in the second of the articles announcing his new agenda, Dewey proceeded to the interrogation of that structure of meanings; in doing so, he sketched the new logic he understood to be residing in the rationality of nineteenth-century fact. This two-part article, "The Scholastic and the Speculator," was published in the Inlander, not a professional journal, and like "The Present Position of Logical Theory," it was never reprinted in the author's lifetime.[20] Even so, it bears a close reading because it completes the manifesto begun in "The Present Position"—it actually describes the historical stage only mentioned there—and because it powerfully shaped Dewey's subsequent intellectual development by committing him to a periodization of thought in which the seemingly abstract problems governing scientific inquiry or philosophical speculation appeared instead as the practical demands of political-economic development. So conceived, "The Scholastic and the Speculator" is more than the endearing consequence of Dewey's encounter with "the trusts" and their corollary in a "credit economy" by way of Ford; for it identifies modern capitalism as the site on which new epistemological possibilities are being created, and looks accordingly to the ongoing transformation of capitalism for the empirical warrant and indispensable condition of impending intellectual revolution.

Dewey speaks freely and metaphorically in the format of the Inlander—that is, in a manner already foreign to the professional journals. He does not have to struggle to say what is on his mind because he does not have to reconstruct his premises or fear that his audience will be scandalized by political utterance. The piece reads as if it were written for delivery as a public lecture. So we can almost hear and see Dewey warming to the theme of scholasticism introduced in "The Present Position of Logical Theory." Here too he insists that scholasticism has outlasted the social context in which it first emerged, but he now suggests that it represents a constraint on intellectual development because it cannot and does not take its cue from the political-economic posture of postfeudal culture. "The Scholastic was not commercial," in other words. "He did not give and take, take in order to give, and give in order to take; he took all he could get, and gave only under compulsion—the compulsion being what we call the Renaissance." The Scholastic was the master of abstraction, "the miser of philosophy"; he was "the man who wanted to save truth lest it should get away." But this "abstraction from life is still going on" because the exuberant episte-mological alternative available in the actual conduct of modern, commercial life has not been recognized as such. "The human mind is still engaged in the process of saving and storing. *It is this saving process of mind,* and not any special act or particular portion of history, which constitutes Scholasticism" (149).

To abstract or save knowledge is to remove thought from its historical setting—from its conditions and its embodiment. The Scholastic, for example, "subtracted Aristotle from life; from the circumstances of time, of place, of social and intellectual life which gave him his meaning, and regarded him *in abstracto*; in the air, that is to say" (148). This false abstraction amounts to theft. "It is taking a thing not out of its apparent relations in order to get it into its real relations, but taking a thing out of relations and keeping it out. Not to put too fine a point upon it, the Scholastic was an embezzler" (149). But Dewey does not so much reject saving as he demands investment. "The commerce of mind with the world requires its fund, its capitalized store, as surely as the commerce in material products." To that extent, the Scholastic's embezzlement of thought had prevented "mental bankruptcy" in the modern age (151). This idle hoard of the Scholastic must now be treated as "the credit of thought"—not as a hedge against the future—and turned to account by philosophical speculation. "Human intelligence has always been gathering in wealth from the wreckage of time and hugging the salvage to itself to set out its full meaning: the *scholastic.* But intelligence must throw its fund out again into the stress of life: it must venture its savings against the pressure of facts: the *speculator*" (152).

In such an account, or rather line of credit, commerce in all its modern permutations comprises the appropriate model of the work of the mind.

"The comparison of thinking with commerce is no forced analogy," Dewey claims. "There is but one commerce: The meeting of Mind and Reality. Sometimes the meeting is of one kind and we call it Thought; sometimes it is of another and we call it Language; sometimes another and we call it Art; sometimes another and we call it Justice, Rightness; sometimes another and we call it Trade. Only because we are such materialists, fixing our attention upon the rigid thing instead of upon the moving act, do we identify the last exchange especially as commerce" (151). Thus Newton's law of gravitation and the Standard Oil Company are analogous attempts at balancing "the credit of thought with the debit of experience." Each represents a risky investment in—that is, a commitment to—a world naturalized and stabilized by thought. "Nature keeps her books by the double entry system, and every venture completed must in time be referred for accounting to the original capital of truth" (152).

Dewey's treatment of *speculation* is not an ironic appropriation of a popular metaphor; as he would say, he does not abstract the word or the activity from its "real relations" to the social movements, economic practices, and political programs of the late nineteenth century, so that he might put it to recondite use. Instead he suggests that the metaphor—the activity of the word—integrates the structure of meanings immanent in the predominantly commercial and increasingly contingent character of the postfeudal social world, especially in the North American extremity of that world. "The Yankee is the great speculator. Undisturbed by the Anglo-purist he continues his great 'guess' upon life. If he ceases in any measure to say 'I guess' it is only because he has gone a step further and learned to say 'I bet' so and so" (152). Dewey also suggests that by the end of the nineteenth century, with the rise of trusts like Standard Oil, the immanent is imminent, the word is finally fleshed out. For the trust is a grand wager on the future which demands coordinated social action in accordance with the still-speculative truth of that future: its masterminds must *create* the reality that will prove its validity.

And so the "thought-speculator"—that is, "the merchant of thought, who, though he both saves and spends, yet neither embezzles nor gambles" (154)—finally appears as the proper alternative to the Scholastic's separation of mind and reality. For within the structure of meanings created by the modern, commercial social world, and more immediately or explicitly by a "credit economy," reality is contingent on, and becomes a product of, the speculation formalized in the marketplace. The "credit of thought" does not, then, represent an immutable or external reality; it cannot because it is a *surplus* of meanings invested in an impending future, a bet on a reality that does not yet exist except as purpose and possibility. "Every thought, every judgment involves a leap forward, a jump, a venture. . . . It always is, and always must remain the individual venture: the stake of self or some part of self against the ongoing stream of life. Every judgment a man passes on life is perforce, his 'I bet,' his speculation. So much of his saved capital of truth he invests in the judgment: 'The state of things is thus and so'" (153). All persons are as artificial as "the trusts" in this sense because every thought leads beyond the necessary, toward the possible, into the symbolic; thoughts as such circulate in a "credit economy," wherein their current cash values or representational properties are uninteresting and unknowable. Every subject position now reproduces the situation of the speculator, who treats the waiting truth of the symbolic as the reality on which he or she must act. For the rationality of nineteenth-century fact resides in the intelligence mobilized or materialized by business enterprise—the rationality that is fully organized and disclosed, however, only in and through "the trusts."

Dewey's sympathy for the devil is not unqualified. He worries, for example, about the souls of the philosophers who bet everything on their own systems and about the character of speculation animated by the hope of private gain. "All the great philosophers have had something of this ruthless adventure of thought, this reckless throwing of the accumulated store of truth. Although the prodigal is always a more attractive figure than the miser, there must still be some better way. Only because thinking has been separated from action, the theorist from the economist in life, has speculation assumed this private form" (154). Even so, the bargain he strikes here will hereafter govern his approach to the political and intellectual possibilities of his time. The structure of meanings residing in the "credit economy" of modern capitalism, as he sees it, leads beyond the given, the necessary, or the natural, and must open onto the political economy of the contingent, where speculation is not the exception but the rule. The "fuller realization of the actual state of social relationships" had, then, to be traced in the phenomenology of the market; for the surplus of meanings representing the future was produced there.

Dewey's liberalism was determined by this hopeful perspective on the metaphorical—that is, the social and epistemological—possibilities generated by the ongoing transformation of capitalism. But his sense of these possibilities was neither utopian nor limited by bourgeois notions of political propriety. After all, the same sense of impending revolution characterized the works and lives of contemporary intellectuals and artists throughout the world. Meanwhile, bourgeois notions of political propriety (like Victorian notions of cultural propriety) were being redefined or repudiated by the growth of populist and socialist movements with large constituencies among small property-holders as well as middle-class intellectuals, and by the emergence of an *haute bourgeoisie* that congregated in the boardrooms of the new museums if not the new corporations.[21]

What finally distinguishes Dewey is the mere resilience of his hope. In 1919, when he returned to the themes first adumbrated in the early 1890s, his sense of impending possibilities was still intact and, more to the point, was still determined by the phenomenology of the market—that is, the historical logic—he had sketched in 1891. I do not mean that Dewey was alone among postwar American intellectuals in treating "the cultivated public and the business public" as parts of a cultural whole that was potentially greater than the sum of these parts. The so-called young intellectuals, especially those schooled in Alfred Stieglitz's prewar circle, were also engaged in the same project. But even though they read Veblen, or perhaps because they did, they were not as cognizant as Dewey of the promise of science and business enterprise, at least not until much later—Lewis Mumford's *Technics and Civilization* (1934) is an attempt to rectify their ignorance—and they tended, therefore, to see the "business public" as an undifferentiated mass of Philistines. Dewey himself was of course one of their fallen idols, in part because he seemed so unambiguous about this promise as to sound to them like a chamber of commerce booster.[22]

At any rate, *Reconstruction in Philosophy* (1920) completes the periodization of thought introduced in 1891.[23] For example, the second chapter, "Some Historical Factors in Philosophical Reconstruction," reiterates and clarifies "The Present Position of Logical Theory" by claiming that "modern industry *is* so much applied science" (41) and conversely that "the needs of modern industry have been tremendous stimuli to scientific investigation" (42). But no matter where we look in this book, we find that Dewey treats philosophy in the same historical manner, as thoughtful answers to the practical questions people could ask at different stages of their social development. Philosophy "originated not out of intellectual material, but out of social and emotional material" (25), he claims at the outset. "It has been occupied with the precious values embedded in social traditions, . . . it has sprung from a clash of social ends and from a conflict of inherited institutions with incompatible contemporary tendencies" (26). Accordingly the third chapter, "The Scientific Factor in Reconstruction of Philosophy," is largely about the intellectual revolution of "the transition period" (66), ca. 1400–1800, through which the closed, finite world of scholasticism was torn open, mechanics became a separate science, and modern industry was born. Here is how the chapter begins: "Philosophy starts from some deep and wide way of responding to the difficulties life presents, but it grows only when material is at hand for making this practical response conscious, articulate and communicable" (53). In the modern epoch, that material is the combination of mechanics and enterprise that produces invention, and, sooner or later, progress. "The whole of nature became a scene of pushes and pulls, of cogs and levers, of motions of parts or elements to which the formulae of movements produced by well-known machines were directly applicable" (69).

If Dewey summarizes his position anywhere, he does so in the fifth chapter, "Changed Conceptions of the Ideal and the Real." It is probably the most forthrightly philosophical chapter of the book. He tries in this setting to distinguish between classical and modern modes of thought.

> In the classical philosophy, the ideal world is essentially a haven in which man finds rest from the storms of life; it is an asylum in which he takes refuge from the troubles of existence with the calm assurance that it alone is supremely real. When the belief that knowledge is active and operative takes hold of men, the ideal realm is no longer aloof and separate; it is rather that collection of imagined possibilities that stimulates men to new efforts and realizations. . . . in the classic view the Idea belongs ready-made in a noumenal world. Hence, it is only an object of personal aspiration or consolation, while to the modern, an idea is a suggestion of something to de done or of a way of doing. (118)

Dewey illustrates the difference by asking how each mode of thought would deal with the discontent provoked by the phenomenological field of space and time—that is, by *distance*. In the classic mode, he claims, the metaphysical reality of distance would be denied, and that would be the end of it (118–19). In the modern mode, on the other hand, the dream of an end to isolation and separation would return to and reshape the phenomenal world. "The idea becomes a standpoint from which to examine existing occurrences. . . . The suggestion or fancy though still ideal is treated as a possibility capable of realization *in* the concrete natural world, not as a superior reality apart from that world. As such, it becomes a platform from which to scrutinize natural events" (120). Insofar as the idea takes on the properties of a method for observing and changing actual existence in line with the possibilities it presupposes, it becomes more fact than fancy—in fact it becomes *invention*. "Invention proceeds, and at last we have the telegraph, the telephone, first through wires, and then with no artificial medium" (120). Under the sign of invention, knowledge becomes experimental. The ideal and the rational cease, therefore, "to be a separate ready-made world incapable of being used as a lever to transform the actual empirical world"; instead they "represent intelligently thought out possibilities *of* the existent world" (121–22).[24]

But as the Scholastic changed his demeanor, "not his inner habit and tendency," and "in seeming to surrender to the scientific man took him captive," so the classical mode of thought survived the transition from feudalism to capitalism which created the modern mode of thought.[25] Its habitat is the world of "educated men, cultivated men in particular," and its form is "contemplative esthetic appreciation" (116–17, 127). And so long as philosophy as such indulges only this classical mode by rejecting the "authorized spirit of science"—that is, the assumption that all knowledge is experimental—the relation between "moral progress" and "economic accomplishments" can be comprehended only as disjuncture (121–25). Dewey already recognizes C. P. Snow's "two cultures" in the making.[26] But if he sees the raw material for the renewed growth of philosophy in the practical conduct of business enterprise, in the structure of meanings produced by the applied science of modern industry, in the mode of thought specific to capitalism, he is not willing to let one culture colonize the other.

> The scientific attitude that has actually proved itself in scientific progress is, as has been pointed out, a practical attitude. It takes forms as disguises for hidden processes. Its interest in changes is in what it leads to, what can be done with it, to what use it can be put. While it has brought nature under control, there is something hard and aggressive in its attitude toward nature unfavorable to the esthetic enjoyment of the world. Surely there is no more significant question before the world than this question of the possibility and method of reconciliation of the attitudes of practical science and contemplative esthetic appreciation. Without the former, man will be the sport and victim of natural forces which he cannot use or control. Without the latter, mankind might become a race of economic monsters, restlessly driving hard bargains with nature and with one another, bored with leisure or capable of putting it to use only in ostentatious display and extravagant dissipation. (127)

Even so, to open the question is to acknowledge the failure of philosophy, to realize that it has treated the "economic accomplishments" of the modern epoch as external to its proper domain. "The causes remain which brought philosophy into existence as an attempt to find an intelligent substitute for blind custom and blind impulse as guides to life and conduct. The attempt has not been successfully accomplished" (126). For the theorist and the economist are still separated. "The improvement in the method of knowing [has] remained so far mainly limited to technical and economic matters" (125). We have in fact changed what and how we know—that is, our selves—by changing the world, by moving beyond feudalism, by inaugurating and developing capitalism (28–76); but these related changes cannot be grasped as possibilities, as the raw materials of moral choices and philosophical discourse, so long as philosophers, unlike the rest of us, treat the contingency residing in capitalism as the negation rather than the condition of knowledge, including knowledge of our selves.

Dewey's distance from the course of contemporary change is measurable in the historical evidence he cites—it is mostly from "the transition period." Perhaps that distance, that long view, explains the resilience of his hope. But now and then the past tense becomes present, and we can hear him speaking directly to his colleagues. One such moment comes midway through the fifth chapter, when he describes the radical shift in the "moral disposition toward change" entailed by the early modern embrace of "the active conception of knowledge." Here he is also prescribing a new regimen for his fellow philosophers and social theorists, a regimen that, if followed by their intellectual heirs, might allow them to see that the world they believe we have lost was never ours, and that the point is, after all, to change it.

> In the degree in which the active conception of knowledge prevails, and the environment is regarded as something that has to be changed in order to be truly known, men are imbued with courage, with what may almost be termed an aggressive attitude toward nature. The latter becomes plastic, something to be subjected to human uses. The moral disposition toward change is deeply modified. This loses its pathos, it ceases to be haunted with melancholy through suggesting only decay and loss. Change becomes significant of new possibilities and ends to be attained; it becomes prophetic of a better future. Change is associated with progress rather than with lapse and fall. Since changes are going on anyway, the great thing is to learn enough about them so that we [might] be able to lay hold of them and turn them in the direction of our desires. (116)

Thoughts and Things in Emersonian Perspective

Only once does Dewey presume to speak *for* a colleague in *Reconstruction in Philosophy*. It is fitting, and in view of my purposes rather convenient, that the colleague is William James and that the work cited is *Pragmatism*.[27] For in Lecture 6 of that key text, the habitat of truth becomes "a credit system" in which "ideas can only be symbols and not copies" of reality (577–79). In *The Meaning of Truth: A Sequel to Pragmatism* (1909), James himself repeatedly claims that the "pivotal part" of *Pragmatism* is this lecture—this account of the truth as the profoundly contingent or functional relation between ideas and their impending objects (823–30, 897–908, 918–36). Each time he does so, moreover, he invokes Dewey, as if the philosophical futures in which he deals will eventually require the endorsement of another "thought-speculator."

James finally turns Whitman's "lesson of reception" to account in *Pragmatism*. Here the phenomenology of the market signifies and authorizes acquiescence to, but also criticism of, the actual state of social relationships; for the "credit system" in which truth circulates now appears as evidence for the expansion of the contingent within the domain of necessity, of political economy itself. To acknowledge that expansion is to acknowledge the fruits of corporate capital; but to criticize existing modes of cognition is to criticize the actual state of social relationships, because by pragmatic criteria the evidence of cognition as such is to be found there, in its practical expression and consequences. This ambiguous stance toward the consequences of nineteenth-century history is not yet an argument about the nature of modern capitalism; but it is now more than an assumption, and it corroborates the position James sketched in the *Talks to Teachers*. Both Lewis Mumford and Richard Rorty—the early dissenter and the contemporary celebrant— overlook these critical and ambiguous dimensions of the pragmatic phenomenology. Mumford, for example, suggests that James's "persistent use of financial metaphors" indicates a certain "smell of the Gilded Age"; it seems he "was only warming over again the hash of everyday experience." Rorty similarly treats pragmatism as the final word on that extremity of history which amounts to bourgeois-liberal democracy. There is of course something to be said for their position. James does in fact grasp everyday experience, or rather its depiction in common sense, as the spontaneous, discursive elements of philosophy; he did give voice to the "moods of the dumb majority." And, like Dewey, he does find a principle of hope in the modern, liberal, broadly progressive outlook forged after the turn of the century.[28]

But I would insist that James's agenda cannot be reduced to an apology for modern capitalism, and thus to an erudite edition of commodity fetishism. I say this not because I follow the intellectual historians in assuming that he was unaware of or uninterested in the ongoing transformation of capitalism, but because I think his agenda must be understood as a vital part of that transformation. Under the sign of pragmatism, the change we know as the transition from proprietary to corporate capitalism loses its pathos; for it treats this change as significant of new possibilities and ends to be attained, not as an ending—as a point of departure rather than a destination, as a transition *to* a social order and cognitive regime in which neither self nor knowledge can be located or stabilized by reference to external necessity.

Before turning to *Pragmatism*, I want to clarify and illustrate these propositions in a way that James would, I think, approve—by invoking Emerson and Whitman. Let me say at the outset of this excursion that I do not claim that James completed his project; only we can do that. He tried to describe a cognitive regime that he believed was evident and yet unknown, inchoate, or incomplete. He tried to give form and durability to what was still shapeless and still only potentially significant in his time. He did not quite succeed because the attempt to describe the new regime as immanent in the actually existing circumstances of his time often begins to sound, at least in retrospect, like a celebration of those circumstances. At those moments, the difference or tension between the real and the rational seems to dissolve, and James appears as the jolly preacher of "pragmatic adjustment" and positive thinking. The radical critics of his time and ours take these moments as the substance of pragmatism, and accordingly dismiss it as a covertly conformist doctrine. That is a mistake, in my view; for the attempt itself—the method, not the result—is what remains significant and useful. Like Whitman, James believed that his way of knowing was the completion or elaboration of possibilities residing in actually existing circumstances; it was in that sense the determinate negation of such possibilities, that is, it contained but recast them, or preserved and annulled them. It was not, then, a radical method, for it aimed to include and transcend, not repudiate and escape, a past that was construed as both an order of ideas and an order of events. Indeed pragmatism might be characterized by its refusal to accept the division of the world into incommensurable orders of ideas and events, with their corresponding methods of logical and causal analysis.

In North America, the lineage of that refusal begins with "Nature" (1837), Emerson's first attempt at a new testament for a new age. The object of investigation here was not what we would recognize as the natural world. Instead, it was externality as such.[29] But Emerson was particularly concerned with the built environment, which he took to mean matter in the form of commodities, acting as incentive to and limit on both thought and will. So conceived, the commodity form was a labor process as well as a product of labor, a means as well as an end, an active, commercial, mechanical attitude toward things as well as things themselves (10–11). The "fearful extent and multitude of objects" (23) created under the sign of the commodity "must be ranked under this name, nature," Emerson claims, because they now compose much of what philosophy considers external to the essential or the spiritual, and thus natural (8).

But he cannot decide where to stand within this field of objects. By his account, there are only two stances available. "The sensual man conforms thought to things; the poet conforms things to his thoughts. The one esteems nature rooted and fast; the other, as fluid, and impresses his being thereon" (31). Emerson is ambivalent because the sensual man, the man who treats "the tree of the poet" as a mere "stick of timber" (9)—that is, as a commodity—still receives "an education in the great doctrine of Use." He knows: "All things with which we deal, preach to us. What is a farm but a mute gospel? The chaff and the wheat, weeds and plants, blight, rain, insects, sun,—it is a sacred emblem from the first furrows of spring to the last stack which the snow of winter overtakes in the fields. But the sailor, the shepherd, the miner, the merchant, in their several resorts, have each an experience precisely parallel and leading to the same conclusion" (26).

There is no exit from the church, in any event. "And neither can man be understood without these objects, nor these objects without man." Even so, the preaching of things has to be interpreted; for "man is an analogist, and studies relations in all objects" (19). Emerson of course wants to study and interpret these relations as if he were the poet. So he begins by stating his faith in the mundane and mechanical means by which "the world becomes, at last, only a realized will,—the double of the man" (11–12, 15, 24–25). Early on in the essay, steam-driven contraptions and legal conventions appear to be the apparatus of Spirit, even though Emerson duly notes that they express a lower order of apprehension, which, in the manner of romantic philosophy, he calls "understanding."[30] For example: "To diminish friction, [man] paves the road with iron bars, and, mounting a coach with a ship-load of men, animals, and merchandise behind him, he darts through the country, from town to town, like an eagle or a swallow through the air. By the aggregate of these aids, how is the face of the world changed, from the era of Noah to that of Napoleon!" (12).

Or again: "What disputing of prices, what reckonings of interest,—and all to form the Hand of the mind;—to instruct us that 'good thoughts are no better than good dreams, unless they be executed!' The same good office is performed by Property and its filial systems of debt and credit. . . . Whilst now it [property] is the gymnastics of the understanding, it is hiving in the foresight of the spirit, experience in profounder laws" (24).

But in the guise of the "Orphic poet" who concludes the essay, and as the author who introduces this poet in the penultimate chapter, he sounds rather doubtful about his ability to impress his being(s) on "the fearful extent and multitude of objects." He has lost his earlier faith. For example: "The world proceeds from the same spirit as the body of man. . . . But it differs from the body in one important respect. It is not, like that, now subjected to the human will" (38).

The function of the poet in "Nature" is to grasp the Spirit at work in the "natural" processes and products of the commodity form, by integrating "unrenewed understanding"—a "despotism of the senses [that] binds us to nature as if we were part of it"—and Reason, which "mars this faith" in the unity of man and nature because it "shows us nature aloof, and, as it were, afloat" (30). By recording his loss of faith in the world as "only a realized will," Emerson has, then, reenacted the history of thought as the development of reason through alienation and abstraction; he has accordingly posed the problem that poetry appears, in both senses of the word, to solve. Neither understanding nor reason, he claims, can place us in the world of commodities as if we belong there because we created it. But in the end the spirit does not move him, and cannot animate that world.

For Emerson the poet is too reasonable and too logical; he wants the repose of silence and distance, and becomes irritable because the world is still under construction. "As we degenerate, the contrast between us and our house is more evident. We are as much strangers in nature, as we are aliens from God. . . . Is not the landscape, every glimpse of which hath grandeur, a face of him? Yet this may show us what discord is between man and nature, for you cannot freely admire a noble landscape, if laborers are digging in the field hard by. The poet finds something ridiculous in his delight, until he is out of the sight of men" (39).

To be out of the sight of the people who create the landscape by their labor, by digging in the field, is to treat the thing—the landscape—as a finished world unto itself. But it is also to make of the thing an abstraction, an artistic device, a symbol "aloof, and, as it were, afloat." In other words, it is to indulge in the fetishism of commodities. Emerson has finally become a "transparent eyeball": the metaphor of vision displaces all other modes of apprehension and accordingly makes the interiors, the histories, of things invisible. The commodity form now includes only the finished product, not the labor process; so its meanings can be determined apart from, or "out of the sight" of, the laborers who made it.

We should recall, however, that Emerson did not begin here, estranged from, and practically mystified by, a commodified world. Nor is it where he would remain. As late as *The Conduct of Life* (1860), he was still striving to make poetry solve the problem of signification that neither understanding nor reason could by itself address. But by then the poetry was appended to the prose, not quoted in the body of the essays: the material and the spiritual occupied separate spheres.[31]

Meanwhile, Whitman made poetry out of the same prosaic materials that had stumped Emerson.[32] He, too, was deeply impressed by the sheer density of everyday objects and events. His catalogue of "the closest simplest things" within the "usual routine" of "Song for Occupations" goes on for four pages, listing the tools and the transactions embedded in the things as well as the things themselves (94–98). Here is how this catalogue ends:

> In them the heft of the heaviest. . . . in them far more than you
>   estimated, and far less also,
> In them, not yourself. . . . you and your soul enclose all things,
>   regardless of estimation,
> In them your themes and hints and provokers . . . if not, the whole
>   earth has no themes or hints or provokers, and
> Never had.
>
> I do not affirm what you see beyond is futile. . . . I do not advise you
>   to stop,
> I do not say leadings you thought great are not great,
> But I say that none lead to greater or sadder or happier than those
>   lead to.
>
> Will you seek far off? You surely come back at last. (98)

There are no meanings, great or small, apart from the things that we make, and that make up the world we inhabit. Our selves, even our souls, are distributed across the face of this landscape, ignoble as it may seem by comparison with what we claim to see beyond it, or with what we "seek far off" on the metaphysical frontier of symbol and Spirit. Yet Whitman is willing to endow the teeming world of objects with a weird life of its own, to take commodity fetishism as his point of departure.

> When the psalm sings instead of the singer,
> When the script preaches instead of the preacher,
> When the pulpit descends and goes instead of the carver that carved the
>   supporting desk,
> When the sacred vessels or the bits of the eucharist, or the lath and
>   plast, procreate as effectually as the young silversmiths or bakers, or
>   the masons in their overalls,
> When a university course convinces like a slumbering woman and child
>   convince,

> When the minted gold in the vault smiles like the nightwatchman's
>   daughter,
> When warrantee deeds loafe in chairs opposite and are my friendly
>   companions. . . . (98–99)

This is a world in which the symbols of religion and property have come to life. Again, it is not what we would recognize as the natural world. It is a world turned upside down, or rather inside out, by the commodity form and its attendant estrangement. And yet even when our products preach to us, as if they were the speaking subjects and we were the inanimate objects of their increasing articulation—even when the commodified world of objects obeys its own logic of reproduction, indeed begins to procreate in the form of capital—Whitman can respond without panic or resignation or bewilderment. For the reversal of cause (subject) and effect (object) impending in postartisanal market society has become the condition, not the limit, of his poem.

> When warrantee deeds loafe in chairs opposite and are my friendly
>   companions,
> I intend to reach them my hand and make as much of them as I do of
>   men and women. (99)

This is the conclusion of "Song for Occupations." Whitman has announced that to treat the symbols or representations of things as if they are themselves living things is not a mistake, so long as we recognize *our* selves in them and through them—so long as we refuse to become Orphic eyeballs, that is, so long as we refuse to produce symbols and "noble landscapes" through abstraction, by taking ourselves out of the sight of living men and women. In effect, Whitman insists that he is Emerson's "sensual man," who hears, and teaches, the mute gospel revealed in the commodity form. But he can treat the curious disjuncture between the substantial and symbolic properties of the commodity form as incentive to the production of meaning, as the stuff of poetry, because he assumes—according to the catalogue of tools and transactions which compose the "usual routine"— that both properties derive from the labor, ultimately from the very bodies, of men and women. That is why these symbols of power smile, and "loafe in chairs," and why Whitman intends to treat them not as strangers, not as the evidence of his estrangement from the "fearful extent and multitude of objects," but as friends to whom he can reach his hand. Like "the closest simplest things," he suggests, they embody images of our selves and so determine how we imagine our selves. In this sense, Whitman's understanding of things is renewed by a revision of Emerson's poetic procedure—not because he conforms thought to things, or reduces one to the other, but because he treats commodities as the embodiment of our selves, as the substantial *and* symbolic forms in which our thoughts appear to us.

Let me try to summarize the argument embedded in this excursion, and then return to James with that in mind. Emerson and Whitman establish the choices available to those who would try to get beyond the Kantian division of the world into incommensurable orders of events and ideas, through which the relation between social or historical circumstances and ethical or aesthetic principles becomes unintelligible, and finally unimportant. The "sensual man" who would conform thought to things, for example, resembles Kant's caricature of the empiricist tradition that arrived in North America as Scottish commonsense philosophy. But Emerson's poet also disturbs Kant's division of the world into mutually exclusive orders of matter and mind, which were accordingly governed by different laws. For the poet recognizes, at least at the outset, that the commodity form is both an event and an idea, an object and a symbol—a use value and an exchange value—and he treats this apparent disjuncture as the occasion for conjecture on the relation between things and thoughts. Whitman goes even further, of course, by rehabilitating the "sensual man," by making him the poet. He, too, is inspired by the apparent reversal of cause (subject) and effect (object) residing in the proliferation of the commodity form—the same reversal that Kant took as his rationale for dividing the world and reinstating an inviolable sphere of subjectivity.[33] Indeed Whitman treats this reversal as his point of departure, but refuses to accept its consequences as anything less than a promising opportunity for thought, for poetry, for politics. He treats the symptoms of commodity fetishism as the elements of a cure.

Both poets move beyond the Kantian divide, then, and propose to reopen if not redraw the space between the order of ideas and the order of events, between thoughts and things. They constitute the North American version of romantic philosophy. But, here as elsewhere, that is a tradition in which stances toward or within the "fearful extent and multitude of objects" are extremely diverse. Emerson's oscillation between the "sensual man" and the poet—his attempt to integrate the three modes of apprehension—recapitulates this diversity, and reminds us that romantic responses to postartisanal market society can take the form of repulsion or, what amounts to the same thing, repose through the abstraction of noble landscapes from their social context. It might also remind us that commodities continue to proliferate and circulate, and the estrangement of market society remains intact, if our response is either repulsion or repose. Whitman would remind us in any event. For he begins where Emerson did, but he denies us these romantic responses. He forces us to treat thoughts and things as indissolubly related, and to treat the commodity form as the site of the transactions between them. In short, Whitman demands that we treat the phenomenology of the market as the phenomenology of spirit. By doing so, he "challenged the abnormal dignity of American letters," as Van Wyck Brooks put it in 1915, and "precipitated the American character."[34]

Even before Brooks, James understood Whitman's post-Kantian yet unromantic response to the commodity form, and tried to make it systematic without resorting to Hegel. Unlike Charles Peirce, he never did invoke the great dialectician except to ridicule the dialectic.[35] But James did grasp the difference between Emerson and Whitman, and used it to remind himself that the latter's stance within "the fearful extent and multitude of objects" could be interpreted as pure tolerance. And he did finally seize on the universal commodity—money—as his indispensable metaphor. In that sense, he did develop the argument Hegel introduced in *The Phenomenology of Spirit*, to the effect that the "harmonious unity" of truth cannot "remain detached from diversity, like a finished article from the instrument that shapes it." Hegel shows that if "to know something falsely means that knowledge is not adequate to, is not on equal terms with, its substance," then all knowledge, every truth, requires falsehood—the disjuncture of symbol and object, say, or of thoughts and things—as the necessary condition of its attainment. The ideal, the harmonious unity, or the impending truth of ethical principles, must then be located in the divisions of time, in historical circumstances. But, as we have seen, this argument turns on the metaphor of money. "Truth and falsehood as commonly understood belong to those sharply defined ideas which claim a completely fixed nature of their own, one standing in solid isolation on this side, the other on that, without any community between them. Against that view it must be pointed out, that truth is not like stamped coin that is issued ready from the mint and so can be taken up and used." Truth is instead like modern surrogates for money, like securities that preserve the original principal by enlarging on it. "The false is no longer false as a moment of the true."[36] James understood this duplicity and contingency of the truth better than anyone else, precisely because the commodity form animated his language and thought. Of course he claimed to have learned the lesson from Whitman and his fellow poets, not from philosophers. But then Hegel claimed a similarly literary lineage. He, too, was trying to finish philosophy.

Let us turn, finally, to James's "lesson of reception." He insists that pragmatism has been available for centuries as a model of mind, language, or thought; but he also claims that until the turn of the twentieth century, it could only be glimpsed as a radical alternative to received tradition (508). Now it is on the verge of becoming a characteristic of Western culture because it can accommodate the new facts of everyday experience, or rather give new significance to that experience. By 1898, "the times seemed ripe for its reception"; a decade later, "the term applies itself to a number of tendencies that hitherto have lacked a collective name" (507). Indeed pragmatism threatens to become the mainstream, the new mode of cognition. "Not until in our time has it generalized itself, become conscious of a universal mission, pretended to a conquering destiny" (508). But what happened? Why did no one notice when Peirce outlined the basic principles of pragmatism in 1878 (507)? What order of events validated his strictly semiotic notion of self and knowledge?[37]

James does not periodize pragmatism except to announce that the times are ripe for it. But he does make "persistent use of financial metaphors" and does therefore situate his agenda within the vernacular of the transition question that confronted his generation. He repeatedly refers to the "cash-value" of words and ideas, as if there is a bottom line—a foundation of truth, a point of rest—in the ledger that records our intellectual transactions; in a similar vein he also cites "our general obligation to do what pays" (e.g., 509, 519, 576–87). Yet he emphatically rejects the notion that the function of mind or consciousness is to copy or represent a fixed, external reality and, by implication, the notion that money is only a means of exchange, that is, a set of symbols that necessarily corresponds to objects "out there" in the "real world" constituted by the products of labor. In effect James is simply claiming that money, as redefined by modern business enterprise, is an appropriate metaphor for mind, language, and thought. For example: "You must bring out of each word its practical cash-value, set it at work within the stream of your experience. It appears less as a solution, then, than as a program for more work, and more particularly as an indication of the ways in which existing realities may be *changed*" (509). But notice that the "cash-value" of language resides in the surplus—not the equivalence or the equilibrium—it produces. This surplus must be reinvested if it is to make a difference, that is, if it is to bear more interest in the future by changing existing realities. "All human thinking gets discursified; we exchange ideas; we lend and borrow verifications, get them from one another by means of social intercourse. All truth thus gets verbally built out, stored up, and made available for every one" (579).

So the financial metaphors lead toward the "credit system" of Lecture 6, in which truths become the provisional representations of moments that do not yet exist "out there" in the "real world," in which speculation as such therefore becomes the normal procedure of consciousness or thought, and in which crisis is signaled by a generalized demand for immediate verification—or redemption in cash—of the symbolic tokens of truth. "Truth lives, in fact, for the most part on a credit system. Our thoughts and beliefs 'pass,' so long as nothing challenges them, just as bank-notes pass so long as nobody refuses them. But this all points to direct face-to-face verification somewhere, without which the fabric of truth collapses like a financial system with no cash-basis whatever. You accept my verification of one thing, I yours of another. We trade on each other's truth" (576–77).

James never apologizes for his financial metaphors because he sees more than the metaphysical pathos that many European philosophers and American social scientists recognized in the contingency, mutability, and "merely psychological reality" introduced and enforced by a modern "credit economy." In fact he welcomes what Georg Simmel, the preeminent European philosopher of money, described as "the contemporary historical dissolution of all that is substantial, absolute and eternal in the flux of things."[38] For in that dissolution James, like Dewey, finds both promise and verification of a mode of cognition in which the distinction between knower and known, self and other, subject and object—or the relation between personality and property, freedom and necessity, consumption and production—must be re-created and embodied in time and in new social forms, not assumed to be fixed, or given by the past. The reality of the romance of the self foretold by Hegel and Whitman is written in this new political economy of the sign, in this radically contingent "credit system" constituted by corporate capitalism. Here symbols become fundamental realities because they correspond to nothing more—or less—than purposes and possibilities to be tested by action in the present; they matter because they make a difference. "Everything here is plastic" (513).[39]

James calls pragmatism a new name for an old way of thinking because he wants it to be recognized as a cognitive regime that both preserves and annuls the past. By his account, it includes earlier regimes by providing answers to questions they raised but could not answer, and moves beyond them by completing them, by raising new questions and designating new facts. "New truth is always a go-between," he notes, "a smoother-over of transitions. It marries old opinion to new fact so as ever to show a minimum of jolt, a maximum of continuity" (513). In this sense, it does not repudiate the past in the name of present doctrine; instead it recasts the relation between past and present doctrine and allows each to invigorate the other. Thus pragmatism is new truth par excellence; for it "unstiffens all our theories, limbers them up and sets them to work. Being nothing essentially new, it harmonizes with many ancient philosophic tendencies. It agrees with nominalism for instance, in always appealing to particulars; with utilitarianism in emphasizing practical aspects; with positivism in its disdain for verbal solutions, useless questions and metaphysical abstractions" (510). Lectures 1 through 5 demonstrate this inclusive character of pragmatism—"this mediating way of thinking" (504)—and clear the stage for the more positive and detailed statement that follows in Lectures 6 through 8.

For James, as for Dewey, the new mode of cognition is either inscribed in the actual state of social relationships or it does not exist. If it does not reside in and flow from these relationships, and so does not have, or become, practical effects in and on the world, it cannot be a genuine, inclusive alternative to existing modes of cognition. "There can *be* no difference anywhere that does n't *make* a difference elsewhere—no difference in abstract truth that does n't express itself in a difference in concrete fact and in conduct consequent upon that fact, imposed on somebody, somehow, somewhere, and somewhen" (508). Since ideas are themselves "parts of our experience," they can "become true just in so far as they help us to get into satisfactory relation with other parts of our experience" (512). Yet James does not bother to demonstrate such propositions by reference to these other parts of experience, by recourse to historical evidence; instead he assumes that his audience has already read the "dissolution of all that is substantial, absolute and eternal" in the flux of a "credit economy" and that it requires not a way of reinstating what has dissolved but a way of expressing, and using, the new relations between obviously and increasingly contingent areas, moments, and elements of social relationships. His "mediating way of thinking" opens, then, onto the future as well as the past; for it allows his listeners to acknowledge and act on the characteristic changes of their time—to treat such change as the condition and template, not the negation, of new truth. But the condensation of historical circumstances in the metaphors of the money question seems almost to deprive his proposed transactions of the cash-basis they need.

The practical test of "this mediating way of thinking," in which James does place contemporary ideas in relation to "other parts of our experience," is not to be found in *The Meaning of Truth* or *A Pluralistic Universe*. In these works, both published in 1909, he is defending the positions taken up in

Pragmatism and is doing so by interrogating modes of cognition from the singular standpoint of the philosopher who admits to the current dilemmas of philosophy. He continues to ignore the typical question of post-Kantian philosophy—how do I know what I know?—and instead asks, what do you say knowledge is, how do you say it, and what, if anything, follows when you do? But the answers are incentives to the revision of philosophical discourse. In "The Moral Equivalent of War" (1910), by contrast, James actually moves beyond this discourse and treats ideas as the embodiment of collective attitudes toward, and social experience of, present circumstances and future possibilities. It is the last installment in his purchase of—or rather on—a grammar that would unify the vocabularies of science and metaphysics, of politics and philosophy, of production and cognition.[40]

Here James suggests that war, "the romance of history," becomes a kind of psychological residue and cultural imperative insofar as the realm of necessity, and with it the need for strenuous exertion in the name of some external, anonymously defined purpose, recede before a "pacific cosmopolitan industrialism" (275–85). By this account, the *idea* of war preserves the extremities of human nature and effort that are no longer necessary, or even possible, under the aegis of modern capitalism; its horrors "are a cheap price to pay for rescue from the only alternative supposed, of a world of clerks and teachers, of co-education and zo-ophily, of 'consumer's leagues' and 'associated charities,' of industrialism unlimited, and feminism unabashed" (276). In other words, the idea of war keeps the "irremediable flatness" of Chautauqua at bay. It is the symbolic landscape on which men can still admire the jagged edges of existence.

To the extent that emancipation from the political-economic imperatives of the past is a genuine cause for concern because it dissolves or challenges the existing, external sources of social structure and individual character—and accordingly demands articulation of new imperatives—the "fear of emancipation" will probably take this weirdly regressive form, that is, this masculine, militaristic form. "The transition to a 'pleasure-economy' may be fatal to a being wielding no powers of defence against its disintegrative influences. If we speak of the *fear of emancipation from the fear-regime*, we put the whole situation into a single phrase; fear regarding ourselves now taking the place of the ancient fear of the enemy" (281).[41] The "hard externality" in which the Other subsists must be reconstituted and reinstated in the idea of war; for it can no longer be imputed to or derived from that area of life and language defined by political economy.

In their "unwillingness to see the supreme theatre of human strenuousness closed" (282), the militarists resemble the man who escaped the Chautauquan enclosure. But of course the content of their romance is repugnant to James. "When whole nations are the armies, and the science of destruction vies in intellectual refinement with the sciences of production, I see that war becomes absurd and impossible from its own monstrosity" (286). He argues their case because his object is to convince his fellow pacifists that the desires of men emancipated from external necessity, from its designation of the Other, will reappear as militarism unless they find an outlet in the idea as well as the experience of socialism—unless socialists rewrite their utopia to accommodate the romance of history now effectively embodied only in the *idea* of war. "I devoutly believe in the reign of peace," James declares, "and in the gradual advent of some sort of a socialistic equilibrium" (286). But he also notes that the extant argument for both reproduces the insipid realism of Chautauqua.

> So long as anti-militarists propose no substitute for war's disciplinary function, no *moral equivalent* of war, analogous, as one might say, to the mechanical equivalent of heat, so long they fail to realize the full inwardness of the situation. And as a rule they do fail. The duties, penalties, and sanctions pictured in the utopias they paint are all too weak and tame to touch the military-minded. . . . our socialistic peace-advocates all believe absolutely in this world's values; and instead of the fear of the Lord and the fear of the enemy, the only fear they reckon with is the fear of poverty if one be lazy. (283–84)

It seems that the socialists take for granted the values produced by a "pacific cosmopolitan industrialism," and seek merely to extend them in space and time. The real opposition and danger to their project apparently derive not from "the luxurious classes," who remain above the fray (290), but from those with "no powers of defence against [the] disintegrative influences" residing in the "transition to a 'pleasure-economy'"—residing, that is, in the rapid expansion or reconstruction of social roles, spaces, and selves determined by the ongoing transformation of capitalism. In this account, a socialist project bound by the categories of necessity, production, and class would be neither reactionary nor revolutionary; instead it would embrace a future to be decided "only gradually and insipidly by 'evolution'" (282). It would in that sense become an adjunct or imitation of "pacific cosmopolitan industrialism," indistinguishable, in the long run, from the project of industrial*ists*.

James's alternative to this realistic sublimation of socialism is to resurrect what his audience as well as later historians would recognize as a form of republicanism, through which "a stable system of morals of civic honor builds itself up" (289). His via media is, then, neither a simple projection of actually existing capitalism (i.e., "pacific cosmopolitan industrialism") nor an outright rejection of the antimodern desires unleashed by and directed against "the transition to a 'pleasure-economy.' " It is an attempt to mediate between them, to contain them both in a future that is greater than the sum of these parts. James's specific proposal sounds as if it were uttered quite recently, but not just because his late-twentieth-century listeners can remember the Peace Corps, Vista, or their precursors from the New Deal; for he treats the category of necessity—or the struggle against nature that seems for better or worse to have defined *human* nature—as something that we must now reinvent, reinstate, and formalize in a kind of political ritual that has cultural, not economic, purposes. In other words, he assumes that the cultural salience of the realm of necessity is something that has to be re-created in time because it is no longer self-evident. It is not invisible; but it is now fully implicated in the historical dissolution of all that is substantial, absolute, and *external* in the flux of things modern.

There is nothing to make one indignant in the mere fact that life is hard, that men should toil and suffer pain. The planetary conditions once for all are such, and we can stand it. But that so many men, by mere accident of birth and opportunity, should have a life of *nothing else* but toil and pain and hardness and inferiority imposed upon them, . . .—*this* is capable of arousing indignation in reflective minds. . . . If now—and this is my idea—there were, instead of military conscription a conscription of the whole youthful population to form for a certain number of years a part of the army enlisted against *Nature*, the injustice would tend to be evened out, and numerous other goods to the commonwealth would follow. The military ideals of hardihood and discipline would be wrought into the growing fibre of the people; no one would remain blind, as the luxurious classes now are blind, to man's relations to the globe he lives on, and to the permanently sour and hard foundations of his higher life. To coal and iron mines, to freight trains, to fishing fleets in December, to dishwashing, clothes-washing, and window-washing, to road-building and tunnel-making, to foundries and stoke-holes, and to the frames of skyscrapers, would our gilded youth be drafted off, according to their choice, to get the childishness knocked out of them, and to come back into society with healthier sympathies and soberer ideas. . . . Such a conscription, with the state of public opinion that would have required it, and the moral fruits it would bear, would preserve in the midst of a pacific civilization the manly virtues which the military party is so afraid of seeing disappear in peace. (289–91)

"And to the frames of skyscrapers": James finally returns to the scene and the narrative standpoint of the romance he wrote (and interpreted) for his audience of college students, the "gilded youth" of the 1890s. Now he speaks in the same voice to his comrades within the socialist movement of the early twentieth century, urging them to visit the same scene and see it as he did, as necessary, heroic, and significant—but as only part of a larger story that has yet to be written.

Modern Subjectivity and Moral Philosophy

Before I turn to the composition and recomposition of that story in the prose works of the young intellectuals—those who saw themselves as characters in the narrative James borrowed from Whitman—I want to sketch the kinds of selfhood and knowledge posited in pragmatism. By doing so, I can provisionally summarize the reconstruction of subjectivity residing in the transition from proprietary to corporate capitalism, and explain why the personality sanctioned by pragmatism seems both sensible and scandalous, both inevitable and impossible.

Perhaps the best way to compress what I want to say about this personality is to note that it is postmodern in the strictest sense. I mean that its theoreticians do not believe that thoughts and things inhabit different ontological orders: they do not acknowledge an external or natural realm of objects, of things-in-themselves, which is ultimately impervious to, or fundamentally different than, thought or mind or consciousness. Accordingly they escape the structure of meanings built around modern subjectivity, which presupposes the self's separation or cognitive distance from this reified realm of objects. More to the point, these theoreticians are not necessarily trapped between the epistemological extremes enabled by modern subjectivity—that is, between *romanticism*, which typically glorifies the "organic" or "subjective" inner self as against the "mechanical" or "objective" circumstances that constitute outward existence; and *positivism*, which typically celebrates the increasing density of that external, thing-like realm of objects as the evidence of progress toward the species' mastery of nature.[42]

Just as modern subjectivity denies any continuity between mind and matter, so it denies, or cannot grasp, any continuity between past and present. For within its structure of meanings, the present always appears as radical departure from the past: the romantics feel they are exiled, and the positivists know they are liberated, from the more transcendent, transparent, or traditional past. Pragmatism gets us beyond this temporal discontinuity of modern subjectivity by positing a personality that is embedded in historical time, and thus is better situated than its predecessors to assess present circumstances and future possibilities in light of—not necessarily in rebellion against—past choices. But note what follows: the postmodern personality sanctioned by pragmatism is a *more* promising bearer of an intelligible morality than the progeny of Enlightenment, simply because it can treat inherited standards, customs, and practices—and the communities that made them possible—as something more than an external constraint on its own content, development, or fulfillment.

To those who assume that postmodernism and moral relativism can and should be equated, this conclusion will sound perverse. To those who assume that, since the advent of capitalism, and more particularly since the emergence of modern-industrial society, the integrity and moral capacity of the human personality have been threatened if not destroyed by economic growth and development, it will sound preposterous. And to those who assume that the articulation of genuine ethical principles and the conduct of moral philosophy require detachment or abstraction from the temporal and the contingent—that is, from particular historical circumstances and communities—it will sound naive.[43] I need, then, to interrogate these assumptions before I can elaborate on the conclusion they would disallow.

I would begin by asking how and why they came to be assumptions. Why does the moral personality or philosopher appear in each case as a figure that remains outside of or immune to the corrupting effects of historical time? If it is self-evident that morality cannot exist independently of the historical contexts in which motives, intentions, and actions become intelligible to both agents and interpreters, how can this suprahistorical figure serve the purposes of moral philosophy? The point of asking these questions, I would emphasize, is not to discover a "mistake" in the construction of the moral personality, but to understand why its architects did not (and do not) see the obvious absence of a temporal dimension as a defect in their design.

Certainly the classical theoreticians of the political order realized in the polis did not see it as a defect. They defined political order as the characteristic innovation of the human species, but believed that it could be maintained only so long as it was projected into space and, conversely, that insofar as it became subject to the vicissitudes of time, it would revolve in a predictable yet irrational cycle of corrupt regimes until conquered by an external enemy. These vicissitudes were consequences of what we would call the division of labor; the dynamic principle of historical time was *commerce*, or, in modern parlance, economic development. So conceived, the significant consequences of historical time were the proliferation of economic interests and social strata, the accumulation and concentration of wealth, the increasing complexities of culture, the appearance of luxury—everything, in other words, that would encourage individuals to forget their obligations to the political community (or to meet them by hiring mercenaries) and to revel instead in the idiocy of private life. To forget or to hire out one's political obligations was to promote the disintegration of one's moral personality as well as the community, however, because that personality derived from, and was inconceivable without, one's location as citizen in the political space of the polis; only there did the recognition of justice, of the common good—which required both attention to and abstraction from one's private interests—become a practical and educative problem for each individual. Thus the consequences of historical time, the products of development, were personal as well as political; indeed the personal was the political, and vice versa, simply because the theoreticians of the polis could not imagine a personality prior to, or detached from, the political community. That is why they could make no meaningful distinction between moral and political philosophy.[44]

The divergence of moral and political philosophy characteristic of Hellenistic cultures, a divergence registered particularly in Stoicism, rabbinic Judaism, and early Christianity, would, then, signify the utter collapse of communities that could serve as plausible standards of political theory and practice—not the disenchantment of the "Machiavellian Moment" or the advent of modernity. These forms of what Hegel called the "unhappy consciousness" are nevertheless prototypes of modern alienation; for they presuppose the absence or irrelevance of *politics*. But they recapitulate the classical treatment of historical time as the venue of the irrational or the ironic. The high theorists of the Christian church, for example, did try to find providential meaning in history, and did define the profane order of events as a more or less linear movement toward apocalypse if not redemption. Even so, they could not specify the relation between the sacred and the profane, the universal and the particular, the ethical and the historical, with any precision or clarity; it necessarily remained a mystery of faith.[45]

The crucifixion eventually became the emblem of that mystery. It functioned not so much as evidence of a unique event in the past—of an intersection between heaven and earth—as figure of an impending future. It was the "occasion" for hope because it was the representation of a promise still to be kept in God's own good time, according to a calendar that human beings must find indecipherable. In this sense, Christendom made the received tradition more poignant. The past now weighed like a nightmare on the minds of the living; for the passage of time signified both the ineradicable division of heaven and earth and the closer approach of the end of days, when life would proceed on earth as it is in heaven.

But this may be a way of saying that the retreat from politics led by the early Christian church made historical time matter in ways it could not and did not under the sign of the polis. Consider the profound change of moral season promoted by the spread of the new Christian doctrines and institutions, through which the ethical principles embodied in the *Iliad* and in Hellenistic cultures were finally repudiated. I do not mean that early converts to Christianity loved their neighbors, or became meek and child-like, or divested themselves of all earthly possessions; merely that they believed they should do so, and that their beliefs were cause and effect of the eclipse of antiquity. The principles that animated these beliefs, and that regulated the broader change of moral season, were equality and charity. In the early church, these principles were integrated by letting the simple criterion of need—as against the rival criteria of birth, office, income, strength, intelligence—govern the distribution of the world's goods. But as that church became a going concern of the postrepublican world, the criterion of need became politically problematic. In the absence of ways to deliver the goods to everyone, that is, in a world permeated by the church but dominated by disease, hunger, and poverty, this criterion had to become local or eschatological. In other words, it had to become either the creed of communities that had withdrawn from the larger society, or, what is practically the same thing, the ideological correlate of faith in an impending apocalypse. The more worldly or realistic alternative to these radical positions (e.g., the alternative outlined by Clement of Alexandria) was a kind of positivist piety that presupposed the permanence of the poor. From each position, however, even from that of the realists, the most mundane of historical circumstances—the distribution of goods—acquired a moral significance it could not have had for the educated observer of late antiquity.[46]

So it was the deepening tension between estrangement from and engagement with the world that characterized the Christian attitude toward historical time. If one could not join God on earth, in this life, then prayer, study, and ritual could supplement but not supplant the love of one's neighbors. The erotic imperative of the Christian dispensation accordingly became worldly or "horizontal" without losing its transcendent meanings—to love God was to love those who must die before they wake in his heaven. Withdrawal from their world in the name of God became sinful. Meanwhile, however, the church fathers were perfecting a figural interpretation of pagan life and history, through which they established "vertical" and providential—not temporal or causal—connections between worldly events. These connections displaced the very proximity of the profane by deducing the particularities of place, time, and cause from the universal designated as divine providence. Ultimately they became the clerisy's warrant for treating earthly existence as prelude to real life in heaven, and for accepting Augustine's claim that "true justice resides only in that commonwealth whose founder and governor is Christ"—only in the City of God, that is, where existential relations of place, time, and cause could not matter, and where the choices and conflicts that require articulation in political terms could not emerge.[47]

This tension between estrangement and engagement was finally resolved by the Protestants' repudiation of the figural currency in which the church had circulated its promises. Protestants understood the value of symbols, as the controversy over transubstantiation demonstrates. Even so, they wanted to reinstate the immediacy of primitive faith—not because they were fond of the simple life but because they assumed that reason and its symbolic or linguistic results were fully implicated in and corrupted by the original fall from grace. To rely on reason, they claimed, was to depend on the Devil for deliverance from evil. So they insisted on a more transparent or spontaneous relation between symbols and events, between words and things, than a figural interpretation of their world would allow. Like the new men of science who believed that the condition of knowledge was their conscious manipulation of the world through experiment, the Protestants believed that the condition of grace was their active production of the world through work—through a "calling." Truth was not something always waiting to be discovered as it was in the beginning; it was to be created and tested by one's expenditure of energy in the here and now.[48]

Of course this kind of direct engagement with the world could become, or permit, a new form of estrangement. To take up a calling in a world that was beyond redemption, for example, was to surrender this life in the name of the next. But that is precisely what Martin Luther demanded of his followers. The world is ruled by the Devil, he claimed, and proved it by reference to the demonic power of money. "Usury lives securely and rages, as if he were God and lord in all lands. . . . In truth the traffic in interest is a sign and a token that the world is sold into the Devil's slavery by grievous sins." More emphatically: "Money is the word of the Devil, through which he creates all things, the way God created through the true word." Merely to follow one's calling was, then, "to take upon oneself and bear the hate of the Devil, of the world, of the flesh, of sins and of death," as Luther reminded his more zealous comrades. "It is not necessary for you, like monks and hermits, to take up a special cross: remain with people and in your calling; there the Devil and the World will lay cross enough upon you."[49]

To engage this world—to be in *and* of it—was to estrange oneself from the paradigm of the moral personality residing elsewhere, in a timeless kingdom of God. The alternative was to be in but not *of* this world, to be "divided up in time," as Augustine put it. To secure the integrity or autonomy of the soul by surrendering only the body to the tyranny of external circumstances was, however, to claim that an unbound interior constitutes the genuine self, the authentically moral personality: *in interiore homine habitat veritas*. As Luther explained this Augustinian principle: "When we consider the inner, spiritual man, and see what belongs to him if he is to be a free and devout Christian, in fact and in name, it is evident that, whatever the name, no outer thing can make him either free or religious. For his religion and freedom . . . are neither bodily nor outward."[50]

Now to constitute the genuine self in this way, as an unbound interior, was to leave the tyranny of external circumstances intact, and to make morality as such both radical—it becomes critique of all "outer things"—and unintelligible, by draining it of any particular, historical content, by placing its possibility beyond, or rather before and after, the accretions of historical time. In this sense, Protestantism is the paradigm of pure modernity, and deserves all the attention it has received from the minions of Marx, Weber, and Freud; for it produces an "empty subjectivity" by detaching self-determination from any particular social content. That is why Luther's criticism of sixteenth-century marriage laws sounds as if it were written in the late eighteenth century by an admirer of Jean-Jacques Rousseau. "There is no hope of a cure unless the whole of the laws made by men, no matter what their standing, are repealed once for all. When we have recovered the freedom of the Gospel, we should judge and rule in accordance with it in every respect." This is strong medicine prescribed by a religious fanatic, not a doctor of philosophy. But Kant, that most rational admirer of Rousseau, wrote almost the same prescription in his *Critique of Pure Reason* (1781). "For whereas, so far as nature is concerned, experience supplies the rule and is the source of truth, in respect to the moral law it is, alas, the mother of illusion! Nothing is more reprehensible than to derive the laws prescribing what *ought to be done* from what *is done*, or to impose upon them the limits by which the latter is circumscribed." No wonder Hegel called Luther the founder of modern philosophy, and tried to find a way beyond the "maximum of terror" embodied in Kant's enlightened account of modern subjectivity.[51]

I have sketched Hegel's new departure elsewhere in this book.[52] Here I want only to suggest that its novelty and power reside in the attempt to treat ethical principles and historical circumstances as commensurable, indeed as immanently related, forms of existence or expression. To put it in the terms of the questions with which I began this inquiry, Hegel treats historical time as the necessary condition for the emergence and realization of the moral personality—that is, of self-consciousness and self-determination. So he is neither a romantic nor a positivist. He plans an alternative to the "system of needs" developing in civil society, where Luther had seen the Devil at work, and where the romantics would find only Philistines; but he builds it on this very site of pure modernity. He also demonstrates that the elaborate empiricism of the Scottish Enlightenment is profoundly metaphysical, thus useless to those interested only in the observable facts of the here and the now; but his critique of the romantics is animated by a materialism more radical than their positivist opponents could imagine. All subsequent attempts to get beyond these epistemological extremes, including the attempt we know as pragmatism, will therefore sound more or less Hegelian.[53]

In fact, Hegel had already repaired the "chief defect" of materialism as Marx defined it in 1845, in the first thesis on Feuerbach. "The object, reality, sensuousness is conceived only in the form of the object [of] perception, but not as sensuous human activity, [not as] practice, not subjectively. . . . Feuerbach wants sensuous objects actually different from thought objects: but he does not comprehend human activity itself as objective." Marx notwithstanding, Hegel did conceive the realm of objects "subjectively," as human activity—as the incessant articulation of desire through work, not merely the products of work—and did comprehend language "objectively," as a deep historical structure that "posits" subjectivity because it *creates* speakers (by using those conventions of speech which they did not themselves invent, they become intelligible speakers), and yet could not exist without them. Thought and will were moments on a continuum, according to Hegel, not different human faculties. If we were to translate that proposition into an American idiom, we would probably say what James did, that if thoughts and things are not quite interchangeable parts of experience, they are certainly to be defined by the contexts in which they acquire meaning. "In one group it ['a given undivided bit of experience'] figures as a thought, in another group as a thing." Or, if we were feeling even more provocative, we would repeat after Peirce, who was paraphrasing Hegel: "Matter is effete mind."[54]

The difficulty of appreciating Hegel's new departure—and of describing the postmodern personality sanctioned by pragmatism as a moral personality—derives, I think, from our inability to imagine an alternative to modern subjectivity which forfeits neither modernity nor subjectivity. The contemporary heirs of the original romantics are those radicals and reactionaries whose critique of "liberal society" and "consumer capitalism" in the name of genuine selfhood usually recapitulates the erudite Luddism of high literary modernists; the heirs of the original positivists are those liberals and conservatives whose defense of private property and "free markets" in the name of individual initiative or autonomy actually promotes the growth of large corporate bureaucracies. One camp would forfeit modernity, the other would forfeit subjectivity; each would do so in the hope of preserving the possibility of a moral personality.

This impasse is testimony to our unconscious embrace of the attitudes toward history residing in previous constructions of that personality. In other words, we are still prisoners of the past inscribed in these constructions; for we still assume that the integrity of the self is threatened, or dissolved, by extension in time as well as space, by historical development. Like Kant's predecessors from the classical and Christian eras, we identify the dynamic principle of historical time as commerce or economic development; so we begin to associate historical time with the development of capitalism, and eventually equate the dynamic and the demonic according to strict Lutheran usage. Like Kant himself, we assume that a rational and secular foundation for morality is secured insofar as we can not only imagine but enact what is impossible—that is, an extrasituational or unconditional moral imperative, which, in turn, presupposes a disembodied self, an Archimedean point undefiled by earthly relations of place, time, and cause.

The apparent exception to this Archimedean rule is the foundation built on the figure of the freeholder, the yeoman, the citizen-soldier, whose freedom (from external domination) and moral personality were guaranteed by his legal title and active relation to real or productive property. The yeoman was a revolutionary figure in the great transition from feudalism to capitalism because he insisted that necessity and freedom were compatible, that freedom could not mean the abolition of all situation, of all particular circumstances or worldly conditions. But the yeoman served as the paradigm of the moral personality precisely because he escaped the vicissitudes of historical time; and he made his escape—he remained innocent of corruption, conflict, even of culture—by virtue of his extension in space, his property. The ancient republic was now reduced to this new man. So long as he occupied his unique *place*, in relation to his property, he could not be corrupted, and a rational, secular foundation for morality could be located in an extrapolitical sphere of noncoercive social relations conducive to self-determination. Hegel suggested as much in his studies of civil society: "Property is the first embodiment of freedom." He went on to argue, however, that by "first embodiment" he meant a first approximation—something like an overture or introduction to a long and unfinished composition. In other words, the history of freedom was complicated but not completed by the new "system of needs" developing within civil society.[55]

The revolutionary figure who presided over this "first embodiment of freedom" still haunts our historical imagination. But he typically appears in the mutilated form of the uncivilized entrepreneur—the Philistine—because the extraeconomic positions and purposes of the original bourgeois citizen seem quaint in the twentieth-century context of corporate capitalism. To be sure, those positions and purposes looked problematic to knowledgeable observers long before the rise of the industrial working class and the modern corporation revised the relation between property and personality. For the meaning of private property was the object of political debate and juridical revision during and after the great transition to modernity in the form of market society, ca. 1400–1800. Since property served in theory and practice as the foundation of the moral personality discovered in that transition, the subject in question, then and thereafter, was the meaning of the modern self, the moral capacity of the bourgeois individual. But my point is that the resources denominated as property cannot function as the groundwork of the moral personality in any meaningful sense if large corporate bureaucracies, not individuals, can establish control of those resources. Insofar as artificial corporate persons can establish (not merely assert) their control of such resources—we should remember that their ability to do so was not clearly decided at the law and in the larger culture until the second decade of the twentieth century—the moral purpose of "economic" activity becomes unintelligible, and intellectuals, among others, acquire a rationale for rethinking the relations between economy, morality, and personality.[56]

Let me try another approach to this same point. The relation between space and time represented by the figure of the freeholder, the yeoman, and the citizen-soldier—that is, the repression or displacement of historical time by space, by new frontiers—cracks under the weight of industrialization in the nineteenth century, and finally collapses with the advent of corporate-industrial capitalism, ca. 1890–1920. At that moment of collapse, the choices available to those who would reconstitute the moral personality were to situate it in historical time—to define the integrity of the self as the consequence of development because it is the activity by which the parts of experience are integrated—or to reclaim the extratemporal space in which the figure of the freeholder, the yeoman, and the citizen-soldier once moved freely and meant more than business. Pragmatism as James sketched it was one version, or effect, of the first choice; so, too, was naturalism as Dreiser defined it. Populism was one version, or effect, of the second choice; high literary modernism was another, although it was not convened until poets cast themselves in the role once reserved for the Gothic freeholder.[57]

In view of the circumstances, which include the available intellectual alternatives, James's choice seems perfectly sensible. But of course it is also scandalous because, from the standpoint of the received tradition, it entails strictly situational ethics. Pragmatists cannot imagine a disembodied self, an Archimedean point undefiled by earthly relations of place, time, and cause; so they cannot imagine an extrasituational or unconditional moral imperative. According to their critics, moral relativism—pure subjectivity—must follow. These critics argue that genuine morality consists of claims (or rules) about what ought to be done which can be generalized beyond any given situation, beyond what is done in that particular historical circumstance.[58] The personality they presuppose as the agent of genuinely moral claims must, then, lack a temporal dimension; indeed that moral personality must occupy, or amount to, an extratemporal space. The cartographers who draw this inner space by intricate inference—these are mainly philosophers—will call it thought, mind, or consciousness. Most other academics and intellectuals will probably call it something else (reason, art, law, culture, personality, human nature, etc.) but will nonetheless use the map because they assume it represents real and significant boundaries between thoughts and things. They will also assume that to dispense with the map, as pragmatists propose, is to adopt the antimetaphysical mechanics of positivism or utilitarianism, and accordingly to preclude any radical criticism of the world as it exists.

The argument between pragmatists and their critics will tend, therefore, to sound like a quarrel between positivists and romantics, especially since the critics themselves typically believe that modern subjectivity contains or exhausts the possibilities of genuine selfhood. If we suppose, however, that pragmatism began as a way of drawing on and arguing with both positivism and romanticism, then we can listen differently, from the beginning, to what the pragmatists have to say. We may finally decide that we are not convinced; but we will know that we have heard something new. When James talks, for example, we will be able to hear an attempt to transcend modern subjectivity, which is necessarily an attempt to redesign the moral personality, the genuine self, by giving it the temporal dimension it so obviously lacked. Of course Hegel had a similar agenda, as Dewey kept reminding his readers until he had crafted his own; so this attempt is not wholly original. It is nevertheless new in an American context because it works, in every sense, by recuperating historical time and past ideas—by insisting on the temporal continuity that modern subjectivity and its constituents cannot imagine.

Surely that inclusive spirit of pragmatism is foreign to the posture of those who defend it by claiming its immunity from the canonical texts, issues, and questions of traditional philosophy or epistemology—by claiming, in effect, that pragmatism and its rivals are simply incommensurable.[59] For to adopt this posture is to agree with those who assume either that the redesign of the moral personality in pragmatism signifies the surrender of subjectivity as such, or that the absence in pragmatism of what philosophers traditionally identified as morality's agent must mean the absence of morality in a world interpreted by pragmatists. These are assumptions that James and Dewey neither made nor endorsed. Poor Dewey spent the late 1920s trying to prove that point to young intellectuals like Lewis Mumford.[60] But James did not receive much criticism along these lines from Mumford's generation of cultural radicals—at least while he was alive he did not—and so did not have to defend himself against the broadcast charge of "utilitarianism," by which the radicals meant the supposed subordination in pragmatism of values to technique, of social norms to technical rules of efficient goods production. In the next two chapters, I would like, therefore, to consider the charge and propose a defense that is consistent with both the idea of the past and the presence of the postmodern in James's pragmatism. I make this case in the belief that doing so is the most promising way to save him from his defenders as well as his detractors.

CHAPTER 9

. . . .

THE ROMANTIC ACQUIESCENCE:

PRAGMATISM AND THE YOUNG

INTELLECTUALS

Young Intellectuals, Then and Now

Until the appearance of Mumford's *Golden Day* in 1926, James was almost exempt from the kind of criticism Dewey had endured since 1917, when he publicly promoted American entry into the world war. In fact, the early critics of pragmatism—Randolph Bourne, Van Wyck Brooks, Harold Stearns—tried to distinguish between a Jamesian pragmatism and an instrumental acquiescence to the reality of war.[1] To be sure, Bertrand Russell had announced in 1909 that pragmatism did not qualify as serious philosophy because it sanctioned faith and beliefs, not reason and real truths. Émile Durkheim had argued along similar lines in his lectures on pragmatism of 1913–14. But both were using James to get at Henri Bergson, who contributed an introduction to the French edition of *Pragmatism* in 1911. And neither paid much attention to Dewey. In the United States, it remained, then, for Mumford to make James a codefendant in an indictment of pragmatism that reached beyond the professional journals.[2]

The narrative strategy Mumford adopted was ingenious. He treated pragmatism as the spirit, the culmination, of the Gilded Age; it was, he claimed, the "attitude of compromise" perfected by the bewildered "children of industrialism" (182, 188, 192). Accordingly he analyzed it anthropologically, as an artifact that required interpretation because it was irretrievably embedded in a cultural milieu that had decayed or disappeared. Pragmatism was then twice removed from the current scene; as the pure expression of an earlier, primitive stage of development, its function was now purely residual, ceremonial, and psychological. Certainly it could not serve the present purpose of cultural renewal. The narrative form of this critique was radical because it consigned James and pragmatism to the dustbin of nineteenth-century history. Its content was more familiar and persuasive because it consisted of long-standing complaints, although these, too, were recast in the heat of Mumford's relentless reduction of pragmatism to the "animus of the pioneer" (186–87).

This debunking method revealed that pragmatism failed as critical doctrine because it never transcended what Mumford had specified in the first chapter as the origins of the American mind—that is, the utilitarian spirit of modern science and of modern Christianity. "The new ideas that James achieved were not so influential as those he accepted and rested upon; and the latter, pretty plainly, were the protestantism, the individualism, the scientific distrust of 'values,' which had come down in unbroken succession from Calvin and Luther, from Locke and Hobbes and Hume and Bentham and Mill" (188). Mumford had simply removed the metaphor from James's equation of pragmatism and Protestantism; by doing so, by taking it literally, he could claim to have shown that pragmatism was deeply implicated in the production of precisely those attitudes and values (or lack of values) that had made American culture a disaster. "The very words James used to recommend pragmatism should make us suspicious of its pretensions" (189).

The historical range and detail of Mumford's argument thickened the description of pragmatism made originally by Bourne, Brooks, and Stearns. In "Letters and Leadership" (1918), Brooks, for example, had identified "our real awakeners" as the servants of power who preached pragmatic adjustment to reality, that is, "the sociologists whose doctrine is the adaptation of man to his environment, the apostles of a narrow efficiency, and the pragmatic and realistic philosophers who stand behind them." These awakeners were influential because they seemed, and claimed, to represent an impending American century: "Their philosophy has been the formulation, the rationalization of the whole spirit of American life at least since the Spanish war." So the future they represented would be disfigured by their inability to distinguish between means and ends. "Social efficiency is the ideal posited by Professor Dewey. But an ideal is an end, and social efficiency is not an end; it is a means towards the realization of human values." In short, pragmatism was inadequate to the task of cultural criticism because it was warmed-over positivism. "It has assumed the right to formulate the aims of life and the values by which those aims are tested, aims and values which, we are led by history to believe, can be effectively formulated only by individual minds not in harmony with the existing fact but in revolt against it." In *Liberalism in America* (1919), Stearns also dwelled on the reversal of means and ends apparently accomplished by pragmatism. But he was even more afraid than Brooks of a future in which pragmatic intellectuals and politicians asked only whether their ideas were effective; for this was a future in which moral relativism reigned. "Pushed to extremes, indeed, it becomes a justification for almost anything. . . . It is a philosophy so enamoured of mingling with the warm living stream of everyday [life] that it turns with ferocity upon any claims for ethical resistance to the main current of events."[3]

Mumford himself quoted Bourne's famous essay on Dewey in concluding his last substantive chapter (265–68). But he seems to have been affected by the elegiac tone of the essay; for he showed Dewey more respect than a "disciple" of James would have any reason to expect. Not that Mumford believed that instrumentalism was an improvement on pragmatism; both remained prisoners of the past that began with the unsettlement of Europe in the sixteenth century. "Mr. Dewey's philosophy represents what is still positive and purposeful in that limited circle of ideas in which the American mind was originally born; he is at home in the atmosphere of protestantism, with its emphasis upon the role of intelligence in morals; in science, with its emphasis upon procedure, technique, and deliberate experiment; and he embraces technology with the same esthetic faith that Mr. Henry Ford embraces it" (256). This faint echo of an earlier passage on James indicates that Mumford had already exhausted his critical vocabulary. He finally admitted as much: "What I have said of William James applies with considerable force to his disciple" (265). In other words: "The deficiencies of Mr. Dewey's philosophy are the deficiencies of the American scene itself: they arise out of his too easy acceptance of the Seventeenth and Eighteenth Century framework of ideas" (261). By this account, pragmatism could not criticize, and did not break with, the historical moment codified in the "utilitarian idealism" of the Enlightenment. As Brooks had suggested, it was not a party to the *romantic* revolt that had defined, and still sustained, the artist's identity under the regime of industrial capitalism. So it was not a part of what the young intellectuals called the usable past.[4]

Until quite recently, most writers on the Left have ratified this verdict. Now a new generation of young intellectuals has begun to reexamine the evidence, and to find that Richard Rorty's enthusiasm for pragmatism can be contagious. But these writers tend to treat Dewey as the central figure in the creation of the pragmatist-progressive tradition, and to be slightly embarrassed by James. At any rate they seem always to deal with him in passing—on their way toward the more tough-minded Dewey—as if he were the demented uncle whose place in the family tree is still in question. Those who do linger with James tend to treat him with the kind of all-purpose affection that obliterates the distinction between dogs and demented uncles, and that finally makes us want to pat him on the head, not listen to him carefully. Perhaps that is why they patronize a pragmatism he would not recognize.[5]

The recent rehabilitation of pragmatism has, then, reversed the relation between James and Dewey which Mumford's predecessors proposed. Where they suggested that James's temperament and ideas would not have allowed mere acquiescence to the "existing fact" of world war or globalized capitalism—that his pragmatism was not strictly instrumental or simply utilitarian—the new generation suggests that it was Dewey, not James, who developed a pragmatism that is something more than respect for results. Mumford's charge of "utilitarian idealism" still stands, therefore, but it applies only to James the mugwump, popularizer, and proselytizer; so conceived, as pitchman, he functions as middleman between the more profound Peirce and the more democratic Dewey. My defense of James becomes more difficult in this setting. For I must take issue with the new lineage in which he appears as conscientious caveman—as the missing link in the emergence of Postmodern Man—yet avoid claiming either that the evolution of pragmatism ends with James or that Dewey deserves debunking and demotion. Unless I am content to enter a plea of incommensurability and move accordingly to set aside the verdict of relativism, I must meanwhile assess the new arguments for pragmatism, but also address the old charges against pragmatism.

In other words, if I am to defend James, I cannot exclude the intergenerational, intertextual evidence that has shaped the reception and the evolution of pragmatism. Let me begin, then, with an exchange of 1927 between Mumford and Dewey which, by all accounts, trivialized their differences, but which has become an important artifact in the rehabilitation of both the young intellectuals and the pragmatist tradition. Casey Blake, for example, uses this exchange to summarize Mumford's increasing alienation from, and cultural critique of, modern American capitalism. Robert Westbrook uses it to defend Dewey's instrumentalism against the indictment of *The Golden Day*—to claim, in fact, that "Mumford's treatment of James [is] less misleading than his criticism of Dewey," because Mumford was criticizing precisely "those features of James's pragmatism to which Dewey most objected." More to the point, Blake and Westbrook agree that Mumford's attack on Dewey in *The Golden Day* is easily deflected because it missed his growing interest in aesthetic values and cultural practices; presumably a defense of James on the same grounds is impossible. "Throughout the

1920s," Blake notes, "Dewey gave increasing attention to the place of art and values in his philosophy of experience." Blake concludes that by 1927 the two antagonists were "exploring complementary themes in American politics, culture, and social thought." Westbrook also stresses the bad timing of the debate. "Mumford advanced his critique at the very moment that Dewey was shifting his attention as a philosopher to an analysis of the value-laden dimensions of human experience (including art) and articulating a social philosophy decidedly different from what Mumford termed 'pragmatic liberalism' and similar, in important respects, to that of Mumford himself."[6]

So Blake and Westbrook simply cede the critical high ground to the young intellectuals. Their defense of Dewey never addresses the crucial question of selfhood or personality which they raise explicitly, by citing Dewey in this connection, or implicitly, by letting Mumford's "humanism" go unchallenged; nor does it address the larger question of how to differentiate between "utilitarian idealism" and the residual scientism of Dewey's outlook. Instead, they promote a kind of "poststructural" pragmatism that is impervious to Mumford's barbs, they assume, because it has finally risen above the parched landscape of politics or philosophy and paid its respects to art, values, and culture. What is truly astonishing about their position is not so much that it makes culture a refuge from and retort to politics—by now this is a typical gesture—as that it takes Mumford's periodization of pragmatism for granted. In effect, Blake and Westbrook argue that until Dewey's "linguistic turn" of the mid-to-late 1920s, pragmatism was as uncivilized as Mumford claimed.

To take issue with their argument, which validates the new lineage of the pragmatist tradition by displacing James and pinning all its hopes on Dewey, is therefore to take issue with Mumford. As preface to this unpleasant task—we might, after all, owe more to Mumford than to Dewey—let me quote something he said in the exchange of 1927. "It is not that we reject Mr. Dewey; that would be ingratitude: but . . . we seek for a broader field and a less provincial interpretation of Life and Nature than he has given us."[7] Just so: it is not that I reject Mumford, for that would be virtually impossible; I seek instead to include his interpretation of our selves, our capacities, in the broader field staked out by pragmatism. I need, then, to demonstrate three propositions. First, Mumford's perspective of the 1920s (and after) was at the romantic extreme of the epistemological positions enabled by modern subjectivity. Second, and consequently, he could not see how pragmatism was anything more than positivism, or anything less than a utilitarian calculus of and capitulation to the external, thing-like world of objects. Third, the pragmatist field is larger and more fertile than the area that Mumford and similarly romantic radicals have cultivated over the years; in fact, it still surrounds them, and, should they be moved to seek "a broader field," it will be their first or last stop on the way out of the old neighborhood.

When I say that Mumford's perspective was romantic, I do not mean simply that he celebrated the "organic" as an attribute of either nature or culture. I also mean that, like Emerson, he could not dispense with an ontological distinction between thoughts and things. Accordingly he assumed that the necessary condition of self-consciousness and self-determination was abstention or release from externality—from the external, thing-like world of objects. He designated the modern form of that externality by the metonym of "the machine," to which he reduced the "entire technological complex" characteristic of capitalism in its "paleotechnic" phase (ultimately the metonym became perfectly synchronic, so that it designated all forms of mechanized and/or bureaucratized state power). The peoples entrapped in this complex were "creatures of the machine system"; they could free themselves only through an education of desire that enabled their return to the organic principles and possibilities of culture.[8]

Students of Mumford will be neither surprised nor offended to hear me call him a romantic—that is how they routinely categorize his perspective of the 1920s and after, unless they are pondering the apparent exception of *Technics and Civilization* (1934). For example, Charles Molesworth summarizes this perspective as "something like a Romantic sense of tragic humanism." Leo Marx notes that the "essential presuppositions of Mumford's thinking derive from the counter-Enlightenment, or what Alfred North Whitehead called, in *Science and the Modern World* (1925), 'the romantic reaction.'" And Casey Blake quite properly denies that Mumford was an "idealist," suggesting instead that his position "is best seen as a highly subjectivist variant of pragmatism that drew on Romanticism as a corrective to perceived weaknesses in Dewey's thought."[9] They may be surprised, however, and perhaps offended as well, to hear me claim that it was precisely his romantic perspective that not only disabled his attempt to transcend the dualisms of the Enlightenment project but reinstated the binary oppositions—between inner and outer, mind and body, reason and desire, subjectivity and objectivity, science and humanism—which he consistently diagnosed as symptoms of the psychological and social disintegration specific to modernity. It was this romantic humanism, in other words, that determined his (mis)reading of pragmatism, and ultimately allowed him to denounce its demolition of the distinction between thoughts and things as if he were Thomas Carlyle attending the birth of the object and the death of the subject under the sign of positivism, not Lewis Mumford witnessing the reconstruction of subjectivity under the prodding of pragmatism.

Mumford, Bergson, Melville

Let us see how the anachronism works. In August 1935, Mumford was preparing to review the first three volumes of Arnold Toynbee's huge history by rereading Oswald Spengler's *Decline of the West* (1918–22). He wrote his friend Brooks that Spengler was "very unsound indeed" on the question of "technics," which of course Mumford himself had just surveyed in his sixth and most ambitious book. But "on the contrasts between the mechanical and the organic in thought," Spengler was "very satisfactory." This remark opened onto a long parenthesis: "Incidentally, the more I think about the machine the more I find myself appreciating Bergson. . . . My own philosophy could be treated as a modification of his, for whereas he draws a distinction between intuition, which is vital, and reason, which is mechanical, and lets it go at that, I go on to point out that the mechanical itself is a creation of life and only when it is perversely divorced from all our experience, including our feeling and intuition, does it become dangerous, that is, anti-vital." The most exquisite irony of this impromptu genealogy is perhaps the most obvious one—that Mumford had arrived at the point James reached in the last few years of his life, when he became Bergson's great admirer. Here is another: Bergson concluded his introduction to the French edition of *Pragmatism* with this preemptive rejoinder to its critics: "People have said that the pragmatism of James was only a form of skepticism, that it lowered truth, that it subordinated truth to material reality, that it advised against and discouraged disinterested scientific research. Such an interpretation will never enter the heads of those who read his work attentively."[10]

Now if Bergson had anticipated Mumford's response to James, or if Mumford had declared his antipathy to Bergson, Mumford's response to James would not be anomalous—surely it would not require explanation by reference to anyone's romantic humanism. But in fact Bergson admired James (and vice versa), and Mumford admired Bergson. So we have to ask how and why Mumford could construct an intellectual genealogy that installed as its locus the bastardized version of pragmatism found in the essentially romantic vision of Bergson. In other words, we have to ask whether Mumford had better reasons than James to admire Bergson. If it turns out that

Bergson and Mumford do have more in common than Bergson and James, we can stop treating the young intellectuals' misreading of pragmatism as a necessary condition of contemporary cultural criticism, and start treating it as a text that requires more interpretation. Once we do, this text might become evidence of an unfinished struggle with and about founding fathers—that is, of a drama in which we function not as critics once removed but as chorus twice rehearsed.

What, then, did Bergson say that Mumford could admire? Is the affiliation Mumford declared legitimate? Bergson has been accused of promoting all sorts of nonsense, but his lasting effect on European intellectual life was much less profound than the polemics of the early twentieth century would suggest. He did shape the movement toward Catholic modernism. He did cause Georges Sorel to read William James, then to write what is still probably the longest appreciation of pragmatism, De l'utilité du pragmatisme (1921). And he did make Carl Jung's mysticism possible. "We ought to be particularly grateful to Bergson," Jung announced in 1916, "for having broken a lance in defence of the irrational." Even so, Bergson's philosophy was always the foil, never the foundation, of intellectual innovation and movement in the first three decades of the century.[11]

The source of his isolation helps to explain Mumford's claim on his intellectual legacy. Bergson argued that philosophy was plagued by analysis—by the diagrammatic or dissecting approach of reason and its scientific armature—but could be cured by intuition, through which knowers entered the known and grasped the real movement of things-in-themselves. The difficulty, Bergson knew, was to explain exactly how intuition supplemented (or locally supplanted) the operations of analysis. "But if metaphysics is to proceed by intuition, if intuition has as its object the mobility of duration, and if duration is psychological in essence, are we not going to shut the philosopher up in exclusive self-contemplation?"[12] Yet he could not specify the form or the method of intuition except to invoke introspection as its paradigm; nor could he describe the content or the result of intuition except to say that, like a work of art, it was immediately recognizable once experienced. In effect, his discovery was incommunicable. So he could inspire but not inform subsequent inquiry into the nature and conditions of knowledge.

Mumford notwithstanding, Bergson's goal was not to break the mechanism of the intellect, although his declamatory style seemed always to be leading him toward the radical solution. Instead, he tried to grasp the intellect as a "bright nucleus" still suspended in and sustained by ineffable human capacities ("elements") that had been repressed in the course of evolution.

> It is the totality of these elements that we must find again and rejoin to the intellect proper, in order to grasp the true nature of vital activity. And we shall probably be aided in this by the fringe of vague intuition that surrounds our distinct—that is, intellectual—representation. For what can this useless fringe be, if not that part of the evolving principle which has not shrunk to the peculiar form of our [vertebrate] organization, but has settled around it unasked for, unwanted? It is there, accordingly, that we must look for hints to expand the intellectual form of our thought; from there we shall derive the impetus necessary to lift us above ourselves.[13]

But Bergson could not argue that intellect and intuition were indissoluble or equally indispensable moments in our apprehension of the world. For he assumed that reason or intellect had already done its necessary work—indeed that it had become a fetter on human development—and that the creative evolution of the future would require the cultivation of the "more extensive power" found at the margins of reason, in the "fringe of vague intuition." So he was less interested in rehabilitating reason than in reducing its scope. "To philosophize means to reverse the normal directions of the workings of thought."[14]

This definition of philosophy, from Bergson's "Introduction to Metaphysics" (1903), resembles those proposed by German and English romantics such as Friedrich Schelling, Samuel Taylor Coleridge, and Thomas Carlyle. For example, Schelling claimed that "all philosophizing consists in recalling the condition in which we were at one with nature"—that is, it consists in the recovery of the moment before or after reason, armed with science, had exiled imagination, separated subject from object, and placed the Absolute beyond reach. In fact, the resemblance between Schelling and Bergson is uncanny, and not simply because each was a kind of boy wonder whose public lectures were major social events, and whose mature philosophical works were greeted with short-term acclaim but long-term neglect. Schelling organized his *System of Transcendental Idealism* (1800) around a notion of intuition that sounds as if Bergson invented it.[15] Intuition, he claimed, discloses "the identity of the conscious and the unconscious in the self, and consciousness of this identity. The product of this intuition will therefore verge on the one side upon the product of nature, and on the other upon the product of freedom." In other words, intuition inhabits the area that is neither particular nor universal. As Bergson put it, "Between these two extreme limits [materiality and eternity] moves intuition, and this movement is metaphysics itself." [16] Schelling was equally insistent, but more aware of the aesthetic imperative at work in his philosophy.

> The whole of philosophy starts, and must start, from a principle which, as the absolute principle, is also at the same time the absolutely identical. An absolutely simple and identical cannot be grasped or communicated through description, nor through concepts at all. It can only be intuited. Such an intuition is the organ of all philosophy.—But this intuition, which is an intellectual rather than a sensory one, and has as its object neither the objective nor the subjective, . . . is itself merely an internal one, which cannot in turn become objective for itself: it can become objective only through the second intuition. This second intuition is the aesthetic. (229 n. 1)

For Schelling, as for Bergson, the work of art was, then, the characteristic content or result of intuition. Bergson, for example, typically demonstrated the existence of intuition either by inference clothed in rhetorical questions or by reference to "literary composition" and the like. Both claimed, moreover, that philosophy had to adopt precisely the form or method (intuition) that produced art. So they proposed not that the domain of philosophy opened onto the domain of art but that the latter should absorb the former. "It is art alone," Schelling concluded, "which can succeed in objectifying with universal validity what the philosopher is able to present in a merely subjective fashion" (232). On this terrain, "the problem of the human personality," as Bergson put it, became the central problem—that is, "the direct contact of the self with the self" became the "privileged case" against which all others would be judged. For the work of art was the work of the artist, of that individual personality in direct contact, through intuition, with the inner sources of his genius. Schelling was emphatic about this: the "primordial self" was the "absolute," the site on which nature and freedom intersected to produce the work of art. But Bergson was even more pointed. "Let us then go down into our own inner selves." He knew there was no place else to turn: "There is at least one reality which we all seize from within, by intuition and not by simple analysis. It is our own person in its flowing through time, the self which endures." [17]

By now we are in a position to see why Mumford declared his affiliation with Bergson, and how it goes much deeper than their common attempt to conscript intuition for the struggle against scientism. It was a way of preserving the sphere of subjectivity—the domain of art—in what his friend Brooks called "an age of reaction." Like Brooks, Mumford embodied, in his work as well as his life, the choices every intellectual faced after 1924. The difference between them was that Brooks was driven mad by this shrunken life of the mind. Between 1920 and 1926, in biographies of Mark Twain, Henry James, and Emerson, Brooks tried desperately to reconvene the extremes of modern subjectivity by trying on its various guises, much as Edgar Allan Poe had done a century before in fictional settings: on the one hand, pure objectivity, the willful loss of self and consciousness in the external, thing-like world of objects, or in the extrarational realm of artistic intuition; on the other, "excessive subjectivity," the annihilation of all externality in the hypertrophy of the ego, the mind's eye. As his life and his prose disintegrated, Brooks became what he said great writers were, "transparent mediums, mirrors . . . through which life freely passes back and forth between the mind and the world": all the antinomies, all the discontinuities, of modern subjectivity were inscribed in his *Life of Emerson* (1926), and then enacted in his subsequent breakdown.[18] Mumford lived them, too, but he was more fortunate, more resilient, more determined. Above all, he was more *removed*. He was too young to have been scarred by the eclipse of the prewar sense of intellectual purpose and possibility or by the postwar loss of intellectual community. He never approached or crossed the "fragile bridge" that had once connected the new radicals among intellectuals and the recently (re)organized working class. Of course it was this very distance from the prewar earthquake that gave Mumford's perspective a novel, critical, cultural edge, and that ultimately spared him from Brooks's "season in hell."[19]

But the same distance made that earthquake seem a late and minor spasm in the post-Enlightenment conflict between romanticism and positivism. From this standpoint—Mumford's standpoint—the problematic of modern subjectivity was never in question; for the choice disclosed to intellectuals who adopted it was between romanticism and the more or less positivist opposition. Mumford was the key figure in defining that standpoint and thus in rehabilitating the romantic extreme of modern subjectivity. In doing so, he chose a lineage that finally affiliated him with Schelling and the larger romantic tradition. He also chose a usable past that would determine the horizon of expectations for most writers on the American Left. They would be able to take his attitude toward pragmatism for granted.

Bergson was a significant part of the lineage Mumford chose because he had already "modernized" the romantic idiom. I have said that Jamesian pragmatism is one version or effect of a choice about how, or where, to locate the moral personality. Bergson's philosophy was another version or effect of the same choice—it, too, was characterized by an attempt to situate that personality in time rather than in extratemporal space. But this time is not historical time. Bergson tried to solve "the problem of the human personality" by developing the notion of "duration," the inner life of the self which is impervious to "conceptual representation" because, as pure mobility, it "excludes all idea of juxtaposition, reciprocal exteriority and extension." So conceived, "duration" becomes an extratemporal order of selfhood in which symbols are neither necessary nor possible, and of which only metaphysical intuition can provide an account. "If there exists a means of possessing a reality absolutely, instead of knowing it relatively, of placing oneself within it instead of adopting points of view toward it, of having the intuition of it instead of making the analysis of it, in short, of grasping it over and above all expression, translation or symbolical representation, metaphysics is that very means. Metaphysics is therefore the science which claims to dispense with symbols."[20]

The intuitive self that inhabits and interprets the extrasymbolic order of "duration" stands, then, somewhere between the figure of the freeholder uncorrupted by historical time and the fully historicized, postmodern personality sanctioned by pragmatism. In this sense, Alfred North Whitehead was correct to claim that Bergson "recurs to Descartes" in attempting to ground the moral personality on an inviolable inner life. Bergson could not imagine that personality as the consequence of "reciprocal exteriority"—in other words, as the "social self" his American counterparts took for granted by 1905—and so he fell back on Descartes. But he defined the inviolable inner life of the genuine self by means of the body (intuition), not the mind (analysis); and he depicted that body, as Whitehead recognized, in medical or clinical terms borrowed from modern physiology. With one stroke, then, he "modernized" the romantic idiom of artistic intuition and renovated a Cartesian account of self-knowledge.[21]

By rehabilitating the romantic extreme of modern subjectivity and aligning himself with Bergson, Mumford, too, fell back on Descartes—or at least on the dualism codified in the ontological distinction between thoughts and things. The self he could imagine became usable and durable insofar as it abstained accordingly from the external, thing-like world of objects, that is, insofar as it was not implicated in and corrupted by the circulation of commodities. This self had to seek its sources of unity or durability in form and in culture—in the kind of "symbolic interaction" that was neither conducted under the sign of the universal commodity nor determined by the rigid protocol of reason, analysis, or logic, "the money of mind." In the late 1920s, Mumford discovered and developed this self in an austere personal life that centered on rustic Amenia, New York, and in an appreciative biography of Herman Melville that became a manifesto of "excessive subjectivity."[22]

Mumford identified so powerfully with Melville that at times the biography begins to sound like autobiography—much as did Brooks's *Life of Emerson*.[23] "In describing Melville's experience and his state of mind," he announced at the outset, "I have taken the liberty of using his own language wherever possible; and I have done this so freely that, except where I have quoted whole passages, I have omitted quotation marks" (vi). In this case, too, the author denied himself any critical distance on his subject by denying that there were any crucial differences between the past and the present which required hermeneutical principles: "It is not that we have to go back to these writers: it is, rather, that we have come abreast of them" (364). Melville could then emerge as the appropriate model for selfhood in the mid-twentieth century because he had found bedrock by digging ever deeper within himself. "The stripping down of Herman Melville's ego, which he began in Mardi and finished in Pierre, was a sloughing away of labels, nicknames, party war-cries, habits, conventions, and acceptances; it was, necessarily, a prelude to that building up of a new ego, a surer and more central, a social and participating self, which is the task of our own time for both men and communities" (367).

This author sculpted a durable self, and not incidentally carved out a space for other, equally authentic selves, by choosing the simple life of the solitary writer. His long-term project was of course interrupted by the Civil War. But Mumford had already claimed that *Moby Dick* was the site of a synthesis still unique in North America. On the one hand, the novel treated science and poetry as commensurable narrative forms. For the first time in American literature, the "respect for fact" that characterized modern culture was "completely wedded to the imagination" (191–92). On the other hand, the novel put the scattered pieces of the human personality back together again but did not, in doing so, simply reinstate the unconsciously parochial unity of an ancient or medieval model.

Moby-Dick, then, is one of the first great mythologies to be created in the modern world, created, that is, out of the stuff of that world, its science, its exploration, its terrestrial daring, its concentration upon power and dominion over nature, and not out of ancient symbols . . . or medieval folk-legends. . . . [It] thus brings together the two disseloved halves of the modern world and the modern self—its positive, practical, scientific, externalized self, bent on conquest and knowledge, and its imaginative, ideal half, bent on the transposition of conflict into art, and power into humanity. (193)

The grammatical ambiguity of this passage—notice how the antecedents seem to divide and begin reproducing, as if they were one-cell organisms—indicates Mumford's profound ambiguity about the possibility of discovering a usable self by projecting it into the modern-industrial world. He was much more comfortable with the possibility of discovering that self by "stripping down" the ego, by removing or releasing it from the divisions and desires necessarily experienced by the personality that is *in* but also *of* this teeming, commodified world. Even so, Mumford was aware that the result could be a dead end. I think that is why he had tried to complicate his notion of a simple, genuine self in an earlier summary passage on *Moby Dick*. "Man's defence lies within himself, not within the narrow, isolated ego, which may be overwhelmed, but in that self which we share with our fellows" (186–87).

Here is the same "social and participating self" to which he would return in the book's epilogue.[24] But it can be shared, and becomes durable, only insofar as it cultivates the better half of the modern self—the introspective, "imaginative, ideal half"—and does not indulge the temptations of the externalized self. "To make that self more solid, one must advance positive science, produce formative ideas, and embody ideal forms in which all men may, to a greater or lesser degree, participate" (187). This more solid self begins to sound like Dr. Jekyll without a laboratory, or Dr. Faustus without the Devil, or, for that matter, Ahab without the white whale; in other words, this solid self begins to sound like a good Victorian gentleman. But that cannot be the model Mumford had in mind. It is more likely that he recalled the roster of prepragmatic thinkers he proposed in *The Golden Day*. "The Hindu guru, the Platonic philosopher, aloof from this struggle [of life], is not virtuous in James's sense; neither is the pure scientist, the Clerk-Maxwell, the Faraday, the Gibb, the Einstein—the activity of all these creatures, what is it but 'idle amusement'?"[25] These thinkers were heroes because they were removed from, and indifferent to, the practical consequences of thought, indeed from the practical life as such.

So, then, was Ahab, one of those true "captains of the spirit [who] must oppose the prudence of Starbuck and the common sense of Stubb" (188). He embodied "excessive subjectivity" because he rose above the objective mass, the dead weight, of the *new* Leviathan, the whale that "stands for the practical life" (187), "the whale of industry and science" (188). Like

Melville, Ahab was a hero for the twentieth century because he rose above the sordid system of needs articulated in modern-industrial civil society: he struck through this mundane, bourgeois mask, through the "sluggish routine" of everyday life and "material existence" (188–89). But Mumford had already suggested that "in battling against evil, with power instead of love, Ahab himself . . . becomes the image of the thing he hates" (186). So he had to adapt Shelley's radical interpretation of Milton's Satan if he was to make Melville's Ahab the hero of *Moby Dick*.[26]

> He represents, not as in the first parable, an heroic power that misconceives its mission and misapplies itself: here he rather stands for human purpose at its highest expression. His pursuit is "futile" because it wrecks the boat and brings home no oil and causes material loss and extinguishes many human lives; but in another sense, it is not futile at all, but is the only significant part of the voyage, since oil is burned and ships eventually break up and men die and even the towers of proud cities crumble away as the buildings sink beneath the sand or the jungle, while all that remains, all that perpetuates the life and the struggle, are their forms and symbols, their art, their literature, their science, as they have been incorporated in the social heritage of man. . . . Life, Life purposive, Life formative, Life expressive, is more than living, as living itself is more than the finding of a livelihood. (189–90)

Mumford's absorption in the romantic attitude he attributed to Melville as well as Ahab was now so complete that the narrator who comes between these two, and who announces Melville's authorial ambiguity, disappeared. And when Ishmael disappeared, so, too, did Mumford's critical distance on his subject. Melville himself did not, and could not, specify the one and only "significant part of the voyage." His respect for brute fact, and his wonder at the meanings embedded in everyday life, were too great; he tried not to rise above these details of "material existence" on the Pequod, but to grasp their significance. That is why he uses Ishmael's voice, among others, to tell Ahab's story—to flesh it out, to bring it down to earth, to make us feel the effects of the indifference to practical consequences which is embodied in Ahab's blindness to everything *except* forms and symbols. Ishmael's mere presence in the text is reminder enough of its author's ambiguity. That he alone lived to tell the story should suggest that we need to hear his side of it.[27]

Mumford must have understood that, since he introduced his general interpretation of *Moby Dick* by claiming that Ahab "lost his humanity in the

very act of vindicating it" (186). But this homily was immediately undermined in three ways. First, Mumford distinguishes between the form and
content of Ahab's tragic end. "His defiance is noble, his methods are ill
chosen." Or again: "[The] evil Ahab seeks to strike is the sum of one's enemies. He does not bow down to it and accept it: therein lies his heroism
and virtue: but he fights it with its own weapons and therein lies his madness" (186). One cannot expect to subdue the "vacant external powers in
the universe"—for example, "the whale of industry and science"—if one is
already implicated in and thus corrupted by them: one can be in but not of
this world (186). Second, Mumford secures Ahab's audition for the hero's
role by advertising the "more solid," genteel self we somehow "share with
our fellows"; as the subsequent, sympathetic treatment of Ahab's mono-
mania makes clear, it is better to be satanic, and solitary, than boring—
better to be altogether aloof from the bourgeois struggle for material existence which occupies, in every sense, "the greater part of the daily round of
humanity" (188). Third, Mumford casts Ahab in the role of Milton's Satan,
the romantics' favorite hero, and gives him a rave review. As the differences between Melville and Mumford disappear—"I have omitted quotation
marks"—so the differences between Ishmael and Ahab, between crew and
captain, become unimportant. Dialogue becomes monologue; and the voice
that resounds in this interpretation is Ahab's.

Technics and Personality

From his standpoint, the "astonishing reversal" that historians find in Mumford's *Technics and Civilization* was more apparent than real, or rather was
no more astonishing than Brooks's periodic reversals of his demented flight
from the "perfect objectivity" of a self without subjectivity.[28] For Ahab had
reprised the role of Faustus as well as Satan; and Mumford had applauded
his performance. So I want to argue that the acceptance in *Technics* of "an
impassive, objective personality type" *completed* Mumford's rehabilitation
of the romantic extreme enabled by modern subjectivity. It contradicts the
"ethical speculations of the Melville biography" only in the sense that the
romantic's retort to positivism or scientism finally validates the positivist's
acquiescence to the "given fact"—I will have more to say about this unintended consequence later—and thus contradicts the ostensible purpose of
romanticism.[29] I do not want to minimize the conflicts contained by Mumford's extraordinary essay; but I do want to show that they are resolved by
recourse to a romantic idiom.

We should note, to begin with, that the original title of *Technics* was "Form and Personality." Like Brooks, Mumford was still exploring the grounds and the possibilities of subjectivity, still trying to find a place for simple, genuine selves. But he had enlarged the scope of the search for a usable self, to include modern machines and mechanical attitudes as well as the organic synthesis of late medieval civilization. The "modern concept of personality" he discovered in the course of writing this book would fascinate him thereafter.[30] We should note, furthermore, that Mumford's declaration of affiliation with Bergson's romantic modernism came *after* the publication of *Technics*, and in the context of a continuing consideration of "the machine." By all means, let us acknowledge that the book he wrote is not the book he set out to write—that it is more ambiguous than we might have expected. But let us also acknowledge that when it was finished, and published, he claimed it was consistent with what came before and after it.

If we ask why he made that claim about *this* book, and if we are not satisfied with answers that cite his immaturity or ignorance—such answers should make us wonder why anyone would take his books of the 1920s seriously—we can then read it as an attempt to transcend the antinomies of modern subjectivity which does not quite succeed. Mumford was clearly disturbed by the antiquarian or reactionary temper of certain antimechanical creeds, and clearly recognized that romanticism could (and sometimes did) devolve into the worship of the archaic and the "raw primitive" (chapter 6). By corroborating a perception of radical discontinuity between past and present, this antimodern attitude reinforced precisely those regressive cultural tendencies that prevented the creative assimilation of "the machine" and its intellectual correlates for authentically organic purposes. In effect, Mumford was cautioning his allies and criticizing himself along lines originally suggested by Waldo Frank, who had argued in a review of *The Golden Day* that to reject the "present interim of the Machine" was to betray any "promise from our past," including the promise of the future made by Emerson, Whitman, Melville, and Lincoln.[31] Here is how Mumford acknowledged the legitimacy of Frank's argument:

In its animus, romanticism was right; for it represented those vital and historical and organic attributes that had been deliberately eliminated from the concepts of science and from the methods of the earlier technics, and it provided necessary channels of compensation. . . . Unfortunately, in its comprehension of the forces that were at work in society the romantic movement was weak: overcome by the callous destruction that attended the introduction of the machine, it did not distinguish between the forces that were hostile to life and those that served it. . . . In its effort to find remedies for the dire weakness and perversion of industrial society, romanticism avoided the very energies by which alone it could hope to create a more sufficient pattern of existence—namely, the energies that were focussed in science and technics and in the mass of new machine-workers themselves. The romantic movement was retrospective, walled-in, sentimental: in a word, regressive. (286–87)

Mumford was apparently inspired by Melville's reintegration of the "dissevered halves" of the world and the self; for *Technics and Civilization* is another attempt to put Humpty-Dumpty back together again. Mumford retained the binary classification of the Melville biography in describing the still-scattered pieces of the whole personality (imaginative-ideal versus practical-scientific); but he tried to be more historically specific about how these corresponded to the "general split in ideas occasioned by the machine," that is, to the opposition between the Romantic and the Utilitarian (285–303). In keeping with his provisional recognition of the limits of romanticism and his larger interest in "Form and Personality," Mumford also tried to accommodate this utilitarian dimension, this prodigal, "externalized self." In other words, he tried to accommodate what he understood to be the equivalent of utilitarianism—pragmatism—as a way of imagining and constructing a usable yet modern self. "In the world of ideas, romanticism and utilitarianism go side by side: Shakespeare with his cult of the individual hero and his emphasis [on] nationalism appeared at the same time as the pragmatic Bacon" (284).

But try as he might, Mumford could not welcome the prodigal home. As we will see, the "objective personality" corresponding to the regimen of the machine remained a foreign body in his prose which was neutralized if not dissolved by a dose of the romantic antidote (284–87, 298, 319–20, 323–33, 359–73). For the whole personality he desired, and designed, was simply the sum of these "objective" and "subjective" parts. He either described the existing relation between them by reiterating the spatial metaphors of paleotechnic science—they "go side by side," as if each was a reaction to the other—or prescribed an improved relation by demanding that the "romantic personality" be certified as the executive branch in a new separation of psychological (and cultural) powers. And this is a way of saying that he could not specify any necessary or immanent or intrinsic relation between these two dimensions of the modern personality because his historical periodization disclosed none. For example: "One is confronted, then, by the fact that the machine is ambivalent. It is both an instrument of liberation and one of repression. It has economized human energy and it has misdirected it. It has created a wider framework of order and it has produced muddle and chaos. It has nobly served human purposes and it has distorted and denied them" (283). Historians have used remarks like this to claim that Mumford momentarily succumbed to "technological determinism."[32] But his metaphor and his meaning were clear enough in context. He merely noted that industrial capitalism constituted evidence for *both* positivists (utilitarians), who would see in technical progress the instrument of liberation from every parochial inheritance, *and* romantics, who would see, in the same movement away from tradition and custom, the mechanical instrument of repression in every sense. On these historical grounds—that is, on the terrain of modern subjectivity—no choice was possible because the extremes were incommensurable. So conceived, or compromised, Mumford's rationale for a reintegrated human personality was a pious wish, a moral imperative, a romantic imprecation.

But he kept trying to grasp the indispensable ethical principle of his argument—the integrity of the personality—as something to be found in the details of technological history. He knew that somehow he had to define the facts in light of this value, and vice versa. "The conclusion is obvious: we cannot intelligently accept the practical benefits of the machine without accepting its moral imperatives and its esthetic forms. Otherwise both ourselves and our society will be the victims of a shattering disunity" (355). Mumford finally declared that in the early stages of the "neotechnic phase," which we now recognize as the second industrial revolution of the late nineteenth and early twentieth centuries, scientists began to define reality more flexibly and more broadly than the "mechanical world picture" of the seventeenth century would have allowed, to include social-cultural qualities and relations; meanwhile, their methods conquered fields of enterprise hitherto conducted by rule of thumb and were, in turn, modified by encounter with "the living organism and human society" (368–73, 216–17). The consequent "conceptual change" of the early twentieth century gave new standing and significance to the organic, as against the mechanical. "Machines, which had assumed their own characteristic shapes in developing independent of organic forms, were now forced to recognize the superior economy of nature" (253). Indeed, Mumford claimed that the "more vital interests" created by this reversal could be observed in "the very structure of machines themselves," for example in the design of airplanes (371, 250–55). We could treat that claim as proof of what one reviewer called the "mysterious animism" of the argument. But we must also realize that it cleared the way for the return of the repressed romantic alternative. To the extent that readers accepted his extraordinary claim as a given fact, Mumford had rational, historical grounds for installing the "romantic personality" as the legitimate successor to, and ruler of, the "objective personality" forged in the paleotechnic crucible. In short, he could deduce *ought* from *is*.[33]

Mumford's call for a return to nature in the name of science was issued in a quasi-clinical language that eventually made romanticism a psychological category as well as a cultural disposition and an intellectual movement (283–87, 298, 319–20, 368). So conceived, romanticism was id-like in its abiding distaste for abstraction, quantification, specialization; but as the excluded, and thus "insurgent," dimension of the human personality, it would become madness with a method. For example: "Romanticism in all its manifestations, from Shakespeare to William Morris, . . . was an attempt to restore the essential activities of human life to a central place in the new scheme, instead of accepting the machine as a center, and holding all its values to be final and absolute. . . . Vital organs of life, which have been amputated through historic accident, must be restored at least in fantasy, as preliminary to their actual rebuilding in fact: a psychosis is sometimes the only possible alternative to complete disruption and death" (286).

By this account, romanticism was a kind of guerrilla movement just waiting for its moment to emerge from the jungles of the collective unconscious, to raze the ego's straitened citadels. But Mumford had already armed it with the instruments of the neotechnic phase; so its impending victory would have more than psychological or metaphorical effects. "As a result of all these advances, one of the major problems for the new technics becomes the removal of the blighted paleotechnic environment, and the re-education of its victims to a more vital regimen of working and living" (248). The revolution he imagined was, then, a simple inversion of the inherited relation between romanticism and utilitarianism, entailing as such the displacement, in every sense, of the paleotechnic interregnum during which "the machine"—"the projection of one particular side of the human personality" (317)—had repressed and mutilated the larger organism.

Even before he spoke of this side in more appreciative terms, Mumford announced that he would not let the romantic insurgent enter a coalition government, and that the opposition—the "objective," utilitarian personality—would be recognized only if it accepted the prime ministry of romanticism. "The most objective advocates of the machine must recognize the underlying human validity of the Romantic protest against the machine: the elements originally embodied in literature and art in the romantic movement are essential parts of the human heritage that can not be neglected or flouted: they point to a synthesis more comprehensive than that developed through the organs of the machine itself" (319–20). So his subsequent appraisal of the "objective personality" sounded like a provisional endorsement at best. Mumford might as well have been a chamber of commerce president preparing to eulogize an organizer from the I.W.W.; he had already denounced what he now had to defend.

For example, toward the end of the chapter on neotechnics, he noted that the "mind-body process" had been clarified by new medical theory and practice. "The dualism of the dead mechanical body, belonging to the world of matter, and the vital transcendent soul, belonging to the spiritual realm, disappears before the increasing insight, derived from physiology on one hand and the investigation of neuroses on the other, of a dynamic interpenetration and conversion within the boundaries of organic structures and functions" (249). Later, in the context of his first approximation of the "objective personality," Mumford reiterated this dictum. "We no longer regard nature as if man himself were not implicated in her, and as if his modifications of nature were not themselves a part of the natural order to which he is born" (329). But he had already expressed an admiration for "the machine" in quite different terms.

> What remains as the permanent contribution of the machine . . . is the technique of cooperative thought and action it has fostered, the esthetic excellence of the machine forms, the delicate logic of materials and forces, which has added a new canon—the machine canon—to the arts: above all, perhaps, the more objective personality that has come into existence through a more sensitive and understanding intercourse with those new social instruments and through their deliberate cultural assimilation. In projecting one side of the human personality into the concrete forms of the machine, we have created an independent environment that has reacted upon every other side of the personality. (324)

Mumford went even further in his second approximation of the "objective personality." Here he noted, "The concept of a neutral world, untouched by man's efforts, indifferent to his activities, obdurate to his wish and supplication, is one of the great triumphs of man's imagination, and in itself it represents a fresh human value" (361). He had earlier insisted that this concept, and the more or less modern world to which it corresponded, contained artistic meaning and significance. "For finally, if nature itself is not an absolute, and if the facts of external nature are not the artist's sole materials, nor its literal imitation his guarantee of esthetic success, science nevertheless gives him the assurance of a partly independent realm which defines the limits of his own working powers" (332–33). But this statement was preceded by a different drawing of the boundary between the natural and the artificial. "External nature has no finally independent authority: it exists, as a result of man's collective experience, and as a subject for his further improvisations by means of science, technics, and the humane arts" (329).

We could of course note these contradictions and pronounce their author momentarily confused. But they are precisely the contradictions that we should expect from someone who has used the epistemological map provided by modern subjectivity to revisit the scene of Emersonian ambivalence. Moreover, they suggest that Mumford was trying to understand how modern science and industry—in a word, capitalism—had complicated the relation between the organic and the mechanical, the romantic and the utilitarian, the subjective and the objective, or, as Emerson and James would have it, between thoughts and things. There can be no doubt that he remembered Dewey's rendering of the "transition period" as the moment when the protoindustrial arts taught us that natural facts were not as inert as they had seemed under the regime of "classical philosophy." Indeed, we could read *Technics and Civilization* as a reply to *Reconstruction in Philosophy*. For Mumford enriched the evidence of incessant invention and technical progress which Dewey had used to broaden the definition of philosophy; but he reached rather different conclusions. Where Dewey claimed that the "structure of meanings" specific to modernity was animated by belief in the fundamentally human nature of the world—thoughts became things under the sign of "invention"—Mumford claimed that it was dominated by belief in the automatic clockwork of a neutral, "external nature." Both recognized the articulation of the human personality in the increase of mechanical processes and devices after 1400; and each cited the mechanical character of modern science as proof of his claims about modern culture. But Mumford saw only symptoms of disease, of the alienated human condition. Dewey saw attempted cures as well.[34]

Mumford could not, then, assimilate "the machine" because he could not explain how or why anyone would want to assimilate the artificial culture of paleotechnic modernity—the "second-hand experiences, the starvation of the senses, the remoteness from nature and animal activity" (248)— let alone the hybrid fruits of corporate-industrial capital (165–99, 210–11, 263–67). He was so committed to what the "more subjective," romantic personality represented that he could not acknowledge its organic relation either to modernity in the form of market society or to its negation in the form of the "objective personality." In fact he insisted that the new "organic approach in thought," which he interpreted as the return of the repressed romantic alternative (364–73), taught a simple lesson—the natural was, after all, superior to the artificial, the abstract, and the mechanical. "We now realize that the machines, at their best, are lame counterfeits of living organisms. Our finest airplanes are crude uncertain approximations compared with a flying duck: our best electric lamps cannot compare in efficiency with the light of the firefly: our most complicated automatic telephone exchange is a childish contraption compared with the nervous system of the human body" (371).

Note that Mumford restricted the meaning of "living organism" to that which recapitulates the natural, the instinctual, and the habitual—to that which lacks purpose because it is unconscious or unreasonable, and which cannot, therefore, characterize human nature. By this rigorously romantic measure, the best work of the great artists would amount to "lame counterfeits" of real Life. Mumford knew that "man's singular ability consists in the fact that he creates standards and ends of his own, not given directly in the external scheme of things, and in fulfilling his own nature in cooperation with the environment, he creates a third realm, the realm of the arts, in which the two are harmonized and ordered and made significant" (317–18). But as this passage demonstrates, he could not imagine a "third realm" of personality, of social and participating selfhood, that was greater than the sum of its "subjective" and "objective" parts. For, like Schelling and Bergson, he did not believe that these parts could be harmonized and ordered and made significant except in works of art, that is, in the intuitive work of those primordial selves called artists; at any rate he did not explain how they could be.

Poiesis *and Politics*

Technics and Civilization failed, then, because it never escaped the Emersonian orbit first plotted in *The Golden Day*. But by saying this, I do not mean to reiterate what I have said about the romantic resolution, or rather annulment, of the antinomies Mumford inscribed in *Technics*. Instead I want to indicate the absence of alienated or abstract social labor in his historical consciousness, and to assess the meaning of that absence. Let me begin by recalling how Emerson had retreated from the position that made the world "a realized will,—the double of the man."[35] He completed that retreat as the Orphic poet in the final chapter of "Nature"; he introduced it in the penultimate chapter. "Is not the landscape, every glimpse of which hath a grandeur, a face of him [God]? Yet this may show us what discord is between man and nature, for you cannot freely admire a noble landscape, if laborers are digging in the field hard by. The poet finds something ridiculous in his delight, until he is out of the sight of men" (39). By Emerson's accounting, the appearance on the horizon of wage laborers only deepens the division between internal and external worlds, between poetic-subjective and legal-objective properties. The life of the mind, not the extension of the body, heals the breach; more precisely, art or culture, not work or social labor, is the instrument by which thought penetrates the "solid seeming block of matter" (34), making it "the double of the man."

> So long as the active powers predominate over the reflective, we resist with indignation any hint that nature is more short-lived or mutable than spirit. The broker, the wheelwright, the carpenter, the toll-man, are much displeased at the intimation. But whilst we acquiesce entirely in the permanence of natural laws, the question of the absolute existence of nature, still remains open. It is the uniform effect of culture on the human mind, not to shake our faith in the stability of particular phenomena, as of heat, water, azote; but to lead us to regard nature as a phenomenon, not a substance; to attribute necessary existence to spirit; to esteem nature as an accident and an effect. (30, cf. 36)

Notice that Emerson conflates all forms of wage labor—unlike most of his contemporaries, he makes no distinction between the "productive" labor of the wheelwright or carpenter and the "unproductive" labor of the broker or the toll-man. He acknowledges a difference between "active" and "reflective" powers which corresponds, at least in retrospect, to a division between manual and mental labor; but he seems to believe that the crucial distinction to be made is between work for wages and work on behalf of spirit as such, and that work for wages postpones or precludes the "effect of culture." If we suppose that this belief does animate the essay, Emerson's insistence on the opposition between the "sensual man" (who "conforms thought to things") and the poet takes on new meaning—it begins to sound like the first match between objective and subjective personalities—and his equation of the broker and the carpenter becomes intelligible. By the same supposition, the retreat recorded in "Nature" is the flight of culture from the invasion of capitalism. The domain of the poet must contract, Emerson claims, as the domain of wage labor expands.

His celebration of material and mechanical progress in the second chapter ("Commodity"), or his study of "relations in all objects" in the fourth chapter ("Language"), would seem inconsistent with this claim. But Emerson's procedure is to naturalize the material, the mechanical, and the artificial. For example: "The misery of man appears like childish petulance, when we explore the steady and prodigal provision that has been made for his support and delight on this green ball which floats him through the heavens. . . . Beasts, fire, water, stones, and corn serve him" (11). Of course, in their natural state, as simple thing or material object, none of these "servants"— not even water—were useful or valuable to human beings. Each was domesticated, transported, transformed, or cultivated by human beings only as it became an essential part of some unnatural ritual or routine; neither the biological functions nor the cultural meanings of these things were given by the things themselves, apart from the shared human purposes that made them significant of social life in the first place. Emerson naturalizes them by reducing them to biological functions. Like Feuerbach, he could grasp them as objects but not as activity. "Nature, in its ministry to man, is not only the material, but is also the process and the result. . . . The wind sows the seed; the sun evaporates the sea; the wind blows the vapor to the field . . . the rain feeds the plant; the plant feeds the animal; and thus the endless circulations of the divine charity nourish man." And so the mechanical is admirable because it imitates the natural. "The useful arts are but reproductions or new combinations by the wit of man, of the same natural benefactors" (11). From this standpoint, which Mumford would adopt to naturalize another industrial revolution, the machine *is* the garden, slightly rearranged.[36]

"Man the Reformer" (1841), the famous lecture to the Mechanics' Apprentices' Library Association of Boston, might also seem a deviation from the claim that the poet must retreat as the proletariat expands.[37] For here Emerson enunciates "the doctrine of the Farm": "Every man ought to stand in primary relations with the work of the world, ought to do it himself, and not to suffer the accident of his having a purse in his pocket, or his having been bred to some dishonorable and injurious craft, to sever him from those duties; and for this reason, that labor is God's education; that he only is a sincere learner, he only can become a master, who learns the secrets of labor, and who by real cunning extorts from nature its sceptre" (152).

He goes on to acknowledge, however, that "the amount of manual labor which is necessary to the maintenance of a family, indisposes and disqualifies for intellectual exertion" (152). Thus "if a man find in himself any strong bias to poetry, to art, to the contemplative life," he must escape the *system* of needs in civil society and prepare himself for the simple life. "That man ought to reckon early with himself, and, respecting the compensations of the Universe, ought to ransom himself from the duties of economy, by a certain rigor and privation in his habits. . . . Let him be a caenobite, a pauper, and if need be, celibate also" (153). That man will become a genuine self by stripping down his desires to the bare essentials.

He will come to know himself, his poetic calling, by abstention from the sluggish routine of everyday life and material existence—that is, by abstention "from the duties of economy" if not "from the advantages of civil society" as such (155). To the extent, then, that Emerson leaves the farm and considers the "secrets of labor" in a wider, urban-industrial setting, he discovers artisans and mechanics, not proletarians. He discovers craftsmen whose production of goods still presupposed their customary level of consumption, not workers whose output and incomes were increasingly and anonymously determined by the capacities of mechanized shops, mills, or factories. The homogeneous time on the job of unskilled wage earners— in other words, abstract or alienated labor—did not qualify as God's education; for it held no secrets. Accordingly it did not even appear in this hymn to artisanal forms of labor.

But Emerson came of age when postartisanal market society was only possible. If he had acknowledged the impending priority of abstract social labor and its corollaries, we would probably say he was remarkably attuned to the political-economic tendencies of the nineteenth century. Mumford came of age when postindustrial market society was already actual; the issue of his time, as he put it in *Technics*, was "the transition beyond the historic forms of capitalism and the equally limited original forms of the machine to a life-centered economy" (303). Moreover, that book was designed to explain the political-economic tendencies of Western civilization from the mid-fourteenth to the mid-twentieth century. So if Mumford had acknowledged the historical importance of abstract social labor and its corollaries, we would have little reason to note the fact. But he did not; instead he recapitulated Emerson's treatment of the conflict between poets and proletarians. And that fact is worth noting.

Mumford's inability to fathom the modern world of work is on proud display in the illustrations he chose to substantiate the novel periodization of *Technics*. There are twelve plates bearing on the paleotechnic phase (ca. 1700–1900) and twenty-four on the neotechnic successor. By my count, twenty-nine people show up in the photographs depicting the neotechnic phase; of these, twenty-seven are passengers or observers of some kind— for example, the figures in the museum-like interior of a Soviet power plant at Plate 15.1—and two are solitary attendants of huge, semiautomatic machines (one tends a cotton-spinning machine, the other an automatic stoker). The only social labor in sight is performed by the stylized steelworkers of a mural by Thomas Hart Benton (Plate 13.2). Now in his prose depiction of neotechnic development, Mumford pointed out that electrification, instrumentation, and automation had "steadily been diminishing the worker's importance in factory production. Two million workers were cast out between 1919 and 1929 in the United States, while production itself actually increased" (228). He also pointed out that the nature of work had changed accordingly. "The worker, instead of being a source of work, becomes an observer and regulator of the performance of the machine—a supervisor of production rather than an active agent" (227). So we might say that Benton's artistic abstraction of social labor corroborates the claims of the text with respect to the decline of socially necessary labor.[38]

But the modern world of work is also missing from the plates on the paleotechnic phase, including those plates purporting to illustrate it. For example, the caption of Plate 7.1 begins, "Typical separation of labor-power and skill: increased efficiency at the price of increased servility of labor." The scene described is an eighteenth-century woodworker's shop, from Diderot's *Encyclopedia*. On the right an adult male works at a lathe; in the foreground at center is a young but fully grown male, presumably an apprentice, who uses a long handle to turn an oversized wooden wheel connected by belts to the lathe at right; in the background another male works at a second lathe driven by a foot treadle. Tools are neatly hung on the walls; light streams in through windows on three sides of the shop, and from the open front door (the point of view is the back of the shop); nothing clutters the floor, not even wood shavings. There is no servility in sight here, and the "increased efficiency" to which Mumford draws our attention remains a mystery because the division of labor we can observe is both rudimentary and momentary (someday the apprentice has to move to the lathe). For this is the same Spartan world of the artisan that Emerson discovered when he tried to decipher the "secrets of labor." In this world, abstract or alienated social labor was absent; in late-eighteenth-century France, as in early-nineteenth-century North America, it signified the sluggish routine of wage slavery.

The set of four *Encyclopedia* plates in which the woodworker's shop appears is entitled "Early Manufacture." Plate 7.2, "Mass-production of bottles," and 7.4, "Child-labor in pin-manufacture," show people actually producing commodities. But the two bottle-makers on view already look like machine-herds: they bend over and reach into an enormous oven stuffed with glass containers of all shapes and sizes. Mumford does not explain what these bottle-makers are doing; instead he explains the cultural functions of glass. In his caption for the child-labor scene, he notes that it was supposed to illustrate Adam Smith's argument on the division of labor, and that such "employment of the coolie labor of children was an essential basis of paleotechnic capitalism." But the scene itself looks like a kindergarten for autistic children: the *Encyclopedia* artist illustrated the principle of the division of labor by giving each of five figures a task unrelated, at least in pictorial space, to any other. In the remaining plates on the paleotechnic phase, no labor of any kind is on view; indeed there are no human figures to be seen except the passengers and observers who will inherit the earth in the neotechnic phase of the narrative.

When we turn from the illustrations to the text of *Technics*, we will notice the same absence of abstract or alienated social labor; or rather we will notice that human beings disappear with the advent of the factory system and its postartisanal forms of labor. For example: "Reduced to the function of a cog, the new worker could not operate without being joined to a machine. Since the workers lacked the capitalists' incentives of gain and social opportunity, the only things that kept them bound to the machine were starvation, ignorance, and fear" (173). Or again, "In so far as the workers were diseased, crippled, stupefied, and reduced to apathy and dejection by the paleotechnic environment they were only, up to a certain point, so much the better adapted to the new routine of factory and mill" (175). In this appearance of homogeneous labor-time, of routinized wage labor, Mumford saw not metaphorical but literal abstraction from real life—from the more transparent and palpable experience available under the preindustrial regime of handicraft, in which *poiesis* contained the connotations of production, labor, or work. "With the starvation of the senses went a general starvation of the mind: mere literacy, the ability to read signs, shop notices, newspapers, took the place of that general sensory and motor training that went with the handicraft and the agricultural industries" (181). No wonder "romanticism avoided the very energies by which alone it could hope to create a more sufficient pattern of existence—namely, the energies that were focussed in science and technics and in the mass of new machine-workers themselves" (287). To draw on those energies would have been to accept the abstraction from real life enforced by modern-industrial capitalism, to repudiate Ahab's interpretation of "human purpose at its highest expression," and ultimately to lose one's self in the belly of the beast, in the sheer mass of the new Leviathan.[39]

Mumford knew better than most other intellectuals that the price of *poiesis* was backwardness. "Individual self-sufficiency is another way of saying technological crudeness. . . . The machine has broken down the relative isolation—never complete even in the most primitive societies—of the handicraft period: it has intensified the need for collective effort and collective order" (280). But he also knew that almost everything he had written, and certainly all of what he still believed about personality or selfhood, was predicated on *poiesis*, that is, on the premodern and indeed ancient notion of the relation between work and its products, or between necessity and freedom. "Work, it is true, is the constant form of man's interaction with his environment, if by work one means the sum total of exertions necessary to sustain life. . . . But work in the form of unwilling drudgery or of that sedentary routine which . . . the Athenians so properly despised—work in these degrading forms is the true province of machines" (279–80). From this standpoint, the only possible justification for abstract or alienated social labor—that is, for the emergence of a paleotechnic proletariat—was that its neotechnic consequences would allow the return of the repressed regime of handicraft. In that future, "external nature" would finally appear as the direct "effect of culture" Emerson had insisted it should be; for it would then appear not as Commodity, not as the work of *homo faber*, not as the product of abstract or alienated social labor, but "as a result of man's collective experience, and as a subject for his further improvisations by means of science, technics, and the humane arts" (329). For the time being, however, in the present that was the foreseeable future, the relation between historical circumstance (form) and ethical principle (personality)—between *is* and *ought*—would be unintelligible if not unspeakable, since socially necessary labor was in fact receding while abstract and alienated labor was not (and could not, so long as capitalism did not simply disappear).

I would, then, suggest that Mumford's "artisanal critique of the industrial separation of art and labor," as one recent admirer puts it, is the *least* promising aspect of his cultural criticism, as it is of ours.[40] For it is precisely what petrified the opposition between Dewey and the young intellectuals in the 1920s and thereafter. Where they saw only objects, only the dominion of dead matter, of past labor, of industrial capital, he saw activity, "invention," the social labor and "moral community" of the factory as well—in other words, he saw what William James had seen from the train to Buffalo. So he grasped the promise of the impending future as fulfillment of, not departure from, the tendencies of the past, or rather as preservation *and* annulment of those tendencies. Dewey's usable past was accordingly broader than that of the young intellectuals, who were, by temperament and method, pretty much confined to celebrating those rare moments of unity and transcendence (the "golden days") which typically figure as the Before and After of history, of modernity, of industrial capitalism, or all of the above; for that reason, he never shared their profound sense of exile from the present, from their own place in time.

But my purpose is not to insist that we must choose between Dewey and Mumford. I have already claimed, and will argue in what follows, that this is not the real choice before us. For now, I want to trace the linkage between the Emersonian commitment to *poiesis*, the prime ministry of romanticism, and the "technocratic" politics at the core of Mumford's best work. In other words, I want to suggest that the self disclosed by his cultural sensibility and historical method is neither social nor participating—that it is instead an isolate, primordial self forged in a "third realm" of the arts, which reproduces the regime of handicraft and preserves in memory "the underlying human validity of the Romantic protest against the machine" by virtue of its detachment from the political economy of abstract or alienated social labor.

The linkage between *poiesis*, romanticism, and technocracy becomes obvious in Mumford's defense of the middle term as an abiding "attempt to restore the essential activities of human life to a central place in the new scheme, instead of accepting the machine as a center" (286). Once upon a time, romanticism was regressive because "life and energy and adventure were at first on the side of the machine: handicraft was associated with the fixed, the sessile, the superannuated, the dying" (285). Under neotechnic auspices, it gained a new lease on life. "The claims of life, once expressed solely by the Romantics and by the more archaic social groups and institutions of society, are now beginning to be represented at the very heart of technics itself" (368). So the return of repressed romanticism signified the repudiation of abstraction and accordingly the restoration of *poiesis*. "When we think and act in terms of an organic whole, rather than in terms of abstractions, . . . we will no longer require from the machine alone what we should demand through a many-sided adjustment of every other aspect of life. . . . Once we cultivate the arts of life directly, the proportion occupied by mechanical routine and by mechanical instruments will again diminish" (425–26, cf. 346–49). In short, the neotechnic transition would reinstate the regime of handicraft. "Automatic machines may conquer an ever-larger province in basic production: but it must be balanced by the hand-crafts and the machine-crafts for education, recreation, and experiment" (416–17).

As we know, Mumford had already argued that the nineteenth-century romantics could not offer an authentic alternative to "the machine" because they had not drawn on the energies available in science and technics, or in "the mass of new machine-workers" (287). But he did not suggest that their twentieth-century successors should turn to the modern-industrial working class for social or intellectual support of the neotechnic transition; in fact he provided two arguments against doing so. First, the claims of life did not require representation or articulation beyond that found in the nature— the organic telos—of the neotechnic artifacts themselves (250–55, 370–71). Second, and more important, the "mass of new machine-workers" appeared as the site on which the "objective personality" had been constructed. For this mass was uniquely "bound to the machine," that is, to material circumstances, to the mechanical agents of psychological externalization and cultural objectification; as the creature of science and industry, it was deeply sunk in sluggish routine—so deeply that only "captains of the spirit" like Ahab could rouse it. For example: "In the nineteenth century the mass of workers, cowed, uneducated, unskilled in cooperation, were only too willing to permit the capitalists to retain the responsibilities for financial management and production" (418). But nothing had changed since then because the abstraction from life enforced by modern-industrial capitalism had removed the paleotechnic proletariat from the scene of education, that is, from what Emerson had called the "effect of culture": "Until the worker emerges from a state of spiritless dependence there can be no large gain either in collective efficiency or social direction" (418).

Like Emerson, Mumford could not imagine intellectual growth or cultural development under the sign of abstract or alienated social labor. In his view, any departure from the inertia he associated with nineteenth-century workers would appear anomalous or even dangerous, for example as the spastic source of demand for spectacle in politics as in mass sports (303–7, 314–17). In the impending neotechnic transition, that proletarian "objectivity" had, then, to be governed by the "subjectivity" of those who had remained apart from, or had risen above, the domain of political economy, and thus had created a vital "culture of personality," a realm of *poiesis*, in which the legitimate "claims of life" were embodied as works of art, not learned in the course of social labor. The prime ministry of romanticism— its management of the "objective personality"—served this "subjective," but nonetheless political, purpose.

So my claim is not that Mumford's politics suffered from a lack of proletarian focus or sympathies, as if increased attention to the international working class would have dissolved the antinomies of his analysis and aligned him with the authentically progressive forces of his time. It is instead that there is a strong resemblance between the "culture of personality" corresponding to his notion of the genuine self and the high court of the poet convened by the literary Luddites who gave modernism a bad name by looking backward for alternatives to capitalism. In view of this claim, I would propose a change of venue. In other words, I would propose that critics of capitalism acknowledge the limits of romanticism and adopt the perspective(s) of pragmatism. At long last, I turn to a defense of this immodest proposal.

. . . .

CHAPTER 10

THE PAST AND THE

PRESENCE OF THE POSTMODERN

IN PRAGMATISM

Davidson, Dewey, and the Death of the Subject

To complete my argument about the historic meaning and contemporary significance of Jamesian pragmatism, I need to substantiate two propositions introduced in previous chapters. First I need to show how it preserves and annuls modern subjectivity—that is, how it works by drawing on and arguing with both romanticism and positivism, how it establishes the temporal continuity that the constituents of modern subjectivity cannot imagine, and how it constitutes a "larger field" than the romantic reaction codified in the outlook of the young intellectuals. Then I need to show how the pragmatist critique of modern subjectivity authorizes the reconstruction of the moral personality—in other words, how the postmodern personality sanctioned by pragmatism could become the bearer of an intelligible morality.

In my view it is almost self-evident that pragmatism is the first approximation of the postmodern sensibility simply because it transcends modern subjectivity—almost, but not quite. Sometimes changes are so profound—so complete and effective—that we do not recognize them as events that have already occurred. Donald Davidson, the influential philosopher, suggested as much in a 1986 essay entitled "The Myth of the Subjective." Here he noted that the ideas associated with "the relation between the human mind and the rest of nature, [or] the subjective and the objective as we have come to think of them, . . . are now coming under critical scrutiny, and the result promises to mark a sea change in contemporary philosophical thought—a change so profound that we may not recognize that it is occurring."[1] The change he had in mind was the "demise of the subjective" (166) that would derive from the collapse of the ontological division between mind and world, thought and thing, or, as Davidson once put it, scheme and content. "What we are about to see," he claimed, "is the emergence of a radically revised view of the relation of mind and the world" (163).

Meanwhile, he noted, most philosophers would cling to the "myth of the subjective," which he summarized as follows: "Since we cannot be certain what the world outside the mind is like, the subjective can keep its virtue—its chastity, its certainty for us—only by being protected from contamination by the world" (162). According to Davidson, this myth had determined the agenda of modern philosophy. "To a large extent this picture of mind and its place in nature has defined the problems modern philosophy has thought it had to solve" (161). Or again: "Instead of saying it is the scheme-content dichotomy that has dominated and defined the problems of modern philosophy, then, one could as well say it is how the dualism of the objective and the subjective has been conceived. For these dualisms have a common origin: a concept of the mind with its private states and objects" (163). So the impending changes—"these dualisms are being questioned in new ways or are being radically reworked" (163)—would presumably determine a *post*modern agenda in the discipline of philosophy if not in the culture at large.

Davidson's admirers among pragmatists do not label him a postmodern philosopher. Instead they try to depict him (against his wishes) as a new branch on the family tree. They do so on the grounds that "what Davidson added to Dewey is a non-representationalist philosophy of language that supplements, and in some measure replaces, Dewey's non-representationalist account of knowledge."[2] But the fact is that James produced the first version of this account of knowledge in 1904 and 1905, in essays for professional journals which later appeared as parts of either *The Meaning of Truth* (1909) or *Essays in Radical Empiricism* (1912). So the question of whether Davidson's philosophy of language supersedes this account should be addressed by reference to those essays and their impact—on Dewey among others. In 1903, James himself believed that the "Chicago School" led by Dewey was developing an alternative to the modern dualisms of subject and object. In the long run, he would be correct; meanwhile, however, that alternative emerged as a result of his own return to the themes of *The Will to Believe* and the *Talks to Teachers*, which he developed systematically in courses at Harvard after 1897.[3] And it is not as if no one noticed what James was doing. He spent a great deal of time and energy after 1904 simply replying to the critics of "radical empiricism," who believed, with good reason, that pragmatism was its cause and effect. Certainly Dewey and Alfred North Whitehead noticed what he was doing; accordingly they dated "the entailed revolution in our ways of thinking about philosophy" (167), as Davidson names the consequence of "the demise of the subjective," from 1904, when the new *Journal of Philosophy, Psychology and Scientific Methods* published "Does Consciousness Exist?"

In 1925, Whitehead, for example, claimed that the modern epoch in philosophy lasted from 1637, when Descartes's *Discourse on Method* appeared, to 1904, when James's essay appeared.

> It is an exaggeration to attribute a general change in a climate of thought to any one piece of writing, or to any one author. No doubt Descartes only expressed definitely and in decisive form what was already in the air of his period. Analogously, in attributing to William James the inauguration of a new stage in philosophy, we should be neglecting other influences of his time. But, admitting this, there still seems a certain fitness in contrasting his essay, *Does Consciousness Exist*, published in 1904, with Descartes' *Discourse on Method*, published in 1637. James clears the stage of the old paraphernalia; or rather he entirely alters its lighting. . . . The scientific materialism and the Cartesian ego were both challenged at the same moment, one by science and the other by philosophy, as represented by William James with his psychological antecedents; and the double challenge marks the end of a period which lasted for about two hundred and fifty years.[4]

The ways in which Dewey used, cited, and responded to this essay suggest that he concurred with Whitehead's verdict on its historical importance and implications. Between 1905 and 1909, and more often than not in the same *Journal of Philosophy, Psychology and Scientific Methods* which published "Does Consciousness Exist?," Dewey repeatedly invoked James's challenge to the Cartesian ego as the warrant or the occasion for his own arguments on behalf of a radical empiricism. For example, here is how he concluded "The Realism of Pragmatism" (1905): "I speak only for myself, but in giving my hearty assent to what Professor James has said about the nature of truth (see *Journal of Philosophy, Psychology and Scientific Methods*, p. 118, Vol. II), I venture to express the hope that he conceives the matter in much the same way as I have suggested. Certainly it is the obvious deduction from his denial of the existence of consciousness." Dewey announced his affiliation even more forthrightly in private correspondence. In acknowledging James's review of *Studies in Logical Theory* (1903), which appeared in 1904, he declared, "As far as I am concerned I have simply been rendering back in logical vocabulary what was already your own."[5]

A few months earlier, in December 1903, Dewey had taken up a question that he explored initially in the 1890s, while attempting to assimilate James's *Principles of Psychology*. "I have a good mind sometime," he told the author, "to make an inventory of all the points in which your psychology 'already' furnishes the instrumentalities for a pragmatic logic, ethics and metaphysics." Dewey could see *The Principles* as groundwork for the later pragmatist positions because as early as 1894 he had recognized that chapter 10 of this seminal book illustrated "the entire uselessness of an ego outside and behind" experience as such—in other words, it proved what James would argue in 1904 and after, that consciousness did not exist apart from its embodiment. But Dewey had also realized then that James could not entirely dispel the ego, the subject, "the faint rumour left behind by the disappearing 'soul,'" from the pages of *The Principles*, simply because the book was largely written in the 1880s, when it was virtually impossible to move beyond Kant's "transcendental ego" without appearing to accept Herbert Spencer's social science. From this standpoint, the essays of 1904–5 would represent the radical resolution of the ambiguities—or rather the residual dualism—remaining in James's philosophy.[6]

At any rate this is how Dewey treated them when he returned to the question in 1940, in a piece for the same *Journal of Philosophy* that had in its first few volumes featured so much of the early work of the original pragmatists. The title of the piece, "The Vanishing Subject in the Psychology of James," indicates both Dewey's purpose and the antecedents of Davidson's announcement regarding "the demise of the subjective." In concluding, Dewey noted, "Psychological theory is still the bulwark for all doctrines that assume independent and separate 'mind' and 'world' set over against each other." But he went on to point out that the dualism "originally came into psychology from philosophy." He had already shown why James's psychology should be read as symptom and cure of this reciprocal contamination—how *The Principles* contained both "official acceptance of epistemological dualism" and a subversive account of self-knowledge "in which the 'subject' of dualistic epistemology disappears." But Dewey recognized the essays of 1904–5 as the warrant for his reading of *The Principles*, according to which the subversive account of self-knowledge became the privileged truth of that text. "What he finally said in 1904, after he had thrown over his knowing Thought or Consciousness as a mere echo of a departed soul, was, after all, but an expression of ideas put forth in his *Psychology*, freed from hesitation and ambiguity."[7]

Now if we suppose that Davidson is correct to believe that the impending changes in philosophy are profound, even revolutionary, because they would resolve the dualisms specific to the modern epoch by certifying the death of the subject (a.k.a. "the demise of the subjective"), and if we further suppose that Dewey and Whitehead were correct to trace the beginning of this end to James's essays of 1904–5, then we should ask why the subject in question has taken so long to die, and why the cultural revolution residing in the chronicle of its death remains unfinished or unnoticed. The question is worth asking even before we gather evidence of a death foretold from the essays of 1904–5. For the mere resilience of modern subjectivity suggests that it is something more plausible than a myth, and that we might, therefore, want to learn to live with it. With these possibilities in mind, I would answer the question in two ways. First, the expectation that the Cartesian ego will disappear was, and is, no more realistic than the expectation that any given moment of infantile development will disappear insofar as a child grows and matures. The *return* of the repressed is much more likely, for cultures as for personalities, simply because each new moment of development will recall and recast the significance of past moments. In one of the essays on radical empiricism, James quoted Kierkegaard to explain this process: "We live forward, but we understand backward." Moreover, the political economy of the sign specific to corporate capitalism clearly thrives on what social theorists have called desublimation or deterritorialization, that is, on the mobilization of "archaic" desires—these are quite literally forces of production—in the name of intensified subjectivity and increased profitability. So if we do not learn how to complete the transition to a postcapitalist civilization, the impending society of the spectacle will surely teach us how to live backward and understand forward.[8]

Second, and probably more important, the romantic reaction led by the young intellectuals which reinstated modern subjectivity does not constitute a genuine, counterrevolutionary alternative to pragmatist postmodernism unless we begin to treat its separation of mind and world as an ontological condition of human nature, not a product of the historic transition from feudalism to capitalism. Modern subjectivity is not a form of "false consciousness," in other words, which we can exorcise by naming it "the myth of the subjective." For it is a discrete event as well as an idea. It is more real than God in this sense because it happened. As the sources of radical doubt about the evidence of the senses multiplied in the transition period, ca. 1400–1800, and as the immediate, affective links between emotions and environments were blocked or severed, the European ego became a singular "point of view" on or above the world and the body rather than an undivided dimension of both. The problem of perspective—where to position oneself in relation to the world and the body conceived as external objects—accordingly became the metaphor of personal identity as well as the central issue of epistemology and moral philosophy. The modern subject was born, in short, when the logic of the gaze became the paradigm of knowledge. But we should remember that the problem of perspective was quite genuine because this logic both required and accommodated new spaces and greater distances between subject and object—the relationship between human beings and their earthly or embodied environment(s) had in fact changed drastically—and did, therefore, make the nature of reality, and, for that matter, the reality of nature, open questions.[9]

Certainly it was not obvious that the reality in question could be apprehended from *any* point of view or subject position. So anxiety about the subject's position in relation to the world became anxiety about the subjective as such, and that in turn created demand for rules or procedures that would formalize and guarantee its integrity.[10] In retrospect, we can, then, see that the subjective becomes "mythic" only insofar as we treat it as something more or less than historically contingent. To treat it as something more is to mistake it for a transhistorical attribute of human nature, and to assume the ontological priority of the pure self. But to treat it as something less, as Davidson does by denying or forgetting that it was both cause and effect of a historically specific transition to modernity, is to remove philosophical conversation from the conditions and sources of its development.

This last assertion no doubt seems apocalyptic in view of the claims made on Davidson's behalf. So I should explain what I mean before turning to James's rendition of the death of the subject. Davidson's most enthusiastic and effective champion is Richard Rorty, who insists that "the point of edifying philosophy is to keep the conversation going rather than to find objective truth."[11] If we suppose that he is correct, we will be led to the conclusion that there is not, and cannot be, a significant difference between doing philosophy and doing history. At any rate that is where I am led by the following logic. To make this claim, Rorty must assume that fact and value are indissoluble, and consequently that there is no independent body of fact on which rival accounts of the same phenomena can draw in deciding the superiority of one over another. Thus each account becomes incommensurable with all others. To adopt the metaphor of conversation, each voice becomes unintelligible to all others. If the point of philosophy is to keep this conversation going, philosophers must, then, have some criteria according to which new voices are admitted and old voices are permitted to remain— but that is only another way of saying that they must have some criteria according to which participants in the conversation can evaluate rival accounts of the same phenomena by making them commensurable accounts. Without such criteria, there is no conversation because everything becomes opinion: the facts of the case change as each participant yields to the next.[12]

But as Alasdair MacIntyre has shown, the only way to articulate such criteria is by recourse to historical consciousness and method. For if there is no independent body of fact on which rival accounts can draw, the best available account must be the one that includes its rivals, that preserves and annuls its predecessors by showing *why* they have no satisfactory answers for the questions they have raised in the normal course of their development, and by showing *how* these questions can be addressed from within a new and more inclusive account. The "why" is prior to the "how" in every sense because the commensurability and then the superiority of a new account become evident only insofar as its proponents can demonstrate that its predecessors have become incoherent or inadequate according to their own standards. So these proponents of the new account must situate their demonstration in the narrative time of historical explanation, where the incoherence and inadequacy of rival accounts become conditions of intellectual progress, that is, where "the false is no longer false as a moment of the true."

Davidson's position denies this historiographical entailment of "edifying philosophy," and indeed happily excludes its rivals from the conversation by treating them as creatures of a myth. By Rorty's own definition, therefore, Davidson does not qualify as a philosopher. But then Rorty also argues in favor of adjourning philosophy as such. So I would go further and say that, by denying this edifying entailment, Davidson has reinstated the figure of those final or "objective truths" he and Rorty ridicule in other contexts. For if we cannot specify the limitations of modern subjectivity except by suggesting that its constituents are irrational, we have claimed, in effect, not merely that our postmythic account is incommensurable with its predecessors, but that the conversation connecting us to people with whom we differ *due to historical circumstances* cannot, and need not, be continued. We have claimed, again in effect, that the final truth in this respect is already ours. But we will be at a loss to explain how or why we have come to believe what we do about subject and object, except by reference to some innate capacity of mind to represent this new truth. As a result, we will tend to believe that our rivals have not retired to the dustbin of history because they are incapable of acknowledging the truth as we represent it. We will be mystified or offended, in other words, by those who disagree with us on the issue of modern subjectivity, especially if they claim that their position is both rational and truthful. And so the truth in question will become precisely what Davidson and Rorty insist it is not—a timeless object to which good ideas should correspond.

Does Consciousness Exist?

Let us turn, finally, to James's essays of 1904–5, to see if we can find the primary sources of a postmodern pluralism, a radically pragmatic empiricism, that will permit the annulment *and* preservation of modern subjectivity, and so will let us live less anxiously with it. By all accounts, then as now, the key essay is "Does Consciousness Exist?" It is a convenient consensus for my purposes, because here James sounds as if he were trying to convince not just his contemporaries, but Emerson as well. In preparation for his address at the Emerson centenary of May 1903, James had reread the collected works. But he prolonged this reckoning by using the first installment of his new "metaphysical system" to explore the meaning and significance of the binary opposition between thoughts and things which dominated the Emersonian vision.[13] In fact he begins by quoting from an unnamed text that could be "Nature." " 'Thoughts' and 'things' are names for two sorts of object, which common sense will always find contrasted and will always practically oppose to each other" (1141, also 1145, 1148, 1153–54). Then James equates the "thought" of common sense and the "consciousness" of philosophy; having done so, he can announce the imminent death of the "transcendental ego" that represents subjectivity.

I believe that "consciousness," when once it has evaporated to [the neo-Kantian] estate of pure diaphaneity, is on the point of disappearing altogether. It is the name of a nonentity, and has no right to a place among first principles. Those who still cling to it are clinging to a mere echo, the faint rumour left behind by the disappearing "soul" upon the air of philosophy. . . . For twenty years past I have mistrusted "consciousness" as an entity; for seven or eight years past I have suggested its non-existence to my students, and tried to give them its pragmatic equivalent in realities of experience. It seems to me that the hour is ripe for it to be openly and universally discarded. (1141–42)

So much for the dualisms on which Emerson the Orphic poet and philosopher had settled. But James does not claim that there are no thoughts; instead he insists that the notion of "consciousness" and its more or less "subjective" bearers are unnecessary to explain the existence and effects of thoughts. "There is, I mean, no aboriginal stuff or quality of being, contrasted with that of which material objects are made, out of which our thoughts of them are made." Thoughts are real, in other words, because "there is a function in experience which thoughts perform." This function is knowing, through which the "portions" of the "one primal stuff in the world"—pure experience, the "instant field of the present"—are related; but knowing is only "a particular sort of relation" between parts of pure experience, in which knower and known are continuously reconstituted by new alignments of thought and thing, not subject and object (1142, 1151).

James proposes, then, to discard the neo-Kantian version of the theorem that "experience is indefeasibly dualistic in structure" (1142), not to deny any distinction between mind and matter or soul and body. He objects to the subject-object dualism that inevitably accompanies the notion of consciousness as toasted by "belated drinkers at the Kantian spring"; for it somehow subsists outside of time, and so cannot move, change, or develop. "Souls were detachable, had separate destinies; things could happen to them. To consciousness as such nothing can happen, for, timeless itself, it is only a witness of happenings in time, in which it plays no part" (1143). In this sense, James suggests that philosophical dualism has a history, of which "neo-Kantism" is the highest stage (1142). He cites G. E. Moore (of Cambridge-Bloomsbury fame) and Paul Natorp as representatives of that stage, in which philosophers cannot define or describe "consciousness"— " 'it seems to vanish,' " says Moore—and yet insist that it remains after "mental subtraction" removes the content of thought from the agent of thought, thereby distinguishing the known from the knower (1143–44). "Experience, at this rate," James points out, "would be much like a paint of which the world pictures were made," that is, something with a "dual constitution," dividing naturally into particular pigments (content) and universal oil or solvent (consciousness).[14] He then turns to his own argument, which, he notes, "is exactly the reverse of this" (1144).

> Experience, I believe, has no such inner duplicity; and the separation into consciousness and content comes, not by way of subtraction, but by way of addition—the addition, to a given concrete piece of it, of other sets of experiences, in connection with which severally its use or function may be of two different kinds. The paint will also serve here as an illustration. In a pot in a paint-shop, along with other paints, it serves in its entirety as so much saleable matter. Spread on a canvas, with other paints around it, it represents, on the contrary, a feature in a picture and performs a spiritual function. Just so, I maintain, does a given undivided portion of experience, taken in one context of associates, play the part of a knower,

of a state of mind, of "consciousness"; while in a different context the same undivided bit of experience plays the part of a thing known, of an objective "content." In a word, in one group it figures as a thought, in another group as a thing. And, since it can figure in both groups simultaneously we have every right to speak of it as subjective and objective both at once. (1144–45)

Things like paint acquire meanings and significance—they become the particular contents of experience—only in terms of human purposes or thoughts. So far the neo-Kantian account might work. But such purposes or thoughts are not given or revealed by "consciousness" as such, that is, by a subject conceived as prior or external to the particular contents of experience, by a mind or self that is somehow exempt from the vicissitudes of time. At any rate this is the substance of James's retort to "neo-Kantism" in Section 2 of the essay. Here it becomes obvious that he wants above all to situate "the function of knowing" in historical time, and accordingly to overcome by *explaining*—to preserve by reinterpreting—the inherited dualisms of subject and object.

James notes that "the whole philosophy of perception," which I take to mean epistemology, "has been just one long wrangle over the paradox that what is evidently one reality should be in two places at once, both in outer space and in a person's mind" (1145–46). He has already encouraged the reader to relive the experience of seeing *and* perceiving the room in which he sits—that is, to experience the room as thing, as "a physical object, his actual field of vision," but also as thought, as "those self-same things which his mind, as we say, perceives" (1145). So the paradox is close by, and not at all abstruse or abstract. One way to solve it is by recourse to the strictly spatial metaphors of geometry. "The puzzle of how the one identical room can be in two places is at bottom just the puzzle of how one identical point can be on two lines. It can, if it be situated at their intersection." But the experience of the room is plainly more complex than an intersection that occurs in a merely logical or mathematical universe. "If the 'pure experience' of the room were a place of intersection of two processes, which connected it with different groups of associates respectively, it could be counted twice over, as belonging to either group, and spoken of loosely as existing in two places, although it would remain all the time a numerically single thing" (1146). The question then becomes, "What are the two processes, now, into which the room-experience simultaneously enters in this way?" James believes that the answer appears when we acknowledge the dimension of *time* to which the geometer's point must be indifferent. "One of them is the reader's personal biography, the other is the history of the house of which the room is part" (1146).

These become the temporal grounds on which he thinks he can recast and recuperate dualism.

> As "subjective" we say that the experience represents; as "objective" it is represented. What represents and what is represented is here numerically the same; but we must remember that no dualism of being represented and representing resides in the experience *per se*. In its pure state, or when isolated, there is no self-splitting of it into consciousness and what the consciousness is "of." Its subjectivity and objectivity are functional attributes solely, realized only when the experience is "taken," *i.e.*, talked-of, twice, considered along with its two differing contexts respectively, by a new retrospective experience, of which that whole past complication now forms the fresh content. (1151)

The problem of perspective—how to paint "the world pictures" from the modern, neo-Kantian standpoint of a timeless subject—is now complicated, but not displaced, by the attitude of retrospection. For the world of pure experience "is only virtually or potentially either object or subject." It becomes a purpose, a state of mind, a "reality intended," as we begin acting on it in time, that is, as we begin *adding to it* by "the doubling of it in retrospection" (1151). But even in its simplicity and unity, "the immediate experience in its passing is always 'truth,' practical truth," because it is not yet a state of mind that stands corrected or confirmed by retrospection (1151). For the time being, it is all we have.

By complicating the problem of perspective in this manner, James identifies three orders of truth or reality. There is the practical truth residing in the "instant field of the present." There are the truths we learn backward by adding, retrospectively, to the practical truth of immediate experience. And then there is "truth absolute and objective." This third order of truth is final in every sense because its condition is the end of time. "If the world were then and there to go out like a candle, [the immediate experience] would remain truth absolute and objective, for it would be 'the last word,' would have no critic, and no one would ever oppose the thought in it to the reality intended" (1151). So the only truths of which we can speak and be aware are those provisional, second-order truths we can represent as they emerge in the narrative time of historical consciousness and explanation. We can come to know the practical truth of immediate experience by acting on it, by adding to it the second-order truths of retrospection. But we cannot know the absolute truth—we cannot hear the last word on any subject—until the end of time.

Subject-object dualism is, then, a functional distinction that becomes intelligible *as* a historical phenomenon because it *is* a historical phenomenon. It is only *in retrospect* that an experience can be disaggregated. "In its pure state, or when isolated, there is no self-splitting of it into consciousness and what the consciousness is 'of'" (1151). But it does not follow that these divisions of time represent falsehood from which we must flee. James insists instead that they are the condition of the only truths we can know. That is why he claims that his account can preserve dualism by reinterpreting it. "The dualism connoted by such double-barreled terms as 'experience,' 'phenomenon,' 'datum,' '*Vorfindung*'—terms which, in philosophy at any rate, tend more and more to replace the single-barreled terms of 'thought' and 'thing'—that dualism, I say, is still preserved in this account, but reinterpreted, so that, instead of being mysterious and elusive, it becomes verifiable and concrete. It is an affair of relations, it falls outside, not inside, the single experience considered, and can always be particularized and defined" (1145).

So the resolution of the ambiguity residing in *The Principles* was not as radical as Dewey supposed; for modern subjectivity and its attendant dualisms do not simply vanish from this account. James does of course object to the neo-Kantian version of the subject. In his view, it was both unnecessary as a bulwark of selfhood or morality against the encroachments of pure experience and incapable of serving as such in its "thoroughly ghostly condition." But we should not confuse his farewell to this owl of Minerva with a farewell to owls. He wants to transcend modern subjectivity by annulling *and* preserving it; that is why he refuses to treat it as the unfortunate mistake of his unenlightened predecessors. As usual, James is trying to find the middle ground on which he can reconcile "previous truth and novel fact"; as always, he finds that place in time, between *now* and *then*.

In the second of the essays collected under the rubric of radical empiricism, "A World of Pure Experience," he explores the same area; in doing so, he completes the critique of modern subjectivity, and introduces the metaphors as well as the arguments that would reappear in *Pragmatism*.[15] James concludes, for example, by claiming that a philosophy of pure experience is analogous to a mosaic, because the spaces between the pieces are no less important parts of the composition than the pieces themselves. "Life is in the transitions as much as in the terms connected; often, indeed, it seems to be there more emphatically" (42). For the passage beyond a given moment will make earlier moments significant or not. "These relations of continuous transition experienced are what make our experiences cognitive. . . . When one of them terminates a previous series of them with a sense of fulfillment, it, we say, is what those other experiences 'had in view.' The knowledge, in such a case, is verified, the truth is 'salted down.' " But verification is unusual precisely because it constitutes an ending, not a transition. "Mainly, however, we live on speculative investments, or on our prospects only. But living on things *in posse* is as good as living in the actual, so long as our credit remains good. It is evident that for the most part it is good, and that the universe seldom protests our drafts." The metaphor works here, at the conclusion of an argument about the centrality of time in self-knowledge, because credit is the future tense of money. "In this sense we at every moment can continue to believe in an existing *beyond*" (42–43, cf. 39–40).

James keeps stopping to summarize, to emphasize that time is the key to his argument. For example, "According to my view, experience as a whole is a process in time, whereby innumerable particular terms lapse and are superseded by others that follow upon them by transitions which, whether disjunctive or conjunctive in content, are themselves experiences, and must in general be accounted at least as real as the terms which they relate" (31–32). Indeed he insists that timeless knowledge is impossible if not inconceivable, for "every later moment continues and corroborates an earlier one": "In this continuing and corroborating, taken in no transcendental sense, but denoting definitely felt transitions, *lies all that the knowing of a percept by an idea can possibly contain or signify*. Wherever such transitions are felt, the first experience *knows* the last one. Where they do not, or where even as possibles they cannot, intervene, there can be no pretence of knowing. . . . Knowledge of sensible realities thus comes to life inside the tissue of experience. It is *made*; and made by relations that unroll themselves in time" (29).

James recalls, but also amplifies, the argument of "Does Consciousness Exist?," by suggesting that the "cognitive relations" connecting the terms, or the discrete moments, of experience, and thereby constituting knowledge as such, are prospective as well as retrospective. The actual, the necessary, and the present are defined, then, by the virtual, the possible, and the pending—that is, by what they are not but could, or will, become. "Until established by the end of the process, [an idea's] quality of knowing . . . could still be doubted; and yet the knowing really was there, as the result now shows" (34). But the virtual, the possible, and the pending are themselves implicated in the reality of time—the "existing *beyond*" they represent is still in and of this world. James's illustration underscores the profanity of his position. "Just so we are 'mortal' all the time, by reason of the virtuality of the inevitable event which will make us so when it shall have come" (34). Because human beings know that their bodies decay in the fullness of time, they treat every life as a death foretold: they define themselves by reference to an ending they cannot predict.

"A World of Pure Experience" completes the argument of "Does Consciousness Exist?" by showing that our departure from neo-Kantian rationalism does not deliver us unto a "Humian type of empiricism" (22). James knew that David Hume was one of the first philosophers to write as if the enunciation of ethical principles and the analysis of historical circumstances were not antithetical enterprises—as if the goal of philosophy was to understand the relation between the universal and the particular, not to assume that one was the primary reality from which the other could be deduced and criticized.[16] But James also knew that Hume's project failed because it could not go far enough, and became a way of denying the significance of universals as such, that is, of treating the whole as the simple sum of its parts. "Empiricism is known as the opposite of rationalism. . . . [It] lays the explanatory stress upon the part, the element, the individual, and treats the whole as a collection and the universal as an abstraction" (22). Radical empiricism fulfills the promise of Hume's project, then, by treating the perceived relations or transitions *between* the moments or parts of experience as if they were themselves real, true, and vital. "To be radical, an empiricism must neither admit into its constructions any element that is not directly experienced, nor exclude from them any element that is directly experienced. For such a philosophy, *the relations that connect experiences must themselves be experienced relations, and any kind of relation experienced must be accounted as real as anything else in the system*" (22).

As James annuls and preserves the legacy of Kant in "Does Consciousness Exist?," so he preserves and annuls the legacy of Hume in "A World of Pure Experience." He argues that the rationalist recourse to "trans-experiential [i.e., suprahistorical] agents of unification, substances, intellectual categories and powers, or selves," was the "natural result" of an empiricism in which "conjunctive relations" between experiences did not appear as "fully coordinate" with the more obvious discontinuities. Insofar as empiricists continue to "insist most on the disjunctions," and accordingly do not recognize the activity that unifies or integrates the parts of experience as itself a form of experience, a more or less rationalist, neo-Kantian retort to Hume is therefore plausible. But insofar as empiricists do recognize such activity as a directly experienced element of life, they will have transcended Hume and made the rationalists' invocation of extratemporal agency—for example, of "consciousness"—unnecessary. *"Radical empiricism*, as I understand it, *does full justice to conjunctive relations*, without, however, treating them as rationalism always tends to treat them, as being true in some supernal way, as if the unity of things and their variety belonged to different orders of truth and vitality altogether" (23).

If the whole is the sum of its parts by this account, the parts now include the relations between them; and these relations—the "relations that unroll themselves in time"—determine the meanings of the parts by plotting their cognitive positions. It follows that the elements, moments, or terms of experience cannot be detached from their relations to one another, and that the whole, of which they are virtual, possible, and pending parts, defines or constitutes them as such. In other words, the universal is something we *experience*, as a lived relation—it is a concrete and intrinsic dimension of the particular, not a metaphysical abstraction or heuristic device that we must superimpose on our experience. For it emerges in time, and only in time. "This bare relation of *withness* between some parts of the sum total of experience and other parts, is the fact that ordinary empiricism over-emphasizes against rationalism, the latter always tending to ignore it unduly. Radical empiricism, on the contrary, is fair to both the unity and disconnexion. It finds no reason for treating either as illusory. It allots to each its definite sphere of description, and agrees that there appear to be actual forces at work which tend, as time goes on, to make the unity greater" (24).

James is, then, claiming that the vicissitudes of time are the necessary condition of the self's integrity as well as knowledge. And he is fully aware of how extraordinary that claim must sound to those educated by the Western philosophical tradition. "The conjunctive relation that has given most trouble to philosophy is *the co-conscious transition*, so to call it, by which one experience passes into another when both belong to the same self" (25). Individuals change with time, of course, but that is no reason, James suggests, to insist that the self is only an agenda of appetites, a "bundle of sensations," a perfectly discontinuous and externally determined object that is accordingly incapable of moral judgment.[17] For it is change—the experience of transition from one state to another—that makes the articulation of "conjunctive relations" between the parts of experience possible and necessary. "Personal histories are processes of change in time, and *the change itself is one of the things immediately experienced*. 'Change' in this case means continuous as opposed to discontinuous transition. But continuous transition is one sort of conjunctive relation" (25).

James now puts all his cards on the table, and announces that he is proposing to rewrite the agenda of philosophy, by making it the study of these changes, these "continuous transitions" that mobilize, or become, the forces of unity in our selves. "To be a radical empiricist means to hold fast to this conjunctive relation [i.e., to 'continuous transition'] of all others, for this is the strategic point, the position through which, if a hole be made, all the corruptions of dialectics and all the metaphysical fictions pour into our philosophy" (25). In other words, if we know that the integrity of the self resides in and flows from its experience of time, of change, of development, we have no reason either to depend on suprahistorical "agencies of union" for the groundwork of truth and morality, or to assume that the habitat of the moral personality must be something other than historical time. We have every reason to believe instead that the discovery of universal ethical principles entails the understanding of particular historical circumstances, and vice versa, or, to be more precise, that an ethical principle becomes "universal"—that is, it transcends the historical circumstances under which it was enunciated—only insofar as we can imagine how it might be embodied or applied under historical circumstances that differ significantly from those under which it was enunciated. To make this imaginative leap, we need of course to acknowledge the force and weight of these significant differences. But we also need to explain how and why they do not preclude what James calls continuity—we need to explain how and why we can treat different historical epochs as commensurable. To do so is to situate our selves and our arguments in the narrative time of historical explanation, where transitions are, or can be, continuous.

The critique of modern subjectivity is now complete; for James has shown that the integrity of the self requires not immunity from but immersion in pure experience. By his account, the fall into time and space and desire is the necessary condition of the moral personality, because it elicits and establishes "conjunctive relations" through which we can apprehend our development in time as continuity, and can project ourselves into a future that is consistent with our pasts. So he has changed the subject in every sense. But James has neither ignored nor repudiated modern subjectivity and its attendant dualisms; he has instead contained them within his more inclusive account. For example, James draws on positivism in its empiricist incarnation as a way of avoiding purely verbal or logical solutions, of reducing the volume of abstract, metaphysical cant about the universal; but he also insists that the whole is greater than the sum of its parts, that the "conjunctive relations" leading us beyond the instant field of the present already constitute a concrete universal from which we can learn something useful—that is, applicable—about truth and morality. In short, he shows that by its own criterion of direct experience, empiricism is incomplete and incoherent unless it acknowledges the perceived relations that connect and transcend the discrete elements of experience.

James's debt to romanticism is less obvious, because he is impatient with anyone who would treat desire as the antithesis of reason. By and large, the romantics of the nineteenth and twentieth centuries have followed the positivists in assuming that reason and desire are antithetical; but they have always chosen desire—in the form of the natural, the organic, the female, the bodily, and the intuitive—over reason, because they have normally associated reason with the new Leviathan, the bourgeois "system of needs," brought forth by modern science and industry. Even so, romanticism and positivism produce the same results; for to choose between reason and desire as if they were mutually exclusive modes of apprehension is to repress and mutilate one or the other, and accordingly to make the differences between them unimportant. At that point, where reason and desire become practically identical, we can have no rational and communicable grounds on which to oppose those desires we find distasteful or destructive, and no reason to modulate our own desires for the sake of an ideal or purpose that cannot be realized immediately. This is the irony James excludes from his studies in the development of the postmodern personality by insisting that reason and desire are indissoluble, not indistinguishable.

But those studies do challenge the principle of analysis, the "brain that divides" wholes into parts, forests into trees, and selves into mere sensations. For James believes that our minds can be understood, and redeemed, only by acknowledging their origins in, and continuous collaboration with, our bodies. Here, for example, is how he concludes "Does Consciousness Exist?": "The stream of thinking (which I recognize emphatically as a phenomenon) is only a careless name for what, when scrutinized, reveals itself to consist chiefly of the stream of my breathing. . . . breath moving outwards, between the glottis and the nostrils, is, I am persuaded, the essence out of which philosophers have constructed the entity known as consciousness" (1157–58). James is, then, completing the resurrection of the body which romantics have defined as their goal since 1800. But unlike the romantics, he refuses to corroborate the reported ascension of the resurrected body, or to worship it as a higher standard of truth than the mind. For to adopt the romantic position, and to invert the positivist specification of the relation between body and mind, is to leave intact the original, ontological divide that eventually petrifies as the dualisms of value and fact, desire and reason, object and subject. James tries instead to *preserve* the difference between these terms by *changing* its status and function within his new system, by treating it in the same way he treats the difference between things and thoughts—that is, as a contingent, historical phenomenon.

Pragmatism as a Postrepublican Frame of Acceptance

The task that remains is to show how this pragmatist critique of modern subjectivity authorizes the reconstruction of the moral personality. I must begin by recalling the arguments of previous chapters, for they will become essential to the argument hereafter. In chapter 8, I claimed that the relation between space and time represented by the figure of the freeholder, the yeoman, and the citizen-soldier—that is, the repression of historical time by space, by new frontiers—collapses with the advent of corporate-industrial capitalism, ca. 1890–1920. Accordingly I suggested that the choices available to those who would reconstitute the moral personality were to situate it in historical time or to reclaim the extratemporal space in which the figure of the freeholder, the yeoman, and the citizen-soldier once moved freely. I concluded that pragmatism as James sketched it was one version, or effect, of the first choice, and that populism and high literary modernism were different versions, or effects, of the second choice. I went on in chapter 9 to demonstrate that the romantic reaction led by Lewis Mumford was another version or effect of the second choice. And in this chapter, I have shown that the problem of perspective and the metaphors of space—for example, painting "the world pictures" from the neo-Kantian standpoint—are complicated but not displaced by the pragmatist attitude toward history and its corresponding metaphors of time.

So conceived, the meaning of pragmatism is clear enough. But its significance will not be until we assess it in terms of the Atlantic republican tradition through which those metaphors of time became idiomatic elements of the North American political vernacular. We must then turn to J.G.A. Pocock's monumental history of that tradition. As I understand it, his purpose was to explain "the curious extent to which the most postmodern and post-industrial of societies [the United States] continues to venerate pre-modern and anti-industrial values, symbols, and constitutional forms, and to suffer from an awareness of the tensions between practice and morality." Pocock named this curious veneration a "quarrel of the self with history." He claimed that even in the twentieth century it typically appears as an obsessive concern with "the threat of corruption," because North Americans "inherited rhetorical and conceptual structures which ensured that venality in public officials, the growth of a military-industrial complex in government, other-directedness and one-dimensionality in individuals, could all be identified in terms continuous with those used in the classical analysis of corruption"—that is, with those used in the civic humanist tradition founded by Aristotle, rehabilitated by Machiavelli, Harrington, and Montesquieu in the sixteenth and seventeenth centuries, revised by the Commonwealthmen of eighteenth-century England, and reinvigorated by the revolutionaries of North America. By the classical account, corruption in all its guises was the inevitable effect of the republic's descent into secular time, the region of commerce, accumulation, luxury, and vice. But the eighteenth-century version of civic humanism also lacked a middle term between the static utopia anchored by civic virtue—that is, by a majority of freeholding citizens—and the developmental dynamic of the market economy, which, by permitting speculation and by enforcing the concentration of wealth and "natural power," would eventually corrupt private citizens as well as public officials. The private manipulation of paper money, and more particularly of public credit, accordingly signified the logic of historical time construed as *commerce*.[18]

Since the revolution that founded the nation was transacted under the sign of civic humanism, "American metahistory has remained the rhetoric of a spatial escape and return, and has never been that of a dialectical process." In other words, North Americans have remained profoundly skeptical about modern-industrial capitalism because they have understood it in terms of the Atlantic republican tradition, as a threat to both civic virtue and the "moral stability of the human personality." But they have also remained profoundly cynical about their capacity to transform or transcend modern-industrial capitalism, because in the history of capitalism as such they have seen nothing more than irony, nothing less than "movement away from the norms defining that [moral] stability." So Pocock's argument finally and inadvertently converges on that of Louis Hartz. For he suggests in concluding that what is missing from American political culture is not socialism but the "ethos of historicist socialism": "When we speak of historicism, we mean both an attempt to engage the personality and its integrity in the movement of history, and an attempt to depict history as generating new norms and values. The underlying strength of historicism is . . . this sense of the secular creativity of history, its linear capacity to bring about incessant qualitative transformations of human life; but the paradox of American thought—on the other hand, the essence of socialist thought—has been a constant moral polemic against the way in which this happens."[19]

From Pocock's standpoint, the end of the Machiavellian moment in

North America would, then, presuppose an alternative to the metahistorical "rhetoric of a spatial escape and return," that is, a way of treating historical time as the medium in which virtue becomes a lived experience, a concrete universal. This alternative would have to address "the concern for the moral stability of the human personality"—the concern that animates "the quarrel of the self with history"—by demonstrating that such stability emerges only in time, and develops only as a social, historical phenomenon. Insofar as it completed that demonstration, and yet remained critical of capitalism, this alternative would amount to the "ethos of historicist socialism"; for it would have freed American thought, and by the same token socialist thought, from the antimodernist irony that still regulates both, and would accordingly recognize in the development of capitalism the necessary condition of a passage beyond class society.

As I see it, this postrepublican alternative is pragmatism. Between 1897 and 1910, in working out his new philosophical system and sounding out its political implications, James does in fact try to end, or at least to mediate, the "quarrel of the self with history," and to describe a socialism that does not merely validate a "pacific cosmopolitan industrialism." Again, he does not complete his project. He knew he could not. "It may perhaps be enough for me," he said in April 1905, "to indicate the beginning of the road to follow."[20] Nevertheless I would claim that, then as now, he came closer than most of his critics to the destination Pocock calls the "ethos of historicist socialism." I say this not only because James advocates "some sort of socialistic equilibrium" in his search for a moral equivalent of war, but also because the essays on radical empiricism formalize the insights of the *Talks to Teachers* by identifying the moral personality with the liminal figures who had hitherto appeared only at the margins, as the Other, in modern political theory.

In both the republican and the liberal variations on the theme of modern political theory, these were the figures of the proletariat. Early modern political theorists in the Anglo-American world treated the distribution of property within civil society as the deep structure of the history legible in the manipulation of public credit. They assumed that the distribution of property determined the balance of social power between estates, and that property was the means to, and the foundation of, the self-determining personality. They accordingly expressed their concern for the moral stability of the human personality in the language of political economy, as if it were a social question to be addressed by the study and the disposition of property. Disciples of both Montesquieu and Locke believed, for example, that those who lacked property—those who had to sell their ability to produce goods and services for wages—also lacked moral substance and political capacity because they were subject to external domination by their employers. Unlike the freeholder, the yeoman, the citizen-soldier, or, for that matter, the merchant, these proletarians had no place, no fixed location, either in the body politic or in civil society; they could not escape the vicissitudes of time because they were creatures of necessity.[21]

Indeed the transatlantic revolutionaries of the late eighteenth century gave a new inflection to the familiar difference between rich and poor by claiming that its characteristic form in modern, commercial society was a class division and that, as such, it would prove to be the central threat to republican government. In this sense, they used the figure of the proletariat to represent the vicissitudes of modern times. For example, in June 1787, at the constitutional convention, James Madison pointed out that a mere increase of population would make leveling more likely, because the majority of that increase would be composed of the creatures of necessity. "An increase of population will of necessity increase the proportion of those who labour under all the hardships of life & secretly sigh for a more equal distribution of its blessings. These may in time outnumber those who are placed above the feelings of indigence. According to the equal laws of suffrage, the power will slide into the hands of the former." So the question was, could that outcome be prevented without giving up on popular government? "How is this danger to be guarded against on republican principles?"[22] Was there a middle term between the static utopia of agrarian virtue still personified by the yeoman and the dynamic dystopia of modern commerce now personified by the proletariat?

Madison addressed these questions in a long comment on Jefferson's proposed constitution for Virginia. Here he offered a close reading of recent history which stressed the contradiction between the theory of republican government and the inner articulation of modern civil society. In the 1770s, he noted, there was no fundamental conflict over the "two cardinal objects of Government, the rights of persons and the rights of property," presumably because all components of the revolutionary coalition agreed that property and liberty were indissoluble. "In the existing state of American population and American property, the two classes of rights were so little discriminated that a provision for the rights of persons was to include of itself those of property, and it was natural to infer from the tendency of republican laws that these different interests would be more and more identified." But in retrospect, it was clear that the men of property were becoming a minority. "Experience and investigation have however produced more correct ideas on this subject. It is now observed that in all populous countries, the smaller part only can be interested in preserving the rights of property." Even the frontier would one day recapitulate the class division of the settled areas. "It must be foreseen that America and Kentucky itself will by degrees arrive at this State of Society; that in some parts of the Union a very great advance is already made towards it."[23]

In August 1787, again in convention, Madison reiterated this prophecy. "In future times a great majority of the people will not only be without landed, but any other sort of, property." North America was not yet as "populous" as comparable countries and therefore not yet as divided or contentious. "The United States have not reached the stage of Society in which conflicting feelings of the Class with, and the Class without property, have the operation natural to them in Countries fully peopled." But the "Class without property" was still an inevitable threat to liberty and justice. As such, it was also a threat to the moral stability of the human personality. For if property served as the foundation of the self-determining personality, and if the moral stability of the human personality presupposed self-determination, then the proletariat represented the dissolution of all foundations. That is probably why Marx called it the universal class. That is certainly why Madison treated it as the dupe of ambition or the instrument of wealth, but not as an agent in its own right; in his view, it could not know, let alone realize, its own intentions. "If all power be suffered to slide into hands not interested in the rights of property which must be the case whenever a majority fall under that description, one of two things cannot fail to happen; either they will unite against the other description and become the dupes and instruments of ambition, or their poverty and dependence will render them the mercenary instruments of wealth. In either case liberty will be subverted, in the first by a despotism growing out of anarchy, in the second, by an oligarchy founded on corruption."[24]

When modulated by Madison, what Pocock defines as both the paradox of American thought and the essence of socialist thought—that is, the moral polemic against "the secular creativity of history"—begins to sound like a more local and pointed polemic against the moral implications of the particular historical event we know as the rise of the working class. In other words, it begins to sound like a protest against proletarianization construed as the loss of the human personality's foundation or fixed location in space, *in property*, and thus as the loss of its moral substance or stability. I would, then, suggest that the polemic at the heart of American and socialist thought is, after all, the critique of domination as it develops under capitalism— of the "natural power" exercised by the "Class with property" in a market society—rather than the quarrel of the genuine self with the dynamic of history epitomized by commerce. For that polemic typically represents the loss of subjectivity not as the price of entanglement in the enticements of commerce, but as the loss of control over the property in one's capacity to produce values through work.

With few exceptions, twentieth-century critics of capitalism in the United States have assumed that their task is to reiterate this moral polemic against proletarianization by reclaiming the legacy of the nineteenth-century radicals, Populists, and socialists who normally cited the "original intent" of the founders. But to adopt that Emersonian attitude toward history is to assume that intellectual growth or cultural development is impossible under the sign of abstract or alienated social labor, and to mourn the loss of subjectivity from the standpoint of "those who are placed above the feelings of indigence," as if the fate of subjectivity—not of the modern subject determined by the dialectic of Enlightenment—is at issue. By merely reiterating the moral polemic against proletarianization, twentieth-century critics of capitalism in the United States have placed that subject beyond the scope of their critique; and so they have validated the practice if not the theory of possessive individualism.

To accept proletarianization as a historical fact that is beyond criticism would, then, be to accept the loss of *modern* subjectivity—better known as the death of the subject—without protest or mourning. Within this comic "frame of acceptance," as Kenneth Burke would call it, the central question becomes how to *change* the subject of modern political theory and practice by rethinking the sources of subjectivity and self-determination. For as Burke insists, frames of acceptance "draw the lines of battle—and they appear 'passive' only to one whose frame would persuade him to draw the lines of battle differently." [25] To accept proletarianization in this spirit would be to accept neither the hierarchies of class society nor the eclipse of subjectivity as such; it would instead be to grasp in the rise of corporate capitalism and its attendant forms of solidarity the possibility of transcending the antinomies of modern subjectivity, and accordingly to recognize the prototypes of a postmodern subjectivity in the "social self" and the "artificial person" sanctioned or validated by corporate capitalism. But that would be to end "the quarrel of the self with history" by treating the integrity of the self as a social and historical phenomenon that finally becomes legible in the order of events we know as the twentieth century.

In the United States, the comic frame of acceptance that integrates these attitudes toward history and subjectivity has gone by the name of pragmatism, or, as Lewis Mumford would have it, "the pragmatic acquiescence." Burke would probably say that Mumford mistakenly equated acceptance and passivity. But the important truth conveyed by Mumford's label is that pragmatists dispense with the moral polemic against proletarianization. They accept the social consequences of that historic process as the premise of their thinking about the meaning and the moral stability of the human personality. I do not mean that pragmatism promotes a proletarian morality (whatever that may be), or gives priority to the principle of class. Instead I mean that pragmatism, at least as James understood it, comes closer to the "ethos of historicist socialism" than Mumford's "artisanal critique" of capitalism would allow, because it gives up the ghost of the freeholder, the yeoman, and the citizen-soldier but does not surrender the genuine self or the moral personality to the empiricists and positivists who would define it as a series of responses to external stimuli. It precludes the romanticization of bourgeois society—of that proto-industrial moment in which capital and labor have not yet begun to divide up the spoils of modernity—but does not authorize the repudiation of the past. So it becomes a promising way of conceiving the transition to a postmodern, postindustrial, and perhaps post-capitalist society as "continuous," that is, as the extrapolation of tendencies observable in corporate capitalism.

Rorty, Relativism, and the Problem of History

But the question of relativism remains. Does pragmatism amount to eru-dite expedience, as Mumford and many others have insisted? Does it annul modern subjectivity only to make the moral personality unthinkable? I have already suggested that the postmodern personality sanctioned by prag-matism may be a more promising bearer of an intelligible morality than the progeny of Enlightenment. I want to explore this possibility in light of recent controversies in philosophy, and to demonstrate accordingly that pragmatism transcends relativism by reconstructing the moral personality. To do so, however, is to proceed as if relativism is something more than a red herring. I need, therefore, to show that relativism is a question worth serious consideration before I can show how pragmatism addresses it.

Richard Rorty, Hilary Putnam, and Donald Davidson, the most promi-nent of contemporary philosophers with pragmatist pretensions or sympa-thies, have tended to dismiss the question of relativism in three ways. The relativist, they claim, is at least inconsistent and probably incoherent; for he holds that no point of view is more justifiable or rational than any other, yet maintains the point of view which amounts to relativism. They also claim that the fear of relativism—whether it is formalized as metaphysical realism or not—signifies an attachment to a "correspondence" theory of truth and thus reinstates the absurd and unattainable standard of "objectivity." Finally, they claim that the so-called incommensurability thesis (according to which we cannot rationally choose one theory over another because each theory convenes a different domain of fact) becomes a philosophical problem only insofar as we assume that there must be universal criteria and procedures for establishing truth or certainty—insofar, that is, as we assume the need for epistemology. Here is how Rorty puts it: "Thus epistemology proceeds on the assumption that all contributions to a given discourse are commensurable. . . . By 'commensurable' I mean able to be brought under a set of rules which will tell us how rational agreement can be reached on what would settle the issue on every point where statements seem to conflict." [26]

To my mind these are unsatisfying ways of addressing the question because they treat relativism as a matter of logic, not history. As Alasdair MacIntyre and Charles Taylor have shown, relativism is another name for the empty subjectivity produced by the modern condition—it is the predicament "of those who inhabit a certain type of frontier or boundary situation," as MacIntyre puts it, that is, of those who can begin to create social roles for themselves by choosing or changing the communities with which they will identify. [27] In this light, Rorty's response to his critics is a non sequitur; for it ends any conversation about how to choose (or change) these communities by foreclosing any criterion except "ethnocentrism." Indeed he writes as if Creon's response to Antigone were the last word on the choices available to us. Here is an example from Rorty's *Philosophy and the Mirror of Nature*: "For epistemology, to be rational is to find the proper set of terms into which all the contributions [to the 'conversation of mankind'] should be translated if agreement is to become possible. . . . Epistemology views the participants [in the conversation] as united in what Oakshott calls an *universitas*—a group united by mutual interests in achieving a common end. Hermeneutics views them as united in what he calls a *societas*—persons whose paths through life have fallen together, united by civility rather than by a common goal, much less a common ground." [28]

Notice that the *societas* through which we are supposed to keep the conversation going is an accident of history: these are people who, like preschool siblings or the inhabitants of a medieval village, have been assembled by circumstances they did not create or choose. Is Rorty, then, saying that the participants in the postepistemological "conversation of mankind" will resemble well-mannered children or premodern peasants because they are united by nothing more than custom and civility? It seems to me that he is, and that the absent cause of this absurd effect is Rorty's displacement of historical time.

Relativism must appear to these people—to children and to premodern peasants—precisely as it appears to Rorty, as a "pseudo-problem." For these people do not choose their social roles and political obligations; they do not, and cannot, adjudicate among rival goods as a matter of course because the contours of their lives are largely determined by custom, tradition, and authority from which there is no obvious appeal, and to which there is no practical alternative. These are people who have not yet entered historical time as we know it in the modern world, as the medium in which we remain true to ourselves by intentionally *changing* our selves and our world. So they cannot yet know what it means to confront choices where the rapid increase of social roles as well as the technological compression of space and time have already made the consequences of their choosing easily imaginable if not measurable. They cannot yet know what it means to separate themselves from their communities, and what it means to choose or to create social roles unlike those prescribed by their families or villages; accordingly they do not treat such local prescriptions as the citizen of the modern world learns to treat them—that is, as true for these particular communities, not all communities regardless of time and place. In sum, they are not relativists because they cannot be relativists: they do not occupy the borderlands that come with the territory of modernity, and so cannot see themselves settling in one place or another as the result of choosing one place over another. They are ethnocentric, but not because they choose to be.

Rorty offered an earlier version of his criterion of ethnocentrism in "Dewey's Metaphysics," an essay from 1977 which he cites to substantiate the concluding argument of *Philosophy and the Mirror of Nature*. Here he insisted that "no man can serve both Locke and Hegel," a dictum he explained as follows: "What Green and Hegel had seen, and Dewey himself saw perfectly well except when he was sidetracked into doing 'metaphysics,' was that we can eliminate epistemological problems by eliminating the assumption that justification [of our claims to knowledge] must repose on something other than social practices and human needs." Rorty is less provocative than he supposes; for this statement is unexceptionable so long as he acknowledges that it entails, in turn, the justification of "social practices" and the interrogation of "human needs." But he does not acknowledge that entailment. To be more precise, he does not acknowledge that this project of justification and interrogation requires the kind of historical consciousness that permits us to learn from past experience—that is, *from people who did not share our beliefs*. Instead Rorty proceeds as if this project presupposes the kind of suprahistorical criterion he has already ridiculed. For example: "Nobody can claim to offer an 'empirical' account of something called 'the inclusive integrity of experience,' . . . if he also agrees with Hegel that the starting point of philosophic thought is bound to be the dialectical situation in which one finds oneself caught in one's own historical period—the problems of the men of one's time."[29]

In "Solidarity or Objectivity" (1985), the final formulation of the criterion of ethnocentrism, Rorty is even more strident about the radical discontinuity of historical time. "We Western liberal intellectuals should accept the fact that we have to start from where we are. . . . This lonely provincialism, this admission that we are just the historical moment that we are, not the representatives of something ahistorical, is what makes traditional Kantian liberals like Rawls draw back from pragmatism." Again Rorty writes as if the "social practices" and "human needs" to which we must refer in justifying our claims to knowledge do not themselves require justification because they are by definition local, particular, and historically specific; they are prefigurative, or self-evident, and as such are not subject to retrieval and reconsideration in light of historical experience. They serve in this sense as his groundwork or foundation, or, as he would have it, his "starting point." But the logic of his inquiry cannot lead beyond that point because it precludes or denies the possibility of any *continuities* between the social practices of different civilizations, or for that matter of comparable civilizations at different stages of development; in effect, such practices are incommensurable. For example:

> [The realist] attributes to the pragmatist a perverse form of his own attempted detachment, and sees him as an ironic, sneering aesthete who refuses to take the choice between communities seriously, a mere "relativist." But the pragmatist, dominated by the desire for solidarity, can only be criticized for taking his own community too seriously. He can only be criticized for ethnocentrism, not for relativism. To be ethnocentric is to divide the human race into the people to whom one must justify one's beliefs and the others. The first group—one's *ethnos*—comprises those who share enough of one's beliefs to make fruitful conversation possible.[30]

So Rorty energetically excavates the suprahistorical foundations of traditional metaphysics only to replace them with the prefigurative social practices—that is, the local, particular customs or traditions—of communities to which we happen to belong. As he frames it, there can be no alternative to these practices *except* within the edifice of "objectivity" erected on those suprahistorical foundations. But sooner or later, we will have to abandon the dubious shelter of "objectivity"; at that moment, Rorty suggests, we must begin to rebuild our knowledge on an ethnocentric acceptance of these local, particular, prefigurative social practices. "Either we attach a special privilege to our own community, or we pretend an impossible tolerance for every other group" (29). Relativism "is merely a red herring" because it presupposes this pretense of detachment from our own place, time, and community; in short, it presupposes the Archimedean point of epistemology (29–30).

I want to emphasize that by Rorty's account, our choices about the communities that shape us *cannot* be made rationally, in view of the consequences, because the communities in question are assumed to be either accidental or incommensurable; we cannot know the consequences until we have made the choice, he suggests, for they will not appear as such until we have chosen the community and adopted the paradigm that constitute them as consequences. In effect, Rorty is saying that we cannot transcend "the historical moment that we are." But this, too, would be unexceptionable, if he proceeded to acknowledge that the historical moment we are always contains, or implies, the moments we were and will become, in what James called the "existing beyond." From someone who claims a Hegelian lineage, that acknowledgment would seem natural and necessary. But it never appears. Instead, Rorty insists on his "lonely provincialism." For example, "The pragmatists' justification of toleration, free inquiry, and the quest for undistorted communication can only take the form of a comparison between societies which exemplify these habits and those which do not, leading up to the suggestion that nobody who has experienced both would prefer the latter" (29). Notice that the "comparison between societies" by which we must justify our habits is not a procedure that would reveal the continuity or commensurability of these different societies; it is instead a way of defining the choice between them as the realization of historical discontinuity—that is, as the result of a conversion experience, a gestalt switch, or a paradigm shift. By this account, a comparison of significantly different communities, societies, or paradigms does not, and cannot, let us acknowledge the provisional or *relative* truth of each.

I would, then, claim that Rorty's constant invocations of Hegel tend to mislead us; for they let us assume that his project is animated by the kind of historical sensibility that permeated the Hegelian critique of Enlightenment, of modernity, and of modern subjectivity. The fact is that Rorty treats relativism in the same way that Davidson treats the dualism of subject and object—as a myth that requires debunking, not as a decisive and produc-

The Postmodern in Pragmatism : 283

tive moment in the development of self-consciousness which deserves our serious attention. He does not believe that "the false is no longer false as a moment of the true," as Hegel did. He cannot imagine how his philosophical agenda might annul and preserve—that is, *include*—the problem of relativism because he does not acknowledge any continuity between his agenda and the agenda determined by epistemology: in his view, they are mutually exclusive paradigms, not historically determined possibilities that constitute a larger, cultural matrix.

These claims would not be criticisms if Rorty did not want to cloak himself in the historicist mantle. But he does want to, as, for example, in "Postmodernist Bourgeois Liberalism" (1983): "The moral justification of the institutions and practices of one's group—e.g., of the contemporary bourgeoisie—is mostly a matter of historical narratives . . . rather than of philosophical metanarratives." Here the context of comparison becomes temporal if not historical; and the choices produced by that context are accordingly more complicated than those Rorty allows in promoting solidarity over "objectivity." In fact, he acknowledges that relativism might be understood as a synonym for the moral condition of pure modernity, because the process of modernization lengthens what Norbert Elias calls "the chains of social action and interdependence." Rorty notes, for example: "Morality is, as Wilfred Sellars has said, a matter of 'we-intentions.' Most moral dilemmas are thus reflections of the fact that most of us identify with a number of different communities and are equally reluctant to marginalize ourselves in relation to any of them. This diversity of identifications increases with education, just as the number of communities with which a person may identify increases with civilization."[31]

By acknowledging the consequences of "civilization" in this fashion, Rorty has acknowledged the historical fact of relativism. By his own account, relativism now appears as something more than a mistake and less than a myth; for the need to grasp the provisional or relative truth of different communities is presumably an effect of the "diversity of identifications" which characterizes the advent of modern society. How, then, can he continue to dismiss it as a red herring or a "pseudo-problem"? He can if he assumes that there is no way to explain or narrate the transitions from one community, society, or paradigm to another because these transitions are disjunctures that eradicate the traces of their predecessors and rivals.

But if Rorty makes that assumption, he can appeal only to aesthetic criteria or anecdotal evidence in justifying the paradigm shift he desires. On the one hand, he cannot appeal to what his interlocutors or critics take to be rational grounds, rules of evidence, scientific principles, or historical facts;

for he will assume that these are reconvened by every paradigm shift, and by every transition from one community or society to another. On the other hand, he will have no reason to explain or justify his beliefs except by appeal to aesthetic criteria; for he has not only abolished the distinction between the form and the content of justification—what is tasteful must be true and vice versa—but has also made it impossible to think of historical time as the continuum in which the justification of actually existing social practices becomes meaningful. That is why Rorty cannot simply announce that the moral justification of such practices is "mostly a matter of historical narratives." He has to add a parenthetical explanation that becomes the bottom line: "The principal backup for historiography is not philosophy but the arts, which serve to develop and modify a group's self-image by, for example, apotheosizing its heroes, diabolizing its enemies, mounting dialogue among its members, and refocusing its attention" (200).

I would claim accordingly that Rorty's dismissal of relativism is an effect of his Foucauldian displacement of historical time, and that so long as we take this displacement for granted, we cannot take relativism any more seriously than Rorty does. To test these claims, we need, then, to ask whether a different approach to historical time would permit a different treatment of relativism. Can we speak of continuities in historical time, and, if so, can we say that they produce both the problem of and a solution to relativism? Can we verify transitions from one community, society, or paradigm to another which do not eradicate their predecessors and rivals? If so, do such continuities and transitions let us interrogate the Nietzschean notion of "genealogy," from which Michel Foucault and his admirers—including Rorty—have learned that "history becomes 'effective' to the degree that it introduces discontinuity into our very being"?[32]

Answers to these questions could be construed not as anomalies that require the revision of Rorty's pragmatic paradigm but as evidence that is constituted by its rival, the "epistemological" paradigm. For example, what looks like continuity from the standpoint of historiography convened by epistemological assumptions may look like discontinuity when seen through a "genealogical" grid that repudiates the form and the content of the "history of ideas." So my last question must be, can we make these standpoints commensurable? In other words, can we complete Rorty's account by replacing the historical continuity it displaces? If so, we may have found a way of addressing our own transition question; for in that event, we have found a way to tell stories in the form of history which would allow for a future that is neither inevitable return to nor radical break with the past.

The Postmodern in Pragmatism : 285

Let me begin with the question of continuities in historical time. It is a question that is both logical and historical, but also personal and political, because our answers to it will be determined by our definitions of *revolution*. At any rate it is clear that Rorty's historical sensibility presupposes Thomas Kuhn's account of scientific revolutions. By that account, the paradigm shift that renews "normal science" is the consequence of an epistemological crisis so profound that even the unacknowledged background beliefs which constitute a community's common sense become the terms of ideological conflict; the transition to the new paradigm—that is, the scientific revolution—is complete when all traces of the old are eradicated because every background belief has been reconstituted in the transition, by the new paradigm. By Kuhn's definition, then, *revolution* is, or requires, a repudiation of received tradition and a radical break with the past.[33]

I do not mean to suggest that Kuhn changed the way social scientists and the larger public thought about revolutions. I would suggest instead that he clarified a definition that was already available. Since the seventeenth century, the left wing of revolutionary movements—from the Levellers and Diggers to the antifederalists and abolitionists, from the Jacobins to the Bolsheviks—has insisted that the goal of revolution as such is to break with the past by repudiating received political tradition. Since the early nineteenth century, conservatives in the Burkean mold have also identified the modern Left with the project of revolution so conceived; they have accordingly confirmed what the Left has claimed on its own behalf, and have contributed to a consensus that leaves its definition of revolution intact. But the fact remains that revolutionary movements have always been larger than their "cutting edges" on the Left, and have faltered or failed insofar as their leaders have forgotten that. The seemingly irrational cycles of economic reform and cultural revolution in late-twentieth-century China and Cuba, for example, are symptoms of the impasse impending where the Left treats itself as a miniature or representation of the revolutionary movement as such. So, too, is the debacle of state socialism in Eastern Europe.[34]

In the United States, this political reduction has never worked. As a result, social scientists tended, until quite recently, to claim that Americans have had little or no revolutionary experience—that their revolution was an exceptionally dignified and tranquil affair, signifying nothing in terms of social conflict and political change. But the point is not that we now know better because the social historians have demonstrated the reality of the radicalism residing in the American Revolution. For we could always turn to the epoch of Civil War and Reconstruction for evidence of revolutionary discontinuity comparable to anything in the European transition to modernity. The point is that both acts of the American revolution made a difference because the finished script incorporated received tradition by rewriting the past; as directed by those who played the leading roles, that script also accommodated a cast that was more variegated and less radical than the antifederalists and the abolitionists would have tolerated. The second act of this revolutionary drama made sense of the first because its principal playwrights were not interested in an escape from the past; at any rate they could not imagine how it would be effected without irreparable damage to the prospects for popular government.

Abraham Lincoln is the best example of what I am getting at here. Between his Peoria speech of October 1854 and the presidential campaign of 1860, he moved away from *both* the radical and the conservative positions on the question of slavery, each of which was convened by assuming that the Declaration of Independence represented the ethical principles of the revolutionary struggle and the Constitution represented the historical compromises of the revolutionary settlement. To the "cotton conservatives" who argued that it was unrealistic to criticize constitutionally and historically determined institutions like slavery from the moral high ground afforded by the Declaration, Lincoln replied, "If the negro is a *man*, why then my ancient faith teaches me that 'all men are created equal'; and that there can be no moral right in connection with one man's making a slave of another." To the radicals and abolitionists who argued that the historical development determined by the Constitution was just so much departure from the ethical principles of the Declaration, he replied, in debate with Stephen A. Douglas and more forcefully in the Cooper Union speech of February 1860, that these two documents had to be read as scenes from the same unfolding drama.[35]

Thus Lincoln's position precluded compromise on the issue of slavery in the territories because it derived from the ethical principles of the Declaration; yet it treated the Constitution as both legitimate source of and historical limit on the political innovation that would be required by the abandonment of compromise. In this sense, Lincoln demanded neither acceptance of actually existing institutions nor a return to an uncorrupted state of nature; so he was neither a conservative nor a radical. He was a revolutionary because he recognized that the choice his generation faced was not between the discontinuity of radical political change and the continuity of the republic still defined by the Constitution. He recognized, in other words, that the United States could remain true to its original principles and purposes only by changing radically, so that the condition of republican continuity had become revolutionary *dis*continuity. To put it another way, Lincoln understood that received political tradition had become incoherent, in part because there was no common standard by which Americans could assess or adjudicate their differences on slavery. As he saw it, his task was to reconstitute that tradition by retelling the story of the founding, by producing a narrative of that epochal event and its consequences which would make the founders newly intelligible to his generation. As history, that narrative was completed in the Cooper Union speech; as drama, it was completed at Gettysburg in 1863.[36]

Lincoln's revolutionary achievement was, then, to show that the past (the founding) and the present (the crisis of the Union) were continuous and comparable moments in the historical development of the United States. So the definition of *revolution* to be inferred from his achievement is neither a repudiation of received tradition nor a radical break with the past. By this account, revolution is, or requires, a reconstruction of received tradition which explains or settles the conflicts that compose the tradition, and which, by recognizing and regulating significant new conflicts, becomes the ligature of another tradition. By this definition, a successful revolutionary movement would claim to have *restored*, not revoked, historical continuity, and would be able to make that claim after having conducted the most radical political experiments.

But if we can say that historical continuity is evident even in the cataclysms of modern revolution, we can also say that paradigm shifts cannot be what Kuhn and Rorty assume them to be—that is, moments of almost total discontinuity, when, as MacIntyre puts it, "everything is put in question simultaneously." We can accordingly take James's advice and begin to acknowledge the continuities as well as the discontinuities of historical time. We can stop behaving "as if the unity of things and their variety belonged to different orders of truth and vitality altogether," and instead try to be "fair to both the unity and disconnexion" that we discover in our lives and our pasts.[37]

Insofar as we do take James's advice and acknowledge these continuities in historical time, we can also begin to see that they produce the problem of relativism. Here we need only note that in the absence of such perceived continuities, relativism is inconceivable; for in that case, we would experience the world in profiles, and would never have to reconcile discordant beliefs, to choose among rival goods, or to simplify a growing "diversity of identifications." In this world, our situations could not be liminal—we could not "live forward but learn backward" because every choice would create a unique moment of almost total discontinuity. Choosing to identify with one community over another, for example, would not pose any special problems because identification with its "we-intentions" would forthwith make other intentions and other communities not merely incommensurable but irretrievable. Such choices would neither allow nor require the consideration of our previous and potential identifications; for we would not experience ourselves as a continuum constituted in as well as by change or transition. And so we would never find ourselves in the position of having to choose, on rational grounds, between two communities whose respective "we-intentions" are incompatible, yet equally intelligible and rational (where "on rational grounds" means simply "with good reasons," and good reasons are those that acknowledge but do not appeal to or rely on my fears or desires, and so persuade me by reference to purposes and standards which are not necessarily mine—in the sense that I did not invent them—but with which I can agree). In short, we could never become relativists.

But of course we do, and should be glad of it. For if we cannot attribute rationality to communities that do not already share our beliefs, we cannot learn from them (and vice versa) by studying our differences. In cases of conflict, moreover, we will have no way to persuade them because we will have abjured the possibility of any common purposes and corresponding standards of rationality. The "determined inhabitants of space" as well as the "pious descendants of time"—this is Foucault's distinction—should, then, fear a world from which historical continuity and therefore relativism are absent, because that is a world in which political conflicts cannot be mediated or settled without coercion. It is a world in which truths are plural but inert, because they are not subject to interrogation and revision as a result of conflict between communities that do not yet share enough beliefs to make conversation immediately fruitful.[38]

Transitive Subjects

How, then, do we recognize the fact of relativism without accepting it as the final truth? In other words, can we say that our acknowledgment of continuities in historical time produces a solution to as well as the problem of relativism? My own answer derives from—or just is—my interpretation of radical empiricism. If I am right to claim that James has discovered the possibility of concrete universals in the continuities of historical time, I can then claim that he has posited a transhistorical standard of rationality by which to criticize or justify actually existing or impending social practices. These universals and the standard they produce are emphatically not "something ahistorical," as Rorty labels the alternatives to "the historical moment that we are." For the terrain on which James situates his system is the *incomplete present*, the middle ground between "previous truth and novel fact," where the transitions we experience are "like a thin line of flame advancing across the dry autumnal field." James adds: "In this line we live prospectively as well as retrospectively. It is 'of' the past, inasmuch as it comes expressly as the past's continuation; it is 'of' the future in so far as the future, when it comes, will have continued it." He is even more impatient than Rorty with any metaphysical repression of historical time; but he also understands, and demonstrates, that every moment, every event, becomes intelligible only in retrospect or prospect, in the "continuous transitions" between them, which he calls "conjunctive relations" or simply "change in time."[39]

I have already noted that James was quite insistent on this "strategic point." He believed that philosophy regressed insofar as it treated change in time as undeniable evidence of discontinuity. For in that case, philosophers and others would tend to invoke suprahistorical "agents of unification"— "substances, intellectual categories and powers, or selves"—as a way of explaining wholes that were obviously greater than the sum of their parts. "To be a radical empiricist means to hold fast to this conjunctive relation of all others [i.e., to the 'continuous transition,' the self's experience of 'change in time'], for this is the strategic point, the position through which, if a hole be made, all the corruptions of dialectics and all the metaphysical fictions pour into our philosophy." James believed that the transcendental ego was already afloat on the "rationalist" or neo-Kantian current of his time. But he was aware that the metaphysical fictions of empiricism flowed from the same source. "The plain conjunctive experience has been discredited by both schools, the empiricists leaving things permanently disjoined, and the rationalists remedying the looseness by their absolutes or substances" (26). So I do not think James would be surprised to hear that these fictions resurfaced in the late twentieth century.

I do think he would be surprised to hear, from Richard Rorty among others, that the central metaphysical fictions of ordinary empiricism—the "higher principles of disunion," as James called them—were authorized by pragmatism. For he understood pragmatism as the "mediating way of thinking" that became possible and necessary in the passage beyond the discontinuities of modern subjectivity, that is, in the passage beyond "rationalism" (Kant) and empiricism (Hume) which he first explored in the essays on *radical* empiricism. These essays recast the history of philosophy, and set the stage for pragmatism, in two ways. First, they demonstrate that the debate between "rationalism" and empiricism presupposes agreement on the significance of the discontinuities inscribed in modern subjectivity: "The plain conjunctive experience has been discredited by both schools." In this sense, James shows that the tradition, or the continuum, of modern Western philosophy consists of conflicts over the implications of these discontinuities, and that this tradition makes the conflicts of the mid-eighteenth and the late nineteenth centuries commensurable. Second, these essays demonstrate that it is only from the standpoint of James's proposed departure that the tradition in question becomes intelligible—and remains useful—as a continuum of conflicts over the core issues of subjectivity. In other words, he preserves the received tradition in philosophy by producing a new narrative in which traditional conflicts are explained *and* annulled. He does not so much break with the past as rewrite it.

James concludes the second section of "A World of Pure Experience" with a playful rejoinder to his critics. "If we insist on treating things as really separate when they are given [i.e., experienced] as continuously joined, invoking, when union is required, transcendental principles to overcome the separateness we have assumed, then we ought to stand ready to perform the converse act. We ought to invoke higher principles of disunion also, to make our merely experienced disjunctions more truly real" (26–27). If we deny the reality of any and all conjunctive relations or continuous transitions, James declares, we can bridge the gaps with the transcendental egos, categories, and substances of "rationalism," or "invoke higher principles of disunion" to elevate the significance of "merely experienced disjunctions"; either way, we have become metaphysicians. But he clearly did not expect empiricists "to perform the converse act," to invent a metaphysics of absence in which the empty subjectivity of modern life became an ontological property of human life; for he could not imagine a metaphysical empiricism through which the discontinuities of modern subjectivity became something more than historical facts, that is, something like "higher principles." In short, James could not imagine the metaphysics of absence that would finally determine Foucault's interpretation of Nietzschean "genealogy."

In the late twentieth century, we can, of course, study such a metaphysics, because the "higher principles of disunion" which regulate Foucault's "genealogical" approach to European history also animate Kuhn's account of scientific revolution and accordingly authorize Rorty's displacement of historical time. But it is obviously incompatible with radical empiricism and pragmatism *as James understood them*; for these "higher principles of disunion" presuppose the discontinuities of modern subjectivity and their correlate in the model of epistemology. I would therefore claim that Rorty's critique of this model can be completed only insofar as we replace the historical continuity he has hitherto displaced. Let me try a more sequential and syllogistic approach to the same point. By now it is clear that Rorty's defense of pragmatism derives from his critique of epistemology; it is also clear that the premise of his critique is the elevation of "merely experienced disjunctions" to the status of "higher principles of disunion." But if James is correct to claim that these principles permit or enforce an epistemological model, then Rorty's defense of pragmatism will be incoherent; for it will covertly reinstate what it overtly rejects.

And yet if we agree with James *and* Rorty in thinking that a critique of epistemology is a necessary preface to pragmatism, our question will be how to make Rorty's defense of pragmatism coherent in its own terms. So we will ask not how to prevent the return of repressed dualisms but how to reinterpret the dreamwork of Cartesian doubt in the terms James proposed, "so that, instead of being mysterious and elusive, it becomes verifiable and concrete"; in other words, we will ask how to treat the discontinuities of modern subjectivity as historical events rather than "higher principles of disunion." To answer such questions, we must sooner or later turn to the essays in radical empiricism; for it is here that James demonstrates the significance of continuities in historical time.

I have already explained how that demonstration works. Let me now return to the question of why it matters. In the first two essays of 1904–5, James shows that subjectivity can survive its expulsion from the private Eden of the inner self. The choice before us, he claims, is not between objectivity and subjectivity as such; that is, we need not choose between the creature of circumstance in which there is neither temporal nor moral continuity and the pure self in which morality abides as abstention from the vicissitudes of time. For these are the choices determined by philosophers (e.g., Hume and Kant) who assume that the solvent of subjectivity— and accordingly of the moral personality—is historical time. Once we drop that assumption, as James demands, things look different. For example, we might then say that if we situate the self in historical time, it has a better chance of becoming a moral personality. At any rate that is what I would say on the basis of the following passage from "A World of Pure Experience":

> in passing from one of my own moments to another the sameness of object and interest is unbroken, and both the earlier and the later experience are of things directly lived. There is no other *nature*, no other whatness than this absence of break and this sense of continuity in that most intimate of conjunctive relations, the passing of one experience into another when they belong to the same self. And this whatness is real empirical "content" just as the whatness of separation and discontinuity

is real content in the contrasted case. Practically to experience one's personal continuum in this living way is to know the originals of the ideas of continuity and sameness, to know what the words stand for concretely, to own all that they can ever mean. (26)

By this account, the self is not just in the transitions—it just is the transitions. It is the *context* within which changes and choices become intelligible and meaningful texts; it is the activity by which these parts of experience are convened as commensurable and significant moments or events, to be understood only in (or as) a temporal relation to each other. The integrity of the self resides, therefore, in the retrospective integration of these moments, in the knowledge that is "made by relations that unroll themselves in time" (29). This integrity is, moreover, the guarantee of the postmetaphysical system James wants to build. In other words, radical empiricism, and presumably pragmatism as well, are predicated on the integrity of the self so conceived. "This is the strategic point, the position through which, if a hole be made, all the corruptions of dialectics and all the metaphysical fictions pour into our philosophy." But the integrity of the self—the ethical principle that serves as premise and purpose of all moral philosophy—now appears as the consequence, not the casualty, of historical development. In short, the moral personality is now conceived as the daughter of time.

James was generally suspicious of "universals" because they were the inflated currency in which neo-Kantian "rationalists" circulated their claims on the truths that remained exempt from time. So when he cites "the originals of the ideas of continuity and sameness," as he does here, or when he announces that "there appear to be actual forces at work which tend, as time goes on, to make the unity [i.e., the self's integration of the parts of experience] greater" (24), we should take note—we should realize that, for James, these are large investments of linguistic resources. At the very least we should realize that "continuity" or "unity" are the postmetaphysical equivalents of the "substances, intellectual categories and powers, or selves" from which philosophers and theologians have customarily deduced a universal standard of moral judgment. James is of course interested in a transhistorical standard of rationality, not a universal standard of moral judgment. That is why (and how) words like "continuity" point beyond the "lonely provincialism" of the particular historical moment: they indicate that every such moment—every change and every choice in the here and now—acquires its meaning and significance only in the context of other moments from the "existing beyond." What these words "stand for concretely," then, is this historical context, this unfolding relation between here and there, now and then, actual and potential, which the self constructs, *or rather becomes*, in time.

So the notion of the self has the same central or causative function in the systems of Kant and James. The difference is of course that in the latter's system, the self is a social relation or context, not a substance removed from the vicissitudes of time. In this sense, James refuses to make Kant's "existential" distinction between empirical selves and moral agents—by his account, our embodiment in time and space is the condition of morality.[40] Even so, the self produced by radical empiricism and endorsed by pragmatism is no less an absent cause than Kant's "transcendental ego"; for it is neither character nor event in the story it tells or enables. I do not mean that James defines the self as an omniscient narrator who stands above or outside the discrete events of pure experience. I mean instead that he treats the self as the discourse that develops *between* these events, letting us interpret them as scenes from an unfinished story.

The moral of the story told or enabled by such a transitive subject would be that there is no exit from historical time—not even in the discontinuities of modern revolution—except through the "rhetoric of spatial escape and return" that frames every horizon as yet another new frontier. So we could not read this story for the happy endings and boyish beginnings that arrive as radical break from or inevitable return to the past; nor could we read it for insight into "character," construed either as the real estate of moral properties or as the obvious origin of dramatic narratives. From the standpoint of modern subjectivity, therefore, this story would be unintelligible at best. If it then became a popular story, as it did, for example, in *Sister Carrie*, and if we wanted to make cultural sense of its popularity without resort to nostalgia for the good old days—that is, without exiling ourselves from our own time—we would have to learn how to read it from the standpoint of postmodern subjectivity afforded by the essays in radical empiricism. And this is a way of saying that if we want to read for the ending of the story we call the twentieth century, we should begin where James did, with questions rather than assumptions about the shapes of the future.

NOTES

CHAPTER ONE

1. J. M. Keynes, "Economic Possibilities for Our Grandchildren," *Nation and Athenaeum*, October 11, 18, 1930, reprinted in *Essays in Persuasion* (New York: Norton, 1963), pp. 358–73, here 373; Alec Marsh, "The Money Question and the Poetry of Ezra Pound and William Carlos Williams" (Ph.D. diss., Rutgers University, 1992).

2. Ralph Waldo Emerson, "The Poet," in *Selections from Ralph Waldo Emerson*, ed. Stephen E. Whicher (Boston: Houghton Mifflin, 1957), pp. 222–41, here 238.

3. To be more precise, my interpretation of the model is based primarily on my understanding of Karl Marx, *Capital*, 3 vols., trans. Ernest Untermann (Chicago: Charles Kerr, 1906–7); of idem, *Theories of Surplus Value*, 3 vols. (Moscow: Progress Publishers, 1968), references to which will hereafter appear in the text; and of Michal Kalecki, *Studies in the Theory of Business Cycles, 1933–1939*, trans. Ada Kalecka (New York: A. M. Kelley, 1966), esp. pp. 26–33; Anatol Murad, "Net Investment and Industrial Progress," in Kenneth Kurihara, ed., *Post-Keynesian Economics* (New Brunswick: Rutgers University Press, 1954), pp. 227–50; Martin J. Sklar, "On the Proletarian Revolution and the End of Political-Economic Society," *Radical America* 3 (1969): 1–41; Sydney Coontz, *Productive Labour and Effective Demand* (New York: A. M. Kelley, 1966), pp. 66–158; Michio Morishima, *Marx's Economics: A Dual Theory of Value and Growth* (New York: Cambridge University Press, 1973). In the same connection, I would also cite Nicholas Kaldor's *Essays on Economic Stability and Growth* (London: Duckworth, 1961), esp. pp. 103–19, 177–92, 213–300; Shigeto Tsuru, "Keynes versus Marx: The Methodology of Aggregates," in Kurihara, ed. *Post-Keynesian Economics*, pp. 320–44; and Alexander Erlich, "Notes on Marxian Model of Capital Acccumulation," *American Economic Review* 57 (1967): 599–615.

4. The elevation of "concentration" to a regulative principle of analysis and periodization is evident, I believe, in the more or less Marxist accounts of David P. Levine, "The Theory of the Growth of the Capitalist Economy," *Economic Development and Cultural Change* 24 (1975): 47–74; Joseph Steindl, *Maturity and Stagnation in American Capitalism* (New York: Monthly Review Press, 1976); Paul Baran and Paul Sweezy, *Monopoly Capital* (New York: Monthly Review Press, 1965); and James O'Connor, *The Fiscal Crisis of the State* (New York: St. Martin's, 1973).

5. See, for example, the volumes issued by the National Bureau of Economic Research under the rubric of the Conference on Income and Wealth, *Studies in In-*

come and Wealth, esp. vols. 24 (Princeton: Princeton University Press, 1960) and 30 (New York: National Bureau of Economic Research, 1966), which feature the contributions of Robert Gallman and Stanley Lebergott. Cf. notes 15 and 18 below.

6. W. Arthur Lewis, *The Theory of Economic Growth* (Homewood, Ill.: Irwin, 1955), p. 214.

7. The distinction between consumption and investment as sources of growth and/or demand is revivified under the auspices of the Keynesian revolution, but sometimes to the extent that investment is practically displaced, at least in theory, as a source of growth; at that point, the neoclassical paradigm, from which Keynes fought to free himself and his contemporaries, reasserts itself, and "consumers' sovereignty"—the change in consumer preferences enabled by rising per capita incomes—becomes the heir apparent in the province of growth theory. For example, see Richard A. Easterlin, "Growth of the American Economy," in M. E. Falkus, ed., *Readings in the History of Economic Growth* (New York: Oxford University Press, 1968), pp. 171–222, esp. 190–92, wherein "differing income elasticities of consumer demand" are designated as the critical source of economic change and growth.

8. See Coontz, *Productive Labour*, pp. 93–112; Donald J. Harris, "On Marx's Scheme of Reproduction and Accumulation," *Journal of Political Economy* 80 (1972): 505–22; Howard Sherman, "Marxist Models of Cyclical Growth," *History of Political Economy* 3 (1971): 28–55; Martin Bronfenbrenner, "The Marxian Macroeconomic Model: Extension from Two Departments," *Kyklos* 19 (1966): 201–18; and Wilhelm Krelle, "Marx as a Growth Theorist," *German Economic Review* 9 (1971): 122–33.

9. Cf. Morishima, *Marx's Economics*, pp. 3, 8, 38–39, 70, 82–89, 92–93, 97–98, 102–3. My disagreement with Morishima's central contention—that Marx's model "performs badly because he assigned different and asymmetric roles to the capitalists of departments I and II in the accumulation of capital" (p. 7)—will become clear in my own presentation of that model; but my disagreement only emphasizes my debt to this brilliant book. For Morishima's elaboration of the point, see pp. 119–22, 125, 146; for an example of how influential his view has become among those sympathetic to Marx, see M. C. Howard and J. E. King, *The Political Economy of Marx* (Harlow, Eng.: Longman, 1975), pp. 193–94. An early and particularly forceful version of the counterargument that assumes the "priority of Department I" is V. I. Lenin, *The Development of Capitalism in Russia* (1899), vol. 3 of the *Collected Works* (Moscow: Progress Publishers, 1960), pp. 43–69.

10. See Walt Rostow, *The Stages of Economic Growth* (New York: Cambridge University Press, 1960); idem, *The Process of Economic Growth* (New York: Cambridge University Press, 1952), chaps. 4, 12–13; A. O. Hirschman, *The Strategy of Economic Development* (New Haven: Yale University Press, 1958), chaps. 4–7; Lewis, *Theory of Economic Growth*, esp. chaps. 5–6; Simon Kuznets, *Six Lectures on Economic Growth* (Glencoe, Ill.: Free Press, 1959), pp. 29–35, 69–81; David S. Landes, *The Unbound Prometheus* (New York: Cambridge University Press, 1969), chaps. 1–4; and W. G. Hoffmann, *British Industry, 1700–1950*, trans. W. O. Henderson and W. H. Chaloner (Oxford: Oxford University Press, 1955), pp. 29–35, 206–13.

11. C. B. Macpherson's analysis of "simple market society" captures the peculiar ambiguity of this stage: see *The Political Theory of Possessive Individualism: Hobbes to Locke* (New York: Oxford University Press, 1962), pp. 50–55. So, too, does the notion of "proto-industrialization," for which see F. F. Mendels, "Proto-industrialization: The First Phase of the Industrialization Process," *Journal of Economic History* 32 (1972): 241–61, and Peter Kriedtke, Hans Medick, and Jurgen Schlumbohm, *Industrialization before Industrialization: Rural Industry in the Genesis of Capitalism*, trans. Beate Schempp (New York: Cambridge University Press, 1981), chaps. 2, 6.

12. Cf. W. G. Hoffmann, *The Growth of Industrial Economies*, trans. W. O. Henderson and W. H. Chaloner (Manchester: University of Manchester Press, 1958), pp. 31–35; Hirschman, *Strategy of Economic Development*, pp. 111–12; Landes, *Unbound Prometheus*, pp. 47–52; E. W. Gilboy, "Demand as a Factor in the Industrial Revolution," in R. M. Hartwell, ed., *The Causes of the Industrial Revolution in England* (New York: Barnes & Noble, 1967), pp. 121–38. Gilboy's essay was originally published in 1932; she makes most of the arguments we now associate with Neil McKendrick, but her claims to historiographical significance are quite modest by comparison with his.

13. See Neil McKendrick, John Brewer, and J. H. Plumb, *The Birth of Consumer Society: The Commercialization of Eighteenth-century England* (Bloomington: Indiana University Press, 1982), esp. pp. 10–35 of McKendrick's introduction; also Joan Thirsk, *Economic Policy and Projects: The Development of a Consumer Society in Early Modern Europe* (Oxford: Clarendon Press, 1978); Jackson Lears, "The Stabilization of Sorcery: Antebellum Origins of Consumer Culture," forthcoming as a chapter in his *Fables of Abundance: American Advertising and American Culture, 1820–1970*; and Jean-Christophe Agnew, "Coming Up for Air: Consumer Culture in Historical Perspective" (paper presented at the Organization of American Historians meeting, St. Louis, March 1989). Cf. Marx, *Capital* 1:627, 648–52, 667, on the complicated relation between consumption and accumulation, e.g., at 651: "But the progress of capitalist production not only creates a world of delights; it lays open, in speculation and the credit system, a thousand sources of sudden enrichment. When a certain stage of development has been reached, a conventional degree of prodigality, which is also an exhibition of wealth, and consequently a source of credit, becomes a business necessity. . . . Luxury enters into capital's expenses of representation." Notice that here Marx says expenses of *representation*, not production.

14. Insofar as growth is animated by the proletarianization of agricultural populations and urban working-class formation—that is, insofar as growth is led by the consumer goods sector—the failure to recognize any contradiction between accumulation and consumption is both understandable and reasonable. Marx's indictment of classical political economy on this count is nonetheless essential to an understanding of subsequent patterns and theories of growth: see *Capital* 1:644–48, 2:414–52, 504–10, 552–70, and *Theories of Surplus Value* 1:89–150. Also see Kenneth R. May, "The Structure of Classical Value Theories," *Review of Economic Studies* 17 (1950): 60–69.

15. Almost all modern theories of growth do, in fact, emphasize the role of capi-

tal formation or rates of investment: see F. H. Hahn and R.C.O. Mathews, "The Theory of Economic Growth: A Survey," *Economic Journal* 74 (1964): 779–902, and Moses Abramovitz, "Economics of Growth," in B. F. Haley, ed., *A Survey of Contemporary Economics* (Homewood, Ill.: Irwin, 1952), pp. 132–78, esp. 146–76. In "The New View of Investment: A Neoclassical Analysis," *Quarterly Journal of Economics* 76 (1962): 548–67, Edmund S. Phelps suggests that the doubts about the correlation between capital formation and growth which surfaced in the mid-1950s were laid to rest by the early 1960s. I am not so sure. In any event, there can be little doubt that capital formation played a leading role in the economic history inspired or sponsored by the National Bureau of Economic Research, ca. 1949–66, much of which was later generalized as the "new economic history." For good examples of this history, see Lance E. Davis, "Capital and Growth," in Lance E. Davis et al., *American Economic Growth: An Economist's History of the U.S.* (New York: Harper & Row, 1972), pp. 280–310, and Lance E. Davis and Robert E. Gallman, "Capital Formation in the United States in the Nineteenth Century," *The Cambridge Economic History of Europe*, 7 vols. (Cambridge: Cambridge University Press, 1978), 7:1–69 and endnotes at 495–503.

16. See John W. Kendrick, *Productivity Trends in the United States* (Princeton: Princeton University Press, 1961), pp. 134–70; D. Creamer, S. P. Dobrovolsky, and I. Borenstein, *Capital in Manufacturing and Mining: Its Formation and Financing* (Princeton: Princeton University Press, 1960), pp. 3–106; John H. Lorant, *The Role of Capital Improving Innovations in American Manufacturing during the 1920s* (New York: Arno, 1975); John E. LaTourette, "Potential Output and the Capital-Output Ratio in the United States Private Business Sector, 1909–1959," *Kyklos* 18 (1965): 316–32; idem, "Sources of Variation in the Capital-Output Ratio in the United States Private Business Sector, 1909–1959," ibid., 635–51; Richard B. DuBoff, "Electrification and Capital Productivity: A Suggested Approach," *Review of Economics and Statistics* 48 (1966): 426–31; and B. F. Massell, "Capital Formation and Technological Change in United States Manufacturing," ibid. 42 (1960): 182–88.

17. Peter Temin, "Manufacturing," in Davis et al., *American Economic Growth*, pp. 418–67, here 449; Hirschman, *Strategy of Economic Development*, pp. 104–16. Cf. Douglass C. North, "Industrialization in the United States," in *Cambridge Economic History of Europe* 6:673–705, here 694.

18. Since the late 1950s, the regulative assumptions of labor force studies have been increasingly derived from a different but related model, through which the crucial principle of disaggregation becomes the binary opposition of goods production versus services, or of public sector versus private sector. Victor Fuchs of the National Bureau of Economic Research and Eli Ginzburg of Columbia University are two of the most prominent theorists associated, respectively, with these views, which Daniel Bell eventually integrated into the notion of "post-industrial society." For examples of the approach based on the distinction between primary and tertiary production or agricultural and industrial occupations, see Stanley Lebergott, "Labor Force and Employment, 1800–1960," in Conference on Research in Income and Wealth, *Studies in Income and Wealth*, vol. 30, *Output, Employment, and Productivity in the United States after 1800* (New York: National Bureau of Economic

Research, 1966), pp. 117–204; idem, *Manpower in Economic Growth* (New York: McGraw-Hill, 1964); Daniel Carson, "Changes in the Industrial Composition of Manpower since the Civil War," in Conference on Research in Income and Wealth, *Studies in Income and Wealth*, vol. 11 (New York: National Bureau of Economic Research, 1949), pp. 46–134; Clarence D. Long, *Labor Force under Changing Income and Employment* (Princeton: Princeton University Press, 1958); and Gladys L. Palmer and A. R. Miller, "Occupational and Industrial Distribution of Employment, 1910–1950," *Manpower in the United States* (New York: Harper, 1954), pp. 83–92. On the political imperatives that informed theories of growth in the 1950s and after, see Henry J. Bruton, "Contemporary Theorizing on Economic Growth," in Bert F. Hoselitz, ed., *Theories of Economic Growth* (Glencoe, Ill.: Free Press, 1960), pp. 239–98.

19. On the reception given Hoffmann's studies (which are cited above at notes 10 and 12), see J. D. Gould, *Economic Growth in History: Survey and Analysis* (London: Methuen, 1972), pp. 414–21; but cf. also Pei-Kang Chang, *Agriculture and Industrialization* (Cambridge: Harvard University Press, 1949), and Seymour Shapiro, *Capital and the Cotton Industry in the Industrial Revolution* (Ithaca: Cornell University Press, 1967), chap. 1 and appendices 2–8, for examples of periodization drawn from Hoffmann. See G.L.S. Shackle, *The Years of High Theory: Invention and Tradition in Economic Thought, 1926–1939* (New York: Cambridge University Press, 1967), on the theoretical revolution of the interwar period and its relation to received wisdom. I should point out that Shackle does not suggest any lineage connecting Marx and his innovating economists, and does not include Kalecki in his pantheon of "high theorists."

20. Joan Robinson, "Kalecki and Keynes," *Problems of Economic Dynamics and Planning: Essays in Honour of Michal Kalecki* (Warsaw: PWN-Polish Scientific Publishers, 1964), pp. 335–41, here 338; cf. Lawrence R. Klein's similar remarks in ibid., 181–91.

21. The original version of Roy Harrod's "formal dynamics" is "An Essay in Dynamic Theory," *Economic Journal* 49 (1939): 14–33; see also his *Towards a Dynamic Economics* (London: Macmillan, 1948), pp. 1–34, 63–100. Cf. E. D. Domar, *Essays in the Theory of Economic Growth* (New York: Oxford University Press, 1957), esp. "Capital Expansion, Rate of Growth, and Employment," pp. 70–82, "Expansion and Employment," pp. 83–108, and "A Soviet Model of Growth," pp. 223–61. For an example of how the Harrod-Domar model gets applied by economists, see John E. LaTourette, "Technological Change and Equilibrium Growth in the Harrod-Domar Model," *Kyklos* 17 (1964): 207–26. The most exhaustive treatment of the relation between the Marxian and the Harrod-Domar models is probably Karl Kuhne, *Economics and Marxism*, trans. Robert Shaw, 2 vols. (New York: St. Martin's, 1979), 2:265–82; but see also Harris, "Marx's Scheme of Reproduction," pp. 517–20. Tsuru is quoted from "Keynes versus Marx," p. 328.

22. On the critical significance of Keynes's disaggregation of income, see Alvin Hansen, *A Guide to Keynes* (New York: McGraw-Hill, 1953), pp. 25–35, 117–25. On the precedents in question, see Carl P. Parrini and Martin J. Sklar, "New Thinking about the Market, 1896–1904: Some American Economists on the Theory of Investment and Surplus Capital," *Journal of Economic History* 43 (1983): 559–78; James

Livingston, "The Social Analysis of Economic History and Theory: Conjectures on Late-Nineteenth Century American Development," *American Historical Review* 92 (1987): 69–95; and Ronald Meek, "Marginalism and Marxism," in R.D.C. Black et al., eds., *The Marginal Revolution in Economics* (Durham, N.C.: Duke University Press, 1973), pp. 233–45. A. K. DasGupta is quoted from "Marx and Keynes," in his *Phases of Capitalism and Economic Theory* (Delhi: Oxford University Press, 1983), pp. 57–63, here 60; cf. also "Marx and Modern Economics," in ibid., pp. 64–72, and Domar's comparison of G. A. Feldman (the economist whose two-sector Marxian model informed Soviet planning after 1928) and Keynes in "A Soviet Model of Growth," pp. 228–36.

23. See Morishima, *Marx's Economics*, pp. 20–21; Tsuru, "Keynes versus Marx," p. 324; and Sklar, "On the Proletarian Revolution," pp. 9–11. Kalecki's "Keynesian" claim that wage cuts would not necessarily restore profitability, and thus could not solve the problem of unemployment by generating increased demand for labor through greater investment, was in fact derived from this Marxian insight into the dual character of labor costs. In effect he argued that wage cuts would reduce demand for consumer goods, which would then lead to overproduction in Department II and eventually to a generalized overproduction crisis as the capitalists of Department II, dismayed by falling demand and prices, canceled orders for new means of production from Department I. In this format, I cannot engage the "value controversy" of the 1970s and 1980s in which Ian Steedman's *Marx after Sraffa* (London: New Left Books, 1977), played such a provocative role. But I suppose that I do need to insist on the significance of Marx's labor theory of value. In my view, it is indispensable if we are interested in explaining profit as something more than monetary sleight of hand, and as something other than an illegitimate deduction from the sum of value created by "productive labor." I agree, then, with J. E. King, who points out that Marx's so-called detour through value was made to explain how wage laborers can be exploited by an exchange of equivalents (and who also notes that Steedman's charge of redundancy—"Anything that can be expresed in terms of value magnitudes can be expressed without them"—is contradicted by his approval of Morishima's analysis of surplus labor): see J. E. King, "Value and Exploitation: Some Recent Debates," in I. Bradley and M. Howard, eds., *Classical and Marxian Political Economy: Essays in Honor of Ronald L. Meek* (New York: St. Martin's, 1982), pp. 157–87. So I must disagree with Herbert Gintis and Samuel Bowles, with Ernesto Laclau and Chantal Mouffe, and with Gayatri Chakravorty Spivak, all of whom treat the labor theory of value as if it were the key to the Marxist critique of capitalism and therefore the pivot on which socialist politics has necessarily (or unfortunately) turned. Spivak claims that "to set the labor theory of value aside is to forget the textual and axiological implications of a materialist predication of the subject" ("Scattered Speculations on the Question of Value" [1985], *In Other Worlds: Essays in Cultural Politics* [London: Routledge Kegan Paul, 1988], pp. 154–75, endnotes at 292–97, here 172). I cannot see how this claim makes any historical or political sense unless we ignore the many "materialist predication[s] of the subject" (for example, the early Protestant predications) which are not animated by or derived from *the* (Marxian?) labor theory of value. Nor can I see why we should be defending a "materialist predication" against its presumably "idealist" alternatives,

rather than trying to get beyond this dualism. Laclau and Mouffe cite the authority of Gintis and Bowles in claiming that Marxists "had to resort to a fiction" when enunciating their "general law of the development of the productive forces" and submitting "all the elements intervening in the productive process to its determinations"—that is, when reducing everything to an instance of the economy. This "fiction," which not incidentally functioned as the generative principle of the labor theory of value, turns out to be the argument that labor power was a commodity (Ernesto Laclau and Chantal Mouffe, *Hegemony and Socialist Strategy: Towards a Radical Democratic Politics* [London: Verso, 1985], pp. 75–85, citing Herbert Gintis and Samuel Bowles, "Structure and Practice in the Labor Theory of Value," *Review of Radical Political Economics* 12 [1981]: 1–26). I agree with Laclau and Mouffe that "workers' resistance to certain forms of domination will depend upon the position they occupy within the ensemble of social relations, and not only in those of production" (p. 85), but I cannot agree that Marx's labor theory of value prevents our study of this ensemble (see, for example, my remarks, in chapters 3 and 7 below, with respect to the priority of the principle of class). The argument that Gintis and Bowles muster is in any case more complicated than Laclau and Mouffe have acknowledged; indeed I would say that Gintis and Bowles's revision of the labor theory of value is more complicated than it needs to be because it serves too many political purposes. They claim that "the usual formulations of the value of labor provide no basis for conceptualizing an alliance of the overlapping but distinct groupings: producers of labor-power [i.e., household labor] and wage workers" (17). I take this to mean that the labor theory of value does not specify the relation between the principles of gender and class. I would of course agree, but I do not see why we should expect so much of the theory in question. Gintis and Bowles argue that labor-power cannot be understood as a commodity because the household labor that produces it is not abstract labor allocated according to market criteria. "Thus the significant role of home-produced noncommodity use values involved in the production of labor-power invalidates the designation of labor-power as the product of abstract labor and therefore as a commodity" (12). To ignore these home-produced use values is, then, to ignore the subjection of women within the patriarchal household. "By collapsing the terms value of labor-power and labor time socially necessary to reproduce the worker the Marxian theory of value commits itself to the result that while wage workers are exploited, house workers are not" (12). I cannot follow this logic, for two reasons. First, Marx did draw our attention to the "historical and moral element" in the determination of the value of labor-power—that is, to what Gintis and Bowles call "noncommodity use values." Second, there was no doubt in the nineteenth century that women were subject to exploitation by men in the patriarchal household; but that exploitation did not require a great deal of explanation because men and women did not confront each other as formal equals who exchanged equivalents in the market. Capitalists and wage-laborers did so confront each other, as formal equals, but by all accounts their relation produced an asymmetry of power. If we treat Marx's theory of value as an attempt to explain this asymmetry—nothing more, nothing less—rather than a unified theory of exploitation on which to ground socialist/democratic politics as such, we can stop placing too many political hopes on it.

24. Cf. Coontz, *Productive Labour*, p. 93: "Marxian economic theory postulates a rise in the capital-labour ratio, i.e., sector [Department] I grows more rapidly than sector II. The implications are as follows: (1) cet. par., a falling rate of profit and (2) a decrease in labour's share of national income." See also Kriedtke, Medick, and Schlumbohm, *Industrialization before Industrialization*, pp. 53–54, 135–60, and E. A. Wrigley, "The Process of Modernization and the Industrial Revolution in England," *Journal of Interdisciplinary History* 3 (1972): 225–59, esp. 237ff., on the tendencies toward reversion to "natural economy" even within "proto-industrial" or modernizing societies.

25. Lewis, *Theory of Economic Growth*, p. 208. I should point out that the numbers or proportions, about which much fuss has been made, are not very important; the context in which the remark makes sense is Lewis's "Economic Development with Unlimited Supplies of Labour," *Manchester School* 22 (1954): 139–91, esp. 155–60. Here he points out that saving increases relatively to national income in the course of an industrial revolution "because the incomes of the savers increase relatively to the national income"; that is, an industrial revolution causes and requires a shift in income shares toward profits. "Our problem then becomes what are the circumstances in which the share of profits in the national income increases?" Also Rostow, *Stages of Economic Growth*, pp. 7–8, 20, 37–46; Jeffrey G. Williamson, "Watersheds and Turning Points: Conjectures on the Long-Term Impact of Civil War Financing," *Journal of Economic History* 34 (1974): 636–61, and "Late-Nineteenth Century American Retardation: A Neo-Classical Analysis," ibid. 33 (1973): 581–607; Coontz, *Productive Labour*, p. 97. Cf. Kaldor, "Characteristics of Economic Development," in *Essays*, pp. 233–42, esp. 234–38; John R. Hicks, *A Theory of Economic History* (Oxford: Clarendon Press, 1969), pp. 142–45; Gould, *Economic Growth in History*, chap. 3, esp. pp. 142–57; Landes, *Unbound Prometheus*, pp. 78–79, 105, 121; and Robert E. Gallman, "Commodity Output, 1839–1899," in Conference on Research in Income and Wealth, *Studies in Income and Wealth*, vol. 24, *Trends in the American Economy in the Nineteenth Century* (Princeton: Princeton University Press, 1960), pp. 13–67, here 38 n. 40 (but cf. Gallman's later criticisms of the Rostow-Lewis position, in *Cambridge Economic History* 7:3–7).

26. Rostow, *Stages of Economic Growth*, pp. 20–21; Abramovitz, "Economics of Growth," pp. 161–62. To my knowledge, there is no dissent from these sentiments among economists except in the practical, inarticulate form of ignorance enforced by mathematical aptitude and professional standards. But cf. Stanley L. Engerman and Robert E. Gallman, "U.S. Economic Growth, 1783–1860," in Paul Uselding, ed., *Research in Economic History*, vol. 8 (Urbana: University of Illinois Press, 1982), pp. 1–46, here 5–8.

27. See E. Nelle, "Theories of Growth and Theories of Value," *Economic Development and Cultural Change* 16 (1967): 15–26, and A. Bhaduri, "On the Significance of Recent Controversies on Capital Theory: A Marxian View," *Economic Journal* 79 (1969): 532–39.

28. Cf. Sklar, "On the Proletarian Revolution," pp. 9–10; Harris, "Marx's Scheme of Reproduction," p. 511; and David M. Gordon, Richard C. Edwards, and Michael Reich, *Segmented Work, Divided Workers: The Historical Transformation of Labor in the U.S.* (New York: Cambridge University Press, 1982), pp. 79–85.

29. For examples, see the works cited at note 14 above and in chapters 3–4 below, among which are Wassily Leontief, "Machines and Man," in *Essays in Economics* (New York: Oxford University Press, 1966), 187–99; R. A. Gordon, "Investment Opportunities in the U.S. before and after World War II," in Erik Lundberg, ed., *The Business Cycle in the Post-War World* (London: Macmillan, 1955), pp. 283–310; Harry T. Oshima, "The Growth of U.S. Factor Productivity: The Significance of New Technologies in the Early Decades of the Twentieth Century," *Journal of Economic History* 44 (1984): 161–70; Steindl, *Maturity and Stagnation*, chap. 9; Alvin Hansen, *Fiscal Policy and Business Cycles* (New York: Norton, 1941), esp. pp. 13–65, 261–88, 341–65; Simon Kuznets, *National Income—A Summary of Findings* (New York: National Bureau of Economic Research, 1946), p. 53; Murad, "Net Investment and Industrial Progress," pp. 237–47, citing figures from Simon Kuznets; Joseph M. Gillman, *The Falling Rate of Profit* (London: Dobson, 1957), pp. 36–41, 52–61, 66–81, 139–42; Maurice Dobb, "Some Features of Capitalism since the First World War," *Capitalism, Development, and Planning* (New York: International Publishers, 1967), pp. 34–47; Charles L. Schultze, *National Income Analysis* (Englewood Cliffs, N.J.: Prentice-Hall, 1964), table 17, p. 120; Lewis Corey, *The Decline of American Capitalism* (New York: Covici, Friede, 1934), chaps. 11–16.

30. Karl Marx, *Grundrisse: Foundations of the Critique of Political Economy*, trans. Martin Nicolaus (Baltimore: Penguin, 1973), pp. 704–6.

31. Ibid.

32. See esp. Hansen, *Fiscal Policy*; Gordon, "Investment Opportunities"; and Steindl, *Maturity and Stagnation*; see also Joseph M. Gillman, *Prosperity in Crisis* (New York: Marzani & Munsell, 1965), chaps. 9–14, for an able summary (and interesting application) of the stagnation thesis.

33. Marx, *Theories of Surplus Value* 2:406.

34. Sklar, "On the Proletarian Revolution," pp. 5–18. This argument implies that corporate capitalism is less wasteful than proprietary capitalism because its centralizing and integrating tendencies permit the economization of resources; hence the argument contains a criticism of Steindl and others who would cite the retarding effect of quasi–monopoly power on rates of investment. To put it in the terms proposed by Phelps, under corporate capitalism, "technical progress is organizational in the sense that its effect on productivity does not require any change in the quantity of the inputs" ("New View of Investment," p. 549). Cf. Alvin Hansen, *The American Economy* (New York: McGraw-Hill, 1957), p. 7: "Taylorism and the so-called rationalization movement, being capital-saving developments, started the downturn in the ratio of capital to output which has characterized the last three decades." Joseph Schumpeter's claim that the 1920s represented an elaboration of tendencies already visible at the turn of the century can be taken in the same spirit. So, too, can Alfred Chandler's claim that it is "within the enterprise that much of what economists call the 'residual' [the proportion of output that cannot be explained by the quantitative growth of input] is created" (*Cambridge Economic History* 7:71).

35. Sklar, "On the Proletarian Revolution," pp. 9–10. While Schumpeter's notion of the " 'Industrial Revolution' of the Twenties" (see his *Business Cycles*, 2 vols. [New York: McGraw-Hill, 1939], 2:732–94) retains a certain utility in describing and deciphering the economic changes of the period 1900–1930, if only because it

assesses the extraordinary technical advances concentrated in these decades, it cannot address the new significance of the consumer goods sector in economic growth, ca. 1910–40; thus it cannot explain as much as Ronald Edsforth believes it does in his *Class Conflict and Cultural Consensus: The Making of Mass Consumer Society in Flint, Michigan* [New Brunswick: Rutgers University Press, 1987])—to be more precise, it cannot explain the making of mass consumer society.

CHAPTER TWO

1. E. D. Domar, "A Soviet Model of Growth," in *Essays in the Theory of Economic Growth* (New York: Oxford University Press, 1957), pp. 223–61, here 236.

2. On access to financial resources, see Glenn Porter and Harold C. Livesay, *Merchants and Manufacturers: Studies in the Changing Structure of Nineteenth-century Marketing* (Baltimore: Johns Hopkins University Press, 1971), chaps. 1–7.

3. See, for example, Douglass C. North, "Industrialization in the United States," in *The Cambridge Economic History of Europe*, 7 vols. (Cambridge: Cambridge University Press, 1978), 6:673–705, here 680, 705, and his *Economic Growth of the United States, 1790–1860* (New York: Norton, 1961), p. 176; Thomas C. Cochran, "Did the Civil War Retard Industrialization?" *Mississippi Valley Historical Review* 48 (1961): 197–210; Stanley L. Engerman, "The Economic Impact of the Civil War," *Explorations in Economic History*, 2d ser., 3 (1966): 176–99; Stanley Lebergott, *The Americans: An Economic Record* (New York: Norton, 1984), pp. 233–48. North undermines his own argument about the irrelevance of the Civil War by claiming that the "critical element" in the success of American manufacturing was "attaining a market large enough to permit the vertical disintegration [hence specialization] of firms" (6:676); if he is correct, as I think he is, he should acknowledge the crucial role of the Civil War in creating a home market—that is, a unitary, continental market—for goods manufactured in the United States. Lebergott similarly undermines his argument by pointing out that "risk declined once the Civil War had demonstrated that the nation would not be split apart" and that, with the decline of risk, investment in longer-lived fixed capital became reasonable (pp. 350–51). Cochran's argument is essentially liberal piety: the costs of war were terrible indeed, especially in the South; but to acknowledge that fact is not to answer the question he raises. Effective rebuttal of Engerman is to be found in Jeffrey G. Williamson's "Watersheds and Turning Points: Conjectures on the Long-Term Impact of Civil War Financing," *Journal of Economic History* 34 (1974): 636–61. A more recent version of the North-Cochran thesis is Roger L. Ransom, *Conflict and Compromise: The Political Economy of Slavery, Emancipation, and the American Civil War* (New York: Cambridge University Press, 1989), chap. 8; in my view, it is no more persuasive than its predecessors.

4. There is no point in citing the already vast literature on the question of the household economy (or "mode of production," as some of the contestants in the debate would have it). But I should note that I share the doubts of Christopher Clark, Charles Post, and Bryan D. Palmer regarding the insularity of household economies, and that what Post seems to ignore is the difference between agricul-

ture in the Ohio River valley, ca. 1820–50, and on the prairies, ca. 1844–60; in other words, until the pattern of internal migration changes in the late 1830s and early 1840s, the position of Michael Merrill, James Henretta, and James O'Connor is not all that indefensible (although it does lead toward a peculiarly populist politics that locates the source of resistance to capitalism outside the sphere of market exchange, and thus writes off the political possibilities of populations that happen to reside in the advanced capitalist nations of the twentieth century). See Christopher Clark, "Household Economy, Market Exchange, and the Rise of Capitalism in the Connecticut Valley, 1880–1860," *Journal of Social History* 13 (1979): 169–89; Charles Post, "The American Road to Capitalism," *New Left Review* 133 (1982): 30–51, esp. pp. 38–44; Bryan D. Palmer, "Social Formation and Class Formation in North America, 1800–1900," in David P. Levine, ed., *Proletarianization and Family History* (London: Academic Press, 1984), pp. 229–309, here 239–44, 261–63; and Jeremy Atack and Fred Bateman, *To Their Own Soil: Agriculture in the Antebellum North* (Ames: Iowa State University Press, 1987), chap. 12.

5. See North, *Economic Growth*, chaps. 9–11; George Dangerfield, *The Era of Good Feelings* (New York: Harper & Row, 1952), pp. 107–20, 448 n. 52; John Mack Faragher, *Sugar Creek: Life on the Illinois Prairie* (New Haven: Yale University Press, 1986), pp. 62–72; Percy Bidwell and John I. Falconer, *History of Agriculture in the Northern United States, 1620–1860* (New York: P. Smith, 1941), chaps. 12–13, 19–21, 24, 26. Albert Fishlow rejects North's contention that the slave South was the crucial source of demand for western agricultural produce, because about 80 percent of the northern produce received at New Orleans was reexported: see Albert Fishlow, "Antebellum Interregional Trade Reconsidered," *American Economic Review* 59 (1964): 352–64; cf. Bidwell and Falconer, *History of Agriculture*, pp. 309–10. But it is possible that both North and Fishlow are correct because each is dealing with a different period. Until the emergence of prairie farming, markets for northwestern farmers, such as they were, did lie more or less downriver; thereafter, the pattern of trade shifted. But even after this momentous shift of the early 1840s, the "butternut" regions of the lower Ohio River valley were still oriented toward the South, in economic and in cultural terms. That orientation helps explain the strength of the Democratic Party in these regions into and through the 1860s. Clement Vallandigham and George Pendleton, for example, were successful Ohio politicians whose constituencies centered in the southern hills of the state, not in the northern end of the Western Reserve.

6. See esp. Atack and Bateman, *Their Own Soil*, chaps. 5, 10–13; Clarence H. Danhof, "Farm-Making Costs and the 'Safety Valve': 1850–1860," *Journal of Political Economy* 49 (1941): 317–59; and Paul A. David, "The Mechanization of Reaping in the Ante-Bellum Midwest," in Henry Rosovsky, ed., *Industrialization in Two Systems: Essays in Honor of Alexander Gerschenkron* (New York: Wiley, 1966), pp. 3–39. See also Richard K. Vedder and Lowell E. Gallaway, "Migration and the Old Northwest," in D. C. Klingaman and R. K. Vedder, eds., *Essays in Nineteenth Century Economic History* (Athens: Ohio University Press, 1975), pp. 159–76; Bidwell and Falconer, *History of Agriculture*, pp. 270–77, 283–99; Allan G. Bogue and Margaret Beattie Bogue, " 'Profits' and the Frontier Land Speculator," *Journal of Economic History* 17 (1957): 1–24; Robert E. Gallman, "Commodity Output, 1839–

1899," in Conference on Research in Income and Wealth, *Studies in Income and Wealth*, vol. 24, *Trends in the American Economy in the Nineteenth Century* (Princeton: Princeton University Press, 1960), tables A-1, A-2; *Historical Statistics of the U.S.* (Washington, D.C.: GPO, 1954), series K-158, p. 285; and North, *Economic Growth*, pp. 114–18.

7. See Faragher, *Sugar Creek*, pp. 173–90, 202–8; Bidwell and Falconer, *History of Agriculture*, pp. 251–56; Isaac Lippincott, *A History of Manufactures in the Ohio Valley to the Year 1860* (1914; reprint, New York: Arno Press, 1973), pp. 152–54; Blanche Evans Hazard, *The Organization of the Boot and Shoe Industry in Massachusetts before 1875* (Cambridge: Harvard University Press, 1921), pp. 82–83, 94–102, 112–14; Alan Dawley, *Class and Community: The Industrial Revolution in Lynn* (Cambridge: Harvard University Press, 1976), pp. 74–78; Alfred D. Chandler, Jr., *The Visible Hand: The Managerial Revolution in American Business* (Cambridge: Harvard University Press, 1977), p. 77; Victor S. Clark, *History of Manufactures in the U.S., 1607–1860* (Washington, D.C.: Carnegie Institution, 1916), pp. 519–21; Thomas E. Leary, "Industrial Ecology and the Labor Process: The Redefinition of Craft in New England Textile Machinery Shops, 1820–1860," in Charles Stephenson and Robert Asher, eds., *Life and Labor: Dimensions of Working-Class History* (Albany: State University of New York Press, 1986), pp. 37–56; and Paul F. McGouldrick, *New England Textiles in the Nineteenth Century* (Cambridge: Harvard University Press, 1968), pp. 19–20, 38, 139–53.

8. Chandler, *Visible Hand*, pp. 49, 75–78; cf. Peter Temin, *Iron and Steel in the Nineteenth Century* (Cambridge: MIT Press, 1964), chaps. 1–4, and Louis C. Hunter, "Influence of the Market upon Technique in the Iron Industry of Western Pennsylvania up to 1860," in A. W. Coats and R. Robertson, eds., *Essays in American Economic History* (New York: Barnes & Noble, 1969), pp. 87–112.

9. On demand for and sites of machinery, see Post, "American Road," p. 48, and Peter F. Temin, "Manufacturing," in Lance E. Davis et al., *American Economic Growth: An Economist's History of the U.S.* (New York: Harper & Row, 1972), pp. 418–67, here 434. On the sources and character of antebellum urbanization, see Stuart M. Blumin, *The Urban Threshold* (Chicago: University of Chicago Press, 1976), chaps. 1–6; W. R. Brock, *Conflict and Transformation: The United States, 1844–1877* (Baltimore: Penguin, 1973), pp. 131–34; Karen Halttunen, *Confidence Men and Painted Women: A Study of Middle-class Culture in America, 1830–1870* (New Haven: Yale University Press, 1982), pp. 33–43; and esp. Jeffrey G. Williamson, "Ante-Bellum Urbanization in the American Northeast," *Journal of Economic History* 25 (1965): 592–608, the amplified version of which is "Urbanization in the American Northeast, 1820–1870," in Robert W. Fogel and Stanley L. Engerman, eds., *The Reinterpretation of American Economic History* (New York: Harper & Row, 1971), pp. 426–36. Adna Ferrin Weber, *The Growth of Cities in the Nineteenth Century* (New York: Macmillan, 1899), pp. 21–26, argues that the rate of urbanization peaked in the 1840s, but does not distinguish between regions, as Williamson does, and ignores towns of less than eight thousand inhabitants. On the concurrent disintegration or transformation of rural cultures in the eastern states, see Thomas Dublin, *Women at Work: The Transformation of Work and Community in Lowell, Massachusetts, 1826–1860* (New York: Columbia University Press, 1979), pp. 28,

42, 50, 175–76; Dawley, *Class and Community*, pp. 134–42; Mary P. Ryan, *Cradle of the Middle Class: The Family in Oneida County, New York, 1790–1865* (New York: Cambridge University Press, 1981), pp. 52–65, 148–55, 165–68; Whitney R. Cross, *The Burned-Over District* (New York: Harper & Row, 1965), pp. 55–87; and Bidwell and Falconer, *History of Agriculture*, pp. 247–73, 307–11, 322–36, 412–16, 448–52.

10. See Temin, *Iron and Steel*, pp. 51–82, esp. 68–70; Kenneth Warren, *The American Steel Industry: A Geographical Interpretation* (Oxford: Clarendon Press, 1973), pp. 12–14, 21, 27–35; and Robert W. Fogel and Stanley L. Engerman, "A Model for the Explanation of Industrial Expansion during the Nineteenth Century: With an Application to the American Iron Industry," *Journal of Political Economy* 77 (1969): 306–28. For evidence that "metropolitan industrialization" on the seaboard and the midcentury boom in consumer goods industries are, and should be treated as, the same historical event, see Sean Wilentz, *Chants Democratic: New York City and the Rise of the American Working Class, 1780–1850* (New York: Oxford University Press, 1984), pp. 27–36, 110–29, and tables 9–13 at pp. 403–5, and Bruce Laurie and Mark Schmitz, "Manufacture and Productivity: The Making of an Industrial Base, Philadelphia, 1850–1880," in Theodore Hershberg, ed., *Philadelphia: Work, Space, Family, and Group Experience in the Nineteenth Century* (New York: Oxford University Press, 1981), pp. 43–92, esp. tables 1, 3, 8–9 and related text at pp. 44–68.

11. Dorothy S. Brady, "Consumption and the Style of Life," in Davis et al., *American Economic Growth*, pp. 61–89, demonstrates the narrow limits of our knowledge of consumption. See otherwise Robert Gallman, "Estimates of American National Product Made before the Civil War," *Economic Development and Cultural Change* 9 (1961): 397–412, table 5 at 412, and George Rogers Taylor, *The Transportation Revolution, 1815–1860* (New York: Harper & Row, 1951), p. 325.

12. See Alvin H. Hansen, "Factors Affecting the Trend of Real Wages," *American Economic Review* 13 (1925): 27–42, table 2 at 32; Edith Abbott, "The Wages of Unskilled Labor in the United States," *Journal of Political Economy* 13 (1905): 321–67, esp. 353 ff; Bidwell and Falconer, *History of Agriculture*, pp. 274–77; Donald R. Adams, "The Standard of Living during American Industrialization: Evidence from the Brandywine Region, 1800–1860," *Journal of Economic History* 42 (1982): 903–17, esp. 914–15; Blumin, *Urban Threshold*, pp. 58–63, 105–22; Clifford E. Clark, Jr., "Domestic Architecture as an Index to Social History: The Romantic Revival and the Cult of Domesticity in America, 1840–1870," *Journal of Interdisciplinary History* 6 (1976): 33–56; Fred W. Peterson, "Vernacular Building and Victorian Architecture: Midwestern American Farm Homes," ibid. 12 (1982): 409–27; Vincent J. Scully, Jr., *The Shingle Style and the Stick Style*, rev. ed. (New Haven: Yale University Press, 1971), pp. xxiii–lix; Faragher, *Sugar Creek*, pp. 188–90; Ryan, *Cradle of the Middle Class*, pp. 147–50, 199–200; Edgar W. Martin, *The Standard of Living in 1860* (Chicago: University of Chicago Press, 1942), pp. 97–123, 189–91; and esp. Ralph Andreano, "Trends in Economic Welfare, 1790–1860," in Ralph Andreano, ed., *New Views on American Economic Development* (Cambridge: Harvard University Press, 1965), pp. 131–67, here 150–57, esp. table H at 154–55.

13. As David S. Reynolds suggests in *Beneath the American Renaissance* (Cambridge: Harvard University Press, 1988), the relation between popular or vernacular

culture and the canonical literature of the 1850s is both closer and more complicated than most studies of either have acknowledged. Both levels of American culture were certainly animated by this new sense of increasingly permeable boundaries between self and Other or home and marketplace—on which see chapter 6 below but also Nina Baym, *Woman's Fiction: A Guide to Novels by and about Women in America, 1820–1870* (Ithaca: Cornell University Press, 1978), esp. pp. 27–50.

14. Roy P. Basler, ed., *Abraham Lincoln: His Speeches and Writings* (Cleveland: World Publishing, 1946), pp. 342–43.

15. Henry C. Carey, *The Past, the Present, and the Future* (1847, 1872; reprint, New York: A. M. Kelley, 1967), pp. 98–103, quoted from 365. "In some respects, [the black woman] certainly is not my equal," Lincoln declared in his speech of June 26, 1857, on the *Dred Scott* decision, "but in her natural right to eat the bread she earns with her own hands without asking leave of any one else, she is my equal, and the equal of all others" (Richard Current, ed., *The Political Thought of Abraham Lincoln* [Indianapolis: Bobbs-Merrill, 1964], p. 88). Cf. Allen Kaufman, *Capitalism, Slavery, and Republican Values: Antebellum Political Economists, 1819–1848* (Austin: University of Texas Press, 1982), chap. 3; Paul K. Conkin, *Prophets of Prosperity: America's First Political Economists* (Bloomington: Indiana University Press, 1980), pp. 284–90.

16. Horace Greeley quoted in Eric Foner, *Free Soil, Free Labor, Free Men: The Ideology of the Republican Party before the Civil War* (New York: Oxford University Press, 1970), p. 22; Abraham Lincoln from Roy P. Basler, ed., *Collected Works of Lincoln,* 8 vols. (New Brunswick: Rutgers University Press, 1953), 1: 412–13. See also Michael Holt's discussion of the tariff in *Forging a Majority: The Formation of the Republican Party in Pittsburgh, 1848–1860* (New Haven: Yale University Press, 1969), pp. 139–45, 178–82, 192–205; on Lincoln and the tariff, see G. S. Boritt, *Lincoln and the Economics of the American Dream* (Memphis: Memphis State University Press, 1978), pp. 101–17.

17. The ambiguous position of the older, commercial elites is captured in Philip Foner, *Business and Slavery* (New York: Russell & Russell, 1942); Leonard Richards, *Gentlemen of Property and Standing: Anti-Abolition Mobs in Jacksonian America* (New York: Oxford University Press, 1970); and Iver Bernstein, *The New York City Draft Riots* (New York: Oxford University Press, 1990), e.g. at pp. 132–45.

18. See Leonard Curry, *Blueprint for Modern America: Non-Military Legislation of the First Civil War Congress* (Nashville: Vanderbilt University Press, 1968), pp. 182–93, 199, 206 (quote from here); A. M. Davis, *The Origins of the National Banking System* (Washington, D.C.: GPO, 1910), pp. 63–64; Paul Trescott, *The Rise of Commercial Banking* (New York; McGraw-Hill, 1963), pp. 50–53; Robert Sharkey, *Money, Class, and Party: An Economic Study of Civil War and Reconstruction* (Baltimore: Johns Hopkins University Press, 1959), pp. 31–45; and Stanley Coben, "Northeastern Business and Radical Reconstruction: A Re-examination," *Mississippi Valley Historical Review* 46 (1959): 67–90, here pp. 68–78.

19. Cf. Sharkey, *Money, Class, and Party,* pp. 49–54; Curry, *Blueprint for Modern America,* pp. 10–35, 182–205; David Montgomery, *Beyond Equality: Labor and the Radical Republicans, 1862–1872* (New York: Knopf, 1967), chap. 2, esp. pp. 59–66,

71, 73–78, 86–87; W. R. Brock, *An American Crisis: Congress and Reconstruction, 1865–1867* (New York: Harper & Row, 1962), chap. 3, esp. pp. 54, 73, 93.

20. See Sharkey, *Money, Class, and Party*, pp. 63–90, 272–75; Coben, "Northeastern Business," pp. 81–82, 87–88; Brock, *American Crisis*, pp. 217–19, 237–39; and Montgomery, *Beyond Equality*, pp. 352–56.

21. See Brock, *American Crisis*, pp. 219–20; cf. Coben, "Northeastern Business," p. 86: "Most large investors, instead of being concerned over the difficulties of investing in the South, turned their attention to the many lucrative opportunities elsewhere—in Minnesota timberlands, Michigan iron and copper mines [the Mesabi range was opened to rail traffic in 1867], Pennsylvania coal and oil, and railroads in almost every state." Cf. note 24 below.

22. Esp. Williamson, "Watersheds and Turning Points"; but also J. Willard Hurst, *Law and the Conditions of Freedom in the Nineteenth-Century United States* (Madison: University of Wisconsin Press, 1956), pp. 79–80; Reuben A. Kessel and Armen A. Alchian, "Real Wages in the North during the Civil War: Mitchell's Data Reinterpreted," *Journal of Law and Economics* 2 (1959): 95–113; and Rufus S. Tucker, "The Distribution of Income among Income Taxpayers in the United States, 1863–1935," *Quarterly Journal of Economics* 52 (1938): 547–87.

23. See works cited at note 18 above and Porter and Livesay, *Merchants and Manufacturers*, pp. 125–26.

24. See Vincent P. Carosso, *Investment Banking in America* (Cambridge: Harvard University Press, 1970), pp. 11–32; Fritz Redlich, *The Molding of American Banking: Men and Ideas*, 2 vols. (1951; reprint, New York: Johnson Reprint, 1968), 2:355–69; Edward G. Kirkland, *Industry Comes of Age, 1860–1897* (Chicago: Quadrangle, 1967), pp. 52–67; and Carter Goodrich, *Government Promotion of American Canals and Railroads, 1800–1900* (New York: Columbia University Press, 1960), pp. 184–89, 196–98, 268–70.

25. Porter and Livesay, *Merchants and Manufacturers*, pp. 116–30; Margaret G. Myers, *The New York Money Market* (New York: Columbia University Press, 1931), pp. 46–48, 315–25.

26. See Coben, "Northeastern Business," pp. 78 n, 86ff.; Brock, *American Crisis*, pp. 219–20; Goodrich, *Promotion*, pp. 186–89; Sharkey, *Money, Class, and Party*, pp. 265–66, 274; but esp. Irwin Unger, *The Greenback Era: A Social and Political History of American Finance, 1865–1879* (Princeton: Princeton University Press, 1964), pp. 47, 159–60. Henry C. Carey was part of a successful lobbying effort on behalf of the tariff and the greenbacks in the immediate postwar period; see his *Reconstruction—Industrial, Financial, and Political: Letters to the Hon. Henry Wilson, Senator from Massachusetts*, in *Miscellaneous Works* (Philadelphia: H. C. Baird, 1872).

27. Unger, *Greenback Era*, pp. 166–67, 269–84, 325–26.

28. Ibid., p. 167. Unger is of course determined to demonstrate that all conflicts over monetary policy were meaningless—that each position in every debate was irrational, venal, and/or unrelated to the larger issues of Reconstruction. But since the evidence always overwhelms the argument, the book remains useful.

29. Cf. Sharkey, *Money, Class, and Party*, pp. 192–219; Montgomery, *Beyond*

Equality, pp. 352–56, 424–46; Chester McArthur Destler, *American Radicalism, 1865–1900* (New London: Connecticut College, 1946), pp. 34–43.

30. See Robert Gallman, "Gross National Product in the United States, 1834–1909," in Conference on Research in Income and Wealth, *Studies in Income and Wealth*, vol. 30, *Output, Employment, and Productivity in the United States after 1800* (New York: National Bureau of Economic Research, 1966), pp. 3–76, here table 4 at p. 15; also his "Commodity Output," table 1 at p. 16 (gainful workers); Robert Gallman and Lance E. Davis, "Capital Formation in the U.S.," in *Cambridge Economic History of Europe* 7:1–69, 495–503, here table 11 at p. 28 (quote from here) and related text at 25–30; Williamson, "Watersheds and Turning Points," p. 652, table 6 at p. 656 and related text at 655–57, table 7 at p. 660; W. G. Hoffmann, *Growth of Industrial Economies*, trans. W. O. Henderson and W. H. Chaloner (Manchester: University of Manchester Press, 1958), table 1 at p. 7; Kessel and Alchian, "Real Wages in the North"; Tucker, "Distribution of Income," pp. 562–77.

31. See chapter 4 for a more elaborate version of this argument; the preliminary version was introduced in my *Origins of the Federal Reserve System: Money, Class, and Corporate Capitalism, 1890–1913* (Ithaca: Cornell University Press, 1986), pp. 33–48.

32. Cf. Leon Fink, "The New Labor History and the Powers of Historical Pessimism," *Journal of American History* 75 (1988): 115–36; Karen Orren, "Organized Labor and the Invention of Modern Liberalism in the U.S.," *Studies in American Political Devlopment* 2 (1987): 317–36. John Bates Clark is quoted from *The Philosophy of Wealth* (Boston: Ginn & Co., 1887), pp. 108–9.

33. Cf. Raymond Williams, *The Country and the City* (New York: Oxford University Press, 1973), pp. 121–25; Eric Auerbach, *Mimesis: The Representation of Reality in Western Literature* (Garden City, N.Y.: Doubleday, 1957); Jacques LeGoff, *Time, Work, and Culture in the Middle Ages*, trans. A. Goldhammer (Chicago: University of Chicago Press, 1980), pp. 53–86, 90, 108–11, 118–21, 125–30; Hannah Arendt, *The Human Condition* (Chicago: University of Chicago Press, 1958), pp. 12–16, 30–37, 81–93, 107 n, 127 n, 223–28, 289–95, 303–20.

34. Cf. Bernard Bailyn, *The Ideological Origins of the American Revolution* (Cambridge: Harvard University Press, 1967), esp. chaps. 2–3; C. B. Macpherson, *The Political Theory of Possessive Individualism: Hobbes to Locke* (New York: Oxford University Press, 1962), chap. 3; J.G.A. Pocock, "Civic Humanism and Its Role in Anglo-American Thought," in his *Politics, Language and Time* (New York: Atheneum, 1971), pp. 80–103. On the "mechanical" aesthetic standards of early bourgeois society, see Lewis Mumford, *The Golden Day* (New York: Horace Liveright, 1926), chap. 1; Ian Watt, *The Rise of the Novel* (London: Chatto & Windus, 1960), esp. chaps. 1–3, 6; and Auerbach, *Mimesis*, pp. 347–82.

35. On this Marx and Weber agreed: see Karl Marx, "Introduction," *A Contribution to the Critique of Political Economy* (New York: International Publishers, 1967), pp. 188–217, here 210, and Max Weber, "Capitalism and Rural Society in Germany," in Hans Gerth and C. Wright Mills, eds., *From Max Weber* (New York: Oxford University Press, 1946), pp. 363–85.

36. J.G.A. Pocock points out that in postfeudal society, property was assumed to be the material foundation of personality as such and in relation to government.

Given that assumption, the concentration of productive property in large business enterprise was a genuine threat to republican politics and popular government; the apocalyptic tone of populist rhetoric was, then, neither fortuitous nor ridiculous. See J.G.A. Pocock, "The Mobility of Property and the Rise of Eighteenth-Century Sociology," *Virtue, Commerce, and History* (New York: Cambridge University Press, 1985), pp. 103–24. The telegraph operator and the machinist are quoted from U.S. Congress, Senate, Committee on Education and Labor, *Report of the Committee of the Senate upon Relations between Capital and Labor and Testimony Taken by the Committee*, 48th Cong., 2d sess., 1885, S. Rept 1262, 1:138, 760.

37. The republican tradition is now a field unto itself, wherein lively debate flourishes. What is often missing in the debate, however, is a grasp of the political economy of republicanism; this is all the more surprising in view of the fact that everyone agrees republicanism emerged as the political culture of a preeminently political-economic society, that is, of bourgeois society. A larger dose of C. B. Macpherson is therefore in order. In North America, the premise of the variable discourse we know as republicanism was that the majority's control of or access to productive property guaranteed each individual's discretion in the use of his property and the development of his personality—in short, equality was the condition of liberty. That the ideology of Northern victory in the Civil War was a peculiarly vigorous form of republicanism and that, so invigorated, it became a cultural constraint on capital accumulation, are the conclusions I draw from Foner, *Free Soil*; Brock, *American Crisis*; Sharkey, *Money, Class, and Party*; Montgomery, *Beyond Equality*; Edmund Wilson, *Patriotic Gore* (New York: Farrar, Straus & Giroux, 1962), pp. 91–115; William L. Barney, *Flawed Victory* (New York: Praeger, 1975), chaps. 2, 5; and from the recent studies of the Knights of Labor, e.g., Leon Fink, *Workingmen's Democracy: The Knights of Labor and American Politics* (Urbana: University of Illinois Press, 1984). I do not suppose that republicanism was the only cultural tradition available in late-nineteenth-century North America. Instead I assume that the mobilization of the majority during the Civil War gave it the vital character of common sense—in other words, that the republican form acquired new religious and metaphorical content between 1850 and 1870, and thus became more accessible and essential to most Americans, even, or rather especially, in their daily lives.

38. See T. J. Jackson Lears, *No Place of Grace: Antimodernism and the Transformation of American Culture, 1880–1920* (New York: Pantheon, 1981); Paul Boyer, *Urban Masses and Moral Order in America, 1820–1920* (Cambridge: Harvard University Press, 1978), part 3; Neil Harris, "Introduction," *The Land of Contrasts, 1880–1901* (New York, 1970), pp. 1–28; E. Digby Baltzell, *The Protestant Establishment* (New York: Random House, 1964), chap. 5; Francis G. Couvares, *The Remaking of Pittsburgh: Class and Culture in an Industrializing City, 1877–1919* (Albany: State University of New York Press, 1984), pp. 33–37; John Higham, *Strangers in the Land*, 2d ed. (New York: Atheneum, 1970), chaps. 3–4; and Edward Kirkland, *Dream and Thought in the Business Community* (Chicago: Quadrangle, 1967), chap. 1. I am not suggesting that capitalists were Social Darwinists to a man—merely that the social ethic they inherited was as significant as the competitive struggle itself in maintaining division among capitalists. On these divisions, see, e.g., Unger, *Greenback Era*; Allen Weinstein, *Prelude to Populism: Origins of the*

Silver Issue (New Haven: Yale University Press, 1970), pp. 265–85; and Joseph A. Wall, *Andrew Carnegie* (New York: Oxford University Press, 1970), pp. 330–35, 612–18. Carroll Wright is quoted from his testimony in *Relations between Capital and Labor* 3:432.

39. See Helen Lefkowitz Horowitz, *Culture and the City: Cultural Philanthropy in Chicago from the 1880s to 1917* (Lexington: University of Kentucky Press, 1976), chaps. 1–5, esp. pp. 68–69, 101–17; Boyer, *Urban Masses and Moral Order*, chap. 12; Neil Harris, "The Lamp of Learning," in A. Oleson and J. Voss, eds., *The Organization of Knowledge in Modern America, 1860–1920* (Baltimore: Johns Hopkins University Press, 1979), pp. 430–39, and "The Gilded Age Revisited: Boston and the Museum Movement," *American Quarterly* 14 (1962): 545–66; Paul Finkelman, "Class and Culture in Late-Nineteenth Century Chicago: The Founding of the Newberry Library," *American Studies* 16 (1975): 5–22; and Theodore L. Low, *The Educational Philosophy and Practice of Art Museums in the United States* (New York: Columbia University Press, 1948), pp. 9–39. Lyman Gage is quoted from his *Memoirs* (New York: House of Field, 1937), pp. 68–69. That his recollection was consistent with the historical record of reform in Chicago is demonstrated in Richard Schneirov, "Class Conflict and Municipal Reform in Chicago," in John Jentz, ed., *German Workers in Industrial Chicago* (DeKalb: Northern Illinois University Press, 1984), pp. 183–205.

40. Christopher Lasch, Neil Harris, Jackson Lears, and (to a lesser extent) E. Digby Baltzell follow the lead of Edith Wharton in suggesting that the regeneration or rehabilitation of the upper class after the mid-1880s was essentially "antimodern" in origin if not effect—that the new ruling class invented itself by accident, as it were, in attempting to evade or explain away the implications of modern-industrial civilization in the United States (see esp. Christopher Lasch, "The Moral and Intellectual Rehabilitation of the Ruling Class," *The World of Nations* [New York: Norton, 1973], pp. 80–99, but also Lears, *No Place of Grace*, pp. 107–17, 301). In my view, the argument has two weaknesses. First, it is too narrow in its focus on a few obvious men of the upper class. Second, and more important, the argument assumes but does not demonstrate that the appropriation of Old World traditions and models is evidence of a desire to escape from industrial capitalism. The assumption may work in the case of Henry Adams; it does not for most other members of the upper class. For the new men of capital were quite selective about the lessons they drew from Ruskin; and in any event Ruskin himself rejected a mindless "medievalism" (cf. Horowitz, *Culture and the City*, chap. 1, and Raymond Williams, *Culture and Society* [Garden City, N.Y.: Doubleday, 1960], p. 159). Moreover, they were careful to conjoin Renaissance architectural models and serious presentations of the mechanical, the industrial, and the scientific when they staged the great fairs of the late nineteenth century; they spent a great deal of time, energy, and money improving or "modernizing" the higher learning in North America; they promoted the development of sophisticated theory that explained the cycles of a specifically modern economy; and they understood and advertised the new corporations as the device by which middle-class social mobility would be reconstituted under modern-industrial conditions. The new men of capital were trying, in short, to civilize the machine, to give modern capitalism an appropriate culture, an ideal form, an ade-

quate theory. That they selected ancestors and traditions from the Old World is not surprising in view of the fact that they could find no usable past within the cultural tradition(s) of the lower classes. At any rate, it seems to me that the emphasis on the accidental, irrational, and antimodern aspects of the transformation in question makes it difficult to recognize the real differences between the American and the European versions of industrial capitalism, or to acknowledge the achievement of Americans in creating a society and a culture which repressed the antimodern *yet bourgeois* tendencies that would give European fascism its deadly dynamism.

41. Henry James, *The American Scene* (New York: Harper & Bros., 1907), pp. 153, 177–80.

42. Ibid., pp. 184–86; the phrase "grope of wealth" is from p. 159. See Frederic Cople Jaher, *The Urban Establishment* (Urbana: University of Illinois Press, 1982), pp. 251–72, regarding the relation between the new men of capital and New York's cultural institutions.

43. Again I am drawing on Williams, *The Country and the City*, in aligning these oppositions with the perceived contradiction between production and consumption. See Alasdair MacIntyre, *After Virtue* (Notre Dame: University of Notre Dame Press, 1981), chap. 3, on the "consuming aesthete" as a typical character or social role in modern Western culture; MacIntyre not incidentally uses the work of Henry James to illustrate his argument.

44. Cf. my treatment of the money question in *Origins of the Federal Reserve*, pp. 90–94, and in chapters 6 and 8 below. See also Henry George, *Progress and Poverty*, 50th anniversary ed. (New York: Robert Schalkenbach Foundation, 1939), pp. 266–71. My conjectures on the monetary corollaries of late-nineteenth-century political languages have been shaped by Marc Shell, *Money, Language, and Thought* (Berkeley: University of California Press, 1982), and by my reading of the Chicago Historical Society's bound collection of political pamphlets from the period, the sixty-three volumes of which contain dozens if not hundreds of cheap, popular publications on the money question. Most of the authors I have encountered clearly understood the larger cultural implications of their positions on the meaning and functions of money.

45. See my "Social Analysis of Economic History and Theory: Conjectures on Late-Nineteenth Century American Development," *American Historical Review* 92 (1987): 69–95, here 87–95, for fuller discussion and documentation.

46. Ronald L. Meek, "Economics and Ideology," *Economics and Ideology and Other Essays* (London: Chapman & Hall, 1967), pp. 196–224, here 208. This notion of a composite or "social self" is deeply embedded in the new economics of the late nineteenth century—indeed it is what finally makes the marginalist theory of demand coherent, or rather what allows economists to distill the unruly molecular forces of individual desire into the usable organic compounds of consumer demand (and they use this language to describe their peculiar alchemy). For example, see Clark, *Philosophy of Wealth*, pp. 37–39, 46, 55, 81, 89, 95–96, 175–78; Arthur T. Hadley, *Economics* (New York: Putnam's, 1896), pp. 69–70; and Simon Patten, "The Effect of the Consumption of Wealth on the Economic Welfare of Society" (1886) and "The Scope of Political Economy" (1893), *Essays in Economic Theory*, ed R. G. Tugwell (New York: Knopf, 1924), pp. 1–8, 178–94. But the notion of a "social self"

is also the animating principle and legacy of the cultural transformation expressed in, but not exhausted by, Theodore Dreiser's fiction, William James's philosophy, and the new *physical* complexity of popular culture, ca. 1890–1920. So we can and should treat the marginalist revolution in economics as one level or dimension of a broader cultural-intellectual movement that establishes the overlapping agendas of modernist and postmodern discourses in the twentieth century.

47. David A. Wells and Charles A. Conant are cited in my "Social Analysis of Economic History and Theory," pp. 72–73. I would now modify the argument in light of what I have since learned about (and from) the marginalists' broader, but still preeminently political, concerns—for which see the paragraphs that follow this note and chapter 3 below.

48. See Richard C. Tedlow, "Creating Mass Markets" (paper delivered at the Annual Meeting of the Organization of American Historians, St. Louis, March 1989); Chandler, *Visible Hand*, pp. 218–28; Gunther Barth, *City People* (New York: Oxford University Press, 1980), chaps. 3–4, esp. pp. 64–65, 70, 121–47; John William Ferry, *A History of the Department Store* (New York: Wiley, 1960), chaps. 3–4; *Golden Book of the Wanamaker Stores: Jubilee Year, 1861–1911* (Philadelphia: Wanamaker, 1911), esp. books 1, 3, and 4 (the last announces the coming of the "Informative Age" in advertising); Boris Emmet and John E. Jeuck, *Catalogs and Counters: A History of Sears, Roebuck & Co.* (Chicago: University of Chicago Press, 1950), chaps. 2–7; Edward Hungerford, *The Romance of a Great Store* [Macy's] (New York: R. M. McBride, 1922), pp. 7–61; Lloyd Wendt and Herman Kogan, *Give the Lady What She Wants!: The Story of Marshall Field & Co.* (Chicago: Rand McNally, 1952), pp. 41–215; and Neil Harris, "Museums, Merchandising, and Popular Taste: The Struggle for Influence," in I. Quimby, ed., *Material Culture and the Study of American Life* (New York: Norton, 1978), pp. 140–74, here 143–54, and "The Drama of Consumer Desire," in O. Mayr and R. Post, eds., *Yankee Enterprise* (Washington, D.C.: Smithsonian Institution, 1981), pp. 189–216.

49. William Howard Shaw, *Value of Commodity Output since 1869* (New York: National Bureau of Economic Research, 1947), table 2-1, here pp. 113–24. Cf. Hoffmann, *Growth of Industrial Economies*, table 27, p. 96, showing the relation between net output of the capital goods and the consumer goods industries in the United States.

50. See Dorothy Ross, "Socialism and American Liberalism: Academic Social Thought in the 1880s," *Perspectives in American History* 11 (1977–78): 5–79. On Clark's career and influence, see J. H. Hollander, ed., *Economic Essays Contributed in Honor of John Bates Clark* (New York: Macmillan, 1927), esp. essays by Hollander, pp. 1–5, Frank H. Fetter, pp. 136–56, and E. R. A. Seligman, pp. 283–320. Clark quoted from *Philosophy of Wealth*, p. iii.

51. Clark, *Philosophy of Wealth*, pp. 1–31; quotations taken in order from pp. 3, 15, 21, 31. On the labor theory of value, see more generally pp. 22–28 and chap. 5, pp. 70–90; on mental and manual labor, see pp. 11–21; on the sublimation of the physical and the correlation between the physical and subaltern classes, see pp. 26–31, 38, 42–54.

52. Ibid., chap. 7, pp. 107–25; see esp. p. 115 for the approach and avoidance of

the original problem; see pp. 120–25 and chaps. 8, 10–11, pp. 126–48, 174–220, for the periodization of centralization and solidarity.

53. Ibid., pp. 130, 127, 21. On effective utility, see esp. pp. 78–86; on capital, see chap. 7.

54. Meanwhile, however, Clark had written "Capital and Its Earnings," a sixty-one-page essay that appeared as *Publications of the American Economic Association* 3, no. 2 (1888). Here he distinguished between "concrete" and "pure" capital, or between capital goods and the continuum of ownership that constitutes the social power of capital; in effect, he defined capital in terms of investment, as a function. This "little monograph wears the mien of pure theory," as Frank Fetter points out, and in that sense represents Clark's break from the language and logic of *Philosophy of Wealth* (Frank A. Fetter, "Clark's Reformulation of the Capital Concept," in Hollander, *Economic Essays*, p. 143).

55. J. B. Clark, *The Distribution of Wealth* (New York: Macmillan, 1899), p. 4.

56. Ibid., esp. pp. 53, 83–84, 169–71, 180–82, 356–67. The marginal product(ivity) of labor is treated separately, most pointedly at pp. 106–15.

CHAPTER THREE

1. In chapters 3 and 4, especially in the first sections of each chapter, I am drawing on, but also revising, my "Social Analysis of Economic History and Theory: Conjectures on Late-Nineteenth Century American Development," *The American Historical Review* 92 (1987): 69–95. Elsewhere in these chapters I am assuming that Martin J. Sklar's concept of "disaccumulation" is immediately relevant to my argument about an "age of surplus," although I am proposing that the passage beyond relations of production is perceived and studied before the 1920s by a broader range of artists, intellectuals, and writers than he acknowledges; see his "On the Proletarian Revolution and the End of Political-Economic Society," *Radical America* 3 (1969): 1–41, now revised and published as "Some Political and Cultural Consequences of the Disaccumulation of Capital: Origins of Postindustrial Development in the 1920s," *The United States as a Developing Country* (New York: Cambridge University Press, 1992), pp. 143–96. John Bates Clark is quoted from *The Philosophy of Wealth* (Boston: Ginn & Co., 1887), pp. 108–9; Henry Sidgwick from Francis A. Walker, "The Source of Business Profits," *Quarterly Journal of Economics* 1 (1887): 265–88, here 265; Francis A. Walker from *The Wages Question* (New York: Holt, 1877), p. 248, and from "Source of Business Profits," p. 268. On Sidgwick as a significant moral philosopher of the late nineteenth century, see James T. Kloppenberg, *Uncertain Victory: Social Democracy and Progressivism in European and American Thought, 1870–1920* (New York: Oxford University Press, 1986), pp. 30–35, 47–48, 123–44, 185–87. On the meta-theoretical qualities of Clark's work, see Wesley C. Mitchell's survey, "Economics 1904–1929," *The Backward Art of Spending Money and Other Essays* (1937; reprint, New York: A. M. Kelley, 1950), pp. 386–415, here 399–400, and J. H. Hollander, "John Bates Clark as an Economist," in J. H. Hollander, ed., *Economic Essays Contributed in Honor of John Bates Clark* (New York: Macmillan, 1927), pp. 1–5.

2. J. H. Hollander, "The Residual Claimant Theory of Distribution," *Quarterly Journal of Economics* 17 (1903): 261–79, here 271, 270; cf. Simon Patten, "The Conflict Theory of Distribution," *Yale Review* 17 (1908): 156–84. On Walker's remarkable career and influence, see Sidney Fine, *Laissez-Faire and the General Welfare State* (Ann Arbor: University of Michigan Press, 1956), pp. 73–79, and more recently Dorothy Ross, *The Origins of American Social Science* (New York: Cambridge University Press, 1991), pp. 77–85, 95–97.

3. Walker, "Source of Business Profits," 288. See also J. B. Clark, *The Distribution of Wealth* (New York: Macmillan, 1899), pp. viii, 3–4, 127–35, 180–84, 356–66; John R. Commons, *The Distribution of Wealth* (1893; reprint, New York: A. M. Kelley, 1963), chap. 4; Simon Patten, "Professor Walker's Theory of Distribution," *Quarterly Journal of Economics* 4 (1889): 39–49, and "The Political Significance of Recent Economic Theories," *Annals of the American Academy of Political and Social Science* 32 (1908): 82–94; and Frank A. Fetter, "Clark's Reformulation of the Capital Concept," in Hollander, *Economic Essays*, pp. 136–56. For the more general background of late-nineteenth-century controversies in economic theory, see Fine, *Laissez-Faire*, chap. 7; Ross, *American Social Science*, chap. 4; Joseph Dorfman, *The Economic Mind in American Civilization*, 5 vols. (New York: Viking, 1946–59), 3 : 82–305; Mark Blaug, *Economic Theory in Retrospect* (Homewood, Ill. : Irwin, 1962), chaps. 8–11, esp. pp. 277–83; and R.D.C. Black et al., eds., *The Marginal Revolution in Economics* (Durham, N.C. : Duke University Press, 1973), esp. C.D.W. Goodwin, "Marginalism Moves to the New World," pp. 285–304, and George Stigler, "The Adoption of the Marginal Utility Theory," pp. 304–20.

4. See Maurice Dobb, *Capitalist Enterprise and Social Progress* (London: G. Routledge & Sons, 1925), part 1, chaps. 2–6; Charles A. Tuttle, "The Entrepreneur Function in Economic Literature," *Journal of Political Economy* 35 (1927): 501–21, and "A Functional Theory of Economic Profit," in Hollander, *Economic Essays*, pp. 321–36; Joseph A. Schumpeter, *History of Economic Analysis* (New York: Oxford University Press, 1954), pp. 893–98. The lineage of modern capital theory is traced to American origins in, for example, L. L. Pasinetti, "Switches of Technique and the 'Rate of Return' in Capital Theory," *Economic Journal* 79 (1969): 508–31; P. Garegnani, "Heterogenous Capital, the Production Function, and the Theory of Distribution," *Review of Economic Studies* 37 (1970): 407–36; and Joan Robinson, "The Meaning of Capital," *Contributions to Modern Economics* (New York: Academic Press, 1978), pp. 114–25. I should note here that, for all its deficiencies, the labor theory of value did not require a separate account of income distribution: see Lawrence R. Klein, "Theories of Effective Demand and Employment," in David Horowitz, ed., *Marx and Modern Economics* (New York: Modern Reader, 1968), pp. 138–75, and A. Bhaduri, "On the Significance of Recent Controversies on Capital Theory: A Marxian View," *Economic Journal* 79 (1969): 532–39.

5. Lionel Charles (Lord) Robbins, *The Evolution of Modern Economic Theory* (Chicago: Aldine, 1970), p. 19; cf. Frank H. Knight, *Risk, Uncertainty, and Profit* (New York: Houghton Mifflin, 1921), pp. 109–14.

6. Alfred Marshall, *Principles of Economics*, Variorum ed., 2 vols. (London: Macmillan, 1961) 1: 48; Hollander, "Theory of Distribution," 279. See Walker's refer-

ences to Arthur T. Hadley and Marshall in "Source of Business Profits," pp. 272 n, 275 n, and Marshall's reply to Walker in *Quarterly Journal of Economics* 1 (1887): 477–80.

7. Arthur T. Hadley, *Economics: An Account of the Relations between Private Property and Public Welfare* (New York: Putnam's, 1896), pp. 371–72. On Hadley's central importance in and seminal contributions to the political-economic debates of the 1890s (and after), see Carl P. Parrini and Martin J. Sklar, "New Thinking about the Market, 1896–1904: Some American Economists on the Theory of Investment and Surplus Capital," *Journal of Economic History* 43 (1983): 559–78. On the problem of class struggle from the standpoint of the new economists, see Ross, *American Social Science*, pp. 98–122; an earlier and more provocative version of this argument is her "Socialism and American Liberalism: Academic Social Thought in the 1880s," *Perspectives in American History* 11 (1977–78): 5–79.

8. In other words, the economists ignored neither the fact of class struggle nor the popular appeal of socialism; they simply did not believe that socialism, which they defined as state ownership of the means of production, was the solution to class struggle.

9. This is tricky. Modern liberals, especially modern liberal intellectuals, used to divide the political world into the tripartite sectors of business, labor, and the public. When crisis struck, as for example during World War I or in the 1930s and 1940s, this division became a way of imagining the consent of "the people" aggregated according to function rather than disaggregated into the atomic particles of freely contracting individuals. But it never became the regulative principle of political obligation. Cf. William Appleman Williams, *The Contours of American History* (Cleveland: World Publishing, 1961), pp. 358–60, 384–85, and Ellis Hawley, "Herbert Hoover, the Commerce Secretariat, and the Vision of an Associative State," *Journal of American History* 61 (1973–74): 116–40.

10. C.D.W. Goodwin quoted from "Marginalism Moves to the New World," in Black et al., *Marginal Revolution*, pp. 298–99. On corporate "rationalization" as a broad-gauged strategy, see my *Origins of the Federal Reserve System: Money, Class, and Corporate Capitalism, 1890–1913* (Ithaca: Cornell University Press, 1986), chaps. 1–2, which draws, of course, on Alfred D. Chandler, Jr., *Strategy and Structure: Chapters in the History of the American Industrial Enterprise* (Cambridge: MIT Press, 1962), pp. 24–41, and *The Visible Hand: The Managerial Revolution in American Business* (Cambridge: Harvard University Press, 1977), chaps. 5–11.

11. Jeremiah Jenks, "The Economic Outlook," *Dial* 10 (1890): 252–54, here 252. Cf. Robbins, *Modern Economic Theory*, pp. 18–19, and Schumpeter, *Economic Analysis*, pp. 900–17. See David I. Green "Pain-Cost and Opportunity Cost," *Quarterly Journal of Economics* 8 (1894): 218–29, for the original American version of a theory of cost that went beyond the notions of "abstinence" and "waiting" as explanation of entrepreneurial income. On the problem of fixed costs in the competitive context of the 1890s, see Naomi R. Lamoreaux, *The Great Merger Movement in American Business, 1895–1904* (New York: Cambridge University Press, 1985), esp. chaps. 2–3. Jeremiah Jenks summarized his important studies of the 1880s and 1890s in *The Trust Problem* (New York: McClure, Phillips & Co., 1900); mean-

while, he served as counsel to the U.S. Industrial Commission convened by Congress in 1898 and later served as a member of Theodore Roosevelt's Commission on International Exchange: see Parrini and Sklar, "New Thinking about the Market."

12. Hollander, "Theory of Distribution," p. 278. Cf. chapter 4 below, but also my *Origins of the Federal Reserve*, chap. 2.

13. Quotations from Richard Wightman Fox and T. J. Jackson Lears, "Introduction," *The Culture of Consumption: Critical Essays in American History, 1880–1980* (New York: Pantheon, 1983), pp. ix–xvii, here xii (page references in text hereafter). The equation of commodity form and consumer society is obvious, for example, in Neil McKendrick et al., *The Birth of Consumer Society* (Bloomington: Indiana University Press, 1982); Grant McCracken, *Culture and Consumption* (Bloomington: Indiana University Press, 1988); and T. H. Breen, " 'Baubles of Britain': The American and Consumer Revolutions of the Eighteenth Century," *Past and Present* 119 (1985): 73–104. But see also note 14 below.

14. Georg Lukács, "Reification and the Consciousness of the Proletariat," *History and Class Consciousness*, trans. Rodney Livingstone (Cambridge: MIT Press, 1971), pp. 83–222, here 100. On reification as an "enabling myth" of professionalization among intellectuals, see Bruce Robbins, "The East Is a Career: Edward Said and the Logics of Professionalism," in Michael Sprinker, ed., *Edward Said: A Critical Reader* (Oxford: Blackwell, 1992), pp. 48–73, here 67–68. See also note 40 below and William Leiss, *The Limits to Satisfaction* (Toronto: University of Toronto Press, 1976), which informs Jean-Christophe Agnew, "The Consuming Vision of Henry James," in Fox and Lears, *Culture of Consumption*, pp. 65–100 and endnotes at 221–25 (see esp. 222 n. 9), and "Coming Up for Air: Consumer Culture in Historical Perspective" (paper presented at the Conference on Global Americanization, Florence, November 1989); T. J. Jackson Lears, "From Salvation to Self-Realization: Advertising and the Therapeutic Roots of the Consumer Culture," in *Culture of Consumption*, pp. 5–38 and endnotes at 213–18, and "Beyond Veblen: Rethinking Consumer Culture in America," in Simon J. Bronner, ed., *Consuming Visions: Accumulation and Display in America, 1880–1920* (New York: Norton, 1989), pp. 73–97; Rachel Bowlby, *Just Looking: Consumer Culture in Dreiser, Gissing, and Zola* (London: Methuen, 1985), p. 26; Fredric Jameson, "Reification and Utopia in Mass Culture," *Social Text* 1 (1979): 130–48, and "Postmodernism and Consumer Society," in Hal Foster, ed., *The Anti-Aesthetic: Essays on Postmodern Culture* (Port Townsend, Wash.: Bay Press, 1983), pp. 111–25.

15. John Dewey quoted from "The Scholastic and the Speculator," part 2 (1892), in Jo Ann Boydston, ed., *The Early Works of John Dewey*, 5 vols. (Carbondale, Ill.: Southern Illinois University Press, 1969), 3: 151–54, here 151. For my attempt at a pragmatist treament of the commodity form under corporate capitalism, see part 2, below.

16. See C. B. Macpherson, *The Political Theory of Possessive Individualism: Hobbes to Locke* (New York: Oxford University Press, 1962); J.G.A. Pocock, "The Mobility of Property and the Rise of Eighteenth-Century Sociology," *Virtue, Commerce, and History* (New York: Cambridge University Press, 1985), pp. 103–24, "Early Modern Capitalism—the Augustan Perception," in E. Kamenka and R. S. Neale, eds., *Feudalism, Capitalism, and Beyond* (London: Edward Arnold, 1975), pp. 62–83, and *The*

Machiavellian Moment: Florentine Political Thought and the Atlantic Republican Tra-dition (Princeton: Princeton University Press, 1975), chaps. 13–15; Jean-Christophe Agnew, *Worlds Apart: The Market and the Theater in Anglo-American Culture, 1550–1750* (New York: Cambridge University Press, 1986). Cf. Walter Benn Michaels, "Romance and Real Estate," *Raritan* 2 (1983): 66–87, and Howard Horwitz, "The Standard Oil Trust as Emersonian Hero," ibid. 6 (1987): 97–119.

17. Those who believe that the preceding paragraphs are a caricature of writers on the Left should consult Christopher Lasch's monumental—and moving—attempt to rehabilitate populism by giving it an intellectual lineage connecting Thomas Car-lyle, Ralph Waldo Emerson, William James, and Lewis Mumford: *The True and Only Heaven: Progress and Its Critics* (New York: Norton, 1991), esp. pp. 206–25, 282–352, 529–32. On the invention and recognition of the "social self," and for my placement of James vis-à-vis the populist tradition, see chapters 7–8, below. The best general, historical treatments of the "social self" are Marshall J. Cohen, *Charles Horton Cooley and the Social Self in American Thought* (New York: Garland, 1982), and David W. Noble, *The Paradox of Progressive Thought* (Minneapolis: University of Minnesota Press, 1958).

18. See Livingston, *Origins of the Federal Reserve*, chaps. 3–5.

19. The "social surplus" is a phrase Simon Patten uses in *The Theory of Prosperity* (New York: Macmillan, 1902). The populist perspective on these matters can be sampled in Norman Pollack, ed., *The Populist Mind* (Indianapolis: Bobbs-Merrill, 1967), parts 1-2, pp. 3–327; the best general study of populism as an ideology is Bruce Palmer, *"Man Over Money": The Southern Populist Critique of American Capitalism* (Chapel Hill: University of North Carolina Press, 1980).

20. See Patten, *The New Basis of Civilization* (New York: Macmillan, 1907), esp. pp. 9–27, 121–43. I do not quite understand why Daniel M. Fox believes that "most of Patten's contemporaries ignore[d] his most original and compelling ideas" (*The Discovery of Abundance: Simon Patten and the Transformation of Social Theory* [Ithaca: Cornell University Press, 1967]), pp. 146–47). For Patten was neither an original nor a systematic thinker. He was a phrase-maker rather than a writer: he expressed what was evident yet unknown to many observers of the American scene, who used Patten's words to give their own thoughts a wider currency. For examples, see Van Wyck Brooks, *America's Coming-of-Age* (1915), reprinted in *Three Essays on America* (New York: Dutton, 1934), pp. 9–112, here 32–33; Mary Roberts Coolidge, *Why Women Are So* (1912; reprint, New York: Arno Press, 1972), p. 146; and William James, "The Moral Equivalent of War" (1910), in Henry James, Jr., *Memories and Studies* (New York: Longmans Green, 1911), pp. 267–96, here 281–87. See also chapter 8 n. 41 and related text below.

21. Wesley C. Mitchell, "The Backward Art of Spending Money," *Backward Art*, pp. 3–19, here 5, 17–18; cf. Richard T. Ely, *Studies in the Evolution of Industrial Society* (London: Macmillan, 1903), chap. 8; Walter Lippmann, *Drift and Mastery: An Attempt to Diagnose the Current Unrest* (1914; reprint, Madison: University of Wisconsin Press, 1985), pp. 128–31. On Mitchell's significance as a social theorist and his direct influence on the evolution of economic theory in the United States, see Simon Kuznets, "The Contribution of Wesley C. Mitchell," *Institutional Economics: Veblen, Commons, and Mitchell Reconsidered* (Berkeley: University of California

Press, 1963), pp. 95–122, and Arthur F. Burns, *The Frontiers of Economic Knowledge* (Princeton: Princeton University Press, 1954), pp. 61–106. Cf. also Dolores Hayden, *The Grand Domestic Revolution: A History of Feminist Designs for American Homes, Neighborhoods, and Cities* (Cambridge: MIT Press, 1981), chaps. 9–11, and Ruth Schwartz Cowan, *More Work for Mother: The Ironies of Household Technology* (New York: Basic Books, 1983), chaps. 4–5, on the movement to socialize familial functions.

22. See Jeremiah Jenks, "The Character and Influence of Recent Immigration," *Questions of Public Policy*, Page Lecture Series, Sheffield Scientific School, Yale University (New Haven: Yale University Press, 1913), pp. 1–40, esp. 26–29. On the systematic study of unemployment beginning in the second decade of the new century, see William M. Leiserson, "The Problem of Unemployment Today," *Political Science Quarterly* 31 (1916): 1–24 (note that Leiserson, a student of John R. Commons's who would become the chairman of the National Labor Relations Board in 1939, cited Patten's *New Basis* at p. 10 n. 1); Alexander Keyssar, *Out of Work: The First Century of Unemployment in Massachusetts* (New York: Cambridge University Press, 1986), pp. 262–71; and David Montgomery, "The 'New Unionism' and the Transformation of Workers' Consciousness in America, 1909–1922," *Workers' Control in America* (New York: Cambridge University Press, 1979), pp. 91–112, here 102.

23. The question in recent party battles and electoral struggles, for example, is not whether but how government will spend. In 1992, George Bush promised to give priority to measures that would promote private investment, not to abolish government spending, whereas Bill Clinton simply ignored, or rather adjourned, the distinction between private and public investment.

24. Lippmann, *Drift and Mastery* (page references in text hereafter). William Leuchtenburg's "Introduction," pp. 1–14, is quite good at putting Lippmann in context and explaining why he was such a central figure: "He speaks directly to us because he conveys that sense of first impressions of a newfound world which is our own universe" (p. 13). See also David A. Hollinger, "Science and Anarchy: Walter Lippmann's *Drift and Mastery*," an essay from 1977 reprinted in Hollinger's *In the American Province* (Bloomington: Indiana University Press, 1985), pp. 44–55 (endnotes at 196–99), and better yet, "The Problem of Pragmatism in American History," an essay from 1980 reprinted in ibid., pp. 23–43 (endnotes at 191–96), wherein Hollinger notes that *Drift and Mastery* "was a vehicle for precisely the combination of hopes and aspirations found in the classic texts of the pragmatist philosophers" (p. 40); cf. also Ronald Steel, *Walter Lippmann and the American Century* (New York: Vintage, 1980), chaps. 3–7, and Charles Forcey, *The Crossroads of Liberalism: Croly, Weyl, Lippmann, and the Progressive Era, 1900–1925* (New York: Oxford University Press, 1961), chaps. 3–5.

25. Floyd Dell, who was a leader of what Henry F. May calls the prewar rebellion (he became an associate editor of the *Masses* in 1912), made a similar argument in *Love in the Machine Age* (New York: Farrar & Rinehart, 1930); for that matter, so did Patten, in *New Basis*, pp. 126–29, 150–56.

26. James, "Moral Equivalent," pp. 276, 285; Edward Devine, "The Economic Function of Woman," *Annals of the American Academy* 5 (1894): 45–60, here 52

(cf. also his *Economics* [New York: Macmillan, 1902], chaps. 5–7). Devine was one of the Columbia professors who arranged the lectures that would become Patten's *New Basis*; see Daniel Fox's "Introduction" to the Harvard University Press edition of *New Basis* (Cambridge, 1968), pp. vii–xlv, here xxxiii–xxxiv. My thanks to Joe Broderick for bringing Devine to my attention.

27. See, for example, Eli Zaretsky, *Capitalism, the Family, and Personal Life* (New York: Harper & Row, 1976), chaps. 1–3; Ann Douglas, *The Feminization of American Culture* (New York: Norton, 1977); and Mary P. Ryan, *Cradle of the Middle Class: The Family in Oneida County, New York, 1790–1865* (New York: Cambridge University Press, 1981), chaps. 4–5.

28. William James, "Pragmatism: A New Name for Some Old Ways of Thinking" (1907), in *Writings 1902–1910*, comp. Bruce Kuklick (New York: Library of America, 1987), pp. 481–624, here 520–21. Frank Lentricchia ponders this usage in a brilliant essay, "The Return of William James," *Ariel and the Police* (Madison: University of Wisconsin Press, 1987), pp. 103–33, here 125–26. Cf. chapters 7–8, 10, below, on the reconstruction of subjectivity residing in James's rendition of pragmatism.

29. Cf. Radoslav Selucky, *Marxism, Socialism, Freedom* (New York: St. Martin's, 1979), chap. 7, esp. pp. 190–94; Adolf A. Berle, Jr., and Gardiner C. Means, *The Modern Corporation and Private Property* (New York: Macmillan, 1932), book 2, chaps. 5–7, and book 4; and Adolf A. Berle, Jr., *Power without Property* (New York: Harcourt, Brace & World, 1959), esp. chaps. 2–4.

30. See my treatment of the "moral personality" in chapters 8 and 10 below, which is both appreciation and critique of Pocock's achievement in *The Machiavellian Moment*. The key text for addressing the questions raised by the "feminization" of character in the twentieth century is Genevieve Lloyd, *The Man of Reason: "Male" and "Female" in Western Philosophy* (Minneapolis: University of Minnesota Press, 1984); but cf. also Ruth Bloch, "The Gendered Meanings of Virtue in Revolutionary America," *Signs* 13 (1987): 37–58.

31. See Steel, *Lippmann*, pp. 62–84, and Lippmann's letter to Carl D. Thompson, October 29, 1913, on the limits of municipal socialism, in Bruce Stave, ed., *Socialism and the Cities* (Port Washington, N.Y.: Kennikat, 1975), pp. 184–96. In describing what would become *The New Republic* to Van Wyck Brooks, Lippmann noted that the publication would "be socialistic in direction, but not in method, or phrase or allegiance": Lippmann to Brooks, February 5, 1914, Van Wyck Brooks Papers, Special Collections, Van Pelt Library, University of Pennsylvania, Philadelphia. There is abundant evidence of this agnosticism regarding relations of production and the priority of class. Its rhetorical form is a preference for "people" over "workers" in designating the constituency of socialism, as Kenneth Burke's speech to the American Writers' Congress in 1935 demonstrates. Cf. Frank Lentricchia, *Criticism and Social Change* (Chicago: University of Chicago Press, 1983), pp. 21–38, and as proof that I am not jousting with a straw man, Fredric Jameson, "The Symbolic Inference; or, Kenneth Burke and Ideological Analysis," in H. White and M. Brose, eds., *Representing Kenneth Burke* (Baltimore: Johns Hopkins University Press, 1982), pp. 68–91.

32. On the cultural politics of the young intellectuals, see chapters 7 and 9 below

and citations therein; meanwhile, see esp. Henry F. May, *The End of American Innocence* (New York: Knopf, 1959; Chicago: Quadrangle, 1964), part 3; Bram Dijkstra, *The Hieroglyphics of a New Speech: Cubism, Stieglitz, and the Early Poetry of William Carlos Williams* (Princeton: Princeton University Press, 1969); and Casey Nelson Blake, *Beloved Community: The Cultural Criticisms of Randolph Bourne, Van Wyck Brooks, Waldo Frank, and Lewis Mumford* (Chapel Hill: University of North Carolina Press, 1991), chap. 3.

33. Brooks, *America's Coming-of-Age*, pp. 33, 34–35.

34. Ibid., pp. 78–83. In *Beloved Community*, chaps. 1–2, Blake suggests that a "feminine ideal" animated the young intellectuals' notion of "personality." My argument is consistent with this suggestion, but I have tried to explain the confusion of spheres in the terms used by the intellectuals themselves, that is, by situating the familiar "decline of Victorian culture" in the larger transition from proprietary to corporate capitalism. See also Andreas Huyssen, "Mass Culture as Woman: Modernism's Other," *After the Great Divide: Modernism, Mass Culture, Postmodernism* (Bloomington: Indiana University Press, 1986), pp. 44–62 and endnotes at 225–27; Carroll Smith-Rosenberg, "The New Woman as Androgyne: Social Disorder and Gender Crisis, 1870–1936," *Disorderly Conduct* (New York: Oxford University Press, 1985), pp. 245–96 and endnotes at 324–49; and Klaus Theweleit, *Male Fantasies*, trans. Stephen Conway, Erica Carter, and Chris Turner, 2 vols. (Minneapolis: University of Minnesota Press, 1987, 1989), esp. 1:63–228 and 2:3–61. All three authors argue that, as Huyssen puts it, "fear of the masses in this age of declining liberalism [the late nineteenth and early twentieth centuries] is always also a fear of woman, a fear of nature out of control, of fear of the unconscious, of sexuality, of the loss of identity and stable ego boundaries in the mass" (p. 52). They are quite convincing, of course, but as I try to show in my reading of Lippmann, and of Dreiser's *Sister Carrie* in chapter 6 below, we should not ignore, or dismiss as fetishism, the "imaginary femininity" of so many male writers in the formative period of our own time, ca. 1890–1930. For the truth of the matter is that the female can and does become the standard or model of subjectivity insofar as the commodification of social life is enacted as the completion of proletarianization, and the "social self" accordingly emerges as the practical alternative to the modern subject in the male proprietor; "imaginary femininity" then becomes a way of thinking through the reconstruction of subjectivity which may well be fetishistic—think of the endless variations on the essentialist theme—but which nonetheless points beyond the status quo. For example, thanks to Jacques Lacan, Juliet Mitchell, and Jacqueline Rose, we can now see that psychoanalysis is the result of Freud's "imaginary femininity"; as Rose puts it in *Sexuality in the Field of Vision* (London: Verso, 1987), "The history of pychoanalysis can in many ways be seen entirely in terms of its engagement with this question of feminine sexuality" (p. 51); cf. Juliet Mitchell, *Women: The Longest Revolution* (New York: Pantheon, 1984), pp. 221–77, 295–313, 322–24. We might also see that the "homoerotic unconscious of the phallogocentric economy" to which Luce Irigaray and Judith Butler draw our attention (see Irigaray, *This Sex Which Is Not One*, trans. Catherine Porter [Ithaca: Cornell University Press, 1985], pp. 170–97, and Butler, *Gender Trouble: Feminism and the Subversion of Identity* [London: Routledge Kegan Paul, 1990], pp. 38–43) is complicated if

not superseded by the polymorphous perversity of the "credit economy" on which corporate-industrial capitalism thrives (see chapters 6 and 8 below). At any rate I would propose that we explore this possibility in light of the available historical evidence; my guess is that insofar as we do, Irigaray's claims about twentieth-century capitalism ("The economy—in both the narrow and broad sense—that is in place in our societies thus requires . . . that men be exempt from being used and circulated like commodities" [p. 172]) will sound increasingly anachronistic because they ignore the social fact and cultural consequences of proletarianization.

35. Nancy Cott, *The Grounding of Modern Feminism* (New Haven: Yale University Press, 1988), p. 9.

36. This paragraph is my way of making peace between the social theories and historical methods that are at war in Ernesto Laclau and Chantal Mouffe, *Hegemony and Socialist Strategy* (London: Verso, 1985); it is also a way of understanding Marx's claim that he did not invent class analysis. Cf. chapter 7 below. There is an interesting debate on the centrality of the workplace, relations of production, and the significance of class in "Symposium on David Montgomery's *Fall of the House of Labor*," *Labor History* 30 (1989): 93–137; see esp. Montgomery's reply to his critics, pp. 125–37. For a different but related argument on the declining salience of class, see Allen Kaufman with Lawrence Zacharias and Marvin Karson, *The End of Managerial Ideology?* (New York: Oxford University Press, forthcoming), chaps. 1–5.

37. See chapter 1, "Making Use of Marx"; Marx quoted here from *Grundrisse: Foundations of the Critique of Political Economy*, trans. Martin Nicolaus (Baltimore: Penguin, 1973), pp. 704–5.

38. See chapter 8 below; cf. Mary Parker Follett, *The New State: Group Organization the Solution of Popular Government* (New York: Longmans Green, 1918), esp. part 1; Jessie Taft, *The Woman Movement from the Point of View of Social Consciousness* (Chicago: University of Chicago Press, 1916); George Herbert Mead, *Mind, Self, and Society*, ed. Charles W. Morris (Chicago: University of Chicago Press, 1962), part 3, pp. 135–226 (these are lectures given at the University of Chicago in 1927 and 1930); Josiah Royce, "Self Consciousness, Social Consciousness, and Nature" (1895, 1899), in John J. McDermott, ed., *The Basic Writings of Josiah Royce* (Chicago: University of Chicago Press, 1969), pp. 423–61. I should note here that Mead was a student of Royce's at Harvard (1887–88) and that Taft was a student of Mead's at Chicago (her *Woman Movement* was her dissertation: see Rosalind Rosenberg, *Beyond Separate Spheres: Intellectual Roots of Modern Feminism* [New Haven: Yale University Press, 1982], pp. 131–46). John Dewey and Mead were colleagues at Michigan and Chicago; Royce and William James were colleagues at Harvard. It is also worth noting here that Royce, the great admirer of Hegel (see chapter 6 n. 27), was the inventor of the phrase "Beloved Community."

39. See part 2 below; in chapter 6, I argue that literary naturalism was a key moment in this change of subject around the turn of the century.

40. In other words, my diagnosis is this: the repression of the social self is completed when the American critics of consumer culture—whose intellectual lineage includes the critics of "mass culture"—announce their affiliation with the Frankfurt School. The linguistic twists and turns can be sampled in Max Horkheimer

and Theodor Adorno, *The Dialectic of Enlightenment*, trans. John Cumming (New York: Herder & Herder, 1972), pp. 39, 141–54; David Riesman et al., *The Lonely Crowd: A Study of the Changing American Character* (New Haven: Yale University Press, 1950), esp. pp. 13–26, 31–35, 115–74, 212–24, 235–70, 285–314, 368–73; T. J. Jackson Lears, *No Place of Grace: Antimodernism and the Transformation of American Culture* (New York: Pantheon, 1981), pp. 34–41 (note the use of Riesman at pp. 34–37); idem, "From Salvation to Self-Realization"; idem, "The Ad Man and the Grand Inquisitor: Intimacy, Publicity, and the Managed Self in America, 1880–1940," in George Levine, ed., *Constructions of the Self* (New Brunswick, N.J.: Rutgers University Press, 1992), pp. 107–42; and idem, "Making Fun of Popular Culture," *American Historical Review* 97 (1992): 1417–26. The study of—or rather the obsession with—character types links the Frankfurt School and American social scientists such as Riesman, C. Wright Mills, Hans Gerth, Robert Merton, and Daniel Bell. Eric Fromm is the writer who mediates between these worlds in the 1940s; Riesman, for example, notes that the concepts deployed in Fromm's *Man for Himself* (New York: Holt & Rinehart, 1947) played a "germinal role" in the development of his own typology of "inner" versus "other-direction" (*Lonely Crowd*, p. 173). But perhaps "mediation" in this obvious and palpable sense was unnecessary. For in the same year that Riesman's discursive, anecdotal study appeared, so, too, did a more empirical typology of the American character: Theodor Adorno et al., *The Authoritarian Personality* (New York: Harper, 1950). The key passages in Adorno's own contribution to this huge volume are, I believe, at pp. 744–52, where he defends the method of character typology by reference to the psychological homogenization at work in mass culture. "People form psychological 'classes,' inasmuch as they are stamped by variegated social processes. This in all probability holds good for our own standardized mass culture to even higher a degree than for previous periods. . . . In other words, the critique of typology should not neglect the fact that large numbers of people are no longer, or rather never were, 'individuals' in the sense of traditional nineteenth-century philosophy" (p. 747). So my friend Jackson Lears is addressing straw men when he suggests, "American historians might begin acknowledging that writers as elusive as Adorno cannot merely be used as punching bags for populist self-validation" ("Making Fun," p. 1421). For no one doubts that Adorno and his comrades of the Frankfurt School are complicated (if not elusive) figures. Our question must be not how complicated they are but whether their complications can help us think through the emergence of a postmodern subjectivity, with all that implies for the meanings of "reason" and "character." Can they, or do they, acknowledge that the relation between desire and reason is not, or need not be, antithetical? Can they, or do they, treat selfhood or individuality or character as the function of social solidarity and the daughter of time? My answer is no, they are not much help, at least with respect to these questions. Moreover, I would be surprised by a reading of Horkheimer and Adorno (or of Marcuse) which permitted another answer (Habermas is, I think, a separate case, as are the American writers—Riesman and Mills—who were most profoundly influenced by the Frankfurt School). The "non-heroic residue of tragedy" is a phrase from Northrop Frye used, to persuasive effect, by Hayden White in assessing the aesthetic origins and historiographical effects of irony—see his *Metahistory: The Historical Imagination in Nineteenth-Century Europe* (Baltimore: Johns Hopkins University Press, 1973), esp. pp. 230–33, 371–76.

41. See John Dewey, *Outlines of a Critical Theory of Ethics* (1891; reprint, New York: Greenwood, 1969), pp. 137, 150–51, 176–79; cf. also chapter 8 below, and Neal Coughlan, *Young John Dewey* (Chicago: University of Chicago Press, 1975), chap. 6. Robert Westbrook's treatment of Dewey at this stage of his career—in *John Dewey and American Democracy* (Ithaca: Cornell University Press, 1991), part 1— is less interesting than Coughlan's, probably because it is less speculative in every sense. I borrow the notion of "frame of acceptance" from Kenneth Burke, *Attitudes Toward History*, rev. ed. (Boston: Beacon Press, 1957), part 1, and would insist, following Burke, Hegel, and Hayden White, on the importance of comedy in transcending the ironic mode of historical consciousness; cf. White, *Metahistory*, chap. 2, esp. pp. 93–123.

CHAPTER FOUR

1. See David A. Wells, *Recent Economic Changes* (New York: Appleton, 1889), pp. v–vi, 84–86, 406–22; cf. Edward Atkinson, *The Industrial Progress of the Nation* (1889; reprint, New York: Arno Press, 1973), pp. 111–21; Carroll D. Wright, *Industrial Evolution of the United States* (New York: Flood & Vincent, 1897), pp. 222–27, and "Cheaper Living and the Rise of Wages," *Forum* 16 (1893): 221–28, which is in part a review of *Retail Prices and Wages, Report by Mr. Aldrich from the Committee on Finance*, 52d Cong., 1st sess., July 19, 1892, S. Rept 896, 3 vols. (Washington, D.C.: GPO, 1892). See also Willard Thorp, *Business Annals* (New York: National Bureau of Economic Research, 1926), pp. 103, 131–37, for evidence that Wells, Atkinson, and Wright defined the tendency of economic development no differently than their counterparts in the late-nineteenth-century business community.

2. Clarence D. Long, *Wages and Earnings in the United States, 1860–1890* (Princeton: Princeton University Press, 1960), p. 112; cf. Sidney Weintraub, *An Approach to the Theory of Distribution* (Philadelphia: University of Pennsylvania Press, 1958), pp. 53–54, and A. L. Marty, "Diminishing Returns and the Relative Share of Labor," *Quarterly Journal of Economics* 67 (1953): 615–18.

3. See John W. Kendrick, *Productivity Trends in the United States* (Princeton: Princeton University Press, 1961), tables A-20, A-21, and A-23 at pp. 331–32, 338; Stanley Lebergott, *Manpower in Economic Growth* (New York: McGraw-Hill, 1964), pp. 524, 528; U.S. Bureau of Economic Analysis, *Long-Term Growth, 1860–1970* (Washington, D.C.: GPO, 1973), part 5, charts 18 and 20 at pp. 107, 109; Bernard Weber and S. J. Handfield-Jones, "Variations in the Rate of Economic Growth in the U.S.A., 1869–1939," *Oxford Economic Papers*, n.s., 6 (1954): 101–32, here esp. pp. 104, 121; and E. C. Budd, "Factor Shares, 1850–1910," in *Trends in the American Economy in the Nineteenth Century* (Princeton: Princeton University Press, 1960), tables C-4, C-5 at p. 398. Cf. also W. I. King, *The Wealth and Income of the People of the U.S.* (1915; reprint, New York: Johnson Reprint Co., 1969), pp. 158–207; Charles B. Spahr, *An Essay on the Present Distribution of Wealth in the United States* (Boston: T. Y. Crowell, 1896), pp. 95–109; and for more recent,

comprehensive solutions of late-nineteenth-century puzzles, Rendig Fels, *American Business Cycles, 1865–1897* (Chapel Hill: University of North Carolina Press, 1959), and Jeffrey G. Williamson, *Late-Nineteenth Century American Development: A General Equilibrium History* (New York: Cambridge University Press, 1974), esp. chap. 5. On capital endowment per worker, see Long, *Wages and Earnings*, pp. 61–64; on management initiatives, see Daniel Nelson, *Managers and Workers: Origins of the New Factory System in the United States, 1880–1920* (Madison: University of Wisconsin Press, 1975), pp. 34–54; Alfred D. Chandler, Jr., *The Visible Hand: The Managerial Revolution in American Business* (Cambridge: Harvard University Press, 1979), pp. 271–75; Joseph Litterer, "Systematic Management: The Search for Order and Integration," *Business History Review* 35 (1961): 461–76; and Leland H. Jenks, "Early Phases of the Management Movement," *Administrative Science Quarterly* 5 (1960): 421–47.

4. On empire as a solution to the late-nineteenth-century crisis of "overproduction," see the "revisionist" works of the "Wisconsin School" in which Fred Harvey Harrington and William Appleman Williams were the headmasters; for example, Walter LaFeber, *The New Empire* (Ithaca: Cornell University Press, 1963), chaps. 2–4, and Thomas McCormick, *China Market* (Chicago: Quadrangle, 1962). Carl P. Parrini and Martin J. Sklar, two other Wisconsin-trained historians, break beyond this revisionist formulation by showing that the key question in the problematic of anticolonial empire was investment—see their "New Thinking about the Market, 1896–1904: Some American Economists on the Theory of Investment and Surplus Capital," *Journal of Economic History* 43 (1983): 559–78. In the late nineteenth and early twentieth centuries, economists have a great deal to say about empire; see, for examples, Jeremiah Jenks, *The Trust Problem* (New York: McClure & Philips, 1900), p. 112; John Bates Clark, remarks recorded in *Chicago Conference on Trusts* (Chicago: National Civic Federation, 1899), p. 407; and Charles A. Conant, *The U.S. in the Orient* (1901; reprint, Port Washington, N.Y.: Kennikat, 1971). On the reform of the banking sytem and the idea of empire, see my *Origins of the Federal Reserve System: Money, Class, and Corporate Capitalism, 1890–1913* (Ithaca: Cornell University Press, 1986), pp. 111–18.

5. Arthur T. Lyman quoted from U.S. Congress, Senate, Committee on Education and Labor, *Report of the Committee of the Senate upon Relations between Capital and Labor and Testimony Taken by the Committee*, 48th Cong., 2d sess., 1885, S. Rept 1262, 1:450; cf. Carroll D. Wright at 1:426 and Terence V. Powderly, quoting William Vanderbilt, in "The Army of Unemployed," George E. McNeill, ed., *The Labor Movement: The Problem of To-Day* (New York: M. W. Hazen Co., 1887), pp. 575–84, here 577.

6. On skilled workers' control of machine production, see, for example, David Montgomery: "Workers' Control of Machine Production in the Nineteenth Century," *Labor History* 17 (1976): 485–509; *Workers' Control in America* (New York: Cambridge University Press, 1979); and *The Fall of the House of Labor: The Workplace, the State, and American Labor Activism, 1865–1925* (New York: Cambridge University Press, 1987), chaps. 1, 4–5. See also Katherine Stone, "The Origin of Job Structures in the Steel Industry," *Radical America* 7 (1973): 19–64; Francis G. Couvares, *The Remaking of Pittsburgh* (Albany: State University of New York Press,

1986), chap. 2; Melvyn Dubofsky, "The Origin of Western Working Class Radicalism, 1890–1905," *Labor History* 7 (1966): 131–54; Irwin Yellowitz, "Skilled Workers and Mechanization: The Lasters," ibid. 18 (1977): 197–213; John Laslett, *Labor and the Left, 1880–1924* (New York: Basic Books, 1970), pp. 152–59; and Robert Ozanne, *A Century of Labor-Management Relations at McCormick and International Harvester* (Madison: University of Wisconsin Press, 1967), pp. 16–28. John Frey quoted from Robert Hoxie, *Scientific Management and Labor* (New York: Appleton, 1915), pp. 132–37 (cf. notes 18–19 below); the machinist, John Morrison of New York, quoted from *Relations between Capital and Labor* 1:763.

7. See David M. Gordon, Richard C. Edwards, and Michael Reich, *Segmented Work, Divided Workers: The Historical Transformation of Labor in the United States* (New York: Cambridge University Press, 1982), pp. 97–98, 147, 257–58 n. 29, and works cited at note 3 above.

8. On strikes and their meanings in this period, see P. K. Edwards, *Strikes in the United States, 1881–1974* (New York: St. Martin's, 1981), pp. 84–114; David Montgomery, "Strikes in Nineteenth Century America," *Social Science History* 4 (1980): 81–104, esp. 88–93; and the *Twenty-First Annual Report of the U.S. Commissioner of Labor: Strikes and Lockouts, 1881–1905* (Washington, D.C.: GPO, 1906), pp. 56–64, 70–77. On solidarity across class lines, the work of Herbert Gutman and his students is indispensable; for example, Herbert Gutman, *Work, Culture, and Society in Industrializing America* (New York: Vintage, 1976), esp. the title essay from 1973 at pp. 3–78 but also the pieces based on local and state records, "Trouble on the Railroads in 1873–74" and "Two Lockouts in Pennsylvania, 1873–74," at pp. 295–343, esp. 307–12, 340–41; and idem, "The Workers' Search for Power," in H. Wayne Morgan, ed., *The Gilded Age* (Syracuse: Syracuse University Press, 1970), pp. 31–53. Cf. also Daniel J. Walkowitz, *Worker City, Company Town* (Urbana: University of Illinois Press, 1982), pp. 192–94; Leon Fink, *Workingmen's Democracy* (Urbana: University of Illinois Press, 1983), pp. 25–33, 50–56, 19–26, 221–23; and Nick Salvatore, *Eugene V. Debs: Citizen and Socialist* (Urbana: University of Illinois Press, 1982), pp. 31–34, 72–73, 122, 128.

9. Frank Vanderlip to Ferdinand Baumgarten, August 8, 1904, Vanderlip Papers, Rare Book and Manuscript Library, Columbia University, New York; on the social consequences and capacities of the corporations, see also my "Social Analysis of Economic History and Theory: Conjectures on Late-Nineteenth Century American Development," *American Historical Review* 92 (1987): 69–95.

10. Stephen P. Corliss quoted from *Chicago Conference on Trusts*, p. 137; for related citations, see Livingston, "Social Analysis of Economic History and Theory," n. 31.

11. Jeremiah Jenks quoted from his *Trust Problem*, pp. 34–36. On the consensus with respect to the adaptive potential of combination, see vols. 1 and 13 of the U.S. Industrial Commission's *Reports* (Washington, D.C.: GPO, 1901); *Proceedings of the American Economic Association* 9 (1900); and the special issue of the *Annals of the American Academy: Corporations and the Public Welfare* (1900). On the implications of Sherman Act jurisprudence in the mid-1890s, see William Letwin, *Law and Economic Policy in America* (Chicago: University of Chicago Press, 1965), pp. 144–52, 161–67; Charles W. McCurdy, "The *Knight* Sugar Decision of 1895 and the

Modernization of American Corporation Law," *Business History Review* 53 (1979): 304–42, esp. 328ff.; and Martin J. Sklar, *The Corporate Reconstruction of American Capitalism, 1890–1916: The Market, the Law, and Politics* (New York: Cambridge University Press, 1988), chap. 3.

12. James J. Hill quoted from James H. Bridge, ed., *The Trust: Its Book* (1902; reprint, New York: Arno Press, 1972), p. 100. This was a typical trope in the rhetoric of "combination"; for other examples, see Sidney Sherwood, "Influence of the Trust in the Development of Undertaking Genius," *Proceedings of the American Economic Association* (1900), pp. 163–76, and Livingston, "Social Anaylsis of Economic History and Theory," pp. 83–87.

13. Charles R. Flint, "Industrial Consolidations: What They Have Accomplished for Capital and Labor," *North American Review* 172 (1901): 664–77, here 675. On Flint's importance in the merger wave of 1898–1902, see Thomas R. Navin and Marian V. Sears, "The Rise of a Market for Industrial Securities, 1887–1902," *Business History Review* 29 (1955): 105–38, here 129–35.

14. Flint quoted from "Business Situation in the United States and the Prospects for the Future," *North American Review* 172 (1901): 381–93, here 385; cf. his remarks recorded in U.S. Industrial Commission, *Report on Trusts and Industrial Combinations* (Washington, D.C.: GPO, 1901), p. 92, and remarks of his colleagues in *Report and Proceedings of the Joint Committee of the [New York] Senate and Assembly Appointed to Investigate Trusts* (Albany, N.Y.: N.p., 1897), e.g.: H. O. Havemeyer, president of the American Sugar Refining Co., pp. 121–22; John E. Searles, treasurer of the American Coffee Co., pp. 438–40; E. B. Thomas, president of the Erie Railroad, pp. 1017–20; and Edwin R. Holden, vice-president of the Delaware, Lackawanna and Western Railroad, p. 1049. Flint himself testifies twice, at pp. 456–61 and 530–36. Carroll Wright is quoted from *Thirteenth Annual Report of the U.S. Commissioner of Labor: Hand and Machine Labor*, 2 vols. (Washington, D.C.: GPO, 1899), 1:115.

15. Vanderlip to James Phelan, January 30, 1903, Vanderlip Papers. Vanderlip's perspective here helps explain both accommodation and conflict between organized labor and corporate capital in the twentieth century; so it might help clarify if not adjudicate the remaining differences between the historians of labor and the historians of corporate liberalism.

16. *Hearings before Special Committee of the House of Representatives to Investigate the Taylor and Other Systems of Shop Management under Authority of H. Res. 90, 1912*, reprinted as "Taylor's Testimony before the Special House Committee" in Frederick Winslow Taylor, *Scientific Management* (New York: Harper, 1939), quoted remarks from pp. 88, 29.

17. Ibid., pp. 29–30, 15, 56, 76.

18. W. L. Mackenzie King quoted from "The Four Parties to Industry," an address to the Empire Club of Toronto, March 13, 1919, reprinted in Lyman P. Powell, ed., *The Social Unrest: Capital, Labor and the Public in Turmoil*, 2 vols. (New York: Review of Reviews Co., 1919), 1:35, 34; Taylor from "Testimony," p. 45. On King's importance, for example in devising the "Rockefeller Plan" of 1915 and the Jersey Standard program of 1918–19, which established the new patterns of labor relations under the regime of "welfare capitalism," see Irving Bernstein,

The Lean Years: A History of the American Worker, 1920–33 (Boston: Houghton Mifflin, 1960), pp. 157–69. On organized labor and scientific management more generally, see Milton J. Nadworny, *Scientific Management and the Unions, 1900–1932* (Cambridge: Harvard University Press, 1955), and Daniel Nelson, "Scientific Management, Systematic Management, and Labor, 1880–1915," *Business History Review* 48 (1974): 479–500.

19. John Frey's remarks from Hoxie, *Scientific Management and Labor*, pp. 132–37. Cf. Montgomery, *House of Labor*, chaps. 4–5.

20. On the Populists and "productive labor," see Bruce Palmer, *"Man Over Money": The Southern Populist Critique of American Capitalism* (Chapel Hill: University of North Carolina Press, 1980), chaps. 1–4, and Steven Hahn, *The Roots of Southern Populism: Yeoman Farmers and the Transformation of the Georgia Upcountry, 1850–1890* (New York: Oxford University Press, 1983), esp. chaps. 3, 7; see also chapter 8 below.

21. Quotations from *Relations between Capital and Labor* 1:138, 775. Cf. the testimony of Robert D. Layton, grand secretary of the Knights of Labor, in ibid., pp. 5–37, esp. 5, where Layton explains, "Of course, it is necessary if you employ labor, even to the smallest extent, to handle more or less capital, but in the sense in which 'capitalist' is generally understood, we have not any capitalists in our organization." Layton also makes it clear that "men who are at the head of large establishments" are not admitted to the Knights. See also the remarks of John Keogh, ibid. 3:487.

22. Cf. Salvatore, *Eugene V. Debs*, esp. chaps. 7–8; Stuart B. Kauffman, *Samuel Gompers and the Origins of the A.F. of L.* (Westport, Conn.: Greenwood, 1975); Marc Karson, *American Labor Unions and Politics* (Carbondale: Southern Illinois University Press, 1958), chap. 8; L. Levine, "Syndicalism in America," *Political Science Quarterly* 28 (1913): 451–79; Selig Perlman, *A Theory of the Labor Movement* (New York: Macmillan, 1928), chaps. 1, 5–7; and Selig Perlman and Philip Taft, *Labor Movements: 1896–1932*, vol. 4 of John R. Commons et al., *History of Labor in the United States* (New York: Macmillan, 1935).

23. On real wages, compare Paul A. Douglas, *Real Wages in the U.S., 1890–1926* (Boston: Houghton Mifflin, 1930), against Albert Rees, *Real Wages in Manufacturing, 1890–1914* (Princeton: Princeton University Press, 1961)—by either account, the rate of real wage growth after 1895 fell by at least half from 1884 to 1894. On productivity and "factor shares," that is, the distribution of income between labor and capital, see Frederick C. Mills, *Economic Tendencies in the U.S.* (New York: National Bureau of Economic Research, 1932), pp. 29–46, 132–38, 153–61, 188–200; Kendrick, *Productivity Trends*, pp. 134–70 and tables A-20, A-21, A-23 at pp. 331–32, 338; and Weber and Handfield-Jones, "Variations in the Rate of Economic Growth," esp. figures 1 and 7 at pp. 104, 121.

24. Roberto Mangabeira Unger, *False Necessity: Anti-Necessitarian Social Theory in the Service of Radical Democracy* (New York: Cambridge University Press, 1987), p. 337. Note that in the chapter immediately following this remark, Unger takes up the defense of the "small-holding alternative" to the "centralized factory" and the "multi-divisional enterprise"—that is, the populist alternative to corporate-industrial capitalism. This defense takes a more empirical, monographic form in North American social-labor history, but it is no less pointed.

25. E. S. Meade, "Financial Aspects of the Trust Problem," *Annals of the American Academy* 16 (1900): 345–403, here 356; cf. Livingston, *Origins of the Federal Reserve*, part 1, esp. pp. 53–55. I borrow the term "social death" from Orlando Patterson, *Slavery and Social Death: A Comparative Study* (Cambridge: Harvard University Press, 1982), but I use it here in a much weaker sense than his analysis of slavery requires.

26. See Navin and Sears, "Rise of a Market for Industrial Securities," 116–36; U.S. Department of Commerce, Bureau of the Census, *Manufactures 1905* (Washington, D.C.: GPO, 1907), table 8, p. liv, table 14, p. lxi; W. L. Thorp, *The Integration of Industrial Operation* (Washington, D.C.: GPO, 1924), table 30, p. 76; John Moody, *The Truth about the Trusts* (Chicago: Moody Publishing Co., 1904), p. 486; Luther Conant, Jr., "Industrial Consolidations in the United States," *Journal of the American Statistical Association*, n.s., 7 (1901): 207–26; and Ralph L. Nelson, *Merger Movements in American Industry, 1895–1956* (Princeton: Princeton University Press, 1959), pp. 6, 40, 71–105. Alfred Chandler is quoted from "The Large Industrial Corporation and the Making of the Modern American Economy," in Stephen E. Ambrose, ed., *Institutions in Modern America* (Baltimore: Johns Hopkins University Press, 1967), pp. 71–101, here 74. On the comparative scale of the property transfer, see Sklar, *Corporate Reconstruction*, chap. 1.

27. See chapter 7 below for more discussion of this question. Common stockholders have no inviolable legal claim on the assets of corporations in the event of dissolution or bankruptcy—only a right to payment of dividends in proportion to shares held *if* a dividend is declared; in this sense, the separation of ownership and control is already enacted in the financial reorganizations that summarize mergers and set the stage for vertical integration. On the connection of bureaucracies and large-scale private enterprise, cf. Max Weber, "Bureaucracy," in Hans Gerth and C. Wright Mills, eds., *From Max Weber* (New York: Oxford University Press, 1946), pp. 196–244, esp. 215–16, 221; Walter Lippmann quoted from *Drift and Mastery: An Attempt to Diagnose the Current Unrest* (1914; reprint, Madison: University of Wisconsin Press, 1985), p. 43.

28. See chapter 7, note 17, and related text; cf. C. B. Macpherson, *The Political Theory of Possessive Individualism: Hobbes to Locke* (New York: Oxford University Press, 1962), chap. 4; R. H. Tawney, *Harrington's Interpretation of His Age* (London: Humphrey Milford, 1941); and on the decisive event in the transition from feudalism to capitalism, the transfer of control over agricultural production to rent-paying commoners, Maurice Dobb, *Studies in the Development of Capitalism*, rev. ed. (New York: International Publishers, 1963), chap. 2.

29. The circulation of authors and ideas is pretty remarkable in the late 1920s; the "two cultures" that C. P. Snow worried about had not yet taken shape. Place of publication for all these works is New York. To my mind, the most provocative studies of the young intellectuals in the 1920s are still Martin J. Sklar, "On the Proletarian Revolution and the End of Political-Economic Society," *Radical America* 3 (1969): 1–41, now revised and published as "Some Political and Cultural Consequences of the Disaccumulation of Capital: Origins of Postindustrial Development in the 1920s," *The United States as a Developing Country* (New York: Cambridge University Press, 1992), pp. 143–96, and Warren I. Susman, *Culture as History:*

The Transformation of American Society in the Twentieth Century (New York: Pantheon, 1984), part 1; but Casey Nelson Blake's new book, *Beloved Community: The Cultural Criticisms of Randolph Bourne, Van Wyck Brooks, Waldo Frank, and Lewis Mumford* (Chapel Hill: University of North Carolina Press, 1991), makes us see their work in a new light. My own attempt to come to terms with Lewis Mumford, and with Blake's argument, is chapter 9, below.

30. Joseph Schumpeter's *Business Cycles*, 2 vols. (New York: McGraw-Hill, 1939), is a perfect example of what I mean—see chap. 14 in volume 2, which contains the famous subsection on "The 'Industrial Revolution' of the Twenties," pp. 753–94, but see also pp. 803–6 regarding employment and productivity trends after 1919. Cf. also Henry A. Wallace, *Technology, Corporations, and the General Welfare* (Chapel Hill: University of North Carolina Press, 1937), and Rexford G. Tugwell, *The Industrial Discipline and the Governmental Arts* (New York: Columbia University Press, 1933), pp. 11–64. Here is how Tugwell concludes his preface: "I believe, myself, that we are within a stone's throw of the end of labor—as labor, not as willing and cooperative activity. We know how to make machines do nearly everything. Only defective social mechanisms prevent the consummation of the trend toward the abolition of employment" (p. 7).

31. See chapter 1; Peter Temin quoted from Lance E. Davis et al., *American Economic Growth: An Economist's History of the United States* (New York: Harper & Row, 1972), p. 449. Cf. David Weintraub (an economist who would find employment with the Works Progress Administration), "Effects of Current and Prospective Technological Developments upon Capital Formation," *Proceedings of the American Economic Association* (1933), pp. 15–33: "The capital-equipment industries grew at an even faster rate than industrial production. . . . Since the number of persons engaged in the production of capital goods became a larger and larger proportion of the total gainfully occupied population, consumers' demand, and, consequently, all production became increasingly dependent upon developments in the capital goods industries" (p. 15).

32. On the proportions of the labor force in the two sectors, I have used Department of Commerce, Bureau of the Census, *14th Census of the United States, 1920*, vol. 8: *Manufactures 1919* (Washington, D.C.: GPO, 1923), table 32, p. 146: "Summary for 14 General Groups of Industries: 1919, 1914, 1909, 1904, 1899"; *Abstract of the Twelfth Census of the United States, 1900* (Washington, D.C.: GPO, 1902), tables 156 and 157 at pp. 324–25; *Abstract of the Eleventh Census, 1890* (Washington, D.C.: GPO, 1894), table 2, pp. 112–23; and *A Compendium of the Ninth Census* (Washington, D.C.: GPO, 1872), table 65, pp. 604–15, and table 99, pp. 800–811, to test W. G. Hoffmann's estimates in *The Growth of Industrial Economies*, trans. W. O. Henderson and W. H. Chaloner (Manchester: University of Manchester Press, 1958), pp. 67–101. But see also Tillman M. Sogge, "Industrial Classes in the United States 1870 to 1950," *Journal of the American Statistical Association* 49 (1954): 251–53, and the works cited at chapter 1, note 16, above. On the pace of mechanization, see Harry Jerome, *Mechanization in Industry* (New York: National Bureau of Economic Research, 1934), tables 15–19 and related text at pp. 216–26.

33. See Richard B. DuBoff, "The Introduction of Electric Power in American Manufacturing," *Economic History Review*, 2d ser., 20 (1967): 509–18, and "Electri-

fication and Capital Productivity: A Suggested Approach," *Review of Economics and Statistics* (1966), 426–31; Warren D. Devine, Jr., "From Shafts to Wires: Historical Perspective on Electrification," *Journal of Economic History* 43 (1983): 347–72; and Harry T. Oshima, "The Growth of U.S. Factor Productivity: The Significance of New Technologies in the Early Decades of the Twentieth Century," ibid. 44 (1984): 161–70. I would note here that "fractionalization" of power presupposes a new division of labor in which management has prerogatives it did not have so long as skilled workers controlled machine production, and that periodic use of power presupposes corporate control of supply, or production rather than price cycles. I should also note that I share Paul S. Adler's doubts about Harry Braverman's deskilling thesis, although my doubts are derived from a different source in the Hegelian tradition; see Adler's brilliant essay "Marx, Machines, and Skill," *Technology and Culture* 31 (1990): 780–812.

34. Quoted remarks and calculations from J. Stephen Jeans, ed., *American Industrial Conditions and Competition: Reports of the Commissioners Appointed by the British Iron Trade Association* (London: British Iron Trade Association, 1902), pp. 230, 317–20. On steelworkers in this period, see Stone, "Origin of Job Structures in the Steel Industry," and David Brody, *Steelworkers in America: The Nonunion Era* (Cambridge: Harvard University Press, 1960), chaps. 3, 7–12.

35. See Stephen Meyer III, *The Five Dollar Day: Labor Management and Social Control in the Ford Motor Company, 1908–1921* (Albany, N.Y.: State University of New York Press, 1981), chaps. 2–3, esp. pp. 47–64; Ralph C. Epstein, *The Automobile Industry: Its Economic and Commercial Development* (Chicago: University of Chicago Press, 1928), pp. 30–33, 41–53; David Gartman, *AutoSlavery: The Labor Process in the Automobile Industry, 1897–1950* (New Brunswick: Rutgers University Press, 1986), pp. 60–62, 68–70, 74, 102–14, 129–35; and Montgomery, *House of Labor*, pp. 233–35.

36. On turnover and management's consequent drive to colonize or "modernize" working-class neighborhoods and character structures through "human relations," counseling, company unions, and personnel departments, see Montgomery, *House of Labor*, pp. 239–44; Meyer, *Five Dollar Day*, chaps. 4–7; Bernstein, *Lean Years*, pp. 157–88; Loren Baritz, *The Servants of Power: A History of the Use of Social Science in American Industry* (New York: Wiley, 1965), esp. chaps. 7–8; and Lizabeth Cohen, *Making a New Deal: Industrial Workers in Chicago, 1919–1939* (New York: Cambridge University Press, 1990), chap. 4. Quoted remarks from National Industrial Conference Board, *Mergers in Industry* (New York: National Industrial Conference Board, 1929), p. 20, and Siegfried Giedion, *Mechanization Takes Command* (1948; reprint, New York: Norton, 1969), p. 118.

37. Quotations from Gartman, *AutoSlavery*, pp. 72–73, 77, 109–10, 114, 120; see also Mortier W. La Fever, "Workers, Machinery, and Production in the Automobile Industry," *Monthly Labor Review* 19 (October 1924): 1–26.

38. See Jerome, *Mechanization in Industry*, chaps. 2–3, 5–6; Oshima, "Growth of U.S. Factor Productivity," esp. 163–66; and Alfred D. Chandler, Jr., on the notion of "throughput," in *The Coming of Managerial Capitalism: A Casebook on the History of Economic Institutions* (Homewood, Ill.: Irwin, 1985), case 16, pp. 396–423. On the significance of an absolute decline in the labor force of the capital goods

sector, Sklar, "On the Proletarian Revolution," discussed in chapter 1, is the key text; but see also Sydney Coontz, *Productive Labour and Effective Demand* (New York: A. M. Kelley, 1966), pp. 141–58, and related works cited in chapter 1, notes 1 and 6, above.

39. On capital-output ratios, see Kendrick, *Productivity Trends*, pp. 164–70; D. Creamer et al., *Capital in Manufacturing and Mining: Its Formation and Financing* (Princeton: Princeton University Press, 1960), part 1, pp. 3–106, esp. chap. 3; John E. LaTourette, "Potential Output and the Capital-Output Ratio in the United States Private Business Sector, 1909–1959," *Kyklos* 18 (1965): 316–32, and "Sources of Variation in the Capital-Output Ratio in the United States Private Business Sector, 1909–1959," ibid., 635–51; and Evsey D. Domar, "The Capital-Output Ratio in the U.S.: Its Variation and Stability," in F. A. Lutz and D. C. Hague, eds., *The Theory of Capital* (New York: St. Martin's, 1961), pp. 95–117. On net investment, see Anatol Murad, "Net Investment and Industrial Progress," in Kenneth Kurihara, ed., *Post-Keynesian Economics* (New Brunswick: Rutgers University Press, 1954), pp. 227–50; Simon Kuznets, *National Income: A Summary of Findings* (New York: National Bureau of Economic Research, 1946), p. 58; Robert A. Gordon, "Investment Opportunities in the U.S. before and after World War II," in Erik Lundberg, ed., *The Business Cycle in the Post-War World* (London: Macmillan, 1955), pp. 283–310; Thomas C. Cochran, *The American Business System* (Cambridge: Harvard University Press, 1957), pp. 24–25, citing Kuznets and Raymond Goldsmith; and Harold Vatter, "The Atrophy of Net Investment and Some Consequences for the U.S. Mixed Economy," *Journal of Economic Issues* 16 (1982): 237–53. On innovation and/or technical change versus investment as the source of growth, see Robert Solow, "A Contribution to the Theory of Economic Growth," *Quarterly Journal of Economics* 70 (1956): 65–94; Solomon Fabricant, "Resources and Output Trends in the U.S. since 1870," *American Economic Review* 46 (1956): 5–23; and Benton F. Massell, "Capital Formation and Technological Change in United States Manufacturing," *Review of Economics and Statistics* 42 (1960): 182–88.

40. On the possibility of a new political universe, see, for example, Tugwell, *Industrial Discipline*, chap. 6; on the new functions of wages and the vestigial character of profits, see ibid., chap. 7, esp. p. 183, and, more pointedly, Sklar, "On the Proletarian Revolution," pp. 5–18. See otherwise, for examples, John R. Arnold's four-part series "The Trend of Consumption," *Annalist* 32 (a financial periodical published by the New York Times Co.): September 28, 1928, pp. 472–73; October 5, 1928, pp. 511, 514; October 19, 1928, pp. 608–9; November 30, 1928, pp. 852–53. Arnold was later cited as an authority on manufacturing capital and output: see Creamer et al., *Capital in Manufacturing and Mining*, p. 204. Also Leo Wolman, "Consumption and the Standard of Living," and Frederick C. Mills, "Price Movements and Related Industrial Changes," both in President's Conference on Unemployment, Committee on Recent Economic Changes, *Recent Economic Changes in the United States*, 2 vols. (New York: National Bureau of Economic Research, 1929), 1:13–78, 2:603–55; Mills, *Economic Tendencies*, pp. 269–91; Paul H. Douglas, *The Theory of Wages* (New York: Macmillan, 1934), chap. 8; and Maurice Leven et al., *America's Capacity to Consume* (Washington, D.C.: Brookings Institution, 1934).

41. Stuart Chase, *Men and Machines* (New York: Macmillan, 1929), p. 147; Wes-

ley C. Mitchell, "A Review," in *Recent Economic Changes* 2:841–910, here 878. Cf. G. E. Barnett, *Machinery and Labor* (Cambridge: Harvard University Press, 1926); Elizabeth Faulkner Baker, *Displacement of Men by Machines: Effects of Technological Change in Commercial Printing* (New York: Columbia University Press, 1933); Lewis Corey, *The Decline of American Capitalism* (New York: Covici, Friede, 1934), chaps. 11–15; Archibald MacLeish, "Machines and the Future," *Nation*, February 8, 1933; Jerome, *Mechanization in Industry*, chap. 10; David Weintraub, "The Displacement of Workers through Increase in Efficiency and Their Absorption by Industry, 1920–31," *Journal of the American Statistical Association* 37 (1932): 383–400; Schumpeter, *Business Cycles* 2:803–6; Mills, *Economic Tendencies*, pp. 416–23; Lewis Mumford, *Technics and Civilization* (New York: Harcourt, Brace & World, 1934), pp. 227–28 (also chap. 8: "Orientation"); and "Digest of Material on Technological Changes, Productivity of Labor, and Labor Displacement," *Monthly Labor Review* 27 (November 1932): 1031–57.

42. See George Soule (the former editor of the *New Republic* and a participant in debates on "technocracy" in the early 1930s), *Prosperity Decade: From War to Depression, 1917–1929* (New York: Harper & Row, 1947, 1968), chaps. 6–8, esp. pp. 121–30, 146–47, and Michael A. Bernstein, *The Great Depression: Delayed Recovery and Economic Change, 1929–1939* (New York: Cambridge University Press, 1988), chap. 5. Cf. Ralph G. Hurlin and Meredith B. Givens, "Shifting Occupational Patterns," in the President's Research Committee on Social Trends, *Recent Social Trends in the United States*, 2 vols. (New York: McGraw-Hill, 1934), 1:268–324; Solomon Fabricant, *Employment in Manufacturing, 1899–1939* (New York: National Bureau of Economic Research, 1942), table B-1, pp. 182–214; John P. Henderson, *Changes in the Industrial Distribution of Employment, 1919–59*, University of Illinois Bureau of Economic and Business Research Bulletin #87 (Urbana: University of Illinois Press, 1961).

43. See John H. Lorant, *The Role of Capital-Improving Innovations in American Manufacturing during the 1920s* (New York: Arno Press, 1975), esp. chaps. 2–3; Spurgeon Bell, *Productivity, Wages, and National Income* (Washington, D.C.: Brookings Institution, 1940), appendix F, pp. 281–300; and U.S. Federal Trade Commission, *Report on Motor Vehicle Industry, Pursuant to Joint Resolution No. 87*, 75th Cong., 3d sess., 1939, pp. 6–11.

44. See Gordon, "Investment Opportunities," table 3, p. 298; Creamer et al., *Capital in Manufacturing and Mining*, pp. 132–34; Wassily Leontief, "Machines and Man" (1952), in *Essays in Economics* (New York: Oxford University Press, 1966), pp. 187–99; Joseph M. Gillman, *The Falling Rate of Profit* (London: Dobson, 1957), pp. 74–81; Lowell J. Chawner, "Capital Expenditures for Manufacturing Plant and Equipment—1915 to 1940," *Survey of Current Business* (March 1941), pp. 9–15; and Rexford G. Tugwell, *Industry's Coming of Age* (New York: Harcourt, 1927), chap. 4.

45. Evans Clark, *Financing the Consumer* (New York: Harper & Bros., 1930), pp. 2–5, 193–96 (quoted at 4, 3, 193); on the volume of consumer credit, see chap. 2. Cf. Roland S. Vaile and Helen G. Canoyer, *Income and Consumption* (New York: Holt, 1938), chaps. 6–8, 13–14; William H. Lough, *High-Level Consumption* (New

York: McGraw-Hill, 1935), chap. 2, appendix A ("Base Tabulations of Consumers' Spendings and Withholdings, 1909 to 1931"), pp. 236–47, and appendix E ("Estimates of Consumers' Borrowings"), pp. 308–17; E.R.A. Seligman, *The Economics of Instalment Selling*, 2 vols. (New York: Harper & Bros., 1927), 1:107–17; and Melvin T. Copeland, "Marketing," in *Recent Economic Changes* 1:321–424, here 390–402.

46. I ignore the possibility of higher wages at a given level of employment because the degree of unionization does not then affect the argument, and because zero labor-force growth is an extremely unlikely event.

47. Edmund S. Phelps, "The New View of Investment: A Neoclassical Analysis," *Quarterly Journal of Economics* 76 (1962): 548–67, here 549; cf. Alvin H. Hansen, *The American Economy* (New York: McGraw-Hill, 1957), p. 7. Stuart Chase is quoted from *The Economy of Abundance* (New York: Macmillan, 1934), p. 274. For background on Chase, who was part of "the revolt of the engineers," and believed, accordingly, that the bankers and other middlemen were to blame for the debacle of the 1930s, see Robert B. Westbrook, "Tribune of the Technostructure: The Popular Economics of Stuart Chase," *American Quarterly* 32 (1980): 387–408. On the dynamism of the consumer goods sector, see esp. Bernstein, *Great Depression*, chaps. 2–4, 6.

48. Martha L. Olney, *Buy Now, Pay Later: Advertising, Credit, and Consumer Durables in the 1920s* (Chapel Hill: University of North Carolina Press, 1991); Bernstein, *Great Depression*.

49. Olney, *Buy Now, Pay Later*, pp. 47–54, 57–61, 182–87, quoted from pp. 47, 182, 51. When Olney notes that consumers had to save to buy durables with cash, readers have to wonder how, or why, people saved in order to save; see pp. 63, 102, 105, 133, 181, e.g., p. 63: "If credit financing becomes available, it decreases the amount of saving necessary to purchase an expensive good, allowing a household to make its purchase sooner." Cf. note 50 below.

50. See ibid., chap. 2; Soule, *Prosperity Decade*, pp. 116, 122; Wolman, "Consumption," 1:51–70; Robert S. Lynd, "The People as Consumers," in President's Research Committee, *Recent Social Trends* 2:857–911, esp. 889–906; and J. F. Steiner, "Recreation and Leisure Time Activities," ibid., 912–57. On income distribution in the 1920s, see note 53 below, but for immediate purposes, see Charles F. Holt, "Who Benefited from the Prosperity of the Twenties?," *Explorations in Economic History* 14 (1977): 277–89. The argument on the scope and character of the "consumer durables revolution," which Olney's book is meant to settle (see *Buy Now, Pay Later*, pp. 57–61), was started by Harry T. Oshima, "Consumer Asset Formation and the Future of Capitalism," *Economic Journal* 71 (1961): 20–35 and was kept alive by Thomas F. Juster and Robert E. Lipsey, "A Note on Consumer Asset Formation in the United States," ibid. 77 (1967): 834–47. Olney, Juster, and Lipsey end up on Oshima's side of the argument, but they do not observe the distinction between profit and utility which he introduces as a way of avoiding the conflation of investment and consumption (see Oshima, "Asset Formation," pp. 25–27). By equating spending on consumer durables and investment, they claim not merely that consumer expenditure compensates for declining investment but also that

the differences between consumption and (saving or) investment are insignificant. So they cannot grasp what Oshima does—that the transition to consumer-driven growth in the 1920s was a great watershed in the development of capitalism.

51. Bernstein, *Great Depression*, pp. 39, 27, 40, 31. My correspondence with Professor Bernstein indicates that the contradictions in the argument to which I have drawn attention were imposed by the exigencies of publication; they do not in any case affect the extraordinary importance of his book, which is simply the best study we have of the Great Depression. My remarks should be read as a revision, not a rejection, of Professor Bernstein's argument.

52. Quotation from Chase, *Economy of Abundance*, p. 278. See otherwise Soule, *Prosperity Decade*, pp. 122–24, 155, 320–21; Bell, *Productivity, Wages, and National Income*, chap. 3, esp. pp. 27–34; Leven et al., *Capacity to Consume*, chap. 3; Holt, "Prosperity of the Twenties," table 3 at p. 283; Harold G. Moulton et al., *Capital Expansion, Employment, and Economic Stability* (Washington, D.C.: Brookings Institution, 1940), pp. 18–29, 36; Charles P. Kindleberger, *The World in Depression, 1929–1939* (Berkeley: University of California Press, 1973), pp. 108–13; and W. W. [?] Riefler to Dr. Miller, May 11, 1932, Adolph C. Miller Papers, Box 13, Library of Congress, Washington, D.C.

53. See Soule, *Prosperity Decade*, pp. 276–87; Holt, "Prosperity of the Twenties," table 3 at p. 283; and Riefler to Miller, Miller Papers. On the growth of white-collar, "lower-salaried" employees, and the income effects, see Sogge, "Industrial Classes," p. 252; Seymour Melman, "The Growth of Administrative Overhead in Manufacturing Industries in the United States, 1899–1947," *Oxford Economic Papers*, n.s., 3 (1951): 62–112, table 2 at p. 66; and Jim Potter, *The American Economy between the World Wars* (New York: Wiley, 1974), pp. 56, 66. In "Relative Income Shares in Fact and Theory," *American Economic Review* 47 (1959): 917–42, a summary of and original contribution to the literature on income distribution, Irving B. Kravis concludes, "Much of the increase in the labor share observed in the data for the half century [ca. 1900–1950] was attributable to the growth in relative importance of government employment" (p. 928). I take this to mean that the volume of employment determined by private investment would not have promoted either a comparable "increase in the labor share" or a comparable increase in consumer expenditures.

54. H. W. Arndt, *The Economic Lessons of the Nineteen-Thirties* (London: Oxford University Press, 1944), pp. 50–67, quoted from p. 62. Cf. Potter, *Economy between the World Wars*, pp. 135–40; Kuznets, *National Income*, pp. 52–55, esp. table 16 at p. 53; Creamer et al., *Capital in Manufacturing and Mining*, table 6 at p. 25 and pp. 130–43, 154–55. On consumption expenditures more generally in the 1930s, see U.S. National Resources Committee, Industrial Committee, *Consumer Incomes in the U.S.: Their Distribution 1935–36* (Washington, D.C.: GPO, 1938), and *Consumer Expenditures in the U.S.: Estimates for 1935–36* (Washington, D.C.: GPO, 1939), which are put in historical perspective by the U.S. Department of Labor, *How American Buying Habits Change* (Washington, D.C.: GPO, 1959), chap. 2, pp. 25–55, and chap. 10, pp. 217–42. On the ideological struggle within both the Roosevelt administration and the coalition composing the Democratic Party over the political meaning and economic significance of consumption, see Steve Fraser,

"The 'Labor Question,'" and Alan Brinkley, "The New Deal and the Idea of the State," both in Steve Fraser and Gary Gerstle, eds., *The Rise and Fall of the New Deal Order, 1930–1980* (Princeton: Princeton University Press, 1989), pp. 55–84, esp. 68–71, and 85–121, esp. 87–98; also Rexford G. Tugwell, "Consumers and the New Deal" (an address to the Consumers League of Ohio, Cleveland, May 11, 1934), *The Battle for Democracy* (New York: Columbia University Press, 1935), pp. 268–86; and two general surveys of the conflicts developing within a proto-Keynesian paradigm: Robert M. Collins, *The Business Response to Keynes, 1929–1964* (New York: Columbia University Press, 1981), chaps. 1–3, and Theodore Rosenof, *Patterns of Political Economy in America* (New York: Garland, 1983), part 1.

55. Chase, *Economy of Abundance*, p. 277; Leven et al., *Capacity to Consume*, p. 116. Quoted remarks on relief from Cohen, *Making a New Deal*, pp. 271–72; cf. Joe William Trotter, Jr., *Black Milwaukee: The Making of an Industrial Proletariat, 1915–45* (Urbana: University of Illinois Press, 1985), pp. 161–62.

56. See Simon Patten, *Essays in Economic Theory*, ed. Rexford G. Tugwell (New York: Knopf, 1924). Tugwell describes his personal relationship and intellectual affiliation with Patten in *To the Lesser Heights of Morningside: A Memoir* (Philadelphia: University of Pennsylvania Press, 1982), pp. 43–49, 132–38; note also the remarks at pp. 155–61 on the role of Dewey's instrumentalism in Tugwell's inflection of Patten's "surplus economy." A more sober, biographical account is Rexford G. Tugwell, "Notes on the Life and Work of Simon Nelson Patten," *Journal of Political Economy* 31 (1923): 153–208. When I say that Tugwell was a typical "technocrat," I mean not that he was closely associated with Howard Scott's Technical Alliance and its echoes in the 1930s (on which see William E. Akin, *Technocracy and the American Dream* [Berkeley: University of California Press, 1977]) but that he had more faith in economic planning than in public opinion; cf. Ellis Hawley, *The New Deal and the Problem of Monopoly* (Princeton: Princeton University Press, 1966), pp. 43–46.

CHAPTER FIVE

1. See Morton White, *Social Thought in America: The Revolt Against Formalism*, rev. ed. (Boston: Beacon Press, 1957); H. Stuart Hughes, *Consciousness and Society: The Reorientation of European Social Thought, 1890–1930* (New York: Vintage, 1961); and Henry F. May, *The End of American Innocence: A Study of the First Years of Our Own Time, 1912–1917* (New York: Knopf, 1959; Chicago: Quadrangle, 1964). But see also Eric F. Goldman, *Rendezvous with Destiny: A History of Modern American Reform* (New York: Vintage, 1952); Paul F. Boller, Jr., *American Thought in Transition: The Impact of Evolutionary Naturalism, 1865–1900* (Chicago: Rand McNally, 1969); Larzer Ziff, *The American 1890s: Life and Times of a Lost Generation* (New York: Viking, 1966); Lee Benson, *Turner and Beard: American Historical Writing Reconsidered* (Glencoe, Ill.: Free Press, 1960); R. Jackson Wilson, *In Quest of Community: Social Philosophy in America, 1860–1930* (New York: Oxford University Press, 1968); Nathan I. Huggins, *Harlem Renaissance* (New York: Oxford University Press, 1970); Houston A. Baker, Jr., *Modernism and the Harlem Renais-*

sance (Chicago: University of Chicago Press, 1987); August Meier, *Negro Thought in America, 1880–1915* (Ann Arbor: University of Michigan Press, 1963); Hazel V. Carby, *Reconstructing Womanhood: The Emergence of the Afro-American Woman Novelist* (New York: Oxford University Press, 1987); and David Levering Lewis, *When Harlem Was in Vogue* (New York: Oxford University Press, 1989).

2. See, for example, T. J. Jackson Lears, *No Place of Grace: Antimodernism and the Transformation of American Culture, 1880–1920* (New York: Pantheon, 1981); Lewis Erenberg, *Steppin' Out: New York Nightlife and the Transformation of American Culture, 1890–1930* (Chicago: University of Chicago Press, 1981); also Lary May, *Screening Out the Past: The Birth of Mass Culture and the Motion Picture Industry* (New York: Oxford University Press, 1980); and Roy Rosenzweig, *Eight Hours for What We Will: Workers and Leisure in an Industrial City, 1870–1920* (New York: Cambridge University Press, 1983). But cf. Michel Foucault, *The Archaeology of Knowledge*, trans. A. M. Sheridan Smith (New York: Pantheon, 1972), esp. pp. 166–77, for an argument on behalf of "transformation" as against "change," "progress," "evolution," etc.

3. See Angus Campbell et al. of the Survey Research Center at the University of Michigan, *The American Voter* (New York: Wiley, 1960); Philip Converse, "The Nature of Belief Systems in Mass Publics," in David Apter, ed., *Ideology and Discontent* (Glencoe, Ill.: Free Press, 1964), pp. 206–61; Daniel Bell, *The End of Ideology* (Glencoe, Ill.: Free Press, 1960); Richard Hofstadter, *The Age of Reform: From Bryan to F.D.R.* (New York: Vintage, 1955); David Riesman et al., *The Lonely Crowd* (New Haven: Yale University Press, 1950); Sheldon Wolin, *Politics and Vision: Continuity and Innovation in the Western Political Tradition* (Boston: Little, Brown, 1960); Hannah Arendt, *The Human Condition* (Chicago: University of Chicago Press, 1958), and *On Revolution* (New York: Viking, 1963); C. B. Macpherson, *The Political Theory of Possessive Individualism: Hobbes to Locke* (New York: Oxford University Press, 1962); and C. Wright Mills, *The New Men of Power* (New York: Oxford University Press, 1948), *White Collar: The American Middle Classes* (New York: Oxford University Press, 1951), *The Power Elite* (New York: Oxford University Press, 1959), and *The Sociological Imagination* (New York: Oxford University Press, 1959). See also Hans Gerth and C. Wright Mills, eds., *From Max Weber* (New York: Oxford University Press, 1946), and *Character and Social Structure: The Psychology of Social Institutions* (New York: Oxford University Press, 1953); Talcott Parsons, *The Social System* (Glencoe, Ill.: Free Press, 1951), and "Introduction" to Max Weber, *The Theory of Social and Economic Organization*, trans. and ed. Talcott Parsons (New York: Oxford University Press, 1974); Robert Merton, *Social Theory and Social Structure*, rev. ed. (Glencoe, Ill.: Free Press, 1957); Robert Bierstadt, *Power and Progress: Essays on Sociological Theory* (New York: McGraw-Hill, 1974), two-thirds of which is the work of 1937–1960; William Appleman Williams, *The Contours of American History* (Cleveland: World Publishing Co., 1961); and Thomas Kuhn, *The Structure of Scientific Revolutions* (Chicago: University of Chicago Press, 1962). We should also bear in mind that this was the moment at which Norman O. Brown and Herbert Marcuse reinvented psychoanalysis as a philosophy of history.

4. See Mills, "On Reason and Freedom," *Sociological Imagination*, pp. 165–76, and Hofstadter, *Age of Reform*, pp. 215–56.

5. See Roberto Mangabeira Unger, *Knowledge and Politics* (New York: Free Press, 1975), chap. 3: "The Unity of Liberal Theory," pp. 104–44.

6. On the turn toward social and cultural history, see, e.g., William J. Bouwsma, "From History of Ideas to History of Meaning," *Journal of Interdisciplinary History* 12 (1981): 279–91, and Robert Darnton, "Intellectual and Cultural History," in Michael Kammen, ed., *The Past before Us: Contemporary Historical Writing in the U.S.* (Ithaca: Cornell University Press, 1980), pp. 327–54. The exemplar of the turn in question is of course Clifford Geertz, "Ideology as a Cultural System," in Apter, *Ideology and Discontent*, pp. 47–76. Ralph Ellison examines the "physical complexity" of African-American culture in "Richard Wright's Blues," an essay from 1945 reprinted in his *Shadow and Act* (New York: Random House, 1964), pp. 77–94; see also "Twentieth Century Fiction and the Black Mask of Humanity" (1953), ibid., pp. 24–44, and "Change the Yoke and Slip the Joke" (1958), ibid., pp. 45–59. In the same critical connection, see Albert Murray's brilliant studies of the blues, *Stomping the Blues* (New York: Vintage, 1976), and *The Hero and the Blues* (Columbia: University of Missouri Press, 1982).

7. For example, see Rosenzweig, *Eight Hours*, parts 3–4; Erenberg, *Steppin' Out*; John F. Kasson, *Amusing the Million: Coney Island at the Turn of the Century* (New York: Hill & Wang, 1978); Kathy Peiss, *Cheap Amusements: Working Women and Leisure in Turn-of-the-Century New York* (Philadelphia: Temple University Press, 1986); and Lawrence Levine, *Highbrow/Lowbrow: The Emergence of Cultural Hierarchy in America* (Cambridge: Harvard University Press, 1988).

8. For examples of the new cultural history at its best, see Alan Trachtenberg, *The Incorporation of America* (New York: Hill & Wang, 1982), and T. J. Jackson Lears, "The Concept of Cultural Hegemony," *American Historical Review* 90 (1985): 567–93. Roberto Mangabeira Unger is quoted from his *False Necessity: Anti-Necessitarian Social Theory in the Service of Radical Democracy* (New York: Cambridge University Press, 1987), p. 337 and cf., more generally, pp. 277–340.

9. Among the intellectual historians, James T. Kloppenberg comes closer than anyone else to recognizing that the idea of socialism regulated the political and intellectual discourse of Europe and North America, ca. 1890–1920; but he also comes close to writing as if the liberal tradition reinvigorated by "The Philosophy of the Via Media" was the gravitational center of the late-nineteenth-century intellectual universe, around which alternatives to liberalism—alternatives such as socialism— necessarily moved in orbit: see James T. Kloppenberg, *Uncertain Victory: Social Democracy and Progressivism in European and American Thought, 1870–1920* (New York: Oxford University Press, 1986), for example at pp. 163–75.

10. For example, Goldman, *Rendezvous with Destiny*, chap. 5; Boller, *American Thought in Transition*; and Kloppenberg, *Uncertain Victory*, part 1.

11. For example, see White, *Social Thought*, chaps. 2–4; but see also James Longenbach, *Modernist Poetics of History: Pound, Eliot, and the Sense of the Past* (Princeton: Princeton University Press, 1987); Stephen Kern, *The Culture of Time and Space, 1880–1918* (Cambridge: Harvard University Press, 1983), chaps. 1–4;

and Donald G. Lowe, *History of Bourgeois Perception* (Chicago: University of Chicago Press, 1982), chap. 6.

12. For example, see Marshall J. Cohen, *Self and Society: Charles Horton Cooley and the Idea of Social Self in American Thought* (New York: Garland, 1982); Casey Nelson Blake, *Beloved Community: The Cultural Criticisms of Randolph Bourne, Van Wyck Brooks, Waldo Frank, and Lewis Mumford* (Chapel Hill: University of North Carolina Press, 1990); and Kloppenberg, *Uncertain Victory*, chaps. 3, 5, 8; but the more interesting work done here is by philosophers and literary critics, e.g., Bruce Wilshire, *William James and Phenomenology: A Study of "The Principles of Psychology"* (Bloomington: Indiana University Press, 1968), esp. chap. 6; Vincent M. Colapietro, *Peirce's Approach to the Self: A Semiotic Perspective on Human Subjectivity* (Albany: State University of New York Press, 1989), esp. chap. 4; and Richard Poirier, *The Renewal of Literature: Emersonian Reflections* (New York: Random House, 1987), esp. chap. 5.

13. For example, see Sidney Fine, *Laissez-Faire and the General Welfare State: A Study of Conflict in American Thought, 1865–1901* (Ann Arbor: University of Michigan Press, 1956); Arnold J. Paul, *Conservative Crisis and the Rule of Law* (Ithaca: Cornell University Press, 1960); Robert McCloskey, *American Conservatism in the Age of Enterprise* (Cambridge: Harvard University Press, 1951); William J. Letwin, *Law and Economic Policy in America: The Evolution of the Sherman Antitrust Act* (Chicago: University of Chicago Press, 1965); J. Willard Hurst, *The Legitimacy of the Large Business Corporation in the Law of the U.S.* (Charlottesville: University of Virginia Press, 1970); and Hans. B. Thorelli, *The Federal Antitrust Policy: Origination of an American Tradition* (Baltimore: Johns Hopkins University Press, 1955). The new benchmark for studies in the redefinition of property at the law in this period is Martin J. Sklar, *The Corporate Reconstruction of American Capitalism, 1890–1916: The Market, the Law, and Politics* (New York: Cambridge University Press, 1988).

14. For example, May, *End of American Innocence*, parts 2–3; Rosalind Rosenberg, *Beyond Separate Spheres: Intellectual Roots of Modern Feminism* (New Haven: Yale University Press, 1982); Christopher Lasch, *The New Radicalism in America, 1889–1963: The Intellectual as a Social Type* (New York: Vintage, 1965); Richard Hofstadter, *Anti-Intellectualism in American Life* (New York: Viking, 1962), parts 3–4, 6.

15. For example, see Peiss, *Cheap Amusements*; Erenberg, *Steppin' Out*; and Lears, *No Place of Grace*.

16. For example, see Levine, *Highbrow/Lowbrow*, chap. 3; Rosenzweig, *Eight Hours*, parts 3–4; Richard Jules Oestreicher, *Solidarity and Fragmentation: Working People and Class Consciousness in Detroit, 1875–1900* (Urbana: University of Illinois Press, 1986); and Paul Boyer, *Urban Masses and Moral Order in America, 1820–1920* (Cambridge: Harvard University Press, 1978), part 3.

17. For example, see Kasson, *Amusing the Million*; May, *Screening Out the Past*; Peiss, *Cheap Amusements*; Erenberg, *Steppin' Out*; Rachel Bowlby, *Just Looking: Consumer Culture in Dresier, Gissing, and Zola* (London: Methuen, 1985); and the indispensable essays of Neil Harris, now collected as *Cultural Excursions: Marketing*

Appetites and Cultural Tastes in Modern America (Chicago: University of Chicago Press, 1990).

18. For example, see Warren I. Susman, *Culture as History: The Transformation of American Society in the Twentieth Century* (New York: Pantheon, 1984), and Richard W. Fox and T. J. Jackson Lears, eds., *The Culture of Consumption: Critical Essays in American History, 1880–1980* (New York: Pantheon, 1983).

19. For example, see Lawrence Goodwyn, *Democratic Promise: The Populist Moment in America* (New York: Oxford University Press, 1976); Steven Hahn, *The Roots of Southern Populism: Yeoman Farmers and the Transformation of the Georgia Upcountry, 1850–1890* (New York: Oxford University Press, 1983); Herbert G. Gutman, *Work, Culture, and Society in Industrializing America* (New York: Vintage, 1977), and *Power and Culture: Essays on the American Working Class*, ed. Ira Berlin (New York: Pantheon, 1987); Leon Fink, *Workingmens' Democracy: The Knights of Labor in American Politics* (Urbana: University of Illinois Press, 1983); David Montgomery, *The Fall of the House of Labor: The Workplace, the State, and American Labor Activism, 1865–1925* (New York: Cambridge University Press, 1987); Michael Denning, *Mechanic Accents: Dime Novels and Working Class Culture in America* (London: Verso, 1986); and Michael E. McGerr, *The Decline of Popular Politics: The American North, 1865–1928* (New York: Oxford University Press, 1986). Insightful surveys of the state of the art in social-labor history are Leon Fink, "The New Labor History and the Powers of Historical Pessimism: Consensus, Hegemony, and the Case of the Knights of Labor," with comment following by Jackson Lears, John P. Diggins, George Lipsitz, Mari Jo Buhle and Paul Buhle, and rejoinder by Fink in *Journal of American History* 75 (1988): 115–61, and Leon Fink, "Looking Backward: Reflections on Workers' Culture and Certain Conceptual Dilemmas within Labor History," in J. Carroll Moody and Alice Kessler-Harris, eds., *Perspectives on American Labor History: The Problems of Synthesis* (DeKalb: Northern Illinois University Press, 1990), pp. 5–29.

20. For example, see Rosenberg, *Beyond Separate Spheres*; Linda Gordon, *Woman's Body, Woman's Right: Birth Control in America*, rev. ed. (New York: Penguin, 1990), chaps. 5–10; Nancy F. Cott, *The Grounding of Modern Feminism* (New Haven: Yale University Press, 1988); Mari Jo Buhle, *Women and American Socialism, 1870–1920* (Urbana: University of Illinois Press, 1981); Dolores Hayden, *The Grand Domestic Revolution: A History of Feminist Designs for American Homes, Neighborhoods, and Cities* (Cambridge: MIT Press, 1981), chaps. 7–12; Aileen S. Kraditor, *The Ideas of the Woman Suffrage Movement, 1890–1920* (1965; reprint, Garden City, N.Y.: Doubleday, 1971); William L. O'Neill, *Everyone Was Brave: A History of Feminism in America*, rev. ed. (New Brunswick: Transaction Books, 1989); William Leach, *True Love and Perfect Union: The Feminist Reform of Sex and Society* (New York: Basic Books, 1980); and David Kennedy, *Birth Control in America: The Career of Margaret Sanger* (New Haven: Yale University Press, 1970).

21. See White, *Social Thought*; May, *End of American Innocence*; Wilson, *In Quest of Community*; Kloppenberg, *Uncertain Victory*; and Fine, *Laissez-Faire*; see otherwise Bruce Kuklick, *The Rise of American Philosophy: Cambridge, Massachusetts, 1860–1930* (New Haven: Yale University Press, 1977), and Thomas L. Haskell,

The Emergence of Professional Social Science: The American Social Science Association and the Nineteenth-Century Crisis of Authority (Urbana: University of Ilinois Press, 1977).

22. See George Santayana, "The Genteel Tradition in American Philosophy," *Winds of Doctrine: Studies in Contemporary Opinion* (1913; reprint, New York: Harper, 1957), pp. 186–215, here 204. See also his "William James," in Richard Colton Lyon, ed., *Santayana on America* (New York: Harcourt, Brace & World, 1968), pp. 73–88. On pragmatism and the young intellectuals, see chapter 9 below.

23. See Peiss, *Cheap Amusements*; Rosenzweig, *Eight Hours*; Kasson, *Amusing the Million*; Gutman, *Work, Culture, and Society*; and Goodwyn, *Democratic Promise*; see otherwise Carroll Smith-Rosenberg, *Disorderly Conduct: Visions of Gender in Victorian America* (New York: Oxford University Press, 1986).

CHAPTER SIX

A different version of this chapter is forthcoming in a collection of essays on Dreiser and naturalism edited by Miriam Gogol. My thanks to Professor Gogol for her help in shaping my argument.

1. See Hans Robert Jauss, "Literary History as a Challenge to Literary Theory," *New Literary History* 2 (1970): 7–37, here 11. See also Istvan Soter, "The Dilemma of Literary Science," ibid., 85–100, and on the ironies of historicism across the curriculum, see, for example, Quentin Skinner, "Meaning and Understanding in the History of Ideas," *History and Theory* 8 (1969): 3–53; David Carroll, "The Alterity of Discourse: Form, History, and the Question of the Political," *Diacritics* 13 (1983): 65–83; Peter U. Hohendahl, "On Reception Aesthetics," *New German Critique* 28 (1983): 108–46; Fredric Jameson, "Marxism and Historicism," *New Literary History* 11 (1979): 41–73; Alasdair MacIntyre, "The Relationship of Philosophy to Its Past," in Richard Rorty, J. B. Schneewind, and Quentin Skinner, eds., *Philosophy in History* (New York: Cambridge University Press, 1984), pp. 31–48; and Michael Sprinker, "The Current Conjunture in Theory," *College English* 51 (1989): 825–31.

2. For evidence that our generation of critics has rediscovered the literary event called naturalism, see the special issue on Dreiser of *Modern Fiction Studies* 23 (1977); Eric J. Sundquist, ed., *American Realism: New Essays* (Baltimore: Johns Hopkins University Press, 1982); Donald Pizer, *Twentieth-Century American Literary Naturalism* (Carbondale: Southern Illinois University Press, 1982); Philip Fisher, *Hard Facts: Setting and Form in the American Novel* (New York: Oxford University Press, 1985), pp. 6–7, 12–13, 20–21, 128–78; June Howard, *Form and History in American Literary Naturalism* (Chapel Hill: University of North Carolina Press, 1985), esp. pp. 41–50, 99–102, 107–11, 115, 150–51, 155; and Rachel Bowlby, *Just Looking: Consumer Culture in Dreiser, Gissing, and Zola* (London: Methuen, 1985), esp. pp. 1–65.

3. Since narrative forms are embedded in the history of writing, to retrieve one from the dustbin of literary usage, Barthes suggests, is "an act of historical solidarity." He elaborates on the point in a way that informs all subsequent literary

historicisms: the choice of form, he claims, establishes a "relationship between creation and society" and entails a "literary language transformed by its social finality." Thus writing as such is "essentially the morality of form, the choice of that social area within which the writer elects to situate the Nature of his language" (Roland Barthes, *Writing Degree Zero*, trans. A. Lavers and C. Smith [London: Cape, 1967], p. 14). So conceived, form is both a result and a definition of history. The choice of one over another is determined in the first place by availability, by the range of forms the history of writing has placed at the disposal of writers. But that choice defines the scope of what may be represented, without apology or explanation, as real, plausible, or consequential events—that is, it defines the historical or usable past and so anticipates, or prepares us for, a certain future. Since modern fiction "is constructed in a zone of contact with the incomplete events of a particular present," as Mikhail Bakhtin insists, it necessarily opens onto a future and indeed "begins to feel closer to the future than the past, and begins to seek some valorized support in the future" (Mikhail Bakhtin, *The Dialogic Imagination*, trans. C. Emerson and M. Holquist, ed. M. Holquist [Austin: University of Texas Press, 1982], pp. 33, 26). The morality of form, I would then say, simply is this anticipatory arena where actuality and possibility, past and present, are allowed to collaborate on a history of the future. Hence to suggest that form or genre should be treated as the "immanent ideology" or the "political unconscious" of fictional discourse, as Fredric Jameson does in *The Political Unconscious: Narrative as a Socially Symbolic Act* (Ithaca: Cornell University Press, 1981), is not to remint the reductionist coinage of base and superstructure; it is instead to suggest that *form* is to fictional discourse what *paradigm* is to nonfictional discourse—that is, a historically specific protocol that naturalizes an observable reality and constitutes a social relation between practitioners (writers) and their potential publics.

4. The interdisciplinary agreement on the 1890s as the overture to our own time is apparent, for example, in Richard Rorty, *Consequences of Pragmatism* (Minneapolis: University of Minnesota Press, 1982); John Higham, "The Reorientation of American Culture in the 1890s," in John Weiss, ed., *The Origins of Modern Consciousness* (Detroit: Wayne State University Press, 1965), pp. 25–48; and T. J. Jackson Lears, *No Place of Grace: Antimodernism and the Transformation of American Culture, 1880–1920* (New York: Pantheon, 1981). See also Charles Child Walcutt, *American Literary Naturalism: A Divided Stream*, 2d ed. (Minneapolis: University of Minnesota Press, 1973). Walcutt's approach to naturalism is consistent with my more limited attempt to situate one of Dreiser's novels within the problematic of cultural change in the late-nineteenth-century United States, for in chap. 1, esp. pp. 10–23, he suggests the following: (1) the American Dream resides in the overthrow of the dualism centering in the antinomy of desire and reason (or body and mind), which animates the Western intellectual tradition as such and which is codified in modern liberal psychology; (2) the poetics of this Dream are most clearly articulated in what he calls the monism of transcendentalism—in what most of the rest of us, following Van Wyck Brooks, Lewis Mumford, and F. O. Matthiessen, would probably call the dialectics of the American Renaissance; (3) American literary naturalism is an effort to get beyond the same fundamental dualism, and thus may be construed as a major reinterpretation of the American Dream and a

literary agenda that derives from the earlier Renaissance; and (4) naturalism, as the extremity of realism, is pervaded by a perceived contradiction between "optimism and pessimism, freedom and determination, will and fate, social reformism and mechanistic despair"—thus it is one manifestation of the "divided stream of transcendentalism" because it fails to reinstate the original "transcendentalist union of reason and instinct" (pp. 12, 15). Although Walcutt's subsequent readings of naturalist novels are not as provocative and insightful as this introductory argument, the book seems to me a brilliant success because it illuminates the cultural context within which the intellectual extremity of the naturalist literary agenda begins to make sense. My only criticism of Walcutt is that he does not take his own insights seriously enough. For example, at p. 22 he notes, "Naturalism involved a continual search for form." If he is correct—and I think he is—it becomes necessary to explain and defend, not merely mention in passing, Frank Norris's seemingly bizarre claim to the effect that romance is the necessary formal antidote to realism under modern conditions (see Frank Norris, *The Responsibilities of the Novelist* [1901; reprint, Garden City, N.Y.: Doubleday, 1928], pp. 163–68). And this of course is one way to describe what I am trying to accomplish in the case of *Sister Carrie*, the exemplary naturalist novel that, in my view, transcends the dualism Walcutt decries without denying the possibilities produced in and by a dualizing epoch.

5. See Harold Bloom, *Poetry and Repression* (New Haven: Yale University Press, 1976).

6. Ibid., pp. 135–42, 235–93.

7. Van Wyck Brooks, *America's Coming-of-Age* (1915), reprinted in *Three Essays on America* (New York: Dutton, 1934), pp. 78–89; D. H. Lawrence, *Studies in Classic American Literature* (New York: N.p., 1923), chaps. 10–12; Lewis Mumford, *The Golden Day* (New York: Horace Liveright, 1926), chap. 3, and *Herman Melville* (New York: Harcourt, Brace & Co., 1929).

8. William Dean Howells, *Literary Friends and Acquaintances* (Bloomington: Indiana University Press, 1968), pp. 101–2. These remarks appeared originally in *Harper's Monthly* of November 1895, as "Literary Boston Thirty Years Ago."

9. E. H. Cady, ed., *W. D. Howells as Critic* (Boston: Routledge Kegan Paul, 1973), p. 100.

10. My point of departure is Richard Brodhead's insightful "Hawthorne among the Realists: The Case of Howells," in Sundquist, *American Realism*, pp. 25–41.

11. William Dean Howells, *A Modern Instance* (1882; reprint, Bloomington: Indiana University Press, 1977), p. 361; cf. Lears, *No Place of Grace*, pp. 36–41, on the moral questions raised by acknowledgment of a discontinuous self in the late nineteenth century.

12. Halleck's positions on the relation between extension in space or time and the intelligibility of morality are essentially Kantian; see, for example, Immanuel Kant, *Groundwork of the Metaphysic of Morals*, trans. H. J. Paton (New York: Harper & Row, 1964), p. 125, and *Critique of Pure Reason*, trans. N. K. Smith (New York: Oxford University Press, 1965), pp. 313, 464–79 [A 318–19, 533–57]. Cf. Hegel's emphatic dissent, for example in *The Philosophy of Right* (1821), trans. T. M. Knox (New York: Oxford University Press, 1953): "By this means alone [i.e., "securing for this, its external condition, the rationality of which it is capable"] does mind be-

come at home with itself within this pure externality. There, then, mind's freedom is existent and mind becomes objective to itself in this element which is implicitly inimical to mind's appointed end, freedom" (paragraph 187, addition, p. 125).

13. Cady, *Howells as Critic*, pp. 310–11, cf. p. 102.

14. On desire as the cunning of reason, see G. W. F. Hegel, *The Phenomenology of Mind* (1807), trans. J. B. Baillie (1931; reprint, New York: Harper & Row, 1967), pp. 218–25; Norman O. Brown, *Life against Death: The Psychoanalytical Meaning of History* (Middletown, Conn.: Wesleyan University Press, 1959), chaps. 8–12; Jacques Lacan, *Speech and Language in Psychoanalysis*, trans. Anthony Wilden (Baltimore: Johns Hopkins University Press, 1968), esp. part 3, "Interpretation and Temporality," pp. 53–87; Alexandre Kojève, *Introduction to the Reading of Hegel*, trans. James Nichols, ed. Allan Bloom (Ithaca: Cornell University Press, 1969), esp. pp. 37–41; and Joel Kovel, *The Age of Desire* (New York: Pantheon, 1981), esp. chaps. 6, 10, 12. On Walt Whitman's equation of self and Other ("I and the Abyss"), see Bloom, *Poetry and Repression*, pp. 251–66, and Lewis Hyde, *The Gift: Imagination and the Erotic Life of Property* (New York: Pantheon, 1979), pp. 163–79.

15. On the convergence of artistic, literary, and intellectual agendas at the turn of the century, see, for example, Bram Dijkstra, *The Hieroglyphics of a New Speech: Cubism, Stieglitz, and the Early Poetry of William Carlos Williams* (Princeton: Princeton University Press, 1969); John Berger, *The Success and Failure of Picasso* (New York: Pantheon, 1965), pp. 47–83; Lester H. Cohen, "Locating One's Self: The Problematics of Dreiser's Social World," *Modern Fiction Studies* 23 (1977): 355–68; Donald Lowe, *History of Bourgeois Perception* (Chicago: University of Chicago Press, 1983), chap. 6; Stephen Kern, *The Culture of Time and Space, 1880–1918* (Cambridge: Harvard University Press, 1984); and Sanford Schwartz, *The Matrix of Modernism* (Princeton: Princeton University Press, 1985).

16. Bruce Wilshire's brilliant account of William James's "phenomenological" breakthrough in *The Principles of Psychology* (1890) might stand as a summary of the unfinished cultural revolution I am sketching here: "Clearly James is impressed by the fact that every thought is part of a personal, and apparently private, consciousness. . . . But the upshot of Chapter Ten is that the self is not a sealed container full of intrinsically private thoughts. It is as if the self were blasted open and distributed across the face of the lived-world. . . . There is total reversal: the problem is not how thoughts can be public but how they can be private" (Bruce Wilshire, *William James and Phenomenology: A Study of "The Principles of Psychology"* [Bloomington: Indiana University Press, 1968], p. 125). I do not mean to suggest that James's *Principles* is the source of a cultural revolution; merely that his phenomenology of the self is one symptom of a larger ferment to which naturalism contributes by redefining the characters of fiction. I will be elaborating on these claims in chapters 7–10; meanwhile, cf. Warren I. Susman, " 'Personality' and the Making of Twentieth Century Culture," in John Higham and Paul Conkin, eds., *New Directions in American Intellectual History* (Baltimore: Johns Hopkins University Press, 1979), pp. 212–26; John Kasson, *Amusing the Million: Coney Island at the Turn of the Century* (New York: Hill & Wang, 1978), pp. 6–78; Rem Koolhaas, *Delirious New York* (New York: Oxford University Press, 1978), pp. 22–92; Kathy Peiss, *Cheap Amusements: Working Women and Leisure in Turn-of-the-Century New*

York (Philadelphia: Temple University Press, 1986); Henry F. May, *The End of American Innocence, 1912–1917* (New York: Knopf, 1959); Lewis Erenberg, *Steppin' Out: New York Nightlife and the Transformation of American Culture, 1890–1930* (Chicago: University of Chicago Press, 1981); William R. Leach, "Transformations in a Culture of Consumption: Women and Department Stores, 1890–1925," *Journal of American History* 71 (1984): 319–42; and Eli Zaretsky, *Capitalism, the Family, and Personal Life* (New York: Harper & Row, 1976), pp. 68–76.

17. Again, see Norris, *Responsibilities of the Novelist*, pp. 163–68.

18. Northrop Frye, *The Anatomy of Criticism* (Princeton: Princeton University Press, 1957), pp. 304, 105–6, 136–43, and *The Secular Scripture: A Study of the Structure of Romance* (Cambridge: Harvard University Press, 1976), pp. 47–53; Jameson, *Political Unconscious*, pp. 112–13. Cf. *Howells as Critic*, pp. 81–83, 97–103, 299–313. See also Richard Chase, *The American Novel and Its Tradition* (Garden City, N.Y.: Doubleday, 1957), pp. 12–28, wherein the author argues that romance—or rather its "two streams," one committed to some version of verisimilitude, the other to Gothic adventure verging on science fiction (see pp. 18–20)—defines the American novel as such. This argument is compelling, and it is consistent with my own, I believe, but it does not address the critical question it raises: why, in the late nineteenth century, do American writers have to rediscover, reclaim, and rework the romance form?

19. See Frye, *Anatomy*, p. 193, and *Scripture*, pp. 53–54; cf. Bakhtin, *Dialogic Imagination*, pp. 41–83.

20. Julian Markels, "Theodore Dreiser and the Plotting of Inarticulate Experience," *Massachusetts Review* 2 (1961): 431–48, reprinted in *Sister Carrie*, ed. Donald Pizer (New York: Norton, 1970), pp. 527–41. Cf. Warren French, "John Steinbeck: A Usable Concept of Naturalism," in Y. Hakutani and L. Fried, eds., *American Literary Naturalism: A Reassessment* (Heidelberg: University of Heidelberg Press, 1975), pp. 122–35, but regarding *Sister Carrie*'s inarticulate characters, see pp. 125–27; also see Walcutt, *American Literary Naturalism*, p. 191: "The movement of the novel does not depend upon acts of will by the central figures." I am using the Bantam paperback edition of *Sister Carrie* (New York, 1972) and will hereafter cite page references in the text.

21. Markels, "Inarticulate Experience," pp. 531–32.

22. Walter Benn Michaels, "*Sister Carrie*'s Popular Economy," *Critical Inquiry* 7 (1980): 373–90. Cf. Cohen, "Locating One's Self," p. 366: "The material world becomes the mirror of Carrie's personality."

23. See Michaels, "*Sister Carrie*'s Popular Economy"; cf. Leo Bersani, *A Future for Astyanax* (Boston: Little, Brown, 1976), esp. chap. 2, "Realism and the Fear of Desire," pp. 51–88. Bersani's treatment of Proust at pp. 84–88 reminded me of Dreiser and so may be said to have incited my rereading of *Sister Carrie*.

24. On the transition from rhetoric to style and its implications, see Barthes, *Writing Degree Zero*, pp. 44–52, and Percy Lubbock, *The Craft of Fiction* (New York: Viking, 1957), pp. 251–54.

25. See Jameson, *Political Unconscious*, pp. 113–19, for discussion of the ethical binary at the core of romance.

26. In "Sin and the City: The Uses of Disorder in the Urban Novel," *Centen-*

nial Review 16 (1972): 203–20, Alan Rose suggests that Carrie's outlook shows no maturation or development; French, "John Steinbeck," concurs. Cf. also Neil Harris, "The Drama of Consumer Desire," in O. Mayr and R. Post, eds., *Yankee Enterprise* (Washington, D.C.: Smithsonian Institution, 1981), pp. 189–216, esp. 195–97, where *Sister Carrie* is found to be rather "traditional" in its doubts about the spiritual dividends of commodity fetishism. My argument is closer to that of Markels, "Inarticulate Experience," and Howard, *Form and History*, pp. 101–7.

27. See William James, "Does Consciousness Exist?" (1904), in *Writings 1902–1910*, comp. Bruce Kuklick (New York: Library of America, 1987), pp. 1141–58, here 1152. See chapter 10 below for my reading of this essay. I would insist that the revolt against dualism which characterizes American thought in the 1890s, and which both derives from and leads toward a rediscovery of Hegel's *Phenomenology*, should not be treated as an "anticipation" of the late-twentieth-century intellectual revolution that is animated by French appropriations of Hegel, simply because those French appropriations are themselves predicated on the earlier discoveries of the Americans. To put this another way, the American assimilation of Hegel, ca. 1890–1919, figures largely in the lineage of Alexandre Kojève's lectures of the 1930s on *The Phenomenology*, which have since informed and inspired every attempted renovation of Western philosophy, including the influential attempts of Maurice Merleau-Ponty and Jacques Derrida. In that sense, when we turn to recent interpretations and applications of Hegel, all of which owe something to the French appropriations that begin with Kojève, we are *returning* to the moment of philosophical discovery and innovation that defines the cultural-intellectual ferment of the American 1890s (and after). For one of Kojève's acknowledged precursors is Jean Wahl, whose study of Anglo-American philosophy, and more particularly the "pluralism" of Josiah Royce and James, decisively shaped his subsequent interpretation of Hegel in *Le malheur de la conscience dans la philosophie de Hegel* (1929; reprint, New York: Garland, 1984), which according to George L. Kline was the "first serious twentieth-century European study devoted mainly to Hegel's *Phenomenology*" (George L. Kline, "The Existential Rediscovery of Hegel and Marx," in E. N. Lee and M. Mandelbaum, eds., *Phenomenology and Existentialism* [Baltimore: Johns Hopkins University Press, 1967], pp. 113–38, esp. 117–20). A different approach to the same imposing figures in recent and contemporary French philosophy reveals the critical influence of James on Edmund Husserl, thus on Merleau-Ponty and, at another remove, on Derrida—for which approach see Wilshire, *William James*, and James M. Edie, *William James and Phenomenology* (Bloomington: Indiana University Press, 1987), esp. pp. 19–48. For evidence of the centrality of Hegel and Hegelian formulations in American thought of the 1890s and after, see, aside from John Dewey's works of the period (e.g., *Outlines of a Critical Theory of Ethics* [n.p., 1891], pp. 188–211), the following works: Justus Buchler, ed., *Philosophical Writings of Peirce* (New York: Dover, 1955), pp. 266–67, 322, 365–66; Manley Thompson, *The Pragmatic Philosophy of C. S. Peirce* (Chicago: University of Chicago Press, 1953), p. 180; Josiah Royce, *The Spirit of Modern Philosophy* (Boston: Houghton Mifflin, 1892), pp. xv, 202–19, 492–506 (in its original version, Royce's chapter on Hegel at pp. 190–227, where he singles out *The Phenomenology* as the "best" and "deepest" of Hegel's works, was a public lecture at Harvard, which was

first published in the *Atlantic Monthly*), and *Lectures on Modern Idealism* (New Haven: Yale University Press, 1919), pp. 136–212 (these lectures, on "Post-Kantian Idealism," were originally delivered at Johns Hopkins in 1906); Darnell Rucker, *The Chicago Pragmatists* (Minneapolis: University of Minnesota Press, 1969), p. 60 n; and Marshall J. Cohen, *Charles Horton Cooley and the Social Self in American Thought* (New York: Garland, 1982), pp. 99–124, 148–63.

28. See Bakhtin's "Forms of Time and Chronotope in the Novel," *Dialogic Imagination*, pp. 84–258.

29. See Daniel G. Hoffman, *Form and Fable in American Fiction* (New York: Oxford University Press, 1961), chaps. 1–2; David Grimsted, *Melodrama Unveiled: American Theater and Culture, 1800–1850* (Chicago: University of Chicago Press, 1968); Nathan Huggins, *Harlem Renaissance* (New York: Oxford University Press, 1970), chap. 6; and David R. Roediger, *The Wages of Whiteness: Race and the Making of the American Working Class* (London: Verso, 1991), chaps. 5–6.

30. See chapter 2 above, and Nina Baym, *Woman's Fiction: A Guide to Novels by and about Women in America, 1820–1870* (Ithaca: Cornell University Press, 1978), pp. 27–40, 45–50, 110–233.

31. Herman Melville, *The Confidence-Man* (1857; reprint, New York: New American Library, 1964), pp. 75, 190.

32. Nathaniel Hawthorne, *The Blithedale Romance* (1852; reprint, New York: Norton, 1958), pp. 27–28, 116; on Miles Coverdale's direction of the play, see pp. 143, 146, 170–73, 176, 178, 206, 208, 236.

33. Ibid., pp. 249–50.

34. As I will suggest in what follows, the habitat of this theatrical self in "real life" was the new world described in modern advertising and embodied in the department store. If this world was not entirely new when Dreiser wrote his first novel—there is now a huge debate over the periodization of consumer culture—its boundaries and population were certainly much larger in the 1890s than in the 1840s. As Leach points out, between 1890 and 1915 the "desire to show things off, to publicize or to advertize whatever American capitalism yielded, marked a critical moment in the formation of a new culture of consumption" ("Transformations," p. 326); cf. Harris, "The Drama of Consumer Desire," and Neil Harris, "Museums, Merchandising, and Popular Taste: The Struggle for Influence," in I. Quimby, ed., *Material Culture and the Study of American Life* (New York: Norton, 1978), pp. 140–74, here 143–54. In this format, I cannot contest the plausibility of dating consumer culture from the antebellum period; but I would point out that the possibility of such periodization rests on the pattern of early industrialization (in the United States, ca. 1800–1850), which is invariably accomplished through the development, in fits and starts, of consumer goods industries (e.g., food, textiles, shoes), entailing as such the expansion of a working class that spends what it gets in wages; the commercialization of agriculture and the concomitant enlargement of expenditures by farm households for commodities hitherto appropriated via barter or home production; and the relative decline of profits in the capital goods sector, although effective demand for the output of this sector is sustained by profits generated in the consumer goods sector. In other words, early industrialization is driven by the

increase of consumer demand, or the relative increase of labor's share of national income, and this pattern has led many historians to date consumer culture from the 1840s or even earlier. As I suggest in chapters 1 and 2 above, it is in my view a mistake to propose that a "culture of consumption" emerged then. For the articulation of such a culture presupposes the breakdown of a household economy and the extrusion of females from the household, so that, as Ellen DuBois points out, they begin to "participate directly in society as individuals, not indirectly through their subordinate positions as wives and mothers" (Ellen DuBois, "The Radicalism of the Woman's Suffrage Movement," in Anne Phillips, ed., *Feminism and Equality* [New York: New York University Press, 1987], pp. 127–38, here 131).

35. Michaels, "*Sister Carrie*'s Popular Economy," pp. 384–86.

36. On Hawthorne's attempt "to locate a point of intersection between home and marketplace," see Mark Seltzer, *Henry James and the Art of Power* (Ithaca: Cornell University Press, 1984), pp. 191–92. Dreiser's commentary from "Haunts of Nathaniel Hawthorne," *Truth* 17 (September 21–28, 1898), reprinted in Yoshinobu Hakutani, ed., *Selected Magazine Articles of Theodore Dreiser* (Rutherford, N.J.: Fairleigh Dickinson University Press, 1985), pp. 57–66, here p. 58.

37. See Karl Marx, *Capital: A Critique of Political Economy*, trans. Samuel Moore and Edward Aveling, 3 vols. (Chicago: Charles Kerr, 1906), 1:141–42, and *Grundrisse: Foundations of the Critique of Political Economy*, trans. Martin Nicolaus (Baltimore: Penguin, 1973), pp. 141–74, 196–236; Marc Shell, *Money, Language, and Thought* (Berkeley: University of California Press, 1982), pp. 5, 19, 105–11, and *The Economy of Literature* (Baltimore: Johns Hopkins University Press, 1978), chaps. 1–3; and Lester K. Little, *Religious Poverty and the Profit Economy in Medieval Europe* (Ithaca: Cornell University Press, 1978), chaps. 1–4, 10.

38. See George Rogers Taylor, *The Transportation Revolution* (New York: Harper & Row, 1951), p. 325; in 1846, these amounts were about the same as they had been in 1837 and, indeed, were lower than in 1839.

39. J.G.A. Pocock, "The Mobility of Property and the Rise of Eighteenth-Century Sociology," *Virtue, Commerce, and History* (New York: Cambridge University Press, 1985), pp. 103–24; cf. William Reddy, *Money and Liberty in Modern Europe: A Critique of Historical Understanding* (New York: Cambridge University Press, 1987), chaps. 3–4, and Marx, *Grundrisse*, pp. 223–26.

40. See my *Origins of the Federal Reserve System: Money, Class, and Corporate Capitalism, 1890–1913* (Ithaca: Cornell University Press, 1986), chaps. 3–5, esp. pp. 90–94, and Edward Bellamy's *Looking Backward, 2000–1887* (1887; reprint, New York: New American Library, 1960), chap. 22, to which I was led by Howard Horwitz's brilliant essay "To Find the Value of X: The Pit as Renunciation of Romance," in Sundquist, *American Realism*, pp. 215–37. The quoted remark is attributed to Doctor Leete, the character who acts as the novel's interlocutor. Interestingly enough, the context of this remark is Leete's analysis of late-nineteenth-century economic crises: like many pro-capitalist economists of that period, he defines the "credit system" as both cause of chronic crisis and effect of capitalist development. He is Bellamy's witness at the birth of what Jean Baudrillard calls the "political economy of the sign," or the "third phase" of political economy, which not

incidentally coincides with the rise of "monopolistic capitalism" or "finance capital." See Jean Baudrillard, *The Mirror of Production*, trans. Mark Poster (St. Louis: Telos Press, 1975), pp. 119–29.

41. Cf. Leach, "Transformations," p. 325: "Department stores seemed as if they were not stores at all but theatrical havens, imaginative mediums that depended on the existence of commodities and that transcended them at the same time." On advertising, see the essays by Jackson Lears, Christopher Wilson, and Jean-Christophe Agnew in Richard W. Fox and T. J. Jackson Lears, eds., *The Culture of Consumption* (New York: Pantheon, 1983), pp. 1–100; Merle Curti, "The Changing Concept of Human Nature in the Literature of American Advertising," *Business History Review* 41 (1967): 335–57, esp. pp. 337–51; and Earnest Elmo Calkins, *Modern Advertising* (New York: Appleton, 1905), pp. 7–13. On the marginalist revolution in economic theory, see my "Social Analysis of Economic History and Theory: Conjectures on Late-Nineteenth Century American Development," *American Historical Review* 92 (1987): 69–95 and works cited therein.

42. But the difference between these worlds is crucial. In *Sister Carrie*, desire creates a character or personality capable of abstraction (thus community) and introspection (thus individuality) because it projects her into particularity, into a heterogeneous time and space of objects and others. In the world of advertising, desires are focused on a world of particular objects to create generic consumers who will demand those objects. In this sense, the relation between the particular and the universal posited in *Sister Carrie* is reversed or effaced in advertising, because it seeks to enclose the desires it evokes within the particular commodity forms produced by a market economy.

43. Ann Douglas, *The Feminization of American Culture* (New York: Norton, 1977); cf. also Lears, *No Place of Grace*, which has the same import; Donald Meyer, *The Positive Thinkers* (Garden City, N.Y.: Doubleday, 1965), p. 125; and Brooks, *Coming-of-Age*, pp. 78–79.

44. Jean-Christophe Agnew, "The Consuming Vision of Henry James," in Fox and Lears, *Culture of Consumption*, pp. 65–100 and endnotes at pp. 221–25, esp. p. 222 n. 9, where, having cited William Leiss, *The Limits to Satisfaction* (Toronto: University of Toronto Press, 1976), Agnew states, "The following analysis is deeply indebted to Leiss's work." My quotations are from Leiss, *Limits*, pp. 25, 90. Thomas Haskell's interrogation of the assumption that now animates most historical studies in the United States—that capitalism and character are incompatible—is irrelevant to my argument because he cedes the territory after 1850: see his "Capitalism and the Origins of Humanitarian Sensibility," *American Historical Review* 91 (1985): 339–61, 547–66.

45. I am quoting from Honoré de Balzac, *Father Goriot* (New York: Airmont, 1966), pp. 166, 21, 133, 91–93, except at this last passage (p. 94), where I have substituted my own translation from Honoré de Balzac, *Oeuvres Completes: La Comedie Humaine, Etudes de Moeurs: Scenes de la vie privee*, vol. 6 (Paris: L. Conrad, 1912–40), p. 338 (page references to the Airmont edition hereafter cited in text).

46. Dreiser quoted in Richard Lingeman, *Theodore Dreiser: At the Gates of the City, 1871–1907* (New York: Putnam, 1986), p. 235.

47. Cf. MacIntyre, "The Relationship of Philosophy to Its Past."

48. Hegel, *Phenomenology*, p. 98; cf. Marx, *Grundrisse*, pp. 221–36. I am adopting and adapting the ambitious argument of Shell, *Money, Language, and Thought*, pp. 126–50.

49. Hegel, *Phenomenology*, pp. 81, 98–99; the last passage is quoted from the translation given by Shell, *Money, Language, and Thought*, p. 149. The affinity between Hegel and Freud might be explained by their convergence on this notion that the source and condition of truth is the disjuncture between words and actual events (a disjuncture experienced by every infant born into language at the moment of the loss of the Other), which becomes conjuncture only in the form of stories that lead beyond the actual, toward the symbolic.

50. See Sandy Petrey, "The Language of Realism, the Language of False Consciousness: A Reading of *Sister Carrie*," *Novel* 10 (1977): 101–13; cf. Cathy N. and Arnold E. Davidson, "Carrie's Sisters: The Popular Prototypes for Dreiser's Heroine," *Modern Fiction Studies* 23 (1977): 395–407, esp. 404ff.

51. Michaels, "*Sister Carrie*'s Popular Economy," pp. 388–90.

CHAPTER SEVEN

1. William James, *Talks to Teachers on Psychology and to Students on Some of Life's Ideals* (New York: Henry Holt, 1929); this is a reprint of the 1900 edition, with a preface dated 1899 (hereafter page references will be cited in the text). I want to record my debt to James Gilbert's *Work without Salvation: America's Intellectuals and Industrial Alienation, 1880–1910* (Baltimore: Johns Hopkins University Press, 1977), chaps. 14–15, which led me to these extraordinary lectures, and to David A. Hollinger's seminal essay "The Problem of Pragmatism in American History," *Journal of American History* 62 (1980): 88–107, which challenged his readers to situate the order of ideas we call pragmatism in the order of events we call the Progressive Era—in effect, to periodize pragmatism.

2. On the significance of the romance form, see chapter 6, "The Subject of Naturalism." James actually spent a week at the Chautauqua campgrounds, from July 23 to July 29, 1896; on the twenty-fourth, according to the program preserved in the William James Papers (bMSAm 1092.9) at the Houghton Library of Harvard University, he lectured there on "Psychology and Relaxation." His soporific stint at Chautauqua is recorded in letters to his wife, Alice James, each of which contains some reference to "tepidity," "charmless goodness and seriousness," etc. In the James Papers, see William James to Alice James, July 22, 23, 24, 26, 27, 29, 31, 1896 (he writes from the Atheneum Hotel in Chautauqua between the twenty-third and the twenty-ninth). The red pencil marks on certain passages in these letters indicate that James used them in rewriting "What Makes a Life Significant?" for publication in 1899, and that he revised the *Talks to Teachers* after he delivered the address of June 1896 that was published in 1897 as "The Will to Believe." But there is no reference, in subsequent letters, to the sky-scaling epiphany on the train to Buffalo. In my view, this "absence" makes the story more meaningful, because James has used what seems to be a fictional epiphany to interpret a factual, verifiable week at Chautauqua. I would also note that James was revising the *Talks to Teachers* at the

same time (ca. 1895–98) he began working through the ideas that would become the seminal essays of 1904–5; see note 3 in chapter 10 below.

3. James declares his solidarity with the socialist movement in "The Moral Equivalent of War" (1910), in Henry James, Jr., ed., *Memories and Studies* (New York: Longmans Green, 1911), pp. 265–98, here 286; but he is also critical of that movement: see pp. 283–87, and chapter 6 below.

4. See chapter 2 above, but also Hannah Arendt, *The Human Condition* (Chicago: University of Chicago Press, 1958), chaps. 3–4; C. Wright Mills, *White Collar: The American Middle Classes* (New York: Oxford University Press, 1951), pp. 215–28; Jean Baudrillard, *The Mirror of Production*, trans. Mark Poster (St. Louis: Telos Press, 1975), esp. pp. 21–67; and works cited at note 12 below.

5. The phrase "grope of wealth" is from Henry James, *The American Scene* (New York: Harper & Bros., 1907), p. 159. On the nature—or the absence—of the self in James's *Principles of Psychology*, see Bruce Wilshire, *William James and Phenomenology* (Bloomington: Indiana University Press, 1968), chap. 6, and John Dewey, "The Vanishing Subject in the Psychology of James," *Journal of Philosophy* 37 (1940): 589–99. Cf. my treatment of radical empiricism in chapter 10 below.

6. See Michael Denning, *Mechanic Accents: Dime Novels and Working-Class Culture in America* (London: Verso, 1986), chap. 8.

7. William James, "Address at the Emerson Centenary in Concord," May 25, 1903, in James, *Memories and Studies*, pp. 19–34, here 32. Cf. Kenneth Burke, *Attitudes toward History*, rev. ed. (Boston: Beacon Press, 1961), pp. 14–16.

8. Cf. Lewis Hyde, *The Gift: Imagination and the Erotic Life of Property* (New York: Pantheon, 1979), pp. 163–79, and M. Wynn Thomas, *The Lunar Light of Whitman's Poetry* (Cambridge: Harvard University Press, 1987), chaps. 2–4.

9. In "The Genteel Tradition in American Philosophy," George Santayana claimed that James "had a prophetic sympathy with the dawning sentiments of the age, with the moods of the dumb majority" (from George Santayana, *Winds of Doctrine* [1913; reprint, New York: Harper, 1957], pp. 186–215, here 204). I would note that Santayana's claim qualifies as criticism of James's philosophy only if we assume that "the moods of the dumb majority" are necessarily antithetical to philosophical truths. Walt Whitman is quoted from F. O. Matthiessen, *American Renaissance: Art and Expression in the Age of Emerson and Whitman* (New York: Oxford University Press, 1941), p. 541.

10. See part 1 above, esp. chapters 3–4, on the problem of consumer culture. The now-standard treatment of the "culture of consumption" is Richard W. Fox and T. J. Jackson Lears, eds., *The Culture of Consumption* (New York: Pantheon, 1983); but cf. Jean-Christophe Agnew's fine essay, "Coming Up for Air: Consumer Culture in Historical Perspective," *Intellectual History Newsletter* (1991); also Joe Broderick, "The Discovery of the Consumer as a Social Force: The Consumers' Leagues and Their Reform Strategies" (paper presented at the Rutgers Center for Historical Analysis, May 5, 1992), and works cited at notes 13–14, 40 in chapter 3 above. For examples of references to "consumer capitalism," Rachel Bowlby, *Just Looking: Consumer Culture in Gissing, Zola, and Dreiser* (London: Methuen, 1985), pp. 6, 30, and Frank Lentricchia, *Ariel and the Police* (Madison: University of Wisconsin Press, 1987), p. 149.

11. See Raymond Williams, *The Country and the City* (New York: Oxford University Press, 1973), pp. 121–25.

12. I am restating my claim from chapter 3, that the *priority* of the principle of social class is not an ontological or transhistorical dimension of human experience but a product of the development of capitalism and, accordingly, that to insist on the *priority* of class is not to criticize but to validate capitalism. These claims are derived from my reading of Henri Lefebvre, *The Sociology of Marx*, trans. Norbert Guterman (New York: Pantheon, 1968), esp. chap. 4. On class as the product of struggle as such, see Adam Przeworski, *Capitalism and Social Democracy* (New York: Cambridge University Press, 1985), chap. 2. On class as the product of ideological and other struggles after 1848, see chapter 2 above and works cited therein, particularly those by Eric Foner, David Montgomery, Leonard Richards, and Robert Sharkey; cf. also my "Politics, Ideology, and the Origins of American Revolutions," *Socialist Revolution* 36 (1977): 7–36, esp. pp. 11–18, 29–33, and Dolores Hayden, *The Grand Domestic Revolution: A History of Feminist Designs for American Homes, Neighborhoods, and Cities* (Cambridge: MIT Press, 1981), pp. 5–53 and endnotes at 310–16. Hayden points out that nineteenth-century "communitarian socialism" was a broad and variegated social movement which divided, after midcentury, into a Marxian socialist wing that gave priority to the category of class by emphasizing industrial labor and a "material feminist" wing that gave priority to the category of gender by emphasizing domestic labor. On the salience of race and gender as well as class in the ideological struggles of the 1840s and after, see Joel Porte, *Representative Man: Ralph Waldo Emerson in His Time* (New York: Oxford University Press, 1979), pp. 247–82; David Leverenz, *Manhood and the American Renaissance* (Ithaca: Cornell University Press, 1989); David S. Reynolds, *Beneath the American Renaissance* (Cambridge: Harvard University Press, 1988), part 3; Michael T. Gilmore, *American Romanticism and the Marketplace* (Chicago: University of Chicago Press, 1985); George Forgie, *Patricide in the House Divided: A Psychological Interpretation of Lincoln and His Age* (New York: Norton, 1979); Nina Baym, *Woman's Fiction* (Ithaca: Cornell University Press, 1978), pp. 27–50, 110–233; and James Oakes, *The Ruling Race: A History of American Slaveholders* (New York: Knopf, 1982).

13. The literature on professionalism is now enormous, but most of it takes the kind of debunking approach that obscures the social mobility and intellectual possibilities determined by professionalization. Two brilliant exceptions to this rule are Roberto Unger's treatment of the principle of role and its correlates in *Knowledge and Politics* (New York: Free Press, 1975), pp. 164–74, 315–17, and Bruce Robbins's introduction to *Intellectuals: Aesthetics, Politics, Academics* (Minneapolis: University of Minnesota Press, 1990), pp. ix–xxvii, which is part of a larger project on the politics of professionalization, *Secular Vocations* (London: Verso, 1993). On nation and feminism as the strictly modern (or postmodern?) forms of race and gender, see Harold Cruse, *The Crisis of the Negro Intellectual* (New York: William Morrow, 1967); Houston A. Baker, Jr., *Modernism and the Harlem Renaissance* (Chicago: University of Chicago Press, 1987), pp. 71–98; August Meier, *Negro Thought in America, 1880–1915* (Ann Arbor: University of Michigan Press, 1963), chaps. 7–9, 14; and Nancy Cott, *The Grounding of Modern Feminism* (New Haven: Yale University Press, 1987), pp. 1–50. My parenthetical question about the new forms

of race and gender is not merely rhetorical. To address it, we must follow Cornel West's lead, by asking whether Du Bois's notion of "dual consciousness" is a post-Emersonian approximation of what we now call the "de-centered self." See West, *The American Evasion of Philosophy: A Genealogy of Pragmatism* (Madison: University of Wisconsin Press, 1988), pp. 138–50.

14. See chapter 8 for a fuller treatment of these questions and their bearing on intellectual innovation; cf. my "Reply to Gerald Berk," *Journal of Policy History* 3 (1991): 85–89.

15. Cf. Richard Poirier, *Robert Frost: The Work of Knowing*, 2d ed. (Palo Alto: Stanford University Press, 1990), p. 233: "Frost was disinclined to see modern life as in any significant degree different from what life had ever been because he did not recognize that he lived in a period in which the structurings implicit for at least five hundred years had, by the slow processes of economic, political, and social acculturation, at last become unmistakably grotesque." James did, I think, recognize the grotesque quality of modern subjectivity; at any rate, I think that is why he compares (but does not equate) pragmatism and Protestantism in concluding lecture 3 of *Pragmatism* and in a letter to his brother Henry of May 4, 1907, for which see Henry James, Jr., ed., *The Letters of William James*, 2 vols. (Boston: Little, Brown, 1920), 2:279. On Henry Adams and the meaning of his Gothic obsessions, there is now some potentially interesting debate among historians, for the beginnings of which see T. J. Jackson Lears, *No Place of Grace: Antimodernism and the Transformation of American Culture, 1880–1920* (New York: Pantheon, 1981), pp. 262–97 and endnotes at 360–63, and Cecelia Tichi, *Shifting Gears: Technology, Literature, Culture in Modernist America* (Chapel Hill: University of North Carolina Press, 1987), pp. 137–68. Historians have not yet acknowledged that working-class inflections of the Gothic—for example in the image of the Knights of Labor—might be as complicated as Adams's approach to Chartres; a brilliant exception to this rule is Denning, *Mechanic Accents*, chap. 9. Nor have they recognized that the increasing popularity of the Gothic romance, which often appeared in the form of utopian literature, might signify something more than nostalgia; but see Kenneth M. Roemer, *The Obsolete Necessity: America in Utopian Writings, 1888–1900* (Kent, Ohio: Kent State University Press, 1976); John L. Thomas, *Alternative America* (Cambridge: Harvard University Press, 1983); and F. C. Jaher, *Doubters and Dissenters: Cataclysmic Thought in America, 1885–1918* (Glencoe, Ill.: Free Press, 1964). On the new museum culture, see part 1, chapter 2, above. "Modernization" emerges as theory and practice in this formative period—that is, as both periodization in and professionalization of the social sciences. In fact, the idea of modernity in history, political science, sociology, and economics is inseparable from the articulation of academic departments, professional standards, and organs of communication; which is to say that these diciplines were convened by a new division of labor that was, in turn, predicated on the results—the circulation of theories as well as commodities after 1880—and the prospects of international development determined by the ongoing transformation of capitalism.

16. To my mind, Maurice Dobb, *Studies in the Development of Capitalism*, rev. ed. (New York: International Publishers, 1963), is still the best general treatment of the "transition question." Dobb of course relies on Marx for his periodization. But

see also R. H. Tawney, *Harrington's Interpretation of His Age* (London: Humphrey Milford, 1941); C. B. Macpherson, *The Political Theory of Possessive Individualism: Hobbes to Locke* (New York: Oxford University Press, 1962), esp. chaps. 3–4; T. H. Aston, ed., *The Brenner Debate* (New York: Cambridge University Press, 1986); E. A. Wrigley, "The Process of Modernization and the Industrial Revolution in England," *Journal of Interdisciplinary History* 3 (1972): 225–59; and, for a different perspective on Harrington which is nonetheless consistent with my argument about the transition to modernity, J.G.A. Pocock, *The Machiavellian Moment: Florentine Political Thought and the Atlantic Republican Tradition* (Princeton: Princeton University Press, 1975), pp. 383–400.

17. I tried out these ideas on the "transition question" of our time in "On Alfred Chandler and the Business of History" (paper delivered at the second annual meeting of the Society for the Advancement of Socio-Economics, Washington, D.C., March 17, 1990); the session was chaired by William Becker and included papers by Louis Galambos and Alfred D. Chandler, Jr. I worked the same ideas into a graduate seminar I taught in the spring of 1990. The relevant texts from the pantheon of scholars are Max Weber, *The Theory of Social and Economic Organization*, trans. and ed. Talcott Parsons (New York: Oxford University Press, 1974), esp. pp. 226–28, 243–59, 275–78; Hans Gerth and C. Wright Mills, eds., *From Max Weber* (New York: Oxford University Press, 1946), pp. 196–209; Adolf A. Berle, Jr., and Gardiner Means, *The Modern Corporation and Private Property* (New York: Macmillan, 1932); William Appleman Williams, "The Age of Corporation Capitalism," *The Contours of American History* (Cleveland: World Publishing Co., 1961), pp. 343–478; Martin J. Sklar, *The Corporate Reconstruction of American Capitalism, 1890–1916: The Market, the Law, and Politics* (New York: Cambridge University Press, 1988); and three works by Alfred D. Chandler, Jr.: *Strategy and Structure* (Cambridge: MIT Press, 1962), pp. 26–51; *The Visible Hand: The Managerial Revolution in American Business* (Cambridge: Harvard University Press, 1977), chaps. 9–14; and *Scale and Scope: The Dynamics of Industrial Capitalism* (Cambridge: Harvard University Press, 1990). On the historiographical significance of Sklar's work, see my "How to Succeed in Business History without Really Trying: Remarks on Martin J. Sklar's *Corporate Reconstruction of American Capitalism*," *Business and Economic History*, 2d ser., 21 (1992): 30–35.

18. James B. Weaver, *A Call to Action* (1892), excerpted in George B. Tindall, ed., *A Populist Reader* (New York: Harper & Row, 1966), pp. 60–79, here 71–72. On the recruitment of managerial talent and the new relation between business enterprise and education, see Chandler, *Scale and Scope*, pp. 82–89, and Olivier Zunz, *Making America Corporate, 1870–1920* (Chicago: University of Chicago Press, 1990), chaps. 2–5.

19. Walter Lippmann is quoted from his *Drift and Mastery* (1914; reprint, Madison: University of Wisconsin Press, 1985), pp. 43–45. On the young intellectuals and their compatriots, see, in addition to the works cited at note 13 above, Christopher Lasch, *The New Radicalism in America, 1889–1963: The Intellectual as a Social Type* (New York: Vintage, 1965); Henry F. May, *The End of American Innocence* (New York: Knopf, 1959), esp. part 3; Daniel Aaron, *Writers on the Left* (New York: Avon, 1959), part 1; Rosalind Rosenberg, *Beyond Separate Spheres: Intellectual*

Roots of Modern Feminism (New Haven: Yale University Press, 1982); and Casey Nelson Blake, *Beloved Community: The Cultural Criticisms of Randolph Bourne, Van Wyck Brooks, Waldo Frank, and Lewis Mumford* (Chapel Hill: University of North Carolina Press, 1990). See also chapter 9 below.

20. On the social purposes of the corporate reconstruction, see James Livingston, "The Social Analysis of Economic History and Theory: Conjectures on Late-Nineteenth Century American Development," *American Historical Review* 92 (1987): 69–95. Phelps is quoted from "The New View of Investment: A Neoclassical Analysis," *Quarterly Journal of Economics* 76 (1962): 548–67, here 549; cf. Alfred Chandler's formulations in *The Cambridge Economic History of Europe*, 7 vols. (New York: Cambridge University Press, 1978), 7:71, and in "The Emergence of Managerial Capitalism," case 16 of Alfred Chandler, Jr., and Richard S. Tedlow, *The Coming of Managerial Capitalism* (Homewood, Ill.: Irwin, 1984), pp. 396–422. On the proportionate decline of socially necessary labor and its implications, the key text is Martin J. Sklar, "On the Proletarian Revolution and the End of Political-Economic Society," *Radical America* 3 (1969): 1–41, now revised and published as "Some Political and Cultural Consequences of the Disaccumulation of Capital: Origins of Postindustrial Development in the 1920s," *The United States as a Developing Country* (New York: Cambridge University Press, 1992), pp. 143–96; cf. my use of this text in chapters 1 and 4. Meanwhile, for empirical examples, see Przeworski, *Capitalism and Social Democracy*, chap. 2; Seymour Melman, "The Rise of Administrative Overhead in Manufacturing Industries in the United States, 1899–1947," *Oxford Economic Papers*, n.s., 3 (1951): 62–112; Wassily Leontief, "Machines and Man," *Essays in Economics* (New York: Oxford University Press, 1966), pp. 187–99; and Harry T. Oshima, "The Growth of U.S. Factor Productivity: The Significance of New Technologies in the Early Decades of the Twentieth Century," *Journal of Economic History* 44 (1984): 161–70.

21. See, for example, John H. Lorant, *The Role of Capital Improving Innovations in American Manufacturing in the 1920s* (New York: Arno Press, 1975); Richard B. DuBoff, "Electrification and Capital Productivity: A Suggested Approach," *Review of Economics and Statistics* 48 (1966): 426–31; R. A. Gordon, "Investment Opportunities in the U.S. before and after World War II," in Erik Lundberg, ed., *The Business Cycle in the Post-War World* (London: Macmillan, 1955), pp. 283–310; and Michael A. Bernstein, *The Great Depression: Delayed Recovery and Economic Change* (New York: Cambridge University Press, 1988), chaps. 2–7. For more detailed discussion and documentation, see chapters 1, 3–4, above.

22. Marx quoted from *Grundrisse: Foundations of the Critique of Political Economy*, trans. Martin Nocolaus (Baltimore: Penguin, 1973), pp. 704–05.

CHAPTER EIGHT

1. See chapters 2–3 and the works cited at notes 2, 9 below.

2. See Chester MacArthur Destler, *American Radicalism, 1865–1900* (New London: Connecticut College, 1946), esp. chaps. 2–4, 8–11; John D. Hicks, *The Populist Revolt* (Minneapolis: University of Minnesota Press, 1931), pp. 81–95; Lawrence

Goodwyn, *Democratic Promise: The Populist Moment in America* (New York: Oxford University Press, 1976), chaps. 6–8 (endnotes at pp. 637–53) and appendix A, pp. 565–70, 693–94; Victoria Hattam, "Economic Visions and Political Strategies: American Labor and the State, 1865–1896," *Studies in American Political Development* 4 (1990): 82–129; David Montgomery, *Beyond Equality: Labor and the Radical Republicans, 1862–1872* (New York: Knopf, 1967), chaps. 6–11; Gerald N. Grob, *Workers and Utopia: A Study of Ideological Conflict in the American Labor Movement, 1865–1900* (Evanston, Ill.: Northwestern University Press, 1961), chaps. 2–7; Robert Sharkey, *Money, Class, and Party: An Economic Study of Civil War and Reconstruction* (Baltimore: Johns Hopkins University Press, 1959), chaps. 3, 5; and Walter T. K. Nugent, *Money and American Society, 1865–1880* (New York: Free Press, 1968), chaps. 4–7, 16–17.

3. See James Livingston, "The Social Analysis of Economic History and Theory: Conjectures on Late-Nineteenth Century American Development," *American Historical Review* 92 (1987): 69–95, and Martin J. Sklar, *The Corporate Reconstruction of American Capitalism, 1890–1916: The Market, the Law, and Politics* (New York: Cambridge University Press, 1988), chap. 2.

4. John Bates Clark is the most prominent and influential of the late-nineteenth-century economists seeking to rehabilitate mental labor; see chapter 2 above for a detailed consideration of his achievement in this regard.

5. James Madison is quoted from his "Observations on Jefferson's Draft of a Constitution for Virginia," in Julian P. Boyd, ed., *The Papers of Thomas Jefferson*, 34 vols. (Princeton: Princeton University Press, 1950–), 6:310; Arthur T. Hadley from his *Economics* (New York: Putnam's, 1896), pp. 371–72; on Hadley's critical significance, see Carl P. Parrini and Martin J. Sklar, "New Thinking about the Market, 1896–1904: Some American Economists on Surplus Capital and the Theory of Investment," *Journal of Economic History* 43 (1983): 559–78.

6. On the generalization of the social self, see Marshall J. Cohen, *Charles Horton Cooley and the Social Self in American Thought* (New York: Garland, 1982); David W. Noble, *The Paradox of Progressive Thought* (Minneapolis: University of Minnesota Press, 1958), chaps. 4–8; R. Jackson Wilson, *In Quest of Community: Social Philosophy in the United States, 1860–1920* (New York: Oxford University Press, 1968); and Jean B. Quandt, "From the Small Town to the Great Community: The Idea of Community in the Progressive Era" (Ph.D. diss., Rutgers University, 1970). This notion of the self was evidently verified by observation and experience of solidarity in the late-nineteenth-century labor movement; in addition to note 14 and related text below, see, for examples, my treatment of James in chapter 7 above; Cohen, *Social Self*, pp. 174–86; Noble, *Progressive Thought*, pp. 117–19, 151–52, 169–70; and Laurence Gronlund, *The New Economy: A Peaceable Solution of the Social Problem* (Chicago: Charles Kerr, 1898), pp. 62–72, 89–93 (on Gronlund's importance, see Stow Persons, "Introduction" to Laurence Gronlund, *The Cooperative Commonwealth*, rev. ed. [1890; reprint, Cambridge: Harvard University Press, 1965], pp. vii–xxvi, and Nick Salvatore, *Eugene V. Debs: Citizen and Socialist* [Urbana: University of Illinois Press, 1982], p. 151). It is worth noting here that Gronlund grasped the social self as the site of a new moral philosophy and defined the collectivizing tendency of "the trusts" as the source of that self. "Now the Trust is the womb that

has conceived Collectivism. . . . Now comes Collectivism, and it once more revives the conviction of men's solidarity" (*New Economy*, pp. 35, 62). Surely the social self was central to both pragmatism and feminism of the "Chicago school"—for example, see George Herbert Mead, *Mind, Self, and Society*, ed. Charles W. Morris (Chicago: University of Chicago Press, 1962), part 3, and Jessie Taft, *The Woman Movement from the Point of View of Social Consciousness* (Chicago: University of Chicago Press, 1916), chaps. 2–3. On the related legal questions, see, for example, Roscoe Pound, "The Scope and Purpose of Sociological Jurisprudence II," *Harvard Law Review* 25 (1912): 140–68 ("The conception of law as a securing of interests or a protecting of relations has all but superceded the individualist theory" [p. 143]); John R. Commons, *Legal Foundations of Capitalism* (New York: Macmillan, 1924), chap. 2; John Dewey, "The Historic Background of Corporate Legal Personality," *Yale Law Journal* 35 (1926): 655–73; and more recent treatments: Morton J. Horwitz, "*Santa Clara* Revisited: The Development of Corporate Theory," *West Virginia Law Review* 88 (1985): 173–224; Howard J. Graham, "An Innocent Abroad: The Constitutional Corporate 'Person,'" *UCLA Law Review* 2 (1955): 155–211, reprinted in Howard J. Graham, *Everyman's Constitution: Historical Essays on the Fourteenth Amendment* (Madison: University of Wisconsin Press, 1968), pp. 367–437; Herbert Hovenkamp, *Enterprise and American Law, 1836–1937* (Cambridge: Harvard University Press, 1991), chap. 4; and J. Allen Douglas, "The Problem of Property in the Development of the Corporate Legal Personality" (seminar paper, Department of History, Rutgers University, 1992). Cf. also note 10 below.

7. Cf. James Livingston, *Origins of the Federal Reserve System: Money, Class, and Corporate Capitalism, 1890–1913* (Ithaca: Cornell University Press, 1986), chaps. 3–4.

8. See Marc Shell, *Money, Language, and Thought* (Berkeley: University of California Press, 1982), pp. 5, 19, 105–11; Ann Fabian, *Card Sharps, Dream Books, and Bucket Shops: Gambling in Nineteenth-Century America* (Ithaca: Cornell University Press, 1990), chap. 4; Jonathan M. Lurie, *The Chicago Board of Trade, 1859–1905: The Dynamics of Self-Regulation* (Urbana: University of Illinois Press, 1979), chap. 5; Cedric B. Cowing, *Populists, Plungers, and Progressives: A Social History of Stock and Commodity Speculation, 1890–1936* (Princeton: Princeton University Press, 1965), pp. 5–38; and chapter 6 above.

9. These arguments are based on my reading of the following: John R. Commons et al., *A Documentary History of American Industrial Society*, 10 vols. (Cleveland: A. H. Clark Co., 1910), 9:117–274, esp. the "Platform and Political Action" from the minutes of the 1867 Chicago Congress of the National Labor Union, pp. 175–83; William H. Sylvis (the president of the National Labor Union), "What Is Money?," in James Sylvis, *The Life, Speeches, Labors, and Essays of William H. Sylvis* (1872; reprint, Philadelphia: A. M. Kelley, 1968), pp. 351–87; George E. McNeill, ed., *The Labor Movement: The Problem of To-Day* (New York: M. W. Hazen, 1887), esp. chaps. 17–19, by the editor himself; S. M. Jelley, ed., *The Voice of Labor* (Philadelphia: H. J. Smith, 1888), esp. chaps. 5, 7–9 (chaps. 8–9, pp. 131–48, consist of the report and commentary of a committee appointed by the general assembly of the Knights of Labor held at Richmond in October 1886 "to investigate and report upon the question of hard times"; the committee concluded that "the primal and

general cause of financial and industrial depression, is a suppression of the means of changing titles to the products of labor, and that this blocking of the means of distribution should be remedied by a restoration of the currency of the country" [p. 143]); the Chicago Historical Society's sixty-three-volume collection of nineteenth-century political pamphlets, many of which focus on issues of money (see, for example, vol. 22, in which thirteen of a total of twenty pamphlets from the mid-to-late 1880s address the money question); and the "sound money" debates of the 1890s, on which see Livingston, *Origins of the Federal Reserve System*, chap. 3. But see also Montgomery, *Beyond Equality*, pp. 249–60, 340–56, 426–33, 442–45; David A. Wells, *Robinson Crusoe's Money* (New York: Harper, 1876); Allen Weinstein, *Prelude to Populism: Origins of the Silver Issue* (New Haven: Yale University Press, 1970); Irwin Unger, *The Greenback Era* (Princeton: Princeton University Press, 1964); and Bruce Palmer, *"Man over Money": The Southern Populist Critique of American Capitalism* (Chapel Hill: University of North Carolina Press, 1980).

10. Cf. Fabian, *Card Sharps*, chap. 4; Henry Crosby Emery, *Speculation on the Stock and Produce Exchanges of the United States*, Columbia Studies in History, Economics and Public Law, vol. 7, no. 2 (New York: Columbia University Press, 1896), chaps. 4–5; and Hadley, *Economics*, chap. 4, esp. pp. 105–15. Emery follows Hadley's lead in distinguishing between gambling and speculation and in defending the latter as a necessary element in the development of modern, corporate-industrial capitalism (see pp. 102–6, 149–50); for my purposes, it is also significant that at p. 109 n. 2, Emery cites John Bates Clark's essays of the mid-1890s (on returns to capital as reward for risk), which were integrated and published in 1899 as *The Distribution of Wealth* (see chapter 2 above). On the redefinition of property at the law, see Commons, *Legal Foundations*, chap. 2; J. Willard Hurst, *The Legitimacy of the Business Corporation in the Law of the United States, 1780–1970* (Charlottesville: University of Virginia Press, 1970), pp. 65–68; and Sklar, *Corporate Reconstruction*, part 1.

11. See Livingston, *Origins of the Federal Reserve System*, pp. 91–94.

12. Ibid., chaps. 4–5, esp. pp. 145–49.

13. The best account of Dewey's encounter with Franklin Ford is still Neil Coughlan, *Young John Dewey* (Chicago: University of Chicago Press, 1975), chap. 6; but see also Robert Westbrook, *John Dewey and American Democracy* (Ithaca: Cornell University Press, 1991), pp. 49–58, and Dewey's two letters to William James, June 3 and November 22, 1891, explaining Ford's philosophy and its effect on his *Ethics* of 1891 (see note 14 below), in the William James Papers (bMSAm 1092.9) at the Houghton Library of Harvard University. Dewey is quoted from "The Angle of Reflection," a six-part series in the first volume of the University of Michigan's *Inlander*, in Jo Ann Boydston, ed., *The Early Works of John Dewey*, 5 vols. (Carbondale: Southern Illinois University Press, 1969), 3:195–210, here 206, and from Lewis S. Feuer, "John Dewey and the Back to the People Movement in American Thought," *Journal of the History of Ideas* 20 (1959): 545–68, here 553. In his "Angle of Reflection" series, Dewey sounds very much like the Emerson of "The Poet" (1844): "We have yet had no genius in America, with tyrannous eye, which knew the value of our incomparable materials, and saw, in the barbarism and materialism of the times, another carnival of the same gods whose picture he so admires

in Homer; then in the Middle Age; then in Calvinism" (Stephen E. Whicher, ed., *Selections from Ralph Waldo Emerson* [Boston: Houghton Mifflin, 1957], p. 238).

14. John Dewey, *Outlines of a Critical Theory of Ethics* (1891; reprint, New York: Greenwood, 1969), pp. 176–79 (page references given in the text hereafter). On Hegel and political economy, see Raymond Plant, *Hegel* (Bloomington: Indiana University Press, 1973), pp. 64–72, 87–94, 107–20; Laurence Dickey, *Hegel: Religion, Economics, and the Politics of Spirit* (New York: Cambridge University Press, 1987), part 3; Joachim Ritter, *Hegel and the French Revolution: Essays on the Philosophy of Right*, trans. Richard Dien Winfield (Cambridge: MIT Press, 1982), pp. 63–79, 121–23, 137–42; Manfred Riedel, *Between Tradition and Revolution: The Hegelian Transformation of Political Philosophy*, trans. Walter Wright (New York: Cambridge University Press, 1984), pp. 108–24; Herbert Marcuse, *Reason and Revolution: Hegel and the Rise of Social Theory* (1941; Boston: Beacon Press, 1960), pp. 75–79, 114–17; and Richard Dien Winfield, "Hegel's Challenge to the Modern Economy," in Robert L. Perkins, ed., *History and System: Hegel's Philosophy of History* (Albany: State University of New York Press, 1984), pp. 219–53 (this last piece is obsessively anti-Marxian, but it nonetheless indicates Hegel's interest in and use of modern political economy).

15. Dewey is quoted from "Poetry and Philosophy," a commencement address at Smith College, June 18, 1890, in Boydston, *Early Works* 3:110–24, here 122.

16. Ibid., 113.

17. See Coughlan, *Young John Dewey*; cf. Elizabeth Flower and Murray G. Murphey, *A History of Philosophy in America*, 2 vols. (New York: Putnam's, 1977), 2:822–41.

18. Dewey, "Poetry and Philosophy," 3:123.

19. John Dewey, "The Present Position of Logical Theory," *Monist* 2 (1891): 1–17 (page references in text from *Early Works* 3:125–41).

20. John Dewey, "The Scholastic and the Speculator," *Inlander* 2 (1891–92): 145–48, 186–88 (page references in text from *Early Works* 3:148–54).

21. This was the moment at which the paradigmatic revolutions of the twentieth century (the Mexican, the Russian, and the Chinese revolutions) began in earnest. For an introduction to the transatlantic sense of impending cultural revolution, ca. 1890–1920, see Donald C. Hodges, *The Intellectual Foundations of the Nicaraguan Revolution* (Austin: University of Texas Press, 1982), chap. 2; H. Stuart Hughes, *Consciousness and Society: The Reorientation of European Social Thought, 1890–1930*, rev. ed. (New York: Vintage, 1977); Henry F. May, *The End of American Innocence* (New York: Knopf, 1959); John Berger, *The Success and Failure of Picasso* (New York: Pantheon, 1965), esp. pp. 47–83; Stephen Kern, *The Culture of Time and Space, 1880–1918* (Cambridge: Harvard University Press, 1984); Sanford Schwarz, *The Matrix of Modernism* (Princeton: Princeton University Press, 1985); James Longenbach, *Modernist Poetics of History* (Princeton: Princeton University Press, 1987); Bram Dijkstra, *The Hieroglyphics of a New Speech: Cubism, Stieglitz, and the Early Poetry of William Carlos Williams* (Princeton: Princeton University Press, 1969); James T. Kloppenberg, *Uncertain Victory: Social Democracy and Progressivism in European and American Thought, 1870–1920* (New York: Oxford Uni-

versity Press, 1986); and Donald M. Lowe, *History of Bourgeois Perception* (Chicago: University of Chicago Press, 1982), chap. 6.

22. This project of integrating "the business public and the cultivated public" was the self-appointed task of Van Wyck Brooks, probably the most influential young intellectual of the century's second decade. He is quoted here from *America's Coming-of-Age* (1915), reprinted in his *Three Essays on America* (New York: Dutton, 1934), pp. 15–112, here 78. Dewey's critics, particularly Randolph Bourne but also Brooks, get the benefit of the doubt in Westbrook, *Dewey and Democracy*, chaps. 7–8, and in Casey Nelson Blake's fine new study, *Beloved Community: The Cultural Criticisms of Randolph Bourne, Van Wyck Brooks, Waldo Frank, and Lewis Mumford* (Chapel Hill: University of North Carolina Press, 1991), chap. 5; cf. also Paul Bourke, "The Status of Politics 1909–1919: *The New Republic*, Randolph Bourne, and Van Wyck Brooks," *Journal of American Studies* 8 (1974): 171–202, and Ross Posnock, "Bourne, Dewey, Adorno: Reconciling Pragmatism and the Frankfurt School," *Center for Twentieth Century Studies*, Working Paper No. 4 (Milwaukee: University of Wisconsin, 1989–90), pp. 1–24. Since the object of Bourne's critique was not American entry into the world war but rather war as such, and since Dewey's goals in promoting entry were social-democratic in the best sense (they resemble what we now call multiculturalism), I do not understand why Bourne still gets this benefit of the doubt. My guess is that it expresses our need to romanticize dead radicals. For the relevant texts, see Olaf Hansen, ed., *The Radical Will: Randolph Bourne, Selected Writings 1911–1918* (New York: Urizen, 1977), pp. 307–47, and Jo Ann Boydston, ed., *John Dewey: The Middle Works*, 15 vols. (Carbondale: Southern Illinois University Press, 1976), 11:70–92, 98–106, esp. "Internal Social Reorganization after the War" (1918), pp. 73–86.

23. John Dewey, *Reconstruction in Philosophy* (1920), enlarged ed. (Boston: Beacon Press, 1948), page references in text hereafter.

24. "Invention" is a key word of "The Present Position of Logical Theory"— that is why I think Dewey is struggling in this essay to utter the equivalent of "industrialization." It is worth noting that "invention" is also a key word in the poetry of William Carlos Williams, who was an admirer of Dewey's philosophy and aesthetics; see Alec Marsh, "The 'Money Question' and the Poetry of Ezra Pound and William Carlos Williams" (1993), and Eliza Reilly, "Painting the Pragmatist Personality" (1994), two Rutgers Ph.D. dissertations that illuminate the relation between modernist art and pragmatist philosophies. Meanwhile, we should be reading the seminal work of Richard Poirier, the most recent installment of which is *Poetry and Pragmatism* (Cambridge: Harvard University Press, 1992).

25. Dewey is quoted here from "The Scholastic and the Speculator," 3:148–50.

26. On the two cultures, the "scientific" and the "humanistic," see C. P. Snow, *The Two Cultures and the Scientific Revolution* (New York: Cambridge University Press, 1961).

27. Page references in the text hereafter are to William James, *Writings 1902–1910*, comp. Bruce Kuklick (New York: Library of America, 1987).

28. See Lewis Mumford, *The Golden Day* (New York: Horace Liveright, 1926), pp. 188–92, and Richard Rorty, "Postmodernist Bourgeois Liberalism," *Objectivity,*

Relativism, and Truth (New York: Cambridge University Press, 1991), pp. 197–202. See also chapters 9–10 below on pragmatism according to Mumford and Rorty.

29. I am quoting from *Nature* as it appears in Alfred R. Ferguson, ed., *The Collected Works of Ralph Waldo Emerson*, 3 vols. (Cambridge: Harvard University Press, 1971), 1:7–45 (page references in the text hereafter). My reading of Emerson draws heavily on Michael T. Gilmore, *American Romanticism and the Marketplace* (Chicago: University of Chicago Press, 1985), pp. 13–34; Mumford, *The Golden Day*, chap. 3; Donald E. Pease, *Visionary Compacts: American Renaissance Writings in Cultural Context* (Madison: University of Wisconsin Press, 1987), chap. 6; and Joel Porte, *Representative Man: Ralph Waldo Emerson in His Time* (New York: Oxford University Press, 1979), esp. pp. 247–82. I am not convinced that we should treat Emerson as the founding father of pragmatism—not because I think that Richard Poirier and Cornel West misinterpret him, but because I think that pragmatism is something more (or less?) than a linguistic protocol by which writers evade all fixed forms and unified selves. Cf. my remarks on Howard Horwitz at note 31.

30. On *Verstand* (understanding) and its limitations, see Marcuse, *Reason and Revolution*, pp. 43–49, 105–11, and Charles Taylor, *Hegel* (New York: Cambridge University Press, 1975), pp. 48–49, 66–73, 86, 116–19.

31. See the chapter headings of Ralph Waldo Emerson, *The Conduct of Life* (Boston: Ticknor & Fields, 1860), as well as the chapter entitled "Wealth." But see also Howard Horwitz, "The Standard Oil Trust as Emersonian Hero," *Raritan* 6 (1987): 97–119, wherein the author argues, "Emerson's thought and the organization of the Standard [Oil] Trust responded to common historical problems and anxieties by employing a common logic: the morality of action is justified by the transcendence of personal agency" (p. 99). I am almost persuaded by this argument, in part because it gives new significance to my emphasis on Dewey's use of Standard Oil as an example of the postepistemological mastermind in "The Scholastic and the Speculator." But by Horwitz's account, the common historical problems that elicit the "transcendental logic of agency" are the "anxieties about the dependence of identity on alienable property, fears that fluctuations in the marketplace, and thus in one's property, would effect what William James would call 'vicissitudes in the me'" (p. 106). So conceived, as a "cultural currency" (p. 118) that buys peace of mind because it converts such anxieties to faith (thus effacing the self and eradicating epistemology), the logic in question becomes purely formal, which is precisely what Horwitz insists it is not (pp. 117–19). For it becomes an order of ideas with no intelligible or immanent relation to any order of events except the market as such; and in this it resembles nothing so much as the formal logic economists once ascribed to the competitive markets of the nineteenth century, through which "universal" laws of supply and demand appeared as both the agent of and the apology for social change.

32. See Walt Whitman, "Leaves of Grass" (1855), *Whitman: Poetry and Prose*, comp. Justin Kaplan (New York: Library of America, 1982), pp. 5–145 (page references in the text hereafter). My reading of Whitman has been profoundly shaped by Lewis Hyde, *The Gift: Imagination and the Erotic Life of Property* (New York: Pantheon, 1979), chap. 9, and M. Wynn Thomas, *The Lunar Light of Whitman's*

Poetry (Cambridge: Harvard University Press, 1987), esp. chaps. 2–4. Thomas is quite helpful in analyzing the implications of "postartisanal" market society and the inversion of subject and object impending in that stage of development; but he locates Whitman's critical edge in a celebration of artisanal modes of production rather than where I would, in the diversity of identifications—and in the weird abstractions—afforded by the new industrial stage of development, or rather by the interpenetration of the declining and ascending stages. Alan Trachtenberg's recent lectures and essays on Whitman are even more provocative in their historicizing movement; see, for example, Trachtenberg's unpublished paper "The Politics of Labor and the Poet's Work: A Reading of 'A Song for Occupations.' "

33. On the promise and limits of Kant's project, see Charles Taylor, "Kant's Theory of Freedom," in *Philosophy and the Human Sciences: Philosophical Papers 2* (New York: Cambridge University Press, 1985), pp. 318–37, and *Hegel*, chaps. 6, 14; Alasdair MacIntyre, *After Virtue* (Notre Dame: University of Notre Dame Press, 1981), chaps. 4–6, 16; William R. Galston, *Kant and the Problem of History* (Chicago: University of Chicago Press, 1975); Josiah Royce, *Lectures on Modern Idealism* (New Haven: Yale University Press, 1919), lectures 1–3, pp. 1–86; and Ritter, *Hegel and the French Revolution*, pp. 151–82. I have two reasons for suggesting that the proliferation of the commodity form was the occasion for Kant's division of the world into an order of events and an order of ideas. First, in *The Groundwork of the Metaphysic of Morals*, trans. H. J. Paton, 3d ed. (New York: Harper & Row, 1956), he claims that in the "kingdom of ends"—"a systematic union of rational beings under common objective laws" (p. 101)—"everything has either a *price* or a *dignity*." Dignity cannot be assigned a "market price" or a "fancy price" (*Affectionspreis*) because it has an "intrinsic worth" but no transitive meaning, no instrumental significance. "It is exalted above all price and so admits of no equivalent" (p. 102). By this account, morality has dignity and, indeed, "is the only thing which has dignity," precisely because it does not circulate as a commodity and cannot be represented in terms of money, the universal equivalent. Second, in *The Metaphysical Elements of Right* (1797), Kant distinguishes between "the active and the passive citizen" by claiming that "civil personality" and thus active citizenship are attributes of property holders, not proletarians and other dependents. "Apprentices to merchants or tradesmen, servants who are not employed by the state, minors (*naturaliter vel civiliter*), women in general and all those who are obliged to depend for their living (i.e. for food and protection) on the offices of others (excluding the state)—all of these people have no civil personality, and their existence is, so to speak, purely inherent." Kant sees these figures "as opposed to [those] who can put the products of [their] work up for public sale," that is, who retain their "civil independence" because they sell the products of their labor, not their productive capacities or their labor-power. (From Hans Reiss, ed., *Kant: Political Writings*, trans. H. B. Nisbet, 2d enlarged ed. [New York: Cambridge University Press, 1991], pp. 139–40).

34. Brooks, *America's Coming-of-Age*, p. 82; cf. D. H. Lawrence, *Studies in Classic American Literature* (n.p., 1915, 1923), chap. 12.

35. Peirce invoked Hegel, and not just to irritate James, in "What Pragmatism Is," *Monist* 15 (1905): "The truth is that pragmaticism is closely allied to the Hegelian

absolute idealism" (from C. S. Peirce,"The Essentials of Pragmatism," in Justus Buchler, ed., *Philosophical Writings of Peirce* [New York: Dover, 1955], pp. 251–68, here 266; cf. "The Architecture of Theories" [1891] in ibid., pp. 315–23, here 322, and "Evolutionary Love" [1893] in ibid., pp. 361–74, here 365–66). See also Manley Thompson, *The Pragmatic Philosphy of C. S. Peirce* (Chicago: University of Chicago Press, 1953), p. 180. Until 1903, James was pretty much appalled by Hegel; see, for example, William James, "On Some Hegelisms," *The Will to Believe* (New York: Longmans, Green, 1897), pp. 263–98 (but cf. the preface at p. xiii, where James apologizes for the essay's "superficiality"). My favorite rendition of this attitude is, however, from James, "Absolutism and Empiricism," an essay first published in *Mind* 9 (1884): 281–86 and later reprinted in *Essays in Radical Empiricism* (Cambridge: Harvard University Press, 1976, following the Longmans, Green edition of 1912), pp. 137–43: "Certainly, to my personal knowledge, all Hegelians are not prigs, but I somehow feel as if all prigs ought to end, if developed, by becoming Hegelians" (p. 142). Cf. chapter 10, note 3, below.

36. Quotations in order from G.W.F. Hegel, *The Phenomenology of Mind* (1807), trans. J. B. Baillie (1931; reprint, New York: Harper & Row, 1967), pp. 98, 81, 98, 99; cf. chapter 6 above.

37. On Peirce's semiological notion of the self, see Vincent Michael Colapietro, *Peirce's Approach to the Self: A Semiotic Perspective on Human Subjectivity* (Albany: State University of New York Press, 1989), esp. chap. 4, pp. 66–97.

38. Georg Simmel is quoted from "Anfang einer unvollendeten Selbstdarstellung," an essay cited by David Frisby in his introduction to *The Philosophy of Money*, translated from the second, enlarged edition of 1907 by Tom Bottomore and David Frisby (London: Routledge Kegan Paul, 1978), p. 25; on Simmel's transatlantic significance, see also Max Weber, "Georg Simmel as Sociologist," *Social Research* 39 (1972): 155–63; David N. Levine, ed., *Georg Simmel: On Individuality and Social Forms* (Chicago: University of Chicago Press, 1971); S. P. Altmann, "Simmel's Philosophy of Money," *American Journal of Sociology* 9 (1903): 46–68; and Émile Durkheim's review of the first edition of *Philosophie des Geldes* in *L'annee sociologique* (1900–1901), pp. 140–45.

39. The phrase "political economy of the sign" is from Jean Baudrillard, *The Mirror of Production*, trans. Mark Poster (St. Louis: Telos Press, 1975); see pp. 119–29 and esp. p. 129 n. 9 for Baudrillard's acknowledgment of a correlation between "finance capital" and "floating signifiers."

40. William James, "The Moral Equivalent of War," in Henry James, Jr., ed., *Memories and Studies* (New York: Longmans, Green, 1911), pp. 265–98 (page references in the text hereafter).

41. Here James is paraphrasing and quoting from Simon Patten, *The New Basis of Civilization* (New York: Macmillan, 1907), pp. 9–27, 121–43. Patten was elected president of the American Economic Association in 1907. His remarkably influential book on the passage from the "age of deficit" to the "age of surplus"—from the "pain economy" to the "pleasure economy"—began as a series of lectures in New York City arranged by Edward T. Devine, who had been a student of Patten's at the University of Pennsylvania in the 1890s, and had become general secretary of the New York Charity Organization Society, founder of the New York School

of Social Work, editor of the *Survey* (a leading journal of "social problems"), and Professor of Social Legislation at Columbia University. Patten's book went through eight editions between 1907 and 1923 (see Daniel M. Fox, "Introduction" to the 1968 Harvard University Press edition of *New Basis*, pp. vii–xlv). As I suggest in chapter 3 above, Devine himself was something of a prophet who brought Patten's message of the "economic revolution" to scholars as well as students and social workers—see, for example, Edward T. Devine, "The Economic Function of Woman," *Annals of the American Academy* 5 (1894): 45–60, and Edward T. Devine, *Economics* (New York: Macmillan, 1902), chaps 5–7, on consumption and "social prosperity." Perhaps "influential" is the wrong word with respect to Patten. That all kinds of writers appropriated his terminology of "deficit" and "surplus" without acknowledging the source might indicate instead that he gave apt expression to evident yet unknown social-cultural patterns—that he put into words what many people were already thinking about and acting on. By "all kinds of writers" I mean, for example, Mary Roberts Coolidge *Why Women Are So* (1912; reprint, New York: Arno Press, 1972), p. 146; William M. Leiserson, "The Problem of Unemployment Today," *Political Science Quarterly* 31 (1916): 1–24, here 10 n. 1; Walter E. Weyl, *The New Democracy* (New York: Macmillan, 1912), pp. 191–208 (Weyl, one of the founding editors of the *New Republic*, was also a student of Patten's at the University of Pennsylvania in the 1890s; his book sold almost ten thousand copies); and Brooks, *America's Coming-of-Age*, pp. 32–33—as well as Devine and James (on Coolidge, see Rosalind Rosenberg, *Beyond Separate Spheres: Intellectual Roots of Modern Feminism* [New Haven: Yale University Press, 1982], chap. 7; on Leiserson, a student of John R. Commons's, see Christopher L. Tomlins, *The State and the Unions: Labor Relations, Law, and the Organized Labor Movement in America, 1880–1960* [New York: Cambridge University Press, 1985], pp. 79–82, 204–41). What I find particularly fascinating about James's appropriation of Patten is that it recognizes the reality and the danger of the "disintegrative influences" at work in the so-called pleasure economy; in other words, James recognizes the impending conflict between antimodernist social movements, on the one hand, and socialism, feminism, and "pacific cosmopolitan industrialism" (a.k.a. corporate capitalism) on the other. This is the conflict that, in a European context of class struggle, revolution, and civil war, ca. 1905–23, produced the fascist personality—on which see volume 1 of Klaus Theweleit, *Male Fantasies*, trans. Stephen Conway, Erica Carter, and Chris Turner (Minneapolis: University of Minnesota Press, 1987).

42. As I will use it, "modern subjectivity" is the product of what Alasdair MacIntyre calls the Enlightenment Project of 1630–1850 in *After Virtue*, chap. 4; and it strongly resembles what Charles Taylor calls "modern identity" in an essay of 1981, "Legitimation Crisis?," reprinted in *Philosophy and the Human Sciences*, pp. 248–88 (later expanded into the book cited at note 50 below). But my emphasis on its discontinuities and dualisms derives from my reading of Ritter, *Hegel and the French Revolution*, pp. 59–68; David Kolb, *The Critique of Pure Modernity: Hegel, Heidegger, and After* (Chicago: University of Chicago Press, 1986), chap. 4, esp. pp. 60–65; and Roberto Mangabeira Unger, *Knowledge and Politics* (New York: Free Press, 1975), chaps. 1–3. Cf. Stephen Toulmin, *Cosmopolis: The Hidden Agenda of Modernity* (Chicago: University of Chicago Press, 1990), chaps. 2–3, esp. pp.

108–15; Jonanthan Arac, "Hamlet, *Little Dorrit*, and the History of Character," in Michael Hays, ed., *Critical Conditions: Regarding the Historical Moment* (Minneapolis: University of Minnesota Press, 1992), pp. 82–96; and Friedrich Nietzsche, *On the Advantage and Disadvantage of History for Life*, trans. Peter Preuss (Indianapolis: Hackett, 1980), wherein the "most distinctive property of this modern man" turns out to be "the remarkable opposition of an inside to which no outside and an outside to which no inside corresponds, an opposition unknown to ancient peoples." Nietzsche claims accordingly that knowledge "no longer acts as a transforming motive impelling to action and remains hidden in a certain chaotic inner world which that modern man, with curious pride, calls his unique 'inwardness' " (p. 24; cf. pp. 28–32 and, on the corresponding temporal discontinuities, pp. 13, 41, 62). Two recent collections on historical change in the idea of the self are also helpful in deciphering modern subjectivity: see Michael Carrithers, Steven Collins, and Steven Lukes, eds., *The Category of the Person* (New York: Cambridge University Press, 1985), which interprets Marcel Mauss's essay of 1938, "A Category of the Human Mind: The Notion of Person, the Notion of Self," pp. 1–25; and Thomas C. Heller, Morton Sosna, and David E. Wellbery, eds., *Reconstructing Individualism: Autonomy, Individuality, and the Self in Western Thought* (Palo Alto: Stanford University Press, 1986).

43. Cf. Bernard Williams, *Ethics and the Limits of Philosophy* (Cambridge: Harvard University Press, 1985), p. 1, where a "distinctively philosophical" understanding is defined as "general and abstract, rationally reflective, and concerned with what can be known through different kinds of inquiry." Kant's version of this attitude is the source of *modern* moral philosophy; for example, "Do we not think it a matter of the utmost necessity to work out for once a moral philosophy completely cleansed of everything that can only be empirical and appropriate to anthropology?" (*Groundwork of the Metaphysic of Morals*, p. 57). If I understand the meaning and significance of the "original position" on which John Rawls staked so much in *A Theory of Justice* (Cambridge: Harvard University Press, 1971), it was an answer to Kant's plea. But see Richard Rorty, "The Priority of Democracy to Philosophy" (1988), reprinted in *Objectivity, Relativism, and Truth* (New York: Cambridge University Press, 1991), pp. 175–96, esp. 179–89, for the argument that Rawls should be read as a historicist who is uninterested in a theory of the "moral subject"; and cf. the works cited at note 56 below.

44. See John G. Gunnell, *Political Philosophy and Time: Plato and the Origins of Political Vision* (Chicago: University of Chicago Press, 1968, 1987), esp. chaps. 4–5; Hannah Arendt, *The Human Condition* (Chicago: University of Chicago Press, 1958), chaps. 2, 5; J.G.A. Pocock, *The Machiavellian Moment: Florentine Political Thought and the Atlantic Republican Tradition* (Princeton: Princeton University Press, 1975), chaps. 1–3; Sheldon S. Wolin, *Politics and Vision: Continuity and Innovation in Western Political Thought* (Boston: Little, Brown, 1960), chaps. 1–3; MacIntyre, *After Virtue*, chaps. 10–12.

45. See esp. Karl Lowith, *Meaning in History* (Chicago: University of Chicago Press, 1949), pp. 1–20, 160–207, and endnotes at 225–27, 246–55; but also R. G. Collingwood, *The Idea of History* (London: Oxford University Press, 1946), pp. 31–56.

46. On the historicity of time and the social ethic of the early Christian church, see Wolin, *Politics and Vision*, chap. 4; Erich Auerbach, *Mimesis: The Representation of Reality in Western Literature* (Garden City, N.J.: Doubleday, 1957), pp. 33–43; Rudolph Bultmann, *Primitive Christianity in Its Contemporary Setting*, trans. R. H. Fuller (Cleveland: World Publishing, 1956), pp. 86–93, 175–208; Elaine Pagels, *Adam, Eve, and the Serpent* (New York: Vintage, 1988), chaps. 1–2, 5; John G. Gager, *Kingdom and Community: The Social World of Early Christianity* (Englewood Cliffs, N.J.: Prentice Hall, 1975), chaps. 2, 4; Robert M. Grant, *Early Christianity and Society* (San Francisco: Harper & Row, 1977), chaps. 4–6; Wayne A. Meeks, *The Moral World of the First Christians* (Philadelphia: Westminster Press, 1986), chaps. 2–5; Martin Hengel, *Property and Riches in the Early Church*, trans. John Bowden (London: SCM Press, 1974); Allen Verhey, *The Great Reversal: Ethics and the New Testament* (Grand Rapids, Mich.: Eerdmans Publishing Co., 1984); Alasdair MacIntyre, *A Short History of Ethics* (New York: Macmillan, 1966), chap. 9; and G.W.F. Hegel, *On Christianity: Early Theological Writings*, trans. T. M. Knox (Chicago: University of Chicago Press, 1948), pp. 86–89.

47. On the erotic imperative of the Christian dispensation, see esp. Denis de Rougemont, *Love in the Western World*, trans. Montgomery Belgion (New York: Harper & Row, 1956), book 2; also Bultmann, *Primitive Christianity*, pp. 71–79. On the figural interpretation of secular (historical) time, see Auerbach, *Mimesis*, pp. 55–66, and Lowith, *Meaning in History*, chap. 9. Augustine is quoted from Wolin, *Politics and Vision*, p. 126.

48. The interpenetration of religious, philosophical, and scientific discourses at the dawn of the modern age is the theme of Alexandre Koyré, *From the Closed World to the Infinite Universe* (Baltimore: Johns Hopkins University Press, 1957); E. A. Burtt, *The Metaphysical Foundations of Modern Science*, rev. ed. (Garden City, N.Y.: Doubleday, 1955); and Hans Blumenberg, *The Genesis of the Copernican World*, trans. Robert M. Wallace (Cambridge: MIT Press, 1987). On the new, instrumental conception of reason embodied in both Protestant and scientific practices of the sixteenth and seventeenth centuries, see my "Reflections on 'Romeo and Juliet,'" *Marxist Perspectives* 7 (1979): 50–61; more to the point are MacIntyre, *After Virtue*, pp. 51–53, and Arendt, *Human Condition*, pp. 257–304.

49. See Wolin, *Politics and Vision*, chap. 5, and Norman O. Brown, *Life against Death: The Psychoanalytical Meaning of History* (Middletown, Conn.: Wesleyan University Press, 1959), chaps. 14–15, from which Luther is quoted at pp. 221–22.

50. Augustine quoted from M. H. Abrams, *Natural Supernaturalism: Tradition and Revolution in Romantic Literature* (New York: Norton, 1971), p. 166; Luther quoted from Wolin, *Politics and Vision*, p. 160. On Augustine's principle (*in interiore homine habitat veritas*: "in the inward man dwells truth"), see also Charles Taylor, *Sources of the Self: The Making of the Modern Identity* (Cambridge: Harvard University Press, 1989), chap. 7.

51. Galston, *Kant and the Problem of History*, Kolb, *Critique of Pure Modernity*, and Brown, *Life against Death*, are particularly helpful on these issues. But cf. Marx's own remark on Protestantism in his *Capital: A Critique of Political Economy*, trans. Samuel Moore and Edward Aveling, 3 vols. (Chicago: Charles Kerr, 1906), 1:91. Luther is quoted from Wolin, *Politics and Vision*, p. 143; Kant is quoted from

the *Critique of Pure Reason*, trans. N. K. Smith (New York: Oxford University Press, 1965), p. 313. Here is how Hegel compares Luther and Kant, the founding father of German idealism, in the preface to *The Philosophy of Right* (1821), trans. T. M. Knox (New York: Oxford University Press, 1942): "It is a sheer obstinacy, the obstinacy which does honour to mankind, to refuse to recognize in conviction anything not ratified in thought. This obstinacy is the characteristic of our epoch, besides being the principle peculiar to Protestantism. What Luther initiated as faith in feeling and in witness of the spirit, is precisely what spirit, since become more mature, has striven to apprehend in the concept in order to free and so to find itself in the world as it exists to-day" (p. 12). William James's comparison of pragmatism and Protestantism takes on new meaning in view of Hegel's itinerary: pragmatism begins to sound like Spirit rediscovering itself in the world of the twentieth century. On the terror installed by Enlightenment, see Hegel, *Phenomenology*, pp. 559–610, and *Philosophy of Right*, par. 29, p. 33, par. 258, p. 157, and addition to par. 5, p. 227; cf. also Max Horkheimer and Theodor Adorno, *The Dialectic of Enlightenment*, trans. John Cummings (New York: Herder & Herder, 1972).

52. See chapter 6 above.

53. I am claiming that there is no "young Hegel" from which we may deduce "humanistic" principles that stand as criticism of the "old Hegel," in the manner of Marcuse's *Reason and Revolution*, pp. 169–223—in other words, that there is a certain and significant continuity between *The Phenomenology* and *The Philosophy of Right*. But of course this claim is based on more than my reading of these works; to be specific, it is based on my reading of Ritter, *Hegel and the French Revolution*; Riedel, *Between Tradition and Revolution*; and Kolb, *Critique of Pure Modernity*.

54. For the "Theses on Feuerbach," see *Writings of the Young Marx on Philosophy and Society*, trans. and ed. Lloyd D. Easton and Kurt H. Guddat (Garden City, N.Y.: Doubleday, 1967), pp. 400–402; but cf. Dewey from "The Scholastic and the Speculator": "We are such materialists, fixing our attention upon the rigid thing instead of upon the moving act" (3:151). See otherwise Alexandre Kojève, *Introduction to the Reading of Hegel: Lectures on the Phenomenology of Spirit*, trans. James H. Nichols, Jr., ed. Allan Bloom (Ithaca: Cornell University Press, 1969), pp. 3–70; Kolb, *Critique of Pure Modernity*, pp. 47–49; Trent Schroyer, *The Critique of Domination: The Origins and Development of Critical Theory* (New York: George Braziller, 1973), pp. 54–74; and the sources themselves: Hegel, *Phenomenology of Mind*, pp. 218–40, and *The Philosophy of Right*, pp. 20–36, 122–29, 226 (par. 4–33, 182–98, and addition to par. 4). James is quoted from "Does Consciousness Exist?" (1904) in *Writings 1902–1910*, p. 1145; Peirce is quoted from "The Architecture of Theories," originally published in *Monist* (1891), reprinted in Buchler, *Philosophical Writings*, 315–23, here 322.

55. The works of C. B. Macpherson and J.G.A. Pocock converge here if nowhere else. See C. B. Macpherson, *The Political Theory of Possessive Individualism: Hobbes to Locke* (New York: Oxford University Press, 1962), esp. chaps. 3–4, and works by J.G.A. Pocock: "Early Modern Capitalism—the Augustan Perception," in E. Kamenka and R. S. Neale, eds., *Feudalism, Capitalism and Beyond* (London: Edward Arnold, 1975), pp. 62–83; *The Machiavellian Moment*, chaps. 13–15; and "The Mobility of Property and the Rise of Eighteenth-Century Sociology," *Virtue,*

Commerce, and History (New York: Cambridge University Press, 1985), pp. 103–24. On property and the "system of needs," see Hegel, *Philosophy of Right*, pp. 40–57, 126–34 (par. 40–71, 189–208), quoted from p. 42. On civil society as the sphere of noncoercive social relations, where contract is the paradigm of all transactions between individuals, see Wolin, *Politics and Vision*, chaps. 9–10, esp. pp. 299–314, and Bernard Bailyn, *The Ideological Origins of the American Revolution* (Cambridge: Harvard University Press, 1965), chap. 3.

56. Again, Pocock and Macpherson converge here, on the proposition that arguments over the meaning and functions of property must be understood as arguments about the moral capacity of the modern individual. We are still arguing, of course. For example, see the "Brief of 281 American Historians as Amici Curiae Supporting Appellees [In re: *William L. Webster, et al., v. Reproductive Health Services, et al.*]," *Public Historian* 12 (1990): 57–75, which ends as follows: "Apart from [the] devastating consequences to the lives and health of women, restricting access to abortion will again deny the fundamental legitimacy of women as moral decision-makers." Cf. chapter 8, note 40, below, and Ronald Dworkin, "The Coming Battles over Free Speech," *New York Review of Books*, June 11, 1992, pp. 55–58, 61–64, where the First Amendment appears as the predicate of moral agency and responsibility; Michael J. Sandel, *Liberalism and the Limits of Justice* (New York: Cambridge University Press, 1982), where the "nature of the moral subject" resides in the "antecedent unity of the self," which means that "the subject, however heavily conditioned by its surroundings, is always, irreducibly, prior to his values and ends, and never fully constituted by them" (pp. 15–23, 47–65, 120–22, 133–35, 147–72); and Owen Flanagan, *Varieties of Moral Personality: Ethics and Psychological Realism* (Cambridge: Harvard University Press, 1991), where the "psychological reality of a self-system construed as a substantial unity" becomes the predicate of the moral personality as such (see pp. 255–75). On the anxieties attending the nineteenth-century attachment of individual identity and alienable property, see, more generally, Michael Paul Rogin, *Fathers and Children: Andrew Jackson and the Subjugation of the American Indian* (New York: Knopf, 1975), chaps. 3–4; Walter Benn Michaels, "Romance and Real Estate," *Raritan* 2 (1983): 66–87; and Horwitz, "The Standard Oil Trust as Emersonian Hero."

57. On James's attempt to reconstitute the moral personality by situating it in historical time, see chapter 10 below; on Dreiser and naturalism, see chapter 6 above. Historians and partisans of populism (most historians are partisans) often evoke the "free social space" residing in the "culture of resistance" supposedly created by the Alliance and mourn the passing of the freeholder, because they are searching for what Christopher Lasch calls the "moral equivalent of an earlier form of proprietorship"—that is, a way of reinstating "the principle that property ownership and the independence it confers are absolutely essential preconditions of citizenship" (Christopher Lasch, *The True and Only Heaven: Progress and Its Critics* [New York: Norton, 1991], pp. 16, 223). I had not read Lasch's prodigious (yet unpersuasive) study when I wrote this chapter; I was thinking instead of the new social and labor history on which he relies in defending artisans against innovation. But his argument nonetheless verifies my characterization of the choices available at the turn of the century (for example, see Lasch, *Only Heaven*, pp. 224–25, 302–3,

340–48) and fits my description of contemporary writers on the Left, in chapter 3 above and chapters 9–10 below. See esp. chapter 10, below, on the conflation of the moral polemic against proletarianization and the twentieth-century critique of capitalism; cf. also my "Reply to Gerald Berk," *Journal of Policy History* 3 (1991): 85–89. My friend Marc Manganaro insists that the historical sensibility of high literary modernists is more ambiguous and complicated than my remarks here would suggest; see his important new book, *Myth, Rhetoric, and the Voice of Authority* (New Haven: Yale University Press, 1992), and his earlier collection of essays, *Modernist Anthropology: From Fieldwork to Text* (Princeton: Princeton University Press, 1990). My reply to him has been: yes, the modernists want to write a "poem including history" (on which see Longenbach, *Modernist Poetics of History*), and yes, there is no poem more packed with historical details and references than the *Cantos* (with the possible exception of *The Wasteland*); even so, their sense of the past is quite similar to that of the Populists, simply because they cannot imagine a future without modern subjectivity and its attendant discontinuities—unless they are contemplating the statist alternative that derives from their repudiation of that future. Cf. my discussion of Richard Rorty in chapter 10 below.

58. Cf. note 43 above and chapter 10 below.

59. Richard Rorty makes such a claim in *Philosophy and the Mirror of Nature* (Princeton: Princeton University Press, 1979); again, see chapter 10 below.

60. See Robert Westbrook, "Lewis Mumford, John Dewey, and the 'Pragmatic Acquiescence,'" in Thomas P. Hughes and Agatha C. Hughes, eds., *Lewis Mumford: Public Intellectual* (New York: Oxford University Press, 1990), pp. 301–22 and endnotes at 420–25; also see Blake, *Beloved Community*, pp. 226–27. In chapter 9 below, I suggest that Westbrook and Blake defend Dewey on the wrong grounds and that Mumford can be criticized for acquiescing to the romantic requirements of "authentic" selfhood.

CHAPTER NINE

1. See Randolph Bourne, "Twilight of Idols," *New Republic*, October 1917, reprinted in Olaf Hansen, ed., *The Radical Will: Randolph Bourne, Selected Writings, 1911–1918* (New York: Urizen, 1977), pp. 336–47, here 336, 338, 347; Van Wyck Brooks, "Letters and Leadership" (1918), in *Three Essays on America* (New York: Dutton, 1934), pp. 115–90, here 168–83, esp. 171–72; Harold Stearns, *Liberalism in America* (New York: Boni & Liveright, 1919), chap. 8, esp. pp. 179–84; also idem, *America and the Young Intellectual* (New York: George Doran, 1921), pp. 33, 40, 47. And see also the heartbreaking ten-page letter of Bourne to Brooks, March 28, 1918, in Box 12, Van Wyck Brooks Papers, Van Pelt Library, University of Pennsylvania, Philadelphia, in which Bourne, writing on the occasion of the publication of "Letters and Leadership," denounces the "cult of politics [that] had been inherent in the liberal intellectual's point of view long before the war." In my view, this letter is much more persuasive than the published works from 1917 because it addresses the actual consequences of the war in question, not war as such. Lewis Mumford, *The Golden Day: A Study in American Culture and Experience*

(New York: Horace Liveright, 1926), will hereafter be cited by page number in the text.

2. See Bertrand Russell, *Philosophical Essays*, rev. ed. (New York: Simon & Schuster, 1967), chaps. 3–4, and Émile Durkheim, *Pragmatism and Sociology*, trans. J. C. Whitehouse, ed. John B. Allcock (New York: Cambridge University Press, 1983). Armand Cuvillier's preface to the 1955 French edition of Durkheim's lectures (see pp. xi–xxii) treats James and Dewey as if they were of largely antiquarian interest, not enduring sources of controversy and innovation in European social theory (see, e.g., p. xiii: "Pragmatism now seems rather dull and out-of-date"). Allcock's introduction (pp. xxiii–xli and endnotes at 108–14) is, however, quite good; he explores European interest in pragmatism as if it was something more than an inexplicable digression from serious philosophy and suggests that "the influence of Bertrand Russell's assessment of the movement" accounts for the neglect of pragmatism in the United Kingdom (see 109 n. 3; on the intellectual stage of the United States, I would claim, Mumford plays Russell's role). Durkheim's obsession with James and pragmatism is of course evident in the 1913–14 course of lectures that Marcel Mauss called "the high point of Durkheim's philosophical work" (quoted by Cuvillier in *Pragmatism and Sociology*, p. xi). But it is no less evident in the great work of 1912, *The Elementary Forms of the Religious Life*, trans. Joseph Ward Swain (New York: Free Press, 1965), pp. 26–33, 169–73, 227–30, 235–36, 256–71, 305–8, 362–65, 405–13, 465–96. Here Durkheim insists that his study of totemism serves as a solution to the "problem of knowledge" posed by the either/or choice between Hume and Kant; he insists, in other words, that it serves as a reply to the studies in radical empiricism which James published in 1904–5 (Durkheim read these in English, before they were collected for publication as a book in 1912), not just as an argument with *The Varieties of Religious Experience*, which appeared in 1902. Durkheim borrows the terms of the choice between empiricism and rationalism as James framed it in these studies of 1904–5 (on which see chapter 10 below) but proposes another way of annulling the contradiction, while preserving the difference, between the "two doctrines," by correlating them, respectively, with individuals and society. On these and related matters of Durkheim's debts to both James and Charles Renouvier (the philosopher to whom James turned in curing himself of severe depression in 1872), see Allcock's introduction to *Pragmatism and Sociology*, pp. xxv–xxxiii, and Steven Collins, "Categories, Concepts or Predicaments?: Remarks on Mauss's Use of Philosophical Terminology," in M. Carrithers, S. Collins, and S. Lukes, eds., *The Category of the Person* (New York: Cambridge University Press, 1985), pp. 46–82, here 51–62. Henri Bergson's introduction to the 1911 French edition of *Pragmatism* is chapter 8 of his *Creative Mind*, trans. Mabelle Andison (New York: Greenwood Press, 1968), pp. 248–60. On James and Bergson, see Ralph Barton Perry, *The Thought and Character of William James*, 2 vols. (Boston: Little, Brown & Co., 1935), 2:599–636.

3. Brooks quoted from "Letters and Leadership," pp. 168, 168–69, 170; Stearns quoted from *Liberalism in America*, p. 184.

4. On the young intellectuals and the usable past, see Warren I. Susman, *Culture as History: The Transformation of American Society in the Twentieth Century* (New York: Pantheon, 1984), pp. 7–49, 105–21, and endnotes at 291–99; Martin J. Sklar,

"On the Proletarian Revolution and the End of Political-Economic Society," *Radical America* 3 (May–June 1969): 1–41; Casey Nelson Blake, "The Young Intellectuals and the Culture of Personality," *American Literary History* 1 (1989): 510–34, and *Beloved Community: The Cultural Criticisms of Randolph Bourne, Van Wyck Brooks, Waldo Frank, and Lewis Mumford* (Chapel Hill: University of North Carolina Press, 1990); Christopher Lasch, *The New Radicalism in America: The Intellectual as a Social Type* (New York: Vintage, 1965), and *The Agony of the American Left* (New York: Vintage, 1969), chap. 2; Henry F. May, *The End of American Innocence* (New York: Knopf, 1959), part 3; Daniel Aaron, *Writers on the Left* (New York: Avon, 1960), part 1; Nathan I. Huggins, *Harlem Renaissance* (New York: Oxford University Press, 1970), chaps. 2–5; Houston A. Baker, Jr., *Modernism and the Harlem Renaissance* (Chicago: University of Chicago Press, 1988); Harold Cruse, *The Crisis of the Negro Intellectual* (New York: William Morrow, 1967), pp. 11–95, 115–46; and Rosalind Rosenberg, *Beyond Separate Spheres: Intellectual Roots of Modern Feminism* (New Haven: Yale University Press, 1982), chaps. 5–7. See also Paul F. Bourke's fine essays "The Social Critics and the End of American Innocence: 1907– 1921," *Journal of American Studies* 3 (1969): 57–72, and "The Status of Politics 1909–1919: The New Republic, Randolph Bourne, and Van Wyck Brooks," ibid. 8 (1974): 171–202.

5. To be more specific, the portraits of James in the recent work of Cornel West, Robert Westbrook, and Frank Lentricchia bear little or no resemblance to the James I depict in chapter 5 and chapter 8. I have already suggested that he is not a "bourgeois individualist" as West claims in *The American Evasion of Philosophy: A Genealogy of Pragmatism* (Madison: University of Wisconsin Press, 1989), pp. 65–68; that he is not a "mugwump" as Westbrook claims in "Lewis Mumford, John Dewey, and the 'Pragmatic Acquiescence,'" in Thomas P. Hughes and Agatha C. Hughes, eds., *Lewis Mumford: Public Intellectual* (New York: Oxford University Press, 1990), pp. 301–22 and endnotes at 420–25, esp. 420 n. 4; and that he is not committed to a "quasi-Cartesian subjectivity" as Lentricchia claims in *Ariel and the Police* (Madison: University of Wisconsin Press, 1988), pp. 117–27. I hope to demonstrate hereafter that it is a mistake to affiliate Mumford with pragmatism as Blake attempts in *Beloved Community* or to call James a neo-Romantic as Jacques Barzun does in *A Stroll with William James* (New York: Harper & Row, 1983), pp. 198–202. But I want to emphasize that these works are simply indispensable—my arguments with them should be read as evidence of their originality and importance.

6. See Blake, *Beloved Community*, pp. 226–27; Westbrook, "Pragmatic Acquiescence," p. 301; and Robert Westbrook, *John Dewey and American Democracy* (Ithaca: Cornell University Press, 1991), pp. 130–37, 380–87.

7. The exchange between Dewey and Mumford originally appeared in the *New Republic* of January 5 and 19, 1927; it is reprinted in Gail Kennedy, ed., *Pragmatism and American Culture* (Boston: D. C. Heath, 1950), pp. 49–57 (Mumford is quoted from p. 56). The Lewis Mumford Papers, Special Collections, Van Pelt Library, University of Pennsylvania, Philadelphia, contain two unpublished contributions to this controversy: one (in Box 148, Folder 7125) is an untitled, undated three-page letter to the editor of the *New Republic* (probably from 1927); the other (in Box 149, Folder 7168) is "Mr. Dewey's Critics and Sidney Hook," an eight-page response

to Hook's "John Dewey and his Critics," *New Republic*, June 3, 1931 (reprinted in Kennedy, *Pragmatism and American Culture*, pp. 92–94), which, according to Mumford's handwritten annotation, the editors rejected (interestingly enough, in this second effort, Mumford claims that he "never pinned on Mr. Dewey the tag of the 'pragmatic acquiescence'"). Both contributions indicate that Mumford understood his role in the late 1920s and early 1930s as the curator of intellectual alternatives to pragmatism—in other words, that he understood its appeal and tried to preclude its triumph among left-wing intellectuals. It seems he lost the battle but won the war.

8. See the extraordinary essay by Rosalind Williams, "Lewis Mumford as a Historian of Technology in *Technics and Civilization*," in Hughes and Hughes, *Lewis Mumford*, pp. 43–65 and endnotes at 381–90.

9. See Charles Molesworth, "Inner and Outer: The Axiology of Lewis Mumford," Leo Marx, "Lewis Mumford: Prophet of Organicism," and Casey Blake, "The Perils of Personality: Lewis Mumford and Politics after Liberalism," all in ibid., pp. 241–55, 164–80, 283–300, and endnotes at 414, 401–3, 417–20; cf. also Donald L. Miller, *Lewis Mumford: A Life* (New York: Weidenfeld & Nicholson, 1989), pp. 298–303, and the special issue of *Salmagundi*, no. 49 (1980): "Prophecy Reconsidered, Articles on Lewis Mumford."

10. Mumford to Brooks, August 17, 1935, in Robert Spiller, ed., *The Van Wyck Brooks–Lewis Mumford Letters: The Record of a Literary Friendship* (New York: Dutton, 1970), pp. 117–18; the original is in Box 56, Folder 2, Mumford Papers. Bergson, *Creative Mind*, pp. 259–60.

11. See Jacques Maritain, *Bergsonian Philosophy and Thomism*, 2d ed., trans. Mabelle Andison (New York: Greenwood Press, 1968), and John L. Stanley, ed., *From Georges Sorel: Essays in Socialism and Philosophy*, trans. John Stanley and Charlotte Stanley (New York: Oxford University Press, 1976), pp. 257–90 and endnotes at 354–66 (this is a selection from *The Utility of Pragmatism*). On Bergson, Georges Sorel, and Carl Jung in the intellectual life of early-twentieth-century Europe, see H. Stuart Hughes, *Consciousness and Society: The Reorientation of European Social Thought, 1890–1930*, rev. ed. (New York: Vintage, 1977), pp. 54–61, 90–95, 105–24, 153–82 (Jung is quoted from p. 156); A. E. Pilkington, *Bergson and His Influence: A Reassessment* (New York: Cambridge University Press, 1976); John Stanley, "Editor's Introduction," in Stanley, *From Georges Sorel*, pp. 1–61; and Ernesto Laclau and Chantal Mouffe, *Hegemony and Socialist Strategy* (London: Verso, 1985), pp. 36–42.

12. Bergson, "Introduction to Metaphysics" (1903), *Creative Mind*, pp. 187–237, here 217. According to James, this was "Bergson's most compendious statement of his doctrine"; see William James, *Some Problems of Philosophy* (Cambridge: Harvard University Press, 1979, following the Longmans Green ed. of 1911), p. 53 n. 27.

13. Henri Bergson, *Creative Evolution*, trans. Arthur Mitchell (New York: Modern Library, 1944, following the Henry Holt ed. of 1911), p. 56, cf. pp. 50–104. In the preface, Mitchell thanks James for his "friendly interest" in producing the English translation of "Bergson's most important work."

14. Bergson quoted from ibid., p. 53 (cf. 357–85) and "Introduction to Metaphysics," p. 224.

15. See M. H. Abrams, *Natural Supernaturalism: Tradition and Revolution in Romantic Literature* (New York: Norton, 1971), esp. pp. 172–95, 218–25; Friedrich Schelling is quoted from p. 182. On the inner articulation of German idealism, see also Herbert Marcuse, *Reason and Revolution: Hegel and the Rise of Social Theory* (1941; reprint, Boston: Beacon Press, 1960), pp. 3–29; Charles Taylor, *Hegel* (New York: Cambridge University Press, 1975), part 1; and with regard to the key differences between Schelling, Fichte, and Hegel, see G. A. Kelly, "Notes on Hegel's 'Lordship and Bondage,' " *Review of Metaphysics* 19 (1966): 780–802, and Georg Lukács, *The Young Hegel*, trans. Rodney Livingstone (Cambridge: MIT Press, 1975), pp. 241–94, 423–42.

16. F.W.J. Schelling, *System of Transcendental Idealism*, trans. Peter Heath (Charlottesville: University of Virginia Press, 1978), p. 219 (page references in the text hereafter). Bergson quoted from "Introduction to Metaphysics," p. 221.

17. Bergson quoted from "Introduction to Metaphysics," pp. 200, 236; from "Philosophical Intuition," an address to the Philosophical Congress in Bologna, April 1911, in *Creative Mind*, pp. 126–52, here 147; and again from "Introduction to Metaphysics," p. 192. On Schelling's aesthetics, see F.W.J. Schelling, *The Philosophy of Art*, trans. and ed. Douglas Stott (Minneapolis: University of Minnesota Press, 1989); the editor's introductions at pp. xxvii–lv, 3–19, are quite good because they are animated by resentment of Hegelian hegemony in the domains of both philosophy and aesthetics. On Schelling's broader agenda, see Martin Heidegger, *Schelling's Treatise on the Essence of Human Freedom*, trans. Joan Stambaugh (Athens: Ohio University Press, 1985)—this is a transcript of a lecture course Heidegger gave at the University of Freiburg in 1936—and James Engell, *The Creative Imagination: Enlightenment to Romanticism* (Cambridge: Harvard University Press, 1981), pp. 248–50, 301–27.

18. Brooks quoted here from Blake, *Beloved Community*, pp. 233, 243; on the breakdown, see generally ibid., pp. 229–47, but also James Hoopes, *Van Wyck Brooks: In Search of American Culture* (Amherst: University of Massachusetts Press, 1977), chap. 7. Brooks simply could not reconcile the extreme discontinuities of modern subjectivity; but they were all he had left once he could no longer commit himself to some version of American culture. "A people is like a ciphered parchment," he wrote in 1915, "that has to be held up to the fire before its hidden significances come out" (*America's Coming-of-Age*, in *Three Essays*, p. 109). Ten years later, he could not decipher the American people; and so his life stopped making sense. The manuscript of the Emerson biography was completed in 1926 but was not published by E. P. Dutton until 1932, after Mumford and others (including Eleanor Brooks) had intervened on Brooks's behalf (see Spiller, *Letters*, pp. 56–63, and Hoopes, *Van Wyck Brooks*, pp. 173–78, 188–91). On Poe's experiments of the 1830s, see my "Subjectivity and Slavery in Poe's Autobiography of Ambitious Love," *Psychohistory Review* 21 (1993): 175–96.

19. See Steve Golin, *The Fragile Bridge: Paterson Silk Strike, 1913* (Philadelphia: Temple University Press, 1988); Rebecca Zurier, *Art for the Masses: A Radical Magazine and Its Graphics, 1911–1917* (Philadelphia: Temple University Press, 1988); Bourke, "End of American Innocence," esp. pp. 61–65; Cruse, *Negro Intel-*

lectual, pp. 22–32; May, *End of American Innocence*, pp. 279–329; and Miller, *Mumford*, chaps. 4–6, esp. pp. 101–14.

20. Bergson quoted from "Introduction to Metaphysics," pp. 193–94, 191; cf. 225–30. For a good introduction to Bergsonian intuition, see Leszek Kolokowski, *Bergson* (New York: Cambridge University Press, 1985), chaps. 2–4. Bergson's flight from symbols reminds me of the poetry of William Carlos Williams as Wallace Stevens interpreted it (that is, as antipoetic) but also of the antisymbolic economics of Ezra Pound, for example in "ABC of Economics" (1933) and "A Visiting Card" (1942, 1952), in *Selected Prose, 1909–1965*, ed. William Cookson (London: Faber, 1973), pp. 233–64, 306–65. On these and related matters of interpreting modernism in the political-economic mode, see Alec Marsh, "The Money Question and the Poetry of Ezra Pound and William Carlos Williams" (Ph.D. diss., Rutgers University, 1993).

21. Alfred North Whitehead, *Science and the Modern World* (New York: Mentor Books, 1948), p. 148.

22. See Miller, *Mumford*, chap. 14, and Blake, *Beloved Community*, pp. 260–65.

23. Lewis Mumford, *Herman Melville* (New York: Harcourt, Brace & Co., 1929), page references in the text hereafter.

24. In *Beloved Community*, pp. 263–65, 291–95, Blake emphasizes just this "social and participating self"; I am more doubtful about its resilience and centrality in Mumford's thought.

25. Mumford, *The Golden Day*, p. 190.

26. On Shelley's interpretation of Milton's Satan, see Abrams, *Natural Supernaturalism*, pp. 299–300, and, better yet, William Empson, *Milton's God* (London: New Directions, 1961), which is itself a brilliant variation on this romantic theme.

27. Cf. C. L. R. James, *Mariners, Renegades, and Castaways: The Story of Herman Melville and the World We Live In* (New York: C. L. R. James, 1953), chaps. 1–3, and F. O. Matthiessen, *American Renaissance: Art and Expression in the Age of Emerson and Whitman* (New York: Oxford University Press, 1941), pp. 431–66.

28. Blake, *Beloved Community*, p. 286, and "Politics after Liberalism" in Hughes and Hughes, *Lewis Mumford*, esp. pp. 292–96. Cf. Donald L. Miller, "The Myth of the Machine: Technics and Human Development," ibid., pp. 152–63 and endnotes at 399–401; and see also Christopher Lasch, "Lewis Mumford and the Myth of the Machine," *Salmagundi*, no. 49 (1980): 4–28.

29. See chapter 10 below.

30. See Rosalind Williams, "Mumford as a Historian of Technology," in Hughes and Hughes, *Lewis Mumford*, pp. 43–65 and endnotes at 381–90; also Mumford to Brooks, July 19, 1935, in Spiller, *Letters*, pp. 114–15, and, better yet, Mumford to Brooks, June 21, 1933, in Box 56, Folder 2, Mumford Papers: "By now my book has expanded into three books: one on machines, which covers incidentally the major problems of economics . . . the second on cities, which will cover politics . . . and the third on the Personality, which will bring everything together." In a draft, unpublished preface to Waldo Frank, ed., *America and Alfred Stieglitz* (Garden City, N. Y.: Doubleday, 1935), Mumford concluded on the same note: "The final product of art, however, is not a picture, a poem, a statue, a photograph: the final prod-

uct is a personality" (Box 109, Folder 6641, Mumford Papers). Page references to Lewis Mumford, *Technics and Civilization* (New York: Harcourt, Brace & Co., 1934, 1963), will hereafter be given in the text.

31. See Waldo Frank's review, "Dawn and Dusk," in his collection of essays, *In the American Jungle* (New York: Farrar & Rinehart, 1937), pp. 176–77.

32. See Blake, *Beloved Community*, pp. 279–87.

33. But Mumford deserves credit for discovering what Donald Lowe calls the "perceptual revolution of 1905–15" (Donald M. Lowe, *History of Bourgeois Perception* [Chicago: University of Chicago Press, 1982], chap. 6).

34. The centrality of Francis Bacon in the arguments of both books might suggest that *Technics* was written in response to *Reconstruction in Philosophy*; surely the two books were equally focused on what Dewey called the "transition period," 1400–1800. But Mumford was more likely to associate the period with the "collapse of form"; in this sense, he never moved beyond the paradoxes that dominate his early notes for what became *Technics* (notes in Box 104, Folder 6577, Mumford Papers). For example, a note dated September 3, 1929, reads in part: "The short step from Bacon to *Defoe*. Defoe gives the rationale of the mechanical world: he makes its motives explicit. . . . Science reduces universe to matter & motion: economics reduces social world to goods & money; philosophy to a [story?] of sensations. Custom, tradition, habit, art, poetry become incidental to main business of life." The Mumford who speaks here as if art as such does not express what is evident yet unknown in the present, *in view of* the past, but rather preserves and formalizes folkways (custom, tradition, habit) *from* the past, sounds very much like my colleague Jackson Lears, who, if I am not mistaken, now seems to believe that culture consists in, and that art requires, the retrieval of "things themselves" from the clutches of the commodity form (see, for example, his forthcoming book *Fables of Abundance: American Advertising and American Culture, 1820–1970*, chap. 8). So I would paraphrase Kenneth Burke's characterization of Whitman and James: is not Mumford the noetic replica of Lears?

35. Ralph Waldo Emerson, *Nature* (1837), in Alfred R. Ferguson, ed., *The Collected Works of Ralph Waldo Emerson*, 3 vols. (Cambridge: Harvard University Press, 1971), 1:7–45 (page references in the text hereafter).

36. To my mind, the best treatments of these unnatural acts are Geza Roheim, *The Origin and Function of Culture* (Garden City, N.Y.: Doubleday, 1971), pp. 51–94, and Taylor, *Hegel*, pp. 87–88. Cf. Leo Marx, *The Machine in the Garden* (New York: Oxford University Press, 1964).

37. Ralph Waldo Emerson, "Man the Reformer," in Ferguson, *Collected Works* 1:145–60 (page references in the text hereafter). There is an impending debate between Christopher Lasch, Richard Poirier, and Michael Gilmore on Emerson's attitude toward the market, or rather toward the commodification of labor. I think Poirier and Gilmore are closer to the truth of the matter because they see that Emerson remained ambiguous about the commodity form as such, whereas Lasch designates him as the founding father of the populist tradition that defines proletarianization—the commodification of labor—as the negation of self-determination and thus of democracy. Even so, I think Lasch's argument serves as a salutary reminder of Emerson's essentially artisanal attitude toward work, necessity, and freedom.

See Christopher Lasch, *The True and Only Heaven: Progress and Its Critics* (New York: Norton, 1991), pp. 261–79, 546–51; Richard Poirier, *Poetry and Pragmatism* (Cambridge: Harvard University Press, 1992), chap. 1; and Michael T. Gilmore, *American Romanticism and the Marketplace* (Chicago: University of Chicago Press, 1985), pp. 13–38.

38. On the decline of socially necessary labor after 1919, see esp. Sydney H. Coontz, *Productive Labour and Effective Demand* (New York: A. M. Kelley, 1966), pp. 125–58, and Sklar, "On the Proletarian Revolution," but also chapters 1 and 3 above.

39. In my view, the new social and cultural history finally fails precisely because *poiesis* becomes the regulative principle of its critique of capitalism—on which see chapter 10 below. But see also Lasch, *True and Only Heaven*, chap. 5, in which the author argues that the new social history succeeds as a critique of capitalism precisely because it is regulated by this artisanal principle. On the larger questions of abstract, social labor as against the ancient, artisanal model of *poiesis*, see Manfred Riedel, *Between Tradition and Revolution: The Hegelian Transformation of Political Philosophy*, trans. Walter Wright (New York: Cambridge University Press, 1984), chaps. 1, 5; Hannah Arendt, *The Human Condition* (Chicago: University of Chicago Press, 1958), chaps. 3–4; and an essay that addresses these questions in studying the Frankfurt School: Axel Honneth, "Work and Instrumental Action," *New German Critique*, no. 26 (1982): 31–54. (Like Lasch, Blake, and their compatriots on the American Left, Honneth believes that the standpoint of critique of the division of labor must be artisanal or craft skill, that is, the moment *before* "universal mechanization" under the auspices of scientific management destroys the integrity of the labor process—as he puts it, "moral knowledge [is] embodied in acts of work which maintain their autonomy even in the organizational reality of externally determined work relations" [p. 54]—but his essay is nonetheless illuminating).

40. Blake, *Beloved Community*, pp. 4–9, 140–44, 301–3. Mumford's "artisanal critique" of modern-industrial capitalism is carried to its logical and politically poignant conclusion in Lasch's *True and Only Heaven*.

CHAPTER TEN

1. Donald Davidson, "The Myth of the Subjective," in Michael Krausz, ed., *Relativism: Interpretation and Confrontation* (Notre Dame: University of Notre Dame Press, 1989), pp. 159–72, here 160 (page references in the text hereafter).

2. See John P. Murphy, *Pragmatism: From Peirce to Davidson* (Boulder, Colo.: Westview Press, 1990), pp. 95–98. The quoted remark is from "Pragmatism as Anti-Representationalism," Richard Rorty's introduction to Murphy's book, pp. 1–6, here 5.

3. On James's preparations of 1897–1904, see Notebooks 10, 11, and 12 in the William James Papers (bMSAm 1092.9), Houghton Library, Harvard University, Cambridge, Massachusetts (James understood these journals as parts of a whole; for example, what the Houghton Library calls Notebook 12 begins, "The 'pure experience' hypothesis/Continuation of Book II, p. 35," where "Book II" refers to what

the Houghton Library calls Notebook 11). Notebook 10 contains forty-five double-sided pages, Notebook 11 contains twenty-eight double-sided pages, and Notebook 12 contains fifty-five double-sided pages. Except for the last ten pages of Notebook 12, these writings date from the period 1895–98 and, particularly in 1898, are full of questions and answers that will reappear in the essays of 1904–5. For example, the entry dated April 15, 1898, concludes by claiming that the "portions" of the field of experience "become cognitive only through the field changing into later fields." This passage, which is marked in blue pencil, is from pp. 43–44 of Notebook 12. See also Ralph Barton Perry, *The Thought and Character of William James*, 2 vols. (Boston: Little, Brown, 1935), 2:363–74, and John J. McDermott's indispensable introduction to the Harvard University Press edition of *Essays in Radical Empiricism* (Cambridge, 1976), pp. xi–xlviii. Regarding the "Chicago School" and its relation to radical empiricism, see James, "A World of Pure Experience," in ibid., p. 27 n. 2, and the editorial note (27.34) at p. 167; see also his review, "The Chicago School," *Psychological Bulletin*, January 15, 1904, reprinted in William James, *Writings 1902–1910*, comp. Bruce Kuklick (New York: Library of America, 1987), pp. 1136–40, and Darnell Rucker, *The Chicago Pragmatists* (Minneapolis: University of Minnesota Press, 1969). The 1903 exchange of letters between James and Dewey in the James Papers (esp. William James to John Dewey, March 11, March 23, October 17, 1903) is even more illuminating, for it demonstrates, among other things, that James was thoroughly familiar with Dewey's published work in the professional journals. In his letter of March 23, James wrote: "What you write of the new school of truth both pleases and humiliates me [here James refers to his own letter of March 11, in which he claimed to 'see an entirely new "school of thought" forming']. It humiliates me that I had to wait till I read [A. W.] Moore's article before finding how much on my own lines you were working. Of course I had welcomed you as one coming nearer and nearer, but I had missed the central root of the whole business, and I shall now re-read you (I had read all the articles . . .) and try again a hack [?] at Mead and Lloyd of whom I have always recognized the originality, but whom I have found so far unassimilably obscure. I fancy that much depends on the place one starts out from—you have all come from Hegel . . . , I from empiricism, and though we reach much the same goal it superficially looks different from the opposite sides." Here James finally recognizes that the ungainly hybrid of pragmatism could, and did, thrive on Hegelian grounds. Cf. chapter 8, note 35, above, but also William James, *A Pluralistic Universe* (1909), lecture 3, "Hegel and His Method," in *Writings*, pp. 668–89, and James's weirdly appreciative essay on Benjamin Paul Blood, "A Pluralistic Mystic," in Henry James, Jr., ed., *Memories and Studies* (New York: Longmans Green, 1911), pp. 369–411, here 376–80.

4. Alfred North Whitehead, *Science and the Modern World* (1925; New York: Mentor, 1948), p. 143.

5. See volume 3 of Jo Ann Boydston, ed., *John Dewey: The Middle Works*, 15 vols. (Carbondale: Southern Illinois University Press, 1976). See also works by John Dewey: "Reality as Experience," *Journal of Philosophy, Psychology, and Scientific Methods* 3 (1906): 253–57, here 101–6, esp. 102 n. 1; "The Experimental Theory of Knowledge," *Mind*, n.s., 15 (1906): 293–307, here 107–27, esp. 123 n. 11; "Experi-

ence and Objective Idealism," *Philosophical Review* 15 (1906): 465–81, here 128–44, esp. 142 n. 13; "The Postulate of Immediate Empiricism," *Journal of Philosophy, Psychology, and Scientific Methods* 2 (1905): 393–99, here 158–67, esp. 161 n. 5. "The Realism of Pragmatism" first appeared in ibid., 324–27, and is reprinted in Boydston, *Middle Works* 3:153–57, quoted from p. 156. Dewey's letter to James is quoted in Perry, *Character of William James* 2:526.

6. See Perry, *Character of William James* 2:525, and John Dewey, "The Ego as Cause," *Philosophical Review* 3 (1894): 337–41, reprinted in Jo Ann Boydston, ed., *John Dewey: The Early Works*, 5 vols. (Carbondale: Southern Illinois University Press, 1971), 4:91–95, here 4:95 n. 4.

7. John Dewey, "The Vanishing Subject in the Psychology of James," *Journal of Philosophy* 37 (1940): 589–99, quoted remarks from pp. 599, 596, 598–99.

8. James quotes Kierkegaard in "How Two Minds Can Know One Thing," *Journal of Philosophy, Psychology, and Scientific Methods* 2 (1905): 176–81, the fourth installment in what became the *Essays in Radical Empiricism*, pp. 61–67, here 65 n. 6. On the return of the repressed, see Norman O. Brown, *Life against Death: The Psychoanalytical Meaning of History* (Middletown, Conn.: Wesleyan University Press, 1959), chaps. 3–10; Jean Laplanche, *Life and Death in Psychoanalysis*, trans. Jeffrey Mehlman (Baltimore: Johns Hopkins University Press, 1976), esp. chaps. 2–3. On desublimation and deterritorialization, see Herbert Marcuse, *Eros and Civilization* (Boston: Beacon Press, 1955), esp. chaps. 4, 10; and Gilles Deleuze and Felix Guattari, *Anti-Oedipus: Capitalism and Schizophrenia*, trans. Robert Hurley, Mark Seem, and Helen R. Lane (Minneapolis: University of Minnesota Press, 1983), chap. 3. It is worth noting here that long before the transatlantic rediscovery of Freud in the 1950s, social theorists suggested that the transition to Taylorized capitalism evident in the "trust movement" would mobilize earlier, apparently archaic forms of social-cultural development; for example, see Simon N. Patten, *The New Basis of Civilization* (New York: Macmillan, 1907), p. 91, and Georg Lukács, "Reification and the Consciousness of the Proletariat" (1922), in *History and Class Consciousness*, trans. Rodney Livingstone (Cambridge: MIT Press, 1971), pp. 83–222, here 93.

9. See Norbert Elias, *The Civilizing Process*, trans. Edmund Jephcott, 2 vols. (New York: Pantheon, 1978), esp. chap. 2 (pp. 51–217) of vol. 1 and chap. 2 (pp. 91–225) of vol. 2, but also the "Synopsis" of vol. 2, esp. pp. 270–300; Klaus Theweleit, *Male Fantasies*, trans. Stephen Conway, Erica Carter, and Chris Turner, 2 vols. (Minneapolis: University of Minnesota Press, 1987, 1989), esp. 1:300–363; Norman Bryson, *Vision and Painting: The Logic of the Gaze* (New Haven: Yale University Press, 1983), chaps. 3–6; and Walter J. Ong, *The Presence of the Word* (New Haven: Yale University Press, 1967).

10. See esp. Hannah Arendt, *The Human Condition* (Chicago: University of Chicago Press, 1958), chap. 6; also E. A. Burtt, *The Metaphysical Foundations of Modern Science*, rev. ed. (Garden City, N.Y.: Doubleday, 1955).

11. Rorty quoted from his *Philosophy and the Mirror of Nature* (Princeton: Princeton University Press, 1979), p. 377.

12. The historical logic I follow here is that of Alasdair MacIntyre, "The Relation-

ship of Philosophy to Its Past," in Richard Rorty, J. B. Schneewind, and Quentin Skinner, eds., *Philosophy in History* (New York: Cambridge University Press, 1984), pp. 31–48; but cf. Rorty, *Mirror*, p. 316.

13. Since I have previously quoted "Does Consciousness Exist?" from the Library of America edition of James, *Writings 1902–1910*, pp. 1141–58, I will continue to do so (page references in the text hereafter). On James's preparations for the Emerson centenary, see esp. Notebook 20 in James Papers (bMSAm 1092.9), which is crammed with citations of, excerpts from, and commentary on Emerson's works.

14. If Howard Feinstein's psychoanalytical account of James is credible (and I think it is), this reference to "a paint of which the world pictures were made" is quite significant; for it recasts the language of the "murdered self"—that is, of the painter James once wanted desperately to become. See Howard M. Feinstein, *Becoming William James* (Ithaca: Cornell University Press, 1984), esp. chaps. 7–8. In the journal the Houghton Library calls Notebook 12, "Book III, Seminary of 1897–98, Theoretic psychology [and] Seminary of 1903–4," James reminds himself of the metaphor: "Work the menstruum-simile, in which oil, size, or water stands for consciousness, while the object is made up of pigments held in suspension or solution" (p. 51). This entry is almost certainly from 1903.

15. William James, "A World of Pure Experience," *Essays in Radical Empiricism*, pp. 21–44 (page references in text hereafter).

16. On the question of the relation between particular and universal or parts and wholes, see Roberto Mangabeira Unger, *Knowledge and Politics* (New York: Free Press, 1975), pp. 121–44.

17. This "bundle of sensations" is David Hume's specification of the self; see R. J. Butler, "'I' and Sympathy," *Proceedings of the Aristotelian Society*, supplementary vol. 49 (1975): 1–20.

18. See J.G.A. Pocock, *The Machiavellian Moment: Florentine Political Thought and the Atlantic Republican Tradition* (Princeton: Princeton University Press, 1975), part 3, esp. chaps. 13–15 (pp. 526–52 are particularly relevant to my argument, quoted from pp. 548–49). Like most historians, I have some serious reservations about Pocock's insistence on the centrality of republicanism (of Harrington as against Locke) in the American political tradition. But I think it is pointless to try to prove him "wrong" about the proportionate significance of, say, Daniel Defoe in the reading and political actions of North Americans; for the American Revolution was neither liberal (Lockean) nor republican (Harringtonian): it was both, and was greater than the sum of these parts. Pocock's great achievement is to have illuminated the uneasy relation between modern political theory and practice, by showing how the notion of a moral personality residing in modern ideas about self-determination has mediated between these domains. In view of that achievement, I believe it is almost churlish to criticize him.

19. Ibid., pp. 534–45, 550–51. I say that Pocock and Louis Hartz converge because both prove that Werner Sombart's question about socialism in North America is irrelevant to the political tradition it purports to address. They teach us that what we have to explain is neither the practical absence nor the theoretical emptiness of socialism in the United States (and, for that matter, in western Europe) but rather the blindness of contemporary writers on the Left to the political possibilities that

already exist in the social and economic theories of twentieth-century American intellectuals. I have been arguing in part 2, for example, that the United States may well lack a Marxist intellectual tradition—although the work of Lee Benson in *Turner and Beard: American Historical Writing Reconsidered* (Glencoe, Ill.: Free Press, 1960), should have put even this article of faith in doubt—but it has never wanted for a Hegelian tradition: Peirce and (in his own way) James were right to believe that pragmatism represented the recuperation of this very tradition in North America, long before it became fashionable in continental Europe. My thinking on these matters has been clarified by correspondence and conversation with Martin J. Sklar, who is himself a major theorist of socialism in the United States. Cf. Louis Hartz, *The Liberal Tradition in America* (New York: Harcourt, Brace & World, 1955), esp. part 5.

20. William James, "La notion de conscience," translated as "The Notion of Consciousness" by Salvatore Saladino in *Essays in Radical Empiricism*, appendix 3, pp. 261–71, here 268. This was a communication made at the Fifth International Congress of Psychology in Rome, April 30, 1905, which James described as a "resume" of his series of articles on radical empiricism; the French original is at pp. 105–17.

21. See Arendt, *Human Condition*, pp. 58–73, esp. 62 n. 58, 66 n. 70; Pocock, *Machiavellian Moment*, chaps. 13–14; C. B. Macpherson, *The Political Theory of Possessive Individualism: Hobbes to Locke* (New York: Oxford University Press, 1962), chaps. 3–5; Edmund S. Morgan, *American Slavery, American Freedom: The Ordeal of Colonial Virginia* (New York: Knopf, 1975), pp. 61–69, 236–39, 319–27, 380–87; Isaac Kramnick, *Bolingbroke and His Circle* (Cambridge: Harvard University Press, 1968), chaps. 2–3, 7–9; and David L. Jacobson, ed., *The English Libertarian Heritage: From the Writings of John Trenchard and Thomas Gordon* (Indianapolis: Bobbs-Merrill, 1965), "Cato's Letters" nos. 84 and 94, at pp. 211–24. Cf. also chapter 8, note 56, above.

22. James Madison quoted from his remarks in convention, June 26, 1787, in Max Farrand, ed., *The Records of the Federal Convention of 1787*, 4 vols. (New Haven: Yale University Press, 1911), 1:422–23.

23. James Madison quoted from his "Observations on Jefferson's Draft of a Constitution for Virginia" (1787?) in Julian P. Boyd, ed., *The Papers of Thomas Jefferson*, 34 vols. (Princeton: Princeton University Press, 1950–), 6:308–17, here 310. Madison's observations become all the more poignant when we recall that for the men of his generation, "Kentucky" was a metaphor of social equality and natural plenty as well as a place; for example, John Breckenridge called it "the Eden of America." See Michael Paul Rogin, *Fathers and Children: Andrew Jackson and the Subjugation of the American Indian* (New York: Knopf, 1975), p. 77, and Henry Nash Smith, *Virgin Land: The American West as Symbol and Myth* (Cambridge: Harvard University Press, 1950; Vintage Books ed., New York: Random House, n.d.), pp. 146–49.

24. James Madison quoted from his remarks in convention, August 7, 1787, in Farrand, *Records* 2:203–4, and again from "Observations on Jefferson's Draft," in Boyd, *Papers* 6:310. In *Possessive Individualism*, chap. 3, Macpherson explains how and why the modern proletariat was defined, even in radically democratic political theory and practice, as both "exogenous" and instrumental; but see also works cited at note 21 above. Women were similarly defined, of course, as the works

of Susan Moller Okin, Jean B. Elshtain, Carole Pateman, Genevieve Lloyd, and others demonstrate; see, for example, Genevieve Lloyd, *The Man of Reason: "Male" and "Female" in Western Philosophy* (Minneapolis: University of Minnesota Press, 1984), chaps. 3–5. I have work in progress through which I am trying to explain how and why pragmatism and feminism raise the same questions for political philosophy. My point of departure is Linda J. Nicholson's *Gender and History: The Limits of Social Theory in the Age of the Family* (New York: Columbia University Press, 1986), which shows that the breakdown of a household economy and the consequent entry of females into civil society compose the turning point in the making of a feminist sensibility.

25. Kenneth Burke, *Attitudes toward History*, rev. ed. (Boston: Beacon Press, 1961), pp. 19–44, 92–107, quoted from p. 20. The best reading of Burke I know is Frank Lentricchia, *Criticism and Social Change* (Chicago: University of Chicago Press, 1983); but see also William H. Rueckert, *Kenneth Burke and the Drama of Human Relations*, 2d ed. (Berkeley: University of California Press, 1982).

26. See Hilary Putnam, *Reason, Truth, and History* (New York: Cambridge University Press, 1981), chaps. 5–7; Davidson, "Myth of the Subjective," pp. 163–71; and Rorty, *Mirror*, chap. 7 (quoted from p. 316).

27. See Alasdair MacIntyre, "Relativism, Power, and Philosophy," in Krausz, *Relativism*, pp. 182–204 (quoted from p. 184), and Charles Taylor, *Sources of the Self: The Making of the Modern Identity* (Cambridge: Harvard University Press, 1989), chaps. 2–7, 23–25.

28. If it was not Sophocles who first asked whether the social roles provided by the polis exhausted the possibilities of selfhood, he was the first to ask the question as if the answer had to take the form of a dramatic narrative—that is, a story. See Alasdair MacIntyre, *After Virtue* (Notre Dame: University of Notre Dame Press, 1981), chap. 11. Rorty is quoted from *Mirror*, p. 318.

29. See Richard Rorty, "Dewey's Metaphysics," in Steven M. Cahn, *New Studies in the Philosophy of John Dewey* (Hanover, N.H.: University of Press of New England, 1977), pp. 45–74, here 61–62, 60; cf. Rorty, *Mirror*, p. 368 n. 13. Richard Bernstein, "Philosophy in the Conversation of Mankind," *Review of Metaphysics* 33 (1980): 744–75, is an incisive critique of Rorty's book from which I have learned a great deal. More recent and more strident arguments about Rorty's positions are Sheldon S. Wolin, "Democracy in the Discourse of Postmodernism," *Social Research* 57 (1990): 5–30, and Richard J. Bernstein, "Rorty's Liberal Utopia," ibid., 31–72. But see also Thomas McCarthy, "Private Irony and Public Decency: Richard Rorty's New Pragmatism," *Critical Inquiry* 16 (1990): 355–70, with an exchange between Rorty and McCarthy at ibid., 633–55, and Nancy Fraser, "Solidarity or Singularity?: Richard Rorty between Romanticism and Technocracy," *Unruly Practices: Power, Discourse, and Gender in Contemporary Social Theory* (Minneapolis: University of Minnesota Press, 1989), pp. 93–110. Fraser's essay is particularly insightful and, for my purposes, quite useful; she demonstrates that Rorty is caught between what I have called the extremes of modern subjectivity, that is, between romanticism and positivism (see chapters 8–9 above). Fraser calls these extremes romanticism and pragmatism, as Lewis Mumford did in *Technics and Civilization* (New York: Harcourt, Brace & World, 1934) and as Casey Blake does in "The Perils

of Personality: Lewis Mumford and Politics after Liberalism," in Agatha C. Hughes and Thomas P. Hughes, eds., *Lewis Mumford: Public Intellectual* (New York: Oxford University Press, 1990), pp. 283–300 (endnotes at 417–20), e.g., at 287. Of course I think it is a mistake to equate pragmatism and positivism (or utilitarianism), as Fraser seems to do in reducing pragmatism to "liberal problem-solving"; but her central claim, with which I fully agree, is that a genuinely romantic version of (or a strictly aesthetic argument for) pragmatism is ultimately incoherent.

30. Richard Rorty, "Solidarity or Objectivity," originally in John Rajchman and Cornel West, eds., *Post-Analytic Philosophy* (New York: Cambridge University Press, 1985), pp. 3–19, reprinted in Richard Rorty, *Objectivity, Relativism, and Truth* (New York: Cambridge University Press, 1991), pp. 21–34, here 30 (page references in text hereafter).

31. Richard Rorty, "Postmodernist Bourgeois Liberalism," originally in *Journal of Philosophy* 80 (1983): 583–89, reprinted in Rorty, *Objectivity, Relativism, and Truth*, pp. 197–202, here 200 (page references in text hereafter). Elias is quoted from *Civilizing Process* 2:236; cf. Hegel's analysis of civil society in *The Philosophy of Right*, trans. T. M. Knox (New York: Oxford University Press, 1942), par. 187, p. 124: "Individuals in their capacity as burghers in this state are private persons whose end is their own interest. This end is mediated through the universal which thus appears as a means to its realization. Consequently, individuals can attain their ends only in so far as they themselves determine their knowing, willing, and acting in a universal way and make themselves links in this chain of social connections."

32. Michel Foucault, "Nietzsche, Genealogy, History," in Donald F. Bouchard, ed., *Language, Counter-Memory, Practice: Selected Essays and Interviews*, trans. Donald F. Bouchard and Sherry Simon (Ithaca: Cornell University Press, 1977), pp. 139–64, esp. 146, 150–54, 160–64, here 154; cf. Foucault's "What Is an Author?," in ibid., pp. 113–38, esp. 120–24. On the question of discontinuity, see also the following works by Foucault: "History, Discourse, and Discontinuity," *Salmagundi* 20 (1972): 225–48; *The Order of Things: An Archaeology of the Human Sciences* (New York: Pantheon, 1971), pp. xxii–iii, 125–38, 269–79; and *The Archaeology of Knowledge*, trans. A. M. Sheridan Smith (New York: Pantheon, 1972), esp. part 4, pp. 166–77 (see below for comment on these pages). And see Frank Lentricchia, "Michel Foucault's Fantasy for Humanists," *Ariel and the Police* (Madison: University of Wisconsin Press, 1987), pp. 29–102, here 96–99; E. M. Henning, "Archaeology, Deconstruction, and Intellectual History," in Dominick LaCapra and Steven L. Kaplan, eds., *Modern European Intellectual History* (Ithaca: Cornell University Press, 1982), pp. 153–96, here 157–58, 182–83; and H. D. Harootunian, "Foucault, Genealogy, History: The Pursuit of Otherness," and Isaac D. Balbus, "Disciplining Women: Michel Foucault and the Power of Feminist Discourse," both in Jonathan Arac, ed., *After Foucault: Humanistic Knowledge, Postmodern Challenges* (New Brunswick, N.J.: Rutgers University Press, 1988), pp. 110–37, 138–60, esp. 116–24, 139–40. Cf. Donald M. Lowe's *History of Bourgeois Perception* (Chicago: University of Chicago Press, 1982), which is informed throughout by Foucault's method and sensibility: "The perceptual transformation from bourgeois society to the bureaucratic society of controlled consumption, during the decade of 1905–15, was as fundamental as that from the Renaissance to estate society in the early seven-

teenth century, or that from estate society to bourgeois society in the last third of the eighteenth century. There is no continuity from one period to the next; each is a different world" (p. 109). Yet it seems to me that Foucault's position is more complicated than Lowe—or, for that matter, Harootunian, Balbus, and Rorty—would allow. "It is understandable," he wrote in *The Archaeology of Knowledge*, "that some minds are so attached to all those old metaphors by which, for a century and a half, history (movement, flux, innovation) has been imagined, that they see archaeology simply as the negation of history and the crude affirmation of discontinuity" (p. 173). But note that he was defining the opposition, not designating his own principles, in describing these minds. At any rate, *The Archaeology of Knowledge* does not so much dismiss continuity as demand that it be treated as a historical phenomenon. For example, "For archaeology, the identical and the continuous are not what must be found at the end of the analysis; . . . far from manifesting that fundamental, reassuring inertia which we like to use as a criterion of change, they are themselves actively, regularly formed" (p. 174). What James calls continuous transitions could be defined in these very terms, as "actively, regularly formed." We might then say that Foucault himself tried, not always successfully, to recuperate historical time, and that his followers have stopped trying. But this is pretty much what I said in chapter 9 about Lewis Mumford and his followers on the American Left, namely, by reverting to romanticism, they have reinstated modern subjectivity and its attendant discontinuities. So I am persuaded by Allan Megill's claim that Foucault's work has romantic antecedents: see Allan Megill, *Prophets of Extremity: Nietzsche, Heidegger, Foucault, Derrida* (Berkeley: University of California Press, 1985), chaps. 5–6.

33. See Thomas Kuhn, *The Structure of Scientific Revolutions*, 2d ed. (Chicago: University of Chicago Press, 1970), esp. chaps. 5, 10; cf. Rorty, *Mirror*, pp. 322–56. See also the helpful discussions of Kuhn and his critics in Richard Bernstein, *Beyond Objectivism and Relativism: Science, Hermeneutics, and Praxis* (Philadelphia: University of Pennsylvania Press, 1983), part 2, pp. 52–108 and endnotes at 240–47, and in Alasdair MacIntyre, "Epistemological Crises, Dramatic Narrative, and the Philosophy of Science," *Monist* 60 (1977): 453–72.

34. See Hannah Arendt, *On Revolution* (1963; reprint, New York: Penguin, 1977)), chaps. 4–5; MacIntyre, "Epistemological Crises," pp. 460–61; and Martin J. Sklar, *The Corporate Reconstruction of American Capitalism, 1890–1916: The Market, the Law, and Politics* (New York: Cambridge University Press, 1988), p. 361. In my view, Ernesto Laclau and Chantal Mouffe, *Hegemony and Socialist Strategy* (London: Verso, 1985), is important if only because it acknowledges that revolution is not the exclusive property or project of radicals on the Left. Cf. my "Radicals All!," *Reviews in American History* 16 (June 1988): 307–13.

35. Abraham Lincoln is quoted from "Speech at Peoria, Illinois," October 16, 1854, in Roy P. Basler, ed., *Collected Works of Abraham Lincoln*, 8 vols. (New Brunswick, N.J.: Rutgers University Press, 1953), 2:247–83, here 266. The Cooper Union speech of February 27, 1860, in which Lincoln painstakingly demonstrates the continuity of the Declaration and the Constitution, is in Basler, *Collected Works* 3:522–50. I have made these arguments before, in "Politics, Ideology, and the Origins of American Revolutions," *Socialist Revolution* 36 (1977): 7–36, and in a talk

at a conference on "Free Soil and the Constitution" sponsored by Ripon College in September 1987. In this talk, "Revolutionary Politics in the Electoral Arena: The Constitutional Basis of Lincoln's Appeal," I argued that Lincoln's focus on "no extension"—on the territorial disposition of slavery—was not a paradox, not a devolution from the more principled stance of abolitionism, not merely a concession to a public opinion that valued constitutional procedure. Instead, I claim, the focus on "new countries" made a reenactment of the founding the immediate and practical issue in a way that abolitionism could not, for it returned the electorate to the past without replicating the past; it reinstated the image of new beginnings, the American Adam, but did not propose to escape from the past. So conceived, "no extension" was a trope that recalled, returned, reverted—it was not evasion but revision of the past. My talk at Ripon was invited by Kim Shankman, the political scientist who convened the conference and who deserves my thanks after all these years. But I would like to note that my ideas about Lincoln have been reshaped over the years by conversations with William Burr, Larry Lynn, Martin J. Sklar, Steve Rosswurm, Keith Haynes, Paul Wolman, and Don Shankman—all former members of the DeKalb Socialist Historians Group, with whom I was able to discuss Don E. Fehrenbacher, *Prelude to Greatness: Lincoln in the 1850s* (Palo Alto: Stanford University Press, 1962), and Harry V. Jaffa, *Crisis of the House Divided: An Interpretation of the Issues in the Lincoln-Douglas Debates*, 2d ed. (Garden City, N.Y.: Doubleday, 1959). I should also note that the new book by Garry Wills, *Lincoln at Gettysburg: The Words That Remade America* (New York: Simon & Schuster, 1992), came too late for me to use in writing this chapter.

36. Lincoln always insisted that what we would call "ideological struggle" was central to political innovation where popular government ruled. For example, in the first debate with Douglas on August 21, 1858, at Ottawa, Illinois, he said: "In this and like communities, public sentiment is everything. With public sentiment, nothing can fail; without it, nothing can succeed. Consequently, he who molds public sentiment, goes deeper than he who enacts statutes or pronounces decisions. He makes statutes and decisions possible or impossible to be executed." This molding is precisely what Lincoln took to be his primary responsibility between 1854 and 1865. See Basler, *Collected Works* 3:12–30, here 27. On public opinion as the embodiment of consent, which must serve as the principle of political obligation where the Declaration's commitment to human equality is honored, and on what follows for those who would change public opinion, see Jaffa, *House Divided*, chap. 17.

37. See MacIntyre, "Epistemological Crises," p. 466, and James, "A World of Pure Experience," pp. 23–24.

38. Michel Foucault, "Of Other Spaces," *Diacritics* 16 (1986): 22–27, here 22. On the inevitable resort to power in adjudicating differences between communities when incommensurability becomes the norm of discourse, see MacIntyre, "Relativism, Power, and Philosophy," pp. 200–202. But see also Foucault, "Nietzsche, Genealogy, History," esp. pp. 150–52, which I read as a meditation on this very theme of domination as the predicate of paradigm shifts; as the author puts it, "If interpretation is the violent or surreptitious appropriation of a system of rules, which in itself has no essential meaning, in order to impose a direction, to bend it to a new will, to force participation in a different game, and to subject it to sec-

ondary rules, then the development of humanity is a series of interpretations" (pp. 151–52). In light of Foucault's work, I believe it is worth asking whether the key differences between Nietzsche and James derive from their attitudes toward the logic and language of markets. There is no principle of equivalence in Nietzsche's work—all exchange is unequal, every transaction requires or produces an asymmetry of power. This would not be worth remarking except that he claims that it was in "the sphere of legal obligations, that the moral conceptual world of 'guilt,' 'conscience,' 'duty,' 'sacredness of duty' had its origin," and insists that this sphere of law, contract, and debt developed as the necessary corollary of "the oldest and most primitive personal relationship, that between buyer and seller, creditor and debtor: it was here that one person first encountered another person, that one person first *measured himself* against another." Indeed, Nietzsche goes on to claim, "Setting prices, determining values, contriving equivalences, exchanging—these preoccupied the earliest thinking of man to so great an extent that in a certain sense they constitute thinking *as such.*" So, once primitive societies had "arrived at the great generalization, 'everything has its price; all things can be paid for'—the oldest and naivest moral canon of *justice,*" they had fallen from the innocence of domination and moved toward the position that justice required "good will among parties of approximately equal power." (From F. W. Nietzsche, *On the Genealogy of Morals,* trans. Walter Kaufmann and R. J. Hollingdale [New York: Vintage, 1967], pp. 65, 70, italics in original.) By this accounting—it is not incidentally a parody of Hegel's *Philosophy of Right*—the "second innocence" (*Unschuld*) impending in the decline of faith would be realized when all debts were canceled and all markets adjourned, when *das Schuldgefuhl,* "the guilty feeling of indebtedness," as Kaufmann translates it, would dissolve because money and markets would not serve as the organizing principles of thought (ibid., pp. 90–91); the conscience-stricken human animal would then revert to domination as the natural form of social intercourse.

39. James, "A World of Pure Experience," pp. 42, 23–27 (references in the text hereafter).

40. Cf. Rorty, *Mirror,* p. 382: "The notion that we can get around overconfident philosophical realism and positivistic reductions only by adopting something like Kant's transcendental standpoint seems to me the basic mistake in programs like that of Habermas. . . . What is required to accomplish these laudable purposes is not Kant's 'epistemological' distinction between the transcendental and the empirical standpoints, but rather his 'existential' distinction between people as empirical selves and as moral agents." In a later essay, "The Priority of Democracy to Philosophy" (1988), reprinted in Rorty, *Objectivity, Relativism, and Truth,* pp. 175–96, Rorty suggests, however, that such an existential distinction is pointless because the effect of twentieth-century intellectual innovation "is to erase the picture of the self common to Greek metaphysics, Christian theology, and Enlightenment rationalism." He goes on to claim that we do not need this "model of the human self"; or rather we do not need "the idea that the human self has a center (a divine spark, or a truth-tracking faculty called 'reason') and that argumentation will, given time and patience, penetrate to this center" (pp. 176, 192, 188). He proposes an alternative—"a notion of the human self as a centerless web of historically conditioned beliefs and desires"—but discounts its importance. "If one *wants* a model of the

human self, then this picture of a centerless web will fill the need. But for purposes of liberal social theory, one can do without such a model. One can get along with common sense and social science, areas of discourse in which the term 'the self' rarely occurs" (p. 192). I cannot agree with Rorty in this instance because I agree with him on the priority of democracy to philosophy. I have tried to show, in chapters 8–10, that arguments about the nature of the self and the moral personality are in effect arguments about the meaning and scope of democracy. I would now insist that these arguments are the vernacular in which we discuss and determine the changing relation between public and private spheres of modern life—which is to say that they compose the common sense we need to develop social theory and social science. If "we heirs of the Enlightenment for whom justice has become the first virtue" (p. 182) begin by assuming that beliefs about the needs and capacities of human beings set the limits of public policy and establish the purposes of political deliberation, how can we detach politics from a model of, or debate about, the self? If we derive our sense of justice from our ideas about what each of us deserves, or legitimately desires, why would we want to detach them? If effected, would not that detachment end the evolution of our sense of justice by making new ideas about selfhood—new beliefs about the needs and capacities of human beings—irrelevant to public policy and political deliberation? My point is not that we must have a self with a suprahistorical center, but that we need models of and arguments about the self if we are to have political debate in which justice figures as the "first virtue." In other words, if Rorty is correct about the effect of twentieth-century intellectual innovation, the model of the self contained in the essays on radical empiricism becomes indispensable to the political debates we want to have.

INDEX

· ·